STUDIES IN HINDU LAW AND DHARMAŚĀSTRA

Anthem South Asian Normative Traditions Studies

The **Anthem South Asian Normative Traditions Studies** series features textual studies, thematic analysis and historical reconstructions devoted to the exploration of South Asian normative materials. Committed both to well known normative productions (such as Sanskrit *dharmasūtras* and *dharmaśāstras* and Pāli *vinaya*) and to lesser known vernacular or regional materials, this series aims to enhance the understanding of the many variants assumed by the legal, normative and codifying intellectual discourses in South Asia. This series is under the direction of Patrick Olivelle, Professor of Sanskrit and Indian Religions at the University of Texas at Austin, USA.

Series Editor

Federico Squarcini, University of Florence, Italy

Editorial Board

Patrick Olivelle, University of Texas at Austin, USA
Whitney Cox, School of Oriental and African Studies, UK
Donald R. Davis, Jr, University of Wisconsin-Madison, USA
Timothy Lubin, Washington and Lee University, USA
David Brick, Yale University, USA
Ethan Kroll, Baker & McKenzie LLP, USA
Mark McClish, Birmingham-Southern College, USA

STUDIES IN HINDU LAW AND DHARMAŚĀSTRA

Ludo Rocher

Edited with an Introduction by Donald R. Davis, Jr

ANTHEM PRESS
LONDON · NEW YORK · DELHI

Anthem Press
An imprint of Wimbledon Publishing Company
www.anthempress.com

This edition first published in UK and USA 2014
by ANTHEM PRESS
75–76 Blackfriars Road, London SE1 8HA, UK
or PO Box 9779, London SW19 7ZG, UK
and
244 Madison Ave. #116, New York, NY 10016, USA

First published in hardback by Anthem Press in 2012

British Library Cataloguing in Publication Data
A catalogue record for this book is available from the British Library.

Library of Congress Cataloging in Publication Data
A catalog record for this book has been requested.

ISBN-13: 978 1 78308 315 2 (Pbk)
ISBN-10: 1 78308 315 8 (Pbk)

This title is also available as an ebook.

Contents

Foreword by Richard W. Lariviere 9
Preface 11
Abbreviations 13
Note on the Edition 15
Introduction 17

PART ONE. THE NATURE OF HINDU LAW

Hindu Conceptions of Law 39
The Historical Foundations of Ancient Indian Law 59
Hindu Law and Religion: Where to Draw the Line 83
Law Books in an Oral Culture: The Indian Dharmaśāstras 103
Schools of Hindu Law 119
Changing Patterns of Diversification in Hindu Law 129

PART TWO. GENERAL TOPICS OF HINDU LAW

Ancient Hindu Criminal Law 145
Hindu Law of Succession: From the Śāstras *to Modern Law* 163
Caste and Occupation in Classical India: The Normative Texts 201
Megasthenes on Indian Lawbooks 215
The "Ambassador" in Ancient India 219
The Status of Minors according to Classical Hindu Law 235
Quandoque bonus dormitat *Jīmūtavāhanas?* 249
Notes on Mixed Castes in Classical India 255
Inheritance and Śrāddha*: The Principle of "Spiritual Benefit"* 267

The Theory of Matrimonial Causes According to the Dharmaśāstra 279
Jīmūtavāhana's Dāyabhāga *and the Maxim* Factum Valet 305
The Divinity of Royal Power in Ancient India according to Dharmaśāstra 315
A Few Considerations on Monocracy in Ancient India 331

PART THREE. HINDU LEGAL PROCEDURE

The Theory of Proof in Ancient Hindu Law 361
The Problem of the Mixed Reply in Ancient Hindu Law 395
The Reply in Hindu Legal Procedure: Mitra Miśra's Criticism of the Vyavahāra-Cintāmaṇi 405
"Lawyers" in Classical Hindu Law 417
Anumāna in the Bṛhaspatismṛti 435

PART FOUR. TECHNICAL STUDIES OF HINDU LAW

Possession Held for Three Generations by Persons Related to the Owner 445
The Vīramitrodaya *on the Right of Private Defence* 451
The Technical Term Anubandha *in Sanskrit Legal Literature* 473
The Kāmasūtra*: Vātsyāyana's Attitude toward* Dharma *and Dharmaśāstra* 481
In Defense of Jīmūtavāhana 497
Dāsadāsī 503
The Definition of Vākparuṣya 513
Janmasvatvavāda *and* Uparamasvatvavāda: *The First Chapters on Inheritance in the* Mitākṣarā *and* Dāyabhāga 527
Karma and Rebirth in the Dharmaśāstras 539
Notes on the Technical Term Sāhasa: *"Fine, Pecuniary Penalty"* 565
Avyāvahārika *Debts and Kauṭilya 3.1.1–11* 581
The Sūtra*s and* Śāstra*s on the Eight Types of Marriage* 587
Caritraṃ Pustakaraṇe 597
The Terms Niyukta, Aniyukta, *and* Niyoga *in Sanskrit Legal Literature* 603
The Aurasa *Son* 613
The Introduction of the Gautamadharmasūtra 623

PART FIVE. ANGLO-HINDU AND CUSTOMARY LAW

Indian Response to Anglo-Hindu Law 633
Can a Murderer Inherit his Victim's Estate? British Responses to Troublesome Questions in Hindu Law 643

Foreword

Don Davis has done scholars a great favor. He has collected together in one place much of the work of one of the bright lights of American academia. Prof. Ludo Rocher is a member of the American Philosophical Society, former President of the American Oriental Society, and Chairman of the Board of Trustees of the American Institute of Indian Studies. All significant distinctions in an important career. But what is most compelling, most distinctive, and most enduring about Prof. Rocher's career are two things: (1) his broad, comprehensive, and always rock-solid contributions to our understanding of classical India and (2) his generous, tireless, and effective mentoring of generations of students. Many of the most important Indological positions in the country are held by Prof. Rocher's students. Don Davis is part of that *paramparā* and he has given us the great gift of a reprinting of work whose collective impact has moved Indology forward steadily and consistently for more than 50 years. Those of us who continue to rely on dog-eared and heavily marked up copies of these articles and who have sent students hither and yon to make new copies are grateful for this service.

Future generations of students and scholars will more easily understand the impressive breadth and depth of Rocher's work as a result of this collection. Their value and their validity endure. They are superb examples of what Davis refers to as the "philological particular." The focus and the technical mastery represented by these articles are what give coherence to such breadth of scholarship. We are fortunate to have this collection, but this collection's real impact will be on future generations of scholars who will as a result be more likely to be able to access this important work. Many of the journals that Rocher published in are not available electronically, and the half-life of Festschriften is diminished by the increased dependency of libraries on electronic collections.

We who care deeply for Indology and philological rigor are grateful to Davis and his assistants for making this good work available to us.

Eugene, Oregon
Richard W. Lariviere

Preface

I was inspired to collect Prof. Rocher's writings on Hindu law and Dharmaśāstra in the process of finding and gathering certain of his articles for use in a course on Hindu law. It became apparent that Rocher's fundamental writings were obscured by virtue of their dispersion in a variety of Festschrifts and less popular journals —in contrast to the regularly reprinted editions of works by Lingat and Derrett, perhaps the two other great Western scholars of Hindu law in the mid-to-late 20th century. It was also true that Rocher's ideas had not received adequate attention in the most recent work in the field. To my mind, this was very unfortunate and I felt the problems could best be rectified by making Rocher's works available in a more centralized and readily available format. I hope that this final collection, an incomplete, but more than representative assemblage of Rocher's *Kleine Schriften*, will make the publication of work on Hindu law without an appreciation of Rocher's contributions more and more difficult. The most interesting reward of re-reading Rocher's works and cataloging his ideas has been the challenge they pose to my own writing on the subject, which I had thought was already heavily informed by Rocher's direct and indirect influence on my training.

I have been superbly assisted in the preparation of this collection by three fine graduate students from my department, Torrey Goad, Jeremy Holiday, and John Stavrellis who together completed the laborious task of re-keying all of the included articles from their original contexts. I am especially grateful for Mr. Goad's meticulous attention to diacritical and tabular details. The final edition has an aesthetic coherence and more than a few emendations, corrections, and additions to the articles that would have been impossible without their help.

Finally, I wish to thank Federico Squarcini, Patrick Olivelle and Anthem Press for making this the first volume in the new series, Richard Lariviere for writing the Foreword, Tim Lubin for helpful suggestions for the Introduction, the University of Wisconsin Graduate School and the Wisconsin Alumni Research Foundation (WARF) for a summer research grant to work on the edition, and finally Rosane and Ludo Rocher for their warmth, hospitality, and mentoring.

Madison, Wisconsin
Donald R. Davis, Jr

Abbreviations

ĀpDh	*Āpastamba Dharmasūtra*
AŚ	*Arthaśāstra of Kauṭilya*
BDh	*Baudhāyana Dharmasūtra*
BhG	*Bhagavad Gītā*
BS	*Bṛhaspati Smṛti*
Dnī	*Daṇḍanīti*
Dbhā	*Dāyabhāga* (Jīmūtavāhana)
DbhāKta	*Dāyabhāgavyākhyā* (Kṛṣṇatarkālaṅkāra)
DbhāRca	*Dāyabhāgaṭikā* (Rāmacandra)
DbhāŚnā	*Dāyabhāgaṭikā* (Śrināthа)
DhK	*Dharmakośa*, edited L.S. Joshi
Dkra	*Dāyādhikārakramasaṃgraha* (Kṛṣṇatarkālaṅkāra)
DS	*Devala Smṛti*
Dta	*Divyatattva* (Raghunandana)
DVi	*Daṇḍaviveka* (Vardhamāna)
GDh	*Gautama Dharmasūtra*
GHda	*Mitākṣarā* (Haradatta)
GMka	*Maskaribhāṣya* (Maskarin)
HDhŚ	*History of Dharmaśāstra* (P.V. Kane)
Kdhe	*Kāmadhenu* (Gopāla)
KS	*Kātyāyana Smṛti*
KātŚr	*Kātyāyana Śrauta Sūtra*
Kta	*Kṛtyakalpataru, Vyavahārakāṇḍa* (Lakṣmīdhara)
MBh	*Mahābhārata*
MBhru	*Manusmṛtivivaraṇa* (Bhāruci)
MDh	*Mānava Dharmaśāstra*
MKlū	*Manvarthamuktāvali* (Kullūkabhaṭṭa)
MMdhā	*Manusmṛtibhāṣya* (Medhātithi)

MNda	*Nandinī* (Nandana)
MRa	*Madanaratnapradīpa* (Madanasiṃha)
MRca	*Manubhāvārthacandrikā* (Rāmacandra)
MRvā	*Manvarthacandrikā* (Rāghavānanda)
MSna	*Manvarthanibandha* (Sarvajñanārāyaṇa)
NMS	*Nāradīyamanusaṃhitā*
NMSBha	*Bhāṣya* (Bhavasvāmin)
NS	*Nārada Smṛti*
Pā	Pāṇini's *Aṣṭādhyāyī*
PMā	*Parāśaramādhavīya* (Mādhava)
PMS	*Pūrva Mīmāṃsā Sūtras* of Jaimini
Rkau	*Rājadharmakaustubha* (Anantadeva)
Rām	*Rāmāyaṇa* of Vālmīki
SBE	*Sacred Books of the East*
Sca	*Smṛticandrikā* (Devaṇṇabhaṭṭa)
Sci	*Smṛticintāmaṇi* (Gaṅgāditya)
ŚL	*Śaṅkha-Likhita Smṛti*
SSā	*Smṛtisāra*
Svi	*Sarasvatīvilāsa* (Pratāparūdradeva)
TS	*Taittirīya Saṃhitā*
VaDh	*Vasiṣṭha Dharmasūtra*
Vci	*Vivādacintāmaṇi* (Vācaspati Miśra)
ViDh	*Viṣṇu Smṛti*
ViNpa	*Keśavavaijayantī* (Nandapaṇḍita)
Vma	*Vyavahāramayūkha* (Nīlakaṇṭha)
Vmi	*Vīramitrodaya* (Mitra Miśra)
Vni	*Vyavahāranirṇaya* (Varadarāja)
Vpra	*Vyavahāraprakāśa* (Mitra Miśra)
Vra	*Vivādaratnākara* (Caṇḍeśvara)
Vsā	*Vyavahārasāra* (Dalapatirāja) Nṛsiṃhaprasāda
Vtā	*Vivādatāṇḍava* (Kamalākara)
Vyci	*Vyavahāracintāmaṇi* (Vācaspati Miśra)
VySm	*Vyāsa Smṛti*
YApa	*Aparārka* (Aparāditya)
YBā	*Bālakrīḍā* (Viśvarūpa)
YDh	*Yājñavalkya Dharmaśāstra*
YDka	*Dīpakalikā* (Śulapāṇi)
YMtā	*Mitākṣarā* (Vijñāneśvara)
YMtāBbha	*Bālaṃbhaṭṭī* (Balaṃbhaṭṭā or Lakṣmīdevī)
YMtāSbo	*Subodhinī* (Viśveśvarabhaṭṭa)
YMtāVmi	*Vīramitrodaya* (Mitra Miśra)

Note on the Edition

For this edition of Rocher's principal studies of Hindu law and Dharmaśāstra, all of the original articles have been re-keyed and reformatted according to a standardized system of bibliographic citation and text layout. Beyond presenting an aesthetically coherent text, this process has enabled certain changes and corrections to be made to the original articles, including stylistic changes, corrections of typographical errors, minor authorial modifications, and occasional editorial interventions. Unlike a *Kleine Schriften*, therefore, the original pagination is not preserved, nor was it thought important to indicate in the reformatted text. The standardization process has also altered the number and numbering of the original footnotes, since all the articles now conform to an author-date citation system. This may cause some minor consternation on those rare occasions when one may want to check a reference to an original footnote. The relatively short length of most of Rocher's articles, however, should not make cross-referencing too burdensome, and the advantages gained by reformatting were thought to outweigh the disadvantages. In some cases, conventions from the original article have been preserved for reasons of internal cross-referencing and we have avoided dogmatic editorial changes that might present a false uniformity. Finally, though bibliographic information is given for all the articles included in this edition, a comprehensive bibliography of Rocher's writings has not been included, primarily because it would inevitably be incomplete in view of the fact that Rocher is still publishing. Remaining errors and inconsistencies, inevitable in a work of this size, are the responsibility of the editor.

Introduction

One of the most difficult challenges for any scholar is to master two intellectual traditions at once. European and American scholars of Asia have regularly had to contend not only with the deep intellectual heritage of Europe that sets the terms of discourse for almost all academia, but also with equally complex Indic, Chinese, or Islamic intellectual traditions, and vice-versa. In order to engage academic colleagues, it has always been incumbent to have a firm general grounding in the thought, rhetoric, and style of Western academia, beginning with the Greeks. At the same time, a thorough mastery of one or more Asian languages and Asian intellectual history is also required for any claim to authoritative scholarship to be substantiated and defensible. It has sometimes been too easy for scholars to dabble in the intellectual world of an Asian tradition without seriously and fully immersing themselves and their own thought in the presuppositions, logic, and hermeneutics of their chosen area.

This volume presents the work of one person who has successfully accomplished this difficult task and has imparted both the necessity of such dual mastery and the enthusiasm needed to achieve it to a host of students in over forty years of teaching. Prof. Ludo Rocher studied both law and Indology and received higher degrees in both from the University of Ghent in Belgium. In Europe, he studied Sanskrit with Adriaan Scharpe, Jan Gonda, Barend Faddegon, and C.A. Rylands. He also spent two years in Pune, India studying Indic intellectual traditions, especially Dharmaśāstra, under T.S. Srinivasa Sastri of Deccan College. Beginning in 1966, Rocher became Professor of Sanskrit at the University of Pennsylvania where he taught until his recent retirement. This brief academic pedigree, however, does not do justice to the range of knowledge from which Prof. Rocher has drawn or to which he has contributed.

It is, for instance, impossible to convey to non-Indologists how behind just one of Rocher's sidenotes on India's rich grammatical tradition lie years and years of training with Indian pandits. Conversely, for non-lawyers, it is hard to understand the depth of Rocher's knowledge of Roman and Civil law, because it, like Indian grammar, shows up indirectly and in a supporting role throughout these studies.

The selection of articles presented here, therefore, inevitably distorts to some extent the wider contributions that Rocher has made and the historical development of his ideas. Most, but not all, of the essays collected for this volume were written for Indological journals and make heavy use of the technical vocabulary and philological method found in that field. Presented together, the chapters elide their original contexts and, to some extent, their original purposes. Discerning readers will find patterns of interest and trends in Rocher's work that could be useful, for instance, for examining the field of Hindu law since Indian independence. The main purpose of the present collection, however, is simply to get these essential studies before a wider audience.

In this introduction to a nearly comprehensive collection of Rocher's writings on Hindu law and Dharmaśāstra, I will present an interpretive account of his many contributions to this field, organized around themes that recur in his work. At certain points comparisons and contrasts between Rocher's ideas and those of his Indological colleagues will also be made. The intent of the introduction is not to heap praise upon Rocher or his work (however deserving both may be), but rather to distill the key contributions he has made, both methodological and substantive, to this still important academic field. The broad nature of Rocher's interests in Hindu law and Dharmaśāstra also means that this introduction necessarily comments upon the current state of the field, without pretending to comprehend all the many avenues of investigation, both taken and not yet taken. The result is both a summary review of Rocher's ideas and a critical evaluation of the impact of those ideas on the present study of law, legal texts, and legal history in India.

The Nature of Hindu Law and Its Relation to Dharmaśāstra

If I had to select the most prominent theme in Rocher's understanding of Dharmaśāstra and its relation to Hindu law, it would certainly be his repeated and insistent argument that Dharmaśāstra is first and foremost a scholarly and scholastic tradition, not a practical legal tradition.[1] "Scholarly" and "legal" are not mutually exclusive categories and Rocher does not suggest otherwise. Instead, the distinction he draws points to the intention and purpose of the systematic efforts of the authors of Dharmaśāstra. Did they intend to create books or digests of positive law for use in functioning courts or were they rather concerned with the theological system of the *dharma* tradition, especially after and as articulated in Manu, the quintessential Dharmaśāstra text and the model and touchstone for all later Hindu legal texts (Olivelle 2005)? Even these options do not wholly exclude one another, but Rocher demonstrates time and again the necessity of first understanding the texts from the inside, of trying to recover and imagine the centrality of the theological systematization of *dharma* that Dharmaśāstra contains. Only then can against-the-grain readings that attempt to historicize Dharmaśāstra find a plausible intellectual foundation. Reversing the emphasis was a cardinal mistake of the British appropriation of Dharmaśāstra and remains a methodological approach in a variety of academic and professional legal literature on India.

In one general formulation of this thesis, Rocher states, "This author looks upon the compilers of the Dharmaśāstras primarily as pandits, who worked with a set of data which they tried —very hard, as they ought to— to arrange within a number of acceptable systems. Some of them, totally unknown to us, succeeded in elaborating such systems. From then onward, these systems remained unchanged" (1978: 1301). In his most recent general statement to this effect, Rocher combines the insight that Dharmaśāstra is in the first place a scholarly tradition with the equally important recognition that the work of scholars is not necessarily divorced from reality. Delineating two prevalent, but extreme views of the relation of Dharmaśāstra and law, Rocher writes:

> Either the information [of the texts]... is infinitely broad and detailed, allowing [the scholar] to reconstruct both substantive and adjective law in ancient India with a high degree of accuracy; or the entire corpus of classical Indian law books is untrustworthy and should be dismissed as a source of information on what really was the law of the land. I will suggest... that there is a better and more productive approach... than asking the single question whether or not they describe the law of the land... (1993: 260)

Rocher's solution to this problem is one that echoes in the work of Richard Lariviere and forms the basis for nearly all of my own efforts to situate Dharmaśāstra in history. In Rocher's words again:

[1] Olivelle's regular use of "expert tradition" seems indebted to Rocher here.

> What I wanted to show... is that it is possible, in a culture in which memorization plays an important role in day-to-day life, to have books, the *dharmaśāstras*, that are legal fiction because they were divorced from the practical administration of justice... but which are not for that reason the product of brahminical fantasy. They are books of law —rather, books of laws— containing... "rules and observations" that were, indeed, at some time and in some place "governing the life and conduct of people." (1993: 267)

Rocher's conclusion here is endorsed and elaborated by Lariviere in an important article recently reprinted in the *Journal of Indian Philosophy*'s special issue on *dharma*. Lariviere's critique (2004: 611) therein of an early statement by Rocher (1984) to the effect that commentaries and digests did not represent the law of the land and were "purely panditic, learned commentaries" is forceful, but does not fully negate Rocher's central point about the scholarly and scholastic nature of Dharmaśāstra. In fact, Lariviere's own position has been refined by Olivelle in ways that come closer to Rocher's idea. Olivelle writes, "Dharmaśāstra, however, represents an expert tradition and, therefore, presents not a simple record of customs [Lariviere's putative position] but a jurisprudential reflection on custom [Rocher's position, better expressed]. Custom is taken here to a second order of discourse, a discourse that the native tradition calls *śāstra*." (2004: xxxix, bracketed remarks added). What Rocher's solution does, especially as enhanced by two of his students, is permit the use of Dharmaśāstra for historical studies of law, but only when full recognition is given to the nature of the texts and the commitments of their authors. The solution allows us to negotiate the pitfalls of uncritical acceptance of Dharmaśāstra as history, on the one hand, and total rejection of Dharmaśāstra as panditic fantasy, on the other.

Embedded in this view of the relationship between Dharmaśāstra and Hindu law is an esteem for the intellectual achievement and the hermeneutic and aesthetic beauty of the "system" of Dharmaśāstra as a scholastic tradition. It is not from mere personal fancy that Rocher foregrounds the achievement and integrity of Dharmaśāstra as a prodigious feat of collective human intellect. He is insisting rather that Dharmaśāstra be appreciated on its own terms, no matter how remote its system may seem today. One gleans a sense of Rocher's view from the parenthetical aside in the first quotation above "they tried —*very hard, as they ought to*— to arrange... [emphasis added]." In my view, Rocher reveals here the extent to which he has absorbed the worldview of the authors whose work he admires and struggles to understand. That they "ought to" work very hard signals for a reader the deep engagement with the texts and their ideas that Rocher possesses and also provides some sense of the intellectual and possibly personal transformation in perspective he has experienced as a result of studying Dharmaśāstra and Hindu law. He has begun to think as the transmitters of Dharmaśāstra did. Such intellectual and personal transformations are the core of humanistic scholarship.

An illustrative example of Rocher's appropriation of the Dharmaśāstra modes of reasoning is contained in his short "defense" of the famed Dharmaśāstra commentator Jīmūtavāhana's view of gifts and the transfer of property (1976). Jīmūtavāhana's *Dāyabhāga* has been repeatedly criticized for advocating an incoherent law of gifts (Colebrooke, Kane, Ramaswami, and Derrett are named as accusers) such that a legal gift of property may be effected solely through the act of the donor. In other words, acceptance is allegedly not necessary for a valid gift. Rocher shows how an obsession with viewing Dharmaśāstra as legal codes has led a string of scholars and judges astray. The principal connection missed by others is that Jīmūtavāhana's argument rests on grammatical and not legal argumentation. With reference to three rules from the famed grammarian Pāṇini, Rocher takes us through the logic of Jīmūtavāhana's view of gifts, namely that it is grammatically and hermeneutically[2] unjustifiable to take the single verb *to give* as meaning both *to give and to receive*, with two different agents being implied. Rather, Jīmūtavāhana suggests, *to give* means a legal alienation in favor of someone who can recognize the gift as his and with a concomitant transfer of ownership to that person. *To receive*, then, means not to take ownership (for ownership can only be given), but rather to become aware of ownership, a key element in most legal theories of property in India.[3] This is a technical argument based on subtle rules of grammar that have been ignored by scholars interested only in the legal value of Dharmaśāstra. Of course, as Rocher points out, Jīmūtavāhana's argument dovetails nicely with his "larger ideas on ownership in the joint family property," but it also salvages two essential tools in the exegetical arsenal of Dharmaśāstra commentators, namely grammar and Mīmāṃsā hermeneutics. Jīmūtavāhana implicitly suggests that other commentators must contravene these exegetical principles to construct their theory of gifts. Rocher similarly suggests that modern commentators have allowed a presupposi-

[2] Though not mentioned explicitly by Rocher, the cardinal Mīmāṃsā principle against *vākya-bheda*, or "split of the sentence," seems to be at work here as well. Essentially, this principle means that a single rule should only enjoin one action, not two, i.e. only giving, not both giving and receiving.

[3] For a thorough study of property in India, see Derrett 1962 and the 2010 dissertation by Ethan Kroll from the University of Chicago.

tion, namely that Dharmaśāstras are legal texts like modern legal codes or legislation, to predetermine their interpretation, in this case a very negative judgment, of Jīmūtavāhana's reasoning.

For Rocher, it is imperative that we first understand the internal logic of texts like the *Dāyabhāga* before we begin to make historical judgments about the merits of its particular arguments. It is unfair to accuse Jīmūtavāhana of being a bad lawyer if he was never trying to be a lawyer in the first place. At the root of the problem is the failure of many modern scholars to enter deeply into the intellectual milieu of the authors they study by ignoring cognate disciplines such as grammar and hermeneutics that Dharmaśāstra authors took as fundamental to their work. Superficial readings of texts like Dharmaśāstra can lead then to a host of errors that stem from bringing modern scholarly concerns, especially about law and legal history, to a set of texts that presuppose a different educational background and speak to a different set of experts. It is only after a thorough training in and exposure to the internal Weltanschauung of Dharmaśāstra that one can delineate different kinds of arguments and can tease out ideas that might have social and historical origins from those that pertain to the rules of scholastic discourse and the theology of Dharmaśāstra.

Related to Rocher's view that Dharmaśāstra is foremost a scholarly tradition is his insistence that the subject of Dharmaśāstra is definitively *dharma*, and not law. There are two aspects of this position: 1) that the tradition or "system" of Dharmaśāstra shows remarkable consistency through time (Rocher 1984: 35), and 2) that the subject of *dharma* within Dharmaśāstra is similarly stable and does not become more law-oriented over time. Rocher's term "system" seems to refer simultaneously to both the process of composition and organization of Dharmaśāstras in a strict sense and, equally important, the hermeneutic tradition of interpreting those texts in the form of scholastic commentaries.

Contrary to Lingat and Derrett, Rocher rejects equating "the transition from *śāstra* to commentary with the passage from '*dharma* to law'" (1978: 1303). The commentarial literature in Dharmaśāstra was taken by the British and later scholars to be a refinement of the positions of the early *śāstra* texts in the light of changing historical circumstances and further legal developments. The commentaries were also held to contain more interest in the law itself. More specifically, Rocher shows how the commentators "became looked upon as lawyers, jurisconsults and lawgivers... [whose works] reflected the differing laws of the various regions of India" (1972c: 170) —most famously, Colebrooke's "schools of Hindu law" notion "that the *Dāyabhāga* prevailed in Bengal, whereas the *Mitākṣarā* prevailed in the province of Banaras, later changed into 'the rest of India'" (1972c: 171). It was Colebrooke's identification of the authors of Dharmaśāstra texts and commentaries as "lawyers" that gradually led to a privileging of the more familiarly legal portions of Dharmaśāstra. By contrast, Rocher states, "the commentaries do not in any way attach greater importance to the legal sections of the ancient texts than they do to any other sections of the *dharma*, nor do they treat them in any different way" (1978: 1303).[4] Stated more generally, "the commentators did not aim at introducing any novelties. Their sole purpose was a correct interpretation of the ancient texts as such" (1969: 394). What is at stake here is our understanding of Dharmaśāstra as a scholarly discipline. Rocher's consistent position has been that the commentaries are primarily products of the "system" of Dharmaśāstra (1978: 1301) —a scholarly and scholastic system that demonstrates remarkably stable techniques of interpretation and subject matter over a period of two thousand years or so.

I do not think Rocher is denying absolutely any development of thought or any intrusion of historical context into the Dharmaśāstra (see Rocher 1984). Rather, he is trying to ensure that if one wants to undertake an historical study of Dharmaśāstra —whether concerned with law, religion, ethics, ritual practice, or whatever— then, one should take into account as his/her initial starting point the fact that the commentators of Dharmaśāstra were not lawyers, did not divide their allegiances into schools of thought, and sought *primarily* to provide correct interpretations of earlier texts with hermeneutic techniques that were as old as the tradition itself and that were not *explicitly* concerned to bring the *dharma* in accord with contemporary situations.[5]

Rocher's emphasis on *dharma* as the subject of Dharmaśāstra concerns a related mistake that resulted in the privileging of the

[4] Compare also Rocher (1972a: 194): "It is an error of historical perspective to try to separate the religious element from legal matters in the traditional *Dharmaśāstra*."

[5] Rocher's point here and more generally, namely that Dharmaśāstra is not only a tradition of law, that its authors were not lawyers, and that its contents did not become more legal over time, differentiates him from Derrett, who maintained a typically British view that Dharmaśāstra was indeed the law of the land, even if supplemented by customary law. Derrett occasionally acknowledges the difficulties inherent in historical research using Dharmaśāstra, but ignores Rocher's positions in such a way that his conclusions are subject to the same criticisms that Rocher is making of the mistakes of Jones, Colebrooke, and the other early British Orientalists who mistook Dharmaśāstra for codes of law. Derrett's engagement with Rocher is eclectic, only using Rocher when it serves his point. The more profound insights of Rocher are dismissed: "In several articles and reviews Prof. Ludo Rocher has expressed reservations on this subject" (Smith and Derrett 1975: 419), referring precisely to the question of "the relation between the idealistic precepts of the *dharmaśāstra* itself and day-to-day practice" (ibid.).

vyavahāra division of Dharmaśāstra as the legal section, and a loss of interest in the *ācāra* and *prāyaścitta* divisions.[6] The unity of *dharma* as a combination of the three traditional divisions of *ācāra*, *vyavahāra*, and *prāyaścitta* was lost in the process.[7] K.V. Rangaswami Aiyangar had long ago pointed out the error of treating *vyavahāra* differently (1941: 23), but Rocher has amplified the position by highlighting the related error of treating the commentaries as qualitatively different in orientation and purpose than the *mūla*-texts themselves. This artificial elevation of *vyavahāra* presumes a distinction between religion and law in Dharmaśāstra —an argument supported by Derrett alone among Hindu law scholars.

If Dharmaśāstra is a scholarly discipline in the first place (and not a set of practical laws) and if *dharma* is a unified, but complex subject (that does not become more law-oriented over time), then what does Rocher think is the connection between Dharmaśāstra, *dharma*, and law, if anything? Here Rocher takes his cue from an early Western observer of India, Father Bouchet, a French Jesuit from Pondicherry. Bouchet, like Megasthenes 2000 years earlier, notes that the administration of law in his long acquaintance with India never occurred with reference to law books or written laws of any kind (Rocher 1984: 18). According to Rocher, "The main conclusion to be drawn from Bouchet's letter is that... law was administered on the basis of unwritten maxims, which were transmitted from generation to generation, in the local vernaculars, some of them applicable to the population of the area generally, others to specific groups such as the members of a particular caste only" (1993: 263). Indeed, Rocher refers at several places in his writings to the importance of maxims (see 1978: 1301–1304 and 1984: 34) in the practical law of India. He connects the importance of legal maxims several times with larger questions about orality in India and the unlikelihood of written laws having much impact in such a committedly oral environment (1993, 1994).

Although I have for a long time been frustrated by the maddening vagueness of phrases such as "floating maxims" and "traditional customs," Rocher's points about orality and the role of maxims are difficult to ignore. My own work in fact corroborates

[6] Derrett is probably the best-known perpetrator in this regard. He regularly refers to the *vyavahāra* sections of Dharmaśāstra as the sections dealing with "law as we know it." See, for example, Derrett 1968: 99 and Smith and Derrett 1975: 419. It is only fair to point out, however, that Rocher occasionally allows such slippage in his own work.

[7] This division is traceable to the *Yājñavalkyasmṛti* which is traditionally divided into three sections under these headings.

Rocher's thesis in the sense that the vocabulary of law in medieval Kerala says nothing about *dharma* and Dharmaśāstra directly and only speaks of *ācāra*, *maryādā*, *samaya*, and the like —terms that are closer to, though more specific than, the usual English rendering "custom." Similarly, ethnographic studies have shown the importance and prevalence of maxims (Tam., Mal. *paḻañcol*, *paḻamōḻi*, etc.) in colonial and contemporary India (Srinivas 1952, Dumont 1986). Maxims (Skt. *nyāya*) were also important in classical Dharmaśāstra texts and generally in Indic scholarly traditions (see Sarkar 1909 and Jacob 1911). However, Rocher does not make any connection between vernacular and Sanskritic maxims, nor does he explore the legal usage of either sort of maxim in any detail. To summarize Rocher's vision of law in traditional India, practical law in classical and medieval India did not rely directly on Dharmaśāstra, but rather on unwritten law and custom, captured in an abbreviated form in widespread maxims. Rocher does not elaborate upon this basic understanding because he feels constrained by the state of historical evidence for legal history in India.

With this simple description of practical law in mind, the distinction of Dharmaśāstra from "law-books" and *dharma* from law that Rocher has repeatedly made leads to an inexorable, but still difficult, conclusion. For classical and medieval India, *dharma* and Dharmaśāstra must be distinguished conceptually from Hindu law, at least if we mean by the latter term a practically functioning legal system. It is commonplace among Indologists and even specialists in Dharmaśāstra or Hindu law, including Rocher, to elide this distinction, to chalk it up to unfortunate terminological conflations of a colonial era. The explicit connection of Dharmaśāstra and Hindu law was indeed a link made first by early British administrators and it is proper and possible to speak of Anglo-Hindu law (the usual name for the colonial Hindu law) as derived initially on the basis of translations of Dharmaśāstra and the opinions of court pandits informed by those texts. Scholars occasionally discuss the problem, especially with clear recognition of the British misunderstandings in this regard, but they usually resolve not to fight tradition and accepted scholarly practice (I myself have done this more than once). The fact remains that a rather significant intellectual confusion and a perpetuation of widespread misperceptions of both Dharmaśāstra and Hindu law during the bulk of Indian history results from this intransigent and seemingly innocent pairing.

The question then arises whether it is appropriate to speak of "Hindu law" at all prior to the British coinage of the term. A question few, if any, scholars of classical, colonial, or modern Hindu law have ever bothered to ask is: what makes a legal system or set of legal rules Hindu? The obvious and correct answer must be Dharmaśāstra, but this response begs another question: if connection to or reliance on Dharmaśāstra makes a "system" Hindu, does it also make it law, and more particularly positive law, the "law of the land"? Rocher's response is an emphatic "no," despite the efforts of Kane, Derrett, Lingat, and others to argue, in a more sophisticated formulation of the basic colonial position, that Dharmaśāstra is and always has been the source of Hindu law, regardless of the paucity of evidence to demonstate that argument in those terms.

It would have been interesting and useful if Rocher had gone beyond his attempts to show the primarily scholastic, as opposed to legal, nature of Dharmaśāstra as a tradition. His contribution on this point has been largely negative, consisting of a series of well-argued counter-examples to demonstrate the nature of scholastic reasoning in remarkable technical detail and with great insight into the internal logic of Dharmaśāstra. In other words, Rocher has never offered a positive description of law in practice in classical and medieval India, with the rather vague exception of a reliance on "maxims and customs" already discussed. On this question, a great of deal research remains to be done. In particular, other historical evidence from India —epigraphy, archival materials, literary and other texts— must be examined for details about law and interpreted with an eye to understanding law in practice.[8] Any such research that involves Dharmaśāstra, however, must begin from an appreciation of the nature of the genre as primarily a scholastic tradition and from a deep engagement with the worldview, hermeneutics, and agendas of its authors. The necessity of this methodological and interpretive prerequisite has been the great contribution of Rocher to the study of Hindu law.

Hindu Legal Procedure

It is most interesting to read Rocher's studies of Hindu legal procedure (*vyavahāra*) after reading his general characterizations and topical studies of Hindu law and Dharmaśāstra because one immediately encounters the terminological difficulties in sustaining a discussion of Dharmaśāstra without resort to legal, and often very technical, vocabulary. Given his general view of Dharmaśāstra, one might expect Rocher to employ legal vocabulary only hesitantly when discussing philological or other sub-

[8] Ingo Strauch's recent German translation (2002) of the *Lekhapaddhati* and its annotations sets an excellent precedent for the kind of research that must be done for legal historical studies of India to move forward.

stantive points that emanate from these texts. Unfortunately, the texts themselves demand a legal interpretation in many places and it would be foolish and downright misleading to eschew the vocabulary of law in translating and explaining them.

The topic of legal procedure is discussed in immense detail in Dharmaśāstra, so much so that it becomes difficult to sustain an idea that such procedures were never implemented in courts. We should recall here that a fairly widespread scholarly consensus (Lariviere 2004) views *śāstra* in general as derived from practice, despite the internal view of *śāstra*s themselves that the rules came first and in fact created practice (Pollock 1989). What this means for Hindu legal procedure is that the many details of plaints, replies, judicial inquiries, evidence, bases for judgment, etc. probably have some origin in the actual practices of a court somewhere and sometime, though this history is completely obscured by the rhetorical idiom of Dharmaśāstra. In the almost complete absence of corroborating evidence for the functioning of courts,[9] however, an interpretation of textual descriptions of Hindu legal procedure as being connected to and derived from practice is based upon an educated guess. Moreover, it is also clear that many, perhaps most, elements and developments of Hindu legal procedure in Dharmaśāstra appear not in response to practice and changes in practice, but rather due to the systematizations of scholastic commentary described so forcefully in Rocher's work.

If we examine one of Rocher's best studies of Hindu adjective law as described in Dharmaśāstra, we get a better sense of the difficulties in holding together a view of Hindu law as connected to Dharmaśāstra with a view that attends to its practical manifestations. When it comes to Hindu legal procedure, the latter question is generally avoided by Rocher, who instead offers insightful histories of the textual developments on a number of key points relating to legal process in Dharmaśāstra.

On the question of the mixed reply (*saṃkīrṇottara*) to a plaint, Rocher describes a dramatic change in the permissibility of replying to different accusations of a plaint in different ways, for example, by denying one part while admitting another. Through a close reading of four discussions of the mixed reply in both early and later *dharma* texts, Rocher argues that the tradition generally seems to have passed through four stages of thought on whether mixed replies were permissible. Early authors such as

[9] See Lariviere 1984 for a late practical example of a functioning court that does follow Dharmaśāstra procedures. Given the late date of this *jayapattra*, however, it is conceivable that the adherence to the procedures is an artificial exercise or an invention of tradition.

Kātyāyana reject the mixed reply outright, but the later texts of Harita, Vijñāneśvara, and Vācaspati Miśra progressively interpret the mixed reply, respectively, as only partially permitted, as permitted but productive of separate trials for the distinct replies, and as permitted and judiciable in a single trial (1961: 386).

Rocher draws two conclusions from this change that deserve attention. First, he writes that a focus on the mixed reply serves as "an excellent example of the commentators' strenuous attempts to reconcile into a single harmonious structure the various authoritative texts they found at their disposal, contradictory as they may seem to be at a first glance" and that they "succeeded in bringing about this radical change without in any way detracting from their fundamental conception of the eternal and unalterable *dharma*" (1961: 386). In other words, Rocher's thesis that the system of Dharmaśāstra is always uppermost in the minds of its transmitters is preserved, despite the fact that starkly opposed legal conclusions have been reached and promoted over time. Rocher's understanding of the interpretive developments concerning the mixed reply leads to his second conclusion that "Hindu law has been capable of gradually passing on from a stage of strict and absolute formalism to a basically realistic system where equity and good sense became more and more preponderant" (1961: 387). Here we see a good example, common in the field as already mentioned, of linking a conclusion drawn from Dharmaśāstra as a scholastic tradition with a conclusion about Hindu law and, apparently, Hindu law in practice. To be fair, Rocher leaves the practicality of the change unexplored and does not make any strong or even clear claim that the change was manifest in practical legal contexts. Nevertheless, to use the mixed reply as a window on "Hindu law" implies some measure of practicality underlying the change. In the light of his general view of Dharmaśāstra, how can we explain Rocher's seemingly simple jump from an analysis of *dharma* texts to a claim about Hindu law?

Part of the answer lies in the intended audiences for Rocher's different essays. In his broader studies of the nature of Hindu law and Dharmaśāstra, written for general audiences in legal studies or philosophy, Rocher always emphasizes the limits on simplistic linkages between the two. In his studies that appear in Indological journals, by contrast, Rocher presumes a basic understanding of the relationship of Hindu law and Dharmaśāstra and does not feel compelled to repeatedly and distractingly define terms, when the point or the argument of the essay lies elsewhere. Thus, in the case of the mixed reply, an explicit discussion of the practicality issue would have necessitated an intrusive digression into an essay that is primarily an analysis of an evolution in scholastic interpretations. Most of the essays in this volume must be read with this consideration in mind —Rocher's work is usually intended for Indologists and he assumes prior knowledge of Indic textual and cultural history and Indic categories that allow him to make specific and new arguments without having to reinvent the wheel as a prolegomenon to each of his articles. One might wish that Rocher had taken at least a few more opportunities to clarify the terms and presuppositions he employs, but a good reading of his work demands an appreciation for the different audiences he addresses and a recognition that superficially contradictory statements may appear between his articles largely for this reason.

Another explanation returns to the difficulties of denying absolutely that Dharmaśāstra influenced and was influenced by practical life, both religious and legal. To speak of Hindu law means for Rocher to acknowledge the probable, though difficult to prove, connection of practical law and Dharmaśāstra. Hindu law becomes a provisional label, a purposefully vague designation for a legal reality that is approachable mainly through jurisprudential texts. Rocher views Hindu law as an imagined community, though he might not like the imputation of Anderson's ideas to his own. What the imagined community idea offers in this context, however, is a way of conceptualizing the system of Dharmaśāstra as simultaneously the product of an imaginative scholastic tradition and of a religio-legal reality that only partially conforms to what is imagined.

Hindu legal procedure was a central focus of Rocher's early work and the several articles he has written on the subject collectively articulate both the depth of thinking about adjective law in Hindu jurisprudence and the ingenious use of hermeneutic techniques for reinterpreting procedural issues over time. As with so many other issues in Hindu law, legal procedure in historical practice remains elusive but not totally beyond reach.

Topical and Technical Studies of Hindu Law and Dharmaśāstra

Perhaps the most important single methodological point to be gleaned from Rocher's work is the value of philology. The many articles collected here under the headings of topical and technical studies of Hindu Law attest powerfully to both the potential results and the clear restrictions on possible conclusions that emerge from the careful and informed reading of texts. Two examples from Rocher's many philological studies show the simultaneously widened and narrowed insights yielded by close readings.

Rocher's article on the technical term *anubandha* in Dharmaśāstra reveals the presence of an important legal concept, namely recidivism, in Hindu jurisprudence. *Anubandha* regularly appears in lists of factors to be considered in the determination of punishment. Previous studies —Rocher takes K.P. Jayaswal's as his example— understood *anubandha* in passages such as MDh 8.126 to refer to the cause or motive of a crime. In other words, many scholars had seen *anubandha* as kind of extenuating circumstance or motivation for a criminal act that mitigated the crime, and therefore its punishment, to some extent. Contrary to this interpretation, Rocher demonstrates that the term means "the wrongdoer's inclination or his propensity to committing offence... the internal mental condition of a man which continually puts him up to criminal activity" (1955: 228). Here Dharmaśāstra prescribes that recidivists or habitual offenders should receive harsher punishments, precisely because of their innate proclivity to crime. Though early translators such as Jolly had correctly understood *anubandha*, as Rocher points out, his careful examination of the commentarial glosses, usually some form of *punaḥpunaḥkaraṇam*, "committing [crimes] again and again," considerably clarifies this regularly encountered technical term in Dharmaśāstra and gives the term its proper legal sense.

The second example comes from Rocher's investigation of the opening of the third chapter of the Kauṭilīya *Arthaśāstra*, specifically the meaning of the much-debated phrase *vyāvahārikān arthān* in 3.1.1, "lawsuits arising from (legal) transactions." This section of the AŚ and another passage of Vyāsa/Uśanas became in due course the foundation for an important element of the colonial and modern Hindu law, the specification of a son's responsibility for his father debts. From the time of Colebrooke, a variety of meanings were attributed to debts that were not *vyāvahārika*, ranging from debts made from immoral motives to those incurred through folly or caprice to those that are simply "not usual" (1978: 18). The most widely accepted interpretation in modern Hindu law in fact conforms to Colebrooke's original characterization of *avyāvahārika* debts as "any debt for a cause repugnant to good morals." In this instance, Rocher actually diverges from the traditional commentators who "have restricted themselves to giving examples of *avyāvahārika*" leaving it to contemporary Indian lawyers to "find a common denominator for them" (20). Instead, Rocher proposes a reading that relies on three factors: 1) the syllogistic exposition of the passage where the phrase occurs, 2) the doubled denotation of *vyavahāra* as both general commerce or activity and legal procedure more particularly, and 3) the technical use of the verbs *sidh* and *kṛ* in this context. Rocher's conclusion is remarkably simple: *vyāvahārika* refers in this case to commerce or transactions conducted validly and legally. The opening of the section contains a syllogistic structure of rules, exceptions, and counter-exceptions and employs *vyavahāra* in both of its senses at the same time. Only transactions that are valid and legal are to be entertained by a court, meaning that only transactions meeting prima facie criteria for validity and legality should be moved to the investigative and evidentiary trial phase (*kriyā*). In terms of a son's responsibilities, Rocher views the matter as considered in Vyāsa/Uśanas and in modern Hindu law in straightforward terms: a son should be responsible only for those debts that arise from transactions conducted validly and legally; other claims of debt should be rejected by the court on the grounds that the original transaction was null and void. Through a careful analysis of the language and structure of this old text, Rocher is able to cut through a morass of contemporary errors emanating telescopically from Colebrooke's original rendering. In the process, he eliminates the idea that a father's debt could be nullified on the grounds of immorality, folly, or caprice, each of which begs the question of a standard for judgment. Instead, Rocher argues that the passage merely states the common legal principle that only legally valid debt-claims may be adjudicated in a court and, by extension, directed toward a person's heirs. Other kinds of debt-claims —from illegal gambling, from improper fiduciary arrangements, or from invalid contracts— should not be considered by a court as matters of law.

The conclusions in both of these examples restrict the interpretive sphere in one way and expand it in another. In the case of *anubandha*, the more prevalent interpretation of *anubandha* as a kind of extenuating circumstance or justification, interesting as it would be if it were accurate, is denied or checked by a concomitant expansion of the meaning of the term in the very different direction of repeated offenses and recidivism. Similarly, with *vyavahāra*/ *avyāvahārika* the received interpretation of Colebrooke with its many attendant ambiguities about what is moral is set aside in favor of a simpler explanation that pays attention to the specific language and structural context of the terms and suggests that the real significance of the passage is its expression of a widespread legal principle. In both articles, the philological method is the key to exposing a new, more accurate reading of the text and its wider implications. As is so common in his work, here again it is Rocher's sensitive appropriation of the reasoning and training used and presumed by the authors of Dharmaśāstra that allows him to give a fresh and more plausible interpretation of the texts. Most of the articles collected in this volume fall into this pattern —a methodical presentation of evidence from the Dharmaśāstra tradition ends with a modest conclusion that often attempts to emend previous conclusions.

The Transition from Traditional to Modern Hindu Law

The final contribution of Rocher's that I would like to explore briefly is his view of the transition from traditional to modern Hindu law, both the ideological and the practical aspects of this much-discussed transition. Though I think it hard to dispute that Derrett has made the most comprehensive studies on this question, Rocher brings a different perspective to the problem that is noteworthy. Derrett's work provides very detailed insight into the phases of transition, the principal actors involved, and the ironies and misunderstandings entailed. Occasionally, however, Derrett seems to lack analytical neutrality and becomes quite aggresive in his criticisms of both Indian and British legal opinions. Rocher avoids both the modern apologetics of the nationalist-period writing on Hindu law (exemplified, for instance, in the work of P.V. Kane) and British justifications of the consequences of their colonial policies on law in India.[10] Nationalist writing is characterized by a mission to demonstrate the viability of classical Hindu law, its purportedly modern ideas, and its equal status to other legal systems of the world. British colonial accounts similarly defend the system created and choices made under their political rule. Like Derrett, Rocher criticizes simplistic calls for a return to classical Hindu law and acknowledges forthrightly the mistakes and misunderstandings of the British views of Hindu law.

For example, Rocher (1972b), like Marc Galanter (1972) and others, argues that Hindu law as developed (some would say invented) by the British was a radical departure from traditional Hindu law, but a departure that was readily appropriated by the Indians to the extent that by the time of Independence, it was Indians who were among the most vocal in advocating the preservation of the Anglo-Hindu law. The idea that Anglo-Hindu law was so different was a hard pill to swallow in Britain, for it implied a long series of mistakes and, worse, purposeful distortions of law in India —a direct contradiction of their stated policy to apply native law to the natives. In his capacity as a scholar and not a lawyer, Rocher is concerned with accurate and responsible representation of the history of law in India, not with policy. To this end, he insists that we must be willing to acknowledge differences, changes, and mistakes in the study of Dharmaśāstra and Hindu law, even when these show us or previous scholars in a bad light.

[10] By "nationalist" and "colonial," I do not intend to give these terms any pejorative sense or to suggest an *extraordinary* bias, but rather I am merely indicating an important historical context for the production of scholarship.

At the same time, he sympathizes with modern apologists' efforts to separate religion and law without assenting to their arguments (1972a), to codify Hindu law or pursue a Uniform Code (1984), and to secure a practicable system of law that acknowledges the historical circumstances of India's emergence as an independent and sovereign modern nation (1972b).

One of the best short summaries of the transition from traditional to colonial Hindu law is found in Rocher's presidential address to the American Oriental Society (1987). There he spells out very clearly the main factors involved in the radical changes introduced in the Hindu law tradition by the British, including linguistic obstacles, cultural misunderstandings, flawed translations, the insinuations of case law, and the application of British moral standards. Rocher's main interest in the colonial and modern forms of Hindu law has been the moment of colonial appropriation of the Hindu law, and especially the role of the early Orientalists such as Colebrooke in the transition. Recently, he completed a biography of Colebrooke in collaboration with Rosane Rocher (2011), whose own work on the biographies of early Indologists is essential.

Philology, Humanism, and Orientalism

To summarize Rocher's contributions to the fields of Dharmaśāstra and Hindu law, I would concentrate on three words —philology, empathy, and reserve. Each is related to the other and together they constitute an epitome of the method and values that underlie Rocher's work. As a final observation to this introduction to Rocher's shorter studies, I would like to do what Rocher's reserve and humility would never allow him to do himself— to place his contributions in a larger framework of humanistic scholarship.

Rocher is in many ways proud to be part of a much maligned lineage of Orientalist scholars, whose mastery of Asian languages and texts has for more than thirty years now been attacked by some and defended by others, even as it was attacked by the English Utilitarians over 150 years ago for very different reasons. It may be ironic, but also appropriate, then to bring the ideas of the most famous critic of Orientalism, Edward Said, to bear on Rocher's work, and vice-versa.

It is by now a well-known criticism of Said's thesis that he indiscriminately lumps together all Western study of Asia under his peculiarly broad sense of Orientalism[11] without attending to the very

[11] Said initially defines an Orientalist according to the "most readily accepted designation for Orientalism" as "anyone who teaches, writes about, or

clear denotations of the term in the eighteenth and nineteenth century (Rosane Rocher 1993, Trautmann 1997). Of course, this does not at all vitiate the vital impact of his thesis, but it does create a space for an important distinction between Orientalisms, and specifically a more positive valuation of the work of the self-proclaimed Orientalists. Said's retort to this criticism merely reasserts his fundamental doubt that "Orientalism properly understood can ever, in fact, be completely detached from its rather more complicated and not always flattering circumstances" (1979: 341). No possibility to distinguish the work and attitudes of different persons is acknowledged here; all are equally tainted and convicted by the *ism*: "all academic knowledge about India and Egypt is somehow tinged and impressed with, violated by, the gross political fact" (ibid.: 11). It is precisely the slippage from idea to person that is objected to in this criticism of Said, which Rocher undoubtedly shares. It is ironic and unfortunate that Said's remarks on humanism are at times incommensurate with his remarks on Orientalism for his laudatory descriptions of a humanisitic philology could and should be applied to many, though by no means all, Orientalists:

> Positive knowledge of languages and history was necessary, but it was never enough... The main requirement for the kind of philological understanding Auerbach and his predecessors were tallking about and tried to practice was one that sympathetically and subjectively entered into the life of the written text as seen from the perspective of this time and its author (*eingefüllen*). (1994: xxv)

And more recently:

> ...to be able to understand a humanistic text, one must try to do so as if one is the author of that text, living the author's reality, undergoing the kind of life experiences intrinsic to the author's life, and so forth, all by that combination of erudition and sympathy that is the hallmark of philological hermeneutics. (2004: 92)

I cannot think of a more apt description of the approach to Dharmaśāstra and Hindu law that Rocher takes. But Said's propensity to speak of Orientalism rather than Orientalists precludes the possibility that his vision of humanism and philology might be applied in meaningful and helpful ways to the work and lives of specific scholars. And yet, as I have tried to show with respect

researches the Orient —and this applies whether the person is an anthropologist, sociologist, historian, or philologist..." (1979: 2). Immediately, there are problems with this definition for it is much too broad, imputes a label to social scientists that had been reserved for humanists, and fails to distinguish self-proclaimed appellations from external labels.

to the work of Rocher and as Said's reflections on humanism demand, *serious* engagment with language, history, and text almost automatically produces a transformation in the scholar. By serious, I mean "sympathetic" and "subjective" in Said's sense or hermeneutic in Gadamer's (1975) or even Ricoeur's (1981), i.e. a type of scholarly engagement in which the scholar is always implicated in, convicted by, and impressed with what is being studied.

It is clear that Said's warnings about essentialism and the failure to be self-aware and self-critical in scholarship accuse us all, Rocher not excepted, and it would indeed be remarkable if there were *not* regular slips in thought and expression that reflect the prejudice exposed by Said's sense of Orientalism rather than his sense of humanism. But where is it said that scholars need always to be self-consistent and that one cannot be both Orientalist and humanist, whether the former be taken narrowly or broadly? Rocher, it seems to me, exemplifies just such a scholar, and it strikes me as unimaginable to think that he is the first Orientalist to be also a humanist in Said's sense.

There is one element of Said's humanism which Rocher would not find acceptable, namely the claim that humanism is by nature political, even politically subversive (2004: 71ff.). This claim is the real link between Said's notions of Orientalism and humanism, namely Foucault's idea that power and knowledge are connected in specific historical ways. Readers can judge for themselves whether Rocher's work entails or reifies certain political structures —the judgments are likely to diverge widely. Still, because Said argues that humanism is best pursued through philology, it may be worthwhile to investigate what is meant by philology here.

Recalling for a moment Rocher's reserve, or reluctance to make grand claims or conclusions, it is important to note that the emphasis on broad, general questions in this introduction is precisely the opposite of the methodology advocated and employed in the articles collected here. Rocher prefers short studies of a precise philological point to ruminations on the nature of difficult categories such as Hindu law, and the vast majority of the articles that follow exemplify this preference. It is possible to criticize Rocher, one of the few modern scholars to immerse himself in traditional understandings of Indic texts, for not using that special gift and training to provide surveys and overviews of the Hindu law tradition, but this criticism presumes that Rocher should want to write introductory works and that it is some kind of failure that he did not do so more frequently.[12] Such a view of

[12] Exceptions are, of course, found in Part One of this volume on the nature of Hindu law.

Rocher's work is mistaken, however, because Rocher's approach to scholarship places the greatest value on the particular, not the general. It is here that Rocher, representing the continued heritage of the early Orientalists, diverges most dramatically from the philology advocated by Said. In other words, the choice is a conscious one —an argument expressed and validated through repeated exemplifications, rather than self-critical reflection. Rocher would no doubt find Said's philology to be too insistent on big generalizations and premature in its grand gestures in the absence of the necessary and needed particulars that might enable such speculations. Conversely, Said might find Rocher's philology to be too hesitant to conclude, intellectually unreachable in its technical specificity, and insufficiently self-critical. There are merits in both approaches, though it seems unlikely that a widespread rapprochement will be reached any time soon. And this is really unfortunate, because it is precisely the pejorative and insulting connotation of Orientalism in Said's sense today that prevents a large segment of scholars of South Asia from seeing the value of the philological particular, pursued for so long in the lineage of Orientalists properly so called. Rocher is a master of that Orientalist philology and of the humanism it entails. To read his work without an appreciation of this deep humanism, careful philology, and intellectual humility is to miss an essential part of his contribution to scholarship.

Part One

The Nature of Hindu Law

1

Hindu Conceptions of Law

Any discussion of Hindu conceptions of law has to start with the basic observation that nowhere in the Hindu tradition is there a term to express the concept of law, neither in the sense of *ius* nor in that of *lex*. Not until the arrival of the colonial powers was the concept of law used on the subcontinent, by Europeans and through the medium of European languages. It was not until 1772, the year in which it was decided that, "in all suits regarding inheritance, marriage, caste, and other religious usages or institution" (Acharyya 1914), the Hindus should be governed by their own laws, that an effort was made to study and translate the Sanskrit books in which the Hindu laws were codified. These books happen to be the Dharmaśāstras, treatises on *dharma*. Hence, the equation established by the Western editors and translators of these books was "*dharma-śāstra*" equals lawbook, code, or institute. They also established the equation: *dharma* equals law.[13]

To be sure, Indians have followed this well-established practice.[14] When it comes to expressing the concept of law in modern India through the medium of modern Indian languages, how-

[13] Note, for example, the following titles: *Institutes of Hindu Law, or the Ordinances of Manu* (Jones 1794); *The Institutes of Manu* (Haughton 1825); *Lois de Manou* (Deslongchamps 1830–33); *Yājñavalkyas Gesetzbuch* (Stenzler 1849); *The Ordinances of Manu* (Burnell 1884); *The Laws of Manu* (Bühler 1886); and *The Code of Manu* (Jolly 1887). [Ed. note: one could now add to this list the more recent titles *The Laws of Manu* (Doniger and Smith 1991) and *The Law Code of Manu* (Olivelle 2004), the latter of which at least justifies the usage in self-conscious reflection on this problem].

[14] See, for example, G. Jha, *The Laws of Manu*. Jha began this translation in 1920.

ever, different terms are used. For instance, recent dictionaries of India's official language, Hindi, normally give two terms for law, one borrowed from the Arabic-Persian (Muslim) tradition, *kānūn,* and one from the Sanskrit (Hindu) tradition, *vidhi.* In addition, when the Indian Constitution was translated into Hindi, *vidhi*[15] became the official translation for law, both in the text of the Constitution and in the English-Hindi wordlist published along with it by the Government of India.

The reason why modern Indian languages looked for different terms to express law may, at least in part, have been due to the fact that, in the meanwhile, they had all accepted *dharma* as the Indian equivalent for another concept imported from the West —religion. It is not quite clear when and by whom *dharma* was first used in the restricted sense of religion. One thing is sure, however, it represents a conscious effort to find, for a category that had no equivalent in India, a word from the Indian vocabulary which, even though it was not perfectly identical, came at least closer than any other available term.

Dharma and Law

After the above introductory remarks, this article will now attempt to interpret the data as they emerge from the Hindu tradition. The pivot of the entire system is *dharma,* which is neither religion nor law, and yet crucial for the topic of this article —the Hindu conceptions of law. *Dharma* has been rightly described as "one of those Sanskrit words that defy all attempts at an exact rendering in English or any other tongue" (Kane 1930–62: 1.1). It is therefore essential to approach it from within the Hindu tradition, and describe how classical Hinduism itself understood it.

Dharma[16] is a noun formed with the suffix °*ma*[17] from a root *dhar* or *dhṛ*. The root expresses actions such as to hold, bear, carry, maintain, preserve, keep. Hence, *dharma* is the way in which, or the means by which, one holds, bears, carries, or maintains, and, in accordance with semantic development common in Sanskrit, it means not only the *way* of doing these things, but also *the* way of doing them. *Dharma,* then, is the way in which one ought to hold, bear, carry, or maintain. On a cosmic level, *dharma* is the way in which one maintains everything, the way in which

[15] *Vidhi* is a traditional term, meaning "injunction," referring to those sections of the Vedas that contain actual rules rather than other sections that are merely explanatory.

[16] For bibliographical studies on *dharma,* see Rocher 1965 and Sternbach 1973.

[17] Compare *-men* in Latin *carmen, -ma* in Greek *rheuma.*

the cosmos or the balance in the cosmos, is maintained. At the micro-level, *dharma* is the way in which every constituent element of the cosmos contributes its share to maintaining the overall balance. Each element has its own *dharma,* its *svadharma.* As long as each element of the cosmos performs its specific *svadharma,* the overall balance does not suffer. As soon as an element, however, deviates from its own *dharma,* that is, commits *adharma,* the balance is disturbed.

Theoreticians of *dharma* will, of course, insist on the fact that every cosmic element has its *svadharma.* The sun is supposed to rise in the morning and to set at night; water —the rains— has to arrive at a set time of the year and disappear at another set time. In practice, however, Hindus have primarily paid attention to the *dharma* of human beings. Each individual human being has a *svadharma,* which is determined essentially by two factors: belonging to one of the four stages of life (*āśrama*); and belonging to one of the four social classes (*varṇa*). From these two factors comes the expression, *varṇāśrama-dharma.*

For a better understanding of the Hindu conception of law, one characteristic of the human *dharma* deserves to be pointed out above all. A person's *dharma* regulates all activities, whatever their nature. The *dharma* ordains when the individual shall awaken, how that person shall divide the day, and when the person shall retire at night. The *dharma* rules a person's diet, quantitatively and qualitatively. The *dharma,* of course, regulates the human's relationship to the supernatural powers, and prescribes the rituals and ceremonies by which these relations shall be sustained; it therefore deals with the Hindu's religion. *Dharma* also governs the individual's relations with fellow people; it rules social contacts, many aspects of which belong to the field of law. To put it differently, Hindu law is, together with every other aspect of a Hindu's activities, part of Hindu *dharma.* Hindu rules of law are to be found in the Dharmaśāstras, but these texts also contain a variety of other rules which have little or nothing in common with law.

A first important consequence of the concept of *dharma* is that, in Hinduism, law, religion, and all other topics dealt with in the Dharmaśāstras are inextricably intertwined. All attempts to disentangle the various categories and to label particular concepts or institutions as essentially religious or essentially legal, are bound to force upon them categorizations which are foreign to the Hindu way of thinking.

An example is the implication, in classical Hinduism, of committing what Western society would call a crime: killing a human being; more specifically, killing a member of the highest class, a Brahmin. Not to complicate the description, this examination shall restrict itself to quoting from a single text, the Dharmaśāstra attributed to Manu (Bühler 1886). First, killing a Brahmin is ranked among the four great sins, *mahāpātaka* (MDh 9.235). Subsequently, punishment for great sins is said to be corporal punishment (MDh 9.236): in the specific case of killing a Brahmin, the brand of a headless corpse on the offender's forehead (MDh 9.237). This rule is followed by a number of social implications:

> Excluded from all fellowship at meals, excluded from all sacrifices, excluded from instruction and from matrimonial alliances, abject and excluded from all religious duties, let them wander over (this) earth. Such (persons) who have been branded with (indelible) marks must be cast off by their paternal and maternal relations, and receive neither compassion nor a salutation; that is the teaching of Manu. (MDh 9.238–239)

The text continues that corporal punishment (MDh 9.240) may be replaced by the highest fine, if the killer at the same time performs a variety —too long to enumerate here— of intricate penances described in great detail elsewhere in the text (MDh 11.73–87, 90). Manu then makes the usual distinction between the case in which the crime was committed by a Brahmin and by someone belonging to a lower class; the former has to be less severely punished than the latter (MDh 9.241–42). Finally, in another chapter, the text describes the fate of the killer of a Brahmin in the next rebirth: "The slayer of a Brahmana enters the womb of a dog, a pig, an ass, a camel, a cow, a goat, a sheep, a deer, a bird, a Caṇḍāla, and a Pukkasa" (MDh 12.55).

In short, killing a Brahmin was a transgression of *dharma*, with all the consequences thereof. The transgression implies a criminal element requiring punishment by the king, an element of sin to be expiated by performing penances, and an element of exclusion from one's usual social circles. It is also to be noted that the Hindu penal code is strongly influenced by the caste system. For the same offense a member of a lower class is more severely punished than one of a higher class (a Brahmin is totally exempt from any kind of corporal punishment), with the correlative provision that, for the same offense, punishment is higher or lower depending on whether the victim is of a higher or lower class. Also, Hindu crime extends beyond this life, and is linked to the theory of rebirth.

The extent to which private law was interwoven with other categories cannot be better illustrated than by referring to some of the difficulties which the British judges were to experience when they were called upon to apply the *dharma* texts as legal codes in the Anglo-Hindu law courts. They soon came to the conclusion: "All those old text-books and commentaries are apt to mingle religious and moral considerations, not being positive laws, with rules intended for positive laws."[18] No matter how much they were concerned not to interfere with the religious beliefs of the Hindus —a concern that is expressed over and again in the law reports— they decided that "the Courts are to enforce only rules of positive law and not religious or moral precepts" (Gupte 1947).

One of the simplest applications of this position concerns the validity of adoption. The Sanskrit texts clearly require that, for an adoption to be valid, a particular ritual, called *dattahoma*, has to be performed. The question arose, whether or not the *dattahoma* was a legal prerequisite for adoption, the legal character of which was, of course, never doubted. The dilemma was described as follows:

> In certain circumstances the point might be the subject of a prolonged and very conflicting argument, as the authorities, ancient and modern, are not in accord on the point as to whether this is a legal as well as a religious requisite. There is a danger, on the one hand, of not paying due respect to those religious rites which are observed and followed among large classes of Indian belief, while, on the other hand, the danger must also be avoided of carrying these, except when the law is clear, into the legal sphere, so as to affect or impair personal or patrimonial rights.[19]

The result was that, in Anglo-Hindu courts, the legal act, adoption, was separated from the religious act, *dattahoma*, and that the former was held valid without the latter (Aiyar 1950).

Another, more complex, example involves both adoption and inheritance. The *dharma* texts forbid adoption of an only son. Vasiṣṭha, for instance, allows the father to give, sell, or abandon his son, but adds the proviso, "let him not give or receive (in adoption) an only son" (VaDh 15.2–3). In a case that was to become very influential, the Privy Council reiterated their view that one should not "take for strict law precepts which are meant to appeal to the moral sense," and decided that the adoption of an only son is not null and void under the Hindu law.[20]

Although the *dharma* texts rarely exhibit justification for their statements, the rationale of Vasiṣṭha's rule is clear. The text is obviously concerned about the fact of the natural father who becomes deprived of his only son. The son is, of course, the natural heir of his father. At the same time, however, he is much more than that; he frees his father "from his debt to the Manes" (MDh 9.106, VaDh 11.48), and, after the father's death, he is the only person capable of performing the ritual, called *śrāddha*, which is required for the father to join the ranks of his ancestors. This

[18] *Rao Balwant Singh v. Rani Kishori*, 25 I.A. 54, 69 (1898).

[19] *Bal Gangadhar Tilak v. Shrinivas Pandit*, 42 I.A. 135, 148–49 (1915).

[20] *Sri Balasu v. Sri Balasu*, 26 I.A. 113, 136 (1889).

example not only explains why an only son should not be the object of an adoption; it also shows that what we call inheritance in Hinduism involves far more than the legal rights to an estate.

The Privy Council became acutely aware of the scope of Hindu inheritance when they were faced with a murderer claiming the estate of his victim. The Council stated:

> Before this Board it has been contended that the matter is governed by Hindu Law, and that the Hindu Law makes no provision disqualifying a murderer from succeeding to the estate of his victim, and therefore it must be taken that according to this law he can succeed.[21]

It was seen earlier that the Hindu *dharma* does not condone murder. On the contrary, it is both a crime and a sin. The problem confronting the Privy Council lies elsewhere: who are, according to the *dharma*, those who are disqualified from succeeding to an estate, and, more importantly, what is the underlying justification? Manu has the following enumeration: "Eunuchs and outcasts, (persons) born blind or deaf, the insane, idiots and the dumb, as well as those deficient in any organ (of action or sensation), receive no share" (MDh 9.201). Murderers are not among them. Those listed in the text as "incompetent to receive a share" are individuals who are unable to administer it, and, also, to perform for the deceased the necessary funeral rites. In this case, the Privy Council decided to overrule Hindu law: "The alternative is between the Hindu law being as above stated or being for this purpose non-existent, and in that case the High Court have rightly decided that the principle of equity, justice and good conscience exclude the murderer."[22]

Sources of Law

Another consequence of the Hindu concept of *dharma* is that law shares its basic features with religion and all other categories treated in the Dharmaśāstras. To illustrate this point this article will first present a brief description of these texts, and then it will examine the characteristics of their contents generally and their legal materials in particular.

[21] *Kenchava v. Girimallappa Channappa*, 51 I.A. 368, 372–73 (1924).

[22] Section 25 of the Hindu Succession Act, 1958, states: "A person who commits murder or abets the commission of murder shall be disqualified from inheriting the property of the person murdered, or any other property in furtherance of the succession to which he or she committed or abetted the commission of the murder."

The source materials for our knowledge of classical Hindu *dharma* are primarily the Dharmasūtras and Dharmaśāstras. Although the latter term is also used collectively for both kinds of texts, the principal difference is that the *sūtras* are older, and composed in the succinct and often enigmatic prose style used in many other branches of Hindu learning (such as *Yogasūtras*, *Vedāntasūtras*, and Pāṇini's grammatical *sūtras*). The most important Dharmasūtras are those attributed to Gautama, Āpastamba, Vasiṣṭha, and Baudhāyana (Bühler 1879). They may have been composed between 600 and 300 BC.[23]

The more recent Dharmaśāstras are in verse, in the typical thirty-two syllable distichs called *śloka* or *anuṣṭubh*, which are characteristic not only of the Sanskrit epics but also of learned treatises in many fields such as medicine and architecture.[24]

Closely related to the Dharmaśāstras are the epics and the Purāṇas. Long passages from these texts are devoted to various aspects of *dharma*, including legal topics. In fact, many verses and passages are more or less identical with verses and passages in the Dharmaśāstras. The question of which text, in such cases, is the borrower, and which the one borrowed from, is one that is bound to tempt Western, or Western-trained, philologists. For the present purposes, the solution of these problems is less important than the fact that the same legal materials that occur in the Dharmaśāstras, are also found in epic and bardic literature. The later commentators were to quote from the epics and the Purāṇas, perhaps not as often as from the Dharmaśāstras, but definitely giving all those sources the same legal authority.

The beginning of this century saw the discovery, in South India, of a manuscript of a text which had been known only through a few indirect references. The title of the book is *Arthaśāstra*,[25] it is attributed to an author variously called Kauṭilya or Kauṭalya, and other names, who may have been the minister of Candragupta, the famous Maurya emperor in the third century BC. This book exhibits a large amount of legal materials, and, especially, provides a totally new, detailed account of Hindu

[23] The date of theses texts are, like the dates of most Sanskrit texts, highly uncertain. See Kane 1930–62.

[24] The most important texts of this catagory are attributed to Manu (200 BC–AD 100), Yājñavalkya (AD 100–300), Viṣṇu (AD 100–300), Nārada (AD 100–400), Bṛhaspati (AD 300–500), and Kātyāyana (AD 400–600). There are also numerous minor metrical Dharmaśāstras, some of which have been preserved, often in larger collections, whereas others are known only from quotations in later commentarial literature. Dates are from Kane 1930–62. See note 15; Viṣṇu in Jolly 1880; Nārada and Bṛhaspati in Jolly 1889; Kātyāyana in Kane 1933; Yājñavalkya in Stenzler 1849.

[25] See Shamasastry 1923, Meyer 1929, and Kangle 1965.

administrative law. Indic scholars have rarely been as excited as they were by the discovery of Kauṭilya's *Arthaśāstra*, and in a short period of time a vast scholarly literature on Hindu society and law developed, based on Kauṭilya, using the newly discovered book as their principal source, it being considered superior to the well-known Dharmaśāstras and allied texts. This author shall place the *Arthaśāstra*, as a source of law, in its correct perspective later in this article.

Vedic Basis of Hindu Law

The *dharma* literature does not exist in a vacuum, according to the Hindu tradition. On the contrary, it has a well-determined place within a larger literary framework, with important consequences for the Hindu conception of law. First, the Dharmasūtras each belong directly to one of the branches of the Vedas. Together with other *sūtras*, such as the Śrautasūtras, which regulate the most elaborate ritual, the Gṛhyasūtras, which describe the more modest house ritual, and the Śulbasūtras, which are devoted to the correct construction of the sacrificial altar, the Dharmasūtras form the class of Kalpasūtras. One such Kalpasūtra exists in each branch of the Vedas. Within each branch the *sūtras* attach themselves to the earlier Āraṇyaka, via the Āraṇyaka to the Brāhmaṇa, and ultimately, to the basic Saṃhitā. Thus, the Dharmasūtra attributed to Vasiṣṭha belongs to the *Ṛgveda*, that of Gautama to *Sāmaveda*, and those of Āpastamba and Baudhāyana to the Taittirīya branch of the Black Yajurveda.

The way in which the versified Dharmaśāstras are related to Vedic literature is less clear. An idea, first proposed by Max Müller (1859), and further elaborated by Bühler (1886) in the introduction to his translation of Manu, was that the Dharmaśāstras are versified recasts of earlier and lost prose Dharmasūtras. In this way the *śāstras*, too, belong to specific branches of the Vedas. The Dharmaśāstras attributed to Manu would then belong to the Maitrāyaṇīya branch of the Black Yajurveda, and that attributed to Kātyāyana to the Vājasaneyi branch of the White Yajurveda.

According to a different theory, the Dharmaśāstras came into being at a time when Hinduism was threatened nearly simultaneously by Buddhism and Jainism (vom Bradke 1882). To react successfully against these threats it was felt necessary to eliminate the differences between schools and couch the texts in a more popular and more easily accessible form. The result was that the historical, vertical sequence of *saṃhitā-brāhmaṇa-āraṇyaka-sūtra*, within each branch of the Vedas was replaced with a horizontal cross sequence, each of which specialized in one particular topic across school boundaries, *in casu*: *dharma*.

The important point here is that all the texts on *dharma* derive more or less directly from the Veda. The standard phrase is *vedo dharmasya mūlam*, "the root of the *dharma* is the Veda." Veda and *dharma* are, in many ways, synonymous. This premise has important consequences for the nature of the rules on *dharma* and, hence, for the Hindu conception of law. The Veda was not created by men. It has been revealed by a number of privileged sages who subsequently transmitted it to mankind. The Revelation, (*śruti*) *stricto sensu*, comprehends only the Saṃhitās and Brāhmaṇas, and most often extends to the Āraṇyakas and Upaniṣads. The various *sūtras*, including the Dharmasūtras and Dharmaśāstras, technically belong to a less direct type of revelation, *smṛti*, often translated as "tradition" to distinguish it from revelation. The epics and Purāṇas also belong to this category. This distinction, however, is unimportant for present purposes. The main point to be remembered is that the Veda, and therefore the *dharma*, and, for that reason, law, are, for the orthodox Hindu, perfect, complete, eternal, and, above all, not to be altered through human intervention.

Comprehensiveness of Hindu Dharma and Law

In reality, the situation is far more complex than the above portrays. Even though the useful *Dharmakośa* "Encyclopedia of Dharma,"[26] under most headings, starts its quotations with the extracts from the Vedas, and notwithstanding assertions that the Veda provides information of "considerable importance" on *dharma* (Dharwar 1936), even a casual observer will notice that there are hardly any rules of *dharma* and even less rules of law in the *śruti*.

The extent to which *dharma* has a Vedic basis may be illustrated with the following example. Yājñavalkya lays down as one of the qualifications required of an acceptable bride the necessity for her to have a brother (YDh 1.52–53). Indeed, the *Ṛgveda* points, at least twice, to the low reputation of a woman who has no brother; she is tempted to deviate from the right path because she is unable to acquire a regular husband. In addition, Vasiṣṭha indicates the reason why such a woman is unacceptable as a bride: "[a] maiden who has no brothers comes back to the male ancestors (of her own family); returning she becomes their son" (VaDh 17.16). The text even adds that this fact "is declared

[26] L.S. Joshi ed. (1937–41). It lists, solely in Sanskrit, all the ancient texts, together with extracts from commentaries, relative to specific topics of *dharma*. The legal section is in three volumes.

in the Veda" (VaDh 17.16). From the above example comes the orthodox conclusion that the rules of Yājñavalkya and Vasiṣṭha have a Vedic basis, and that the passages from the *Ṛgveda* are illustrations of their rules in Vedic times.

Elsewhere, at a much higher intellectual level, the tradition does recognize that the *dharma*, taught by the Veda, is far from complete. Primarily the highly sophisticated Mīmāṃsā, has developed a number of fictions to account for the situation. Some of these fictions are extremely technical and scholastic (Sastri 1926). Basically, they all say that the Veda is indeed complete the most developed stage of the texts, this principle leads to detailed regulations on the composition of a court of law, presided over by the king and assisted by a varying number of Brahmins "who are experts on *dharma*." This description of the court is followed by a fourfold treatment of the proceedings. The qualifications, or lack of them, of the plaintiff and the written plaint are followed by equally elaborate discussions of the defendant and his plea. The third section analyzes the various types of evidence, and goes into detail on witnesses, written evidence, possession, oaths, and ordeals. The final section deals, much more briefly, with the verdict, but hardly alludes to its implementation.

In most texts the rules of procedure are set forth on the occasion of the treatment of the first *vivādapada*, literally path or area of dispute. The *vivādapada*s are invariably eighteen in number. Manu enumerates them as follows:

> Of those (titles) the first is non-payment of debts, (then follow), (2) deposit and pledg., (3) sale without ownership, (4) concerns among partners, and (5) resumption of gifts, (6) non-payment of wages, (7) non-performance of agreements, (8) rescission of sale and purchase, (9) disputes between the owner (of cattle) and his servants, (10) disputes regarding boundaries, (11) assault, (12) defamation, (13) theft, (14) robbery and violence, (15) adultery, (16) duties of man and wife, (17) partition (of inheritance), (18) gambling and betting. (MDh 8.4–7)

Rather than discussing the validity of this division of substantive law, it is important, for a proper evaluation of the system, to keep in mind that the number eighteen appears in numerous subdivisions in India.[27] This probably means that whoever conceived the idea of eighteen *vivādapadas* had the number eighteen in mind first, and only later tried to provide eighteen titles. It also explains a later development which first appears in Nārada. The

[27] For example, the *Mahābhārata* has eighteen books, the *Bhagavadgītā* has eighteen chapters, and there are eighteen Purāṇas.

eighteenfold subdivision is not abandoned but the eighteenth title becomes "Miscellaneous," which allows authors to insert there any materials which do not find a place in any of the other seventeen chapters.

One final remark in connection with the theory that the Veda and Vedic *dharma* are comprehensive is in order. However lengthy and detailed the later Dharmaśāstras become in their treatment of law, a number of serious lacunae remain.[28] A recent and carefully produced publication convinced this author more than ever before how little is known about the Hindu laws of taxation in general, and of the laws of specific times and specific places in particular (Jha 1967).[29] It would be equally difficult to draw a clear picture of the laws governing land ownership and land tenure in classical India. The texts occasionally refer to these topics but, for some unstated reason, they fail to go into the same kind of details they provide for other and, from a Western point of view, less important subjects.

Unchangeability of Hindu Dharma and Law

The claim of the tradition that *dharma*, including Hindu law, is uniform and unchanging is even more complex. To be sure, the texts display a rare and fascinating uniformity, given the fact that they have been composed over a period of at least ten centuries and in various parts of the vast Indian subcontinent. There are, however, considerable differences, so much so that one might be inclined to speak of real contradictions.

It is tempting, in cases where one text differs from another, to explain the deviations as local or temporal variations —each text reflective of the situation in the part of India or the historical period in which it was composed. This is no longer an adequate explanation, however, when it is noticed that on various occasions, one and the same text exhibits more than one solution for the same legal question. Thus, Manu's chapter on inheritance begins with the rule: "After the death of the father and the mother, the brothers, being assembled, may divide among themselves in equal shares the paternal (and the maternal) estate..." (MDh 9.104). The rule, however, immediately following, unmistakably states the principle of primogeniture: "(Or) the eldest alone may take the whole paternal estate, the others shall live under him

[28] These missing links were one of the reasons why the British, when they decided to apply the Sanskrit texts as the law of the land, abandoned the older Dharmaśāstras in favor of the later and far more voluminous commentaries.

[29] See also my review of Jha's book in the *Indo-Iranian Journal* 13: 287–89 (1972).

just as (they lived) under their father."[30] Another rule speaks of different shares for the sons: "The additional share (deducted) for the eldest shall be one-twentieth (of the estate) and the best of all chattels, for the middlemost half of that, but for the youngest one-fourth."

Another well known and often discussed example concerns Manu's attitude toward *niyoga* (levirate). The text first states: "On failure of issue (by her husband) a woman who has been authorised, may obtain, (in the) proper (manner described), the desired offspring by (cohabitation with) a brother-in-law or (with some other) Sapinda (of the husband)" (MDh 9.59). The text goes on to discuss whether one or two sons should be begotten, insists that the brother-in-law and the widow should behave even as a father and a daughter-in-law, and lays down the penalty for not doing so. The text then continues without any transition: "By twice-born men a widow must not be appointed to (cohabit with) any other (than her husband); for they who appoint (her) to another (man), will violate the eternal law" (MDh 9.64). It devotes another four stanzas to the stern repudiation of the institution of *niyoga* (MDh 9.65–68).

In addition to offering different solutions for the same problem, the texts explicitly allow specific types of variations. On several occasions, after a particular topic of *dharma* has been expounded, supplementary rules are introduced to be applicable only in cases of *āpad*, which is usually translated as times of distress. The word is never, however, clearly defined. It may, obviously, refer to general calamities, such as floods or droughts, but it definitely also refers to distress involving one or a few individuals. For instance, the texts lay down strict rules on the specific occupations for each social group (*varṇa*), but these are invariably followed by exceptions, as in Manu: "[W]hen a Brahmin cannot live by his own activities as explained earlier, he may live by the duties of a Kṣatriya..." (MDh 10.81). If he cannot subsist as a Kṣatriya, he may live as a Vaiśya (MDh 10.82). These are clearly cases of individual *āpad*, which must have been numerous. An individual's *dharma*, and the law that is applicable, depends to a large extent on his caste. The theory of *āpad*, therefore, must be viewed as an indication that the authors of the *dharma* texts did recognize, to a degree, legal variation and adaptation of the law to differing circumstances.

[30] MDh 9.105. The "(Or)" in Bühler's translation is not present in the Sanskrit text. Also his "may divide" and "may take" might equally have been meant to mean "shall divide" and "shall take"; they translate the same optative form of the verbs as "'shall' live" later in the second stanza.

The theory that *dharma* is eternal (*sanātana*) and unchanging had to be adapted to yet another concept that was very popular in Hinduism. The Hindus, even as the ancient Greeks, and many other civilizations, believe in the succession of four *yugas* (world ages), from the best to the worst. The present time is the *Kaliyuga*, which corresponds to the Iron Age. *Dharma* was perfect in the first age, but it diminished by one fourth in each successive age, with the result that in the *Kali* age, *dharma* stands on one leg only.[31] Consequently a number of practices described in the *dharma* texts have been labeled *Kalivarjyas*, "practices to be avoided in the Kali age" (Bhattacharya 1943). For instance, later Dharmaśāstras have used this criterion to account for earlier contradictory statements on *niyoga*: levirate was a common practice in earlier ages, but it should be avoided in the *Kaliyuga*.

Hinduism believes, first, in the gradual deterioration within each *yuga*, and, second, in the eternal return, with interruptions, of the four ages. The logical conclusion, therefore, is that, for the orthodox Hindu, *dharma* and law are, in fact, subject to continuous change.

Finally, it should be pointed out that the Sanskrit texts themselves recognize unwritten sources of *dharma*. One important source, which often figures in enumerations together with *śruti* and *smṛti*, is variously called *sadācāra* (practices of the good) or *śiṣṭācāra* (practices of the learned). Irrespective of the lengthy scholastic disquisitions which these terms have provoked at a later stage, it is clear that, by introducing this type of unwritten and vaguely defined source of law, the texts wanted to give recognition to a number of practices which they themselves did not explicitly codify. Even more significant is the recognition by the texts, *expressis verbis*, of a wide variety of more specific customs as sources of *dharma*. As early as Gautama's Dharmasūtra, the king, when sitting as judge, is supposed to supplement the *dharma* contained in the *śruti* and *smṛti* with the laws (*dharma*) of specific groups. Thus, it has been stated:

> The laws of countries, castes, and families, which are not opposed to the (sacred) records, (have) also authority. Cultivators, traders, herdsmen, money-lenders, and artisans (have authority to lay down rules) for their respective classes. Having heard the (state of) affairs from those who (in each class) have authority (to speak he shall give) the legal decision. (GDh 11.20–22)

Similar rules are repeated throughout Dharmaśāstra literature. Some texts go even further and provide for separate courts of law, which seem to be considered lower than the royal court,

[31] Sanskrit uses the same term for "one quarter" and "a foot, leg."

but at the same time are supposed to judge members of a group according to rules of law current within that group. For instance, Bṛhaspati states: "For persons roaming the forest, a court should be held in the forest; for warriors, in the camp; and for merchants, in the caravan" (BS 1.25, Jolly). Nowhere in the texts have these specialized laws been described, nor is there any indication of their magnitude or contents. The sole requirement, already mentioned by Gautama and reiterated several times in later texts, is that they not be opposed to the Veda and Vedic *dharma.*

Dharmaśāstra v. Legal Practice

Occasional glimpses into the existence of uncodified and unknown sources of law in Hinduism naturally lead to a basic question: To what extent were the written texts on *dharma* true sources of law? Do the texts actually allow an evaluation of the real attitude of Hindus toward law?

Answers to these questions vary considerably. At one end of the spectrum there are evaluations such as this: "There can be no doubt that the smriti rules were concerned with the practical administration of the law" (Mayne 1950: 2). At the other end, however, there is the opinion most forcefully expressed thus: "It is a profound error to regard the Smritis as complete codes of law or as getting all their 'rules' rigidly enforced by the political authorities of their times" (Das 1914). According to the same author, "Hindu Law was in the main never more than a pious wish of its metaphysically-minded, ceremonial-ridden priestly promulgators, and but seldom a stern reality."

There have been attempts to demonstrate that the *dharma* texts were indeed put to practical use in classical India, and that they do reflect the law of the land. This author refers to an article published under the title: "The Harmonizing of Law With the Requirements of Economic Conditions According to the Ancient Dharmaśāstras" (Sternbach 1942). One example mentioned in this article concerns the rate of interest. All Dharmaśāstras agree on the normal rate of interest, fifteen percent. If the debtor, however, undertakes a long and, by implication, dangerous voyage, the interest is raised to 120% and in case of a voyage overseas, to 200%. Although the texts reflect a logical adaptation of the rate of interest to risk, the very fact that this adaptation is identical throughout the literature proves that the system as such was considered more important than local or temporal differences.[32]

[32] Even Sternbach acknowledged that "from the point of view of law, the Indian law-system can be discussed only as static and not as dynamic law, although

A more elaborate and far-reaching attempt to show the practical use of the *dharma* compares the legal systems as they emerge from the Dharmaśāstras of Manu and Yājñavalkya, and concludes that they reflect two very different economic and social situations. Manu represents the Hindu nation of the Brahmāṇic empire (150 BC); Yājñavalkya echoes the prosperous and liberal Sātavāhana empire (AD 150).[33] A detailed analysis of these arguments would lead this article too far. This discussion shall therefore restrict itself to one example, to point out the danger of the tendency to apply modern concepts to the ancient Hindu lawbooks.

Manu distinguishes three levels of fines: the highest (1000 *paṇas*), the middlemost (500), and the lowest (250). These fines are just one of numerous instances throughout Hindu technical literature where quantitative categories are divided into three, each one following being half as large as the preceding one. Yājñavalkya follows the same system, yet his figures are different: 1080, 540, 270. The difference is attributed to a devaluation of the *paṇa* in the time separating both texts. In reality, Yājñavalkya's sole innovation —and a good one from the traditional point of view— is that he replaced Manu's round figure of 1000 by 1080, a variant on the basic number eighteen which has been met earlier in this study.

The above example probably allows, better than many others, an understanding of the true nature of the Hindu lawbooks. On the one hand, and most fundamental, there is the system. From the texts that have been preserved one can, to a certain extent, follow the development and formation of a number of specific systems. Once a system has been established, however, it is never again altered or abandoned. One example of the static nature of a system is the subdivision of substantive law. Once the basic scheme of eighteen titles is introduced, no later text deviates from it. Another example is that of the three degrees of fines. This author looks upon the compilers of the Dharmaśāstras primarily as pandits, who worked with a set of data which they tried —very hard, as they ought to— to arrange within a number of acceptable systems. Some of them, totally unknown to us, succeeded in elaborating such systems. From then onward, these systems remained unchanged. This stability is the remarkable element in Sanskrit technical literature, and it is not restricted to law and Dharmaśāstras.

there is no doubt that the Indian law, like all other laws, has its gradual development" (1942: 528).

[33] See generally Jayaswal 1930.

On the other hand, there is the equally typical tendency of the Indian pandit to enrich, sophisticate, and beautify the work of his predecessors. This tendency explains why the later Dharmaśāstras are far more detailed than the earlier ones. It explains why Nārada —more correctly, the pandit who compiled the Nārada-Dharmaśāstra— further subdivided the eighteen titles of law into one hundred and thirty-two subtitles. It also explains why Yājñavalkya replaced Manu's highest fine of 1000 *paṇas* by 1080.

Many of the legal prescriptions in the Dharmaśāstras must be more or less literal renditions of the mass of floating versified maxims which were current in India from very early times and in many fields. When the Dharmasūtras are described as the older type of texts, it is sometimes forgotten that many of these *sūtras*, the literary style of the time, incorporate sections of existing maxims in *śloka* meter, the style of the later Dharmaśāstras. It is these maxims which were collected, ordered according to subject matter, elaborated into systems, and enriched with an ever growing number of details in the texts. The fact that two or more maxims provided two or more different solutions for the same problem was no obstacle to their being included in the same texts. An example would be Manu's differing rules on the succession of an estate. It is possible that the differing maxims reflected different local usages. Too modern a view of local usages in ancient India, however, overlooks that these usages were definitely not the usages of North, South, East, or any other province of India. They may, from the beginning, have coexisted within small geographic areas. On the other hand, once they were formulated as maxims, they must, together with numerous other maxims, have started on their intriguing and inexplicable voyage across the width and breadth of the subcontinent.

Next to nothing is known about actual legal practice in ancient India. The texts on *dharma*, as they exist today, edited, published, and easily accessible in bookshops and libraries, were certainly not the most wide-spread sources of law. It must be logically accepted that those Brahmins who knew the texts must have tried also to enforce them, at least to a certain extent, whenever they were called on for advice. It is also logical to accept that, in such cases, the ancient Indian kings and minor executives would not normally and intentionally transgress rules of *dharma*, an attitude which would not only harm them in this existence but also in later incarnations.

More important than the texts were the legal maxims referred to earlier. These maxims, not necessarily in Sanskrit, and perhaps merely via illustrative parables, were much better known, as they are today. To the extent to which the maxims were applied to settle disputes, Hindu *dharma* was indeed a source of law. Finally, there must have been the whole spectrum of customs, the existence of which is, as we have seen, confirmed by the texts. Numerous disputes must have been solved in very definite and constant ways for the sole reason that they had been solved in these ways from time immemorial.[34]

Conclusion: Later Developments

Until now this article has concentrated on the classical period of Hinduism, the time of the Dharmasūtras and Dharmaśāstras. To conclude, a few remarks on later developments are in order. Even though some of the less important Dharmaśāstras may have been composed at a much later period, by about the eighth century AD, possibly a little earlier or later, a new period sets in in the history of Hindu *dharma*. From that time onward the entire literature which has been discussed so far becomes, for about ten centuries, the object of numerous and endless commentaries. A strict distinction is now made between, on the one hand, the *smṛti* which obtains absolute authority, and, on the other hand, its interpretation by the commentators which is subject to continuous discussion, innovation, and improvement. Two types of commentaries should be distinguished: (1) the commentaries *stricto sensu* that explain one particular text, *sūtra* after *sūtra*, or *śloka* after *śloka*, comparing them with select passages from other Dharmaśāstras as they proceed; and (2) the *nibandhas*, often translated as digests, which treat one subject after another, quoting and commenting on ancient texts irrespective of their original contexts.

Opinions again vary on the role that the legal sections of the commentaries and digests played as sources of law. Most modern scholars, Western first, Indian later, believe that the commentators used the ancient texts actually to codify the laws of their respective provinces. The most recent study of classical Hindu law even equates the transition from *śastra* to commentary with the passage "from *dharma* to law" (Lingat 1973).

This author has consistently defended a very different interpretation of the commentarial period of *dharma* literature. The com-

[34] In a letter dated 1714, Father Bouchet, S.J., reported at length on the legal system of the Hindus as he observed it. He said that they did not have written laws, but they did have a number of well established maxims, some of which Father Bouchet treated in detail. Also, he stated they had a wide array of customs and usages, unwritten but transmitted from parent to child, from which they would under no circumstance deviate. Bouchet assured his readers that, against all expectations, the system worked and justice prevailed. Bouchet's description may very well apply to most situations in ancient India.

mentaries *stricto sensu* do not in any way attach greater importance to the legal sections of the ancient texts than they do to any other section of the *dharma*, nor do they treat them in any different way. The commentarial technique is identical throughout. In the digests there are now separate sections on *vivāda*, substantive law, *vyavahāra*, either procedure or procedure and substantive law, and *nīti*, administrative law. Once again, however, these legal sections are not more important nor are they in any way different from the many other sections which, together with them, make up the *nibandha*. The basic misunderstanding of these texts, and a total loss of historical perspective, came about during the colonial period, when the legal sections of the commentaries and digests were edited, translated into English, and used as lawbooks, whereas all other sections were left to be studied by historians of religion or totally neglected.

In this author's opinion the Hindu attitude toward law in these Indian Middle Ages was not different from what it had been in more ancient times. In principle, the *śāstra* was still the theoretical source of law. In practice, maxims and customs were paramount. There was one difference, though. In many parts of India where the Mughul Empire was strong, Muslim law took over from Hindu law, also for Hindus. Some of this author's recent research seems to indicate that in certain areas Hindu law had, for all practical purposes, disappeared at the time when the colonial powers appeared on the scene.

As indicated at the beginning of this Article, in 1772 the British, under the impulse of Governor General Warren Hastings, decided that, in a number of areas of private law, Hindus should be governed by their own laws. The answer to the question where these laws might be found, was predictable: the *śāstra*. The British interpreted this answer literally and elevated, for the first time in Indian history, the Dharmaśāstras *qua* texts to the rank of lawbooks. British judges were given the task of applying laws in the courts, the extent of which they did not know, the language of which they were unable to read, and the general background of which they could not understand. For several years, pandits were appointed to the courts to research the laws governing each case. Dissatisfaction with the system and distrust of the pandits led Sir William Jones to study Sanskrit and translate Manu's Dharmaśāstra. The need to have a complete code of Hindu law led to the compilation, by hired pandits, of new digests, which were subsequently translated into English. The vagueness of these codes in turn created the concept of schools of Hindu law based on the premise, wrong in this author's opinion, that the medieval digests codified the laws of different provinces of India, and that they could be used as such. In short, a slowly growing number of legal sections of commentaries and digests were translated into English, and the British judges applied them, as well as they could, even against occasional odds. For instance, when a party or a lawyer presented the judge with a Sanskrit text which had not yet been translated, it should not therefore be less authoritative. Inevitably, the judges introduced a few changes of their own. They arbitrarily separated law from religion. The commentaries were, relatively speaking, the least ambiguous sources of law, therefore the judges reversed the traditional hierarchy, and stated that the wording of the commentary overrules that of the Dharmaśāstras, and the latter that of the Vedas. They gradually avoided consulting and reinterpreting the translations of Sanskrit texts by making Hindu law into a regular case law, invoking precedent and *stare decisis.* When the Hindu lawbooks appeared to be unacceptable, they overruled them on the grounds of justice, equity, and good conscience.

This description would be irrelevant for the study of Hindu conceptions of law, were it not that the Hindu judges, Hindu attorneys, and the Hindu public at large fully accepted this well-intended but perfectly hybrid system of law created by the British. They accepted it before independence, and they continued to live by it after 1947.

In the meanwhile, a number of basically Western codes had been introduced: the Penal Code (1860); the Indian Evidence Act (1872); the Criminal Procedure Code (1898) ; and the Code of Civil Procedure (1908). For more than a century, in the field of private law, several legislative Acts overruled and abrogated more and more provisions of classical Hindu law. In the years before independence, a serious effort was made to codify Hindu private law. The "Hindu Code Bill," however, never became law, in view of the lack of agreement, even among Indians, on the basic principles upon which private laws applicable to all Hindus should be built. The Indian Constitution was even more ambitious: "The State shall endeavour to secure for the citizens a uniform civil code throughout the territory of India."[35] Today, nearly three decades later, there is no evidence to show that this ideal will be realized in the near future.

[35] Indian Constitution, art. 44 (1955).

2

The Historical Foundations of Ancient Indian Law

It cannot be our intention in the following pages to sketch an image of ancient Indian law as it was really practiced (before law courts, etc.), and then to compare this practiced law with the details of the written law. It is too early and our sources of information are too scarce to take such a chance; in fact, I doubt whether one will ever succeed in finding a satisfactory solution this problem with regard to ancient India. What I want to offer the reader instead are deliberations of a general sort that relate to the question and, insofar as possible, to ascertain the extent to which written sources of law were meant by their authors to play a role in determining legal practice.

Before this, however, some remarks about two factors affecting an investigation of this kind should be taken into consideration: first, the value of the notion of "history" in India; and, second, the Indian conception of the relationship of law and history. It is generally accepted that in ancient India the idea of "history" in the meaning of "chronology" or "accurate dating," practically does not exist. In whatever area of ancient India one works, one always has to contend with Macdonell's conclusion that "History is the one weak spot in Indian literature. It is, in fact, non-existent. The total lack of the historical sense is so characteristic, that the whole course of Sanskrit literature is darkened by the shadow of this defect, suffering as it does from an entire absence of exact chronology" (Macdonell 1900: 10). More specifically, Macdonell points here to the impossibility of dating to within a century even the most famous Indian poets such as Kālidāsa.[36] This problem is

[36] Cf. Winternitz 1922: 3.40–41: "Es ist bezeichnend für die Unsicherheit,

widespread, and we find it also in the law: some will place the so-called *Laws of Manu*[37] in the 2nd century BC, and others will place it in the 2nd century AD.

But when it comes to the law and legal texts more specifically, there is yet another difficulty. Where we especially in law expect historical development, such development according to the Indian conceptions does not exist. For orthodox Hindus law is —for the time being I will equate the Indian term *dharma* with "law"— *sanātana*, i.e. eternal, unchangeable. This conception may seem odd, but in reality it is simply a logical result of the Indian outlook on life in general. The Hindu notices, how all events in the cosmos occur according to strict, unchangeable laws: every day the sun rises to bring warmth on earth, every year the rain breaks out so the harvest will not dry out. To this universe and to this normative regularity belong all living creatures and humanity in particular —as orderly a part as the sun, the rains, etc. Humans, too, as a part of the cosmos, behave according to specific unchangeable norms. It is the totality of these norms that is pointed to by the concept *dharma*. *Dharma* is the law and order, the harmony, the regularity, the fundamental balance, the norm, the proper behavior, the good form, which rules in nature and in the human world (Gonda 1941; 1943).

What is special to humanity is the control over *dharma*, all action without exception, from waking in the morning to sleep in the evening, from birth to death. What a person does should be done according to *dharma*, and one should avoid any disturbance of this *dharma*.

I have said that all actions of a man are bound by his *dharma*. And to this belong not only physical actions such as consuming food and drink, but also all actions of the magico-religious variety, and finally also —and this is what interests us here— his rights and obligations in dealing with his fellow creatures, rights and obligations which I consider to belong to the sphere of law.[38] I will have further opportunity to explore the consequences of this relation between *dharma* and law, but for the moment I will re-

die in der indischen Litteraturgeschichte herrscht, dass die Inder von dem Leben ihres berühmtesten Dichters nichts als Märchen zu berichten wissen, und dass über die Zeit des Kālidāsa die Ansichten sowohl der indischen als auch der abendländischen Gelehrten noch immer um Jahrhunderte auseinandergehen, trotzdem unendlich viel darüber geschrieben worden ist."

[37] The most recent and detailed historical view of ancient Indian legal literature is Kane 1930–62. Cf. also Rocher 1954.

[38] Gonda 1941: 554: In the world of men *dharma* is "the whole complex of traditional, religious-ritual, social, etc. norms, according to the existing regular order of affairs is maintained."

strict myself to a focus on the Hindu conception that, in the lens of *dharma*, law, too, is eternal and unchangeable, i.e. that Hindus are controlled by eternal and unchangeable laws that were set forth in "lawbooks," as the textbooks of *dharma* are usually called.

So much for the conception of law of the orthodox Hindu. But it cannot be denied that an impartial and unprejudiced investigator of Hindu law will also discern an historical development —albeit within the unavoidable restrictions resulting from the lack of an accurate chronology— when investigating the historical foundations of ancient Indian law and its historical development.

In the course of this paper, I will distinguish three periods. It speaks for itself that in the study of *ancient* Indian law the first period especially will attract our attention, but the same ancient Indian law persists after, first, Islamic and, later, European (British) law are established in India. Accordingly, I must add a brief discussion concerning the character of ancient Indian law in the Muslim and British periods.

First Period: The Dharmasūtras and the Dharmaśāstras

The Dharmasūtras and the Dharmaśāstras are in most histories of Sanskrit literature treated in separate chapters about "legal literature."[39] From a practical perspective, this label is undoubtedly responsible, but at the same time it cannot be denied that, from a different point of view, it can impart a wrong impression to the uninitiated. To understand the historical formation of this so-called "legal literature," it is indeed imperative to see it —especially in this first period— in its true shape, namely as a small part of a much bigger whole called the Vedic literature.

The foundation of this Vedic literature are the Vedas themselves, four collections or Saṃhitās of the hymns and prayers to various gods, hymns and prayers that were meant to be recited at the sacrifice and other ritual ceremonies. Already in the Saṃhitās several distinctions manifest themselves; they become part of separate "Vedic schools." In each of these schools, a detailed explanatory literature is added to the Saṃhitās, beginning with the Brāhmaṇas. These detailed prose works vary in content but are primarily intended as explanation and interpretation of the details of the complex sacrificial ritual. The often speculative elements in the Brāhmaṇas in turn inspired the Āraṇyakas and Upaniṣads, in

[39] For examples, see von Schroeder 1887: 734–751; Winternitz 1922: 479–535, who treats Dharmaśāstra and Arthaśāstra in the section "Die wissenschaftliche Litteratur" ; and Keith 1920: 437–449, in which "Civil and Religious Law" forms a section of the chapter about "Scientific Literature."

which metaphysical matters are treated, and which will later become the foundation of the Vedānta philosophy. However, I will not attend here to these speculative offshoots of the Brāhmaṇas, but rather to that other class of texts that are in first place meant to regulate the worldly life of the orthodox Hindu.[40]

The worldly duties of the Hindu, meaning primarily ritual duties, were not systematically treated in the Brāhmaṇas. At most, one finds a few stray references that presuppose a knowledge of the full procedure of the sacrifice and of other duties. Gradually we see that the Vedic schools just mentioned, which further split into new schools, methodically codified these presupposed duties of the Brāhmaṇas. Thus arose the different *sūtras*: the Śrautasūtras, the Gṛhyasūtras and the Śulbasūtras, which are almost completely dedicated to a description of the sacrifice and the sacrificial altar —and finally the Dharmasūtras.

Here we see that in terms of textual history a Dharmasūtra depends directly on a Brāhmaṇa and through that Brāhmaṇa on a Vedic Saṃhitā. With this, the origin of the Dharmasūtras is explained, but we must still investigate the origin of the Dharmaśāstras and their relation to the *sūtras*.

There was a time when the solution to this problem seemed to be found. Max Müller was the first to put forward the hypothesis that, in every Vedic school, the basic prose Dharmasūtra was superseded by a versified Dharmaśāstra. It was Georg Bühler more specifically, in the excellent and detailed introduction to his translation of the *Mānava Dharmaśāstra* (1886: xvii) who bolstered Müller's hypothesis with such convincing evidence that the last word in this case seemed to have been spoken. But it still seemed that Bühler's argument had a few weaknesses. In the first place, one remained unconvinced of the existence of a *Mānava Dharmasūtra*, which was presumed by Bühler in order to demonstrate the passage from *sūtra* to *śāstra* in the school of the Mānavas. And, in the second place, though one could not deny that the Dharmaśāstras bore the names of Vedic schools, they were evidently not restricted in their application to one school alone, but rather to be followed by all Hindus.

[40] von Schroeder 1887: 180: "In den Brāhmaṇa's liefen Erklärung und Bestimmung des Rituals einerseits, und die daran geknünpften und darüber hinausgehenden Speculationen andrerseits noch neben einander. Das Eine war untrennbar met dem Andern verbunden. Die Speculation knüpfte sich an die Ceremonie an, und die Ceremonie gründete sich auf die Speculation und bewies ihr Recht durch diese. Im Laufe der Zeit gehen sie beide aber mehr und mehr auseinander und in der auf die Brāhmaṇas folgenden Epoche finden wir beide gesondert behandelt. Es sind andere Werke, die dem Ceremoniell des Opfers dienen, andere, die dem speculativen Bedürfnis Genüge thun. Dan Erstere übernehmen die Sūtras, das letztere die Āraṇyakas und Upanishaden."

There is much to be said for this theory that was first was articulated, I believe, by von Bradke (1882), and which subsequently was incorporated into the *Literaturgeschichte* of Winternitz (1922: 3.485). The Dharmasūtras each belonged to a specific Vedic school. As proof of this, we are pointed to their esoteric and scientific style, almost algebraic formulas, which was undoubtedly meant to be memorized by students and after that to be understood with the help of oral commentary of the master, the guru. Then, we are told, came a time of crisis for orthodox Hinduism,[41] e.g. through the contemporaneous spread of Buddhism and Jainism. In response, it was necessary not only to eliminate existing disputes between schools but also to put the texts into a new, more popular and easily readable form and in this way to make them accessible to all sophisticated Hindus. The result of this was the replacement of the vertical classification in Vedic schools for the study of one specific Saṃhitā, Brāhmaṇa, Āraṇyaka, Upaniṣad, and the corresponding Sūtras, by a horizontal classification or, as Winternitz says, by "trade schools," in which one specific subject, in our case *dharma* was studied in all its aspects and not according the rules of a single school.

Furthermore, in terms of textual history, the Dharmasūtras, and to some extent the Dharmaśāstras, also depend on the Veda. But there is yet another connection between the oldest law books and the Veda, and this second connection comes to the heart of the "law books" that I examine below.

For a Hindu, the Dharmasūtras and the Dharmaśāstras belong to the category of *smṛti*, "tradition." They are collections of rules that were "remembered" by the ancient sages, and transmitted by them to the rest of humanity. So these texts merit great respect, to which no writing of mere humans can aspire. On the other hand, the *smṛti* is not the ultimate primary source for knowledge of *dharma*. The rules of *smṛti* derive their value by being based on the *śruti*, the "revelation," i.e. the actual Vedas. The Veda is eternal and all-encompassing: it contains all *dharma*, and *dharma* can only be found in the Veda. Nevertheless it remains a fact —and even the most orthodox Hindus admit it— that we find not a single positive rule of *dharma* in the Vedas, as we by contrast find constantly in the *smṛti* literature. To explain this fact, Hindus have given several theories —into which I cannot go further here— but the basic gist of which is that we do not find all *dharma* rules in the Vedas because we only know a part of the Veda.[42]

[41] von Bradke 1882: 472, speaks of "Ereignisse, welche vielleicht die ganze brahmanische Gesellschaftsordung in Frage stellten."

[42] Sankararama Sastri 1926:70: "The very absence of a read Vedic basis for most of the Smṛti rules except by a legal fiction gave rise to widely divergent theories that had swayed the minds of scholars from time to time whose one com-

What does this orthodox opinion of the Vedic basis of Indian law truly mean? In other words, what is the value of the Veda for the knowledge of Indian law?

If one reads Zimmer's *Altindisches Leben* (1879), one sees that as a source of law the Veda teaches us almost nothing. And still Kane claims, not wrongly, that we can glean from the Veda information of "considerable importance" about the basis of law (1936: 2).

An example will clarify this. In the *Yājñavalkyasmṛti* (1.52–53) we read that the bride has to satisfy to several conditions, among others that she has to have a brother. Never should one marry a brotherless bride. So also in the *Ṛgveda*, we see at least two times,[43] how a young girl without a brother is depicted as having a bad reputation: she tends to deviate from what is right, because no one will marry her as lawful wife. In other words, the custom of not marrying a girl without a brother already existed in the time of the *Ṛgveda*, and so the *Yājñavalkyasmṛti* has a Vedic basis here. And there is more. By this time, the custom already had an explanatory origin, found in the *Vasiṣṭha Dharmasūtra* (17.16), as being the danger that a brotherless bride will return to her own family to take the place of her brother, which confirms that Vasiṣṭha too has a Vedic basis.[44]

Our conclusion must be that the Veda teaches us little as a direct source of law, but indirectly shows how later *smṛtis* often codified customs and rules that were practiced or aspired to in the early Vedic period.

Having given first the literary-historical background of the *smṛtis* and an exposition of orthodox opinions about the so-called Vedic basis of the *smṛti*, I will now try to give an answer to the question of what these legal rules in the *smṛti* meant to the real life of a Hindu and if they were truly applied. That this question cannot be immediately answered positively or negatively will become apparent when I compare what others have said about the problem.

On one side is the opinion of N. Chandrasekhara Aiyar: "There can be no doubt that the Smriti rules were concerned with the practical administration of the law" (1950: 2).[45]

mon object was to try their level best to establish a Vedic origin of the Smṛti's." For the different theories, see pp. 70–74.

[43] *Ṛgveda* 1.124.7 and 4.5.5. Cf. also *Atharvaveda* 1.17.1.

[44] This usage is closely connected to the necessity for every male Hindu to have a male offspring who is the only one who can make the obligatory offering after his father's death. When a young man gets married, he normally takes the bride to his own house, so that his son will be born in his family's house. Should he marry a girl who does not have a brother, her (sonless) father can stipulate as follows: "I give you this brotherless girl into marriage; her son will be my son." In this case the (grand)son will not make offerings for his father but for his grandfather on his mother's side. Cf. Kane 1930–62: 3. 647, 657–659.

[45] Cf. Dahlmann 1899: 48–49: "wahrhaft geschichtliche Quellen."

On the other, we have the opinion of Govinda Das: "Hindu Law was in the main never more than a pious wish of its metaphysically-minded, ceremonial-ridden priestly promulgators, and but seldom a stern reality" (1914: 16). And elsewhere: "It is a profound error to regard the Smritis as complete codes of law or as getting all their 'rules' rigidly enforced by the political authorities of their times" (ibid.: 8).[46]

We have here two totally contrasting opinions and so we are forced to make a new investigation of the facts and draw our own conclusion. A first question can help us with this: Given that India was a place —and by the way still is— where tradition is extraordinarily strong, so strong that all change is repulsed systematically and with force, nevertheless, it should astonish us if there really were no development at all. In the law, which Indian society certainly knew, it should be possible to find some marks of this development. And in fact, we find marks of such development in the Dharmasūtras and Dharmaśāstras, of which the first and the last are centuries apart from each other, ten centuries in which the beginning of the common era can be considered the center point.

Arguments of this sort have been made earlier, and two of them should be mentioned here. In one of his many publications Ludwik Sternbach (1942) gives some examples of what he calls "The harmonizing of law with the requirements of economic conditions according to the ancient Indian Dharmaśāstras."[47] One of the clearest examples of this according to Sternbach is interest. Normal interest accrues at 15% per year, a figure that is mentioned in almost all important Dharmaśāstras: Manu, Yājñavalkya, Nārada, Bṛhaspati, etc. Sternbach, however, wants to point especially to the fact that this interest is supposed to increase to 120% a year, if the debtor and/or his property must travel through the jungle, and the interest increases up to 220% if ones travels overseas. I freely admit that these texts express a very practical adaptation of interest to risk. However, the fact that the same interest appears in almost every *smṛti* proves nothing in favor of an evolution of law, or for the adjustment of law to changing economic conditions.

Beyond this, Sternbach does not go much further, and so we turn to a book of K.P. Jayaswal, *Manu and Yājñavalkya: A Compari-*

[46] Cf. Winternitz 1922: 3.479: "sie sind ... von Brahmanen, Priestern und Lehrern für Lehrwecke, nicht etwa als Codices für den praktischen Gebrauch der Gerichtshöfe verfasst"; Maine 1920 [1886]: 14.

[47] It should be noticed that even Sternbach admits: "...from the point of view of law, the Indian law system can be discussed only as a static and not as a dynamic law, although there is no doubt that the Indian law, like all other laws, has its gradual development" (528).

son and a Contrast (1930). Jayaswal compares the Dharmaśāstras of Manu and Yājñavalkya carefully and concludes that both are to be seen as exponents of two radically different economic and social situations. Manu, he says, reflects the psychology of the Hindu nation under Brahmanical rule (ca. 150 BC); Yājñavalkya gives the voice of the prosperous and liberal empire of the Sātavāhanas (ca. AD 150) (ibid.: xx–xxi).

From the fact, for example, that Manu but not Yājñavalkya begins the chapter on *daṇḍapāruṣya* (i.e. physical violence)[48] with the punishment of the Śūdra for assault against a Brahmin, Jayaswal concludes that the author of Manu points towards writing a code that is devoted to a suppression of the Śūdra and an elevation of dignity of the Brahmin.[49] One can thus speak of a deliberate adjustment of the law books to social conditions.

Still I think one must be careful in viewing the contradictions of *smṛti* rules as reflecting actual historical conditions. Take the example of ordeals. Manu knows two: the water and the fire; Yājñavalkya knows five: the balance, the fire, the water, the poison, and the holy water. Is this not sufficient evidence to show that Yājñavalkya, in Sternbach's words, is "a slightly more advanced law book" (1942: 530) than Manu?

A positive answer seems easy,[50] and yet there are also arguments that tend to give us a negative answer. First, I must point out that this "slightly more advanced law book," while describing three more ordeals than Manu, does not know one that Manu does.[51] Second, a few references to ordeals occur already in the *Ṛgveda*, especially to the ordeal of fire, among others, that is not mentioned in Manu and so ought not to be unknown in his time. Third, the appearance of ordeals in the *Ṛgveda* proves the speciousness of arguments claiming that the ancient Dharmasūtras, in which ordeals are not mentioned at all, did not know them (cf. Losch 1927: xxx). Fourth, and last, I must point out that there

[48] Cf. Rocher 1954: 311: *daṇḍapāruṣya* = no. 12 of the "eighteen paths" of *vivāda*.

[49] This example contradicts the criterion formulated by Weber (1868: 54) in connection with the sacrificial fee: "Die Habgier der Brāhmaṇa feiert hier wahrhafte Orgien... 'Je alter, je bescheidener, je spatter, je massloser' —wird vielleicht als ein Criterium hierbei augestellt werden dürfen."

[50] Cf. Stenzler, *Yājñavalkya's Gesetzbuch*, 1849: ix: "Wer z.B. das eigentlichte Recht und das gerichtliche verfahren bei beiden gesetzgebern vergleicht, wird nicht nur im allgemeinen bei Yājñavalkya einen fortschritt zu grösserer schärfe und bestimmtheit wahrnemen, sondern auch in vielen einzelnen punkten, in welchen beide wesentliche verschiedenheiten zeigen, Yājñavalkya's standpunkt als einen späteren erkennen."

[51] [Ed. note: I am unsure to what ordeal Rocher refers here. Both MDh 8.114 and YDh 2.95 mention *agni* (fire) and *apas* (submersion in water).]

are ordeals that were never adopted in the *smṛtis*, not even in the most detailed such as Bṛhaspati and Pitāmaha, who distinguish nine ordeals.

We will limit ourselves to this single example of ordeals, but it would not be difficult to extend the list and illuminate other aspects of the problem. Instead, I will focus later on what all these examples teach us.

First, the lack of rules of positive law in the Dharmasūtras is not limited to the one example of ordeals: it is practically general. If we were forced to construct an image of law on what the ancient "law books" teach us, it would be extremely sparse. Foy[52] in 1895 had already pointed out that positive law originally must have been foreign to the books of *dharma* instruction. And, notwithstanding the sharp attack of Johann Jacob Meyer (1929: ix *et passim*), I believe with Hans Losch that even the relatively late *Yājñavalkyasmṛti* originally contained no positive law. Foy considered the *Manusmṛti* as being the great turning point in the history of Dharmaśāstra, because from then on was adopted an almost complete survey of positive law. This is certainly correct as to the impact of the *Manusmṛti* itself, but, for reasons I cannot discuss here, I am convinced that even in Manu the sections on positive law are a later addition.

A second fact can be learned from examples such as ordeals. Even if a rule of positive law does not appear in the older law books, it does not mean that it did not exist. I do not want to give the impression that all rules found in later *smṛtis* already existed in the time of the Vedas, so many centuries earlier. But what in India must have existed is a mass of unwritten customs that gradually took the shape of somewhat fixed legal maxims.[53]

It is obvious that these customs differed in time and especially in space, and equally obvious that certain of these differences were also reflected when the rules were later codified in the Dharmaśāstras. It seems certain, in the state of the present evidence, that it was the author of one of the later versions of the *Mānava Dharmaśāstra* who chose to codify the rules of positive law.

[52] Foy 1895: 3: "Die Vorschriften über staatliche Einrichtungen und den König, die sich in den Rechtsbüchern finden, gehörten wahrscheinlich nicht zu dem ursprünglichen Plan der Rechtsbücher, sondern sind wie die Zivil- und Kriminalgesetze, erst später hinzugekommen, und auch erst im Laufe der historischen Periode, namentlich seit dem Mānavadharmaśāstra zu grösserer Ausbildung und Ausdehnung gelangt."

[53] Leaning on the existence of these "Memorialverse," Lüders (1917: 349–50) has even tried to prove that the younger versified Dharmaśāstras often contain material that is older than that which was assimilated into the older prose Dharmasūtras.

Once the codification of the *Mānava Dharmaśāstra* was complete, however, how should we understand its relation to the later *smṛtis* —Yājñavalkya, Nārada, Bṛhaspati, Kātyāyana, to name only the most important— in light of the first attempt of the *Manusmṛti*? Are the deviations really to be explained as being purposeful adaptations to changing social circumstances? Deviations exist, undoubtedly, but from the example of ordeals, we have seen that these deviations could have had other causes as well.

I will give one other example, in order to show that the so-called deviations should sometimes be attributed to other unexpected factors, without falling back on changing social or political circumstances.

Manu distinguishes three levels of fine: the lowest, 250 *paṇas*; the middle, 500; and the highest, 1000 —on first sight, a seemingly natural classification, based on the round number one thousand. Yājñavalkya, by contrast, establishes the corresponding fines respectively at 270, 540 and 1080— a seemingly less natural solution. In order to explain the change, must we resort to some complicated explanation of criminal administrarion? We might, if we did not know that the number 18 and all permutations of it, including 108 and 1080, in the whole of Indian literature have a special meaning, so special that already two scholars thought it necessary to devote special studies to it.[54]

The only reason for the deviation in the amount of the prescribed fines is the subtle number speculation by the author of the *Yājñavalkyasmṛti*. Similarly, the classification of legal matters into eighteen titles (Rocher 1954), that is already found in Manu, occurs due to this tendency to use the number eighteen as often as possible.[55] And all later authors considered this division so proper, that they all kept it, even on occasions when we can see clearly how discontent they were to divide their texts into it.

What I want to show relates rather to the whole of the legal literature of this first period under consideration. For many dif-

[54] Scheftelowitz 1931 and Stein 1936.

[55] I differ here from the opinion of Jolly, who finds in the eighteenfold classification of legal material a proof for the thesis that the *smṛti* literature is not the result of a Brahmanical fiction but the codification of actually existing customary law: "Wäre es ein Produkt der Theorie, so müsste zuerst die Schablone und dann erst ihre Ausfüllung entstanden sein. Aber an Manu's achtzehn Klagegründen kann Niemand verkennen, dass sie ein für die altüberlieferten Regeln des Gewohnheitsrechts nachträglich zuerst gemachtes Schema darstellen" (1878: 248). I find this rationalisation *a posteriori* even harder to accept, since Jolly himself in the same study already noticed: "Eine abstracte Richtung, ein Hang zu subtilen, nicht selten haarspaltenden Discussionen und Distinctionen, und ein entschiedener Trieb zu schematisieren, bildet eine hervortechende Eigenthümlichkeit der indischen Arier..." (234).

ferent reasons, one always emphasizes the mutual differences in the *smṛtis*. Those differences do indeed exist, and it is impossible for it to have been otherwise, given not only differences in time of several centuries but also in distance of hundreds or thousands of kilometers. More remarkable than the differences, which only concern details, is the tremendous fundamental unity of all these texts, at least from Manu onwards. This unity cannot possibly have arisen by coincidence: it was the purposeful intention of the authors to maintain unity with Manu insofar as possible.[56] And if I can only point at this striving to maintain unity with the relatively late text of Manu, then it may very well be explained by the fact that he was the first seriously to incorporate the positive law, while his predecessors simply referred to unwritten customs.

With this in mind, the question of the mutual relation of the different law books is answered. But this was merely the preparatory problem in relation to our investigation of whether these texts were once the real authorities of law.

The conclusion I just reached regarding the purposeful unity of the texts would be freely accepted by authors like Govinda Das and Sir Henry Maine, the latter of whom says that the Dharmaśāstras offer "an ideal picture of that which, in the view of the Brahmins, ought to be the law" (1920 [1866]: 17). But before agreeing with Maine, I must consider the practical character of the *smṛtis*. To address this question, I must again digress briefly to give necessary consideration at this moment to a new literary genre, or better: a new legal source.

It was only in the first years of this century, that a manuscript of a work was discovered, which until then only been known in theory—Kauṭilya's *Arthaśāstra*. This discovery would become a watershed moment in the study of the ancient Indian institutions. First and foremost, there was the author, who was known to be the minister of kind Candragupta of the Mauryan dynasty. Here finally we had a work that could be dated accurately to the 4th century BC, a rare event in Sanskrit literature. But there was more, the content was also there. Besides, or better: in opposition to the many Dharmaśāstras, textbooks of *dharma*, we now had an Arthaśāstra, a textbook of *artha*. One will only appreciate the full

[56] The fundamental unity of the *smṛti*, the "tradition," over whole India is, according to Pargiter, explained by the fact that the authors of the *smṛti* texts, the *ṛṣis* or "seers," did not concern themselves with existing political borders, but travelled freely from one region to another. "The rishi was independent; spiritual eminence being his aim, he sought out when young the teaching of a distinguished preceptor and, when he had completed his noviciate, was free to establish his hermitage where he pleased or to seek the patronage of some king who might welcome his ministrations" (Pargiter 1922: 4).

picture, if one knows that the Hindu pursues four goals in life: *dharma*, striving for spiritual welfare; *artha*, striving for material welfare; *kāma*, striving for sexual pleasure; and *mokṣa*, striving for liberation, namely from the cycle of rebirth. From then on, one could no longer study Indian institutions on the basis of the Dharmaśāstra, that were largely a product of Brahmanical fantasy. This source of law was now replaced by the pragmatic, materially focused Arthaśāstra. Here one had for the first time information on the historical positive law from ancient India.

A certain optimism abounded: it was said that all that had been written about Indian law and Indian institutions until then should be rejected as worthless, and it should be revised on the basis of information from the *Arthaśāstra*. But as with most pathbreaking discoveries, there was rather soon a kind of awakening. One of the first results of the extensive literature that arose very soon around the *Arthaśāstra*,[57] was the dispute about its authorship. Characteristic in this connection is for example the attitude of Julius Jolly, who gradually replaced the date of 4th century BC. with the date of 3rd or 4th century AD. Similarly, the certainty of the minister of Candragupta Maurya was replaced by the uncertainty of some author who was to be searched for between the 4th century BC and 4th century AD. In short, about the dating and authorship we were in no better position with the *Arthaśāstra* than we were with the *Manusmṛti*.

If this was the first reassessment the enthusiastic reception of Kauṭilya as the only dated legal source, then I unfortunately have to add another in opposition to the assertion that only the *Arthaśāstra* can teach us something about the law in practice. Undoubtedly, the Arthaśāstra offers us much more as legal source than the Dharmaśāstras: as a handbook of administrative law, it is a unique document in Indian legal history. But it would be wrong —in a view that I, along with with Benoy Kumar Sarkar (1937: 203) and others reject— to oppose the Dharmaśāstra and Arthaśāstra as handbooks of private law and public law, respectively. Besides administrative law, Kauṭilya also treats civil law, criminal law, judicial organization, i.e. exactly the law as we find it in the *smṛtis*.[58] And again we generally compare what the *dharma* textbook and the *artha* textbook say about this same subject. But also, again, we focus too much on the differences.

Ordeals once again came to the forefront. No proof by ordeal in Kauṭilya, it was only in the Dharmaśāstras. See here the fun-

[57] For a survey, see Sarkar 1937: 1. 209–361: "The Kauṭalya Question."

[58] Jacobi 1912: 839: "Man ersieht..., dass beide Materien, Recht und Politik, eng zusammengehörten und wahrscheinlich in derselben Schule gelehrt wurden. Es ist somit wenigstens zweifelhaft, ob es ausschliessliche Schulen des Arthaśāstra gab."

damental difference between both: the Arthaśāstra, the true law, stays with both feet on the ground, and does not recognize supermundane legal proof that the Brahmins might wish for in their Dharmaśāstra.[59] Those who made such claims forgot, however, that ordeals were also missing in the Dharmasūtras, and that they only very hesitatingly enter even in Manu. And they also forgot that this silence cannot alter the fact that ordeals were already known in the Vedic period.

Jolly points for example to another difference: Kauṭilya enjoins spies as "agents provocateurs" to catch criminals. A practice worthy of the Arthaśāstra, indeed, except that Manu knows the system of the spies as well as Kauṭilya.

Therefore, looking for points of difference, one could not see the fundamental similarities. And they are there, as much as the differences. I could point to the similarity in the criminal system, of the fines (250, 500, 1000, just as in Manu), of the organization of the evidence by witnesses, etc., but I want to focus on one specific example. If one expects that the Arthaśāstra will react against privileges afforded to Brahmins in the Dharmaśāstras, surely one of the privileges would be that, whatever the offence, a Brahmin is never to be punished physically. Even for murder, his punishment is limited to simple exile. But, of course, this idea is found not only in the Dharmaśāstra, but also in Kauṭilya.

In short, this new legal source, far from giving a revolutionary image of Indian law, seems with further investigation to contain exactly the same principles as the Dharmaśāstras.[60] The deviations between Dharmaśāstra and Arthaśāstra are not more fundamental than those between the Dharmaśāstras mutually.

To be complete in our investigation of legal sources in this first period I must say something about the Epics and the Purāṇas (the "ancient" chronicles). The *Mahābhārata* calls itself a Dharmaśāstra;[61] and indeed whole sections of *dharma* rules are

[59] Jolly 1913: 94: "...dass er der rājanīti von Anfang an nicht entsprach, sich eines so abergläubischen, jeder Art von Betrug und Täuschung Tür und Tor öffnenden Beweismittels, wie die Gottesurteile, irgendwie zu bedienen."

[60] The question can be asked which of the two, Arthaśāstra or Dharmaśāstra, is the original. It is beyond the scope of this investigation to examine this question point by point. We limit ourselves to presuming that the detailed description of positive law in the Dharmaśāstra must be seen as a reaction to the redaction of the *Arthaśāstra* as independent law book, i.e., it must be explained as a precautionary measure on the part of the Brahmanical Dharmaśāstra authors, so that this subject would not escape to their purview. That they succeeded cannot be denied: "There are literally thousands of manuscripts of Manu, Yājñavalkya and Vasiṣṭha, while there have been found only three manuscripts of Kauṭilya's *Arthaśāstra*" (Ingalls 1954: 45).

[61] Ādiparvan 2.83 —cf. Dahlmann 1895.

incorporated into the *Mahābhārata*, the *Rāmāyaṇa*, and the various Purāṇas. As to the question of the origin of these didactic passages (from the Dharmasūtras, from the Dharmaśāstra, from a common source?), there is as yet no consensus. In this connection, however, I only want to establish that neither the Epics nor the Purāṇas teach us anything that is not already known from other sources.

Having shown through this long investigation the fundamental unity of all our written legal sources, I will close our description of the first period by addressing the question of whether or not this law possessed a historical reality, i.e. if this law was really applied before law courts or not.

One point I have not mentioned: India does not know the concept "law." There is no Sanskrit term to express this concept; there only is *dharma*, which I for convenience equated with "law," but that, as we have already seen, is much broader than our concept "law."

Every orthodox Hindu should live according to the whole body of rules that determine his own *dharma*, his *svadharma*. These rules are determined by his caste, his age, his profession, etc. Everyone's *svadharma* is as it were the "logical consequence" of different *dharmas* that belong to him.

Now, the king also has his *svadharma*, determined by his caste, normally a Kṣatriya, etc. and, being king, he had on top of that to pursue *rājadharma*. But to this *rājadharma* also belongs *vyavahāra*, i.e. adjudication and the title of a section of the *smṛti*, which I would describe as "law."

Just as for ordinary people, striving after one's own *dharma* brings the highest reward and violating it means decline in this life and in the life that follows, so also for a king. The dutiful fulfilling of his *rājadharma* brings great glory for him in this life and the highest blessing after his death; the renouncing of it will destroy his kingdom and bring the greatest humiliation after his death, in the shape of a dishonorable rebirth.[62]

[62] Cf. Gosvamy 1938: 201: "He (= the king) is required to wave the rod of punishment pursuant to the dictates of dharma, or else, he himself shall suffer, if not this world, surely in the next world." —Cf. also Winternitz who, while denying the practical value of the *dharma* works, at certain moments views the "lawbooks" in their function as part of *rājadharma*: "... nur insofern die Rechtsprechung zu den Pflichten der Könige gehört, finden sich auch Abschnitte über das Familienrecht, das Prozessverfahren und über das Zivil- und Strafrecht" (1922: 3.480). Still he is too persuaded as to the exclusively Brahmanical character of these texts to draw the most obvious conclusion, very rightfully as Rangaswami Aiyangar says: "The king was not the fountain of law but he was the fountain of Justice" (1952: 176), and "The king is not competent to make Dharma; he must only discover and enforce or implement it" (178).

The prescriptions are not so strict and rigid that their application seems impossible. Moreover, already in the oldest sources, custom is recognized as a very important source of law[63]: local customs, customs of the caste, customs of the family, etc., are mentioned already in the *Gautamadharmasūtra* as an authoritative source of law, and not one *smṛti* fails to recognize this.

The only condition for the validity of the custom —and this is important— is that it not be contrary to the prescriptions of the Veda, i.e. with the *dharma*. In actual practice, this means that, the custom may not go against the rules described in the Dharmasūtras and Dharmaśāstras. The codified rules functioned as general guidelines, which allowed for very free supplementation by the uncodified customs.

Our conclusion about the first period in Indian Law should be this:

We possess a gradual codification of certain legal rules, which all in principle tried to describe the unchangeable foundation of the *sanātanadharma*. The differences in details may not be explained as a conscious adaptation of the texts to changing social circumstances. But this theoretically unchangeable system is not an abstract game of the Brahmanical mind; it was indeed applied as part of *rājadharma* with religious sanction. This practical application in different places and different times was made possible by the important role ascribed to custom, which could freely included within the structure of the *smṛti* so long as it did not contradict the latter.

Second Period: The Period of the Commentaries and the Nibandhas

The Dharmasūtras and Dharmaśāstras were in all likelihood very early subjects for commentators. We have seen after all that the style of the older Dharmasūtras was such that they were practically not understandable without the simultaneous explanation of a guru. But the second period of Indian law is marked by the fact that, on the one hand, no new *smṛtis* were composed, while, on the other hand, the existing *smṛtis* became the subject of written commentaries. I distinguish here the commentaries proper, in which focus mainly on one specific *smṛti*, and the *nibandhas* in which many *smṛtis* are invoked on equal footing in the argument.

In our current knowledge of the texts, this period begins in the 7th or 8th century AD and stretches to the last years of the 18th century, with some *nibandhas* immediately preceding the third period.

[63] For the custom as a source of law, see Kane 1930–62: 3.825–884; Rocher 1952: 92–95.

One fact must instantly attract our attention. This period roughly coincides with the time of Muslim dominance in India. And also in part with British dominance, but these last two centuries should be seen as distinct from Muslim times —a time, namely, in which the British turned a blind eye to legal practices that were maintained unmodified in the previous period.

The question that we have to solve for the second period of Hindu law is as follows. How can we understand the origin of this huge commentarial literature in the historical framework of Muslim dominance in India and what role did it have in practice?

The first question is: did Muslim rulers continue to permit Hindu law to be applied in radically different historical circumstances?

The editor of the 11th edition of *Mayne's Hindu Law and Usage*, N. Chandrasekhara Aiyar, claims that as in the earlier period, so also in this period of Indian history, Hindu law should be seen as "fully recognized and enforced" (1950: 4).[64] As proof for this statement, he cites, among others, the fact that Akbar's own minister of finance, Ṭoḍaramalla, was the author of a huge and detailed *nibandha*, the *Ṭoḍarānanda*.

Our investigation of the first period led to the conclusion that we *with* Mayne, *against* Govinda Das, should understand the *smṛtis* as actually applied law. When it comes to the second period, however, I can no longer agree with Mayne because he oversimplifies the evidence.

If we follow K.M. Panikkar in one of his many textual notices,[65] we must see the Muslim period in India as one of constant con-

[64] Further on the same page: "Even after the establishment of the Muhammadan Rule in the country, the Smriti Law continued to be fully recognised and enforced" is added a restriction: "During the Muhammadan rule in India, while Hindu Criminal Law ceased to be enforced, the Hindu Civil Law continued to be in force amongst Hindu." The first, general statement, as has been said, relies on the fact that extensive juridical works were written even by ministers of the Muslim emperors. How can this fact be joined with Chandrasekhara's second statement, if we know that the juridical treatises of this period also pay equal attention to criminal law and civil law?

[65] 'Preface' to Vaidya 1948: 1.xv: "During this period, one of the main concerns of Hindu thinkers was the maintenance of their inherited social organisation. The Hindu social structure was facing a grave crisis. The egalitarian conception of Islam and its prosyletising activity had created for Hinduism special problems which could not be overlooked. The reaction of Hindu law-givers to this challenge was in general to make Hinduism more rigid and to re-interpret the rules in such way as to resist the encroachments of Islam. It is perhaps this defensive attitude towards society that is responsible for the orthodoxy of views which is the characteristic of the Dharma Śāstra literature of this period." I cannot agree with Panikkar in declaring that the strongly orthodox character of the lawbooks of the Middle Ages be seen as a reaction to Muslim oppression. See further discussion below.

flict: on the one side, Islam, which tries to expand this influence by force, and, on the other, a form of resistance specific to Hinduism, a less aggressive but tough form of resistance that withstood the invasions of various foreign rulers through assimilation. This resistance of Hinduism, along with constant inner conflicts and discord in the Muslim empire in India, led to the fact that the hold of Islam varied widely in India according to local circumstances, not only across the centuries, but also in each specific moment of history.

First, there was the area that stood under direct control of the central Muslim ruler, initially Delhi's sultan, later on the Mughal emperor. There is no doubt that in this part of India, Hindu law was a dead letter. It is true that we have an ordinance of emperor Akbar from 1586 in which it is said that the Hindus from then on will be judged by learned Brahmins and no longer by Muslim *qāzīs* (Blochmann 1873: 1.205). But Akbar was simply an exception, and it is this exceptional quality that explains the fact, adduced by Mayne, that the *Ṭoḍarānanda* could have been written by the emperor's own minister of finance. But the ordinance also shows that Akbar wanted to put an end to situations in which Hindus were subject to the law of Islam. Moreover, though Akbar did accept a Hindu as minister, this openness was far from total, as may be clearly seen in works such as Abu'l Fazl's *Āīn-i-Akbarī*, in which little good is said about the Hindu minister Ṭoḍaramalla. I must assume that, in such circumstances, Akbar's ordinance did not survive the emperor himself and that already his successor, Jahāngīr, returned to the old system.

The so-called Muslim vassal states, in which the degree of independence was always inversely proportional to the power of the emperor, present the same image of the law as the area controlled by the emperor himself.

Finally, there were also a few Hindu states that in certain border regions managed to minimize the hold of Islam. In these states, Muslim administration was in many ways imitated (Jadunath Sarkar 1924: 3), but Hindu kings still ruled. This rule was in practice often very weak, but still we know it was they —I think here especially of the rulers of Mithilā[66] in the far north— who patronized the authors of the juridical commentaries. It is only at these extreme boundaries of India that I can speak, with K.M. Pannikkar, about a somewhat active resistance of Hinduism.

In the area of law, however, any resistance was expressed over the whole of India in a more passive way, if at all. For that I turn to the juridical works of this period itself.

[66] To get an idea of the unusual measure of literary production in Mithilā (= Tirhut) even in the Muslim period, see Singh 1922.

The question of whether or not these works in some way reflect the changed historical background can immediately be answered with a strong "no." If we only knew the juridical literature from this period, we would not even know that there were Muslims in India at the time.

When I saw K.V. Rangaswami Aiyangar's book *Rājadharma* (1941) for the first time some years ago, I was very skeptical about passages such as: "A study of the variations of opinion among Indian writers on Dharmaśāstra will not disclose much chronological progress of ideas, and so-called 'liberal views' may be found in writers of earlier and so-called 'conservative' learning in those of later times" (36).

To deny in one sentence any development of thought to an extensive literature that spans a period of about ten centuries must surely reflect the author's orthodox impulses. Nevertheless, the more I too looked for that development, the more I had to agree with Rangaswami Aiyangar: the commentarial literature of the 18th century defends exactly the same opinions as those of a thousand years earlier.

In addition, I must now recall our first remarks about this second period, namely the fact that in practice the Hindu law was almost wholly displaced by Islamic law. The two points dovetail nicely and open up a more complete understanding of the character and the historical value of commentarial and *nibandha* literature.

The entire commentarial tradition is totally separated from reality; nor was it ever intended to intervene in the reality of practical law and jurisdiction.[67] In fact, it was impossible to put into practice at that moment. Similar to other extensive commentarial literature about abstract subjects, such as, for example, logic, or Nyāya, the *dharma* literature of the Hindu medieval era is simply another element of Brahmin scholasticism, in which the intention of the pandits consisted solely of interpreting without distinction all the ancient texts to the best of their ability and of preserving the knowledge of them.[68] In saying that the legal literature of this

[67] Here I cannot possibly agree with Chandrasekhara Aiyar 1950:1–2: "Later Commentaries and Digests were equally the exponents of the usages of their times in those parts of India where they were composed. And in the guise of commenting, they developed and expounded the rules in greater detail, differentiated between the Smriti rules which continued to be in force and those which had become obsolete; and in the process, incorporated also new usages which had sprung up."

[68] During a visit to one of the numerous Sanskrit schools in India I had the pleasure of meeting a teacher in one of the classrooms who was teaching one of the ancient law books to his students. And he too spoke of an aspect of the law in practice as guarded by a modern code.

period was totally isolated from its historical context, however, I risk giving the impression that this literature has nothing of interest to offer.[69] To avoid this impression I conclude the argument about the second period by giving a brief outline of these texts.

For the commentators, all Dharmasūtras and Dharmaśāstras belong to *smṛti*, the sacred tradition, which in turn goes back to the Veda, the revelation. In this way, all of these texts have an unquestionable and equal authority which cannot be denied.[70]

In practice, however, there are texts that admit of widely divergent interpretations. Using one and the same *smṛti* text, the authors of the *Mitākṣarā* and the *Dāyabhāga* built totally different laws of inheritance. Where the text according to the author of the *Mitākṣarā* means that the son may claim a part in the ownership of family property simply by his birth, the same text according to the author of the *Dāyabhāga* means ownership arises only at the death of the father.[71]

Things get even more complex if two or more *smṛti* texts seem to contradict. For a commentator, such a contradiction can only exist in appearance, and it is up to him to find the right interpretation that will eliminate the contradiction and support both texts. He was assisted in this task by interpretive rules developed in another school, the Mīmāṃsā. I may take, for example, the simple case of interpretation according to *viṣayabheda*, i.e. different spheres of application. This is invoked, among other places, when two texts concerning the slander of a Kṣatriya prescribe two different punishments. The commentator says that the lesser punishment is to be applied when a Vaiśya is the perpetrator and the greater in the case of a Śūdra.

[69] Some authors have given the wrong impression. For example Jadunath Sarkar 1924: 250–251: "Muslim rule also arrested the growth of the Hindus... In consequence, Sanskrit learning virtually died out of mediaeval India. What little was left of it, was extremely barren and consisted of logical subtleties, elaboration of rituals, new editions of Canon Law, commentaries on old books, and commentaries on commentaries."

[70] It is this fact (*contra* Panikkar, above) which declares the strongly orthodox character of the law books in this period.

[71] Sankararama Sastri 1926: 168: "The very diversity of opinion so frequently met with among the commentaries and digests indicates rather that the author is actuated by a desire to discover a legal warrant for the custums and practices of the province in which he flourished from the original sources than that to interpret the law to the best of his lights." It is indeed true, that the *Mitākṣarā* and the *Dāyabhāga* (and to a lesser extent other *nibandhas* as well) are only binding in certain parts of India, and not in others. But this is not enough reason to suppose that they were originally meant to codify the Common law of the area where their prescriptions were applied later. Sankararama Sastri and others confuse here the *result* of differences of opinions between the commentaries with their *cause*.

Another way to eliminate a contradiction is to consider one rule to be *vidhi*, i.e. a positive injunction, and the other to be *arthavāda*, i.e. an explanatory statement or exhortative exaggeration. For example. according to a specific rule a deposit cannot be lost through adverse possession. If another text classifies deposits with instances of adverse possession, then the commentator will declare that the *smṛti* should not be taken literally, just as the old adage "Take poison, rather than eat in that man's house" does not mean you should actually *take* the poison.

As we see, there was plenty of room for argumentation, but argumentation that relies on factors of personal ability, such as the more or less extensive knowledge of the Mīmāṃsā rules, the sharpness of the mind of the author, etc. The remarkable fact is that each author wanted to surpass the other, with the result being that these so-called juridical commentaries grew into one big academic tournament of subtle argument.[72]

The judgment of this literature by Govinda Das is astonishing: "The attempt of the commentators and the digest writers to deduce a coherent and mutually not contradictory set of laws binding on all Hindus has been a dismal failure and a woeful waste of vast and intricate but misapplied learning" (1914: 27).

I hope, however, to have made at least one thing clear: Govinda Das is totally wrong according to the intentions of these authors.

Third Period: The Anglo-Indian Period

The previous period has already brought us to the end of the 18th century. At that point, two centuries had passed since the December 31, 1600, the day on which Queen Elizabeth granted the monopoly over trade with the East to the East India Company. Initially the British were unconcerned about the laws of India. But the gradual transformation of trading companies into colonial powers created a responsibility for the British to adjudicate disputes between their Indian subjects.

It no doubt speaks in favor of the British that they were not inclined to force their own laws on the Indians. This position was not taken without resistance, however, which I will illustrate here with the help of a fragment from the letter of Sir William Jones to Lord Cornwallis (dated March 19, 1788):

[72] This subtle way of arguing reaches a culmination unknown in Western legal literature, when the juridical authors turn to a new kind of logic that developed about this time in India (the Navyanyāya). The reader is referred, for example, to the discussions about the concept of *svatva* (ownership) in Derrett 1956.

> Nothing indeed could be more obviously just, than to determine private contests according to those laws, which the parties themselves had ever considered as the rules of their conduct and engagements in civil life; nor could any thing be wiser than, by a legislative act, to assure the Hindu and Muselman subjects of Great Britain, that the private laws, which they severally hold sacred, and violation of which they would have thought the most grievous oppression, should not be superseded by a new system, of which they could have no knowledge, and which they must have considered as imposed on them by a spirit of rigour and intolerance. (Cited in Rankin 1946: 17)

Jones's statement testifies to the strange fact that certain historical foundations of ancient Indian law also have to be sought in the 19th and 20th centuries!

Indeed, the first practical result of such a view was that in 1773 a commission of ten pandits was called together to summarize all that is essential of the classical Hindu law in a code.[73] This compendium, which was finished in 1775, was translated into Persian and via Persian translated into English. Thus, the English judges possessed in Halhed's *Code of Gentoo Laws* a first instrument to adjudicate disputes between Hindus. Furthermore, from 1772 onwards pandits were attached to every court, who served as advisors to the British judges on questionable matters of Hindu law, an institution that lasted until 1864. Soon men such as Sir William Jones, Colebrooke, and others learned to read the Sanskrit texts themselves and began to translate them into English. Of course, we must always remember that they were never driven by simple philological curiosity in that all their works were meant to contribute to the practical application of Hindu law in the courts.[74]

Certain aspects of Hindu law the British immediately considered intolerable. In some cases, this concerned rare practices such as *satī*, or widow burning, that were then simply prohibited; in other cases, whole areas of law, such as criminal law, procedural law, etc., were replaced by codes modeled on English law books.[75]

[73] Cf. Halhed 1776: ix: "Nothing can so favourably conduce to these two Points (what is meant: conciliate the Affections of the Natives, or ensure Stability to the Acquisition) as a well-timed Toleration in Matters of Religion, and an Adoption of such original Institutes of the Country, as do not immediately clash with the Laws of Interests of the Conquerors."

[74] Cf. Benfey 1869: 341: "Was den Bestrebungen der Missionäre nicht gelingen sollte, verdankt die Wissenschaft mittelbar dem Handel und unmittelbar, wenigstens zunächts, dem Rechtgefühl, eine Erscheinung, die bis jetzt in der Geschichte der Wissenschaften ganz vereinzelt dastehen möchte." Cf. also Windisch 1917–1920: 33.

[75] So the Indian Penal Code (1860), the Indian Evidence Act (1872), the Code of Criminal Procedure (1898), the Code of Civil Procedure (1908), etc.

What interests us as well is the actual Hindu law as it was applied by courts in India, and this concerned especially laws of marriage, adoption, property, inheritance, etc., in short the whole area of civil law. The British strove diligently in these areas to revive a natural application of the ancient Hindu law —an attempt in which they succeeded in some measure—, but there were still two factors that made this renewal of very short duration.

First, the application of Hindu law by British judges suffered early on from several anomalies, to which I can point only briefly.[76] The British judge, could not, for example, read the Sanskrit texts himself. He had to rely on translations that very occasionally and unfortunately differed in essential places, and which, moreover, encompassed but a small part of the law, so that it often happened that one or the other party, who by chance knew Sanskrit, pled to the judge on the basis of law that the judge did not know, etc. Obviously, such cases have not contributed to certainty in the law.

One might have established this certainty by codifying the Hindu law, but nothing beyond the Hindu Code project has yet been pursued. Even the most orthodox Hindus did not foresee that India would be swept up into a fundamental social, economic and political revolution, with the result that many prescriptions of ancient Hindu law became impossible or undesirable.[77] The idea of a comprehensive codification was mooted, but the Indian Parliament in Delhi has repeatedly passed an array of laws that have gradually killed ancient Hindu law: marriage has become dissolvable, women have gained the same rights to property as men, etc. In fact, in recent years we can no longer speak of Hindu law proper.

* * *

I can summarize as follows:

In the first period we saw how ancient unwritten legal customs were gradually integrated in the *sanātanadharma*, with the

[76] Cf. Goldstücker 1871; Rocher 1952, especially its notes.

[77] Sarma 1941: 15: "…most of these books (= the dharmaśāstras) are only of historical importance now. For Hindu society has naturally changed during all these intervening centuries and many new factors undreamt of by old lawgivers have come into existence. Accordingly many of the old laws have become obsolete. Our society has outgrown them. It would be as impossible for us to order our lives today according to these old laws as for a man of twenty five to wear a coat which was made for him when he was a child of five… All that I can do is to follow the spirit and not the letter of our ancient law-givers." Unhappily this healthy opinion has not prevented other organizations such as the R.S.S. (Rāṣṭrīya Svayaṃsevaka Saṃgha) from pursuing a reintroduction and strict application of the ancient law books.

consequence that in all the textual codifications there is a deliberate intention to maintain this unity. These rules were indeed meant to be applied in practice, an application that was made easier by the widespread recognition that the source of law was unwritten custom.

The second period offers the converse image. In adjudication, Hindu law is replaced by Islamic law. But beyond this, there develops a new kind of legal literature, this time not bent on deliberate intentions toward unity, but rather on a desire of the authors to outdo each other through subtle argumentation.

In the third period, at last, there is under the impulse of the British an effort to re-establish the Hindu Law before the courts and also the works from the second period; but the application of it by non-Hindus and especially the realization of the modern, democratic India seems to have as consequence that this effort will end soon, and, what is more, that it, this time for ever, will be the last.

Translated from the Dutch by Savita de Backer, with editorial emendations.

3

Hindu Law and Religion: Where to Draw the Line

S.V. Gupte's *Hindu Law in British India* enunciates the following general principle:

> *The Courts are to enforce only rules of positive law and not religious or moral precepts.* It will be recalled that the Smritis and the Commentaries and Digests contain a considerable admixture of law and religion. Therefore, in applying the rules contained in the Smritis and the Commentaries and Digests, the principal question is whether a particular rule is a rule of positive law or a religious or a moral precept, for the Courts are concerned with rules of positive law only. (1947: 49)

This statement implies two important points: British Indian law was aware of the existence, within Hindu law, of "a considerable admixture of law and religion," and those who were called upon to apply it thought that they could and should separate the "rules of positive law" from the "religious or moral precepts." What is more, they decided that only the "rules of positive law" had to be taken into account in the Courts, whereas the so-called "religious or moral percepts" need not.

As usual, a rule such as the one mentioned above: "The Courts are to enforce only rules of positive law and not religious or moral precepts," had found its way into textbooks on Hindu law only after having been formulated by some of the more prominent judges or by a bench —often the Privy Council— in a number of specific cases. I shall briefly discuss at least one of these cases, because it will bring us a step closer to the thesis which I propose to defend in this paper. This case in question is *Sri Balusu* v. *Sri*

Balusu,[78] the general subject-matter of which can be summarized in this abstract:

> That appeal had reference to the validity of the adoption of an only son. From the religious point of view this is, in many writings of great authority, forbidden. There was, however, in India, considerable difference in the view as to whether the religious and legal institutions on the subject were co-extensive... The case resuited in the decision that the adoption of an only son is not null and void under the Hindu law.[79]

Coming more specially to the problem of the relation between law and religion, their Lordships made the following statement which was to carry a lot of weight in later history of Hindu law:

> Their Lordships had occasion in a late case[80] to dwell upon the mixture of morality, religion and law in the Smritis. They then said, "All these old text-books and commentaries are apt to mingle religious and moral considerations, not being positive laws, with rules intended for positive laws." They now add that the further study of the subject necessary for the decision of these appeals has still more impressed them with the necessity of great caution in interpreting books of mixed religion, morality and law, lest foreign lawyers accustomed to treat as law what they find in authoritative books, and to administer fixed legal systems, should too hastily take for strict law precepts which are meant to appeal to the moral sense, and should thus fetter individual judgements in private affairs, should introduce restrictions into Hindu society, and impart to it an inflexible rigidity, never contemplated by the original lawgivers. (*Sri Balasu*, 136)

For all practical purposes, that meant that the Privy Council did recognize the mixture of law and religion in the Hindu lawbooks. But, at the same time, they professed that when it came to handling legal cases in the courts, the religious element was of no importance. It could simply be discarded, and the only elements to be taken into consideration were the rules of positive law. Later in the same P.C. judgment we read:

> . . . the British rulers of India have in few things been more careful than in avoiding interference with the religious tenets of the Indian peoples. They provide for the peace and stability of families by imposing limits on attempts to disturb the possession of property and the personal legal status of individuals. With the religious side of such matters they do not pretend to interfere. But the posi-

[78] 26 I.A. 113 (P.C.) (1889).
[79] From *Tilak v. Srinivas Pandit*, 42 I.A. 149 (1915).
[80] *Rao Balwant Singh v. Rani Kishori* 25 I.A. 54,69 (1898).

> tion is altered if the validity of temporal arrangements on which temporal courts are asked to decide is to be made subordinate to inquiries into religious beliefs. (*Sri Balasu*, 139)

So far, I could not agree more. I shall come back to this point again. I fully agree not only with the Privy Council but also with all the Indians and the non-Indians, who held the same opinion in more recent times. In view of the totally changed social and economic circumstances, I think it was good for the Hindu law to sever ties with traditional religion. However, where I can no longer follow the Privy Council and a number of modern authors is where they pose that the making of a neat distinction between religion and law is normal within the traditional framework of the so-called Hindu law. I cannot agree with them when they say that, unless we separate religion and law, we come to a situation "never contemplated by the original law-givers." Nor can I, therefore, subscribe to the following statement made by the Privy Council in *Sri Balusu* v. *Sri Balusu*:

> No system of law makes the province of legal obligation coextensive with that of religious or moral obligation. A man may, in his conduct or in the disposition of his property, disregard the plainest dictates of duty. He may prefer an unworthy stranger to those who have the strongest natural claims upon him. He may be ungrateful, selfish, cruel, treacherous to those who have confided in him and whose affection for him has ruined them. And yet he may be within his legal rights. The Hindu sages doubtless saw this distinction as clearly as we do, and the precepts they have given for the guidance of life must be construed with reference to it. If a transaction is declared to be null and void in law, whether on a religious ground or another, it is so; and if its nullity is a necessary implication from a condemnation of it the law must be so declared. But the mere fact that a transaction is condemned in books like the Smritis does not necessarily prove it to be void. It raises the question what kind of condemnation is meant. (139–140)

I can now proceed to unfold the three faceted thesis of this paper. First is the classical, i.e., pre-British, Hindu law where religion and law were indeed co-extensive. In the second, which covers from the British period up to the present day, more recent examples than *Sri Balusu* v. *Sri Balusu* will be cited. There has been, in this facet, a tendency to separate law from religion. As for the third facet, this distinction between law and religion in modern times is good but to justify it on the ground that in so doing one perpetuates the original situation is to place the history of Hindu law in a false perspective. In reality it is one of these characteristic cases where British Hindu law has sharply departed from the traditional and historical evolution of Hindu law.

I shall try to place this specific case of departure from the spirit of Hindu law in its proper setting towards the end of this paper. At this moment I shall adduce some arguments to show why and how religion and law were and had to be intertwined in what we erroneously call classical Hindu "law."

My first argument is a highly theoretical one. It concerns the very nature of the so-called Hindu law. However, notwithstanding its theoretical character, it is an argument with very practical consequences. Let us for a moment return to the year 1772, when Hastings proclaimed an order which, although born of the intention not to interfere with the law of the Indians, was the basis of all difficulties which the British were to encounter later in this field:

> In all suits regarding inheritance, marriage, caste and other religious usages or institutions, the laws of the Koran with respect to Mohamedans and those of the Shaster with respect to the Gentoos shall invariably be adhered to.

Obviously, the term "Shaster" was a reference to the entire body of what the Hindus call Dharmaśāstra. A short examination of the nature of Dharmaśāstra might be very helpful at this point. It is true that the *Mānava-Dharmaśāstra* became, right from William Jones' translation onward (completed 1793, published 1796), known as "the Laws of Manu"; and the Dharmaśāstras generally were soon to become "the Indian law books." This terminology requires no explanation. The very reason why Jones and others after him tried to read and understand the Dharmaśāstras, the very reason why they undertook to translate these books, was to be in possession of a set of laws which they might then, in application of Hasting's order, administer to Hindus in the Courts.

In reality, the Dharmaśāstras were not treatises (*śāstra*) of law but of *dharma*. Thus, from examining the nature of the Dharmaśāstra, we have now been led to ask the question: what is *dharma*? This is not an easy question at all. As stated by P.V. Kane in the very first sentence of his monumental *History of Dharmaśāstra*, "*Dharma* is one of those Sanskrit terms that defy all attempts at an exact rendering in English or any other tongue" (1930–62: 1.1). In the absence of an adequate English term, we shall try the following definition: *dharma* is the way, the right way of behaving oneself. And this correct behavior is expected of each and every element in the universe and at each and every moment as well. It goes without saying that the Dharmaśāstras are mainly concerned with human behavior, with human *dharma*. But they do treat human *dharma* in all its aspects; no type of human activity can be imagined without there being some prescriptions about it in the Dharmaśāstra. The result is that *dharma* is an extremely vague term, covering a wide range of men's activities, including those which, in our terminology, would be called legal, religious, etc. The result also was that the British courts were very embarrassed by the term, as is clear from *Runchordas* v. *Parvatibhai*:

> A bequest by a Hindu testator of moveable and immovable property to trustees for *dharam* was held void. The objects which can be considered to be meant by that word are too vague and uncertain for the administration of them to be under any control.[81]

After these general remarks on the concept of *dharma* in Hinduism, I shall now advance my first argument for the mixture of law and religion as I see it. Law and religion, together with many other aspects of human behavior, are always treated under a single heading *dharma*. What is more, "law" and "religion" have no independent and separate existence in the texts on *dharma*. There are no Sanskrit terms to translate "law" and "religion." "Law" and "religion" are Western compartments which have been artificially introduced into the Hindu *dharma*. There is and there cannot be a line of separation between both. Whenever or wherever we try to introduce such a line of separation, it is an artificial one, which was non-existent for the authors of the Dharmaśāstras.

Incidentally, I must come back here to one of the statements of the Privy Council quoted above. They said: "All these old textbooks and commentaries are apt to mingle religious and moral considerations, not being positive laws, with rules intended for positive laws." Even a statement thus worded is not completely correct, at least not from the Indian point of view. It adequately describes the nature of Dharmaśāstra as the Western scholar sees it, but it should not make us forget that, to the traditional Indian mind, there are no such categories as "law," "religion," and "ethics" and that, consequently, there can be no question of "mingling" these categories together.

The most accurate way of describing the situation would probably be to accept that while all rules and prescriptions, which were grouped either under "law" or under "religion" or under "ethics," do find their place in the so-called Hindu law-books, they are organic and inseparable parts of a single branch of Hindu learning: *dharma*. It was, therefore, unavoidable that the British, as soon as they started looking for legal prescriptions, came across a number of elements which they considered to be nonlegal. I fully appreciate the problems which the English judges

[81] 26 I.A. 71 (P.C.) (1899), from 23 Bom. 725.

in India were faced with when they made this discovery. But that should not prevent us from attributing their distinction between legal and non-legal rules to a lack of historical perspective.

To this first argument of a more or less theoretical character I shall now add a number of practical examples, which have the additional advantage of not only demonstrating that law and religion are co-extensive, but also of showing how both categories go harmoniously together.

The first series of examples will be chosen from a field of law which the British abolished from an early stage, i.e., the criminal law. The replacement of the ancient Hindu criminal law by a Western code rendered the mixture of law and religion in this field of less concern to the English judges. However, it is, important to show that even in an area in which the influence of religion might be smaller —smaller, for instance, than in the field of family law—, the situation described above manifested itself as strongly as in any other area.

The example, which presents itself immediately is the overall influence of the caste system on the degree and on the kind of punishment to be awarded for a particular offense. Identical offenses call for completely different punishments according to the caste of the perpetrator or the victim. Says Baudhāyana (in Bühler's translation):

> If a Kshatriya or (a man of any) other (lower caste) has murdered a Brahmana, death and the confiscation of all his property (shall be his punishment).
> If those same (persons) slay men of equal or lower castes, (the king) shall fix suitable punishments in accordance with their ability.
> For slaying a Kshatriya (the offender) shall give to the king one thousand cows and besides a bull in expiation of his sin.
> For (slaying) a Vaisya one hundred cows, for (slaying) a Sudra ten; and a bull (must be) added (in each case).
> (The punishment for) the murder of a woman —excepting a (Brahmani) who had bathed after temporary uncleanness— and for the destruction of a cow have been explained by the (rule regarding the) murder of a Sudra. (1.18.19–19.3)

Even less "legal" than this general inequality is the preferential treatment of Brahmins who, whatever be the crime which they commit, are exempt from corporal punishment. Manu lays down the following general rule:

> Manu, the son of the Self-existent (*Svayambhu*), has named ten places on which punishment may be (made in full) in the cases of the three (lower) castes (*varṇa*); but a Brahmana shall depart unhurt (from the country). (8.124, Bühler)

In certain cases the king's jurisdiction over Brahmins is even waived, "for fear that he may rouse their anger." Thus Bṛhaspati (1.27) and Kātyāyana (83):

> (The king) should cause the disputes of ascetics and of persons versed in sorcery and witchcraft to be settled by persons familiar with the three Vedas only, and not (decide them) himself, for fear of rousing their resentment. (Jolly's translation)

For the benefit of those who maintain that the true spirit of practical Hindu law should be gathered not from the Dharmaśāstras but from the more realistic Arthaśāstra, it might be added here that the same verse also occurs in Kauṭilya's *Arthaśāstra* (1.19.32).

Besides the influence of the caste system, a thorough understanding of the nature of ancient Hindu criminal law should also take into consideration the fact that criminal law in ancient India was a duty of the king; in other words, it was part of the *rājadharma*. I have shown elsewhere (Rocher 1955; see chapter 7) that Hindu law gradually developed something which comes very close to what we consider to be criminal law. But that did not prevent the very basis of "criminal law," more specifically the sanction foreseen for the king who was in charge of it, from being unquestionably "religious." Says Manu:

> Let him carefully restrain the wicked by three methods —by imprisonment, by putting them in fetters and by various (kinds of) corporal punishment.
> For by punishing the wicked and by favouring the virtuous, kings are constantly sanctified, just as the twice-born men by sacrifices. (8.310–311, Bühler)

And the term used for 'sanctified' is *pūyante*, which is exactly the one employed to indicate the ritual purification obtained by correctly performing a sacrifice. Once again, a different but equally religious sanction is provided for by Kauṭilya:

> (Carrying out) his own duty by the king, who protects the subjects according to law, leads to heaven; of one who does not protect or who inflicts an unjust punishment, (the condition) is the reverse. (3.1.41, Kangle)

The last few instances also raise another more general question which I can only touch upon in this context, a question however which again clearly illustrates the intimate relation between law and religion. I refer here to the coexistence of crime and punishment on the one hand and sin and penance on the other. For a detailed study of penances in ancient Indian legal literature, I can point to W. Gampert's *Die Sühnezeremonien in der altindischen*

Rechtsliteratur (1939). The general idea seems to be that whoever commits a crime at the same time commits a sin. Thus, in a chapter which for all practical purposes deals with punishments and the way in which they should be inflicted by the king, Manu says:

> The slayer of a Brahmana, (a twice-born man) who drinks (the spirituous liquor called) Sura, he who steals (the gold of a Brahmana), and he who violates a Guru's bed, must each and all be considered as men who committed mortal sins (*mahapātaka*). (9.235, Bühler)

The exact relation between punishment and penance is an extremely complex one, which deserves to be studied in detail. My point here was to show that for acts which we consider to belong to the field of law we are often confronted, sometimes unexpectedly, with "religious" penances, as in this verse by Bṛhaspati:

> If a man seizes somebody's land which had been given to the latter by himself or by somebody else, he becomes a worm in excrement and is burned together with his ancestors. (*Āpaddharma*, 38)

After these few examples from ancient Hindu "criminal law," which have only a historical interest and never came up before the British Courts in India, I shall now proceed to another series of examples which have much more than a purely historical interest; they are cases which the British judges were often actively confronted with.

The Hindu marriage offers an excellent example of "law" and "religion" being interrelated. In his summary of the Hindu law of marriage prior to the passing of the Hindu Marriage Act, 1956, S.V. Gupte (1961) very aptly places at the head of his discussion, as article 1: "Marriage is a 'samskara', or a sacrament." Indeed, until very recently, when the idea of a civil contract appeared, a Hindu marriage was never regarded as a contract at all. It was a *saṃskāra* or, as Gupte puts it, "one of the ten samskaras through which the life of a well-conducted Hindu progresses to its appointed end" (1961: 6). This conception of the nature of marriage led to a few interesting results, some of which I shall try to point out here.

Thus, a Hindu marriage, being a *saṃskāra*, constituted an indissoluble union. To quote again from Gupte in his commentary on article 1:

> The nature of the union constituted by marriage was reflected in the incidents and legal consequences of a Hindu marriage. Thus, for instance, marriage being a samskara was an indissoluble union. (6)

Moreover, although the Hindu law did know the concept of incompetence because of young age (*aprāptavyavahāratva*), this is not applicable to marriage. For the male Hindu belonging to one of the three higher castes, there is, of course, the restriction that his marriage should be preceded by another *saṃskāra*, namely: the investiture with the sacred thread (*upanayana*). But a female Hindu, who is excluded from *upanayana*, can be given in marriage at any age. There is even more: not only does a Hindu father have a right to give his daughter in marriage at a very early age, he has the obligation to do so before she reaches puberty. If he fails to do so, the text of Yājñavalkya applies:

> If a father does not give his daughter in marriage before the age of puberty he incurs the sin connected with the killing of an embryo at each period of menstruation. (YDh 1.64)

The father's obligation to give his daughter in marriage was very well illustrated in the case of *Purshottamdas* v. *Purshottamdas*.[82] The plaintiff, who had been betrothed to the defendant's daughter, claimed that, if the girl was not given in marriage to him, he should be allotted Rs. 25,000 damages for breach of the contract of betrothal. The defendant replied that he could not give his daughter in marriage, because she was not willing to marry the plaintiff. The Court's decision was in favour of the plaintiff:

> This [i.e., the defendant's] argument is based on the proposition that all contracts of betrothal in Hindu families are subject to the implied condition that when the time for the marriage has arrived, the girl is willing to be married. The contract is to give the girl in marriage: that involves the willingness of the girl to be given. But to ask the Court to accept this proposition is virtually to ask the Court to disregard the precepts of Hindu law, which treat the marriage of daughters as a religious duty imposed on the parents and guardians, and to look at the matter from the purely English point of view, which sees in marriage nothing but a contract to which the husband and wife must be consenting parties...

Another aspect of the indissoluble character of marriage is the interdiction for widows to remarry. Says Manu:

> A faithful wife, who desires to dwell (after death) with her husband, must never do anything that might displace him who took her hand, whether he be alive or dead. At her pleasure let her emaciate her body by (living on) pure flowers, roots, and fruit; but she must never even mention the name of another man after her

[82] 21 Bom. L.R. 23 (1897).

> husband has died. Until death let her be patient (of hardships), self-controlled, and chaste, and strive (to fulfil) that most excellent duty which (is prescribed) for wives who have one husband only. (5.156–158, Bühler)

Although the widows interdiction to remarry actually does not require any justification once one accepts the indissoluble nature of marriage, the Indian "law books" found it necessary to also provide for a reward for faithful widows and a sanction for the widows who were not.

Thus in Manu one finds:

> She who, controlling her thoughts, words and deeds, never slights her lord, resides (after death) with her husband (in heaven), and is called a virtuous (wife).
> In reward of such conduct, a female who controls her thoughts, speech and actions, gains in this (life) highest renown, and in the next (world) a place near her husband. (5.165–166, Bühler)

And again:

> But a woman who from desire to have offspring violates her duty towards her (deceased) husband, brings on herself disgrace in this world, and loses her place with her husband (in heaven). (5.161, Bühler)

So far, I have tried to interpret the various aspects of the Hindu marriage against the common background of its being a *saṃskāra* and, as a result, an indissoluble union. At that stage the "religious" factor was the most important one. Perhaps, we should even go one step further. It is quite possible that the nature of the Hindu marriage, in its turn, was a logical consequence of the goal of marriage in Hindu society. And, although the goal of the Hindu marriage too has strong religious overtones, I would dare to suggest that the social factor is by no means completely absent.

Manu has an interesting etymological explanation of the term for wife: *jayā*, one which is much older than the *Mānava-Dharmaśāstra*, since it already occurs in the *Aitareyabrāhmaṇa*:

> The husband, after conception by his wife, becomes an embryo and is born again of her; for that is the wifehood of a wife (*jayā*) that he is born (*jāyate*) again by her. (9.8, Bühler)

In other words, the main purpose of a married woman and, hence, of marriage itself, is the continuation of the father's lineage and the procreation of a son. The importance of having a son has been stressed again and again in Sanskrit literature. I shall again quote two stanzas from Manu:

> Through a son he conquers the worlds, through a son's son he obtains immortality, but through his son's grandson he gains the world of the sun. Because a son delivers (*trāyate*) his father from the hell called *Put*, he was therefore called *put-tra* (a deliverer from *Put*) by the Self-Existent (*Svayambhu*) himself. (9.137–138, Bühler)

There is no doubt that the kind of etymology given here for *putra* is worthless linguistically which is not important for our present purpose. What is important is that it gives us a deep insight into what the ancient Indians apparently considered the basic nature of a son and, consequently, of marriage.

In short, the so-called Hindu law of marriage serves to illustrate the nature of Hindu law generally. One or more fundamental data form the basis of the institution. From these data the authors of the Dharmaśāstras have derived a number of logical conclusions. These conclusions, as we see them, touch upon different fields of human activity: religion, law, etc., but to the Hindu mind they are all one: *dharma*.

The illustration of the importance of a son leads me to another field of family law: inheritance. Here, too, the Hindu concept is completely different from the modern Western point of view, as it largely transgresses the field which we are used to calling law. The distinction can best be illustrated by quoting section 25 of the Hindu Succession Act, 1956:

> A person who commits murder or abets the commission of murder shall be disqualified from inheriting the property of the person murdered, or any other property in furtherance of the succession to which he or she committed or abetted the commission of the murder.

This rule, which may seem evident to us, has to be seen against the background of the nature of inheritance according to Hindu law, and the difficulties encountered by the British while applying it in the Courts. The following is an extract from one of the several cases *Kenchava* v. *Girimallappa Channappa*[83] in which the British judges were confronted with a murderer who claimed his right to inherit from the person he had murdered:

> Before this Board it has been contended that the matter is governed by Hindu Law, and that the Hindu Law makes no provision disqualifying a murderer from succeeding to the estate of his victim, and therefore it must be taken that according to this law he can succeed.
> Their Lordships do not take this view... The alternative is between

[83] 51 I.A. (P.C.) 325 (1924).

> the Hindu Law being as above stated or being for this purpose non-existent, and in that case the High Court have rightly decided that the principle of equity, justice and good conscience exclude the murderer. (372–73)

In the name of justice, equity, and good conscience the British consciously departed from the traditional Hindu law, and they were followed in it by the Hindu Succession Act, 1956. The important fact for the purpose of this paper is that, in classical Hindu Law, a murderer was not disqualified from succeeding to the estate of his victim. The question should then be raised: what were the criteria for disqualification from inheritance? Manu thus enumerated the categories of persons who are normally disqualified:

> Eunuchs and outcasts, (persons) born blind or deaf, the insane, idiots and the dumb, as well as those deficient in any organ (of action or sensation), receive no share. (9.201, Bühler)

There can be no doubt, that a person, in order to qualify for inheritance, must be competent as a *dāyāda*, "a receiver of property." He must be able to receive and exercise his right of property; as such, the competence to inherit implies a number of purely legal qualifications. However, to the Hindu mind inheritance means much more than that, and here we leave the field of law. The person who inherits property from somebody else must also be capable of performing *śrāddha* for the person from whom he inherits. *Śrāddha* is the technical term for funeral rites; as the *Mitākṣarā* puts it: the ceremony by which the deceased ceases to be a ghost (*preta*) and becomes a *pitṛ* (ancestor). This is a purely ritualistic requirement which, to our mind, has nothing to do with the competence to accept property but which, for the Hindu, is inseparably connected with it. To come back to the case of the murderer: he can be fully competent to receive his victim's property, and he can have all the necessary qualifications to perform a perfect *śrāddha*; therefore, he is not *a priori* excluded from the right to inherit. On the contrary, all the categories enumerated in the above quoted stanza from Manu do not have these qualifications.

Another aspect of the law of inheritance which elucidates its composite character is the son's obligation to pay their deceased fathers' debts. Says Nārada:

> The grandsons shall pay the debt of their grandfather which having been legitimately inherited by the sons has not been paid by them; the obligation ceases with the fourth in descent. (1.4, Jolly)

The same text even seems to suggest that this is more or less the main purpose of having sons.

> Fathers wish to have sons on their own account, thinking in their minds: "He will release me from all obligations towards superior and inferior beings." (1.5, Jolly)

In other words, to be one's heir is not just a legal right. The Hindu does not have a *right* to accept the inheritance when the assets are attractive enough and to reject it when the debts are larger than the assets. On the contrary, to be one's heir is an obligation which has to be fulfilled irrespective of the relative importance of debts and assets. The reason for the son's liability to pay his father's debts is clear —and it is not primarily a legal one. In certain respects, it is a moral obligation as is clear from the fact that debts contracted by the father for an immoral purpose escape the son's responsibility. The immoral debts have been listed quite often, and the concept was repeatedly referred to in the British Indian Courts. This is Mayne's enumeration of them (1950: 398):

1. debts due to spirituous liquor;
2. debts due to lust;
3. debts due to gambling;
4. unpaid fines;
5. unpaid tolls;
6. debts due to anything idly promised or promises without consideration or anything promised under the influence of wrath;
7. suretyship debts due as surety for appearance, or for confidence or honesty of another ;
8. commercial debts, and
9. debts that are not '*vyavaharika*'.

Moreover, the son's liability to pay his deceased father's debts is also a religious obligation, or, as the British used to call it, a pious obligation. He has to do so for his father's spiritual welfare, as illustrated by Kātyāyana:

> He who having taken a debt or the like does not pay it back to the creditor (or owner) is born in the (latter's) house as a slave or a servant (for wages), a wife, or a beast. (591, Kane)

This the son has to prevent, as he must also prevent his father's merit from being transferred to his creditors. According to Nārada:

> When a devotee, or a man who maintained a sacrificial fire dies without having discharged his debt, the whole merit of his devotions, or of his perpetual fire belongs to his creditors. (1.9, Jolly)

After marriage and inheritance I propose to add a few examples from the third aspect of Hindu family law: adoption. The subject of adoption has received much attention from the authors of Sanskrit law-books, and it became a much discussed subject in British times. I am personally convinced that the importance of adoption is closely connected with certain aspects of the ambivalent law of inheritance. One of the points in the law of inheritance which puzzled the medieval authors of commentaries and, even more so, the British, was the absence from the ancient Dharmaśāstras of any consistent classification of heirs beyond the immediate descendants. Nothing is more confusing and confused than the attempts which the commentators and the jurists of British times made to set up such classifications. Given the scarce data in the ancient texts, this confusion had to be expected. Unlike a number of scholars who blame the Dharmaśāstras for having neglected this aspect of the law of inheritance, I think that the existing lacuna is a completely natural one. Given the composite nature of the "law" of inheritance, given also the importance of having direct descendants who had to perform the *śrāddha* and to pay their ascendants' debts, families without direct descendants must have been practically unheard of, and rules regulating inheritance beyond direct descendants were uncalled for. The father was given various means to assure himself a son: he was allowed to repudiate a wife who bore him no offspring or female offsprings only, and there was the possibility of adopting a son. Thus, in my opinion, adoption too, and the importance it acquired in Hindu law, fit in harmoniously with a scheme which is much broader than the field of law; all this was *dharma.*

The case of *Sri Balusu* v. *Sri Balusu* has been referred to at the beginning of this paper. The Privy Council decided that "the adoption of an only son was not null and void under the Hindu law," invoking the necessity to separate Hindu law from Hindu religion. However, in doing so, they definitely departed from the Hindu *dharma,* as is clear from the following rules laid down by Vasiṣṭha:

> Man formed of uterine blood and virile seed proceeds from his mother and his father (as an effect) from its cause. (Therefore) the father and the mother have power to give, to sell, and to abandon their (son). But let him not give or receive (in adoption) an only son; For he (must remain) to continue the line of the ancestors. (15.1–4, Bühler)

Both this text and the note added to it by Nandapaṇḍita, the author of the *Dattakamīmāṃsā* that "by doing so both giver and receiver incur the offense of extinction of lineage," seem to confirm my view that the theory of adoption was mainly created to maintain the continuity of sonless families. Adoption was forbidden in cases where it would render a family sonless. It would be difficult to determine the exact nature of the basic factor: whether it is legal, religious or social. In any case, from the basic factor are derived a number of consequences which may seem to be of a different nature to us, but which in reality are all *dharma*.

Another aspect of adoption also clearly demonstrates the connection between law and religion and the processes of the British deviation from it. According to the classical treatises on adoption the ceremony of *dattahoma* is an essential rite to be performed to establish the new filial relation. Thus, according to the *Dattakamīmāṃsā*:

> It is, therefore, established that the filial relation of adopted sons is occasioned only by the (proper) ceremonies. Of gift, acceptance, a burnt sacrament, and so forth, should either be wanting, the filial relation even fails.

When faced with the problem whether the ceremony of *dattahoma* was necessary for a valid adoption or not, the British judges hesitated. In *Bal Gangadhar Tilak* v. *Shrinivas Pundit*[84] it was said:

> In certain circumstances the point might be the subject of prolonged and very conflicting argument, as the authorities, ancient and modern, are not in accord on the point as to whether this is a legal as well as a religious requisite. There is a danger, on the one hand, of not paying due respect to those religious rites which are observed and followed among large classes of Indian belief, while, on the other hand, the danger must also be avoided of carrying these, except when the law is clear, into the legal sphere, so as to affect or impair personal or patrimonial rights.

However, the general rule which gradually developed out of these considerations has been formulated as follows by Mayne:

> Amongst the twice-born classes, the performance of *dattahomam* ceremony is not essential to the validity of an adoption where the adopted son belongs to the same *gotra* as the adoptive father. Whether amongst the twice-born classes in other cases *dattahomam* is or is not absolutely essential to the validity of an adoption is not finally settled. (1950: 238–39)

The relation between "law" and "religion" in Dharmaśāstra became acute again in recent years, first with the Hindu Code Bill, and later with the passing of a number of acts which dealt with aspects of family law. Apparently the separation of law from religion was accepted fairly easily in the fields of criminal law, procedure, torts, and contracts; in these fields the traditional views of Dharmaśāstra were abandoned at an early stage, to be replaced by Codes based upon principles of Western law. Reaction was much stronger when

[84] 42 I.A. 148, 149 (1915).

it came to codifying such fields as marriage, succession, joint family, minority, adoption, and maintenance. The examples in the field of criminal law which I have given above are meant to avoid the possible misunderstanding that criminal law, etc. were not codified earlier because they were not religiously involved, whereas marriage, etc. were. The only difference was that in certain fields the religious involvement was given up more easily than in others.

This is not the place to write the history of the Hindu Code Bill. I merely want to oppose the two conflicting views. On the one hand, it was said that this Hindu law, being deeply involved with religious matters, discriminated against those who, although their beliefs and ways of life had nothing in common with Dharmaśāstra, were nevertheless considered by the courts as Hindus, and, hence, fell within the orbit of the Hindu law. As stated by J.D.M. Derrett:

> Jains, Sikhs, Lingayats, Arya Samajists, Brahmo Samajists, Buddhists and even professed atheists, despising all religion, have to suffer the application to them of the Hindu Law, unless they can prove a custom which exempts them in the relevant context. Those who deny every one of the cardinal doctrines which usually serve to identify Hindus are as much Hindus for this purpose as the most orthodox. (1957: 27)

Those who suffered from this kind of discrimination, together with all others who, for one reason or another, thought that the principles of Dharmaśāstra had to be abandoned in a modern society, pleaded for the creation of a new civil law free from all religious overtones.

At this stage their view was opposed by those who maintained that the *dharma* had its roots in the Veda, and therefore, had the characteristics of a divine revelation. As such, *dharma* was eternal and unchangeable and it could not be replaced by a system of law framed by mortals. K.V. Rangaswami Aiyangar pointed out:

> Medhatithi roundly declared that a king cannot make a law overriding *dharma*... The evidence of history does not disclose any exercise of the alleged regal power of independent legislation. (1941: 23)

and

> He [i.e., the king,] cannot make a new law. The royal edict is merely declaratory, and not innovative. (133)

From statements such as these, it was but one step to replace "the king" by "Parliament," and to say that in modern India, the Parliament had no right to make new laws, i.e., laws overriding the revealed prescriptions of Dharmaśāstra, and having a different nature from its specific combination of law, religion, morality, etc. The orthodox Hindu's reaction to modern legislature was adequately summarized by Derrett:

> The orthodox *sastri* commonly admits that Parliament may pass certain Acts affecting the Hindu Law, with the reservation that in so far as the provisions depart from the received tenor of the Dharmasastra they are not binding on any Hindu conscience, despite the fact that they were approved by his elected representatives, and have mundane force simply by virtue of their binding effect upon the Courts which may be called upon from time to time to administer them.[85]

I fully agree with Derrett (loc. cit.) that:

> It is obviously in India's interests that the traditional (apart from the technically constitutional) capacity of the national legislature to pass valid Acts should be investigated, since the present "split mind" on this topic is injurious to public morale.

I can very well see why, in 1953, he wrote the article from which the preceding quotations have been taken: "The Criteria for distinguishing between Legal and Religious Commands in the Dharmaśāstra" (rpt. in Derrett 1968). But his criteria fail to convince me, and so does his conclusion:

> Although countless rulers since the fourth century AD at the latest have made the "Everlasting Dharma" their aim, it cannot be denied that legislative interference with the law had established a millennium of precedents even before the coming of the British. In these circumstances, the cry of "Religion in danger!" as an obstacle to the reform or reinterpretation of the Hindu law is entirely novel, and constitutes a complete innovation. (62)

Today, it is not 1953 but 1968. In the meanwhile four important Acts have been passed; the Hindu Marriage Act, 1955; the Hindu Succession Act, 1956; the Hindu Adoptions and Maintenance Act, 1956; and the Hindu Minority and Guardianship Act, 1956. The time has come both to appreciate the advantages of the new acts, and to acknowledge the fact that they constitute a real break with the traditional system in which law and religion were intimately mixed together. It is time now to see the relation between the law and the religion in India in its real historical perspective. I shall try to do so by way of conclusion.

First, if we say that law and religion were intimately connected in traditional India, we are correct only if the statement is made from the Western point of view. It would not be accurate

[85] 52 A.I.R. (Journal) (1953).

from the Indian point of view. The ancient Indians did not distinguish between the "law" and the "religion"; for them there was only one category: *dharma.* I suspect that the first line of H. von Glasenapp's *Der Hinduismus* (1922): "In India everything is religion" actually is a translation of a Sanskrit phrase or a phrase in a modern Indian language, saying: "In India everything is *dharma.*" This statement could not have been more correct.

The British —and, more specifically, the British judges in India— tried to draw a line between the religion and the law. They did so for obvious reasons. *Dharma* being based upon extra-legal premises, these premises often led to consequences which were contrary to the British principles of justice, equity, and good conscience. Moreover, in many cases the so-called religious background was discarded because the British were unable to understand its implications, and because it was easier for them to take the so-called legal precepts as they stood.

However, while one can appreciate the reasons that led the British to draw a distinction between law and religion and while one can understand that they could hardly have done otherwise, the fact remains that, by doing so, they departed from the original spirit of the Hindu law. We must object to those judgments —cf., *Sri Balusu v. Sri Balusu*— which maintain that, by distinguishing between law and religion, they were faithful to the intentions of the Hindu law-givers. In reality, the distinction between the law and the religion made by the British judges in India is but one aspect of a much wider phenomenon. Although the English lawyers in India tried very hard to maintain the spirit of the traditional Hindu law, for a number of reasons and from a number of points of view they were unable to do so. The introduction of the principles of justice, equity, and good conscience; the transformation of Hindu jurisdiction into a pure case law; the idea that the "Law book of Manu" is more authoritative than any other law book; the concept that, in case of a conflict between an ancient Dharmaśāstra and a medieval commentary, the opinion of the latter prevails; the introduction into Hindu law of the traditionally unknown institution of wills, etc., are but a few examples showing the involuntary transformation which Hindu law underwent at the hands of the British. There is no reason to criticize this phenomenon, but there is no reason to ignore it either.

Finally, the line drawn by the British has been accepted by a number of jurists in independent India, especially by those who wanted to give India a "modern" legal system, completely divorced from the traditional religion. Personally I consider this approach a very sound one. The present day political, social and economic conditions in India have outgrown the situation for which the principles of Dharmaśāstra were conceived. I fully agree with most of the arguments put forth in this connection by Chief Justice M.C. Chagla in *State of Bombay* v. *Narsu Appa Mali.*[86] In this interesting case it was skilfully maintained that the Bombay Prevention of Hindu Bigamous Marriage Act, 1946 —which declares void all bigamous marriages concluded after the coming into force of the Act— contravened the fundamental rights guaranteed under Articles 14, 15, and 25 of the Constitution —e.g., the right to freedom of conscience and the right freely to profess, practice, and propagate religion— and, therefore, was not valid. The claim was thus summarized by M.C. Chagla, C.J.:

> It has been urged before us that among Hindus the institution of marriage is a sacrament, and that marriage is part of Hindu religion which is regulated by what is laid down in the Sastras. It is further pointed out that a Hindu marries not merely for association with his mate, but in order to perpetuate his family by the birth of sons. It is only when a son is born to a Hindu male that he secures spiritual benefit by having someone who can offer oblations to his own shade when he is dead and to the shades of his ancestors, and that there is no heavenly reason for a sonless man. Therefore, the institution of polygamy is based upon the necessity of a Hindu obtaining sons for the sake of religious efficiency. (778)

Confronted by this claim, Chagla opposed the following principle:

> If religious practices run counter to public order, morality or health or a policy of social welfare upon which the State has embarked, then the religious practices must give way before the good of the people of the State as a whole. (778–79)

And he elaborates:

> It is only with very considerable hesitation that I would like to speak about Hindu religion, but it is rather difficult to accept the position that polygamy is an integral part of Hindu religion. It is perfectly true that Hindu religion recognizes the necessity of a son for religious efficacy and spiritual salvation. That same religion also recognizes for institution of adoption. Therefore, the Hindu religion provides for the continuation of the line of a Hindu male within the frame-work of monogamy. But even assuming that polygamy is a recognized institution according to Hindu religious practice, the right of the State to legislate on questions relating to marriage cannot be disputed. Marriage is undoubtedly a social institution, an institution in which the State is vitally interested. (779)

[86] 59 Bom. L.R. 775 (1951).

I am much more impressed by the very last argument, which was also the first one quoted above: marriage is a social institution and the State has a right to interfere therein, than by the reasoning which tries to prove that polygamy was not a reality in the ancient Hindu *dharma*. It was. To say that it was not only weakens one's position. Moreover, it is an error of historical perspective to try to separate the religious element from legal matters in the traditional Dharmaśāstra. Present-day Hindu law is different from the ancient *dharma*, and there is no reason why we should not say so.

I fear that the thesis of this paper may not be a very popular one. The orthodox cannot agree with it. They may accept my position that religion was an integral part of ancient Hindu law, but they may not approve of my view that the present-day departure from it is advantageous. Nor can the modernists agree with it. They too will say that a new and modern system of law is a necessity. But, my point of view undermines the arguments they employ to get their ideas accepted. However, even if unpopular, I am convinced that the thesis of this paper reflects a historical reality.

4

Law Books in an Oral Culture: The Indian Dharmaśāstras

In 1772 the British authorities in Calcutta decided that, to be fair to the Indians, they should administer to them not British laws, which the Indians did not know and would not understand, but the local Hindu and Muslim laws, which they not only understood but had held in high esteem for centuries.[87]

A fair, humane decision it was; a practical, easy decision it was not. The difficulty was not so much with the Muslims: they had the Quran and the Sharia, and many of the Englishmen who were to administer law to them knew Persian, some even Arabic. The problem was with the Hindus. They too, had law books, but these were in Sanskrit, and of that language no Englishman had any notion whatever.

I will pass over the early British solutions to that problem, since they are not relevant to the point I wish to make. I will just note that, after a few years, some courageous Englishmen came to the conclusion that there was only one way to do it right: they had to learn Sanskrit. That and only that would enable them to read the original texts of the Sanskrit law books, without having to depend on intermediaries, pandits, whom they no longer trusted.[88]

[87] Governor Warren Hastings' *Plan for the Administration of Justice* included a section to the effect that "[i]n all suits regarding inheritance, marriage, caste and other religious usages or institutions, the laws of the Koran with respect to the Mohamedans and those of the Shaster with respect to the Gentoos shall invariably be adhered to." It became law as S. 27 of the Administration of Justice Regulation of 11 April 1780.

[88] Pandits were first attached to the Anglo-Indian Courts in 1772; they continued to act as legal counselors until 1864 when their office was abolished. On the distrust of pandits, see, e.g., Derrett 1968: 243.

The British were told that the laws of the Hindus were contained in books called Dharmaśāstras, i.e., *śāstras* "texts, treatises" on *dharma* "the aggregate of all the rules which a Hindu is supposed to live by."[89] The British also learned that the Dharmaśāstra the Hindus most highly respected was the one attributed to Manu, one of the several ancient sages who are supposed to have composed —rather, "revealed"— treatises on *dharma*.

One of the Englishmen who studied Sanskrit was Sir William Jones, since 1783 a judge in the Supreme Court of Judicature in Calcutta.[90] In 1794 Jones indeed completed and published, in Calcutta, an English translation of the Dharmaśāstra attributed to Manu: *Institutes of Hindu Law: or, the Ordinances of Menu.*

To be sure, Jones' translation, which was "printed by the order of Government," was intended, primarily, to serve the administration of justice. According to Jones, the judge,

> it must be remembered, that those laws are actually revered, as the word of the Most High, by nations of great importance to the political and commercial interests of *Europe*, and particularly by millions of *Hindu* subjects, whose well directed industry would add largely to the wealth of *Britain*, and who ask no more in return than protection for their persons and places of abode, justice in their temporal concerns, indulgence to the prejudices of their old religion, and the benefit of those laws, which they have been taught to believe sacred, and which alone they can possibly comprehend. (Jones 1796, rpt. in Haughton 1825: 2.xxi–xxii; see note 92)

Yet, at the same time Jones, the scholar, expressed an opinion that is particularly important in the context of this essay. Jones was convinced that, by translating Manu, he not only had access to the laws to be applied to Hindus in 1794, but learned from the *Manusmṛti* "that system of duties, religious and civil, and the law

[89] The term Dharmaśāstra, in a general sense, is used for both the Dharmasūtras, which are in prose, and the Dharma-śāstras *stricto sensu*, which are in verse. The individual Dharmasūtras and Dharmaśāstras are also called *smṛtis*, and the entire corpus of these texts is referred to as part of "the" *smṛti* (literally, "memory"), i.e., a form of revelation inferior only to the higher form of revelation contained in the several Vedic texts (*śruti*). I must stress that this entire essay deals with this body of texts only, not with the immense commentarial literature on them, which developed at a later time.

[90] The fact that Jones' decision to study Sanskrit was linked to his distrust of the Court pandits is highlighted in a letter to Charles Chapman, written from the Bengal town of Krishnagar on 28 September 1785: "I am proceeding slowly, but surely, in this retired place, in the study of Sanscrit; for I can no longer bear to be at the mercy of our pundits, who deal out Hindu law as they please, and make it at reasonable rates when they cannot find it ready-made" (Cannon 1970: 683–684).

in all its branches, which the Hindus firmly believe to have been promulgated in the beginning of time by menu" (ibid.: viii).[91]

The *Manusmṛti* continued to attract attention after 1794.[92] Yet, more than a half century would pass before the publication of the translation of a second Dharmaśāstra, the one attributed to Yājñavalkya. This translation was not in English but in German, and it was not produced to be of any service whatever to the administration of justice in India. As the translator, Adolf Friedrich Stenzler (1849: iii), pointed out, the British had turned away from the ancient Dharmaśāstras to other Sanskrit texts that were totally devoted to law and, consequently, more important for the administration of justice.[93]

Stenzler noted that the time had come to make a scholarly study of the entire corpus of Indian law books. He submitted that, once the relative chronology of the texts was established, "[a] comparative study of all these texts is bound to lead to results which will contribute not a little to our understanding of the development of life in India" (Stenzler 1849: Vorrede, iii). One year later he argued even more forcefully and in greater detail that "[i]t is to be expected that a more accurate knowledge of this richly developed branch of Indian literature, which draws on the most varied situations of life, will provide true insights into the history of the Indian people" (Stenzler 1850: 237). Stenzler thus formulated, for the Dharmaśāstra literature as a whole, the same expectation voiced for Manu by Jones much earlier, namely that these texts provide a true picture of the law of the land, i.e., of law as it was actually practiced in classical India.

The same idea appears again and again in later scholarly literature. I will restrict myself to quoting some of its major proponents. Friedrich Max Müller noted, at least as far as the prose

[91] Even though he was to be proved wrong on that account, Jones believed that the *Manusmṛti* was composed as early as 1280 BC.

[92] Jones' translation was reprinted, in England, in 1796, and translated into German in 1797. It was again reprinted, with an edition of the Sanskrit text and new annotations, by Graves Chamney Haughton, in 1825. For these and later editions, see Garland Cannon, *Sir William Jones: A Bibliography of Primary and Secondary Sources* (Amsterdam: Benjamins, 1979), 32–34. The first edition of Manu in France, by Auguste Loiseleur Deslongchamps, appeared in 1830; his 1833 translation was reprinted in 1840.

[93] English translations of other ancient *dharma* texts appeared more than one century after Hastings' *Plan*. Except for a preliminary translation, from manuscripts, of the *Nāradasmṛti* by Julius Jolly (1876), most translations were published, at Oxford, in Max Müller's *The Sacred Books of the East*: *Āpastamba* and *Gautama* (vol. 2, Bühler 1879), *Viṣṇu* (vol. 7, Jolly, 1880), *Vasiṣṭha* and *Baudhāyana* (vol. 14, Bühler, 1882), *Manu* (vol. 25, Bühler, 1886), *Nārada* and *Bṛhaspati* (vol. 33, Jolly, 1889). Many other Dharmaśāstras, some of them known only from quotations in the commentaries, still remain untranslated.

Dharmasūtras —which he considered to be older than the versified Dhamaśāstras— are concerned, that "[t]hey are of great importance for forming a correct view of the old state of society in India" (1859: 134).[94] In 1868 Albrecht Weber expressed the hope that the publication of more *dharma* texts "would spread the kind of light which we can as yet hardly fathom" (Weber 1868: 815–117). Arthur Cole Burnell realized that there were considerable differences between the various Dharmaśāstras, but that was "no reason to believe that these works do not represent the actual laws which were administered" (1868: xiii).[95] Leopold von Schroeder spoke of the Indian law books as being "of the highest importance for the knowledge of public and private relations, nay of any aspect of Indian life and activity" (Schroeder 1887: 734). Willy Foy proposed to use the Dharmaśāstras to draw a picture of royal power which was to be "important for the cultural history of India" (Foy 1895: 4), and Joseph Dahlmann heralded the law books as "truly historical records."[96]

Perhaps most important of all is that Julius Jolly's classic work on *Hindu Law and Custom* (1928 [1896]) and Pandurang Vaman Kane's monumental *History of Dharmaśāstra* (1930–62) were based on the assumption that the legal precepts contained in the texts were real,[97] and that the two standard treatises of modern Hindu law confirm in their introductions that "[t]here can be no doubt that the smriti rules were concerned with the practical administra-

[94] There is a potentially misleading statement by Georg Bühler concerning Müller's views on the versified Dharmaśāstras. In connection with the Dharmasūtras attributed to Āpastamba, Bühler noted: "Their discovery enabled Professor Max Müller, nearly thirty years ago, to dispose finally of the Brahmanical legend according to which Hindu society was supposed to be governed by the codes of ancient sages, compiled for the express purpose of tying down each individual to his station, and of strictly regulating even the smallest acts of his daily life" (*Sacred Books of the East*, 2: ix). What Müller really meant is that the versified *śāstras*, which he considered to be more recent than the prose *sūtras*, should not be used to reconstruct life in earlier Vedic times, for "they likewise admitted the rules and customs of a later age" (1859: 61). Müller did not say that the versified Dharmaśāstras were unreliable sources as far as their own times were concerned.

[95] This is all the more remarkable since Burnell was a close friend of James H. Nelson whose —very different— views on the Dharmaśāstras will be discussed later.

[96] "Der Gesellschaftskunde erschliessen sich seit dem neunten Jahrundert v. Chr. im Bereiche des indischen Rechts wahrhaft geschichtliche Quellen" (Dahlmann 1899: 48). Dahlmann opposed the opinion of Senart; see below.

[97] Jolly refers to the *sūtras* and the *śāstras* as two "stages of Indian legal literature" (2). In Kane's third volume (1946), which is more specifically devoted to the legal aspects of *dharma*, he says: "This work in intention and scope...concerns itself with pointing out what the law of the Smṛtis and writers of medieval digests was" (544).

tion of the law" (Aiyar 1950: 2), and, in connection with Manu, speak of "the systematic and cogent collection of rules of existing law that it gave to the people with clarity and in language simple and easy of comprehension" (Desai 1970 [1966]: 20).

Yet, not everyone agreed. I will mention only in passing the opinion of Thomas Babington Macaulay that "neither as the languages of law nor as the languages of religion have the Sanskrit and Arabic any peculiar claim to our encouragement," and his expectation that, once the Indian Law Commission of 1833, on which he sat, had completed its task, "the shastras and the hadith will become useless" (cited in Phillips 1977: 1411, 1410).[98]

Far more important was the proclamation, as early as 1861, of no less a personage than Sir Henry Sumner Maine that

> [t]he Hindoo Code, called the Laws of Menu, which is certainly a Brahmin compilation, undoubtedly enshrines many genuine observances of the Hindu race, but the opinion of the best contemporary orientalists is, that it does not, as a whole, represent a set of rules ever actively administered in Hindostan. It is, in great part, an ideal picture of that which, in the view of the Brahmins, *ought* to be the law.[99] (14)

Maine put the blame squarely on William Jones: "The opinions of Sir William Jones produced great effects both in the East and in the West...The Anglo-Indian Courts accepted from the school of the Sanscritists which he founded the assertion of his Brahmanical advisers, that the sacred laws beginning in the extant book of

[98] Macaulay wished to go even further: "I would strike at the root of the bad system which has hitherto been fostered by us. I would at once stop the printing of Arabic and Sanskrit books" (Phillips 1977: 1412).

[99] On Maine, see J. Duncan M. Derrett 1959. It is not clear to me whom Maine means by "the best contemporary orientalists." According to Derrett (42) "much of what turns up in Maine" was supplied by James Mill's "disastrous" *History of British India* (first published in 1817). As far as I know Mill did not make any statement similar to Maine's. Speaking about the "endless conceits" of Sanskrit grammatical literature, he said, though, that "[i]t could not happen otherwise than that the Hindus should, beyond other nations, abound in those frivolous refinements which are suited to the taste of an uncivilized people. A whole race of men were set apart and exempted from the ordinary cares and labours of life, whom the pain of vacuity forced upon some application of mind, and who were under the necessity of maintaining their influence among the people, by the credit of superior learning, and, if not by real knowledge, which is slowly and with much difficulty attained, by artful contrivances for deceiving the people with the semblance of it. This view of the situation of the Brahmans serves to explain many things which modify and colour Hindu society" (reprint from the 2nd edition, 1972 [1820]: 1.383–384). Mill also agreed with Francis Wilford that the king lists in the Purāṇas "are the creation of the fancies of the writers" (ibid.: 464).

Manu were acknowledged by all Hindus to be binding on them" (1975 [1886]: 6).[100]

Maine's view found support from various quarters. Both for practical and academic reasons, James Henry Nelson who was active in various locations in South India, was unhappy administering the Hindu law created by Jones and other Sanskrit scholars in faraway Calcutta (on Nelson see Derrett 1961: 354–372). He raised the question, "Has such a thing as *'Hindū Law'* at any time existed in the world? Or is it that *'Hindū Law'* is a mere phantom of the brain, imagined by Sanskritists without law and lawyers without Sanskrit?" (Nelson 1877: 2).

Nelson questioned not only the reliability of the *Manusmṛti* as a source of law, but the existence of Manu himself: "If he at any time existed…, which is most unlikely, Manu cannot be supposed to have set laws to India" (4). And he continued:

> Assuming however, for argument's sake that a man named Manu once existed and set laws to men…, it must…be conceded that he set them only to certain masses of men abiding in and about part of the Punjab, namely to certain *Ārya* tribes or families and in some instances also to certain tribes or families styled *Śūdras*. Now: whether a remnant of any one of those tribes or families still exists in any part of India of course is exceedingly doubtful. And whether a remnant of any one of them existed at any time within the limits of the Madras Province, except perhaps on the Western Coast, is still more doubtful.[101] (Ibid.: 4–5)

Arguments against the Dharmaśāstras also came from one eminent European Sanskrit scholar, the Frenchman Émile Senart. In *Les castes dans l'Inde: Les faits et le système*, Senart was less concerned with the legal sections of the Dharmaśāstras than with their presentation of the four-fold caste system: Brahmin, Kṣatriya, Vaiśya, Śūdra. Yet, the result of his study was damaging to the law books as a whole. Senart contrasted the infinitely complex modern caste system with the relatively simple and structured way in which it appears in the Dharmaśāstras and other classical texts such as the epics. He submitted that the present-day complexities must, to a

[100] At least this much is clear, that Jones, the "orientalist," was one of the principal *bêtes noires* of James Mill.

[101] John D. Mayne, whose *Treatise of Hindu Law and Usage* (1878) was first published one year after Nelson's *View*, admits that "[i]n much that he says I thoroughly agree with him." Yet, "it seems to me that the influence of Brahmanism upon even the Sanskrit writers has been greatly exaggerated, and that those parts of the Sanskrit law which are of any practical importance are mainly based upon usage, which, in substance, though not in detail, is common to both the Aryan and non-Aryan tribes" (vii).

certain degree, go back as far as the time of the ancient texts, and concluded: "What seems certain to me is that neither the epics nor, above all, the *Smṛtis* should be accepted as straightforward and faithful witnesses [*témoins intègres et fidèles*] of contemporary data"[102] (1927 [1896]: 11).

Finally, according to Govinda Das, an Indian Sanskrit scholar, "[i]t is a profound error to regard the *Smritis* as *complete* codes of law or as getting all their 'rules' rigidly enforced by the political authorities of their times" (Das 1914: 8). And he concluded a long discussion with the question: "After all this can one seriously contend that Hindu law was in the main ever more than a pious wish of its metaphysically-minded, ceremonial-ridden priestly promulgators, and but seldom a stern reality?" (16).

In other words, according to a number of reputable scholars the ancient Indian Dharmaśāstras duly and truly described the law of the land; according to other equally reputable scholars they were the product of pure brahmanical fantasy and they tell us only what the Brahmin caste would have liked the law of the land to be. The dilemma this situation makes for the historian of classical Hindu law is obvious. Either the information at his disposal is infinitely broad and detailed, allowing him to reconstruct both substantive and adjective law in ancient India with a high degree of accuracy; or the entire corpus of classical Indian law books is untrustworthy and should be dismissed as a source of information on what really was the law of the land. I will suggest in the following pages that there is a better and more productive approach to understanding the nature and meaning of the Indian Dharmaśāstras than asking the single question whether or not they describe the law of the land and, depending on the answer, concluding that they are or are not reliable law books.[103]

By way of introduction I would like to remind the reader of the signal importance, in India, of memorization. It is well known that the entire system of education in classical, and to a certain extent in modern India, was and is based on learning by rote.[104] From a very early age onward Indians were —and still are— trained to memorize sentences, passages, even books on all kinds of topics, whether learned or trivial.

[102] Senart's view was criticized by Hermann Oldenberg (1897: 268), and by Dahlmann (1899: 49–50): "Der ganze Charakter des aus der Wirklichkeit des Lebens hervorgehenden Rechts schliesst aber jene bewusste Fälschung auf das entschiedenste aus").

[103] This essay supersedes my earlier attempts (1957, 1967, and 1978) at understanding the nature of the Dharmaśāstra.

[104] Hence the emphasis on mnemotechnic devices in books on Indian education. See, for example, Mookerji 1969: 211–215; Rocher 1994.

Numerous Western visitors to India have expressed their amazement at this phenomenon, but I wish to concentrate on two such visitors because they reported not only on the mnemonics of Indians but also on law and law books.

In the first place there is a statement attributed to Megasthenes, the ambassador whom Seleucus Nicator, one of the successors of Alexander the Great, sent to Candragupta, the king of the Mauryas. Megasthenes visited India, perhaps several times, ca. 300 BC. A fragment of his lost *Indica,* as recorded in Strabo's *Geography,* relates the ambassador's surprise that there was so little crime among the Indians, "and that too among a people who use unwritten laws only." "For," he continues, "they have no knowledge of written letters, and regulate every single thing from memory" (Strabo in Jones 1930: 15.1.53, 86–89). Megasthenes must have seen an Indian court of law at work. As a Greek, he was puzzled that the judge did not use any law books; as a Greek, he drew the logical conclusion that, if the judge did, i.e., had to do, without a law book, first, the Indians did not have law books, and, second, they must not have known the art of writing.

Megasthenes was wrong as far as the latter part of his conclusion is concerned. We know that there was writing in India in the time of Megasthenes. Also, one of his predecessors, Nearchus, Alexander's friend and companion, reported that, according to some, Indians "write missives on linen cloth that is very closely woven" (ibid.: 15.1.67, 116–117). But Nearchus did confirm Megasthenes' conclusion that the Indians had no law books: "Nearchus...declares...[t]hat their laws, some public and some private, are unwritten" (ibid.: 15.1.66, 114–115).

Nearchus' and, far more so, Megasthenes' statements on the absence of law books have attracted much scholarly attention. Knowing, as we do, that the Indians had many Dharmasūtras, some of which may go back to 500 BC, the Greek observers must have been misled. According to one explanation, the ancient Indians did have written law books, but they were not needed in the law courts because the judges had memorized them (Schwanbeck 1846: 50–51, n. 48).[105] In the opinion of the latest editor of Megasthenes' fragments, "the laws were indeed mainly unwritten; it was not customary [for Indians] to reduce their sacred books (and the Dharmaśāstras belong to them) to writing" (Timmer 1930: 245). Others, finally, dismissed the statements on the absence of law books in ancient India as one of the many instances

[105] Schwanbeck adds an alternative explanation, namely that "for some reason" (*quadam causa*) Indians call their law books *smṛti* (= *mnênê*, memory). Cf. Rocher 1956–1957, also included in the present volume.

"in which the ignorance of the classical writers is difficult to explain" (Majumdar 1960: xix).

At this point I will introduce a document produced by the second visitor to India whom I announced earlier. It is a letter, sent to a prominent jurist in Paris, by a French Jesuit missionary, from Pondicherry in South India, in 1714. It has been published in several editions of the *Lettres édifiantes et curieuses*, the vast collection of letters written from various Jesuit missions. The writer of the letter is Father Jean Venant Bouchet; except for an introductory paragraph, the long letter is entirely devoted to the administration of law as Bouchet saw it in India, some two thousand years after Megasthenes.[106] Yet, some two millennia after Megasthenes, Father Bouchet's first sentence sounds uncannily familiar: "They have neither codes or digests, nor do they have any books in which are written down the laws to which they have to conform to solve the disputes that arise in their families" (Rocher 1984b: 18). In other words, as astute and inquisitive an observer as Father Bouchet did not see any Hindu law books in 1714, either.

The observations on the absence of law books in settling disputes among Hindus, made by two foreigners visiting India at an interval of two thousand years, raise a number of questions. First, what did the Hindu judicial authorities use instead of law books to settle disputes? Second, where were the Dharmaśāstras, composed from ca. 500 BC onward, of which neither Megasthenes nor Bouchet saw any trace? Third, and most important, what are the Dharmaśāstras which William Jones accepted as representing the law of the land, and which Henry Sumner Maine dismissed as brahmanical fantasy?

On the first question Bouchet leaves no doubt. Echoing Megasthenes' brief remark that unwritten laws among Indians did not entail a higher degree of lawlessness, Bouchet explains, in far greater detail, that absence of law books did not in any way imply absence of justice.

> The equity of all their verdicts is entirely founded on a number of customs which they consider inviolable, and on certain usages which are handed down from father to son. They regard these usages as definite and infallible rules, to maintain peace in the family and to end the suits that arise, not only among private individuals, but also among royal princes. (Ibid.: 18–19)

[106] Although the letter has not remained unnoticed, it has not received the attention it deserves. J.H. Nelson referred to it, especially in "Hindu Law at Madras," (1881). For an annotated English translation, see Rocher, "Father Bouchet's Letter," 1984b.

Bouchet makes it clear that some of these customs were "accepted in all castes," such as the belief that children of two brothers or of two sisters are brothers whereas children of a brother and a sister are cousins, with the result that the latter can intermarry, the former cannot. Other customs on the contrary, are valid within a particular caste only, and customs may vary from caste to caste: "As soon as it has been proven that someone's claim is based on a custom that is followed within the caste, and on common usage, that is enough" (ibid.: 19). Also, whereas the village head is the natural judge in suits arising in his village, "[i]f it is a question related to caste, it is the heads of the castes who decide" (ibid.: 31).

In connection with the fact that these customs were unwritten, Bouchet relates how a European gentleman suggested to him that there must be much injustice in a system in which, unlike Europe, judges were not held in check by written laws.

> I shall not examine here the enormous advantages one pretends to derive from this prodigious multitude of laws; but it seems to me that the Indians are not really to be blamed for not having cared to codify their customs. After all, is it not enough that they possess them perfectly? And, if this is so, what is the good of books? In reality, nothing is better known than these customs: I have seen children ten or twelve years old who knew them perfectly. (Ibid.: 21)

Finally, as to the form in which the customs are memorized and transmitted, Bouchet uses, interchangeably, the terms "maxims," "proverbs," and "quatrains," the latter of which seems to indicate that they were in verse. At one point he more specifically refers to the fact that "they quote a quatrain which is to them more or less what Pibrac's quatrains are to us" (ibid.: 28–29).[107]

Bouchet quotes and comments on several of these maxims. For instance:

> When there are several children in a family, the males alone inherit; the girls have no claim at all to the inheritance. (Ibid.: 38–40)

> If the property has not been divided upon the death of the father, anything that has been acquired by one of the children shall be entered into the common stock and divided equally. (Ibid.: 42–43)

> Adopted children share equally in the estate with the children of their adoptive fathers and mothers. (Ibid.: 43–45)

[107] This is a reference to the collection of moralizing quatrains by Gui du Faur, Seigneur de Pibrac (1529–1584). First published in 1574, they became very popular, and went through numerous editions, with additions.

> The father shall pay all debts contracted by his children; children shall equally pay all debts of their father. (Ibid.: 47–48)

Bouchet's letter ends as follows:

> It is these general maxims, Sir, that serve as substitutes for laws in India; it is these that are followed in the administration of justice. There are other more specific laws which are applicable within each caste. Since these would lead me too far, they shall be the subject of another letter which I will be honored to write you. (Ibid.: 48)

Unfortunately, this other letter does not seem to have been written.

The main conclusion to be drawn from Bouchet's letter is that in the area of India with which he was familiar, and probably in most other areas as well, law was administered on the basis of unwritten maxims, which were transmitted from generation to generation, in the local vernaculars, some of them applicable to the population of the area generally, others to specific groups such as the members of a particular caste only. I often wonder whether, had Bouchet also provided the readings of these maxims in the original vernacular, there would not be ample opportunity to compare them with specific verses, "quatrains," *ślokas*, in the written, Sanskrit Dharmaśāstras.[108]

Turning to the second question I asked earlier, it is quite clear that the Dharmaśāstras were unknown to Bouchet's informants. In fact, they were unaware of, and opposed to, even their own maxims being preserved in writing. Bouchet reports that he inquired why they had not collected their customs in books to consult if needed. "Their answer is that, if these customs were entered into books, only the learned would be able to read them, whereas, if they are handed down orally from generation to generation, everyone is fully informed" (Rocher 1984: 20).

Yet, there are indications that the Dharmaśāstras existed in written form perhaps even at a relatively early date. According to a verse in the *Nāradasmṛti*, the *śāstra* is one of the eight "limbs" of legal procedure, together with the king or chief judge, the as-

[108] For example, Bouchet's first maxim closely resembles a half stanza preserved in the *Baudhāyanadharmasūtra* (2.2.3.46) which declares women to be *adāya* "without a share," an idea which also occurs in earlier Vedic texts (*Taittirīyasaṃhitā* 6.5.8.2: women are *adāyāda*). Cf. even *Ṛgveda* 3.31.2: "The son-of-the-body did not share the inheritance with his sister" (transl. Geldner). The principle referred to in the fourth maxim quoted above is well known in the Dharmaśāstras, and corresponds to what in Anglo-Indian law was to be called the pious obligation.

sessors, the accountant, the scribe, gold, fire, and water (transl. Jolly, Introduction, 1.16). A *śloka* "quatrain" attributed to the lost *Bṛhaspatismṛti* 1.17 prescribes that "the king should cause gold, fire, water, and the codes of the sacred law (Dharmaśāstras, plural) to be placed in the midst of them [i.e., the members of the court], also (other) holy and auspicious things."[109] Two other verses attributed to Bṛhaspati also provide the earliest interpretation and reconciliation of the conflicting views on levirate appearing in the preserved *Manusmṛti* (to which I will return later) (transl. Jolly 24.16–17).

Finally, even Bouchet's informants were vaguely aware of certain laws inscribed on mysterious copper plates, and guarded with care by learned Brahmins in a big tower in the city of Conjeeveram. However, "[s]ince the Moors have nearly entirely destroyed this large and famous town, no one has been able to find out what happened to these plates; the only thing we know is that they contained everything that relates to any caste in particular and the relations which different castes should observe among one another" (Rocher 1984: 20).

In other words, law books, even law books in the vernacular, and, *a fortiori*, Sanskrit law books, were the preserve of the learned, of the select few who were able to read —and write— them. In ordinary legal practice everyone used detached, unconnected maxims.

I can now return to the third question I raised: what exactly are the learned, written Dharmaśāstras?[110] To answer this question I must refer to one of their most salient features, which has helped me greatly to reach the conclusion I present in this essay. The point is that there are, in the Dharmaśāstras, some strange and troubling contradictions, not only between different Dharmaśāstras (Kane 1930–62: 3.866–870), but within one and the same text as well.

For instance, in Manu's section on inheritance there is a verse (9.104) to the effect that, after the death of both parents, the sons get together and divide the inheritance equally. The next verse (9.105), without any transition whatever, enjoins that, after the death of both parents, the eldest son gets everything and the younger sons continue to live under him as they did under their

[109] I must note, though, that this verse is attested in one later digest, Devaṇṇabhaṭṭa's *Smṛticandrikā*, only.

[110] I wish to remind the reader that the conclusions that will follow relate to the ancient Dharmasūtras and Dharmaśāstras only (cf. note 3). The commentaries, which are also part of the Dharmaśāstra literature in its broader sense, raise problems of a totally different nature. See, e.g., my "Schools of Hindu Law," 1972, also included in the present volume.

father. A few verses are then dedicated to praising the greatness of an eldest son. And then, again without transition, Manu 9.112 declares that, when both parents are deceased, the inheritance is divided, but in such a way that the eldest son receives an additional share of 5 percent, the next son an extra share of half of that, etc. In other words, within the brief span of nine verses Manu offers three different ways for sons to deal with the parental inheritance.

Elsewhere Manu 9.57 informs us that, when a husband dies without having a son, his younger brother shall substitute for him and have a son with his elder brother's widow. The text goes into detail on how and when the intercourse shall take place, on how the parties shall behave, etc. All of this clearly indicates that Manu is familiar with the custom of levirate which is also known in other legal systems.[111] But Manu 9.64 then goes on to say that a widow should never have intercourse with anyone other than her husband, including her brother-in-law. Such behavior, the text adds is *paśudharma* "*dharma* of *paśu*s, beasts" (9.66).[112]

Contradictions of this kind occur throughout the *Manusmṛti*, but they are particularly obvious in the ninth book devoted to family law (for other examples, see Lingat 1973 [1967]: 182). Scholars who believed that the Dharmaśāstras were codices representing the law of the land were forced to look for justifications. It has been suggested that contradictory rules in the Dharmaśāstras, as in all revealed Hindu texts, must be interpreted as options (Bühler 1886: xcii–xciii).[113] According to Lingat, "[i]t emerges from these texts that the author of the Code of Manu was hostile" to a number of practices, "but he was confronted by customs too deeply rooted for prohibition to be efficacious. All he could do was to try to discredit them" (1973: 182).[114] In connection with levirate in particular, it has been suggested by some that Manu intended the

[111] The son born of this kind of union is called *kṣetra-ja* "field-born," i.e., born from seed sown in someone else's field. Manu describes his share in the inheritance at 9.120–121.

[112] On the history of *niyoga*, from Vedic times onward, see Emeneau and van Nooten 1991: 481–494.

[113] Hence Bühler introduces Manu 9.105 which makes the entire paternal property devolve on the eldest son with the word "[Or]" which is not present in the Sanskrit text. He also offers an alternate explanation: the fact that the versified *Mānava-Dharmaśāstra* is, in his view, a recast of a lost prose *Mānavadharmasūtra* "alone is sufficient to account for contradictions."

[114] According to Derrett too, "the Rishis are found to acknowledge as existing and worthy of regulation a few institutions which affronted their refined moral senses" (Derrett 1978: 52) and he refers to *niyoga* as a prime example. Seventy years earlier Joseph Kohler used Manu's passage on *niyoga* as "a well-known example" of the fact that *lex posterior derogat priori* is a Western, not an Eastern principle (Kohler 1910: 242).

practice to be allowed for *śūdras*, but forbidden for the three higher classes.[115] Most other explanations tacitly assume that Hindu society moved from a stage in which *niyoga* was common practice to a stage in which it was considered taboo.[116] The verses prohibiting levirate, therefore, "are probably a later addition" (Burnell 1884: E.W. Hopkins' note at 255); they have "obviously been tacked on... at a time when the practice of Niyoga had fallen into disuse" (Jolly 1885: 48), the practice having to be described nevertheless as "being part of the traditional Dharma" (Jolly 1928 [1896]: 121).

Notwithstanding these and other ingenious efforts, by the commentators first, by modern scholars later, to account for the contradictions in the Dharmaśāstras, it is obvious that books that prescribe three different ways of dealing with paternal property, books that first prescribe levirate and then forbid it, are hardly usable in legal practice.

The important but easily overlooked point is that it is normal, that it is a premise, in Hinduism, that what is *dharma* for one is different from what is *dharma* for another. *Dharma*, basically, is accepted custom *(ācāra)*, i.e., custom accepted in a region, in a village, even in a caste or a sub-caste within a village. But all these different customs are *dharma* in their own right.[117] With the single and relatively vague proviso that "they should not be contrary to the Veda," the Dharmasūtras and Dharmaśāstras themselves unanimously accept the validity of practices recognized within a region, a caste, or a family; they provide that customs peculiar to cultivators, traders, herdsmen, money-lenders, artisans, etc., are binding on these various groups (see Kane 1930–62: 3.857–863). In the case of inheritance in particular, a verse in Kauṭilya's *Arthaśāstra* 3.7.40 prescribes: "whatever be the customary law (*dharma*) of a region, a caste, a corporation or a village, in accordance with that alone shall he [i.e., the judge] administer the law of inheritance" (Kangle 1963: 249).[118]

[115] This interpretation based on Manu 9.66 ("the practice is reprehended by the learned of the twice-born classes"), appears as early as Eduard Gans, *Das Erbrecht in weltgeschichtlicher Entwickelung* (1824–1825: 1.77), and has often been repeated.

[116] Typically, see Ludwik Sternbach's introduction to Chakradar Jha's *History and Sources of Law in Ancient India* (1987: vii). I should note that this is also the traditional Indian interpretation, exhibited for the first time in the passage from the *Bṛhaspatismṛti* to which I referred earlier: *niyoga* was allowed in the three earlier world ages, but is forbidden in the present, decadent Kali age.

[117] Marc Galanter rightly pointed out that this is one of the main differences between traditional and modern Indian law which "put[s] forth claims in terms of general rules applicable to the whole society" ("Hinduism, Secularism, and the Indian Judiciary," 1971; reprinted in *Law and Society in Modern India*, 1989: 237).

[118] A nearly identical verse is transmitted as part of the lost *Kātyāyanasmṛti* (Kane 313 [884A]).

In actual dispute settlement each of these customs, or sets of customs, was applied, consistently, in the appropriate circumstances. Members of one area or one group always divided paternal property equally, others unequally, others again did not divide it at all. Among some there was levirate, among others there was not.[119] In India's largely oral culture these area-specific or group-specific rules were transmitted in the form of *Memorialverse*, in the vernacular; and they remained unwritten.[120] The composers of the Dharmaśāstras, on the other hand, compiled treatises on *dharma*, on anything they considered worthy of being recorded as *dharma* with some people, somewhere. They gathered that information in books, in the language of the learned, Sanskrit.

What I wanted to show in this essay is that it is possible, in a culture in which memorization plays an important role in day-to-day life, to have books, the Dharmaśāstras, that are legal fiction because they were divorced from the practical administration of justice —the role they were given in 1772[121]— but which are not for that reason the product of brahmanical fantasy.[122] They are books of law —rather, books of laws— containing "a mass of floating verses of rules and observations" that were, indeed, at some time and in some place "governing the life and conduct of people" (Raghavan 1962: 2.335).

[119] On the practice of levirate in modern India, see Emeneau and van Nooten 1991: 487, based primarily on Karve 1965.

[120] I borrowed the term *Memorialverse* in the context of Sanskrit *dharma* literature from an article by Lüders 1917; reprinted in *Philologica Indica. Ausgewählte kleine Schriften*, 1940.

[121] The question whether Hastings' decision was right or wrong has been the object of much scholarly discussion. Derrett refers to K.V. Venkatasubramania Iyer, according to whom Hastings misunderstood what function the *śāstra* had, when he made it the sole source of law, and adds: "this is not quite certain, but the fact that the doubt can arise is significant" (1968: 288). K. Lipstein's conclusion that the Plan of 1772 "led to the application of rules which were either obsolete or never in force" has to be seen against the background of his opinion that the *śāstra* "was never more than a fiction" (1957: 281).

[122] The argument of "brahmanical fantasy" has been used in other areas as well. Cf. Mill's statement on the Brahmins above. Also, in connection with the *Dhātupāṭha*, a list of some two thousand verbal roots of which more than half have not been met with in Sanskrit literature, it has been suggested that it was "concocted" by the Indian grammarians (Whitney 1884; reprinted in Staal 1992: 142). In fact, the Indian pandits have been accused of inventing the Sanskrit language (Dugald Stewart and Christoph Meiners, quoted in Rosane Rocher 1983: 78).

5

Schools of Hindu Law

"The Dayabhaga school prevails in Bengal; the Mitakshara school prevails in the rest of India...One of the main differences between these two principal schools of Hindu law relates...to the law of inheritance" (Mulla 1970: 45). This statement in a highly respected volume on Hindu law can be found in some form or other in all treatises on Hindu law, in many judicial decisions, etc. In fact, the concept of "schools of Hindu law" has become so universally accepted, that it has rarely been objected to in the past and is hardly ever questioned today. When Julius Jolly presented the Tagore Law Lectures in 1883, he considered that he could dispose of the problem with these words: "The notion of Indian Schools of law has been objected to on general grounds, but these objections have been so well refuted by former Tagore Law Professors that I have nothing to add to their arguments" (Jolly 1885: 17; the two Tagore Law Professors referred to are G.D. Banerjee and R. Sarvadhikari).

Yet, it is a well-known fact that the term "schools" was first applied to Hindu law by H.T. Colebrooke (1765–1836).[123] In a reply to an anonymous critic Colebrooke clearly defends the term as his own invention: "I am yet to learn why schools are to be restricted to matters of taste and the fine arts; or why jurisprudence is not to be taught and studied in schools. Nor am I aware that any more appropriate term can be chosen, when speaking

[123] The fact has been stated repeatedly, usually without any supporting evidence. E.g., Gharpure 1931: 29; Mayne 1950: 54.

of diversity of doctrine, deduced by a varied train of reasoning and interpretation, from the same premises."[124]

I shall show in this paper that there may have been good reasons for Colebrooke to believe in the existence of "schools" of Hindu law. In reality, however, he engrafted upon Hindu law an element which was foreign to it, and, by doing so, he steered Hindu law during the British period and after Independence into a course which was not warranted by its past history.

At the moment when a small group of Englishmen in Calcutta tried their best to understand the structure and arrangement of Hindu law, they were already familiar with Muslim law, in which a "school of law" is a well established concept. It is not impossible that they expected the legal system governing Hindus to be based on similar principles. The author of the anonymous tract, referred to above, casts some doubt on the importance and unity of a "Hindoo law of India" (*Observations* 1825: 167). Colebrooke retorts immediately with a reference to the lack of unity in Muslim law: "When he censured the Hindus for want of uniformity in their laws, he overlooked, among his favourite Mahomedans, the discordance of sects, and discrepancy of doctrine" (Strange 1825: 1.318). In *Ganga Sahai v. Lekhraj Singh*, Mr. Justice Mahmood discusses the division of Hindu law into the *Dāyabhāga* school and the *Mitākṣarā* school, the latter being again subdivided into four sub-schools, for Banaras, Mithila, Maharashtra and the Dravidian country, respectively. He then adds: "There is thus an accidental similarity between the divisions of the Hindu law and the manner in which the various schools of the Muhammedan law are arranged, the two main divisions being the Sunni and the Shia schools, and the former, like the Mitakshara school, being subdivided into the four minor divergencies of Hanafi, Shafi'i, Maliki and Hanbali."[125] In reality, the similarity between Hindu law and Muslim law may have been less accidental than Mahmood, J. considered it to be.

The existence of schools of Hindu law seemed also to be borne out by the Sanskrit texts themselves. In the *Vivādārṇavasetu* (1888: 42), for instance, two opinions are opposed as follows: "...*iti Śrīkṛṣṇatarkālaṃkāra-Smārtabhaṭṭācārya-Jīmūtavāhana-prabhṛtayaḥ; ...iti tu Miśrāḥ*."[126] Halhed's *Code of Gentoo Laws* has for this pas-

[124] *Note* by *Mr. C.*, in Strange 1825: 1.317. The anonymous tract referred to is: *Observations on the Law and Constitution of India...*, 1825.

[125] 9 AIR (1887) 253, at 292. Cf. Fyzee 1955: 23–24, for the four schools of Sunnite law: the Ḥanafī school named after Imām Abū Ḥanīfa, the Medina school of Mālik ibn Anas, the school of Imām Shāfi'ī, and the school of Imām Aḥmad ibn Ḥanbal.

[126] I owe these data to the collation sheets of the *Vivādārṇavasetu* prepared by my wife in view of a critical edition of the text.

sage: "This ordination is according to the *Pundits* of *Meet-hul*; but *Sewàrteh Behtàchàrige, Jeimoot Bàhun,* and *Sirree Kishen Terkàlungkàr,* and others, speak to this effect, *viz...*" (Halhed 1781: 25). The term "Miśrāḥ" indeed refers to Vācaspatimiśra and, more generally, to "the *paṇḍits* of Mithila," whereas the other three names are those of three important "*paṇḍits* of Bengal." Elsewhere in the text the opinions of the *paṇḍits* of Bengal are actually opposed to those of the "Maithilāḥ." For example: "...*iti Śrīkṛṣṇa-tarkālaṃkāra-Smārtabhaṭṭācārya-Jīmūtavāhanādayaḥ prāhuḥ; Maithilās tu...*" (ibid.: 79); and "*Smārta-Jīmūtavāhanādayaḥ prāhuḥ; Maithilās tu... ity āhuḥ*" (ibid.: 80). Even when their opinion is not explicitly opposed to that of others, expressions such as "...*iti Smārta-Dāyabhāgakārādayaḥ*" (ibid.: 83) clearly refer to the specific point of view held by the *paṇḍits* of Bengal.

Śrīkṛṣṇatarkālaṃkāra's widely read commentary on the *Dāyabhāga* refers to the opinion of the "*Prāñcaḥ,*" "the Easterners" (Vidyāsāgara 1893: 6). In this text *Dāyabhāga* 2.27 is said to be a refutation of the opinion of Caṇḍeśvara, another important author from Mithila (ibid.: 35).[127] In the *Dāyadhikāra-kramasaṃgraha,* Śrīkṛṣṇa refers to "Miśrāḥ" (Wynch 1818: 4, 37) and "Maithilāḥ" (39), and he explicitly opposes the *Dāyabhāga* to "Miśrāḥ" (37) and "*Maithilamatam*" (31).

Finally, there are cases in which "the Maithilas" are actually opposed to "the Bengalis." Thus, in Gopālapañcānana's *Dāyabhāganirṇaya*: "*Maithilamate...; ...iti Gauḍāḥ*"; and "*tadabhāve sapiṇḍaka iti Śaṅkhavacane Maithilapāṭhāt, tadabhāve sagotrajā iti Gauḍāḥ*" (text unpublished; data from my own collation sheets). It is clear that these are variants for the far more frequent opposition in the same text: Dāyabhāgakāraḥ *versus* Miśrāḥ.

At this stage the early students of Hindu law committed a fundamental error of interpretation, when they, quite naturally, came to think of the authors of these texts as "jurists," "lawyers," "lawgivers," etc. Halhed refers to the *Vivādārṇavasetu* as "the only work of the kind, wherein the genuine principles of the Gentoo jurisprudence are made public, with the sanction of their most respectable Pundits, (or lawyers)" (Halhed 1781: x). In the preface to the *Digest* Colebrooke speaks of Raghunandana and several other "Hindu Lawyers" (Colebrooke 1874: I, ix). The expression became so generally accepted, that it was never again abandoned. A case in point is the following sentence (written in 1880) by Sar-

[127] The statements by commentators that the *Dāyabhāga* "refutes Caṇḍeśvara," etc. have often misled scholars. They only mean that the *Dāyabhāga* refutes an opinion which happens to occur in the *Vivādaratnākara* etc. The *Dāyabhāga* is not, therefore, more recent than these other texts.

vadhikari, on Medhātithi's commentary on "the laws of Manu": "This *jurisconsult* was not satisfied with the work of a mere expositor; he found new meaning in words which had hitherto escaped the ken of *other practised lawyers.* Manu was certainly the basis of *Medhātithi's law*; but the great commentator knew how to read between the lines, and he gave such an explanation of Manu's texts, that *the inspired lawgiver*, had he arisen again from the dead, would have had great difficulty in recognising them as his own" (1922: 247, italics added).[128]

Once the authors of the commentaries and *nibandhas* became looked upon as lawyers, jurisconsults and lawgivers, it was but one step to draw the conclusion that their works reflected the actual law of the land. Moreover, once the Englishmen ascertained that the commentaries and *nibandhas* had been written in different parts of India, it was obvious that the texts they were studying reflected the differing laws of the various regions of India. For example, according to Colebrooke: "An excellent commentary, entitled *Mitácshará*, was compiled by Vijnyaneswara, a hermit, who cites other legislators in the process of his work, and expounds their texts, as well as those of his author, thus composing a treatise which may supply the place of a regular Digest: it is so used in the province of *Benares*, where it is preferred to other law tracts" (Colebrooke 1874 [1786–97]: xiv).

Colebrooke does not explain the process by which Mitākṣarā law became the law of Banaras. He seems to assume that Mitākṣarā law and Dāyabhāga law are different because of the different interpretations which their authors gave an identical body of *śruti* and *smṛti*, applying to it the rules of interpretation of Mīmāṃsā and Nyāya, respectively.[129] We shall, then, conclude that, in Colebrooke's opinion, the two digests were accepted as the laws of Banaras and Bengal, respectively, at a later stage only.

Once again, the principle established by Colebrooke was so obvious, that it remained unchallenged for nearly two centuries.

[128] For other examples, see, e.g., Mayne 1950: 43, where the *Mitākṣarā* is spoken of as "the work of this great jurist," and the same at 44, where Vijñāneśvara is referred to as "this far-seeing jurist and statesman."

[129] See Strange 1825, 1.314: "The written law, whether it be *sruti* or *smriti*, direct revelation, or traditional, is subject to the same rules of interpretation. These rules are collected in the *Mímánsá*, which is a disquisition on proof and authority of precepts. It is considered as a branch of philosophy; and is properly the logic of law. In the eastern part of India, viz. Bengal and Bahar, where the Vedas are less read, and the *Mímánsá* less studied than in the South, the dialectic philosophy, or *Nyáya*, is more consulted, and is there relied on for rules of reasoning and interpretation upon questions of law, as well as upon metaphysical topics. Hence have arisen two principal sects or schools, which, construing the same text variously, deduce upon some important points of law different inferences from the same maxims of law."

It has been said again and again, that the commentaries and *nibandhas* contain the regional laws of India, and, more specifically, that the *Dāyabhāga* prevailed in Bengal, whereas the *Mitākṣarā* prevailed in the province of Banaras, later changed into "the rest of India." However, Colebrooke's reasoning was forgotten, and the authors of commentaries and *nibandhas* gradually became the actual codifiers of the local customs. It was held in 1870, for instance, that the *Mitākṣarā* "subordinates in more than one place the language of texts to custom and approved usage."[130] Sixty-five years later it was still true that "the commentators, while professing to interpret the law as laid down in the Smritis, introduced changes in order to bring it into harmony with the usage followed by the people governed by that law."[131]

One can think of several reasons, though, why Colebrooke, his contemporaries and successors, might have refrained from calling the authors of the commentaries and *nibandhas* "lawyers" or "lawgivers," and why they might have hesitated to associate the Sanskrit texts with local laws and customs. I shall examine some of these reasons, and then point out how and why they were overlooked.

In the first place, Colebrooke knew but did not pay attention to the fact that the *Mitākṣarā*, "a treatise which may supply the place of a regular Digest," was not composed by a lawyer but by "vijnyaneswara, a hermit" (1874 [1786–1797]: 1.xiv).[132] Nor was he struck by the fact that Vijñāneśvara's *Mitākṣarā* was in fact far more than a legal treatise: "Following the arrangement of his author, he has divided his work into three parts: the first treats of duties; the second of private contests and administrative law; the third, of purification, the orders of devotion, penance and so forth."[133]

In the second place, there was ample opportunity for Colebrooke and others to realize that the authors of the commentaries and *nibandhas* never intended to codify differing local laws

[130] 13 M.I.A. 373, 390 (1870).

[131] *Atmaram Abhimanji v. Bajirao Janrao* 62 I.A. 139, 143 (1935); 39 C.W.N. 646; 68 M.L.J. 673.

[132] See complete quotation above. About Vijñāneśvara, see P.V. Kane 1930–62: 1.288–289. Other authors, following Colebrooke, have not been more consistent. Mayne's Vijñāneśvara, "this far-seeing jurist and statesman" (1950: 170, note 3), at the same time "belonged to the order of ascetics" (43). H.V. Divatia offers the following rationalization: "Law was administered in ancient times by kings, some of whom were themselves great Pandits, assisted by Pandits. These Pandits and commentators on Smṛtis voiced the contemporary public opinion and often anticipated it" (1940: 121).

[133] Notice that Colebrooke was fully aware that "Yajnawalcya, grandson of Viswamitra, is described, in the introduction to his own institutes, as delivering his precepts to an audience of ancient philosophers assembled in the province of *Mithilá*" (ibid.: I, p. xiv).

and customs. Colebrooke knew Halhed's *Code of Gentoo Laws* and its Sanskrit original, the *Vivādārṇavasetu*. He might have noticed that the *paṇḍits* called to Calcutta by Warren Hastings did not distinguish between the law of Bengal, the law of Banaras, etc. He did notice that the learned Jagannātha Tarkapañcānana quoted *all* commentaries and *nibandhas* in his *Vivādabhaṅgārṇava*, without connecting them in any way with different geographical areas. It is surprising that Colebrooke did not ask the obvious question: why did Hastings' *paṇḍits* and Jagannātha compose their digests in the way they did? It is surprising that Colebrooke failed to consider the possibility that the *paṇḍits*' way of composing a *nibandha* was perhaps the only possible and correct way of doing it.

In the preface to the *Digest*, Colebrooke restricted himself to being vaguely apologetic: "Should it appear to him [= the reader] that much of the commentary might have been omitted without injury to the context, or that a better arrangement would have rendered the whole more perspicuous, he will remember that the translator could use no freedom with the text, but undertook a verbal translation of it" (Colebrooke 1874 [1786–1797]: 1.xxi). The real reason for Colebrooke's dissatisfaction with the arrangement of the *Digest* becomes clear fourteen years later, in the preface to the translation of the *Mitākṣarā* and *Dāyabhāga*:

> In the preface to the translation of the Digest, I hinted an opinion unfavourable to the arrangement of it, as it has been executed by the native compiler. I have been confirmed in that opinion of the compilation, since its publication; and indeed the author's method of discussing together the discordant opinions maintained by the lawyers of the several schools, without distinguishing in an intelligible manner which of them is the received doctrine of each school, but on the contrary leaving it uncertain whether any of the opinions stated by him do actually prevail, or which doctrine must now be considered to be in force and which obsolete, renders his work of little utility to persons conversant with the law, and of still less service to those who are not versed in Indian jurisprudence; especially to the English reader, for whose use, through the medium of translation, the work was particularly intended. (Colebrooke 1810: ii–iii)

This quotation points to another contributing factor in the creation of schools of Hindu law: the necessity for the British commercial organization to administer law in its territories. The *paṇḍits* who were requested to write "the digest" of Hindu law which might be used in the Courts produced texts which were judged inadequate for that purpose: "In a general compilation, where the authorities are greatly multiplied, and the doctrines of many different schools, and of numerous authors are contrasted and compared, the reader is at a loss to collect the doctrines of a particular school and to follow the train of reasoning by which they are maintained. He is confounded by the perpetual conflict of discordant opinions and jarring deductions; and by the frequent transition from the positions of one sect to the principles of another" (ibid.: iii., cf. Derrett 1968: 246–247). The necessity to supply British judges in the several Courts of the East India Company with "lawbooks" valid in their respective territories, thus, gave real life to the concept of "schools of Hindu law," the abstract existence of which had been assumed for a number of reasons which I have examined earlier in this paper.

Under these circumstances Colebrooke's immediate goal became "the separate publication of the most approved works of each school," and to exhibit "in an exact translation the text of the author with notes selected from the glosses of his commentators or from the works of other writers of the same school" (Colebrooke 1810: iii).

It is easy to understand why Colebrooke was advised to study and translate Jīmūtavāhana's *Dāyabhāga*. The *Dāyabhāga* had become very important in Bengal; it can be said without exaggeration that most later works produced in Bengal were directly or indirectly commentaries on Jīmūtavāhana's text. Yet, this does not warrant the conclusion that the *Dāyabhāga* became important *because it codified Bengali customs.* There are good reasons to believe that P.V. Kane is right when he assigns Jīmūtavāhana's literary activity to the period between 1090 and 1130 (Kane 1930–62: 1.326). How can it, then, be explained that a text written with the express purpose of giving local customs their place within the framework of the Dharmaśāstra remained practically unnoticed for four centuries? Indeed, Śrīnāthācāryacūḍāmaṇi's commentary was written between 1490 and 1525 (Chakravarti 1915: 351). Besides, Śrīnātha's interest in the *Dāyabhāga* was not that of a practicing lawyer. His activity was confined to his *ṭol* in Navadvīpa, "one of the most important and influential, where brilliant students like Raghunandana and others were carefully trained" (ibid.: 351). The *Dāyabhāga* was studied in *ṭols* —as it is today— not by students who had to be taught the local law of inheritance to prepare them for practice in the Courts, but by traditional disciples who studied *dharma* as one of the branches of Hindu learning.

It is also understandable that the early European students of Sanskrit "law texts," working in Calcutta but with strong intellectual ties in Banaras, looked for another treatise —a single treatise, if possible— to represent the school of Banaras and, at the same time, "all the schools of Hindú law, from Benares to the southern extremity of the peninsula of India" (Colebrooke 1810: iv). Vijñāneśvara's *Mitākṣarā* was the obvious choice. Yet, even

Colebrooke realized that Vijñāneśvara was a hermit, and that he commented on the entire *Yājñavalkyasmṛti*. Besides, he can hardly have been connected with the local laws of the province of Banaras, for he wrote when king Vikramārka or Vikramāditya ruled in the city of Kalyāṇa in Central India (Kane 1930–62: 1.288; Jolly 1885: 12–13).

Very few modern scholars have refused to accept the existence of schools of Hindu law. The objections raised by men like A.C. Burnell and J.H. Nelson[134] have not been given much attention. In general, Colebrooke's schools of Hindu law have been unreservedly accepted. The present paper wanted to point out that Colebrooke's schools of Hindu law are a typical example of a Western interpretation forced upon an existing Indian concept. The interpretation was tempting for a number of reasons: Western administrators came to India with the knowledge of "schools of law" in another Oriental legal system; they found in texts which they erroneously considered as codifications of local laws indications of something which might correspond to schools; and the texts representative of the various schools were much more helpful in the Courts than the "digests" which Indian *paṇḍits* prepared at their request. Yet, the interpretation was incorrect. The Sanskrit texts do not have a technical term corresponding to Colebrooke's schools of law;[135] that meaning was read into a terminology the purpose and background of which were entirely different. A case in point is again Sarvadhikari, one of the principal defenders of the schools of Hindu law. He says: "Vachaspati Misra, the author of the Vivada Chintamani, speaks of '*the legislators of Mithila*, and those of other provinces.' Vivada Chintamani is a work of great authority in the Mithila school; and when we find that a clear distinction is made in it between the lawyers of this and 'others,' we must accept it as a fact that at the time of Vachaspati Misra at least Hindu lawyers were distributed into different schools" (Sarvadhikari 1922: 268). A footnote to this passage refers to Prossonno Coomar Tagore's translation of the *Vivādacintāmaṇi*, p. 169. The discussion there is about the term *kumbha* in a verse by Bṛhaspati. Tagore translates: "According to the *Ratnakara* and others...The legislators of *Mithila* call... Others say that..." Notice that Tagore

[134] See Burnell's preface to his translation of Varadarāja's *Vyavahāranirṇaya*, 1872. Also Nelson: 1887: 179–187, and 1877: 20–27; cf. Derrett 1961: 366.

[135] Sarvadhikari (1922: 269) maintains that "there is a word in Sanskrit which is often used in the same sense in which the word 'school' is employed. The word we refer to is '*Sampradaya*.'" But he has to admit that "in law-treatises, however, the word *Sampradaya* is seldom met with. The distinction between the different schools is there marked by citing the different classes of lawyers according to their generic names."

does not say: "and those of other provinces": this is Sarvadhikari's further interpretation of a translation in which "the legislators of Mithila" already reads more into the text than the Sanskrit original warrants. Vācaspatimiśra himself said: …*iti Ratnākarādayaḥ*;… *iti Maithilāḥ*; *anye tu*… (Jha 1937: 135).

I intend to show elsewhere that even basic differences of opinion such as those existing between the *Mitākṣarā* and the *Dāyabhāga* are the result of differing interpretations of one and the same body of *smṛti* rules. Jīmūtavāhana himself points in that direction, at the outset of the *Dāyabhāga*:

> *Manvādivākyāny avimṛśya yeṣāṃ*
> *yasmin vivādo bahudhā budhānām,*
> *teṣāṃ prabodhāya sa dāyabhāgo*
> *nirūpaṇīyaḥ; sudhiyaḥ śṛṇudhvam.*

That means: the wise have not so far given enough thought to the numerous and seemingly conflicting rules on inheritance proclaimed by Manu and others; as a result they have differed in their overall interpretations of these rules. The *Dāyabhāga* will try to provide a more accurate interpretation by assigning each individual rule its proper place within the whole.

The *Dāyabhāga* may have become extremely successful and may have been the source of a regular school of thought on inheritance. We have no right, however, to accuse the author of dishonesty, and say that he used the ancient *smṛti*s as a pretext to lay down or codify the law of Bengal.

6

*Changing Patterns of Diversification in Hindu Law**

What I intend to do today is to take you through the history of Hindu law, from the earliest times until today, and show you various patterns of diversification as they manifested themselves at different times in history. I would like to show you an area of knowledge, and, at the same time, an area of human behavior: the laws of the Hindus, how the patterns of diversification across the Subcontinent changed in the course of time. There were always good reasons for these changes, and even the most orthodox Hindus have come forward to justify them.

You are, of course, familiar with an institution that, with a term derived from Latin, we call levirate. When I consulted the *Encyclopaedia Britannica* on the subject, I found: "In ancient Hebrew society, when a man died without sons his brother was required to marry the widow in order to provide a 'son' and heir to the dead man, thus perpetuating the paternal line." I also learned that "a sample of 185 primitive societies of the 19th and 20th centuries found that 69% exhibited a preference for some such form of secondary marriage." Finally, the author of the article stated that "a similar custom prevailed among the Vedic Aryans of India (1500 to 1000 BC), among whom the son performed funeral rites for the salvation of his deceased father's soul."

Now let me quote from one of our classical Sanskrit lawbooks:

> On failure of issue (by her husband) a woman who has been authorised, may obtain, (in the) proper (manner prescribed), the

* [Editor's note: This essay was originally delivered as part of the South Asia Seminar at the University of Pennsylvania in 1980–81 and, as a result, lacks certain bibliographic details.]

> desired offspring by (cohabitation with) a brother-in-law or (with some other) *sapiṇḍa* (of the husband).
>
> He (who is) appointed to (cohabit with) the widow shall (approach her) at night annointed with clarified butter and silent, (and) beget one son, by no means a second.
>
> But when the purpose of the appointment to (cohabit with) the widow has been attained in accordance with the law, those two shall behave towards each other like a father and a daughter-in-law.
>
> If those two (being thus) appointed deviate from the rule and act from carnal desire, they will both become outcasts, (as men) who defile the bed of a daughter-in-law or of a *Guru*. (MDh 9.59–60, 62–63, trans. Bühler)

It should be pretty obvious that levirate (*niyoga*) was a recognized institution in ancient India. And, knowing what a son means to a Hindu father, this comes as no surprise. Also, there are parallel passages in other lawbooks that confirm the existence of levirate marriage.

But let us now turn to another legal prescription, and this is where diversification appears for the first time:

> By twice-born men a widow must not be appointed to (cohabit with) any other (than her husband); for they who appoint (her) to another (man) will violate the eternal law.
>
> In the sacred texts which refer to marriage the appointment (of widows) is nowhere mentioned, nor is the re-marriage of widows prescribed in the rules concerning marriage. (MDh 9.64–65, trans. Bühler)

As one modern scholar puts it: these two passages on levirate "flatly contradict" one another. And yet, for the rule forbidding levirate, I could also quote you parallel passages from other lawbooks.

Before I proceed, let me give you one more example of this kind of diversification. One rule of law states that, after the death of their father and mother, the brothers shall get together and divide the paternal estate "in equal shares." But there is another rule: it prescribes that the eldest son alone shall take the entire paternal estate, and that the others shall live under him as they lived under their father. And there is a third rule, which tells us that, before things are divided equally, extra shares should be allotted: one-twentieth of the estate to the eldest son, one-eightieth to the youngest son, and one-fortieth of the estate to all those in between.

Now, what do we do with all this? Undoubtedly there *was* diversification in ancient Hindu law. It is what I will call the first, the earliest pattern of diversification: the diversification within the Dharmasūtras and Dharmaśāstras. For those of you who would like to put a date to it, I am talking here about texts composed in the period from 300 BC until AD 700, give or take a couple of centuries at the beginning and at the end.

Before we go on talking about diversification in the Dharmasūtras and Dharmaśāstras, let us not overlook one other fact, namely, the basic unity underlying all these texts. I have been struck for many years, and I remain so today, by the fact that all these texts, whether they were composed in the north, in the center, or in the south of the subcontinent, and whether they were composed in 300 BC or in AD 700, are based on exactly identical principles. I will give you just one example of this underlying unity. The caste system, of course, plays an important role. Any wrong done to a Brāhmaṇa is punished more severely than the same wrong done to a Kṣatriya, one to a Kṣatriya more severely than one to a Vaiśya, and so on. Conversely, the same offense committed by a Śūdra is punished more severely than were it committed by a Kṣatriya, and so on. And every text makes it clear that there shall be no corporal punishment for a Brāhmaṇa, whatever wrong he does. But I have to talk today about differences, not about identity. And differences there were, no doubt. I have already given you a few examples.

That the ancient Indian lawbooks contain different opinions should not, *a priori*, surprise us. After all, we are dealing here with texts —many texts— composed over a period of at least one thousand years, and in all parts of a not very small subcontinent.

Some of these differences are easily explained. I can easily see that levirate was accepted in some regions of India, but rejected in other parts of the Subcontinent. I can also see that levirate was accepted within some castes, but was against the rules of other castes. In other words, I am convinced that the Dharmasūtras and the Dharmaśāstras reveal some very interesting local, caste, and other kinds of diversity as it existed in ancient India.

I wish that was it, and that we could, in good conscience, move on to the second pattern of diversification in Hindu law. But we cannot. The reason is that both rules on levirate —levirate yes, levirate no— occur in the same lawbook, the famous *Laws of Manu*. And they appear there together, one set of rules immediately following the other. And the differing rules on inheritance —equal partition, primogeniture, and a little extra for the eldest son— are again, all three, from *Manu*, one immediately after the other, without the slightest transition. There is not even a *vā* 'or,' as Bühler's translation in the *Sacred Books of the East* might lead you to believe.

I must be honest with you and warn you that the interpretation I am about to give you of this strange form of diversification within the Dharmasūtras and Dharmaśāstras is entirely my own. We are dealing here with a topic on which the most divergent interpretations have been proposed —and destroyed.[136]

The problem is directly related to a hotly debated issue: what are these so-called ancient Indian lawbooks? It is the opinion of a highly respected volume, Mayne's *Treatise on Hindu Law and Usage* (1950) that "there can be no doubt that these rules were concerned with the practical administration of the law." But here is another opinion: "It is a profound error to regard these texts as complete codes of law or as getting all their 'rules' rigidly enforced by the political authorities of their times." And the same author, Govinda Das (1914), goes on: "Hindu Law was in the main never more than a pious wish of its metaphysically-minded, ceremonial-ridden priestly promulgators, and but seldom a stern reality."

As is usually the case in such circumstances, there is something right in both extreme opinions, and there is a lot wrong in them. Personally, I do not believe that our so-called lawbooks were ever meant to be used as lawbooks, that is, as books in the hands of judges while they decided cases. (The Greek ambassador to the Mauryas, Megasthenes, in the third century BC was surprised that Indian judges used no lawbooks, and he drew the wrong conclusion: people without lawbooks must be people without writing.)

Just a few days ago I read proofs of an article in which I give an annotated English translation of a letter written by a French Jesuit, from South India, in 1714. This Jesuit, Father Bouchet, devotes his entire letter to the administration of justice among the Hindus as he observed it. Father Bouchet tells us, explicitly, that no one uses books to enforce their laws. But every area, and every caste in every area, has its own oral legal maxims, transmitted from generation to generation. Everyone knows these maxims, and lives by them. Or, at least, if someone does not live by them, he is soon forced to do so.

Father Bouchet gives several examples of these oral maxims, and the interesting thing is that they could easily have been taken straight out of *Manu* or any other lawbook. And now I can explain what I think our lawbooks really are: in my opinion they are collections of maxims, gathered together by an individual, or by several individuals in the course of time. These maxims may have come from different areas and from different social groups. From our point of view these maxims often contradict each other, but that is our point of view because we erroneously look upon these

[136] [Editor's note: Rocher considers the argument of the present essay to be superseded by his 1993 article, "Law Books in an Oral Culture," reprinted as Chapter 3 in the present volume.]

texts as lawbooks. There is nothing wrong with them if we take them for what they are: collections of maxims, as many maxims as possible, taken from various castes and whatever other groups.

In fact, all these texts are unanimous in telling us that all customs, even the unwritten customs of all groups —craftsmen, traders, the military, and others— are valid sources of law within the group. The texts even allow these customs to be applied in as many specialized courts. From this it seems to me that there must have been even more diversification of law in India than the written texts have preserved for us.

If only the redactors of the Dharmasūtras and Dharmaśāstras, at least for the rules they did codify, had told us that rule A was applied in area or caste or group X, and rule B in area or caste or group Y. Then the legal historian, and the Indian historian generally, would have been in great shape. But, unfortunately for us, that is where the texts let us down.

So far, I have stressed one side of the coin: the ancient texts do show us some of the diversity that existed in real life: local diversity, caste diversity, or whatever. So far, I have more or less agreed with the opinion of Mayne. But, as I said, there is also something right in the opinion of Govinda Das. What I want to show now is that some of the diversity that we observe in the Sūtras and Śāstras has nothing to do with legal diversity as it existed in real life.

The redactors of these texts were also thinkers in their own right. When I say thinkers, I mean, in this type of text, that they were organizers, or, perhaps better, systematizers. They loved to create systems, and, once a system had been created, it stuck, and it never changed. At least, the basic framework of the system remained unchanged. But within the system, individual authors could play with the details; they could display their personal skills, and make the existing systems smoother and more beautiful. This, then, leads to another category of diversification in the Dharmasūtras and Dharmaśāstras. But this diversification, I believe, had nothing to do with diversity in real life.

For instance, all these texts have a tendency to divide things into three tiers. There are thefts of the highest category, of the middlemost category, and of the lowest category. And the highest is always twice as serious as the middlemost, and the middlemost twice as serious as the lowest. That never changes, but the ranking of various offenses in specific categories is very much up to the taste of the individual author.

Let me come back for a moment to the extra share that the eldest son gets in the inheritance. The fact that the eldest gets an extra share of the inheritance in the amount of one-twentieth is pretty well accepted. But I am less certain about whether or not the addition in *Manu* that the middle son gets one-fortieth (one half of one-twentieth) and the younger one-eightieth (one half of one-fortieth) represents a real diversification.

And I cannot omit my favorite example. All texts recognize three levels of pecuniary punishment, the highest, the middlemost, and the lowest, of course. For *Manu* and a few other texts, the respective amounts are 1000, 500, and 250. However, the *Yājñavalkyasmṛti* has 1080, 540, and 270. Modern scholarship has worked hard to explain this diversification. The famous K.P. Jayaswal proposed that the rupee had been devalued between the time of *Manu* and *Yājñavalkya*. In reality, of course, the author of *Yājñavalkyasmṛti*, whoever that may have been, was simply ingenious. He maintained the system of three levels of fines, but he replaced the noncommittal figure of 1000 by the nearest possible variant of 18: 1080. And the number eighteen is a much more attractive figure than ten, one hundred, and so on. There are eighteen books in the *Mahābhārata*, and the *Mahābhārata* battle lasted eighteen days. There are eighteen chapters in the *Bhagavadgītā*. I could go on and on.

That will do for my first pattern of diversification in Hindu law. I will call this the period of stylized and, unfortunately, noncontextualized diversification.

Let us now pass on to a second pattern of diversification, a very different one, and see how it came about. I am now going to cover a period from, let us say, the eighth or ninth century AD up to nearly the end of the eighteenth century. After about AD 800 or 900, no new Dharmaśāstras were composed.[137] A new genre of legal literature sets in: the commentary —many and long commentaries on the Dharmasūtras and Dharmaśāstras. And the new genre of legal literature sets in motion a new pattern of diversification. It is possible, during the rest of this talk, that I may inadvertently speak of commentaries and of digests. There is a technical difference. The commentary follows one particular ancient text, line by line, occasionally bringing in rules from other ancient texts. The digest, which is my equivalent for *nibandha*, does not follow any particular text, but rather proceeds by subject and quotes from all ancient texts at the discretion of the author. But, basically, commentators and digest writers do the same thing.

It is time now to take you back to the "levirate yes, levirate no" rules in the *Laws of Manu*, and to remind you of Bühler's footnote: these two rules "flatly contradict" each other. That was Bühler's opinion, and you might be tempted to agree with him. But not so the commentators. To speak of contradictions in the *smṛti*

[137] [Editor's note: This claim is questionable and seems to reflect a narrow view of what counted as a Dharmaśāstra. Lariviere 2004 [1997] discusses and criticizes this view in detail.]

literature is, itself, a contradiction in terms. If anything looks like a contradiction, it just means that we have not reached a correct understanding of the texts.

Let us take a few examples, building on the ones I gave earlier. This is how a commentator would approach the diversity in the rules on how to partition an estate. The normal situation is that the partition of an inheritance is done in equal shares among all brothers. But if the younger brothers have a special affection for their elder brother, and for the eldest brother in particular, in that case they can allow an extra share of one-twentieth to the eldest, one-fortieth to the middle ones, and one-eightieth to the younger. And if the oldest alone is capable, physically and mentally, he can take the entire estate, and the others will continue to live under him just as they lived under their father. Now you see there are no contradictions in *Manu*!

There is no problem either with the passages on levirate. Levirate, a commentator will say, was allowed in previous world ages, but it is a practice to be avoided in this miserable Kali Age in which we live at present. The *kalivarjyas*, or "practices to be avoided in the Kali Age," become a most convenient way to explain differences. It was applied so often that an Indian scholar has been able to devote a whole book to the subject.

There were, of course, many other ways to explain the differences of the earlier period. I only gave you a few examples, and avoided the real gems, which only Sanskritists trained in all kinds of very technical literature can appreciate. The various techniques, as such, are less important for my purpose today.

More important is the fact that in their interpretations the pandits were on their own. They could put into their interpretations all their skills and all the learning at their disposal. And those of you who have worked with pandits know that a good pandit's skills are something to behold. Part and parcel of displaying these skills was the absolute liberty to find fault with the interpretations of predecessors or contemporaries, the freedom to say flatly that they were wrong, and to propose one's own, much more ingenious and, therefore, superior interpretation.

And there you have my second pattern of diversification in Hindu law: every commentator starts from the premise that the entire *smṛti* literature is one single harmonious whole. But every commentator proves this premise in his own personal way, and these personal ways are often very different. I will call this second period the period of erudite, panditic diversification.

I will try to illustrate this situation with one example, an example that will acquire historical importance when I come to the third pattern of diversification in a few moments. One commentary on the *Yājñavalkyasmṛti* is the *Mitākṣarā*, composed by

Vijñāneśvara around AD 1100. The chapter on inheritance begins with a long theoretical discussion of the nature of property, ownership, and related concepts. The *Mitākṣarā* argues, on the basis of the ancient texts, that one way of acquiring property is by the simple fact of one's birth. Every person, by the very fact of his being born into the joint family, acquires an undivided right of ownership in the common stock. But there is another text, more or less contemporaneous with the *Mitākṣarā*: Jīmūtavāhana's *Dāyabhāga*, which has an equally long and detailed introduction. This text is totally and exclusively devoted to inheritance. But the *Dāyabhāga*, using, interpreting, and commenting on the same body of Dharmasūtra and Dharmaśāstra materials, comes to the opposite conclusion of the *Mitākṣarā*; the *Dāyabhāga* argues that ownership in joint family property, i.e., the right to dispose of it at pleasure, is in the hands of the head of the family alone. The other members of the joint family have no right of ownership in anything until the head, who is normally their father, dies. Once these basic principles are established, the two texts, the *Mitākṣarā* and *Dāyabhāga*, go on interpreting every other ancient rule in the light of their respective principles. And, as you can imagine, we come to two very different systems of the joint family.

In the *Dāyabhāga* the joint family manager is the sole owner of all joint family property. And since ownership means absolute freedom to do with the property whatever one wants to do with it, the *Dāyabhāga* joint family manager can act alone, without having to consult the other joint family members and to receive their permission to act. In the *Mitākṣarā*, on the other hand, the head of the joint family is very much restricted in what he can do with the joint family property. He is allowed to manage, but he cannot dispose at his own pleasure.

I will come back to the *Mitākṣarā* and the *Dāyabhāga* in a few moments. Their totally different interpretations of the identical texts on ownership and, hence, of joint family management and inheritance are only one example among many. There are numerous cases in which the same body of classical texts has led to opposite interpretations in the period of the commentators. And there are, of course, more than just opposite interpretations. On every topic of law there is, each time, a whole range of possible interpretations, going from one extreme to another. In fact, there are not two commentators —there are many— between whom there is absolute agreement on everything. When I say that no two commentators agree, I must add a small qualification. It is only normal, within the traditional Indian system of education, that some of the diversity in the commentators and digests took on a geographical overtone. A few strong centers developed that specialized in the writing of legal commentaries. One such center flourished in Mithilā, where a number of important authors succeeded each other. Another important area of legal writing was Bengal. This again does not mean that all authors in Mithilā agree all the time and that the later ones just echo the earlier ones. And anyone of you who has worked in Bengal will not be surprised if I say that no Bengali pandit was afraid of making it quite clear that another Bengali pandit was wrong. But there is no doubt that, in all that diversity, there is *some* underlying regional unity. When it comes to such basic principles as the role of the joint family manager, it makes sense to speak of "the" Maithilas and of "the" Bengalis, or Gauḍas as they are called in the texts. But, as far as anything beyond the general principles is concerned, pure individual sophistry prevails.

As time went on, the commentaries became longer and longer. There are more and more predecessors whose opinions have to be quoted, to be either approved or rejected, and, above all, to be improved upon. Let me just describe to you the situation as it presents itself in one of the later digests, Mitra Miśra's *Vīramitrodaya*. This text was composed in the first quarter of the seventeenth century in the Gwālior-Jhansi area. Sometimes Mitra Miśra will cite an old Dharmaśāstra passage and say that he agrees with the interpretation of one or more predecessors —let us say, with Vācaspati Miśra— but that he rejects the interpretation of one or more of the predecessors —let us say, Śūlapāṇi. While commenting on another Dharmaśāstra passage, however, Mitra Miśra will say that Śūlapāṇi is right and that Vācaspati Miśra is wrong. By the way, Vācaspati belongs to Mithilā, and Śūlapāṇi belongs to Bengal. There are other occasions on which Mitra Miśra says, more generally, that "the Maithilas" are right and "the Gauḍas" are wrong, or that "the Gauḍas" are right and "the Maithilas" wrong. But there are also numerous instances in which the later commentator quotes the opinion of two, or three, or more predecessors, fully and in detail, and then simply goes on to the next topic. This situation, in which authors quote several opinions —different opinions, contradictory opinions in Western terms— without saying explicitly which one is right and which one is wrong, leads me quite naturally into a third period of diversity in the history of Hindu law: the diversity introduced, not by the authors of Dharmaśāstras, not by the commentators or digest writers, but by the British.

As you know, in 1772, Warren Hastings obtained that, in a number of matters concerning family law, Muslims should be governed by the law of the Qur'ān and Hindus by the laws of the "Shaster." For judges who did not know Sanskrit, applying Hindu laws to Hindus was more easily said than done.

Translating the "Shaster" *par excellence*, the *Laws of Manu*, was not particularly helpful. Mr. Justice Smith or Brown immediately ran into our first pattern of diversification. Should he allow levirate marriage or not? And how shall he rule when, in a suit on inheritance, son A claimed equal partition, son B an extra share, and eldest son C the entire estate? To deal with such problems as these, Warren Hastings commissioned a full-fledged code of Hindu law. He called eleven pandits to Calcutta, and what they came up with for him was the most traditional composition one can imagine. Exactly like the *Vīramitrodaya*, which I just described, the *Vivādārṇavasetu* —that is the name of the book produced by the eleven pandits— displayed a wealth of Dharmaśāstra rules, accompanied by lengthy quotes from a host of commentaries. But when the British judges in India got hold of the English translation, which was prepared in a hurry, it proved less than useful for them as a basis for their judgements: it was my second type of erudite diversification in all its glory.

And that is when something happened that created the third pattern of diversification in Hindu law. What exactly happened, and how it happened, we do not know. But, in 1810, H.T. Colebrooke came out with a volume entitled *Two Treatises on the Hindu Law of Inheritance*. The two treatises translated in this book were Jīmūtavāhana's *Dāyabhāga* and Vijñāneśvara's *Mitākṣarā*. That is why, a little earlier, I chose these two texts to oppose their views on the power of the joint family manager. And Colebrooke did more. He declared the *Dāyabhāga* the law of the land in Bengal and the *Mitākṣarā* the law of the land all over the rest of India.

The choice of the *Dāyabhāga* I can understand. I can imagine that the British asked the Bengali pandits: What is the most authoritative text on inheritance in Bengal? And they answered: The *Dāyabhāga*. After all, this digest itself had been commented on seven or eight times (some of these commentaries having several subcommentaries of their own) and was probably read in all the *ṭols* (the traditional Sanskrit schools).

But the choice of the *Mitākṣarā* puzzles me. Why not choose a text from the competing school of Mithilā? Why choose a text written in what is now the extreme northeast corner of Karnataka, in the district of Bidar, just east of Maharashtra's Sholapur? I personally think that the lawbook for "the others" did not matter too much. If Colebrooke had been stationed in Bombay or Madras, he would probably have been told that there was one lawbook for Bombay or the Madras area and another for the rest of India. The history of Hindu law under the British —and Hindu law today— would have been totally different. That is why I shall call this period the period of haphazard diversification.

I am convinced that, during the time of the commentaries and digests, these texts did not represent the law of the land. They were purely panditic, learned commentaries on ancient authoritative texts. The fact that they display differences does not mean, as some have proposed, that the commentators adapted the ancient sacred texts to local customs. That would have been pure sacrilege on their part. I can imagine that, whenever a party to a lawsuit went for advice to the pandits, the pandit may have told him what, in his opinion, there was in the texts. But I am also convinced that the lawsuits themselves were decided according to pure local custom, at a lower level, and —let us not forget that this is the "Muslim period"— that lawsuits, even among Hindus, at a higher level were decided according to Muslim law. I have looked hard in Bengal to find applications in the court of the *Dāyabhāga* before 1810, but they are not to be found. It is Muslim law all over. I can also assure you that the many commentaries and subcommentaries on the *Dāyabhāga* do not read like lawbooks at all; they are, as one might expect in Bengal, pure treatises on *navyanyāya*, the school of "new-logic."

In other words, the British raised the Sanskrit commentaries and digests to the status of lawbooks to be used in the courts, a role these texts were never meant to play. It is therefore not only a period of haphazard diversification, it is, at the same time, a period of artificial diversification.

And diversification there was. I have so far only talked about two texts that were made available in translation and assigned to two different parts of the Subcontinent. But the proclamation of 1772 had made the "Shaster," i.e., the entire Sanskrit legal literature, a valid source of law. Consequently, when more commentaries and digests were gradually translated, they too were law, and they had to be assigned to some geographic area in India. Bengal did not allow itself to be affected by all this. The *Dāyabhāga* remained the law of Bengal. But there was still "the rest of India" covered by just the *Mitākṣarā*. That text needed some reinforcement. So gradually "the rest of India" was subdivided into four subschools of the *Mitākṣarā*: the Benares school, Mithilā, Maharashtra, and Dravida, which last had three sub-subschools: Tamil, Karnātaka, and Andhra. Each of these subschools has its own authoritative texts, one of the commentaries or digests, with endless discussions as to what happens when their text conflicts with the all-overriding *Mitākṣarā*.

What gradually happened is that, in the various parts of India, there developed a number of separate and different pyramids, with a High Court or Supreme Court, as they were called in those days, at the top of each. Within the territory of each Supreme Court, the judges tried to establish some kind of uniformity; but the different Supreme Courts gradually grew farther and farther apart. Most apart, of course, was the Calcutta Supreme Court. But, as I said earlier, I am convinced that that is a pure accident of history. Even the Privy Council recognized these distinctions, and never tried to go against them.

Finally, we come to the fourth period in the history of Hindu law. Together with the idea of an independent India came the claim to unify and codify Hindu law. In 1941 a committee was formed, with Sir B.N. Rau as Chairman. As you know, the Hindu Code Bill was hotly debated, but failed. No compromise seemed to be possible between the proponents of further modernization of Hindu law and the advocates of a return to pure Sanskrit law.

The Legislative Assembly was even more ambitious, and inserted in the 1950 Constitution that "It shall be the duty of the State to provide India [not just Hindus!] with a civil code." In the meanwhile there have been important milestones toward the unification of Hindu law: the Hindu Marriage Act (1955), the Hindu Succession Act (1956), the Hindu Minority and Guardianship Act (1956), and the Hindu Adoptions and Maintenance Act (1956). That means, however, that even after 1956, and until today, a number of areas of Hindu law remain uncodified.

These areas of Hindu law continue to be administered according to the system that was essentially created by the British and continued by the courts of independent India. There is no new diversification, and whatever diversification remains is shrinking. I shall therefore call the fourth period the period of residual diversification. How much and how long there will be some kind of residual diversification is hard to predict. But that is a problem to be solved by the Indian Parliament, not by us in the South Asia Seminar.

Discussion

Much of the discussion focused on the scope and detail of the Hindu law texts and the interaction between Hindu law and other legal systems. In response to a question concerning a dispute in Jaipur under the Rājpūts over the rights of the Gauḍīyas to use a certain temple, which also included the question of whether or not the Gauḍīyas were also a sect, the speaker stressed that the Dharmaśāstras never mention issues like this. They granted validity to customs and the laws of distinct groups, leaving each group to apply its own customs. The texts would probably have viewed specific temple laws in the same way, leaving temple authorities free to decide their own cases according to their own custom.

In regard to the absence in the Dharmaśāstras of any mention of specific groups or individuals and their rules, one participant suggested that it might be a question of which texts are being examined. In Mīmāṃsā texts, for example, the same type of issue arises: what is right when; but the authors do talk about individual people and customs.

The fact that diversification in Hindu law arises from textual eclecticism and that there is no sense of sectarian "groupness" in the texts raised the question of whether or not a set of people still argue over a question of doctrine which would distinguish them as a group. The speaker stressed that questions of doctrine definitely remain important. Father Bouchet's letter indicates that certain groups had certain fixed laws.

In response to a question on heresy and its legal consequences according to the Dharmaśāstras, the speaker responded that heresy, as such, is not discussed.

The appeal procedure for Hindu law was also clarified. Any legal question, including one on Hindu law, may go to the Supreme Court on appeal; this court is not limited to constitutional issues. Each case in Hindu law is judged according to its particular school; for instance, the court will say this is a *Mitākṣarā* case or a *Dāyabhāga* case and proceed from there. The Supreme Court is not a centralizing or unifying force.

The speaker also pointed out that Muslim law had a major influence on the development of Hindu law. The schools of Hindu law are the result of people like Colebrooke who were familiar with Muslim law and went to India believing that all Oriental legal systems had schools of law. They looked for such schools of law in the Hindu texts and found them to their satisfaction.

Part Two

General Topics of Hindu Law

7

*Ancient Hindu Criminal Law**

Before starting the discussion of the real subject, a preliminary remark should be made about the term "law" used in the title of this paper. Western people have come to know the *Mānava-Dharmaśāstra* under such titles as Bühler's *The Laws of Manu* (cf. Loiseleur-Deslongchamps 1830 and Jolly 1882–83). For the same Western people, however, this word *law* has a very strictly circumscribed connotation: a law to them is a prescription passed and voted upon in the one or two existing legislative assemblies, approved by the head of the state, be he a king or a president, and to be adhered to by the people immediately after its official publication. It should be remembered, then, that in ancient India there was not such a separate concept as "law." What is called "law" nowadays was merely a very small portion of the much more comprehensive doctrine of *dharma*. In view of this, the learned Dr. P.V. Kane has done well to entitle his voluminous work, of which the fourth volume has been recently published, *History of Dharmaśāstra*, adding in parentheses: "(ancient and medieval *religious* and *civil law*)." Nevertheless if we use the term "law," it simply means that this article is concerned with that part of the Dharmaśāstra the contents of which correspond to the rules of conduct which in modern democracies are passed by the legislative assemblies.

It is of even greater importance, however, that the term "criminal" which has been prefixed to "law," be properly understood. In modern India a certain number of offenses have been treated in

*Address at the Tenth Foundation Day celebrations of the Kuppuswami Sastri Research Institute, 18th Sept. 1954.

the Act of 1860 which is known as the Indian Penal Code, whereas another set of cases which are now still treated according to the principles of ancient Hindu law, will probably very soon be enumerated in the Hindu Code, as soon as Parliament passes the Hindu Code Bill. In most other modern countries, too, the simultaneous existence of a Penal Code and a Civil Code has created a sharp distinction between civil and penal wrongs or between civil and criminal law. The object of this paper is an attempt to make out whether the same distinction also existed in the ancient Hindu law or the Dharmaśāstras.

In order to do this, we first of all have to define the term "crime" and to enumerate the characteristics which distinguish it from the ordinary civil wrong. Much has been written on this subject, but in view of the purpose of this paper I think we may overlook all discussions on minor points and define a crime as follows: If I do not pay a debt to my creditor, I certainly cause him to suffer a financial loss, and this entitles him to appeal to certain authorities appointed for that purpose. Independent judges will hear his plaint, and I will be summoned in order that I too may bring forward all arguments to my defense. In the court my creditor himself is my opponent. The court will pass a written judgment whose primary aim will be the indemnification of my creditor's loss, and it will make over this document to executive officers who will force me to act according to the judge's decision. It is, however, up to my creditor and to him only, to decide whether he should bring the matter before the court or not. The loss he undergoes is limited to his own person; no one else in society suffers from my failure of payment, and if my creditor does not complain with the judges, no one will take action against me. I will not be summoned to appear in the court, and no judgment whatsoever will be passed against me. On the other hand, if I commit manslaughter or if I seriously injure my enemy, the reaction will be completely different. In this case it does not matter whether the victim or his relatives complain before the judges or not. Even if the victim does not want to do so, certain public officers will make up a report *ex officio* and action will be taken against me. As before, I will be summoned before the judges, but in this case the opponent in the court is not my victim but society itself represented by a public prosecutor. The victim will be heard as a witness only. In many modern systems of law the victim does not obtain any indemnification at all if he omits to appoint a representative *ad hoc* who expressly asks for it during the trial. This request may be accepted by the court or not, but even if it is, it only forms a secondary part of the judgment. The main concern of the latter is to fix the adequate action to be taken in the name of society against an act which is considered an encroachment on its well-being or, as it is technically called, a trespass on law and order.

I have given these two examples to show that according to modern conceptions some offenses are considered especially serious, to such an extent that they inflict damage not only on the individual himself but on society as a whole. Against such offenses society takes action *suo motu* even in the absence of an individual plaintiff or even against his will. Such offenses are generally called "crimes." With these considerations in mind, when I found the following footnote in the 11th edition of Mayne's *Treatise on Hindu Law and Usage*: "In the Mauryan age, there were two classes of courts, the Dharmasthiya courts for the administration of civil justice and the Kantakasodhana courts for the trial of offenses and crimes" (1950: 12) —I was surprised to learn that a distinction which I had previously thought to be a modern one was mentioned as applicable to the time of the Mauryas. Therefore, I thought it might be worth while to consult the ancient texts on this matter.

In the ancient texts the subject of *vivāda*, or "substantive law" (as we would call it now, in contrast with *vyavahāra*, or "adjective law") is subdivided into a number of topics or *vivādapadāni*. The exact number slightly varies in the different texts (see Kane 1930–62: 3.249) and sometimes reaches twenty-two such as in Someśvara's *Mānasollāsa* or *Abhilaṣitārthacintāmaṇi*, but by far the most authoritative enumeration is the eighteenfold subdivision of the MDh which is as follows:

1. *ṛṇādāna*: either non-payment of debts or recovery of debts according to the analysis of the *tatpuruṣa* compound as *ṛṇa-adāna* or *ṛṇa-ādāna*.
2. *nikṣepa*: deposit.
3. *asvāmivikraya*: sale by a person who is not the owner of the thing sold.
4. *saṃbhūyasamutthāna*: joint undertakings.
5. *dattasyānapākarma*: resumption of gift.
6. *vetanādāna*: non-payment of wages.
7. *saṃvidvyatikrama*: breach of contract.
8. *krayavikrayānuśaya*: rescission of sale and purchase.
9. *svāminpālavivāda*: disputes concerning the owner and the guardian of cattle.
10. *sīmāvivāda*: boundary-disputes.
11. *vākpāruṣya*: insult.
12. *daṇḍapāruṣya*: assault.
13. *steya*: theft.
14. *sāhasa*: which we will leave untranslated for the moment.
15. *strīsaṃgrahaṇa*: adultery.
16. *strīpuṃdharma*: duties of husband and wife.
17. *vibhāga*: partition and inheritance.
18. *dyūtasamāhvaya*: gambling and betting.

For the moment it would serve no purpose to mention the minor details by which this enumeration of the MDh differs from those in *Yājñavalkyasmṛti*, *Nāradasmṛti*, *Bṛhaspatismṛti*, etc. In view of the note quoted from Mayne's *Hindu Law and Usage*, however, a few words ought to be said regarding a similar subdivision found in the *Kauṭilīya Arthaśāstra*. In this work the whole of the third *adhikaraṇa* is devoted to the cases to be treated by the so-called *dharmasthīya*-courts, and with only a few slight deviations, which are irrelevant here, this book covers all *vivādapada*s treated in the MDh as mentioned before. The fourth *adhikaraṇa*, on the other hand, enumerates another series of cases to be treated by the *kaṇṭakaśodhana*-courts. We will not go into the character of the latter here, but with regard to the third *adhikaraṇa*, viz. the cases to be treated before the *dharmasthīya*-courts, it should be said that it also includes such items as theft, physical injury, etc.[138], which are now certainly considered real crimes. It is, therefore, definitely impossible to maintain that the distinction between *dharmasthīya*-courts and *kaṇṭakaśodhana*-courts in the *Arthaśāstra* corresponds to the distinction civil law/criminal law.

Let us, then, try to detect other distinctions made by the ancient texts. Among the verses of the *Kātyāyanasmṛti* collected by P.V. Kane (1933), one goes as follows:

> *sādhyavādasya mūlaṃ syād vādinā yan niveditam | deyāpradānaṃ hiṃsā cetyutthānadvayam ucyate*
>
> The root of litigation is that which is mentioned by the plaintiff; there are two sources of legal procedure, *viz.* non-rendition of what is due and physical injury. (30)

Another verse of Kātyāyana to the same effect runs as follows:

> *utpādayati yo hiṃsā deyaṃ vā na prayacchati | yācamānāya dauḥśilyād ākṛṣyo 'sau nṛpājñayā*
>
> He who causes physical injury or he who for wickedness does not give back what he owes when his creditor asks for it is to be brought into court by order of the king. (28)

Kane, both in his edition of *Kātyāyanasmṛti* (1933: 123) and in his *History of Dharmaśāstra* (1930–62: 3.259), says that "here there is a clear distinction made between civil disputes (*arthamūla* or

[138] K.P. Jayaswal (1930: 116) correctly stresses the fact that the *dharmasthīya*-courts treat all cases coming under the *vyavahāra* law. I therefore fail to see how he can reconcile this with another statement on the same page concerning the *kaṇṭakaśodhana*-courts, viz. "They were Criminal Courts."

dhanamūla) and in criminal cases (*hiṃsāmūla*)." In other words: the distinction between cases relating to the party's property and cases referring to his person would correspond to the distinction civil law versus criminal law.

Let us first look into the collection of verses from the *Bṛhaspatismṛti* collected by Prof. K.V. Rangaswani Aiyangar (1941). Not only do we find the same division of *vivādapada*s into cases referring to one's property and cases referring to one's self:

dvipādo vyavahāraḥ syāt dhanahiṃsāsamudbhavaḥ (1.9ab)

but it is also said that the former include fourteen topics whereas the latter include only four:

dvisaptako 'rthamūlas tu hiṃsāmūlaś caturvidhaḥ (1.9cd)

The fourteen topics, referring to one's wealth are: *kusīda, nidhi, adeya, saṃbhūyotthāna, bhṛtyādāna, aśuśrūṣā, bhūvāda, asvāmivikraya, krayavikrayānuśaya, samayātikrama, strīpuṃsaṃyoga, steya, dāyabhāga,* and *akṣavedana.* And the four topics relating to one's body are: *vākpāruṣya, daṇḍapāruṣya, sāhasa* or *vadha,* and *parastrīsaṃgraha.* Judging from this enumeration of the topics in the two groups I must confess, that this subdivision comes very close to the distinction between civil and criminal law, but at least one important restriction should be made. Not only chapter XVII of the Indian Penal Code, but as far as I know, most other Penal Codes contain a chapter on "Offenses against Property," and the most important among these "Offenses against Property," viz. theft, which accordingly belongs to the *dhanamūlavivāda*s in the enumeration of Bṛhaspati, would then be a civil matter only.

If we remember the statement that only the more dangerous types of offenses are called "crimes," it might then look as if ancient Hindu law did not consider theft a very serious offense, since it is one of the modern crimes ranged among the civil wrongs. This conception would, however, be very wrong, and I want to give here a few examples to show how serious an offense theft was considered. The treatment of theft in the MDh starts as follows:

paramaṃ yatnam ātiṣṭhet stenānāṃ nigrahe nṛpaḥ | stenānāṃ nigrahād asya yaśo rāṣṭraṃ ca vardhate ||

The king should exert himself to the utmost to punish thieves; for, if he punishes thieves, his fame grows and his kingdom prospers. (8.301)

In the frame of the general context of the eighth *adhyāya* this "utmost exertion" is to be interpreted in such a way that the king should exert himself more with regard to punishing thieves than with regard to punishing any of the other offenses mentioned before and, thus, also more than with regard to *vākpāruṣya* and *daṇḍapāruṣya* which are treated immediately before theft. This way of stressing the necessity of punishing theft in particular has induced Louis Renou to make the following statement: "Le vol est le delit type dont la description sert de base au reste [Theft is the paradigmatic crime whose description serves as a basis for the others]" (1950: 117).

That theft is considered a very important crime, especially in the MDh, is obvious, not only from the verse quoted before, but also from the ampleness with which it has been treated in this most important among the Dharmaśāstras. In the eighth *adhyāya* the topic of theft is introduced by a number of general rules enumerating the merits acquired by the king when he punishes thieves adequately and the sin he incurs when he fails to do so, and immediately after this follow the punishments for a number of specific thefts. But this is not all. In the ninth *adhyāya* the treatment of the eighteen *vivādapada*s concludes with the following verse:

> *udito 'yaṃ vistaraśo mitho vivadamānayoḥ | aṣṭādaśasu mārgeṣu vyavahārasya nirṇayaḥ*
>
> I have described above in great detail how lawsuits brought by litigants and falling with the eighteen avenues of litigation are to be decided. (9.250, trans. Olivelle [Ed.])

This verse should be expected to conclude the long chapter on the *vivādapada*s which was introduced at the beginning of the eighth *adhyāya* with the verse:

> *pratyahaṃ deśadṛṣṭaiś ca śāstradṛṣṭaiś ca hetubhiḥ | āṣṭādaśasu mārgeṣu nibaddhāni pṛthak pṛthak*
>
> Every day in accordance with the standards of the region and those specified in the legal texts, [he should look into] lawsuits that fall individually under the eighteen avenues of litigation. (8.3, trans. Olivelle [Ed.])

But much to our surprise, after this concluding verse, another elaborate treatment of theft follows. It is not the place to go into this inconsistency here, but I think a careful comparison of both passages on theft and a comparison also with other ancient texts on this subject will enable me to throw some light on the structure of the eighth and ninth *adhyāya*s of the MDh. As a matter of fact, these *adhyāya*s contain a few other such inconsistencies in their structure, all of which may be due to the same cause.

After this short deviation on the problem of the structure of the eighth and ninth *adhyāyas* of the MDh, let us now return to our main subject. It remains an undisputed fact that the treatment of theft has played a very important part in the ancient Dharmaśāstra literature, to such an extent even that it quite correctly gave rise to such comments as that of Renou quoted before. If we had no other material than this, it might even look as if the Dharmaśāstras did not draw the distinction between civil and criminal law at all, but rather that one crime was considered separately as being so much more important that it could be contrasted with all other crimes and civil wrongs taken together. However, the fact is that it was not theft which was considered as the very highest possible offense, as might be inferred from the verse of the MDh already quoted. Further on in the same *adhyāya* the following verse is found:

> *vāgduṣṭāt taskarāc caiva daṇḍenaiva ca hiṃsataḥ | sāhasasya naraḥ kartā vijñeyaḥ pāpakṛttamaḥ*

> A man who perpetrates violence should be considered far more evil that someone who is offensive is speech, who steals, or who assaults with a rod. (8.345, trans. Olivelle [Ed.])

According to this verse, the sin incurred by him who commits what is called a *sāhasa* is greater than (1) the sin of a *vāgduṣṭa*, i.e., the person who commits *vākpāruṣya*; (2) the sin of a *taskara* or a thief; (3) the sin incurred by a person who commits *daṇḍena hiṃsā*, which according to the commentators in nothing but another name for *daṇḍapāruṣya.*

This verse is particularly interesting and important for our subject, and it is so in different respects. First of all it distinctly separates one particular offense from all others, and it does so because it is more serious than any other one. The sin connected with *sāhasa* is greater than that connected with any other offense. This point is further explained in the two verses which immediately follow. It is said that the king who pardons the perpetrator of a *sāhasa* quickly perishes and incurs hatred (8.346). And the next verse is as follows:

> *na mitrakāraṇād rājā vipulād vā dhanāgamāt | samutsṛjet sāhasikān sarvabhūtabhayāvahān*

> The king must never release violent men who strike terror in all creatures eyeing either friendship or a large monetary gain. (8.347, trans. Olivelle [Ed.])

Here we see, that the king should not let go perpetrators of *sāhasa* neither for friendship nor for a great increase of wealth.

And the verse explicitly qualifies those perpetrators of *sāhasa* as *sarvabhūtabhayāvahān*, the perpetrators of *sāhasa* cause terror to all citizens. In other words, the result of a *sāhasa* is looked upon not so much from the point of view of the damage caused to the individual victim but more so from the standpoint of the damage done by it to all citizens, i.e. to society as a whole. If we would translate the adjective *sarvabhūtabhayāvahān* very freely, we would say that the perpetrator of a *sāhasa* disturbs law and order. And thus we have traced back in the ancient Hindu law one of the great characteristics of the modern "crime."

But the same verse of Manu (8.345) is also important in another respect. Strictly speaking it does not separate *sāhasa* as being more dangerous than any other *vivādapada*, but it distinctly says that *sāhasa* is more dangerous than *vākpāruṣya*, *steya*, and *daṇḍapāruṣya*. Why does the author not say that the perpetrator of *sāhasa* commits a greater sin than the perpetrators of all seventeen other *vivādapadas*, but only a greater sin than three among the seventeen? The answer is obvious. Among the eighteen *vivādapadas* four are more serious than the other fourteen, and these four are *vākpāruṣya*, *steya*, *daṇḍapāruṣya*, and *sāhasa*. But again among these four, *sāhasa* surpasses the others. In other words, according to the MDh three layers should be distinguished in the eighteen *vivādapadas*: (1) the ordinary offenses, such as non-payment of debts, etc.; (2) above these: *vākpāruṣya*, *daṇḍapāruṣya*, and *steya*; (3) at the top: *sāhasa*.

Now that we have thus established the special place attributed to *sāhasa*, it may not be without interest to look into the definition of this term and the contents covered by it. This will indeed provide us with some very interesting data with regard to the concept of criminal law in the ancient texts. In his translation of Vācaspati Miśra's *Vivādacintāmaṇi* (1942), the late Ganganatha Jha at the beginning of the chapter on *sāhasa* prefixes a note in which he says that, "There is some confusion in the use of this term *sāhasa*." This confusion exists indeed, and I will now try to explain what it consists of. It has already been mentioned that in the MDh *sāhasa* is one of the eighteen *vivādapadas* or "titles of law," just as non-payment of debts, etc., *vākpāruṣya*, *daṇḍapāruṣya*, and *steya*. And with some slight modifications the same can be said about similar distinctions by Kauṭilya, Yājñavalkya, Nārada, Bṛhaspati, etc. Accordingly, in nearly all *dharmanibandhas* too, one will find a separate chapter devoted to *sāhasa*, just as one finds one on non-payment of debts, and on *vākpāruṣya*, *daṇḍapāruṣya*, *steya*, etc.

If we look into that part of the MDh (8.341) which by commentators like Kullūkabhaṭṭa is introduced as *idānīṃ sāhasam āha*, "now he discusses *sāhasa*," we do not find any definition of *sāhasa* at all. The definition of *sāhasa* which is most commonly used by the later authors of *dharmanibandhas* is the one found in the *Nāradasmṛti*:

> *sahasā kriyate karma yat kiñcit baladarpitaiḥ* | *tat sāhasam iti proktaṃ saho balam ihocyate*
>
> Whatever act is performed by force (*sahas*) by persons proud of their strength is called *sāhasa*: *sahas* (force) means strength in this world. (14.1)

It should be noted that even this definition is rather vague: the words "whatever act is performed by force" are indeed open to different interpretations, and consequently in the *nibandhas* not always identical subjects are treated under this heading.

We saw, that in the section on *sāhasa*, no definition has been given in the MDh. But if we look back in the section on theft, we find the punishment for stealing grains, vegetables, roots and fruits prescribed as follows:

> *paripūteṣu dhānyeṣu śākamūlaphaleṣu ca* | *niranvaye śataṃ daṇḍaḥ sānvaye 'rdhaśataṃ damaḥ* (8.331)

That is: The punishment for stealing husked grain, vegetables, roots and fruits is twofold: (1) hundred *paṇas* when the theft is *niranvaya*, and (2) *ardhaśata* (Cf. infra) when the theft is *sānvaya*. These terms *niranvaya* and *sānvaya* have been given different interpretations, but before going into that I should like to quote the next verse:

> *syāt sāhasaṃ tv anvayavat prasabhaṃ karma yat kṛtam* | *niranvayaṃ bhavet steyaṃ hṛtvāpavyayate ca yat*
>
> This act, viz. of taking away grains, etc., if done *anvayavat* and with force (*prasabha*) is called *sāhasa*; if done *niranvaya* and if denied, it is called *steya*. (8.332)

From this verse it is clear, that *sāhasa* and *steya* can cover the same acts under different circumstances: (1) If the act is committed forcibly or violently (*prasabha*) and *anvayavat* or *sānvaya*, it is called *sāhasa*; (2) if it is done *niranvaya* and if the act is denied, it is called *steya*. The distinction could, therefore, easily be drawn if the interpretation of the opposite terms *sānvaya* and *niranvaya* was clear. But, as said before, the commentators themselves are at variance here. Thus, Medhātithi, the earliest commentator on the MDh, gives three possible interpretations:

> 1. *anvayo 'nunayaḥ svāminaḥ prītyādiprayogaḥ* | *yat tvadīyaṃ tan madīyam eveti anayā buddhyāhaṃ pravṛtto, na ced evaṃ tadgṛhāṇa ity evamādivacanaṃ tad yatra na kriyate tan niranvayam*

According to this first interpretation *anvaya* is a conciliatory or a propitiatory statement, an appeal to the affection of the owner. The thief defends himself as follows: "I have acted under the impression that what is yours is really mine; if this is not the case, then take it back." The thief, who behaves thus, has not committed a theft but a *sāhasa*.

The second interpretation according to Medhātithi is as follows:

2. *yena saha kaścid api sambandho nāsty ekagrāmavāsādiḥ*

Therefore the act is *niranvaya*, and therefore theft, if between both parties there is no connection whatsoever, such as residence in the same village, etc. And on the other hand, the act would be *sāhasa* when there is such a connection.

And the third interpretation mentioned by Medhātithi is:

3. *anārakṣaṃ niranvayam | sati tu rakṣake ubhayāparādhād alpo daṇḍaḥ*

Niranvaya means "unguarded," whereas *sānvaya* means "in the presence of a guardian"; in the latter case, the guilt is to be divided between the perpetrator of the *sāhasa* and the guardian.

The same verse of Manu is further found in most *dharmanibandhas*, but their interpretations, though differently worded, can all be ranged under one of the three mentioned. Against all these interpretations, however, a common objection should be raised. In the second of the two verses under consideration (8.332), it could not be stated more clearly that *sāhasa* is the act committed *sānvaya* or *anvayavat*, whereas *steya* is the act committed *niranvaya*. Let us now again consider the punishment prescribed in the verse referring to the taking away of grains, etc.: *niranvaye śataṃ daṇḍaḥ sānvaye 'rdhaśataṃ damaḥ*.

Again it is clear, that (1) when there is no *anvaya*, i.e., in case of theft, the punishment should be *śata*, i.e., one hundred *paṇas*, and (2) when there is *anvaya*, i.e., in case of *sāhasa*, the punishment should be *ardhaśata*. Now, all commentators invariably have understood the word *ardhaśata* as meaning fifty. In this way the crime with *anvaya* (i.e., *sāhasa*), which is to be punished with fifty *paṇas*, is less serious than the crime when committed without *anvaya* (i.e., *steya*), for which the punishment is hundred *paṇas*. And it is this interpretation of *ardhaśata* as fifty which accounts for all three of Medhātithi's interpretations of *sānvaya* and *niranvaya*: all of them try to depict *sānvaya*, i.e., *sāhasa*, in such a way that it becomes less serious than *niranvaya*, i.e., *steya*. In the first interpretation *sāhasa* is less serious, because the perpetrator acted under the impression that he too, was entitled to the object. In the second interpretation, again, in the case of *sāhasa* there is some close connection between perpetrator and victim which makes the offense less serious than in cases where such connection is absent. And in the third interpretation, in the case of a *sāhasa* part of the guilt is attributed to the guardian who was incapable of preventing the offense.

It is against this interpretation of *ardhaśata* and therefore against that of *sānvaya* and *niranvaya* that I feel obliged to take exception. Indeed, by their interpretation of *ardhaśata* as fifty the commentators have created a contradiction in the MDh which is actually not there. At this point it should be remembered that in MDh 8.315 it is explicitly said, that *sāhasa* is more serious than theft. And nevertheless with regard to the taking away of grains, etc., the commentators make *sāhasa* less serious than *steya*. This contradiction is unnecessary: the only thing to be changed is the interpretation of *ardhaśata*. It is not fifty that is meant there, but rather one hundred and fifty. In this way the punishment for *sāhasa* becomes more severe than the punishment for theft.

If it is questioned whether this interpretation is permissible, no better argument can be adduced than another verse from the MDh itself:

> *śataṃ brāhmaṇākṛṣya kṣatriyo daṇḍam arhati | vāiśyo 'py ardhaśataṃ dve vā śūdras tu vadham arhati* (8.267)

For insulting a Brāhmaṇa the following punishments are prescribed: (1) for a Kṣatriya: 100; (2) for a Vaiśya: either *ardhaśata* or 200; (3) for a Śūdra: capital punishment. Here the gradation of the punishments undoubtedly is: 100, *ardhaśata*/200, and capital punishment. That means: 100, 150 (not 50)/200 and capital punishment.

The real difference, then, between *sāhasa* and theft is as follows: (1) *Sāhasa* requires *anvaya-prasabhaṃ karma*. *Anvaya* here means: "in the presence of the owner." It goes without saying that the owner, when present, will not permit the thief to take away his property without some attempt on his part to prevent the theft. Before carrying off his booty the thief will have to break the owner's resistance, and thus the offense inevitably becomes a *prasabhaṃ karma*. This whole crime is called *sāhasa*. (2) If, on the other hand, the owner or his guardian is absent, i.e., *niranvaya*, the element of violence is unnecessary, and the offense is a mere *steya*.

The latter argumentation, although deviating from the main subject, at least has shown that in the ancient texts *sāhasa*, let us say "violence," and *steya* or "theft" have been considered as very closely related, to such an extent that it was possible for commentators to interchange their respective values. Compare in this respect, e.g., the definition of *sāhasa* in Yājñavalkya where *sāhasa* is merely described as theft committed under certain circumstances:

sāmānyadravyaprasabhaharaṇāt sāhasaṃ smṛtam (2.230ab)

In other words: an offense is called *sāhasa*, because it consists in violently taking away *sāmānyadravya*, which according to the *Mitākṣarā* stands for property held in common with other people and for property belonging to other people only.

We have now come very close to the final step in our inquiry into the existence in ancient Hindu law of something equivalent to the modern "criminal"; let us, however, first recapitulate the results obtained thus far. Firstly, in connection with one among the eighteen *vivādapadas*, viz. *sāhasa*, we have learned that it is more serious than three other ones, viz. *vākpāruṣya, daṇḍapāruṣya, steya*, which in their turn are more serious than the fourteen remaining offenses. *Sāhasa* is not only more serious than all of them, but the fact that it is dangerous to law and order is one of the fundamental characteristics ascribed to it. And secondly, another *vivādapada*, viz. theft has been closely connected with *sāhasa*, so closely that there was not always a sharp distinction made between them.

This confusion of *steya* and *sāhasa* has gone so far that one may vainly look for *steya* in the enumeration of the eighteen *vivādapadas* as it is found in the *Nāradasmṛti*. It is true that a chapter on theft is found in an appendix to the NS about which Jolly has said that "There is every reason to consider it as the genuine production of Nārada, or whoever else was the author of the *Nāradasmṛti*" (1889: 6). I agree with Jolly that this additional chapter on theft must be very old, since the *nibandhakāras* quote from it as well as they do from the main NS, and as a matter of fact it also occurs in the shorter recension of the NS known as the *Nāradīyamanusaṃhitā*.[139] This is not the place to go into this subject, but I should only like to call to mind the fact mentioned before, viz. that even in the MDh the treatment of theft shows some inconsistency. There theft was treated as a separate *vivādapada*, but nevertheless after the description of the eighteen *vivādapadas* formally closes, another discussion of theft starts. And this kind of appendix in Manu closely corresponds to the real appendix in Nārada. A careful comparison of these two appendices on the same subject strongly led me to think of later additions in both

[139] Edited in the Trivandrum Sanskrit Series, no. 97.

texts.[140] For the original author of the NS the syncretion of *steya* and *sāhasa* was a fact, and his description of *sāhasa* also intends to cover theft at the same time.[141]

But in the mind of the author of the NS not only was theft covered by *sāhasa* but at the time of the NS the meaning of *sāhasa* had even become broader than that, so as to imply other *vivādapadas* also. This will bring us now to the second meaning of *sāhasa* which I already referred to before. After the general definition of *sāhasa* quoted above (14.1), in the next verse we find the following subdivision:

manuṣyamāraṇaṃ steyaṃ paradārābhimarśanam | pāruṣyaṃ dvividhaṃ jñeyaṃ sāhasaṃ ca caturvidham (14.2)

In other words, the genus *sāhasa* covers the following species:

manuṣyamāraṇa: manslaughter
steya: theft
paradārābhimarśana: adultery
pāruṣyam dvidham: *vākpāruṣya* and *daṇḍapāruṣya*

There is no doubt about the close relationship between the MDh and the NS. Not only is this fact stated in the introduction to the NS itself, but it has also been repeated by all scholars who have studied both texts. If the author of the NS extended the content of the term *sāhasa* to other *vivādapadas*, he must have done so because in his opinion all of these shared in that special characteristic of *sāhasa* mentioned before, viz. that manslaughter, theft, adultery, insult, and assault are more than offenses against individuals, and all of them are *sarvabhūtabhayāvaha*, i.e., they disturb law and order. In short, all of them are crimes.

As far as we know, the author of the NS was the first one to group these offenses formally and explicitly under one heading. Nevertheless even as early as the MDh some traces of this grouping are present to show the way to Nārada. First of all, *vākpāruṣya*, *daṇḍapāruṣya*, *sāhasa*, and *strīsaṃgrahaṇa* form one

[140] This reasoning differs from Jolly's (1889: 6): in his opinion the close correspondence of the Appendix in Nārada and the chapter in the ninth *adhyāya* of Manu pleads for the authenticity of the former. It also differs from Kane's (1930–62: 3.198) who thinks that "Nārada follows Manu... in treating of theft after the eighteen titles have been dealt with."

[141] Compare in this respect, e.g., the contents of Nārada's chapter on *sāhasa* as given by Asahāya on NS Mātṛkā 1.24: "*sāhase*: 1) *sāhasalakṣaṇam*, 2) *sāhasadaṇḍavidhānam*, 3) *ādhicchalasteyam*, 4) *kṣudradravyamadhyamottamavidhānam*, 5–6) *dvividhataskaralakṣaṇam*, 7) *taskarasya vyavakarṣaṇam*, 8) *bhaktāvakāśadānādi*, 9) *cauravidhiḥ*, 10) *sāhasasteyadaṇḍaḥ*, 11) *padena caurānveṣaṇavidhiḥ*, 12) *caurābhāve caurādidravyāpanayanam ceti dvādaśa bhedāḥ*".

group in Manu's enumeration of the *vivādapadas* at the outset of the *adhyāya*:

> *pāruṣye daṇḍavācike* | *steyaṃ ca sāhasaṃ caiva strīsaṃgrahaṇam eva ca* (8.6bcd)

Except for a minor detail, viz. that in the *uddeśa* or enumeration *daṇḍapāruṣya* precedes *vākpāruṣya*, whereas in the course of the book this order has been inverted, which inversion the commentators try to explain away very ingeniously, all these —let us call them "criminal cases"— are treated uninterruptedly for 120 *ślokas* (8.266–385). But not only this: after these 120 verses and before taking up a different subject, we find the following recapitulation which applies to all 120 verses as a whole:

> *yasya stenaḥ pure nāsti nānyastrīgo na duṣṭavāk* | *na sāhasikadaṇḍaghnau sa rājā śakralokabhāk* || *eteṣāṃ nigraho rājñaḥ pañcānāṃ viṣaye svake* | *sāmrājyakṛt sajātyeṣu loke caiva yāśaskaraḥ* (8.386–7)

> That king in whose town there is no thief, no adulterer, no defamer, no man guilty or violence, and no committer of assault, attains the world of Indra. The suppression of those five in his dominions secures for a king paramount sovereignty among his peers and fame in the world.

In the *dharmanibandhas* here and there we find hints at this broader sense of *sāhasa* as contrasted with the other fourteen *vivādapadas*. In general, however, it can be said that most treat the eighteen *vivādapadas* one by one without ranging *vākpāruṣya*, *steya*, and *strīsaṃgrahaṇa* together under one heading *sāhasa*. But among the *dharmanibandhas* there are a few exceptions, in which the "criminal" *vivādapadas* are the only ones discussed.

To be mentioned this respect is, e.g., Keśava Paṇḍita's *Daṇḍanīti*, a very late work, since the author flourished as recently as the second half of the 18th century AD. After an introductory chapter containing the usual eulogy of Daṇḍa, the following subjects are treated: *cauryadaṇḍaḥ*, *strīsaṃgrahaṇadaṇḍaḥ*, *vākapāruṣye daṇḍaḥ*, *daṇḍapāruṣye daṇḍaḥ*, and *kevalasāhase daṇḍaḥ*. Here again we find exactly those *vivādapadas* which were ranged under the term *sāhasa* in the NS. Special attention should, however, be drawn to the last chapter entitled *kevalasāhasa*, i.e., *sāhasa* in its narrower sense. From the addition of the qualification *kevala* it is evident that the author was aware that, after all, his whole book dealt with *sāhasa* in the broader sense. At the beginning of this chapter on *kevalasāhasa* the author quotes Nārada's definition, and then adds: "Although the element *sāhasa* is also present in theft, insult, assault, and adultery, it is treated separately here, because in so far as an offense is based on the application of taking pride in the violence, the punishment should be higher."

More important than this *Daṇḍanīti* is another "criminal *dharmanibandha*," called *Daṇḍaviveka* which was written by Vardhamāna near the end of the 15th century AD (not to be confused with the son of Gaṅgeśa, the author of the *Tattvacintāmaṇi*). Not only does this text contain the most exhaustive treatment of criminal law I have come upon thus far, but there is an extremely important passage in it which deserves to be translated here. The author, Vardhamāna, actually accounts for the fact that he treats only a limited number of *vivādapadas*, and he tries to lay down criteria which distinguish these *vivādapadas* from the others which are not dealt with in his treatise. He first enumerates his topics, and for that purpose slightly modifies the verse in which Nārada gave his fourfold subdivision of *sāhasa*:

> *manuṣyamāraṇaṃ steyaṃ paradārābhimarśanam | dve pāruṣye prakīrṇaṃ ca daṇḍasthānāni ṣaḍ viduḥ* (p. 32, 3–4)

People recognize six bases of punishment: manslaughter, theft, adultery, insult, assault, and then he adds a number six, *prakīrṇa*, which we have not met so far, and about which, therefore, a few words will have to be added afterwards.

On this verse, then, Vardhamāna gives his own commentary. In the usual way of argumentation he starts with an objection (*ākṣepa*): *nanu... iti cet.* The objector says: whenever a dispute comes into court, it is always based on greed, folly, and the like, and one of the parties is to be sentenced either for a false plaint or for a false denial. Therefore punishment is to be inflicted in all cases, including those *vivādapadas* which are not treated here. But Vardhamāna rejects this objection: only those offenses are enumerated here, the perpetrators of which are brought to court even without a plaintiff: they are found out by spies and arrested by the king's servants. And this is the case only with manslaughter etc., but not with non-payment of debts, etc. In other words: those who perpetrate the offenses treated in the *Daṇḍaviveka* are brought to court even without their opponent doing so.

Vardhamāna continues: secondly, the other *vivādapadas* such as non-payment of debts are not offenses by themselves; they only become so if they are denied. That means: as long as you acknowledge that you owe money to your creditor, you do not commit any offense, and the judge can only force you to payment but he cannot inflict any other punishment. He can only do so when the debt is denied.

The third distinction, according to Vardhamāna, is as follows. In the case of manslaughter and the like, the person found out to have committed the crime is summoned to court in order to be punished for the wrong he has committed; the treatment of the case before the judges has as its only purpose the fixing of the amount of punishment. In the case of non-payment of debts and the like, on the other hand, the debtor is summoned to court in order to decide whether he really contracted the debt or not. Even if he did, he is punished only if he denies this.

And the fourth and last distinction is as follows: Manslaughter and the like are necessarily accompanied by a malicious disposition of the mind and, thus, they highly outdo the other offenses which may have been committed by mistake only. Consequently they are more likely to terrorize other people in society and they deserve to be punished more severely.

In this passage from the *Daṇḍaviveka*, we undoubtedly are confronted with an excellent description of a crime, and although originally —as conceived by Nārada— the constituents of *sāhasa*, even in its broader sense, did not cover many topics which one would, e.g., find in the Indian Penal Code, the contents of the *Daṇḍaviveka* have become such that one would hardly fail to trace in it any crime mentioned in the modern Penal Code.

It was the chapter on *prakīrṇaka* or "Miscellaneous" which made it possible for the author of the *Daṇḍaviveka* to cover many types of crimes which could not find their place under the traditional headings. Such a chapter existed in the *Kauṭilīyārthaśastra*; does not appear, at least not in name, in the MDh and the YDh, but from Nārada onward it always forms the last *vivādapada*, and most *nibandhas* also follow this tradition.

As is clear from its mere name, "Miscellaneous," this title was used to cover many and various subjects. The definition generally used by the authors of the *nibandhas* is taken from the NS:

prakīrṇake punar jñeyo vyavahāro nṛpāśrayaḥ (18.1ab)

Then follow three full *ślokas* enumerating some specific offenses, which may be omitted here, and the definition concludes with these words:

na dṛṣṭaṃ yac ca pūrveṣu tat sarvaṃ syāt prakīrṇake (18.4cd)

This latter verse is clear: "and whatever has not been discussed under the other headings shall find its place in the chapter called Miscellaneous." This needs no further explanation as it serves the very purpose of the chapter. The first verse (18.1ab), however, is more difficult to understand: "Under Miscellaneous should be reckoned that kind of trial which is *nṛpāśraya*," literally, which is based on the king. It is impossible here to go into the different interpretations given to this term, and therefore I will limit myself to the interpretation of the *Daṇḍaviveka*, which has come closest to the heart of the matter. Vardhamāna says the following (259–260): Manslaughter and other crimes were actually also "based on the king" in so far as the perpetrator is summoned to court by the king's officers, even if the victim of the crime does not do so. But nevertheless, in the court the victim also is given the opportunity to set out his case. It is only after having heard both perpetrator and victim that the offender is punished by the king. In an offense "based on the king," on the other hand, there is really no other victim than the king himself, since the offense is actively directed against the king. Thus, no other party can be heard except the king's spies and officers who have caught the offender. This absence of plaintiff must have been considered a very important characteristic, since in the *Bṛhaspatismṛti* it is used to contrast the chapter "Miscellaneous" with all other *vivādapada*s which are *vādikṛta*:

> *eṣa vādikṛtaḥ prokto vyavahāraḥ samāsataḥ | nṛpāśrayaṃ pravakṣyāmi vyavahāraṃ prakīrṇakam* (29.1)

> Thus far has been expounded the type of trial in which both parties set forth their standpoints; I will now explain the kind of trial called miscellaneous which is based on the king.

For Nārada this *prakīrṇaka* must have been an adequate outlet for covering so many offenses which in the MDh are scattered all over the eighth and ninth *adhyāya*s, within the regular scheme of the eighteen *vivādapada*s. One of the subjects to be covered is offenses against the king or, as we would say, offenses against the State, which are different from the *sāhasa*s as well as from the other offenses. Nārada gives a few additional examples, and vaguely concludes: "And whatever has not been discussed under the other headings shall also find its place in the chapter called Miscellaneous." This sentence was intended to include all kinds of offenses which do not fall under any of the seventeen *vivādapada*s discussed in the preceding chapters.

What I should like to show is that in the time of the Dharmaśāstras *prakīrṇaka* was separate from all other *vivādapada*s and, therefore, was not a part of criminal law only. The first of these "Miscellaneous Offenses," however, viz. offenses against the king, happens to be a very serious one which also disturbs law and order, and therefore the author of the *Daṇḍaviveka* thought it necessary to include it in his manual of criminal law. But not only did he include the offenses against the State, which are only one out of many miscellaneous offenses; he included the title "Miscellaneous Offenses" itself as a whole, and in this way was able to range under it many other crimes not covered by *sāhasa* even when taken in its broader sense. The author of the *Daṇḍaviveka* has thus limited the term *prakīrṇaka*, which traditionally meant miscellaneous "offenses" in general, to miscellaneous "crimes" only.

8

Hindu Law of Succession: From the Śāstras *to Modern Law*

Outline

0. Introduction
    0.1 The Hindu Succession Act, 1956
    0.2 Overriding effect of the Act
    0.3 Scope of the present paper
1. The Period of the *Smṛtis*
    1.0 General remarks
        1.0.1 Rules on succession from the oldest *Dharmasūtras* onward
        1.0.2 Lack of uniformity in these rules
    1.1 The Hindu joint family
        1.1.1 Extra-legal aspects
        1.1.2 Impact on property
        1.1.3 The manager
    1.2 Partition of joint family property
        1.2.1 During the father's lifetime
        1.2.2 After the father's death
        1.2.3 Different forms of partition
        1.2.4 Partition per stirpes
        1.2.5 A son born after partition
        1.2.6 Reunion
    1.3 Separate property
        13.1 Vasiṣṭha
        1.3.2 Viṣṇu
        1.3.3 Gains of learning
        1.3.4 *Strīdhana*

1.4 Other categories of heirs
1.4.1 Female heir
1.4.2 Other heirs
1.43 Vagueness of the rules
1.5 Disqualified heirs
1.6 Inheritance cannot be rejected
2. The Period of the Commentaries
2.1 Characteristics of the commentaries
2.1.1 Complete systems of inheritance
2.1.2 Divergent systems of inheritance
2.1.3 Ownership by birth v. ownership by inheritance
2.2 Background of these characteristics
2.2.1 General background
2.2.2 Background in the special case of succession
3. The British Period
3.1 Application of the *śāstras*
3.1.1 The *paṇḍits*
3.1.2 Translation of the *Lawbooks*
3.1.3 Colebrooke's *Two Treatises*
3.2 Introdicing new elements
3.2.1 Justice, equity, and good conscience
3.2.2 Case law: *stare decisis, communis error facit ius*
3.2.3 Acts of Parliament
3.3 Examples of changes
3.3.1 The pious obligation
3.3.2. Law of wills
4. The Republic of India
4.1 Continuity
4.2 The Civil Code
4.3 The Hindu Succession Act, 1956
4.3.1 Characteristics
4.3.2 Reception

0.1 On June 17, 1956 the President of India gave his assent to The Hindu Succession Act 1956 (Act No. 30 of 1956). As stated in the Preamble, it is "an Act to amend and codify the law relating to intestate succession among Hindus." Both terms are important: "amend" and "codify." Indeed,

> the law before this Act was the law laid down by the Smritikaras and the commentators as modified by custom and usage and as interpreted and applied by judicial decisions. But the law differed from place to place according to the schools exercising their influence in different parts of India. The present Act has attempted to codify the whole law of intestate succession, making it uniformly applicable to all Hindus, with the result that such differences as arose in the past between the schools of law have now disappeared. (Gupte 1963: 316)

Smṛtikāras, commentators, customs, usage, schools of law, judicial decisions: they all are part of the long and checkered career of the law of inheritance and succession in India, which is now amended and codified by The Hindu Succession Act, 1956 (See also Mulla 1959; Derrett 1957, 1963).

0.2 The exact relationship between the new Act and the situation existing prior to its coming into effect has been explicated in sub-section 1 of its section 4:

> Save as otherwise expressly provided in this Act, —
>
> a) any text, rule or interpretation of Hindu law or any custom or usage as part of that law in force immediately before the commencement of this Act shall cease to have effect with respect to any matter for which provision is made in this Act ;
>
> b) any other law in force immediately before the commencement of this Act shall cease to apply to Hindus in so far as it is inconsistent with any of the provisions contained in this Act.

In other words, even the 1956 Act does not completely abrogate the previous system: existing laws are abrogated in so far as they are inconsistent with the Act, and ancient text, rules, interpretations, customs and usages are no longer valid on the condition that their field is now covered by the rules of the new statute (see Gupte 1963: 352). The result is that a study of the Hindu law of succession through the ages, as we shall undertake it in the following pages, even today has much more than a purely historical value. Even today such an old concept as the pious obligation of sons to pay their fathers' debts —which we shall say more about below— can be called upon in the courts[142]: it has not been abrogated by the mere fact that it has not been dealt with in The Hindu Succession Act, 1956.

0.3 Our main purpose is not to write a history of the law of succession in India: this would hardly be possible in a paper like this. We shall first point out a few characteristics of the ancient Hindu law of succession as they appear from the Dharmasūtras and the Dharmaśāstras. These characteristics will be selected not so much in view of being complete, but in order to bring out more clearly the evolution of the law of succession in the course of the three subsequent periods, i.e., during the period of the commentaries, during the British period, and in the independent Republic of India.

[142] *Modi Nathubhai Motilal v. Chotubhai Manibhal Desai*, A.I.R. Guj. 68 (1962). Those who are less familiar with the classical way of quoting the Indian law cases may be referred to Alexandrowicz 1958.

1. The Period of the Smṛtis

1.0 General remarks

1.0.1 Rules about succession and inheritance appear from the oldest Dharmasūtras onward and their number steadily increases in the more recent Dharmaśāstras. In fact, they are so numerous that it would not be possible here to endeavor to give a complete survey of the rules prevailing at that time.[143]

1.0.2 What is even worse is the fact that the rules contained in the Dharmasūtras and the Dharmaśāstras remain far from revealing a uniform system of succession and inheritance. It is a common feature that one and the same text on *dharma* contains rules which apparently reflect different systems of succession, a feature which is so deep rooted that it has to a large extent determined the course of the more recent history of the law of inheritance among Hindus. We shall have ample opportunity to come back to this point below. In the meanwhile, amidst the numerous and varying rules contained in the ancient Sanskrit texts, we shall restrict ourselves to outlining the general principles underlying the various rules, thereby stressing in particular those elements which we consider to be of importance for a better understanding of the later evolution of the law of succession.

1.1 It would not be possible to describe the ancient Hindu law of inheritance without taking as a starting point the typically Indian form of family organization; we mean: the Hindu joint family (see Bernhöft 1891:1–45 and Kapadia 1958: 204–281).[144] If it is true that present-day legislation tends towards its disruption (infra, 3.3.3), it is equally true that until very recently the Hindu joint family has remained the dominant type of family organization in most parts of India.

1.1.1 The Hindu joint family undoubtedly presents a number

[143] The classical volume on the history of Dharmaśāstra still is Jolly (1896: 47–90), which is equally available in English translation by Ghosh 1928: 102–195. See also Jolly 1885 and Mayr 1873. The most complete presentation of the subject is found in Kane 1930–62: 3.542–824. A useful survey of the history of Hindu law is Sarkar 1958; see also Sen-Gupta 1953: 170–226. For a suggestive study as to the usefulness of the study of Hindu law, see Derrett 1956a.

[144] In October 1965, Günther Sontheimer (now at the Südasien-Institut of Heidelberg University) has been granted the Ph.D. degree at the School of Oriental and African Studies in London with a dissertation on the historical development of the Hindu joint family. [Ed. note: see now Sontheimer 1977].

of extra-legal aspects which we can only briefly refer to here. It presupposes that its members live together under the same roof, it implies the very important factor that meals are take in common, and it is most closely related to the common performance of religious sacrifices.[145] Thus it is in the light of religious practices, namely the common participation in the offering to the dead and, hence, the fact of being connected with the same "sacrificial lump" (*piṇḍa*), that we must interpret what perhaps may be called the oldest definition of the joint family in the Dharmaśāstra:

> Moreover, the great-grandfather, the grandfather, the father, oneself, the uterine brothers, the son by a wife of equal caste, the grandson, (and) the greatgrandson —these they call Sapiṇḍas, but not the (greatgrandson's) son—; and amongst these a son and son's son (together with their father) are sharers of an individed oblation. The sharers of divided oblations they call *sakulya*s. (BDh 1.5.11.9–10, trans. Bühler 1882: 178)[146]

1.1.2 However, as far as succession and inheritance are concerned, the Hindu joint family is above all important because it most fundamentally influences the way in which property is held and, consequently, passed on from one person to the other. "In England ownership, as a rule, is single, independent, and unrestricted. It may be joint, but the presumption is to the contrary. It may be restricted, but only in special instances, and under certain provisions. In India, on the contrary, joint ownership is the rule, and will be presumed to exist until the contrary is proved... Absolute, unrestricted ownership, such as enables the owner to do anything he likes with his property, is the exception" (Aiyar 1953: 305).[147]

The extent to which property is common in a Hindu family is perhaps best expressed, be it indirectly, by Nārada:

> Giving, receiving, cattle, food, houses, fields, and servants must be regarded as separate among divided brothers, and so must cooking, religious duties, income, and expenditure (be kept separate) for each of them. (NS 13.38, Jolly 1889: 199)

[145] See Jolly 1928: 104–106. Cf. NS 13.37: "Among unseparated brothers, the performance of religious duties is single. When they have come to a partition, they have to perform their religious duties each for himself" (trans. Jolly 1889: 198).

[146] It will be seen that, as a rule, reference to Dharmaśāstra texts is through the existing standard translations; the reason is that in an article such as this there is no place for lengthy justifications which new personal translations would very often require.

[147] Cf. West and Bühler 1919: 562: "The normal state of a Hindu family is one of union."

1.1.3 There is no doubt that within the joint family a neat distinction was made between the head of the family on the one hand, and all other members on the other. The distinction has been most strongly expressed by Nārada:

> Three persons are independent in this world: a king, a spiritual teacher, and in all castes successively a householder in his own household... Wives, sons, slaves and other attendants are dependent. The head of the family, to whom the property has descended by right of inheritance, is independent with regard to it. (NS 1.32–34; Jolly 1889: 50–51)

If the family consists of a father and descendants, it is, as might be expected, the father who acts as the head of the joint family.[148] In case the family is composed of brothers without their father being alive, it seems as if it is the eldest brother who takes the place of his father[149]: according to one text at least he may do so even during his father's lifetime, if the latter is decrepit (wasteful?), absent or ill (Hārīta 4.3, quoted in Jolly 1928: 170).

It is, of course, an important —though not an easy— problem to know which were the powers of the head of the joint family; for a reason which will become clear below, we shall, however, postpone its discussion until later in the paper.

1.2 In the meanwhile we shall turn towards another problem, and try to determine, what the texts say about when and how the members of the joint family can proceed towards a partition of the joint family property.

1.2.1 According to Gautama, the sons may "divide the father's estate" during his lifetime, on two conditions: that their mother be past child-bearing age, and that the father desire so (GDh 28.2, Bühler 1879: 299). On the other hand, however, the same author excludes from the funeral meal (*śrāddha*) "(sons) who have enforced a division of the family estate against the wish of their father" (GDh 15.19, Bühler 1879: 255). From that moment onward two conclusions are allowed: either the son did not separate from his father and was excluded merely for having expressed the desire, or the separation did take place, against 28.2, and the son was therefore no longer admitted to the *śrāddha*.[150]

[148] GDh 28.1 (Bühler 1879: 299); ĀpDh 2.6.14.1 (Bühler 1879: 132); MDh 9.104 (Bühler 1886: 345).

[149] GDh 28.3 (Bühler 1879: 299); ĀpDh 2.6.14.6 (Bühler 1879: 133); MDh 9.105 (Bühler 1886: 346); NS 13.5 (Jolly 1889: 190).

[150] Bühler, in a note to his translation (255), mentions the latter altenative only; however, he does so under the influence of Yājñavalkya, or actually Cole-

Āpastamba too, has a *sūtra* on this matter, but it allows of two interpretations leading to completely different results. Bühler (1889: 132) translates:

> He should, during his lifetime, divide his wealth equally amongst his sons, excepting the eunuch, the mad man, and the outcast. (ĀpDh 2.6.14.1)

—implying thereby, as he explicitly says in a footnote, "that Āpastamba intends to exhort householders to make a division during their lifetime, as later they ought to become ascetics or hermits." Colebrooke (1810, *Mitākṣarā* 1.3.6), on the other hand, renders as follows:

> A father, making a partition in his life-time, should distribute the heritage equally among his sons,leaving the father complete liberty as to whether separation should take place during his life-time or not.

Manu in his turn seems to straightly reject the possibility of a separation during the father's lifetime:

> After the death of the father and the mother, the brothers, being assembled, may divide among themselves in equal shares the paternal (and the maternal) estate; for, they have no power (over it) while the parents live. (MDh 9.104, Bühler 345)

whereas Yājñavalkya evidently holds the opposite view:

> When the father makes a partition, let him separate his sons [from himself] at his pleasure, and either give the eldest the best share, or [if he choose] all may be equal sharers. (YDh 2.114, Colebrooke 1810, *Mitākṣarā* 1.2.1)

In later texts the possibility of a partition during the father's lifetime appears again. Thus Nārada:

> When a father has distributed his property amongst his sons, that is a lawful distribution for them (and cannot be annulled), whether the share of one be less, or greater than, or equal to the shares of the rest; for the father is the lord of all. A father who is diseased, or angry, or absorbed by (sinful) worldly interests, or who acts illegally, has not the power to distribute his property (as he likes). (NS 13.15–16, Jolly 1889: 192–93)

and also Bṛhaspati:

brooke (1810, *Mitākṣarā* 1.6.5–11) —an assertion which we shall have to reject on principle below (3.1.3).

> Those (sons) for whom their shares have been arranged by the father, whether equal, less, or greater, must be compelled to abide by such arrangement. Otherwise (if they try to alter the arrangement), They shall be punished. (BS 25.4, Jolly 1889: 373)[151]

1.2.2 If the situation is, thus, not very clear during the father's lifetime,[152] it is hardly more distinguishable what is to happen after the father's death. A first possibility is that the sons remain together and continue the joint family. Thus Gautama:

> Or the whole (estate may go) to the first-born (and) he shall support (the rest) as a father. (GDh 28.3, Bühler 299)

and Manu:

> (Or) the eldest alone may take the whole paternal estate, the others shall live under him just as (they lived) under their father. (MDh 9.105, Bühler 346)

But the sons are entitled, after the death of both parents, to ask to be separated. We would even be inclined to say, with Jolly, that "most authors are however of the opinion, expressly or tacitly, that the death of the father is the only precondition for partition among brothers or collaterals" (Jolly 1928: 179).

Gautama's chapter on inheritance, which has been referred to above in connection with partition during the father's lifetime and in connection with absence of partition at the time of the father's death, quite characteristically commences as follows:

> After the father's death let the sons divide the estate. (GDh 28.1, Bühler 299)

And for Manu too, when he proceeds to "the division of the inheritance," the very first rule is as follows:

> After the death of the father and of the mother, the brothers, being assembled, may divide among themselves in equal shares the paternal (and the maternal) estate: for, they have no power (over it) while the parents live. (MDh 9.104, Bühler 345)

For the sake of those who are less familiar with situations Indian it might not be without interest to add the remark that the

[151] Notice the fact that both Nārada and Bṛhaspati allow the father to proceed to both equal and unequal divisions. We shall come back to this point below.

[152] This shows the relative value of such statements as Jolly's: "If partition took place, as the will is not known in Indian law, the only influence the father could exercise on the determination of the shares was to undertake the partition himself" (1928: 177).

expression "after the father's death" also implies a number of situations other than purely physical death, such as when he withdraws from active life to become a hermit, when he is excluded from his caste, etc.[153]

As a matter of fact certain texts seem to rather encourage the sons to proceed to a separation: indeed, since in the joint family sacrifices are performed in common whereas they are performed individually after separation, the spiritual merit is said to be greater in the latter case. For instance, Gautama declares:

> But in partition there is an increase of spiritual merit. (GDh 28.4, Bühler 299)[154]

1.2.3 In case of separation, however, there are again at least two possibilities. Compare, e.g., Bṛhaspati:

> Partition among coparceners is declared to be of two kinds; one is with attention to priority of birth, the other consists of the allotment of equal shares. (BS 25.7, Jolly 371)

A good number of texts prescribe an unequal partition amongst the brothers. Gautama, e.g., has the following rules:

> (The additional share) of the eldest (son consists of) a twentieth part (of the estate), a male and a female (of animals with one row of front teeth, such as cows) , a carriage yoked with animals that have two rows of front teeth, (and) a bull...
>
> (The additional share) of the middlemost (consists of) the sheep, grain, the iron utensils, a house, a cart there are several...
>
> (The additional share) of the youngest (consists of) the sheep, grain, the iron utensils, a house, a care yoked (with oxen), and one of each kind of (other) animals...
>
> All the remaining (property shall be divided) equally. (GDh 28.5–8, Bühler 299–300)[155]

[153] For examples, cf. NS 13.3 (Jolly 1889: 189): "when the father's sexual desire is extinguished and he has ceased to care for worldly interests"; NS 13.25 (195): "If among several brothers one childless should die or become a religious ascetic...".

[154] To the same effect MDh 9.111 (Bühler 347): "Either let them thus live together, or apart, if (each) desires (to gain) spiritual merit; for (by their living) separate (their) merit increases, hence separation is meritorious," to which Bühler aptly quotes the commentaries of Medhātithi and Kullūka: "each of them has to kindle the sacred fire, to offer separately the Agnihotra, the five great sacrifices and so forth, and hence each gains separately merit."

[155] Cf. MDh 9.112 (Bühler 347). On the whole problem, cf. Radhabinod Pal 1929.

The same Dharmasūtra even indicates several other ways and criteria of dividing property unequally. Thus it is possible to favor the eldest son in a different way:

> Or let the eldest have two shares. And the rest one each. (GDh 28.9–10, Bühler 300)[156]

or, again, even more simply, to allow the elder brothers to make their own choice:

> Or let them each take one kind of property, (selecting) according to seniority, what they desire. (GDh 28.11, Bühler 300)

If a man has several wives, the eldest son is not necessarily the son of the wife whom he married first: several rules again deal with the various possibilities (GDh 28.14–16, Bühler 301).

And Gautama finally also envisages unequal partition in case a man had married women of different classes (*varṇa*):

> Or let the special shares (be adjusted) in each class (of sons) according to their mothers. (GDh 28.17, Bühler 301)[157]

Alongside with these different forms of unequal partition other texts, however, also prescribe equal partition. Thus Manu:

> After the death of the father and the mother, the brothers being assembled, may divide among themselves in equal shares the paternal (and the maternal) estate. (MDh 9.104, Bühler 301)

To the same effect also Yājñavalkya:

> Let sons divide equally both the effects and the debts, after their two parents. (YDh 2.117, Colebrooke 1810, *Mitākṣarā* 1.3.1)

and Nārada:

> Let sons equally divide the wealth when the father is dead. (NS 12.3, Colebrooke 1810, *Mitākṣarā* 1.2.7)[158]

1.2.4 In the special case of a predeceased son the rule is that the shares of grandsons shall be adjusted *per stirpes* and not *per capita*. Says Yājñavalkya:

[156] Cf. MDh 9.117 (Bühler 348).

[157] The *Viṣṇusmṛti* has worked out the various caste combinations in no less than 40 *sūtras* (18.1–40, Jolly 1880: 70–73).

[158] Jolly's translation: "The Father being dead, the sons shall divide the estate *as they ought*" (1889: 189) is due to another interpretation of the term *samam* in the Sanskrit text.

> But among grandsons by different fathers, the allotment of shares is according to the fathers. (YDh 2.120, Colebrooke 1810, *Mitākṣarā* 1.5.1)

and, even more clearly, Viṣṇu states:

> (Coparceners) descended from different fathers must adjust their shares according to the fathers. Let each take the wealth due to his father, no other (has a right to it). (ViDh 17.23, Jolly 1880: 70)

1.2.5 A rule to be mentioned is the one propounded in order to safeguard the rights of a son born after partition (*vibhaktaja*). According to Manu:

> A son, born after partition, shall alone take the property of his father, or if any (of the other sons) be reunited with the (father), he shall share with them. (MDh 9.216, Bühler 378)[159]

1.2.6 Before leaving the subject of partition, mention should be made of the possibility offered to separated members of a joint family to re-unite (the technical term for a re-united coparcener is *saṃsṛṣṭin*). Certain rules seem to contain restrictions upon this possibility —reunion is possible with one's father, brother, and father's brother only;[160] after reunion the alternative of unequal partition is excluded;[161] etc.—, but generally speaking reunited coparceners are said to reestablish exactly the same situation as it existed before partition,[162] although here as elsewhere the later commentators have found ample ground for discussion.

1.3 Although, as we said above, there seems to be a presumption in the joint family that all property is held in common, from a very early age onward this must have been a *praesumptio iuris tantum*, the concept of separate, individual property not being unknown in ancient India.

Even if at least two texts do imply that all earnings of the sons belong to the father, because with respect to their father sons are

[159] See also GDh 28.29 (Bühler 303); ViDh 17.3 (Jolly 68); YDh 2.122.

[160] BS 25.72 (Jolly 381): "He who (having been divided), is again living, through affection, together with his father or brother, or with his uncle even, is said to be reunited with them."

[161] BS 25.73 (Jolly 381): "When brothers formally divided are again living together through affection and arrange a second division, the right of primogeniture does not accrue in that case." See also MDh 9.210 (Bühler 376).

[162] BS 25.76 (Jolly 381): "When two (coparceners) have again established together, they shall mutually inherit their property." For applications thereof, see GDh 38.28 (Bühler 303); MDh 9.212 (Bühler 376); ViDh 17.17 (Jolly 69); YDh 2.138 (Stenzler 1849: 65).

on the same footing with slaves,[163] the general tendency, to an ever increasing extent, is to take into consideration and to deal differently with property earned through the individual efforts of one of the joint family members.

1.3.1 Vasiṣṭha is the only one to prescribe:

> And if one of the (brothers) has gained something by his own (effort), he shall receive a double share. (VaDh 17.51, Bühler 1882: 89)

If we understand the rule correctly, for Vasiṣṭha too, the wealth earned by an individual effort went into the joint family property, but its acquirer was, at a later stage, compensated for his efforts by allotting him a larger —the text says: a double[164]— share than to the other joint family members. If we did not fear to fit our data into a jacket they were not meant for, we would say that Vasiṣṭha represents an intermediary stage in between the above mentioned rule which denies the existence of separate property, and the many rules of later authors where individual property has been fully recognized.

1.3.2 According to the *Viṣṇusmṛti*:

> If a father makes a partition with his sons, he may dispose of his self-acquired property as he thinks best... But in regard to wealth inherited of the paternal grandfather, the worship of father and son is equal. (17.1–2, Jolly 67–68)

Here a distinction is made which will become one of the most frequently used criteria with the later commentators; for them the distinction between an individual's rights to ancestral property and personally acquired property will become most helpful for reconciling śāstric texts which would appear less consonant with each other otherwise.

[163] MDh 8.416 (Bühler 326): "A wife, a son, a slave, these three are declared to have no property; the wealth which they earn is (acquired) for him to whom they belong." Identical with NS 5.41 (Jolly 138).

[164] Later commentators will give a much more elastic interpretation to "a double share": in our opinion, however, the author of the *Vāsiṣṭha-Dharmasūstra* did indeed mean a double share. A similar case is to be found with "a half share" in YDh 2.148; see also *Vyavahāramayūka* (transl. P.V. Kane, 1933: 93): "But it (*strīdhana*) has been given, one half (of a share) should be given (to the wife or wives), since there is a text (Yājñavalkya II. 148) 'but if (*strīdhana*) has been given, one should allot half.' *Ardham* means ' as much as would, together with the strīdhana already given, be equal to the share of a son.' But no share (should be allotted) to that (wife) whose (*strīdhana*) wealth is already in excess of the share (that might justly be hers)."

1.3.3 The concept of separate property has been elaborated more particularly in a few specific fields, one of which is that of "gains of learning" (*vidyādhana*). Nārada at once gives the definition of the term and indicates its limitations:

> A learned man is not bound to give a share of his own (acquired) wealth against his will to an unlearned co-heir, unless it have been gained by him using the paternal estate. (NS 13.11, Jolly 191)[165]

As early as Kātyāyana's Dharmaśāstra, *vidyādhana* apparently had become an often applied concept which became difficult to define (KS 867–873, Kane 1933: 307–309); it will become so more and more during the period of the commentaries and during the British period until the passing of the Hindu Gains of Learning Act (Act XXX of 1930).

1.3.4 Another type of separate property is the well-known *strīdhana* "woman's property." *Strīdhana* has been thus defined by Viṣṇu:

> What has been given to a woman by her father, mother, sons, or brothers, what she has received before the sacrificial fire (at the marriage ceremony), what she receives on supersession, what has been given to her by her relatives, her fee (*śulka*), and a gift subsequent, are called "woman's property" (Strīdhana). (ViDh 17.18, Jolly 69)[166]

We shall not even try within the framework of this paper to set out the rules of inheritance regarding *strīdhana*. They are again far from uniform (see Jolly 1928; Kane 1930–62: vol. 3). Even if, in the absence of daughters, the sons intervened and even if, in the case of a childless woman, the husband and the father intervened as heirs, it is worth noticing that ancient Hindu law re-cognized the existence of a separate woman's property which, if possible, was inherited by the daughters.[167]

Apart from this general rule, however, the divergences in detail are such that *strīdhana* has become one of the favorite topics

[165] See also GDh 28.30 (Bühler 303); MDh 9.206 (Bühler 374); YDh 2.119 (Stenzler 62); ViDh 18.42 (Jolly 74).

[166] See also MDh 9.194 (Bühler 370–371); MDh 9.206 (Bühler 374); YDh 2.119 (Stenzler 66); NS 13.8 (Jolly 190); KS 894–901 (Kane, 316–318); etc.

[167] From GDh 28.24 (Bühler 302) onward it is said that "A woman's separate estate (goes) to her unmarried daughters, and (on failure of such) to poor (married daughters)." See also MDh 9.131 (Bühler 352); ViDh 17.21 (Jolly 70); NS 13.9 (Jolly 191).

with the commentators, so as to evolve into a practically inextricable labyrinth in the case-law of the Anglo-Indian courts (Banerjee 1923), which will be discussed below.

1.4 *Strīdhana* at once raises the problem of women's right to inheritance generally, and, on an even more general level, the right to inheritance of those who are to succeed to a man who dies without leaving male issue.

1.4.1 As far as the female members of the joint family are concerned various tendencies are represented.

On reading Nārada one would feel inclined to think that the male members only took part in partition, whereas female members were simply excluded.[168] Although it seems that even then they were entitled to maintenance —the widow and the unmarried daughters—, and that, moreover, the joint family was responsible for the expense involved in the marriages of the unmarried girls.

But there are also texts which actually reserve shares for the female members at the time of partition. Thus Yājñavalkya when the father makes the partition:

> Wenn er gleiche teile macht, so müssen auch seine frauen gleiche teile bekommen, welchen kein vermögen gegeben ist, weder von ihrem manne noch von ihrem schwiegervate. (YDh 2.115, Stenzler 62)

when partition is made by the sons:

> Wenn sie nach dem tode des vaters teilen, soll auch die mutter einen teil bekommen... Ungeweihete sollen von den früher geweihete brüdern geweihet werden: schwestern ebenfalls, aber so dass die *brüder* ihnen den vierten theil des brudertheiles, geben. (YDh 2.123–124, Stenzler 64–65)[169]

and in case of a man dying without male issue:

[168] We think of such texts as NS 13.25–28 (Jolly 195–196): "If among several brothers one childless should die or become a religious ascetic, the others shall divide his property, excepting the Strīdhana. / They shall make provision for his women till they die, in case they remain faithful to the bed of their husband. Should the women not (remain chaste), they must cut off that allowance. / If he has left a daughter, her father's share is destined for her maintenance. They shall maintain her up to the time of her marriage, afterwards let her husband keep her. / After the death of her lord, the relations of her husband shall be the guardians of a woman who has a son. They shall have full authority to control her, to regulate her mode of life, and to maintain her."

[169] See also ViDh 18.34–35 (Jolly 73); MDh 9.118 (Bühler 348); BS 25.64 (Jolly 379); etc.

> Die frau, die töchter, die eltern und die brüder, ein brudersohn, ein verwandter, ein verschwägerter, ein schüler und mitschüler: ...Wenn von diesen ein früherer fehlt, so sou jedesmal der folgende das vermögen desjenigen empfangen, welcher in den himmel gegangen ist, und keine söhne hinterlässt. Diese regel gilt für alle kasten. (YDh 2.135–136, Stenzler 64–65)

1.4.2 Unfortunately, this clear-cut text of Yājñavalkya with reference to a man deceased without leaving male issue seems to be unique. Apart from the fact that in many other texts women are omitted, we are faced with various classes of heirs, ending normally with the king preceded by such terms as *sapiṇḍas*, *gotrajas*, *bandhus*. *sakulyas*, etc., (Kane 1930–62: 3.732–765) about which the only thing we may say with certainty is that they indicate various degrees of relationship, but which do not allow of any more precise definitions.

Without any fear of exaggeration it may be said that we are in complete uncertainty —if certainty ever existed— about the way partition was arranged in case the deceased left no male offspring. As a matter of fact, the commentators were in no better position than we are; the only difference is that we may express our ignorance, whereas the commentators had to find solutions to the best of their abilities. The whole medieval literature and the Anglo-Indian law as well will greatly suffer from the lack of certainty on this point.[170]

1.4.3 The main reason[171] for the vagueness of the rules of inheritance once one exceeds the direct descendants, in our opinion, is that the cases in which direct descendants were absent were extremely rare. For a number of reasons, religious and otherwise, it was of the utmost importance for a Hindu householder to have at least one son (Kane 1930–62: 3.641–643); we may be sure that in the light of this obligation and the effective means which were put at his disposal to fulfill it —supersession of a wife who bore only daughters or no issue at all, adoption, etc.—, fathers dying without male issue cannot have been very numerous.

1.5 In view of its later history, reference should be made here to the reasons which lead to disqualification of heirs in the śāstric texts. The enumeration of disqualified heirs may slightly vary with

[170] Cf. Gledhill (1954: 594): "In *Mitakshara* law, when there is no agnate claimant, the texts give little assistance, and most of the rules for selecting the relation entitled to suceed are the work of the court."

[171] For other reasons: reversion to the king, rareness of partitions in ancient times, etc. Cf. Jolly 1928: 189.

the individual authors[172] but they all more or less correspond to the following passage from Viṣṇu:

> Outcasts, eunuchs, persons incurably diseased, or deficient (in organs of sense or actions, such as blind, deaf, dumb, or insane persons, or lepers) do not receive a share... They should be maintained by those who take the inheritance... And their legitimate sons receive a share... But not the children of an outcast;... Provided they were born after (the commission of) the act on account of which the parents were outcasted... Neither do children begotten (by husbands of an inferior caste) on women of a higher caste receive a share... Their sons do not even receive a share of the wealth of their paternal grandfathers... They should be supported by the heirs. (ViDh 15.32–39, Jolly 64–65)

1.6 Perhaps there is one other point about ancient Indian inheritance which we should mention here, namely the question of whether the heir has a right to reject the inheritance in case the debts are larger than the assets. As far as direct descendants are concerned the answer can be unqualifiedly negative.

Numerous texts lay down the principle of the son's liability to pay his father's and grandfather's debts. E.g., Viṣṇu:

> If he who contracted the debt should die, or become a religious ascetic, or remain abroad for twenty years, that debt shall be discharged by his sons or grandsons. But not by remoter descendants against their will. (ViDh 6.27–28, Jolly 44–45)[173]

Bṛhaspati, after stating the same principle even more strongly:

> The father's debt must be paid first of all, and after that, a man's own debt ; but a debt contracted by the paternal grandfather must always be paid before those two even. (BS 11.48, Jolly 328)

adds an important exception:

> Sons shall not be made to pay (a debt incurred by their father) for spirituous liquor, for losses at play, for idle gifts, for promises made under the influence of love or wrath, or for suretyship, nor the balance of a fine or toll (liquidated in part by their father). (BS 11.51, Jolly 329)[174]

The background of the son's duty to pay his father's debts

[172] ĀpDh 2.6.14.1, 15 (Bühler 132, 135); GDh 28.40, 43 (Bühler 305, 306); VaDh 17.52–53 (Bühler 89); BDh 2.2.3, 37–40 (Bühler 230); MDh 9.201–202 (Bühler 372–373); YDh 2.140–141 (Stenzler 65); NS 13, 21–22 (Jolly 194); etc.

[173] See also YDh 2.50 (Stenzler 53).

[174] See also (already) MDh 8.159 (Bühler 282).

is undoubtedly extra-legal;[175] this did, however, not prevent the son's "pious obligation" from remaining highly effective up to the modern period.

2. The Period of the Commentaries

2.1 The law of inheritance and succession, as it appears in the commentaries and the *nibandhas*, shows a number of characteristics of its own. Although our only sources are Sanskrit texts which pretend to explain the old treatises which were characteristic of the previous period, there can be no doubt that the incredibly voluminous literature which was produced on succession and inheritance during this period not only had its own significance *in se*, but again revealed a number of principles which were to influence very strongly the development of inheritance among Hindus throughout the British period and even down to the present day.

2.1.1 In the first place, the commentaries and *nibandhas* for the first time make an effort to construct a coherent and complete system of inheritance. Whereas it is extremely difficult, if not impossible, to set up a workable system of inheritance merely by reading one or more Dharmaśāstras, the commentators have tried their best to work this whole mass of *sūtras* and *śāstras* on inheritance into coherent systems which answer the questions one normally wants to find an answer for in a treatise on inheritance. An excellent example of this tendency has already been noticed by Jolly: "only the mediaeval jurists drew up a complete system of successive heirs" (Jolly 1928: 189). As said above, the Dharmaśāstras leave us in absolute uncertainty about the order of succession beyond the direct descendants; the commentators have amalgamated the various rules into more or less coherent and complete systems. Although it would be an exaggeration to say that the systems elaborated by the commentators have solved all the problems and removed all the doubts, their ways of dealing with the classes of heirs are completely different from the data furnished by the old *śāstras*. And the same holds good for the rules about *strīdhana*, *vidyādhana*, etc.

2.1.2 A second characteristic of the commentaries, on inheritance as elsewhere, is that the coherent systems which they con-

[175] As a matter of fact, the idea of the son's continuing his father's personality seems to be of Vedic origin; see also Kullūka's reference to *Aitareya Brāhmaṇa* 7.13, on MDh 9.8: "The husband, after conception by his wife, becomes an embryo and is born again by her" (Bühler 329). For the idea of a son's releasing his father from his "debts" to the manes, see also VaDh 11.48 (Bühler 56), etc.

struct are again far from being uniform. As a matter of fact, it could hardly have been otherwise. For the commentators, the whole aggregate of Dharmasūtras and Dharmaśāstras constitute the *smṛti*, i.e., all these prescriptions have been revealed and, hence, are equally authoritative. However, the inconsistencies, not to say the contradictions, in the old texts are such that according to whether one lays more stress upon some of them than upon others, the emerging picture is a completely different one. Among the numerous commentaries which have been written it would not be possible to find two which have reached agreement on all points concerned. While exposing the theories of the *śāstra*s above we have abstained on purpose to interpret the texts against any historical or other background; we have tried to draw a picture which, although making abstraction of numerous details, more or less corresponded to the one which faced the commentators. We hope it adequately conveyed the confused situation it also conveyed to the commentators.

2.1.3 Out of the numerous differences displayed by the commentaries we shall select one example, which besides being most fundamental is also the one which most profoundly influenced the evolution of the Hindu law of inheritance from the British period onward.

According to a number of commentaries, property is acquired in a way which does not require much comment: person B acquires a right of ownership with regard to a particular object at the moment when the right of person A, with whom B had a particular relation, ceases to exist. To take a concrete example: the sons become the owners of the family property at the moment when the father dies, or when, for some other reason, the latter's right is extinguished.

But there are other commentaries which defend a completely different thesis. They pretend that, at least as far as sons and grandsons are concerned, they acquire a right of ownership in the joint family property because of the very fact of their being their father's son or their grandfather's grandson. That means that their ownership does not succeed to their father's or grandfather's, but that from the very moment of their birth onward they become co-owners of the joint family property with their father or grandfather.

Needless to say that these two theories, when worked out in detail, lead to two completely different systems of succession. Succession after the father's death involves that, as long as the father is alive, the sons have no right whatsoever in the family property; in the other system the sons do have, from their birth onward, a right of ownership as real as that of their father. With the result that, in the former case, the father has an absolute right, whereas in the latter case his powers are curtailed by those of his sons: sale or gift of family property will no longer be the father's concern only, but he will have to ask for his sons' permission before being capable of alienating any family property. Moreover, whereas in the former system the extent of a person's property right is well determined, in the latter system it is subject to continuous changes due to the birth or death of a son, a brother, etc., i.e., one holds and acquires property through mere survivorship.

These few instances must suffice here to show how the medieval commentaries, although working upon an identical set of rules —the whole aggregate of Dharmasūtras and Dharmaśāstras—, have nevertheless constructed upon this common basis a number of legal systems which differed from each other not only in detail but even as far as the fundamental principles are concerned.

2.2 As to the reason why the commentaries are more complete than the *śāstras* on the one hand, and different from each other on the other hand, it has been generally held that the commentators drew additional materials from customary law, and, customary law being very different in the various parts of the country, the results inevitably had to be highly different too.[176]

2.2.1 We unhesitatingly agree that the systems of inheritance as described in the works of the commentators create the impression of being much more realistic and much closer practice than is the case with the ancient Dharmasūtras and Dharmaśāstras. For a number of reasons, however, we fear that this impression may be misleading. First, we want to draw attention to the fact that most of the commentaries were written during the Muslim period of Indian history. Even if it may have been customary with Muslim rulers not to force upon their Hindu subjects the roles

[176] Mayr (1873: 1–2): "die Commentatoren... spätere Rechtsgewohnheiten den alten Autor hineinlasen." J.D.M. Derrett (1961: 40): "The Smritis had been enlivened by commentators who introduced customary elements into their exposition." Even more explicitly, Ramaswami (1961: 329): "The commentators and nibandhkars like Vijnanesvara, Jīmūtavāhana, Mitramisra and Kamalakara had developed the Smriti law by a process of interpretation and adaptation to modern social and economic needs," and he regrets that "the golden age of commentators and glossators is gone." In *Chandika Bakhsh v. Muna Kunwar*, (1901) 24 All. 273, at p. 280. the Privy Council held that a family who had left Gujarat before the *Vyavahāramayūkha* was written was nevertheless governed by it —"In Gujarat the Mayukha is recognised as authority of paramount importance when it differs from the Mitakshara," because "it may well be that... the Mayukha only embodied and defined a pre-existing custom."

of inheritance of their own Muslim law,[177] we cannot get beyond the impression that the non-Muslim inheritance law which the Mohammedans allowed to exist was merely the local or tribal custom, and not the "law of the royal court" which the learned commentaries pretended to represent.

We have shown elsewhere (Rocher 1957) that in our opinion the legal commentaries —and that implies the commentaries on the law of inheritance— have to be interpreted against a completely different background. They were the work of highly learned *paṇḍits*, well versed not only in the Dharmaśāstras but in all other branches of Hindu learning as well: in grammar; in Mīmāṃsā, i.e., the science created for the sake of correctly explaining the ancient sacred texts; in Nyāya, i.e., Hindu logic; etc. These learned pandits sincerely believed in the unity of their ancient sacred law texts, and they have applied all their learning and all their skill to demonstrate the truth of this assertion: each of them even tried to do so more perfectly and more harmoniously than their respective predecessors. They did not need the incentive of making the Dharmaśāstra more applicable to legal practice; the intrinsic value and authority of the texts themselves abundantly justify the commentators' efforts. The fact that they hereby tend to render their own systems more realistic and less formalistic is not peculiar to the law of inheritance.[178]

2.2.2 In the case of the medieval law of inheritance too, we are convinced that the commentators were guided by the same motives, and acted in the same way. In our opinion even such a fundamental difference as the one between right of property by birth and right of property by inheritance finds its origin simply and solely in two different, but from the commentator's point of view equally valid interpretations of the entire aggregate of *śāstric* rules.

A detailed demonstration of our thesis would require much more space than can be reserved to it within the broader context of this article. In short, our impression is that the theory of

[177] We obtained oral confirmation of the possibility of such a state affairs from Professor J.N.D. Anderson. J.D.M. Derrett (1961: 14–17) distinguishes four different types of judicial administration; we agree with him in that the Hindu community during the Muslim period was far from being devoid of law and order, but we have the impression that Derrett attributes a greater importance to the Dharmaśāstra than we would be inclined to do. As to U.C. Sarkar (1958: 200): "Most of the important commentaries were composed during the Mahomedan period. This is a sure indication that Hindu law did not die out during the Mahomedan rule in India," it exactly renders the general point of view which we cannot but think of as an over-simplification.

[178] We found the same phenomenon at work elsewhere, and described it in Rocher 1961: 375–387.

property by birth and the theory of property by inheritance are the inevitable consequence of two different conceptions of the powers of the joint family manager in the old *śāstras*; according to whether one accords priority to either conception of these powers one is bound to be led to either theory of property.

According to a number of texts, such as the passage from Nārada quoted above[179] "the head of the family, to whom the property has descended by right of inheritance, is independent with regard to it." In other words: the "manager" of the joint family property actually is the sole proprietor to the exclusion of all other joint family members who have no right of property at all. Along the same lines reference should be made to the above mentioned texts of Gautama and Manu[180] according to which, after the father's death, the eldest son alone takes the whole estate and "the others should live under him just as (they lived) under their father." When reading these texts and many others to the same effect, it is only natural to conclude to a right of property through inheritance, a right which comes about only at the time when the all powerful head of the joint family disappears and when his right passes on either to another single all powerful "manager" as in the texts of Gautama and Manu above, or to several brothers who in their turn become all powerful "managers" of their respective joint families.[181]

But there are other texts which, when taken together, must lead to a completely different conclusion. First of all, a passage of Manu makes it very clear that the right of the eldest son, i.e., of the person whom one would expect to become the joint family manager, is subject to important limitations:

> An eldest brother who through avarice may defraud the younger ones, shall no (longer hold the position of) the eldest, shall not receive an (eldest son's additional) share, and shall be punished by the king...
>
> All brothers who habitually commit forbidden acts are unworthy of (a share of) the property, and the eldest shall not make (anything his) separate property without giving (an equivalent) to his younger brothers.[182]

Again, with Nārada, the "manager" of the joint family property actually is said to be paid for his services:

[179] NS 1.32, 34 (SBE 33: 50–51). Cf. 1.1.3.

[180] GDh 28.3 (SBE 2: 299); MDh 9.105 (SBE 25: 346): cf. 1.2.2.

[181] MDh 9.104 (SBE 25: 345). Cf. 1.2.1: We say that all these brothers become all powerful "managers," since their sons "have no power... while parents live."

[182] MDh 9.213–214 (SBE 25: 377).

> One who, being authorized to look after the affairs of the family charges himself with the management (of the family property) shall be supported by his brothers with (presents of) food, clothing, and vehicles. (NS 13.34, SBE 33: 198)

According to this last series of texts the joint family "manager" appears as a manager *stricto sensu*, to whom powers have been delegated jointly by the other joint family members. Here each member of the joint family holds a right of property himself, a situation which, when thought through to its final consequences, cannot but lead to the conception of a right of property by birth.

As said above, these few examples are mere indications of a point of view which will have to be elaborated separately. However, the few instances which we did adduce here have been selected on purpose: they not only show that both tendencies are present in the *śāstras*, they also prove that they were present within one and the same Dharmaśāstra. The fact that a particular commentator accorded more weight to either set of texts was a sufficient condition for his adherence to either the theory of ownership by birth or the theory of ownership by inheritance.

3. The British Period

3.1 There is no need for us here to retell once again the story of early British justice in India.[183] Be it sufficient to recall that, in 1772, Hastings directed, that

> In all suits regarding inheritance, marriage, caste, and other religious usages or institutions, the laws of the Koran with respect to Mohamedans and those of the Shaster with respect to the Gentoos shall invariably be adhered to.[184]

Even more than to the important decision that the Indians should not be governed by foreign laws but by their own personal laws, we must, within the framework of this paper, draw attention to the fact that the law to be applied to Hindus was to be the law of the *śāstras*.

It is a problem in itself to make out whether Hastings has been particularly lucky in wording his declaration and whether he actually succeeded in his laudable intention to have the Hin-

[183] One may consult on the subject: Jain 1952; Rankin 1946; Fawcett 1934; Miller 1828; Misra, 1959 (ch. V: "The Administration of Civil Justice," pp. 220–297); Morley 1858; Derrett 1961: 10–52.

[184] Quoted in Derrett (1961: 24–25). Hastings declaration was to become law as S.27 of the Regulation of 11 April 1780.

dus administered by their own and real personal laws. Indeed, "it has been asserted, mainly by sociologists rather than by lawyers, that the insistence of the courts upon receiving advice upon the ancient original sources and commentaries, led to the application of rules which were either obsolete or never in force" (Lipstein 1957: 281). Even if we would hesitate to go as far as the author of this statement[185] we shall surprise nobody if, after having explained above our way of looking at the commentaries, we stress the fact that Hastings' declaration pointed the Hindu law of inheritance into a direction which was certainly not the logical continuation of the past.

For many years to come, the evolution of the Hindu law of inheritance —and personal law generally— will be characterized by an intense effort on the part of the British to learn to know and to apply "the law of the *śāstras*."

3.1.1 We shall only mention in passing the first step which was made in that direction: the appointment of *paṇḍits* whose duty it was to consult the *śāstras* on any topic that came up for consideration in the courts, and actually draw up a decision (*vyavasthā*) which, after translation, had to be pronounced by the judges.[186]

3.1.2 However, it was soon felt that the intervention of the *paṇḍits* was not the ideal solution. The uncomfortable situation of the British judges who had no access themselves to the lawbooks they were to apply and who felt themselves completely at the mercy of their Indian interpreters, gave rise to a growing distrust —partly deserved, partly underserved, no doubt— toward the *paṇḍits*. So much so, that some of the English magistrates were ready to make the considerable effort of learning Sanskrit themselves. One of the earliest pioneers of this kind was William Jones who, in a letter to Charles Chapman, writes:

> I am proceeding slowly, but surely, in this retired place, in the study of Sanscrit; for I can no longer bear to be at the mercy of our pundits, who deal out Hindu law as they please, and make it at reasonable rates when they cannot find it ready-made. (Teignmouth 1835: 45–46)[187]

[185] We would not dare to say that the system of the *śāstras* "never" was in force, nor call it "a system of law which was never more than a fiction" (Lipstein 1957). In our opinion the period of non-application of the *śāstra* was restricted to the Muslim period; cf. Rocher 1957.

[186] This institution was introduced in 1772, and remained in effect until 1864 when their office was abolished.

[187] Jones was indeed very strongly opposed to the *paṇḍits*' presence in the Courts, as is clear from a letter to Cornwallis (19 March 1788): "I could not with

Thus came about the first English translations of the old Hindu lawbooks. William Jones' translation of the *Manusmṛti* (1794) had already been preceded by N.B. Halhed's *A Code of Gentoo Laws, or, Ordinations of the Pandits*, first published in 1776,[188] and was to be followed by what is usually called *Colebrooke's Digest* (1798).[189]

3.1.3 As far as succession and inheritance are concerned, twelve years after the completion of the *Digest* Colebrooke writes as follows: "A very ample compilation on this subject is included in the Digest of Hindu Law prepared by Jagannātha under the directions of Sir William Jones. But copious as that work is, it does not supersede the necessity of further aid to the study the Hindu Law of inheritance. In the preface to the translation of the Digest, I hinted an opinion unfavorable to the arrangement of it, as it has been executed by the native compiler. I have been confirmed in that opinion of the compilation since its publication" (1810: ii).

And Colebrooke goes on, introducing the new but extremely far reaching concept of "schools" of Hindu law of inheritance, thus: "and indeed the author's method of discussing together the discordant opinions maintained by the several schools, without distinguishing in an intelligible manner which of them is the received doctrine of each school, but on the contrary leaving it uncertain whether any of the opinions stated by him do actually prevail, or which doctrines must now be considered to be in force and which obsolete, renders his work of little utility to persons conversant with the law, and of still less service to those who are not versed in Indian jurisprudence, especially to the English reader, for whose use, through the medium of translation, the work was particularly intended" (ibid.).

an easy conscience concur in a decision merely on the written opinion of native lawyers in any case in which they would have the remotest interest in misleading the Court."

[188] In May 1773 eleven *paṇḍits* in Calcutta began to compose a Sanskrit treatise, according to specifications given by Hastings. "The work was called Vivādārṇavasetu, or 'bridge across the ocean of litigation,' and it acquired soon afterwards the alternative title *Vivādāṇavabhañjana* 'breakwater to the ocean of litigation,' implying thereby that the certainty now for the first time offered to litigants in the Company's territories would put some check upon the appalling flood of cases which inundated the courts" (Derrett 1961: 85). The Sanskrit text was then translated into Persian and, from Persian, into English by N.B. Halhed.

[189] The composition of the original Sanskrit text. Jagannātha's *Vivādabhaṅgārṇava* "ocean of resolutions of disputes." had been supervised (1788–1794) by W. Jones. It was, however, completed only after Jones' death and was, therefore, translated not by Jones himself but by H.T. Colebrooke.

Hence Colebrooke's decision, rather than to compile and publish a new compilation,[190] to translate two existing treatises: Vijñāneśvara's *Mitākṣarā* and Jimūtavāhana's *Dayabhāga*. "They are the standard works of the Hindu law in the schools of Benares and Bengal respectively" (ibid. ii–iii).

The *Two Treatises on the Hindu Law of Inheritance, Translated by H.T. Colebrooke, Esquire* (1810) from whose preface the preceding quotations have been drawn is again one of the landmarks which have greatly determined the development of the Hindu law of inheritance.

We shall only casually mention here the fact that it is mainly the *Two Treatises* which is responsible for the fact that during the British period —and after it— the *Mitākṣarā* and the *Dāyabhāga* and, hence, the whole commentarial literature has become more authorative than the original *sūtras* and *śāstras* (Rocher 1952). Even setting aside our theory that the *sūtras* and *śāstras* had real authority, certainly much more than the commentaries, the fact remains that in the eyes of the commentators themselves their own works were mere explanations of and, therefore, less authorative than the revealed *śāstras*. From now onward these evaluations will be reversed.[191]

A second, and even more spectacular result of the *Two Treatises* is that, for a century and a half, the Hindu law of inheritance

[190] "In a general compilation, where the authorities are greatly multiplied, and the doctrines of many different schools, and of numerous authors are contrasted and compared, the reader is at a loss to collect the doctrines of a particular school and to follow the train of reasoning by which they are maintained. He is confounded by the perpetual conflict of discordant opinions and jarring deductions; and by the frequent tradition from the positions of one sect to the principles of another. It may be useful then, that such a compilation should be preceded by the separate publication of the most approved works of each school. By exhibiting in an exact translation the text of the author with notes selected from the glosses of his commentators or from the works of other writers of the same school, a correct knowledge of that part of the Hindu law, which is expressly treated by him, will be made more easily attainable, than by trusting solely to a general compilation. The one is best adapted to preparatory study; the other may afterwards be profitably consulted, when a general, but accurate knowledge has been thus previously obtained by the separate study of a complete body of doctrine" (Colebrooke 1810: iii–iv).

[191] We cannot insist too strongly upon the false perspective in which this situation has placed the historical study of Hindu law generally. From the British period onward "Hindu law," has become the law of the commentaries, and, as far as inheritance is concerned, "Mitākṣarā law" and "Dāyabhāga law." The old śāstric rules are no longer considered as prescriptions which, during a particular period of Indian history, had an existence of their own; in other words: one looses sight of the fact that the interpretation of a specific śāstric rule in the *Mitākṣarā*, the *Dāyabhāga*, or any other commentary, is one out of many, and that it does not necessarily correspond to the intentions of the original author. For an example of this anomaly, cf. section 1.2.1 above, note 9.

has been bifurcated into two sections: *Dāyabhāga* law for Bengal, and *Mitākṣarā* law for the rest of India. It is true that both texts are representative of the two main tendencies referred to above: right by birth or right by inheritance, but if Colebrooke had been advised to translate two other treatises, the now classical division into *Dāyabhāga* and *Mitākṣarā* laws might never have existed.[192]

Finally, whatever texts have been translated at a later date,[193] they have all been considered as representing sub-schools of the main twofold division.

3.2 Although the British judges were now in a far better position than before, once again the situation mainly and gradually showed its shortcomings.[194]

3.2.1 We shall not insist here upon the deficiencies of the translations as such.[195] Far more important is the fact that the

[192] In view of our opinion about the highly theoretical value of the commentaries, we even doubt whether the "schools" themselves were not an invention of Colebrooke —or his informant. We were pleased to find partial confirmation of this opinion with Derrett even though he does not share our ideas about the commentaries: "It was laid down by the Privy Council that no researches should be made into what the *ṛṣis* probably meant, but that, where consistent with justice and equity, the view of the most approved local commentators should be followed [*Collector of Madura v. Moottoo Ramalinga*, (1868) 12 Moore's Ind. App. 397, 436]. If however those views were not practised they should nevertheless be ignored. This approach secured the supremacy of a few celebrated commentaries, and their fortuitous localisation. Far more credit was placed in their unsupported statements than was really justifiable" (Derrett 1956a: 240–241).

[193] The other translations throughout the 19th century have been the following:

1. 1818 *Dāyādhikārasaṃgraha* (P.M. Wynch).
2. 1821 *Dattakacandrikā* (J.C.C. Sutherland).
3. 1821 *Dattakamīmāṃsā* (J.C.C. Sutherland).
4. 1827 *Vyavajāramayūka* (H. Borrodaile).
5. 1851 *Smṛticandrikā* (J.F. Thomas).
6. 1863 *Vivādacintāmaṇi* (P.C. Tagore).
7. 1874 *Dāyatattva* (G.C. Sarkar).
8. 1881 *Sarasvatīvilāsa* (Th. Foulkner).

At present the Sanskrit texts on inheritance can most easily be consulted either in Stokes 1965 (contains nos. 2. 3, 4, plus *Mitākṣarā* and *Dāyabhāga*), or in Setlur 1911 (contains all above mentioned texts together with several others).

[194] On the difficulties arising from the use of Sanskrit texts as sources of law, cf. Derrett (1961: 32–37), with numerous references to the cases. Cf. also the contemporary complaint of Th. Goldstücker (1871).

[195] A good example is offered in *Apaji Narhar v. Ramchandra*, (1892) 16 Bom. 29 (F.B.). The question raised was whether under *Mitākṣarā* law a son can in the lifetime of his father sue his father and uncles for a partition of the immovable family property and for possession of his share therein, the father not assenting thereto. The relevant passage of the *Mitākṣarā* has been thus translated by Cole-

Sanskrit texts, even in translations, remained foreign to the English judges who knew neither the original language nor the general principles upon which this strange system had been built. Says the Privy Council:

> At the same time it is quite impossible for us to feel any confidence in our opinion, upon a subject like this, when that opinion is founded upon authorities to which we have access only through translations, and when the doctrines themselves, and the reasons by which they are supported, or impugned, are drawn from the religious tradition, ancient usages, and more modern habits of the Hindus, with which we cannot be familiar.[196]

The main result of this situation was, that the judges looked elsewhere for fundamental principles upon which to construe the Hindu personal law: "Following the practice of early Charters of the East India Company, and acknowledgeng the need to supply a fundamental law which would guide judges where regulations and personal laws failed, secs. 60 and 93 of the Regulation of 5th July 1781 referred the judges to Justice, Equity and Good Conscience."[197]

It goes without saying that the application to Hindu law of inheritance of the English principles of justice, equity and good conscience led to situations which, as compared with pure Hindu law, may be called incongruous. Among many possible examples

brooke (1.5.3): "If the father be alive and separate from the grandfather, or if he have no brothers, a partition with the grandson would not take place since it has been directed that shares shall be allotted in right of the father, if he be deceased; or, admitting partition to take place, it would be made according to the pleasure of the father, like a distribution of his own acquisitions: to obviate this doubt the author says: —'It is well known that the ownership of father and son is the same in land which is acquired by the grandfather, or in a corrody or in chattels [which belonged to him].'" When relying on this translation the answer to the above question is "no," and this actually was the opinion of the majority and, hence, of the F.B. Only one judge, who knew Sanskrit, objected to Colebrooke's rendering and opposed it to Jolly's translation which is indeed the correct one: "Supposing the father to be divided (from his co-parceners) or to have no brothers, shall the estate, which has been inherited from the grandfather, not be divided at all with the grandson in that case, because it has been directed that shares shall be allotted in right of the father if he is deceased (and not otherwise); or, admitting partition to take place (in that case), shall it be instituted by the choice of the father alone? In order to remove the two doubts, which might be thus entertained, the author says: ...".

[196] *Rungama v. Atchama*, Moore's I.A. 1. 97–98 (P.C.).

[197] Derrett (1961: 25), referring to Duncan 1785. On the influence of English common law in India generally, cf. Anantanarayanan and Subba Rao 1957: 118–127; Venkataraman 1957: 156–179; O'Malley 1941; Lindsay 1941: 107–137. On the concepts of justice, equity and good conscience, cf. Derrett 1962; Anderson 1963: 114–153.

we shall only refer to the disqualification of a murderer from succeeding to his victim's estate. In 1924 the Privy Council laid down:

> Before this Board it has been contended that the matter is governed by Hindu Law, and that the Hindu Law makes no provision disqualifying a murderer from succeeding to the estate of his victim, and therefore it must be taken that according to this law he can succeed.
>
> Their Lordships do not take this view... The alternative is between the Hindu Law being as above stated or being for this purpose non-existent, and in that case the High Court have rightly decided that the principle of equity, justice and good conscience exclude the murderer.[198]

3.2.2 To an extent which is perhaps difficult to evaluate, two factors led to another departure from the classical Hindu law. The fact that judges trained in England were called upon to apply texts of law which were all but inaccessible to them naturally led to a situation in which consultation of the law books was avoided whenever possible, to be replaced, from an early date onward,[199] by the English rule of judicial precedent.

The decisions of the High Courts in each province became binding on all subordinate courts within their territorial jurisdiction whereas High Courts themselves were bound to follow the decisions of the Privy Council. Although a certain degree of uniformity was thus attained, the Privy Council continued to recognize the idea of "schools" of Hindu Law, and accepted the fact that similar cases were dealt with in quite different ways in the various High Courts. In other words, the Hindu law of inheritance, although relatively uniform within each province, remained far from uniform throughout the whole of British India.

Not only was the principle of judicial precedent largely restricted to the provinces; it also led to a new departure from the old law. Indeed, the English law of judicial precedent included such maxims as *stare decisis* and *communis error facit ius*. As a result, in a number of cases the courts have deviated consciously from the established principles of Hindu law, for the sole reason and with the sole justification that older decisions had deviated from them before.[200]

[198] *Kenchava v. Girimallappa Channppa*, (1924) 51 I.A., 368, 372–373.

[199] "If not earlier, at least after the amalgamation of the *muffassal* and towns systems of Courts in 1861" (Gledhill 1954: 578).

[200] The application of *stare decisis* is the only aspect of Anglo-Indian law where we would agree —to some extent— with some severe Indian critics of the legal system during the Brltish period. We cannot agree with those who generalize and state that, from the *Bālambhaṭṭī* onward (1760–1780), "about this time the petrifying influence of the British Courts of justice began to fall upon

Thus, when in *Sheo Shankar Lal v. Debi Sahai*[201] the restrictions of disposition imposed on a woman are said to be equal whether she inherits from a male or a female and that none of these possessions pass on to her own heirs, the decision apparently goes against the dispositions of the *Mitākṣarā* according to which such possessions should be considered to be *strīdhana*, and, hence, pass on to the woman's daughters. But, the decision was based upon the fact that the *Mitākṣarā* had not been followed by various High Courts and that, therefore, *communis error facit ius*.[202]

3.2.3 Alongside the purely judge-made law referred to so far, mention must also be made of the introduction into Hindu law of inheritance of another element which had been completely foreign to India before; we mean: the passing of a number Acts which normally abrogated the old law as far as the topics they deal with are concerned. None of these Acts bears on inheritance directly and exclusively, but they nevertheless strongly influence the whole apparatus of succession. The main Central Acts (Gupte 1963: 352–353) which come into consideration will be briefly referred to.

a. The Caste Disabilities Removal Act, 1850

So much of any law or usage now in force within the territories subject to the Government of the East India Company as inflicts to any person forfeiture of rights or property, or may be held in any way to impair or affect any right of inheritance, by reason of his or her renouncing, or having been excluded from the communion of, any religion, or being deprived of caste, shall cease to be enforced as law in the Courts of the East India Company, and in the Courts established by Royal Charter within the said territories.

b. The Special Marriage Act, 1872

Sec. 24: Succession to the property of any person professing the Hindu, Buddhist, Sikh or Jaina religion, who marries under this Act, and to property of the issue of such marriage, shall be regulated by the provisions of the Indian Succession Act, 1865.[203]

Hindu law" (Das 1906: 5). In our opinion the petrifying influence began much earlier than the British; moreover, during the British period Hindu law did not fail to undergo an important change *sui generis*.

[201] (1903) 30 I.A., 202 (qtd. in Ramaswami 1961: 319–329).

[202] As we shall see below, the maxim *communis error facit ius* was also invoked to justify the introduction of wills.

[203] This Act was entirely based on English law. Cf. Stokes 1887–88: 295–484. For its successor. the Indian Succession Act, 1925, cf. Basu 1957.

c. The Hindu Inheritance (Removal of Disabilities) Act, 1928

After what has been said above about disqualification of heirs, it will be appreciated when the Act provides that:

> Notwithstanding any rule of Hindu law or custom to the contrary, no person governed by the Hindu law, other than a person who is and has been from birth a lunatic or idiot, shall be excluded from inheritance or from any right or share in joint family property by reason only of a disease, deformity, or physical or mental defect.

It should be noticed, however, that the Act applies to persons governed by *Mitākṣarā* law only, not to those governed by *Dāyabhāga* law.

d. The Hindu Law of Inheritance (Amendment) Act, 1929

The Act considerably changes the order of heirs at the death of a person governed by *Mitākṣarā* law. In between the father's father and father's brother take place:

– son's daughter, daughter's daughter and sister, who were not heirs before the Act in any *Mitākṣarā* school except in Madras and Bombay, and

– sister's son, who only belonged to the bandhu class.

e. The Hindu Women's Right to Property Act, 1937

The main dispositions of this very important Act, which applies to all schools, may be summarized as follows: when a Hindu dies intestate, his widow is entitled, with regard to the deceased husband's separate property, to a son's share; with regard to the deceased husband's interest in a Hindu joint family property, she will have the same interest as he himself had. She will have the same right of claiming partition as a male owner, but her interest shall be a limited one, known as a Hindu women's Estate —which means that her right to alienate the *corpus* is restricted in the same way as that of a manager,[204] and that, on her death, it passes on to her husband's heirs.

[204] As a result of all this, in 1954 Gledhill could write as follows: "It is interesting to note that this Act was called in aid, though, it is submitted, the logic is not obvious, by the Nagpur High Court recently to support a decision that a woman might be manager of a joint family [*Commissioner of Income Tax v. Lakshminarayana*, A.I.R. (1949) Nag. 128], but this decision caused the Madras High Court, with its traditional devotion to the *Mitākṣarā*, almost to throw up its hands in hor-

The legislation, as far as it relates to inheritance, even though it is not very extensive, introduces a number of novelties the general background to which may be summarized as follows: "The obvious direction of this legislation is departure from the notion of joint family towards the conception of a new social unit comprising the husband and wife and their children, with rules of inheritance based on the degree of affection, irrespective of sex, deemed to exist between the deceased and the heirs" (Gledhill 1954: 595).[205]

3.3 Having reviewed the various elements which contributed towards shaping the Anglo-Indian law of inheritance, we shall now briefly point out a few of the main changes which the Hindu law of inheritance underwent in the course of this period.[206]

3.3.1 Apart from a number of other changes —"The courts had no patience with the law of reunion (*saṃsṛṣṭi*), because it was controversial and obscure" (Derrett 1963: 243)—, "possibly the most curious perversion of *Mitākṣarā* joint family law is the change in the doctrine of pious obligation" (Gledhill 1954: 583).

The doctrine of pious obligation as such was maintained: the sons remained liable to pay their fathers' debts. Moreover, even a number of more specific old rules were regularly adhered to; thus the son was not responsible for debts which were *avyāvahārika* "tainted," i.e. due to the father's criminal or immoral conduct.

On the other hand, however, the pious obligation underwent at least two fundamental changes. First, the British judges could not accept a situation in which a son would be obliged to discharge his father's debts beyond the extent of the assets devolving from the latter. But against this restriction stands an equally obvious extension. If a son was liable to pay all —or most of— his father's debts, the British judges saw no reason why this obligation should arise after the father's death only. As a result, the courts began to make use of the old principle of the pious obligation to give to the father, during his own lifetime, a right to alienate his son's interest in order to purge his debt himself. But

ror [*Radha* v. *Income Tax Commissioner*, A.I.R. (1950) Mad. 538]. The Nagpur decision is, however, a straw which shows the way the wind is blowing" (1954: 588).

[205] This change is the more interesting since, here too, the legislation passed by the Parliament of Independent India seems to continue rather than to reverse this tendency.

[206] For more numerous examples in the various fields of Hindu law, cf. Gledhill 1954: 581–588 (the law of the joint family); 588–591 (marriage); 591–593 (adoption); 593–595 (inheritance); 596 (impartible estates), 596–600 (wills), 600–601 (religious and charitable endowments), 601–602 (caste questions). The classical treatise on the Anglo-Hindu law of inheritance is Sarvadhikari 1922.

the courts were unanimous in requiring that the father could alienate his son's interest only for debts which were "antecedent," i.e., contracted before and independently of the alienation. Thus, it has been ruled by the Privy Council in the famous Brij Narain's case:

> If he [i.e., the father] purports to burden the estate with a mortgage, then unless that mortgage is to discharge an antecedent debt, it would not bind more than his own interest. Antecedent debt means antecedent in fact as well as in time, that is to say, the debt must be truly independent and not part of the transaction impeached.[207]

3.3.2 Whereas the doctrine of the pious obligation is an excellent example of how ancient institutions were maintained but with a fundamental change in their contents, we must now also mention an example of how the Anglo-Indian period enriched Hindu law through the introduction of completely new institutions. The example concerns the law of wills (Phillips and Trevelyan 1914).

Although it has been maintained that at least one verse from the old Dharmaśāstra "makes a very near approach to the modern conception of a will" (Kane 1930–62: 3.817),[208] we would personally not hesitate to subscribe to the opinion that "the will is not known in Indian law" (Jolly 1928, 177): not only none of the numerous written documents can be identified with a testament (Kane 1930–62: 3.816), but the situation in ancient Hindu law is such that a will was not often called for.[209]

Aided perhaps by the fact that the Indians were not completely unfamiliar with wills after a few centuries of Muslim occupation, aided moreover by the Hindus' willingness to assimilate any extraneous element into their own system, the English soon succeeded in introducing a full scale law of wills. After a hesitating start (Kane 1930–62: 3.816–818)[210] Hindu wills were fully recognized by the Privy Council on the basis of the above mentioned maxim *communis error facit ius.*[211]

[207] *Brij Narain v. Mangal Prasad,* (1923) 46 All. 95, at p. 96 (P.C.).

[208] The stanza referred to is KS 566.

[209] Cf. Maine (1930: 213–214), in Chapter VI (The Early History of Testamentary Succession): "In Hindoo law there is no such thing as a true will. The place filled by Wills is occupied by Adoptions... Both a Will and an Adoption threaten a distortion of the ordinary course of Family descent, but they are obviously contrivances for preventing the descent being wholly interrupted when there is no succession of kindred to carry it on."

[210] Strange (1825: 1.253–267; 2.405–441) already has a chapter "On the testamentary Power."

[211] *Beer Pertab v. Rajender Pertab,* (1867) 12 Moore's I.A. 37, 38: "It is too late to contend that, because the ancient Hindu treatises make no mention of wills, a

The Hindu Wills Act, 1870 was based entirely upon the same principles and required exactly the same formalities as the English Wills Act, 1837: the will had to be in writing, the testator had to sign or affix his mark, there had to be two attesting witnesses, etc. As a matter of act, the opinion expressed by a modern Indian author: "It is obvious that the modern Hindu law of wills is purely the creation of judges and is based mainly on the English law on the topic"[212] is so true, that: "The courts in India accustomed to resort to English decisions when doubts arose occasionally applied rules of interpretation laid down in the English cases in construing wills in the Indian language" (Setalvad 1960: 69). It is a most interesting feature to see the Judicial Committee of the Privy Council react against this "almost absurd" tendency.[213]

4. The Republic of India

The evolution of the Hindu law of inheritance in post-independence India is again not understandable without an adequate insight in the pre-independence situation.

4.1 In the first place, there is an important element of continuity. Until only a few years ago one was entitled to say: "Up to the present, Indian independence has produced no change in the direction of the evolution of the law; on the contrary, the development during the British period in India seems to have been accelerated" (Gledhill 1954: 580). The reason for this interesting phenomenon is a very simple one, though it may not be im-

Hindu cannot make a testamentary disposition of his property. Decided cases, too numerous to be questioned, have determined that the testamentary power exists, and may be exercised, at least within the limits which the law prescribes to alienation, by gift *inter vivos*."

[212] Cf. Ramaswami (1961: 328).

[213] *Norendra Nath Sircar v. Kamatbesini Dasi*, (1896) 23 Cal. 563 (PC), p. 572: "To construe one Will by reference to expressions of more or less doubtful import to be found in other Wills is, for the most part, an unprofitable exercise. Happily that method of interpretation has gone out of fashion in this country. To extend it to India would hardly be desirable. To search and sift the heap of cases on Wills which cumber our English law Reports in order to understand and interpret Wills of people speaking a different tongue, trained in different habits of thought and brought up under different conditions of life, seems almost absurd." *Din Tarini Debi v. Krishna Gopal Bagchi*, (1909) 36 Cal. 149, p.156: "The rule of construction in a Hindu as in an English will, is to try and find out the meaning of the testator, taking the whole of the document together, and to give effect to its meaning. In applying the above principle Courts of Justice in this country ought not to judge the language used by a Hindu, according to the artificial rules, which have been applied to the language of people, who live under a different system of law, and in a different state of society."

mediately evident to the legal historian who is not familiar with Indian situations. The fact is that Anglo-Indian law is —and has become more and more— a law made, not by Englishmen, but by Indians. Most of the judges responsible for the application of Hindu law before independence were Hindus; a great number of these Hindu judges had attained a remarkably high level of professional ability (Derrett 1961: 38). And when independence came, either the then living judges carried on, or they were replaced by a younger generation who followed the footsteps to their illustrious predecessors (ibid.: 12).[214]

4.2 On the other hand, however, and although we may say without fear of exaggeration that the Anglo-Indian judicial system brought to India a degree of certainty and of law and order which had never been reached before,[215] the fact remains that the system displayed a number of shortcomings which did not pass unnoticed.

The objection which is most strongly brought to the fore against Hindu law as it existed before and just after independence was its lack of unity. To the already existing arguments of the *śāstras* being applied without the slightest uniformity,[216] of the different High Courts diverging farther and farther from each other,[217] etc. was now added an argument drawn from the national pride of a newly independent nation. As K.M, Munshi put it during the Constituent Assembly Debates:

> Religion must be contained to its proper sphere, and the rest of life regulated and unified so that we can become a strong and consolidated nation. Our first problem is national unity. We must

[214] "The judges of modern India correspond in point of personnel to a large extent with their independence counterparts, and much of their work illustrates tendencies born and confirmed under British influence; they would not wish it otherwise, so far as one can tell. To cite post-Independence cases as authorities on Anglo-Hindu law is in order in nine situations out of ten" (Derrett 1961: 38). For a number of distinguished Indian judges who at the same time excel in śāstric knowledge, see ibid.

[215] "The British nation is proud of having administered justice to oriental peoples with impartiality integrity, conscious of the Roman example. These qualities were thought to have been lacking before the British period, and to the extent to which British standards are respected since British rule ceased that heritage is usually considered a ground for pride" (Derrett 1961: 10).

[216] A characteristic verdict is that of Burnell (1884: xlv): "As the text has been so often referred to by the courts of India, and the ultimate Court of Appeal, the Privy Council in England, it might be expected that some useful help would be got from the law reports; but this is not the case. Most of the cases decided are evidently wrongly decided."

[217] Cf. above, 3.2.2.

be able to say "By our way of life and our personal law, we are a strong and consolidated nation."[218]

It is this desire towards a unified personal law, symbol of national unity, which led to the most important novelty in personal law generally and law of inheritance in particular, namely the inscription into the Constitution of article 44:

> The State shall endeavour to secure for all citizens a uniform civil code throughout the territory of India.

4.3 This is not the right place to retrace the long and chequered history of the Hindu Code Bill;[219] we must proceed immediately to the end of the story, to say that the ideal of an overall Hindu Civil Code has been abandoned at the moment. But an important step forward was made, about ten years ago, by the introduction of four separate Acts of Parliament which, if taken together, already codify a considerable portion of Indian Law. They are:

1. the Hindu Marriage Act, 1955 (Act No. 25 of 1955);
2. the Hindu Succession Act, 1956 (Act No. 30 of 1956);
3. the Hindu Minority and Guardianship Act, 1956 (Act No. 32 of 1956);
4. the Hindu Adoptions and Maintenance Act, 1956 (Act No. 78 of 1956).

Within the context of this study we shall concern ourselves merely with the Hindu Succession Act, 1956,[220] which we already mentioned at the very outset of the paper.

4.3.1 In principle, we may now say that all Hindus[221] enjoy a uniform law of inheritance (sec. 2):

> This Act applies —
>
> (a) to any person, who is Hindu by religion in any of its forms or

[218] *Constituent Assembly Debates*, pp. 547–548, quoted by Gledhill (1954: 603).

[219] The demand for codification is much older than the Constitution. As early as 1892, F.R. Bhikaji published his *Hindu Law in Bombay: A Plea for its Codification* (cf. Derrett 1961: 46). For the argument pro and contra the Civil Code, see Derrett (1957: 189–190).

[220] For the objectives and reasons of the bill when it was introduced (Bill No. xiii of 1954). Cf. *Gazette of India Extraordinary* (Part II, S. 2) dated 26 May 1954.

[221] "The majority community is Hindu, a term sufficiently broad to include persons of the widest variety of belief and practice, or of no beliefs of a religious character whatever. They now make up about 300 millions, and it is a basic

developments, including a Virashaiva, a Lingayat follower of the Brahmo, Prarthana or Arya Samaj;

(b) to any person who is a Buddhist, Jaina or Sikh by religion and

(c) to any other person who is not a Muslim, Christian, Parsi or Jew by religion, unless it is proved that any such person would not have been governed by the Hindu law or by custom or usage as part of that law in respect of any of the matters dealt with herein if this Act had not been passed.

The Act does recognize testamentary succession, in section 30 (1):

> Any Hindu may dispose of by will or other testamentary disposition any property, which is capable of being so disposed of by him in accordance with the provisions of the Indian Succession Act, 1925, or any other law for the time being in force and applicable to Hindus.

As will be clear from the remarks made about wills above, sec. 30 (1) does not create the possibility for a Hindu to dispose of his property by testament. This possibility had been recognized for a long time. The importance of sec. 30 (1) is that, for the first time, statutory recognition is given to the power of a Hindu by will or testamentary document to dispose of property which is capable of disposition (Gupte 1963: 445).

The old law was changed with regard to disqualified persons. From now onward, according to section 28:

> No person shall be disqualified from succeeding to any property on the ground of any disease, defect or deformity or save as provided in this Act, on any other ground whatseover.

Here too, the tendency toward changing the traditional situation[222] had manifested itself during the Anglo-Indian period,[223] but for the first time the new conception is officially enacted.

The classes of heirs are finally well defined, be it in an unexpected way. Indeed, "most systems of intestate succession make clear distinctions between descendants, spouse, ascendents, and collaterals. It comes as an equal shock to those accustomed to the Civil Law types and to those familiar with Anglo-American

theory of the Acts which form the nucleus of the Code that they have enough in common basically to rest content with a single civil law in matters of marriage, divorce, guardianship. adoption, joint family, maintenance and testamentary and intestate succession" (Derrett 1957: 189–211).

[222] Cf. above, 1.5.

[223] For the specific case of a murderer, cf. 3.2.1.

types of distribution to find that the Act mixes the classes apparently without any rational arrangement, and without precedent" (Derrett 1956: 495).

A Schedule added to the Act divides the heirs into two classes:

Class I: Son; daughter; widow; mother; son of predeceased daughter; daughter of a predeceased daughter; widow of a predeceased son; son of a predeceased son of a predeceased son; daughter of a predeceased son of a predeceased son; widow of a predecececeased son of a predeceased son.

These heirs take first (sec. 8) and simultaneously and to the exclusion of all other heirs (sec. 9):

I. Father.
II. (1) Son's daughter's son, (2) son's daughter's daughter, (3) brother, (4) sister.
III. (1) Daughter's son's son, (2) daughter's son's daughter. (3) daughter's daughter's son, 4) daughter's daughter's daughter.
IV. (1) Brother's son, (2) sister's son, (3) brother's daughter, (4) sister's daughter.
V. Father's father; father's mother.
VI. Father's widow; brother's widow.
VII. Father's brother: father's sister.
VIII. Mother's father; mother's mother.
IX. Mother's brother; mother's sister.

These heirs take in the absence of class I (sec. 8): moreover, those in the first entry shall be preferred to those in the second entry, etc. (sec. 9).

In the absence of heirs in both classes the succession goes to the agnates and, in their absence, to the cognates of the deceased (sec. 8).

A most prominent motive behind the Act was undoubtedly to place women upon an approximately equal footing with men with regard to property rights.[224] An excellent example of this tendency is offered by Section 6 of the Act. This section does recognize devolution of property by survivorship under *Mitākṣarā* law:

When a male Hindu dies after the commencement of this Act, having at the time of his death an interest in a Mitakshara coparcenary property, his interest in the property shall devolve by survivorship upon the surviving members of the coparcenary and not in accordance with this Act.

[224] According to Derrett (1956: 488), this motive was even stonger than the "tidying up" of "the disordered and inconsistent mass that were the rules of Anglo-Hindu law, though this academic aim was present."

But the section comprehends an important proviso:

> Provided that, if the deceased had left him surviving a female relative specified in class I of the Schedule or a male relative specified in that class who claims through such female relative, the interest of the deceased in the Mitakshara coparcenary shall devolve by testamentary or intestate succession, as the case may be, under the Act and not by survivorship.

In 1955–56, when it was the intention to also codify joint family law, the principle of *Mitākṣarā* coparcenary was maintained: the coparceners would obtain by survivorship and not by inheritance an already existing interest in the joint family property. The widow, the widow's daughter, and the daughter's son would not acquire anything except a right of maintenance. Due to the proviso, however, the situation has changed completely: as soon as there are any of these privileged female relations, they have a right of succession which prevails over the right by survivorship of the agnates. They have a right of their own, and are no longer dependent on the mercy of the decedent's agnates.

4.3.2 As to the reception of the Hindu Succession Act. 1956, it is too early yet to prophesy its future career. There is no doubt that an orthodox minority even today considers the new law as "grossly contravening the Hindu axioms and beliefs,"[225] but we do not hesitate to subscribe to the judgment of our friend, Professor Derrett, to whose works this article owes so much and who, more than anybody else, has followed step by step the judicial activity in India during the latest few decades: be it for a negative reason —"it has already been pointed out that, however odd a modern statute law of succession to deceased Hindus might turn out to be, the preexisting law was immeasurably worse"— the situation seems to be such that "the general public who are affected by it seem at present neither overtly nor violently dissatisfied" (Derrett 1956: 485).

[225] Deshpande (1943: 151), speaking about the proposals of the Hindu Law Committee.

9

Caste and Occupation in Classical India: The Normative Texts

This is a general study of the relation between caste and occupation according to the normative texts of ancient India. The sources on which this study is based are not new. All Sanskrit texts that will be quoted in this paper are available in English translations which have been read —and relied on— by several generations of scholars. Yet, to understand fully the Sanskrit sources, existing translations not only often prove inadequate; they are in many cases misleading. I shall, therefore, present my own translations for all sources, and supplement them with a commentary whenever necessary.

I shall throughout this paper use the word "caste" to translate the Sanskrit term *varṇa*. Even though this translation is inadequate, any other English equivalent —which would necessarily amount to a lengthy circumlocution— would make the translations from Sanskrit unnecessarily cumbersome.

I shall distinguish between two sets of norms: the strict norm and the pliable norm. This distinction is not made by the texts, at least not explicitly. Yet, it is clear that the authors envisage a twofold situation: the normal situation, in which the strict norm applies, and the —less desirable— abnormal circumstance, which requires the replacement of the strict norm by the pliable norm.

The Strict Norm

Several texts describe the way in which the creator of the universe assigned different occupations to the members of the four castes. The *Manusmṛti* alone exhibits two similar passages on this subject: one in the first chapter, on creation (1.87–91), and one in the tenth chapter, on caste (10.74–131). I shall quote a section of the latter passage, and compare the data from other Dharmasūtras and Dharmaśāstras in my comments and footnotes.

Manu first lists (10.75) the six activities (*karman*) of the Brāhmaṇa: "Teaching (*adhyāpana*), studying (*adhyayana*), performing his own sacrifices (*yajana*), performing sacrifices for others (*yājana*), giving gifts (*dāna*), receiving gifts (*pratigraha*): these are the six activities of a Brāhmaṇa."[226] The next stanza (10.76) draws an interesting distinction; it singles out three activities of the Brāhmaṇa, and labels them his "means of livelihood" (*jīvikā*): "Three of these six activities are his means of livelihood: performing sacrifices for others, teaching, and receiving gifts from the pure." Neither Āpastamba nor Baudhāyana make this distinction, nor does Manu in his first chapter. Vasiṣṭha does not make it for the Brāhmaṇa (2.14), but he does for the Kṣatriya and Vaiśya. Gautama adopts a different procedure: he first (10.1) lists —without using a generic term— the three activities of the twice-born: studying, sacrificing, giving gifts, and then adds "additional" (*adhika*)[227] ones for the Brāhmaṇa (10.2), the Kṣatriya (10.7) , and the Vaiśya (10.49).[228] The separation is complete in the *Viṣṇusmṛti*, which first (2.4–9) gives the *dharma*s of the four castes, and then (2.10–15) their *vṛtti*s, an often used synonym for *jīvikā*. Manu then states (10.77–78) that the three activities which constitute the *jīvikā* of the Brāhmaṇa do not apply in the case of a Kṣatriya or Vaiśya: "Three obligations (*dharma*) are not transferable[229] from the Brāhmaṇa to the Kṣatriya: teaching, performing sacrifices for others, and, thirdly, receiving

[226] The same six "activities" of the Brāhmaṇa are exhibited elsewhere, although with some interesting terminological variants which will be mentioned below: ĀpDh 2.5.10.4–5; GDh 10.1–2; VaDh 2.13–14; BDh 1.10.18.2; ViDh 2.5,9,11; MDh 1.88; YDh 1.1 18. Āpastamba adds three other items: inheritance etc., gathering ears of corn (*śiloñcha)* and anything left unclaimed (*aparigṛhīta*). I have no explanation to offer as to why Viṣṇu omits *dāna* (see note 238).

[227] The term *adhika* also occurs in ĀpDh 2.5.10.6, 7, and YDh 1.118.

[228] GDh 10.3 adds: *pūrveṣu niyamas tu.* I cannot agree with Bühler's translation (1879: 224): "But the former (three) are obligatory (on him)." I would prefer: "The former three are restricted (scil. to the twice-born)," i.e., they do not apply to Śūdras.

[229] The expressions "are not transferable" (10.77) and "shall not be transferred" (10.78) translate the Sanskrit technical terms *nivarante* and *nivarteran,* respectively. The procedure of *nivṛtti* is common in the interpretation of Sanskrit *sūtra* style. It means that a word or words occurring in a particular *sūtra* cease to have effect in the following *sūtra.* It is tempting —but not therefore justifiable— to conclude from this that our present *Manusmṛti* is based on an earlier text in *sūtra* style. ĀpDh 2.5.10.6 has as similar expression: *parihāpya* "leaving aside."

gifts. Similarly, they shall not be transferred to the Vaiśya; such is the rule. For Manu, the creator, does not prescribe these obligations for either one of these."

The three means of livelihood, which cannot be transferred to the Kṣatriya and Vaiśya, are replaced by other means of subsistence (10.79): "As far as their livelihood (*ājīvana*) is concerned, the Kṣatriya carries weapons;[230] the Vaiśya to trade, cattle, and agriculture. But their obligations (*dharma*) are: giving gifts, study, and personal sacrifices (*ijyā*)." By and large the other normative texts agree with Manu. As far as the Kṣatriya is concerned,[231] they probably put more stress on his being the "protector" of the kingdom and its citizens; for the Vaiśya[232] several texts mention an additional activity: *kusīda* "lending money on interest."

The last stanza of this sequence (Manu 10.80) points out that certain occupations are more commendable than others: "Among the specific activities (*karman*) of each one (scil. of the three highest castes) the most distinguished are: for the Brāhmaṇa, concentrating on the Veda: for the Kṣatriya, affording protection; for the Vaiśya, business." The purpose of the stanza is clear; each one of the three higher castes has several possible *jīvikā*, and one of them is more distinguished (*viśiṣṭa*) than the others. The verse is apparently well in its place, after an enumeration of the *jīvikā* of the three twice-born castes. Yet, the reader of the original text cannot fail to be struck by the fact that none of the means of livelihood which are singled out as more commendable occurs in the pre-

230 "The Kṣatriya carries weapons" is a tentative but inadequate translation of the Sanskrit compound *śastrāstrabhṛttva*. Bühler translates: "to carry arms for striking and for throwing." In view of the highly structured composition of Manu's text on caste and occupation, I venture to propose a different interpretation. The Brāhmaṇa has three means of livelihood, and so has the Vaiśya; the text makes it very clear that the Śūdra, as opposed to the three higher castes, has only one (see below). We may therefore expect that the text lists three means of livelihood for the Kṣatriya: *śastra* + *astra* + *bhṛttva* "weapons for striking" + "weapons for throwing" + "supporting, protecting (scil. the other (castes)." I realize the boldness of this interpretation; however, Baudhāyana, to whom Manu is closer than to any other earlier text, is the only one to list three means of livelihood for the Kṣatriya.

231 ĀpDh 2.5.10.6; GDh 10.7–8 (*rājan* instead of Kṣatriya); VaDh 2.17 (*rājanya* instead of Kṣatriya); ViDh 2.12; YDh 1.119. BDh (1.10.18.3) is the only one who lists three different means of livelihood: weapons (*śastra*), protection (*bhūtarakṣaṇa*), and *kośa*. The commentator explains at length the other two elements, but is silent on *kośa*. It normally refers to the king's treasury, but is unexpected here as Manu's *astra*.

232 The means of livelihood are mentioned in ĀpDh 2.5.10.7 and BDh 1.10.18.4. *Kusīda* is added to them in GDh 10.49, VaDh 2.19, YDh 1.119, and ViDh 2.13. The latter adds a fifth item: *yonipoṣaṇa*, which is unclear, and normally interpreted as growing or protecting seeds.

ceding lists. We can only speculate about this stanza eventually being a later insertion into the text; the terms themselves, which I have tried to translate as literally as possible, have given rise to very different interpretations.[233]

The Śūdra is not mentioned in Manu 10.74–80, but his position is clearly stated in Manu 1.91: "One single activity did the Lord assign the Śūdra: ungrudging service (*śuśrūṣā*)[234] to all the aforementioned castes."

The Śūdra obviously occupies a very special place in the occupation system. He is excluded from *yajana, adhyayana,* and *dāna,* which are not merely obligations, but at the same time rights which entail preternatural[235] benefits. The Sanskrit text of Manu 1.91 contains a few elements, the impact of which is difficult to render in an English translation. It is made clear that none of the multiple activities of the three higher castes apply to the Śūdra; he has but one task only, and a totally different one: *śuśrūṣā.* It is also made clear his service should be to all three castes mentioned in the three preceding stanzas. Finally, although Manu does not say so explicitly, the Śūdra's *śuśrūsā* belongs to the category of *jīvikā* "means of livelihood."[236] Yet, the Śūdra too is entitled to some kind of preternatural benefit, namely by perform his service *anasūyayā* "without spite, without envy, without grudge." Less obvious —and less often pointed out— is the fact that the position of the Brāhmaṇa in the occupational framework is equally special. Translations into Western languages conceal the undoubtedly intentional connection between the Brāhmaṇa's three means of livelihood (*jīvikā*), and

[233] "Concentrating on the Veda" translates the Sanskrit term *vedābhyāsa* which, in this context, should refer to *adhyāpana* "teaching the Veda", but which more often indicates "studying the Veda." "Business" is my interpretation of the term *vārttā.* The commentators on Manu present various interpretations, covering from one to three of the Brāhmaṇa's means of livelihood. It is clear, however, that the text wants to refer to only one of them.

[234] The Śūdra's "service" to the higher castes is also referred to in GDh 10.56, VaDh 2.20, and BDh 1.10.18.5. These three texts use the same term: *paricaryā,* which means "service, attendance," with the additional idea of "honour, worship." Manu replaces *paricaryā* by *śuśrūsā,* literally "the desire to listen to, the desire, to obey," and, hence, "willingness or readiness to obey." The term *śuśrūsā* also occurs in ViDh 2.8 and YDh 1.1118.

[235] "Preternatural" is an inadequate translation of *adṛṣṭārtha.* Kullūka, one of the commentators on the *Manusmṛti,* appropriately calls the means of livelihood *dṛṣṭārtha* "having a visible, tangible goal," and, consequently, labels the other obligations *adṛṣṭārtha* "having an invisible extra-mundane goal."

[236] Gautama, after mentioning the duty of the Śūdra: "Service to the higher castes"' (10.56), adds: "he should seek his livelihood (*vṛtti*) from them" (10.57). Similarly VaDh: "Serving them is the only means of livelihood (*vṛtti*) allowed to a Śūdra" (2.20). ViDh alone ranks *dvijaśuśrūsā* among the *dharmas.*

the other three *dharmas*. The six activities prescribed for the Brāhmaṇa actually form three binaries:

adhyayana : adhyāpana,
yajana : yājana,
dāna : pratigraha,

The terms *adhyāpana* and *yājana* are the respective causative forms of *adhyayana* and *yajana*. If *adhyayana* means "studying the Vedas," a*dhyāpana* literally means "making (scil. others) study the Vedas," and, hence, "instructing others in the Vedas." Similarly, *yajana* means "performing sacrifices for one's own benefit," whereas *yājana* means "making others perform sacrifices for their own benefit," and, consequently, "acting as the officiating priest in a sacrifice meant for —and paid by— another person." The third pair, *dāna* and *pratigraha*, are not etymologically related; but their meanings are. Whereas *dāna* means "gift, the act of giving," *pratigraha* literally means "taking back, taking again, taking in one's own turn." In fact, *pratigraha* in Indian society is not a mere passive acceptance of gifts; it implies a moral obligation on the part of the benefactor, imposed on him by the personality of the beneficiary. Hence, here too, *pratigraha* is, in reality, nothing else than *dāpana*, the causative form of *dāna*.[237]

In short, the Śūdra is divorced from the three preternatural activities —and preternatural benefits— of the higher castes; he has some kind of preternatural benefit of his own, but this is merely an accessory to the way in which he fulfils his sole *jīvikā*: *śuśrūṣā*. At the other end, the Brāhmaṇa, like the Kṣatriya and the Vaiśya, has three activities, plus his own specific *jīvikās*. But, in his case, the *jīvikās* have no other purpose than to provide an outlet for the preternatural activities of his fellow Brāhmaṇas and, especially, the Kṣatriyas and Vaiśyas. Consequently, the Kṣatriyas and Vaiśyas are the only two castes who have preternatural obligations and practical obligations which are basically different. They share with the Brāhmaṇas the benefits of *adhyayana*, *yajana*, and *dāna*; they share with the Śūdras an independent,

[237] The binary *dāna/pratigraha* is common to all texts on *dharma*, except that ĀpDh 2.5.10.4 uses the parallel form *pratigrahaṇa*, and that it is missing in Viṣṇu's unusual grouping of the six activities. The pair *adhyayana/adhyāpana* presents two variants: VaDh 2.14 replaces *adhyayana* by the compound *svādhyāyādhyayana*, and GDh 10.2 is alone to have *pravacana* instead of *adhyāpana*. Finally, *yājana* occurs in all texts —the reading *yajana* in VaDh 2.14 is erroneous—, but its counterparts are *yajña* in ĀpDh 2.5.10.4 and VaDh 2.14, and *ijyā* in GDh 10.1 and YDh 2.118 (cf. also MDh 10.79).

full-fledged *jīvikā*. The strict norm is summarized in Table 1.[238]

Table 1

	karman					
	(dharma)			jīvikā		
Br	adhyayana	yajana	dāna	adhyāyana	yājana	pratigraha
Kṣa	↓	↓	↓	śastrāstrabhṛttva		
Vai	↓	↓	↓	vaṇik	paśu	kṛṣi
Śū	anasūyayā śuśrūṣā					

The Pliable Norm

It is a well known fact that the assignment of different sets of activities to the four castes at the same time implies a rank ordering. Manu (1.87) refers to an idea which is as old as the *Ṛgveda*, when he introduces the sequence 1.88–91 as follows: "The very resplendent one, to protect the entire creation, assigned activities separately to his mouth, arms, thighs, and feet." It is again impossible to bring out in translation a number of essential points which the Sanskrit text naturally suggests to the reader. "To protect" implies the important idea of guarding, safeguarding, preserving. To maintain the proper order in the created world, the Creator assigned to the four castes which emanated from the head, arms, thighs, and feet of the Puruṣa respectively (cf. *Ṛgveda* 10.90.12), four distinct sets of activities. The text underscores the fact that these sets of activities are distinct (*pṛthak*), and the verb

[238] The only text that deviates considerably from the general scheme is the *Viṣṇusmṛti* (2.415). Details have been referred to elsewhere in this paper. I shall now add a survey of its entire system:

– Brāhmaṇa (a) *dharma: adhyayana, yajana, adhyāpana*
(b) *vṛtti: yajana, pratigraha*
– Kṣatriya (a) *dharma: adhyayana, yajana, śastranityatā*
(b) *vṛtti: kṣititrāṇa*
– Vaiśya (a) *dharma: adhyayana, yajana, paśupālana*
(b) *vṛtti: kṛṣi, gorakṣa, vānijya, kusīda, yonipoṣaṇa*
– Śūdra (a) *dharma: dvijātiśuśrūsā*
(b) *vṛtti: sarvaśilpāni*

translated as "assigned" (*akalpayat*) also implies a distributive assignment.[239] The stanza (1.92) following immediately after the sequence 1.88–91 reiterates the idea of rank ordering involved in the four *varṇas* and, consequently, in their respective sea of occupations: "Puruṣa is purer above his navel; therefore Svayambhū declared that his mouth is purest of all."

Given this frame of reference, it is normal that living by the specific occupation prescribed for one's own caste is the ideal situation. Manu (10.97) says so explicitly: "The obligations of one's own group, poorly done, are better than those of another group, perfectly executed; for as soon as one lives by the obligations of another group, one is excluded from his own."[240] Yet, Manu and authors on *dharma* display an unexpectedly large number of rules dealing with members of one caste living by the occupations reserved for other castes. The relation between the two sets of rules, which I have called the strict norm and the pliable norm, respectively, raises a number of interesting problems which I shall now investigate.

First, the rule that a person of lower birth shall not live by the activities reserved for a man of higher birth seems to be absolute. Says Manu (10.96): "If a man of lower birth,[241] out of greed, lives by the activities of one of higher birth, the king shall confiscate all his property, and banish him immediately." Notice the assumption on the part of the author, that upward occupational mobility is motivated by "greed" (*lobha*). "Greed" should not be taken here in its restricted sense of looking for material gain; it also implies the desire for other privileges connected with membership in a higher caste.

There is, however, one exception, provided for by Manu (10.99–100): "When a Śūdra cannot earn a living by serving the twice-born, he may, if he risks to lose his son or his wife, live by the activities of artisans. He shall practice those activities of artisans and those types of handicrafts, by which the twice-born are best served." To be sure, the activities of artisans (*kārukakarman*) and handicrafts (*śilpa*) are not listed by Manu among the occupations of any caste. *Śilpa* is one of the possible means of livelihood in the long passage on Śūdras in Gautama (10.60), and Viṣṇu mentions, in his list of means of livelihood: "For the Śūdra,

[239] GDh (10.66) concludes the section on caste and occupation with the rule: "Each caste shall serve those that are of a higher rank." "Serve" is expressed by means of *pari-car*, a root which is used for the activity of the Śūdra only.

[240] The text says: *patito jātitah*, literally: "fallen from his *jāti*." It is one of those cases, in which *jāti* seems to be nothing more than a synonym of *varṇa*.

[241] "Of lower birth" translates as *adhamo jātyā*, "low by *jāti*." It is possible that *jāti* is again a direct synonym of *varṇa*.

all kinds of handicrafts" (2.14). Yet, Manu's intention is clear: in case of emergency the Śūdra, like the members of the other three castes —see below— shall be given the opportunity to turn to the occupations of another caste. In his case, he shall be allowed to adopt some of the means of livelihood of the Vaiśya,[242] with the proviso that he shall select those occupations of the Vaiśya which are closest to his strict norm: *śuśrūṣā*.

On the contrary, all texts agree that a member of a higher caste is, under certain circumstances, authorized to adopt the lifestyle of those of the immediately lower caste. The circumstances in which this normally happens is called *āpad*, an ill-defined term meaning "time of distress." Viṣṇu (2.15) formulates the general principle: "In times of distress the means of livelihood of each caste are those of the immediately lower one."[243] Manu does not have the general rule, but he does give the specific examples. After discussing the regular occupations of the Vaiśya, he continues (10.95): "A Kṣatriya, who has fallen in to misfortune, may live by all this; but under no circumstances shall he take upon himself a superior livelihood."[244] Similarly, the Vaiśya may live the life of a Śūdra. Manu (10.98): "A Vaiśya, who cannot live by his own obligations, may also exist by the occupation of a Śūdra. He should avoid forbidden activities, and abandon this situation as soon as he is in a position to do so." This stanza stresses two elements which appear repeatedly in the sources, and which illustrate the twofold restrictions of downward occupational mobility according to the normative texts. First, the member of a higher caste living by the occupations of a lower caste shall abstain from "forbidden activities." The commentators on Manu 10.98 restrict themselves to giving examples: the Vaiśya should not eat the leavings of others, he should not eat forbidden food, etc. More important is the underlying principle: a member of a higher caste adopting the lifestyle of a lower caste should under no circumstances indulge in *akāryāṇi* "things which he should not do." Second, the member of a higher caste adopting the lifestyle of a lower caste "should abandon this situation as soon as he is in a position to do so." In other words, occupational mobility should be temporary; it is allowed only if, and as long as, one is not able to live by one's own occupations. No normative text envisages the

[242] YDh (1.120) clearly states that, if a Śūdra is unable to earn a living by serving the twice born, "he may become a merchant, or live by various kinds of handicrafts, (scil. always) keeping in mind the welfare of the twice-born."

[243] VaDh (2.22) omits the qualification *āpadi* "in time of distress," and simply states: "If they are unable to live by their own obligations...".

[244] "A superior livelihood" translates Sanskrit *jyāyasīṃ vṛttim*; VaDh (2.22–23) opposes *pāpīyasīm* and *jyāyasīm*.

situation in which a member of a particular caste decides, for the rest of his life, to adopt the lifestyle of another caste.

In accordance with this general principle, a distressed Brāhmaṇa may live as a Kṣatriya. According to Manu (10.81): "If a Brāhmaṇa cannot live by his own activities as explained earlier, he may live by the duties of a Kṣatriya; for the latter is next to him in rank."[245] But for the Brāhmaṇa another question is raised: what is to happen if he cannot maintain himself even by living as a Kṣatriya? Can he then also live as a Vaiśya? The answers vary. In the chapter on the treatment of witnesses, Manu (8.102) seems to condemn this practice: "Brāhmaṇas who tend cattle, who are traders, artisans, actors, servants or money-lenders, should be treated like Śūdras."

However, in the regular chapter on caste occupations Manu (10.82) clearly extends the rule allowing the member of a caste to live by the occupations of the immediately lower caste to the occupations of the two lower ones in the case of a Brāhmaṇa: "If one asks, 'What will happen if he is unable to subsist by the occupations of both highest castes,' the answer is, 'He may live by the means of livelihood of the Vaiśya, practicing agriculture and tending cattle.'" The special construction used in this stanza: "If one asks..." seems to indicate that the question whether or not a Brāhmaṇa could be allowed to live the life of a Vaiśya was debatable.[246] Yet, the answer leaves no doubt. In fact, Baudhāyana, who (2.2.4.16) extends the lifestyle of a Kṣatriya to a Brāhmaṇa in a way which is very similar to Manu's (10.81), states (2.2.4.19) without alluding to a possible debate: "The livelihood of a Vaiśya may be adopted, because he is next in rank (scil. after the Kṣatriya)."

On the occasion of Manu 10.98, I have already referred to the twofold restrictions which are an inherent part of the pliable norm in the texts on *dharma*. These restrictions are especially prominent in the sections that allow a Brāhmaṇa to live as a Kṣatriya and, even more so, in those that make it possible for him to live as a Vaiśya. The temporal restriction is stressed by Yājñavalkya (3.35): "In times of distress a Brāhmaṇa may

[245] BDh (2.2.4.16) expresses the same idea, but he continues (2.2.4.17): "Gautama says that this should not be allowed; for the obligations of Kṣatriyas are too violent for Brāhmaṇas." Yet, GDh (7.6) does allow the Brāhmaṇa who cannot subsist by his own occupations, to adopt those of the Kṣatriya: he also states elsewhere (7.25) that "when his life is in danger, even a Brāhmaṇa may take up arms." On this apparent contradiction, see Bühler (1879: lii).

[246] The Sanskrit construction: "...*iti cet*, ...," is extremely rare in texts such as the *Manusmṛti*. Its appropriate place is in technical literature, in prose, where the words quoted before *iti cet* contain the position of a real or imagined objector, which is subsequently refuted.

live by the activities of Kṣatriya or even those of Vaiśya; as soon as this period is over, he shall purify himself and return to his own activities."[247] Far more attention has been paid to the selectivity restriction: even though the Kṣatriya and, eventually, the Brāhmaṇa are allowed to earn a living by means of activities which the strict norm reserves for the Vaiśya, they have to avoid several aspects of this kind of occupation. With regard to agriculture Manu (10.83) immediately introduces a restriction which is valid both for the Brāhmaṇa and Kṣatriya: "If a Brāhmaṇa, or even a Kṣatriya, lives by the occupations of a Vaiśya, he shall by all means avoid agriculture that causes many injuries and that is dependent on others."[248] Baudhāyana (2.2.4.20–21) proposes a twofold restriction for the Brāhmaṇa: if he ploughs, he should do so before his first meal; he should use two uncastrated bulls whose noses have not been pierced, coaxing them frequently, but not striking them with a goad.[249]

Trade is not mentioned in Manu 10.82. It is clear, however, that the stanza intends to refer to all means of livelihood of the Vaiśya, including trade. Says Manu (10.85): "If (scil. a Brāhmaṇa) abandons the perfect fulfillment of his obligations because his means of livelihood become insufficient, he may increase his possessions by selling goods traded by Vaiśyas,[250] making however the following exceptions." The selectivity restriction is, in the case of trade, even more elaborate than for agriculture. In fact, Manu devotes most of the following nine stanzas (10.86–94) to a detailed enumeration of the various commodities which a Brāhmaṇa should not sell, even in times of distress. Most other texts on *dharma* follow the same pattern: they briefly state that the Brāhmaṇa is allowed to trade, but supplement this principle with

[247] The Sanskrit text is ambivalent. It means either that the Brāhmaṇa shall return to what is his own "path," or that he shall throw away "on the road" whatever he has gained by acting as a Kṣatriya or Vaiśya.

[248] If this interpretation is correct, MDh 10.83 excepts certain types of agriculture from the general rule 10.82. It is also possible that 10.83 was meant to emphasize the disadvantage of agriculture generally, and originally represented the view of the other school of thought referred to in 10.84: "Some say that agriculture is a good thing; yet, this means of livelihood should be despised by the good; the wooden instrument with iron point hurts the earth and the beings in the earth."

[249] Similarly, VaDh 2.32.

[250] "Goods traded by Vaiśyas" translates Sanskrit *vitpaṇya*. *Paṇya* literally means "that which ought to be traded, that which is fit to be traded." In this case: "by Vaiśyas." Similarly, ĀpDh (1.7.20.10–11) states that the Brāhmaṇa may sell *paṇyas*, but should avoid *apaṇyas* "objects which he ought not to trade in." It is interesting to notice that the name for the object of trade invariably derives from a verbal root *paṇ*, whereas the names for trader (*vaṇij*) and trade (*vāṇijya*) always derive from a root *vaṇ*. Both are obviously related, but not interchangeable.

lengthy lists of exceptions.[251] The time restriction appears most clearly in Āpastamba (1.7.21.3–4): "He should not be more eager than necessary (to act as a trader). Once he is able to resume his normal livelihood, he should abstain (from living like a Vaiśya)." Manu (10.93) stresses the sanction rather than the restriction: "If a Brāhmaṇa sells any kind of marketable goods of his own free will,[252] he will within seven days reach the status of a Vaiśya."

To be complete I must also refer to a rule by Gautama (7.73), who quotes the opinion of "some," that a Brāhmaṇa may even adopt the lifestyle of a Śūdra, if and when his life is in danger. Gautama himself (7.22) seems to reject this opinion.

Table 2

Means of livelihood	Strict norm	Pliable norm			
		Downward mobility		Upward mobility	
		+	extension	–	exception
adhyāyana yājana pratigraha	Brāhmaṇa				
śastrāstrabhṛttva	Kṣatriya	Brāhmaṇa			
vaṇik paśu kṛṣi	Vaiśya	Kṣatriya	Brāhmaṇa		Śūdra
śuśrūṣā	Śūdra	Vaiśya			

The essential features of the pliable norm are summarized in Table 2. It shows that there are basically two types of exceptions to the strict norm. First, all castes may, under certain circumstances, live by the means of livelihood of the immediately lower caste. In one case only this rule can be extended: the Brāhmaṇa may

[251] E.g., ĀpDh: principle 1.7.20.10–11, exceptions 1.7.20.11–1.7.21.2; GDh: principle 7.7, exceptions 7.821; VaDh: principle 2.24, exceptions 2.24–39; YDh: principle 3.35, exceptions 3.36–40.

[252] GDh 10.5 reads as follows in Bühler's translation (1879: 225): "Agriculture and trade (are) also (lawful for a Brāhmaṇa) provided he does not do the work himself." From this translation Bühler draws a far-reaching —modernistic— conclusion: "These rules which allow Brāhmaṇas to be gentlemen farmers and sleeping partners in mercantile or banking firms, managed by Vaiśyas, do not occur in other Smṛtis. But they agree with the practice followed at present in many parts of India...". In reality, Gautama allows the Brāhmaṇa to engage in agriculture and trade, if they are *asvayaṃkṛta* "not done of his own free a will, at his own initiative; without their being forced on him by unfavourable circumstances." Thus, GDh 10.5 expresses the same idea as MDh 10.93.

eventually, and with restrictions, live the life of a Vaiśya. Second, no caste is allowed to live by the means of livelihood of a higher caste, with one exception; the Śūdra may eventually live the life of a Vaiśya. Practically speaking, this means:

(1) the lifestyle which, under the strict norm, is that of the Kṣatriya, may also be adopted by one other caste: the Brāhmaṇa;

(2) that of the Śūdra may also be followed by one other caste: the Vaiśya;

(3) the way of life of the Vaiśya may, under different circumstances and in different ways, be adopted by all four castes;

(4) the lifestyle of the Brāhmaṇa is the only one which, under no circumstances, may be shared by any other caste.

It is tempting to speculate on the relationship between the strict norm and the pliable norm. Why first construe a strict system of occupational rules, to have it followed immediately by such a large number of exceptions and counter-exceptions that of the original system very little remains? To ask this question means to raise the problem of the nature of the ancient Indian "law books" generally. Did they actually codify the practices and customs of their times, or are they merely a kind of "natural law" describing the ideal situation irrespective of what happened in everyday life? The most natural and most logical solution seems to be, that the strict norm indeed represents the ideal situation, whereas the pliable norm stands for the "law givers" adapting their rigid principles to a reality which failed to conform to them. There may be some truth to this point of view, although I would then expect the different texts to display a wide variety of rules within the pliable norm, according to the social systems of their times and the specific areas of the subcontinent in which they were composed. In reality, the rules of the pliable norm are as uniform as those of the strict norm. Without proposing it as a solution for the entire problem, I do want to raise a point which is often overlooked by modern interpreters of the classical Indian "law books." The composers of these texts must have been conscious of the fact that their subject was *dharma* and, by definition, *dharma* is eternal and unchangeable. Besides, *dharma* is perfect and all-inclusive. As a result, the various Dharmasūtras and Dharmaśāstras, while working with identical basic principles, differ in their treatments of caste and occupation only in so far as some are more successful in presenting a perfect and all-inclusive system, others less. I hope to have shown, from such examples as the terminology of the six obligations of the Brāhmaṇa, that the most perfect, harmonious, and complete system is that of the *Manusmṛti.* Manu's ability to arrange his subjects harmoniously and exhaustively, not his originality, accounts for its being considered by the tradition as the foremost among the texts on *dharma.*

10

Megasthenes on Indian Lawbooks

The Greek author Strabo (quoted by Timmer 1930, from Strabo XV 1.53) has preserved a statement of Megasthenes, the Greek ambassador to Candragupta Maurya, according to which theft was an extremely rare phenomenon in the India which he visited.

And the quotation continues: "..., *agraphois kai tauta nomois chrōmenois oude gar grammata eidenai autous, all aēo mnēmēs ekasta dioikeisthai.*"

The latest editor of the fragments of Megasthenes' *Indica*, B.C.J. Timmer, thereby following her predecessors, translates as follows: "..., and this notwithstanding the fact that they use unwritten laws. For they do not know the script, but they administer everything from memory" (1930: 240–41).

Many a page has been written to discuss the possible date of the introduction of writing in India, but at least it seems to be well established now that writing *was* known in India by the time when Megasthenes lived at the court of Candragupta Maurya.

Consequently, we fully agree with Timmer when she argues that Megasthenes' statement on this point must be false: "No doubt, Megasthenes' opinion that the Indians did not know writing was a misunderstanding" (245).

However, Timmer pleads extenuating circumstances in favor of Megasthenes' apparent inconsistency. Indeed, she says, it was a misunderstanding "based upon the fact that Megasthenes *rightly observed* that the laws were unwritten and that oral tradition played such an important part in India" (245). According to Timmer, "the laws were indeed mainly unwritten; it was not customary with the Indians to reduce their sacred books (and the Dharmaśāstras belong to them) to writing" (245).

Moreover, in a footnote to the latter sentence reference is made to Winternitz (1908: 1.28ff.). In this paragraph of the great history of Sanskrit literature, after a lengthy discussion as to when writing began to be used in India for literary purposes, Winternitz concludes as follows: "After all this it is, then, probable that in ancient times there had been no written books in India" (32).

Winternitz has chosen his words extremely cautiously: he does not unhesitatingly maintain that in ancient times (that means: not even in the time of Patañjali, 2nd century bc) writing was definitely not used for literary purposes; he only takes into consideration the probability that for a number of reasons (which have been adduced at 32–33), for a long time the Brāhmī-script, though known and used for other purposes, was not made use of to preserve the sacred texts.

This cautiousness is not without reason. Actually, the whole theory is based on a mere *argumentum ex silentio*. Not a single ancient text, not even the *Mahābhāṣya* in the 2nd century BC, refers to their having been written down in manuscripts. This *argumentum ex silentio* has been interpreted in two different ways:

> (1) Some say, that writing *was* used for literary purposes from an early date, but written books were of very little importance and they had very little authority as compared with oral tradition.
>
> (2) Others pretend that, if writing had been used for literary purposes, it would be impossible not to find even a single reference to such use in the texts.

In other words: the absence of evidence or at least the negative evidence of the *argumentum ex silentio* has, thus, led to two completely opposite conclusions. It is perfectly sound that, in the absence of any positive evidence, both these possibilities should be given an equal chance. And it is even equally sound, as Winternitz does, to feel oneself more attracted to either of them on the basis of an abstract, but objective, argumentation.

To the student of Megasthenes' text, however, it might be tempting to actually decide in favor of the second alternative; and this also seems to have been the case with Timmer, who interprets Megasthenes' statement about the absence of written laws as a positive argument in favor of Winternitz's second hypothesis. It is, therefore, the purpose of the present article to warn against using the words of the Greek author as a decisive piece of evidence for the hypothesis that the Indians did not know written laws at least by the end of the 4th century BC.

It is not unlikely at all that an ambassador living at the court of the Maurya king had often been in a position to attend a trial presided over by the king himself or by his appointed judges. On such occasions he may well have been impressed by the fact that these judges did not permanently have written codes at hand for easy reference; on the contrary, they continually quoted the law from memory without any reference to a written text.

Supposing this had been the case, was it, therefore, a sufficient reason to immediately come to the conclusion, that all written codes of law and writing in general were simply non-existent? Shall we, then, presume that Megasthenes never witnessed any other striking instance of the extraordinary capacity of the Indian mind when it comes to knowing whole books by heart without any help of a written text? Be it sufficient to say that, in that case, a foreign visitor to India in this very 20th century might equally well be led to the same conclusion!

However, the truth is that there is no need at all to accept that the Greek ambassador drew such a rash and illogical conclusion. For his statement becomes far less rash and less illogical, if we only take the trouble to investigate the real source of the wording of the Greek text. Imagine Megasthenes on some occasion or other (e.g., *after* having attended a trial as described above) questioning a judge in Pāṭaliputra about the origin of the Indian laws, and about the place where these laws were being preserved. To such a question the Indian judge undoubtedly replied: *smṛtau*, or perhaps *smaraṇe*. Of course, the interpreter or Megasthenes himself must have been perfectly familiar with the usual meaning of the word *smṛtiḥ* or *smaraṇam*: "memory." When, thus, the Indian judge himself was understood to say that all his laws had to be preserved *en mnēmē*, i.e., that all law was to be administered "according to memory": *apo mnēmēs dioikeisthai* to the Greek mind this ascertainment necessarily involved that no written lawbooks were available at all.

As Timmer said, "Megasthenes' opinion that the Indians did not know writing was a misunderstanding." But —and that is where we have to differ from Timmer— this misunderstanding was *not* based on the fact that Megasthenes "rightly observed" that the laws were unwritten. It only proves that Megasthenes has never *seen* an actual lawbook, but does *not* prove anything as to whether written lawbooks existed or not.

In reality, Megasthenes' so-called correct observation that the laws were unwritten is based on still another misunderstanding, the origin of which is again perfectly well traceable, in so far as it was the result of sheer coincidence. As we saw, it is but natural that a foreigner like Megasthenes or even a non-educated Indian interpreter (who may have been some merchant) should have understood the expression of the *dharmaśāstrī* that the laws were preserved "*smṛtau*" in its usual sense of "in memory," and that he accordingly rendered it as *ev uvnun*.[253] On the other hand, for the *dharmaśāstrī* himself (as for anybody who is acquainted with the Indian sacred lore) the technical term *smṛtiḥ* is so common that he will not even have thought it necessary to further elucidate this particular meaning of the word, the more because the Greek ambassador too seemed to be able to readily have at hand a corresponding term in his own language.

This misunderstanding is a sheer coincidence indeed. For, if the question as to where the sacred prescriptions were preserved had by chance not been put with reference to the "laws" but, e.g., to the Vedas, though equally much unwritten and remembered, we may be sure that the Indian informant's reply would have been different. In that case he would certainly not have answered *smṛtau* but *śrutau*, a term for which it would have been much more difficult to find a common and easily intelligible Greek equivalent. Megasthenes might, then, have put some further questions on the subject, and he consequently might have been made to understand the correct meaning of the technical terms *śrutiḥ* and *smṛtiḥ*. He might even have learned something definite about the existence or non-existence of written texts of the *śrutiḥ* and *smṛtiḥ*, and, in that case only, his statement might have turned out to be a unique and reliable piece of evidence on a problem which, as it is, has not through Megasthenes' words been carried any farther than the undecided alternative posed by Winternitz.

[253] This is an excellent example of Timmer's most pertinent note according to which the use of interpreters (Strabo mentions a case where no less than three were necessary) always creates the possibility of misunderstandings of any kind: "Even the intervention of a single interpreter may have been the source of many errors. And also in the case where a conversation could be held without an interpreter, e.g. in Persian, there would still have remained the difficulty that neither party at the same time understood the Indian language and Greek, with the result that the terms used may have lost their original meaning in the intermediary language —an element which we should well consider, when the words used by Megasthenes do not cover the Indian concepts" (Timmer 1930: 45–6)!

11

The "Ambassador" in Ancient India

Introduction

In Brussels the author of the present paper often visits a building, at the gate of which, in beautiful Devanāgarī characters, the words "Bhāratīya Dūtavāsa" have been inscribed on a copperplate. It is, literally translated, the "Residence of the Indian *Dūta*," i.e., the "Ambassador," as can be derived from the English words added below: "Embassy of India." The well-known fact that the word *dūta* has been selected as the modern Hindi equivalent for the English *Ambassador* needs no further comment, but, since the word ultimately belongs to Sanskrit vocabulary, it may be asked whether the *dūta* in ancient India was in any way the forerunner of the present-day Indian ambassador.

Of course, diplomacy and the diplomatic agents, one of whom is the present Ambassador for India in Belgium, are quite modern institutions. "...The word [sc. diplomacy] was first used in England as late as 1796 by Burke. The need for such a term was, indeed, only then beginning to be felt; for, though in a sense as old as history, it was only in quite modern times, even in Europe, that diplomacy developed into a uniform system, based upon generally recognized rules and directed by a diplomatic hierarchy having a fixed international status" (*Encyclopedia Britannica* 7, 1947: 404). Nevertheless, in the following pages a brief attempt will be made to collect and to interpret a number of references to the ancient *dūta*, in order to show that the practice of the king's sending an envoy to another monarch was definitely not unknown in ancient times.

Were there Permanent Embassies in Ancient India?

The first point to be raised is the question whether the office of the ancient Indian *dūta* was a permanent one or not. In other words: did the ancient Indian *dūta* already resemble his modern namesake in that he was accredited to another ruler's court for a long time continuously?

In recent works on the subject there seems to be a tendency to reject the permanent character of the *dūta*'s services. Some of the arguments which have led to this conclusion may be summed up as follows:

> 1. "The system of accrediting ambassadors permanently from one court to another is *too modern* to have existed in those ages" (Viswanatha 1925: 64).
> 2. "Permanent embassies were, it would appear,...probably *unnecessary* even in the time of Kauṭilya" (ibid.: 65). Indeed, "as Megasthenes says, there was the second department of Chandragupta's municipal administration which looked after the foreigners. This was apparently to discharge the duties of a special diplomatic office" (ibid.: 65, n. 1. On the *astunomoi*, cf. infra).
> 3. "It is doubtful whether there were permanent resident embassies in vogue in ancient times," since "the Sanskrit word for ambassador, *dūta*, literally means a *messenger* and suggests that he visited the foreign court for a particular purpose or mission" (Altekar 1955: 295).

The reader will at once notice that all these statements —and many others of a similar nature— are actually based upon no textual or any positive evidence whatsoever. The main historic instance where we might expect at least to find some direct evidence on this point is that of Megasthenes. As a matter of fact, Megasthenes' example may seem an interesting one for a twofold reason: not only was he an actual envoy sent to an Indian court by a non-Indian ruler, but he also compiled a literary work on his mission to India. Unfortunately, even there the Greek keywords according to which "he often came to Sandracottus" are such that they have been taken to refer to a permanent embassy (Schwanbeck) and to a non-permanent embassy (Timmer) as well (for the whole problem, see Timmer 1930: 6–7). It must be said that, on reading the Greek text, we personally would rather feel inclined towards the latter interpretation.

In this respect it definitely is a most remarkable —though somewhat unfortunate— coincidence that exactly the same ambiguity found in the Greek text also occurs in a passage from Kauṭilya's *Arthaśāstra*. Just as the Greek words: "he *often* came to Sandracottus," may refer either to a number of separate missions from one court to the other or to several audiences of an ambassador permanently residing at the foreign court, in the same way Kauṭilya's words, "in the whole circle of states (*maṇḍala*) he should post envoys *continuously*," (Shamasastry 1924: 305.1–2) leave us in doubt as to whether the envoys should reside abroad permanently or return there on various occasions.

Under these circumstances we prefer to abstain from making any general statement about the permanent or non-permanent character of the ancient Indian "embassies." Our extremely modest contribution to this problem will be reduced to pointing out below a couple of instances which seem to show that some prescriptions on the *dūta* must have been meant by their authors to apply to "ambassadors" sent off for very specific missions only.[254]

Definition of the Dūta

As soon as we try to trace a definition of the technical term *dūta* in Sanskrit literature, it becomes necessary also to introduce to the reader a second term (which happens to be found under two forms, viz. *cara* and *cāra*). Both terms, e.g., simultaneously occur in a verse from the YDh (1.328cd), where it is said that the king "should, then, see his *caras* and send off his *dūtas*":[255]

paśyec carāṃs tato dūtān preṣayen mantrisaṃgataḥ ||

The *Mitākṣarā*, while commenting upon this verse, proposes the following definitions *per oppositionem*: 1) "*Caras* are those who are sent to another ruler's country in order to find out the situation there; *they move about secretly* under the disguise of wandering mendicants, ascetics, and the like." 2) On the contrary, "*dūtas* are those who *openly* go back and forth to another king."

Elsewhere, the mutual relation of both terms has been represented somewhat differently. Thus, in the *Kāmandakīyanītisāra* (12.32) the *dūta* is considered to be a particular sub-type of the *cara*:

prakāśāś cāprakāśāś ca caras tu dvividhaḥ smṛtaḥ |
aprakāśo'yam uddiṣṭaḥ prakāśo dūta ucyate ||

In other words: there are two kinds of *caras*, the open and the secret one; of these two, the open *cara* is called *dūta*.

[254] Cf. Viswanatha 1925: 64, n. 1: "Dr. Shama Sastri informs me that the word *Ubhayavetana* denotes (an) ambassador permanently accredited to a foreign court." However permanent the services of the *ubhayavetana* may have been, he definitely ranks among spies and, therefore, falls beyond the scope of this article.

[255] The last word of the verse remains untranslated here. We will have the opportunity to come back to it below.

It is not the right place here to enter into a discussion about the ultimate origin of this distinction of open and secret spies. Let us merely remind the reader of the fact that this is not the only instance of a subdivision into *prakāśa-* and *aprakāśa-* subclasses of the same category of people. Students of Hindu law will be reminded of the subdivision of thieves into *prakāśa-* and *aprakāśa-taskaras*, etc.

Still, however closely related both officials may have been, and even though an occasional reference to the "spy" (*cara*) may be necessary, the present article will be limited to an inquiry into the nature and the functions of the "envoy" (*dūta*) only.[256] This limitation is the more justified since it creates an opportunity to counteract the prevailing tendency more and more to neglect the *dūta* in favor of the *cara*, not only in the Sanskrit texts themselves, but even more so in modern studies on the subject. The "discovery" of Kauṭilya's theory of spies so thoroughly impressed its modern students and so happily supported their thesis of ancient Indian Machiavellianism, that they started losing sight of the other type of royal messenger who was the *dūta*.

Three Kinds of Envoys

With their usual inclination towards subtle subdivisions, the ancient authors distinguish three kinds of *dūtas*. They are, according to the passage from the *Mitākṣarā* quoted above (on YDh 1.328cd): 1) one who is *nisṛṣṭārtha*, 2) one who is *saṃdiṣṭārtha*, and 3) one who is *śāsanahara*.[257]

With perfect clearness the author of the *Mitākṣarā* defines these three types of *dūtas* in the following terms:

1. A *dūta* is *nisṛṣṭārtha*, when, while expounding his king's affairs, he has authority, at his own responsibility to adapt his words to the circumstances.

[256] Notice that the close relationship of the "envoy" and the "spy," as indicated in the *Kāmandakīyanītisāra*, does not seem to be a phenomenon which is peculiar to ancient India only. According to the *Encyclopedia Britannica* ("espionage"), as quoted by P.V. Kane in modern times too, "an ambassador is often nothing more than an honourable spy acting under the protection of the law of nations" (1930–62: 3.129).

[257] In order not to run the risk of falsely identifying words which, being introduced at so different times and in so different parts of the world, may well have been meant to cover completely different connotations, we do not follow those who propose for these terms translations taken from the various grades of modern diplomatic personnel. As a matter of fact, we shall see that nothing very definite at all can be said about this threefold subdivision. To those who do not understand Sanskrit, the sense of the terms will become sufficiently clear from the discussion to follow.

2. A *dūta* is *saṃdiṣṭārtha*, when he communicates to the other king just as much as he has been told himself (sc. without making any alterations of his own accord).
3. He is *śāsanahara*, when he carries along with him a royal decree (sc. without having to say anything himself). As a matter of fact, this latter definition seems to imply that the former two types of *dūtas* did *not* carry written messages (though they may, of course, have carried some kind of written credentials).

As stated before, these definitions are perfectly clear. They quite logically correspond to the etymological sense of the terms used, so much so that we would hardly have expected them to be worded otherwise, and they apparently do not raise any problem. Still, when a commentator like Vijñāneśvara amplifies the mere term *dūta* found in the text of Yājñavalkya to such an extent as to present us with a threefold subdivision, we have a right to know the authoritative source (*śruti, smṛti*, etc.) for his doing so.

At this stage of our inquiry we shall have to turn to Kauṭilya's *Arthaśāstra*. In this remarkable text (Shamasastry 1924: 30.3–5) we are confronted with the same threefold subdivision. Just one small divergence should be noticed: the second kind of *dūta*, instead of being called *saṃdiṣṭārtha*, as was the case in the *Mitākṣarā*, is termed *parimitārtha*. Yet, as far as the etymological interpretation is concerned, this term is perfectly synonymous with the one used by Vijñāneśvara and, therefore, does not present any difficulty.

It is another problem whether the definitions of the *Mitākṣarā* too, are found in the *Arthaśāstra* as well. Let us, then, examine what has been said in the latter concerning the threefold subdivision:

1. A *dūta* is *nisṛṣṭārtha*, when he has been provided with *amātyasaṃpad*.
2. He is *parimitārtha*, when he is one quarter less.
3. He is *śāsanahara*, when he is one half less.

It needs no further comment that the whole problem is reduced here to determining the sense of the term *amātyasaṃpad*: the three kinds of *dūtas* have, indeed, been described as having full *amātyasaṃpad*, three quarters or half of it, respectively.

The term *amātyasaṃpad* not only also occurs in other places of the AŚ, but it seems to have been a real technical term for which Kauṭilya has provided us with an extensive definition (15.2–5). Since we shall have to come back to this definition below, at present we shall not go beyond stating a most remarkable fact: differently from the *Mitākṣarā*, Kauṭilya's definitions of the three kinds of *dūtas* have nothing to do whatsoever with their respective powers, but they rather refer to the qualifications required of these high officials. Actually, Kauṭilya's words can hardly be said to be *definitions* of the various *dūtas*: the term *amātyasampad* is not exclusive to the *dūta*; it has also been used not only with regard to the *amātya*, as is natural, but equally so with regard to the *sārvādhyakṣa* (68.2) and the *lekhaka* (70.19).

All this inevitably must lead us to the conclusion that the AŚ can hardly have served as the direct or unique source of the *Mitākṣarā*. Unless Vijñāneśvara could consult another source, unknown to us, we are left with the vague conjecture that he of his own accord —with good reason, as we shall see below— has interpreted three terms[258] which were perspicuous enough by themselves but which had remained undefined in the AŚ.[259]

Qualifications of the Dūta

Long lists of qualifications required in an envoy have been set out in various texts, one of them having been summarized by the general term *amātyasampad* in the AŚ. As said before —and as is clear from the word itself— the qualifications thus referred to are not peculiar to the *dūta* only; they have been required in several high officials. But there also exist other lists of qualifications specifically meant for the envoy (e.g. MBh 5.37.25, 12.86.27; Rām 2.100.25; MDh 7.63–64; MatP 215.12–13; *Kāmandakīyanītisāra* XII passim).

Anybody who has become more or less familiar with such enumerations, knows that the items contained therein are often vague and susceptible to various interpretations, most of which the commentators have not failed to discuss at great length. However interesting a detailed analysis of this matter might be, it cannot be gone into at present. It must be hoped that the following brief survey will at least give some idea of the high standards required in the envoy:

1. By birth, the envoy should belong to the *jānapada*[260] and he should be of good family.
2. Physically, he should be of good health and free from diseases; he should be strong and capable of bearing severe hardships.
3. Intellectually, the envoy should be a man of solid learning:

[258] Thereby for some reason or other replacing the word *parimitārtha* by its synonym *saṃdiṣṭārtha*.

[259] For the benefit of those interested in the composition of Kauṭilya's AŚ, it should be added that the three categories of *dūtas* introduced by Kauṭilya are a strange example of a subdivision which is introduced without having anywhere else in the AŚ been made use of.

[260] *Jānapada* is one of these much discussed terms by Kauṭilya. In this case it might merely mean that the envoy should be a citizen of the state, i.e., he should not be a foreigner.

he should be well-versed in the traditional sciences (*śāstras*), but he should also have acquired a practical knowledge of the foreign country, its language, etc. Moreover, in order to fulfill his duties successfully, it is required that he should be clever and dexterous.

4. From the moral point of view, he should have a good character, he should be truthful, honest, and not liable to be won over by others. He should be patient and steady without, on the other hand, being obstinate, arrogant, or stubborn.
5. Finally, in his dealings with others he should be kind and amiable, so as not unnecessarily to raise any inimical feelings. It goes without saying that an envoy should be eloquent in order that he might in all cases convince the foreign king. During his conversation with the latter he should prove to be an expert psychologist, inasmuch as he should be able to draw the necessary conclusions from the king's gestures, from the expressions on his face, and, in general, from all outward hints that might be indicative of his inward feelings.

The Envoy's Departure

Very little is known about the departure of the *dūta*. One single detail has been mentioned in the text of Yājñavalkya quoted above (1.328d), viz. that the king should send off (*preṣayet*) his envoys *mantrisaṃgata*.

The latter expression is at least ambiguous. It leaves us in doubt:

1. Either the king's "meeting his ministers" is to take place at the very moment of the departure of the *dūta*. If so, the *dūta* should obtain his instructions from a council composed of the king and his ministers.
2. Or the said meeting should take place some time before the departure of the envoy. In that case the envoy should not necessarily be present at the deliberations. The latter should be held only in order to prepare the message to be carried by the *dūta*.

As a matter of fact, it is the latter alternative which proves to be the more plausible one. Indeed, if we compare a reference from MDh (7.153), there the *dūtasaṃpreṣaṇa* has been enumerated among those items which the king should "think of," which he should "concentrate upon," either privately or in his council of ministers. In other words, the *dūta* himself has nothing to do at all with the meeting of the council referred to by Yājñavalkya. The latter is meant only to *prepare* his departure.

In connection with the preceding verses of Manu and Yājñavalkya, let us now turn to the initial sentence of the chapter on the *dūta* in the AŚ. It consists of two words only, both of them, however, being equally enigmatic: *uddhṛtamantro dūtapraṇidhiḥ*.

If we confined ourselves to consulting their translation by Shamasastry: "Whoever has succeeded as a councilor is an envoy" (2nd ed. 1923: 31), we might even be convinced that they cannot have any connection whatsoever with the point under consideration. J.J. Meyer's translation sounds completely different: "Ist er mit der Beratung im Reinen, dann kommt die Massnahme mit dem Gesandten" (Meyer 1925: 34.19–20). Not only does this make a much better sense, but in our opinion it also comes much closer to the actual sense of the Sanskrit text.

For a better understanding of the term *uddhṛtamantra*, it might not be without interest first of all to draw attention to the fact that this compound evidently refers to the same act already indicated by the above mentioned *mantra-saṃgata* in the YDh: the object of the envoy's missions should, indeed, be discussed beforehand in a council of ministers. Furthermore, the root *uddhṛ* in this connection should not cause any difficulties to those acquainted with the Sanskrit literature on legal procedure. Is it not a common expression that lawsuits too should be *uddhṛta* by the king in accordance with the *dharma* (cf. NS, *Mātṛkā* 1.32)? As has been rightly interpreted by one of the commentators, this means that the case should "be decided accurately" [cf. *Vyavahāracintāmaṇi*, ed. Rocher, no. 13 + note (171)].

We would, then, understand the whole sentence as follows: the king should secretly[261] communicate his orders to the envoy and send him off after the resolution (*mantra*) has been duly clarified (sc. in his council of ministers).

Incidentally, if it is true that a council should thus be held before every envoy's departure, this is one of the reasons that make us infer that the authors were thinking not so much of a permanent but rather of a specific "embassy."

Arrival at the Foreign Court

Again, at least something can be said about the *dūta's* audiences with the foreign king. The latter, when receiving the envoy, should, indeed, be surrounded by his council of ministers.

Thus, Kauṭilya: *mantripariṣadā sāmantadūtaṁ...gacchet*, "he (the king) should approach the envoy of the neighbouring king, together with his assembly of ministers" (45.2–3).

The reader will notice that this statement occurs in the chapter entitled *ātmarakṣitaka*, i.e., on the personal safety of the king.

[261] The idea of secrecy so much inheres in the root *pra-ni-dhā* (cf. Meyer 1925: 380.25–26), that sometimes *praṇidhi* has become a synonym for "spy" itself (e.g., MDh 7.153).

Still, it is the safety *of the deliberations* which has been meant in the first place, for, even if it was to be feared that the envoy might try to kill the king, the ministers would not in any case be adequate protection against such physical violence.

The presence of the king's ministers was even considered important enough not to be omitted in the description of the arrival of Rāma's envoy Aṅgada at the court of Rāvaṇa: there too, the latter heard the envoy's message *sāmātya*, "in the presence of his ministers" (Rām 6.41.76).

One more thought might well be given consideration in this matter. Megasthenes refers to a class of Indian officers called *astunomoi*, divided into six bodies of five. "…Those of the second (body) attend to the entertainment of foreigners. To these they assign lodgings, and they keep watch over their mode of life by means of those persons whom they give to them for assistants. They escort them on the way when they leave the country, or, in the event of their dying, forward their property to their relatives. They take care of them when they are sick, and, if thy die, bury them" (Smith 1905: 200).

Agreed that we are completely ignorant as to the duties of the *astunomos* with regard to the very particular type of foreigner that is the envoy, still it is at least not impossible that he actually was concerned with the audiences of the envoy too. If it is correct that there existed a striking similarity[262] between the duties of the Indian *astunomos* as described above and the Greek officer called *proxenos*,[263] it might not be without interest to learn about the *proxenos* that "it was (also) his duty to present to the authorities and public assembly of his native city the envoys who were sent from time to time from the State which had made him their *proxenos*, and to promote the objects of such missions by his personal influence with his fellow-citizens" (Smith 1905: 201, after Newton: 1883).

The Envoy's Prerogatives

There can be little doubt that the nature of the messages carried by the *dūta* was such as not always to please the king to whom they were delivered. If the above mentioned story of Aṅgada's message to Rāvaṇa (Rām 6.41.77–81) is typical example of the usual envoy's language, we should not be surprised that the *dūta's* life sometimes was in real danger.

[262] Or even more so if it is true that the Indian *astunomos* is the only Indian officer showing traces of Hellenistic influence (cf. Smith 1905: 200).

[263] The *proxenos* was a citizen living in his native town or state but at the same time acting as an officer for the ruler of a foreign town or state.

In order to secure the personal safety of the *dūta*, the following prescription has been laid down:

> Never should the king in any calamity whatsoever kill an envoy; the killer of an envoy, together with his companions, goes to hell. If the king, who desires to follow the duties of the Kṣatriyas, kills an envoy who reports what he has been told to, his ancestors are burdened with the sin for killing an embryo. (MBh 12.86.25–26)

However sacred the person of the envoy may, thus, have been, it seems to have been thought wise in due time to remind the displeased king of this privilege. How else can we account for the following sentence found in the AŚ:

> To him (i.e. to the king who is displeased with his message) he should say: "Envoys actually are their kings' mouthpieces, yours and the others' as well. Therefore, if they speak as they have been told, notwithstanding the fact that weapons have been raised against them, even the lowest among them should not be killed. How much less, then, the *Brāhmaṇa*! Theirs are the words of somebody else. Such are the envoys' duties." (30.15–17)

In this connection, attention should be drawn to another passage from Kauṭilya (31.9), where we are informed as to what the envoy should do:

> *kāryasyāsiddhāv uparudhyamānas.*

In other words, to quote Shamasastry: "If he has not succeeded in his mission," the envoy should be "detained."[264]

Whatever slight variations there may have been in the interpretations of the term *uparudhyamāna*, as proposed by the various translators and commentators, it seems, at least, to be unanimously accepted that the envoy could be subjected to some restrictions with regard to his right to free movement, whether it be actual detention or not.

However, while reading the chapter on the *dūta* in the light of this interpretation, some doubts have occurred to us with regard to the correctness of the latter.

First of all, when being *uparudhyamāna*, the envoy should put to himself a number of questions regarding the possible origin of the *uparodha* which he has been subjected to. And after this inquiry, he is left with the choice between at least two alternatives:

> *vased apasared vā.*

[264] Shamasastry 1923: 33. Similarly, Meyer: "Gluckt seine Sendung nicht und wird er (vom fremden Herrscher) zuruckgehalten..." (37.6–7).

Unless we are seriously mistaken, this must mean: "either he should stay, or he should retreat." Would it, then, be thinkable that the person who is to make this choice, is one under detention or, at least, under custody of some kind or other?

The doubt raised by this apparent inconsistency in the text has led us towards investigating the sense of the various forms of the root *uparudh* occurring in Kauṭilya. Without being able here to set out in detail the results of this investigation, let it be said at once, that the idea of "hindrance" naturally being present everywhere, there is no reason whatsoever why we necessarily should interpret the term as implying an actual "detention."

Finally, though the existing translations "If he has not succeeded in his mission," etc., seem to have largely contributed towards scholars' definitely accepting the reading *kāryasyāsiddhau*, i.e., *kāryasya asiddhau*, it would be wrong to overlook the fact that another reading too, has been found, viz. *kāryasya siddhau*. In view of the quite common —and understandable— scribes' errors of the type *kāryasyāsiddhau-kāryasya siddhau*, it is not even possible *a priori* to decide in favor of either of them (Trivandrum Sanskrit Series, No. 79: 81.1).

Still, there are at least two arguments which make us feel rather sympathetic towards the somewhat neglected reading *kāryasya siddhau*:

1. The first argument is taken from the doctrine of textual criticism. Indeed, there can be no doubt that in texts of this kind the reading which we would prefer is the *lectio difficilior*.[265] In other words: we can much more easily imagine a less intelligent or a less attentive scribe to change *kāryāsya siddhau* into the much more common *kāryasyāsiddhau*, than *vice versa*.

2. The second argument directly touches upon the very sense of the expression. If the text reads *kāryasya asiddhau*, the situation of *uparodha* is bound to be the result of this failure; the inconsistency caused by such interpretation has been pointed out above. On the contrary, when we consider the reading *kāryasya siddhau* as the original one, the text quite naturally means: "when he is hindered in the fulfillment of his undertaking," first he should try to detect the reason behind the hindrance and, then, he should decide either to stay on or to retreat.

[265] Those who may not be familiar with this purely philological principle should be referred to Katre 1954: 72.

Let it, however, be said that, in the present state of our knowledge, we do not want to impose this interpretation as final. It is nothing but another humble attempt to remove one of the numerous stumbling blocks in the AŚ.

If we, thus, have thought it necessary to reject the generally accepted interpretation according to which this passage from Kauṭilya refers to the *dūta*'s imprisonment, we do not, thereby, mean to say that the envoy was in all cases free from any punishment whatsoever. As a matter of fact, we do possess positive evidence to the contrary. In a passage from the *Rāmāyaṇa* (5.52.13cd–15), it has been said that the *dūta* should under no circumstances be *killed* (*vadha*), but other punishments are not at all excluded. The four examples which have been explicitly mentioned as such are: mutilation of the body, whipping, shaving the head, and branding.

Moreover, even the said prohibition to kill an envoy cannot have been applied as universally as it might appear from the above *Rāmāyaṇa* passage. Of course, elsewhere the author of the *Rāmāyaṇa* again reiterates the same rule (6.20.18), but at the same time he adds the following exception:

> But the envoy who conceals his king's thought to express his own ideas instead, he being an envoy saying-things-he-ought-not-to-say, deserves to be killed.

And the same exception also occurs in the *Mahābhārata* (5.70.7cd).

Kauṭilya himself refers to a different case where the envoy might also be subjected to some kind of punishment: when he has delivered an unpleasant message, the envoy, though officially not yet dismissed, would do better to retreat, and he should do so for fear of *bandha* or *vadha*, i.e. —probably— detention or death. If he does not retreat, he might be detained (31.18–19).

The Envoy's Activities

The task of the envoy has been summed up in one single compound as follows:

> *dūte saṃdhiviparyayau* [sc. *āyattau*] (MDh 7.65d)

i.e., according to Bühler's translation: "peace and its opposite (war) depend on the ambassador."

The same idea has, then, been further developed in the next *śloka*:

> For the ambassador alone makes (kings') allies and separates al-

> lies; the ambassador transacts that business by which (kings) are disunited or not. (MDh 7.66)

Once again, it seems to us as if the preceding *śloka*s must have been written with a view to an envoy who was sent to another king's court whenever a question of peace or war was to be dealt with, i.e., an envoy who was sent for a very specific purpose.

It goes without saying that the first duty to be fulfilled by the envoy while at the foreign king's court was the delivery of his message. Again and again we have been told that the envoy should do so *yathokta*, i.e., "as he has been told himself." However, if it is true that "peace or its opposite depended on the ambassador," it must be that his speaking *yathokta* cannot have been taken too strictly. Not only must we accept that some envoys at least were given authority to speak as they themselves thought fit under the circumstances —thereby merely observing some general directives—, but we now also understand why commentators like Vijñāneśvara considered themselves authorized to propose a definition for the *nisṛṣṭārtha* type of envoy without there being any apparent source for it in the *smṛti*.

So much for the delivery of his own message. But the king expects much more from his envoy: he expects him to bring back a lot of useful information which may serve as guidance for his own future policy. While at the foreign court itself,

> With respect to the affairs let the (ambassador) explore the expression of the countenance, the gestures and actions of the (foreign king) through the gestures and actions of his confidential (advisers), and (discover) his designs among his servants.[266]

A very similar rule is found in the AŚ (30.12–14). It says that, whenever the envoy notices the following signs on the part of the other king, he may infer him to be loyal: (1) kindness in his speech, on his face, and in his eyes, (2) hospitable reception of the envoy's words, (3) inquiry about pleasant things, (4) participation in referring to (his own king's?) virtues, (5) allowing him a seat near the throne, (6) respectful treatment, (7) calling to mind pleasant items and (8) showing confidence. If he detects the opposite signs, he must know the king to be displeased. It is in the latter case that the envoy should, for safety's sake, stress the above mentioned fact that his words are not his but his master's!

After all this, our picture of the envoy's duties would still be incomplete, if we failed to mention the fact that at the same time

[266] Thus Bühler's translation of MDh 7.67. Some slightly different interpretations may be compared to Bühler's footnote *ad hoc*.

the *dūta* should avail himself of the opportunity of his presence in foreign territory to keep an open eye on a number of other things. The few sentences of Kauṭilya treating this aspect of the envoy's activities (30.9–10, and 31.2–7) present a number of problems which we propose to deal with on another occasion. In general it can be said that he should examine the sites in view of a possible future war, the country's resources, etc., and that he should not hesitate at all to appeal to spies or to any rapscallion that could be useful to this end.

On the contrary, he should be extremely cautious not to divulge any information of that kind relating to his own country. In order not to run such risks, he is strongly advised to keep aloof of "wine and women," since both of these are likely to make his tongue looser than it should be (31.7–9 and 31.1–2).

Conclusion

The preceding notes on the ancient *dūta* certainly have not exhausted the subject. However, it is hoped that they will have sufficed to show that in ancient India too, there existed some kind of a diplomatic agent, who sometimes has been represented to be a modern invention only. More generally speaking, we may, thus, subscribe to the conclusion already drawn by V. Ramaswami: "Ever since the Aryans began to organize their common life in political units they felt the need of some system of rules to regulate their intercommunity relations" (Ramaswami 1948: 43). We even fully agree with the same learned author's words that "international law is not a monopoly of Europe." Unfortunately, we have to disagree when it comes to his conclusion that "roots of international law" —i.e., international law as we know it today— "are to be traced far back in India's past." Whatever be said about it, modern international law *is* a creation of modern history, and its foundations happen to have been laid mainly in Europe; it does not go back to ancient India, as little as it would go back to ancient Greece or Rome.

No doubt, we do understand how Indian scholars have, for sentimental reasons, been led to statements of this kind at a time when a certain class of Europeans came over to their country to impress them with the absurd idea of European superiority in all fields. It was but natural that they felt injured and that they reacted by trying to show that, in reality, it was India that was in many respects superior to the invaders' homeland. But, at present, things have changed. Independent India is no longer subjected to any European domination. The idea of one people being superior to another is now dead. But inasmuch as it is no longer tolerable for European scholars to work from any such baseless racial or national prejudices, there is no longer room on the Indian side to compensate this tendency by letting sentiment get the better of scientific objectivity. Let all of us, on equal terms and as true friends, cooperate towards reaching scientific truth which, as it is, is difficult enough to attain.

Rather unexpectedly —though perhaps not quite inappropriately— we have been induced to conclude this paper on ancient Indian international political relations by a note on present-day international scientific understanding.

12

The Status of Minors according to Classical Hindu Law

Defintion of Minority

The text which has been used most often to define minority in classical Hindu law is a passage from the *Nāradasmṛti* (1.35), which Jolly translates as follows:

> A child is comparable to an embryo up to the eighth year. A youth, who has not yet reached the age of sixteen, is called Pogaṇḍa.

According to the generally accepted interpretation of this passage, minority ends at the time when the young man reaches his sixteenth year, and the Sanskrit technical term for a minor is *pogaṇḍa* (e.g., Kane 1933: 297: "'*pogaṇḍa*' means a minor who has not attained the 16th year"). Although this interpretation is basically acceptable, a number of remarks are necessary to avoid possible misunderstandings.

Remark 1.

The first remark concerns the accuracy of Jolly's translation. Although its Sanskrit original does not seem to present any major difficulties, it shares at least one feature with most other Sanskrit texts: they lend themselves to translations into modern Western languages, which, without being positively incorrect, do not accurately convey the meaning of the Sanskrit original. Jolly's interpretation of NS 1.35 is a fair example of this kind of translation. In reality Nārada says:

> Up to the age of eight years a child (*śiśu*) is similar to an embryo; up to the age of sixteen, he is a boy (*bāla*), and is also called *pogaṇḍa*.

Even this translation needs to be interpreted to the reader who has no access to the Sanskrit text. Nārada states, first, that until he is eight years old, a *śiśu* has no more rights or duties than he had as an unborn embryo. Between the ages of eight and sixteen, however, he is a *bāla*. *Bāla*, as an adjective, means: "young, childish," and, as a noun: "child, boy." Yet, to the Indian reader *bāla* at the same time suggests the idea of "strong, capable." The latter half of the text, therefore, means: between the ages of eight and sixteen the child has strength and capability, and, yet, he is also called *pogaṇḍa*. The etymology of this term is unknown; in other contexts it seems to indicate: "not full-grown," perhaps "missing a limb" (see Mayrhofer 1963: 2.344).

Remark 2.

The second remark concerns the status of the young man after he reaches the age of sixteen. Kātyāyana (844cd) refers to this situation as follows, according to Kane's translation:

> ...and in the case of men they attain understanding of affairs at the sixteenth year.

That means, that at the age of sixteen the young man becomes *vyavahārin*, literally: "capable of valid activities or business." The more common term is *vyavahārajña* "knowing transactions, competent to transact valid business." There is no doubt that the transition from being *avyavahārajña* "not knowing transactions" to *vyavahārajña* is the principal criterion which in Hindu law separates minority from majority. The same opposition is sometimes also expressed by means of two related terms: *prāptavyavahāra* "one who has reached (the right age to conduct) transactions," as against *aprāptavyavahāra* for him "who has not reached" that age.[267]

In the verse which follows the one quoted earlier Nārada (1.36) adds an interesting detail:

> Afterwards he is no longer a minor and independent, in case his parents are dead. While they are alive he can never acquire independence, even though he may have reached a mature age. (Tr. Jolly)

"He is no longer a minor" is Jolly's free translation of *vyavahārajña*. The text shows that, according to Nārada, majority implies independence only if the parents are dead. As long as the

[267] In other circumstances, the term *aprāptavyavahāra* can have a different meaning. YDh 2.243, for example, uses it to refer to a person involved in a lawsuit "who has not reached (the end of) the proceedings."

parents are alive, the major son remains dependent on them, irrespective of his age.

Remark 3.

A few words must be added here in connection with the majority of women. All the texts quoted so far use masculine nouns to refer to minors and majors. This may or may not be accidental. We have at least one source in which women are said to become *prāptavyavahārā* at a different age than men. Thus, Kauṭilya (3.3.1), as translated by Kangle:

> A woman twelve years of age attains majority, a man when sixteen years of age.

Whereas men who become *prāptavyavahāra* are at least independent in case their parents are dead, the Hindu law texts make it clear that women cannot become independent under any circumstances. Viṣṇu (25.13) lists among the duties of a woman:

> To remain subject, in her infancy, to her father; in her youth, to her husband; and in her old age, to her sons. (Tr. Jolly)

Similarly, Manu (9.3):

> Her father protects (her) in childhood, her husband protects (her) in youth, and her sons protect (her) in old age; a woman is never fit for independence. (Tr. Bühler; similarly MDh 5.147–48)

The fact that the case of women is, thus, totally different from that of men, leads me to suggest that the terms *vyavahārajña* and *prāptavyavahāra* also refer to basically different situations, when used for the two sexes. A stanza by Manu (9.88) says:

> To a distinguished, handsome suitor (of) equal (caste) should (a father) give his daughter in accordance with the prescribed rule, though she have not attained (the proper age). (Tr. Bühler)

The expression used for "though she have not attained" is *aprāptā*. It obviously refers to the same period of the girl's life which Gautama (18.21) has in mind:

> A girl should be given in marriage before (she attains the age of) puberty. (Tr. Bühler)

This text literally says: "before (the beginning of) menstruation." Kauṭilya (4.12.1, 3) refers to the same dividing line in a woman's life, in another context, and with different but related adjectives: *aprāptaphalā* "one who has not reached (the proper age to have) offspring," and *prāptaphalā* for the girl who has reached that age. Kangle translates:

> For one violating a maiden of the same varṇa who has not yet attained puberty,...Of one violating a maiden who has reached puberty,....

In view of all this evidence, I suggest that, in the case of women, the expression *prāptavyavahārā* at the age of twelve refers to their "having reached the proper age for marriage and childbearing."

Remark 4.

All ancient texts unanimously mention the age of sixteen as the time at which a man reaches majority. However, the later commentators could not help noticing and discussing a possible ambiguity. Nārada (1.35) says that a child is a *bāla* "up to his sixteenth year," and Kātyāyana (844) states that a man becomes a *vyavahārin* "in his sixteenth year." The question is: does majority start at the beginning or at the end of the sixteenth year? Since I cannot treat the commentaries exhaustively elsewhere in this article, I shall restrict myself with regard to this question, and merely state that both theories have found their advocates. It is particularly interesting to notice, that the divided opinions of the medieval commentators are reflected in the decisions of the Anglo-Hindu law courts: it was held in Bengal that minority ends at the end of the fifteenth year, whereas the Bombay and Madras courts were generally in favor of the completion of one's sixteenth year (HDhS 3.574, n. 1081 a).

Remark 5.

Sanskrit has also developed a term to refer to those who have become too old to transact business. Parallel to *aprāptavyavahāra* for those who have not yet reached the proper age, *atītavyavahāra* indicates those "who have gone beyond" the proper age to conduct business. For instance, after having described how the relatives should protect minors in case of inheritance, Baudhāyana (2.2.3.37) continues:

> Granting food, clothes, (and shelter), they shall support those who are incapable of transacting legal business (tr. Bühler),

with the understanding that Bühler's "those who are incapable" really means: "those who are no longer capable."[268]

[268] Bühler's erroneous translation is due to the fact that he wrongly considers those enumerated in the following rule (2.2.3.38) as a further specification of *atītavyavahāra* in 2.2.3.37. In reality, Baudhāyana prescribes food and shelter for (1) those who are *atītavyavahāra*, and (2) those who are blind, etc.

The Minor's Inability to Make Valid Contracts

Since the minor is *avyavahārajña* or *aprāptavyavahāra*, it follows that any *vyavahāra* "business, contract" made by him is invalid. This principle has been expressed in many texts. Kauṭilya (3.1.12) associates transactions made by an *aprāptavyavahāra* with those made by an *atītavyavahāra*:

> (Transactions) other than these shall not succeed, also those concluded by ... a minor or a person grown too old for doing business. (Tr. Kangle)

According to Nārada (1.39) there is no difference between transactions concluded by a *bāla*, and those by any other kind of dependent person:

> If a boy or one who possesses no independence transacts anything, it is declared an invalid transaction by persons acquainted with the law. (Tr. Jolly)

This rule is important, for it shows that the major but yet dependent son has no more right to engage in a transaction than the minor. In fact, after having declared invalid all transactions by wives and slaves, Nārada (1.30) continues:

> If a son has contracted any business without authorization from his father, it is also declared an invalid transaction. A slave and a son are equal in that respect. (Tr. Jolly)

Manu (8.163) also declares that a transaction by a *bāla* "does not succeed." His text is interesting, because the long enumeration of those who are unable to make contracts suggests very clearly to which other categories of persons the *bāla* is assimilated:

> A contract made by a person intoxicated, or insane, or grievously disordered (by disease and so forth), or wholly dependent, by an infant or very old man, or by an unauthorized (party) is invalid. (Tr. Bühler)

Yājñavalkya (2.32) presents a very similar enumeration.

Since a minor cannot make valid contracts generally, he is *a fortiori* not qualified to make any contract in particular. The *bāla* is, therefore, listed as an unauthorized party to a number of specific contracts. For instance, according to Kauṭilya (3.11.16):

> The suretyship of a minor is void in law. (Tr. Kangle)

The fact that the minor son is not liable to pay his deceased father's debts will be treated later in this article.

Criminal Liability of the Minor

A number of texts contain references to the *bāla* in their discussions on the concept of guilt, and its repercussions on penance and punishment. Haradatta's commentary on Gautama (2.6), and Vijñāneśvara's commentary on Yājñavalkya (3.243) present the following stanza, which the latter attributes to Angiras:

> One more than eighty years old, and a child less than sixteen years of age deserve only a half penance, and so do women, and sick persons.

Vijñāneśvara adds other similar quotations, one by Sumantu:

> Before the age of twelve and after the age of eighty, penance is reduced to one half for men, to one quarter for women,

and one by Viṣṇu:

> One half of the regular penance should be imposed on women, elderly people, and the sick, one quarter on children; this rule applies to all types of sins.

Both commentators then continue with the following quotation, attributed to Śaṅkha in Vijñāneśvara's text:

> For one between the ages of five and eleven penance shall be done by his teacher, father, brother, or friend. For one younger than that there is neither crime nor sin; he shall, therefore, neither be punished by the king, nor shall he undergo penance.

This principle of reduced guilt, and, hence, reduced liability and punishment for minors has been applied in several specific circumstances. According to Kauṭilya (4.13.25–26) the minor should not be punished for causing an accident:

> When the driver is a minor, the owner if in the carriage is to be fined [literally: punished]...if the owner is not there, the person in the carriage or the driver if he has attained majority. The king shall confiscate a carriage driven by a minor or one without a man it. (Tr. Kangle)

Manu (9.282–83) prescribes a reduced punishment for a minor who pollutes the highway:

> But he who, except in a case of extreme necessity, drops filth on the king's high-road, shall pay two kārsāpaṇas and immediately remove (that) filth. But a person in urgent necessity, an aged man,

> a pregnant woman, or a child, shall be reprimanded and clean the (place); that is the settled rule. (Tr. Bühler)

Another text by Manu (9.230) reserves a special type of punishment for *bālas*:

> On women, infants, men of disordered mind, the poor and the sick, the king shall inflict punishment with a whip, a cane, or a rope and the like. (Tr. Bühler)

The *raison d'être* of this rule is not clear. It may be another application of the principle of reduced guilt, but it is also possible that it provides the king with a substitute for a fine, which he is not allowed to charge against the property of a minor. The latter interpretation imposes itself, if the rule is supposed to be read in conjunction with the immediately preceding one (9.229):

> But a Kṣatriya, a Vaiśya, and a Śūdra who are unable to pay a fine, shall discharge the debt by labour; a Brāhmaṇa shall pay by installments. (Tr. Bühler)

Unfortunately, the problem of context in this kind of text can no longer be solved. The Indian commentators invariably accept the solution which fits their own purpose. The historian of Hindu law has to confine himself to mentioning both alternatives.

Protection of the Minor's Person

There are a few texts which refer to the sale or gift of a child. Āpastamba (2.6.13.11) forbids this practice:

> The gift (or acceptance of a child) and the right to sell (or buy) a child are not recognized. (Tr. Bühler)

Kauṭilya (3.13.1–5) seems to draw a distinction between *ārya* and *mleccha* children. The Sanskrit text presents a number of problems of interpretation, which cannot be discussed here. Kangle translates as follows:

> For one selling or keeping as a pledge a minor Ārya individual except a slave for livelihood, the fine is twelve paṇas for a kinsman in the case of a Śūdra, double that in the case of a Vaiśya, three times in the case of a Kṣatriya, four times in the case of a Brahmin. For a stranger, the lowest, the middle and the highest fines and death are the punishments (respectively), also for purchasers and witnesses. It is not an offense for Mlecchas to sell an offspring or keep it as a pledge. But there shall be no slavery for an Ārya in any circumstances whatsoever. Or, after keeping

> as a pledge an Ārya when the family has bound itself in times of distress of Āryas, they shall, on finding the redemption-amount, redeem first the minor or one who renders help.

Kauṭilya (3.13.13) also provides for special protection for the offspring of an *ārya* father who has sold his own person:

> The progeny of one who sells himself shall be known as Ārya. (Tr. Kangle)

It is not clear how the references that prohibit the alienation of minors, relate to another set of rules describing the different —mostly twelve— kinds of sons. One of these is the *krītaka* "the son bought." Manu (9.174) defines him as follows:

> If a man buys a (boy), whether equal or unequal (in good qualities), from his father and mother for the sake of having a son, that (child) is called a (son) bought. (Tr. Bühler)

The "son bought" appears in all the major texts (Kane 1930–62: 3.645), including Kauṭilya's. Āpastamba seems to stand alone in recognizing no other type of son than the *aurasa*, the son of a husband and wife of the same caste; as indicated earlier, he is also the one who prohibits the sale or purchase of children.

The minor enjoys yet another kind of personal protection. In Nārada's text (Introduction 1.52–54) the *aprāptavyavahāra* figures among those whom the king cannot summon to appear in court, and who cannot be subjected to *āsedha*, an ill-defined right of restraint that can be exercised by a plaintiff against a prospective defendant:

> One about to marry; one tormented by an illness; one about to offer a sacrifice; one afflicted by a calamity; one accused by another; one employed in the king's service; cowherds engaged in tending cattle; cultivators in the act of cultivation; artisans, while engaged in their own occupations; soldiers, during warfare; one who has not yet arrived at years of discretion; a messenger; one about to give alms; one fulfilling a vow; one harassed by difficulties; a person belonging to any of these categories must not be arrested, nor shall the king summon him (before a court of justice). (Tr. Jolly)

Protection of the Minor's Property

A large number of passages from the Dharmasūtras and Dharmaśāstras refer to property owned by minors (*bāladhana*). The principle that *bāladhana* ought to be protected is already formulated by Gautama (10.48):

> The property of infants must be protected until they attain their majority or complete their studentship. (Tr. Bühler)

Vasiṣṭha makes a similar statement, and adds (16.9):

> But if (a minor) comes of age, his property must be made over to him. (Tr. Bühler)

Although neither text explicitly states who is responsible for the protection of the child's property, we know that the intended grammatical subject in all such sentences is the king.[269] Kauṭilya (2.1.26) probably refers to the same situation, although he might also have thought of actual maintenance of minors by the king, as suggested by Kangle's translation:

> And the king should maintain children, aged persons and persons in distress when these are helpless, as also the woman who has borne no child and the sons of one who has (when these are helpless).

If this interpretation is correct, Kauṭilya (2.1.27) differs from Gautama and Vasiṣṭha in so far as he entrusts the actual protection of the property of minors to the village elders rather than to the king:

> The elders of the village should augment the property of a minor till he comes of age, also the property of a temple. (Tr. Kangle)

A text by Manu (8.27) is so similar to that by Gautama, that we are probably entitled to read the former's more specific definition of the minor's property as "inherited property" back into the —more ancient— latter:

> The king shall protect the inherited (and other) property of the minor,[270] until he returned (from his teacher's house) or until he has passed his minority. (Tr. Bühler)

Manu does not state how the king should exercise this protection. However, he lists (8.28) a number of analogous cases:

> In like manner care must be taken of barren women, of those

[269] ViDh 3.65 states explicitly: "The king must protect the property of minors, of (blind, lame or other) helpless persons (who have no guide), and of women (without a guardian)" (tr. Jolly).

[270] I am not convinced that the expression "the inherited (and other) property of the minor" is an accurate translation of the Sanskrit original. The text literally reads: "inherited property (*riktha*) such as *bāladhana* and other."

> who have no sons, of those whose family is extinct, of wives and widows faithful to their lords, and of women afflicted with diseases (tr. Bühler),

and adds (8.29):

> A righteous king must punish like thieves those relatives who appropriate the property of such females during their lifetime. (Tr. Bühler)

We may, therefore, assume that the punishment for thieves also applies to the relatives who appropriate the inherited property of minors.

The fact that, in reality, the relatives are in charge of the minors' shares is made clear in several texts. Thus, Baudhāyana (2.3.36):

> Let them carefully protect the shares of those who are minors, as well as the increments (thereon). (Tr. Bühler)

Kātyāyana first states (844ab) that actual partition can only take place among persons who are of legal age:

> Partition is ordained among (coparceners) who have attained (years of) understanding of worldly affairs (tr. Kane),

but he also provides (845) for the share of minors:

> The property (share in the joint estate) of those who have not attained years of discretion, being made free from expenses, should be kept (by other coheirs) with their (the minors') relatives and friends; the same should be done (to the shares) of those who have gone abroad. (Tr. Kane)[271]

Kauṭilya has a similar statement of principle (3.5.19):

> There is partition only among those who have attained majority (tr. Kangle),

and he too, makes it a point (3.5.20) to protect the shares of minors, with some interesting variants:

> They shall deposit with the mother's kinsmen or village elders,

[271] Cf. also KS 845 A: "All (coheirs) should protect the share of the (coheir) who has gone abroad; and his share of the ancestral estate should be guarded by the relatives, if his sons are minor or if he be dead. After him his minor (sons) should partition the wealth according to their shares" (tr. Kane).

> the share of those who have not attained majority, clearing it of debts, till they come of age, also the share of one who is away on a journey. (Tr. Kangle)

Nārada (2.15) refers to an unspecified person who takes a wealthy minor into his house —if the interpretation of his commentator, Asahāya, is correct— in the chapter on deposits:

> He who fails to restore a deposit, and he who demands what he never deposited, shall both be punished like thieves, and shall be made to pay a sum equal (in amount to the value of the deposit)....If a man takes charge of a wealthy boy, the law is also the same. (Tr. Jolly)

Kātyāyana (552) mentions a far-reaching application of the protection of the property of minors; he exempts minors from the general obligation of the Hindu son to pay his deceased father's debts:

> (A son need) never pay (the debt of his father) when the father is dead, if he (the son) has not attained years of discretion. But when the proper time (to pay the debt) comes, he must pay according to the law, otherwise his forefathers may remain in hell. (Tr. Kane)

The meaning of "the proper time" seems to be explained[272] in another verse by Kātyāyana (553):

> If (a son) has not reached (years of) discretion, he, though independent, is not liable for the debt (of the father). (Real) independence is understood to belong to one who is senior and seniority is due to the (attainment of) certain qualities and age. (Tr. Kane)

If this interpretation is correct, the son does not have to pay his deceased father's debts before the age of sixteen; as soon as he reaches that age, the "pious obligation" applies to him to the same extent to which it applies to the son who is a major at the time of inheritance.

Property of minors is also exempt from another general rule of Hindu law; the minor does not lose his title by prescription. Manu's general rule (8.147):

[272] I say: "seems to be explained," because the same stanza occurs in NS (1.31), in a totally different context: the minor's inability to contract valid debts *of his own*. This is Jolly's translation: "A youth who, though independent, has not yet arrived at years of discretion, is not capable of contracting valid debts. (Real) independence belongs to the eldest son (only); (the right of) seniority is based on both capacity and age." This is another example to show how identical Sanskrit texts can be used by the commentators to apply to different situations.

> (But in general) whatever (chattel) an owner sees enjoyed by others during ten years, while, though present, he says nothing, that (chattel) he shall not recover (tr. Bühler),

is restated in the next stanza (8.148), but idiots and minors are introduced as exceptions:

> If (the owner is) neither an idiot nor a minor and if (his chattel) is enjoyed (by another) before his eyes, it is lost to him by law; the adverse possessor shall retain that property (tr. Bühler),

and the infant figures again in a more complete list of exceptions (8.149):

> A pledge, a boundary, the property of infants, an (open) deposit, a sealed deposit, women, the property of the king and the wealth of a Shrotriya are not lost in consequence of (adverse) enjoyment. (Tr. Bühler)

For similar rules, see GDh 12.37, YDh 2.24–25, BS 7.29, KS 330, and AŚ 3.11.13 and 3.16.30.

Conclusion

The preceding discussion is based on all texts from the Dharmasūtras, Dharmaśāstras, and Kauṭilya's *Arthaśāstra*, in which the *bāla* —eventually, *pogaṇḍa*— is explicitly referred to. Other texts were not taken into consideration. For example, texts bearing on sons born after partition were not discussed, because their rights are those of sons, not of minors. Thus, Manu (9.216):

> But a son, born after partition, shall alone take the property of his father, or if any (of the other sons) be reunited with the (father), he shall share with them. (Tr. Bühler)

For the same reason I did not include rules concerning sons, in which their minority or majority is irrelevant, or in which it is not explicitly stated that they refer to sons less than sixteen years old. Thus, Kātyāyana (573):

> If a woman who has a son forsakes her son, though quite able (to bear the burden of the family), then depriving her of her strīdhana wealth, the son should pay off his father's debt (with it). (This is the view of) Manu. (Tr. Kane)

The more interesting point for this study is the recognition by ancient Hindu law of an age group too young to be subjected to the regular rules of law. Unlike modern legal systems, Hindu law has not laid down *a priori* the principle that minors should be protected, and formulated its rules according to that premise. Nowhere in the ancient Hindu "lawbooks" has a selection been reserved to treat the rights and duties of minors systematically and exhaustively. But the texts are numerous enough to show that the *bāla* is a well established category; he "does not know the right procedures," and, as a result, his liability for wrongdoing is diminished, and, wherever possible, his person and property deserve special protection.

13

Quandoque bonus dormitat *Jīmūtavāhanas*?

The Problem

Jīmūtavāhana's *Dāyabhāga* twice quotes the same verse from the *Bṛhaspatismṛti* (K.V. Rangaswami Aiyangar's ed. 26.9):

pitror abhāve bhrātṝṇāṃ vibhāgaḥ sampradarśitaḥ |
mātur nivṛtte rajasi jīvator api śasyate ||

After the death of both parents, division of the property among brothers has been ordained (to take place). It may take place even in their lifetime, if the mother be past child-bearing. (Trans. Jolly 25.1)

Immediately after the first citation (2.2) Jīmūtavāhana comments:

nāsya vacanasya pitṛdhanagocaratvam.

This text does *not bear on partition of their father's property.* (Trans. Colebrooke; emphasis added)

Following the second citation of the same Bṛhaspati verse, the *Dāyabhāga* (3.11) has this comment:

nivṛttarajaskāyāṃ mātari jīvantyāṃ vibhāgasya mātṛdhanāgocaratvānupapatter ubhayābhāvoktavibhāgasyaiva jīvator apīty apikāreṇa śastatvakīrtanād ubhayor abhāve bhrātṛvibhāgaḥ pitṛdhanagocara evāvadhāryate.

Since partition while the mother is living cannot be relative to the mother's particular property, and since the authorised partition after the demise of both parents, which is indicated by the particle in the phrase "even while they are both living," is thus pronounced to be proper; partition among brothers after the death of parents *is evidently relative to the father's property.* (Trans. Colebrooke; emphasis added)

There is nothing in the notes to Colebrooke's translation to signal a possible inconsistency. Śrikṛṣṇatarkālaṃkāra (at Dbhā 3.11), on the other hand, saw a problem and found it necessary to defend Jīmūtavāhana:

pitṛdhanagocara eva iti: pitāmahadhanasyāpi pituḥ svatvavattvāt pitṛdhanatvena tasyāpi saṃgrahaḥ. evakāreṇa mātṛdhanamātravyavacchedaḥ. tenāsya vacanasya na prāguktapitāmahadhanagoc aratvavirodhaḥ.

That means that, according to Śrīkṛṣṇa, since the father is also the owner of ancestral property, it too, is included under "the father's property." When Jīmūtavāhana says here that BS 26.9 applies to the father's property "only" [*eva*], his sole purpose is to prevent the text from applying to the mother's property. "In this way, Dbhā 3.4 does not contradict its earlier statement that BS 26.9 applies to ancestral property."

Yet Śrīkṛṣṇatarkālaṃkāra's interpretation does not do away with Jīmūtavāhana's earlier, categorical statement that BS 26.9 does *not* apply to the father's property. Either Jīmūtavāhana was inconsistent, or we have to try to understand him better than has been done so far.

BS 26.9 in Dayabhāga, Chapter Three

The third chapter of the *Dāyabhāga* opens with the statement that, even though the death of the father gives his sons a right of ownership in his property, full brothers ought to delay partition until after the death of their mother.

In support of this statement Jīmūtavāhana refers to MDh 9.104 quoted elsewhere in the *Dāyabhāga* (1.14):

ūrdhvaṃ pituś ca mātuś ca sametya bhrātaraḥ samam |
bhajeran paitṛkam riktham anīśās te hi jīvatoḥ ||

After the death of the father and the mother, the brothers, being assembled, may divide among themselves in equal shares the paternal (and maternal) estate, for, they have no power (over it) while the parents live. (Trans. Bühler)

Jīmūtavāhana next rejects the interpretation that sons should wait to divide their father's property until after *his* death and to divide their mother's property until after *her* death. He demonstrates that MDh 9.104 and a number of similar texts do not bear on maternal property. One of the texts cited in this context is BS 26.9.

The Bṛhaspati text and Jīmūtavāhana's comments have been introduced above. Consistent with his interpretation at Dbhā 2.2 to which I will return, Jīmūtavāhana states that the reference to the mother being beyond menopause makes it impossible for the second half of BS 26.9 to refer to partition of maternal property. The particle *api* in the second half implies that the first half of the verse cannot bear on maternal property either. At that point Jīmūtavāhana draws the conclusion:

ubhayor abhāve bhrātṛvibhāgaḥ pitṛdhanagocara evāvadhāryate.

I agree with Śrīkṛṣṇa (also quoted above) that Jīmūtavāhana uses the term *pitṛdhana*, perhaps ambiguously, for any kind of property that comes to sons *from* and *through* their father, and that includes both paternal and ancestral property.

However, the main point to remember is that, in chapter three, Jīmūtavāhana is interested in the first half of BS 26.9: the fact that sons ought to wait until their mother's death does not refer to partition of maternal property.

BS 26.9 in Dayabhāga, Chapter Two

Chapter two of the *Dāyabhāga* deals with partition of ancestral property. Right at the start of the chapter (2.1) Jīmūtavāhana cites BS 26.9 and sets out to prove that it is relevant to this kind of partition. Although he does not quote any predecessor holding a different position, he states his own view rather aggressively. He immediately zeroes in on the expression *nivṛtte rajasi* in the Bṛhaspati text, and uses it to prove two things.

First, the rule that partition can take place only after the mother's menopause cannot apply to the sons' paternal property. Indeed, MDh 9.216 = NS 13.44, which state that a son born *after partition* inherits from his father, imply that a father *is allowed* to partition his property with his sons prior to his wife's menopause. If BS 26.9 meant that paternal property can be divided *after* the mother's menopause only, the Manu and Nārada texts would become inoperative, for at that time it is no longer possible for the father to have another son.

Second, partition after the mother's menopause cannot refer to the mother's own property, for that could leave her without anything for the rest of her life.

The next two paragraphs (Dbhā 2.3–4) merely add that, besides the mother being beyond menopause, partition of ancestral property during the parents' lifetime also requires the father's willingness to do so.

At paragraph 2.5 Jīmūtavāhana then continues as follows:

ataḥ pitror abhāva ity ekaḥ kālaḥ.

Colebrooke translates: "Hence [since such is the import of Bṛhaspati's text] the decease of both parents is one period [for the partition of the grandfather's estate]." Both passages in brackets are, according to a footnote, based on Śrīkṛṣṇatarkālaṃkāra's commentary on the *Dāyabhāga*. In reality, Śrīkṛṣṇa has far more than that; he was obviously ill at ease with the initial word *ataḥ* which is supposed to establish a cause to effect relationship between what precedes and the new paragraph. He first provides the interpretation referred to by Colebrooke:

ata iti: yato Bṛhaspativacanasya na pitṛdhanaviṣayatvam ata ity arthaḥ.

That means: since the Bṛhaspati text does not apply to paternal property, therefore.

He, however, also adds an alternative explanation:

athavā yato 'patyasambhāvanābhāvaḥ pitur icchāsahakṛta eva vibhāganimittaṃ na tu svātantryeṇa ata ity arthaḥ.

Or else it means: since the impossibility of having children is a sufficient reason for partition only if the father is willing whereas they cannot do it on there own initiative, therefore.

The reason for Jīmūtavāhana's uneasiness is that, in reality, *ataḥ* at the beginning of paragraph 2.5 does not draw any conclusion either from 2.2 or 2.3–4. Paragraph 2.2 commented on the second half of BS 26.9, paragraph 2.3–4 constituted a mere digression on the necessity of the father's willingness to partition the property, a condition which is not mentioned in the second half of BS 26.9.

Following what I called his rather aggressive commentary on the second half of BS 26.9, with *ataḥ* Jīmūtavāhana now, for the first time in chapter two, turns his attention to the first half of the verse. And he does so in 2.5–6 which belong far more closely together than their separation into two separate paragraphs might suggest. If I may be allowed to translate *ataḥ* very freely, I would say: "So far so good, but let us come back to BS 26.9 and see what the first half of the verse teaches us."

The first half of BS 26.9 says that one possible time for partition is after the death of *both* parents [*pitror abhāve*]. Jīmūtavāhana now raises the question: what does the use of the dual *pitror* mean here? The first part of his answer is as follows:

> *sodarabhrātṝṇāṃ pitṛdhanavibhāgo 'pi mātur abhāva eva kāryaḥ.*

Colebrooke translates: "a division of the father's estate among brothers of the whole blood ought [in strictness (from Maheśvara's commentary)] to be made only after the decease of the mother."

In this one important word remains untranslated: *api*. What Jīmūtavāhana really wants to say is that, when partition is delayed until after the father's death, any group of full brothers must postpone, until after their respective mother's death, not only partition of ancestral property, but partition of their father's property as well [*api*].

Then follows the second part of Jīmūtavāhana's answer:

> *na tu mātṛdhanavibhāgārthaṃ mātur abhāvasyopādānaṃ jīvator apīty asya mātṛdhana-gocaratvānupapatteḥ anyadhanagocaratvam avaśyaṃ vācyaṃ tena yatraiva vibhāge pitror abhāvo nimittaṃ tatraiva jīvator apīty apiśabdena jīvanasyāpi śastatvakīrtanāt na mātur abhāvo mātṛdhane vyākhyeyaḥ.*

Colebrooke translates:

> The mention of the mother's demise does not here imply partition of her goods: since the phrase "even while they are both living" cannot relate to the mother's separate property. It must be understood as relating to the property of another person; for the legality of partition in the instance of survival is there propounded (as appears from the word even), in the same case in which the demise of both parents was declared a reason of distribution. The death of the mother must not be expounded as relative to her goods.

Colebrooke failed to do full justice to the initial words *na tu*. What Jīmūtavāhana means to say is that, "on the other hand," even though the dual *pitror* includes the mother, the first half of BS 26.9 does not apply to the mother's property. The word *api* in *jīvator api* places *jīvator* and *pitror abhāve* on the same level. So, even as the dual *jīvator* does not imply that the second half of BS 26.9 also applies to maternal property, in the same way the dual *pitror* does not imply this.

The second half of BS 26.9 was discussed at Dhbā 2.2–4, the first half at 2.5–6. Only now follows Jīmūtavāhana's final conclusion:

> *tasmāt pitāmahādidhanasyāpi pitror abhāva ity ekaḥ kālaḥ. tathā mātur nivṛtte rajasi pitur icchāta ity aparaḥ.*

Colebrooke: Therefore the death of both parents is one period for partition of an estate inherited from a grandfather or other ancestor, and the other is by the choice of the father when the mother is past child-bearing.

A less literal rendering might read as follows:

In conclusion [*tasmāt*], as far as ancestral property is concerned, there are two possible times of partition.
(1) Even as with the father's own property (a topic discussed in chapter one), ancestral property too [*api*] can be divided after the death of both parents.
(2) Ancestral property can be also divided while both parents are still living, provided (a) that the mother is beyond menopause, and (b) that the father is willing.

Conclusion

There is no doubt that, when one reads the *Dāyabhāga* carefully, one cannot help halting before Jīmūtavāhana's twofold interpretation of BS 26.9. Yet, notwithstanding some imprecision and ambiguity, his position vis-à-vis the Bṛhaspati text is clear and consistent. I have summarized it above in a free rendering of Jīmūtavāhana's conclusion [Dhbā 2.7].

The main reason why Jīmūtavāhana has been misunderstood has been the failure by his readers to follow the three separate stages in his interpretation of BS 26.9 in the second chapter of the *Dāyabhāga.*

1. Here as elsewhere in the *Dāyabhāga* a reference to a *vacana* is not necessarily a reference to the entire text. The expression *asya vacanasya* at Dbhā 2.2 shows convincingly that a rule prescribing partition by sons in their parents' lifetime but after the mother's menopause "does not bear on partition of their father's property." He does not mean to say that partition after the parents' death does not bear on paternal property.
2. Here as elsewhere in the *Dāyabhāga* Jīmūtavāhana uses the word *ataḥ*, not to draw a conclusion from an immediately preceding passage, but rather to cut away from it and return to a topic that was temporarily abandoned to deal with some urgent matter or just to indulge in a digression.
3. Here as elsewhere in the *Dāyabhāga* Jīmūtavāhana reserves the use of *tasmāt* to bring discussions, often long discussions, to a close, and draw the final conclusion.

14

Notes on Mixed Castes in Classical India

§1. The so-called "mixed castes" in classical India have been studied in the past. The most comprehensive collection of data appears in P.V. Kane's *History of Dharmaśāstra* (1930–62: 2.69–104).[273] In this paper I want to return to the original texts on which these data are based, schematize some of the materials, and try to draw certain conclusions. The texts are the Dharmasūtras, the early Dharmaśāstras, and Kauṭilya's Arthaśāstra, as follows:

- GDh, 4.16–21 (Stenzler's edition, Bühler's translation) = 4.14–17 (Ānandāśrama edition);
- BDh 1.16.6–8 + 1.17.3–8 (Hultzsch's edition, Bühler's translation) = 1.16.7–8 + 1.17.2–8 (Kashi edition);
- VaDh 18.1–6, 8–9;
- ViDh 16.2–6;
- MDh 10.6, 8–9, 11–12, 16–17;
- YDh 1.91–95;
- AŚ 3.7.20–30.

It should be noted that one Dharmasūtra, that of Āpastamba, does not discuss the matter of mixed castes.

§2. On the other hand, Gautama gives two sets. A first set is followed by a second one, introduced by: "Some say…" The interesting point is that not only the content but also the way of

[273] The text of this article was written before the publication of Brinkhaus 1978. Brinkhaus treats the texts in far greater detail, but pays less attention to general trends which are the prime concern of this paper.

presentation in both sets are totally different; I shall return to this point later (§29).

§3. Baudhāyana also introduces mixed castes twice, one after the other. The situation is far more confused in this treatise, and considerable text-critical research will be required to solve the problem. The first passage follows immediately after the rules on the number of wives members of the four *varṇas* are allowed to have: from four to one. After a few rules which are difficult to understand Baudhāyana exhibits a second set of *sūtras* on mixed castes. Although the presentation in both cases is quite different, the contents are nearly identical, with one exception (§19), one omission in the first set (§9), and one uncertainty (§§9, 24).

§4. Consequently the following analysis is based on nine different descriptions of mixed castes. Reference to them will be as follows:[274]

Gautama	G^1
	G^2
Baudhāyana	B^1
	B^2
Vasiṣṭha	Va
Viṣṇu	Vi
Manu	M
Yājñavalkya	Y
Kauṭilya	AŚ

§5. There are, of course, two basically different types of mixed marriages, in both of which the husband is the point of reference. If he marries a woman of a lower *varṇa* than his own, the marriage is *anuloma*; if he marries a woman of a higher *varṇa*, the marriage is *pratiloma*.

The Brāhmaṇa can conclude an *anuloma* marriage in three different degrees:

with a Kṣatriya woman:	A^1b
with a Vaiśya woman:	A^2b
with a Śūdra woman:	A^3b

274 [Ed. note: Slightly modified abbreviations for Sanskrit texts are used in the tables contained in this chapter.]

There are two degrees of *anuloma* for a Kṣatriya:

with a Vaiśya woman:	A^1k
with a Śūdra woman:	A^2k

There is only one degree of *anuloma* for the Vaiśya:

with a Śūdra woman:	A^1v

Conversely, there is one possible degree of *pratiloma* marriage for a Kṣatriya:

with a Brāhmaṇa woman:	P^1k

Two degrees of *pratiloma* are possible for a Vaiśya:

with a Kṣatriya woman:	P^1v
with a Brāhmaṇa woman:	P^2v

And there are three degrees of *pratiloma* for a Śūdra:

with a Vaiśya woman:	P^1s
with a Kṣatriya woman:	P^2s
with a Brāhmaṇa woman:	P^3s

§6. All together there are, thus, twelve different cases of primary mixed castes, i.e., those that come into being as a result of marriages the parties to which belong to two of the four original *varṇa*s. Some of the texts on which this study is based discuss a smaller or larger number of secondary mixed castes, i.e., those that come into being when one or both parties to the marriage belong(s) to one or two primary mixed castes. This article will not concern itself with secondary mixed castes; they will only be referred to occasionally in direct relation to one or the other of the primary mixed castes. Table 1 presents a complete picture of the twelve primary mixed castes as they appear in the nine versions of the texts mentioned earlier (§4).

§7. The most striking fact in Table 1 is that there is absolute unanimity in all nine versions for one situation only:

P^3s = *caṇḍāla.*

That means that all texts agree on the name of the worst case of primary mixed marriage: the single highest degree of *pratiloma.*

§8. As might be expected, a nearly equally strong unanimity appears in the single highest degree of *anuloma*: A^3b. However, in this case there is one exception. Viṣṇu's general approach to *anuloma* (§23) apparently did not tolerate exceptions, not even for *anuloma,* in the third degree. Moreover, G^1 and G^2 call A^3b *pāraśava,* B^1 *niṣāda,* both terms evidently being interchangeable:

B^2	"*niṣāda*; some say: *pāraśava,*"
M	"*niṣāda* who is called *pāraśava,*"
Y	"*niṣāda* or also *pāraśava,*"
AŚ	"*niṣāda* or *pāraśava.*"

A similar statement by Vasiṣṭha will be discussed later (§22).

§9. Besides P^3s and A^3b there is quasi-unanimity in one other case:

P^1k = *sūta.*

B^1 is the only version in which *sūta* is absent. It lists eight *pratilomas*: *āyogava, māgadha, vaiṇa, kṣattṛ, pulkasa, kukkuṭa, vaidehaka,* and *caṇḍāla.* Three of these are explained immediately as secondary mixed castes:

vaiṇa	=	A^2k (*ugra*) x Kṣatriya
pulkasa	=	A^3b (*niṣāda*) x Vaiśya
kukkuṭa	=	Vaiśya x A^3b (*niṣāda*)

This leaves only five primary *pratilomas*. Even though all manuscripts used so far by editors of Baudhāyana seem to confirm this situation, I cannot accept that a *sūtrakāra* would have neglected to mention the sixth *pratiloma*: *sūta.* I therefore include it, in parentheses, in Table 1.

Table 1

	Brāhmaṇa *F*	Kṣatriya *F*	Vaiśya *F*	Śūdra *F*
Brāhmaṇa *M*		Brāhmaṇa B^1 B^2 AŚ b-sadṛśa M Kṣatriya Vi savarṇa G^1 mūrdhāvasikta G^2 Y ambaṣṭha Va A^1b	Vaiśya Vi ambaṣṭha B^1 B^2 M Y AŚ niṣāda G^1 bhṛjjakaṇṭha G^2 ugra Va A^2b	Śūdra Va pāraśava G^1 G^2 niṣāda B^1 pāraśava/niṣāda B^2 Va M Y AŚ A^3b
Kṣatriya *M*	sūta G^1 G^2 (B^1) B^2 Va Vi M Y AŚ P^1k		Kṣatriya B^1 B^2 AŚ k-sadṛśa M Vaiśya Vi māhiṣya G^2 Y ambaṣṭha G^1 Va A^1k	Śūdra Vi ugra B^1 B^2 Va M Y AŚ dauṣmanta G^1 yavana G^2 A^2k
Vaiśya *M*	vaideha (ka) B^1? B^2 Vi M Y AŚ kṛta G^1 māgadha G^2 rāmaka (romaka) Va P^2v	māgadha G^1 M Y AŚ pulkasa Va Vi āyogava B^1? B^2 dhīvara G^2 P^1v		Vaiśya B^1 v-sadṛśa M Śūdra Vi AŚ rathakāra B^2 karaṇa G^2 Y ugra G^1 ambaṣṭha Va A^1v
Śūdra *M*	caṇḍāla G^1 G^2 B^1? B^2 Va Vi M Y AŚ P^2s	kṣattṛ B^1? B^2 M Y AŚ vaidehaka G^1 pulkasa G^2 vaiṇa Va māgadha Vi P^2s	āyogava G^1 Vi M Y AŚ māgadha B^1? B^2 vaideha G^2 antyavasāyin Va P^1s	

§10. The reason why P^1k is unanimous has to be different from that of the unanimity in the two extreme cases: P^3s and A^3b. Even though Kauṭilya (3.7.29) states that the *sūta* as P^1k is different from the *sūta* who recites the *purāṇa*s, I suggest that the question be reconsidered. Together with some of the other terms exhibited in Table 1 —*rathakāra*, *kṣattṛ*, *niṣāda*, *māgadha*, *ugra*, *āyogava*— *sūta* appears already in Vedic texts (Kane 1930–62: 2.43–44). It is at least surprising that of all these terms *sūta* alone has attained an unquestioned status among the mixed castes. I intend to come back to this problem in another publication.

§11. In all other cases than the three discussed so far terminology varies greatly from one version to the other. Ten terms occur only once:

G^1	*kṛta*	: P^2v
	dauṣmanta	: A^2k
	savarṇa	: A^1b
G^2	*dhīvara*	: P^1v
	bhṛjjakaṇṭha	: A^2b
	yavana	: A^2k
B^2	*rathakāra*	: A^1v
Va	*antyavasāyin*	: P^1s
	rāmaka (*romaka*)	: P^2v
	vaiṇa	: P^2s

Four of these are used elsewhere for secondary mixed castes: *antyavasāyin* (ibid.: 2.71), *yavana* (ibid.: 2.92–93), *rathakāra* (ibid.: 2.94), and *vaiṇa* (ibid.: 2.95).

§12. Six terms are far better represented, but with up to two, three, or even four different meanings:

āyogava	P^1s	: G^1 Vi M Y AŚ
	P^1v	: B^1? B^2
pulkasa	P^2s	: G^2
	P^1v	: Va Vi
ambaṣṭha	A^1k	: G^1
	A^1bkv	: Va
	A^2b	: B^1 B^2 M Y AŚ

ugra	A¹v	: G¹
	A²bk	: Va
	A²k	: B¹ B² M Y AŚ
vaidehaka	P¹s	: G²
	P²s	: G¹
	P²v	: B¹? B² Vi M Y AŚ
māgadha	P¹v	: G¹ M Y AŚ
	P²v	: G²
	P¹s	: B¹? B²
	P²s	: Vi

§13. Terms occurring in more than one text and used with only one meaning are rare:

kṣattṛ	P²s	: B¹? B² M Y AŚ
māhiṣya	A¹k	: G² Y
mūrdhāvasikta	A¹b	: G² Y

§14. The only distinction which is strictly maintained throughout is that between *anulomas* and *pratilomas*: not a single term is used for any of the categories of A in one text and for any type of P in another. We shall now examine some characteristics which are proper to either basic category.

§15. First, *anuloma* as a generic type is considered superior to all species of *pratiloma*. Viṣṇu, who adopts a uniform and relatively lenient attitude toward all *anulomas* (§23), labels *pratilomas* as a whole: "despised by the Āryas." Manu (10.10) has a general derogatory term for P: *apasada*. And Yājñavalkya concludes his brief passage on mixed castes by calling *pratiloma* and *anuloma* "worse" and "better," respectively.

§16. Second, Table 2 clearly shows that the *anulomas* are normally given before the *pratilomas*. There is only one straight exception: Va, and one case —G²— in which A and P —plus the regular marriages— are incorporated following the four vertical columns of Table 1.

§17. Finally, one important feature sets all *anulomas* apart from all *pratilomas*: all six sub-categories are, at least in certain texts, considered not as mixed castes but as members or assimilated members of one of the four *varṇas*.

§18. There can be no doubt that of all types of primary mixed castes A^1, as a group, was considered least objectionable. As shown in Table 2 they are listed first and together in three versions: G^1, B^2, and M.

§19. Both B^1 and B^2 display the most lenient approach to A^1, at least in two cases out of three. In both A^1b and A^1k the offspring retain their fathers' *varṇas*: Brāhmaṇa and Kṣatriya, respectively. This sequence is strangely interrupted by B^2 in the case of A^1v, where the offspring is called *rathakāra*. The term occurs nowhere else as the name of a primary mixed caste: (§11). It is used once more by Baudhāyana (1.5.9). "The *snātaka* may accept uncooked food from Brāhmaṇas, Kṣatriyas, Vaiśyas, and *rathakāras*," which seems to indicate a lower status than that of a Vaiśya. It is interesting to notice that Yājñavalkya mentions only one type of secondary mixed caste: *rathakāra*, corresponding to the offspring of A^1k and A^1v.

§20. Kauṭilya's treatment of A^1 bears a strange resemblance to that of B^2: A^1b = Brāhmaṇa and A^1k = Kṣatriya as in B^1 and B^2, but A^1v = Śūdra as against B^2: A^1v = *rathakāra*.

§21. Manu, although less lenient, also has no special names for the three cases of A^1. He consistently considers them *sadṛśa* "assimilated" to their fathers' *varṇas*.

§22. At this stage I should like to combine the special position of A^1 generally (§§18–21) with the equally special treatment of the single case of A^3 (§8) to propose an interpretation for Va 18.8–9. The Sanskrit text reads:

> *ekāntarādvyantarātryantarāsu jātā brāhmaṇakṣatriyavaiśyair ambaṣṭhograniṣādā bhavanti. śūdrāṇāṃ pāraśavaḥ.*

Bühler's translation is equally ambiguous: "(Children) begotten by Brāhmaṇas, Kṣatriyas, and Vaiśyas on females of the next lower, second lower, and third lower castes become (respectively) Ambaṣṭhas, Ugras, and Niṣādas. (The son of a Brāhmaṇa and) of a Śūdra woman (is) a Pāraśava."

Table 2

G^1	A^1b	A^1k	A^1v	A^2b	A^2k	A^3b	P^1k	P^1v	P^1s	P^2v	P^2s	P^3s
G^2	bb)P^1k	P^2v	P^3s	A^1b (k	k) P^1v	P^2s	A^2b	A^1k (v	v) P^1s	A^3b	A^2k	A^1v(ss
B^1	A^1b	A^1k	A^1v	A^2b	A^2k	A^3b	see §§9,24					
B^2	A^1b	A^2b	A^3b	A^1k	A^2k	A^1v	P^1s	P^2s	P^3s	P^1v	P^2v	P^1k
Va	P^3s	P^2s	P^1s	P^2v	P^1v	P^1k	see §§22					
Vi	mother's *varṇa*, see §23						P^1s	P^1v	P^2s	P^3s	P^2v	P^1k
M	A^1b	A^1k	A^1v	A^2b	A^3b	A^2k	P^1k	P^1v	P^2v	P^1s	P^2s	P^3s
Y	A^1b	A^2b	A^3b	A^1k	A^2k	A^1v	P^1k	P^2v	P^3s	P^1v	P^2s	P^1s
AŚ	A^1b	A^1k	A^2b	A^3b	A^2k	A^1v	P^1s	P^2s	P^3s	P^1v	P^2v	P^1k

Since *sūtra* 8 includes a marriage of a Brāhmaṇa with a woman of the "third lower caste," it already refers to A^3b. In this respect it coincides with *sūtra* 9, which is not a different case as Bühler's translation might make us believe. In reality, *pāraśava* in *sūtra* 9 and *niṣāda* in *sūtra* 8 refer to the same mixed caste. If so, *ambaṣṭha* and *ugra* refer to the three cases of A^1 and the two cases of A^2, respectively. My interpretation of *sūtra* 9 is radically different from Bühler's which also does not do justice to the genitive *śūdrāṇām*: "For Śūdras he —the *niṣāda*— is *pāraśava*." Stated differently, Śūdras call *pāraśava* the mixed caste that others label *niṣāda*. Thus interpreted Va 18.9 is a welcome contribution to the problem discussed above (§8).

§23. Viṣṇu is lenient in a different way. For him all A^1 have the —lower— *varṇa*s of their mothers; but, on the other hand, he extends his leniency to all *anuloma*s:

A^1b	Kṣatriya
A^2b A^1k	Vaiśya
A^3b A^2k A^1v	Śūdra

The principle is applied so strictly that it even overrules the unanimity elsewhere for A^3b: *pāraśava* or *niṣāda* (§8).

§24. The treatment of *pratilomas* in the texts shows fewer general trends than we have been able to discern in the case of the *anulomas*. The only two special cases of *caṇḍāla* and *sūta* have been discussed earlier (§§7, 9). Unlike in the case of *anulomas*, nothing distinguishes the three less serious cases of P^1 from the two more serious instances of P^2. In one version —B^1— it is not even possible to assign with certainty the five (§9) terms mentioned for *pratilomas*. Since B^1 generally agrees with B^2 elsewhere, and because its *pratiloma* terminology corresponds to that of B^2, I have, in Table 1 arranged the five terms for *pratilomas* in B^1 according to those of B^2, followed by question marks.

§25. Looking back at the sources on primary mixed castes one cannot help being struck by the fact that no two single versions are identical. Mixed castes is not one of those subjects which, once they had been laid down by one authority, was invariably adhered to by all others. There is, thus, a fundamental difference between the four basic *varṇas* and the mixed castes to which their combinations give rise.

§26. This does not mean that the system of mixed castes did not develop a number of invariables of its own. The most obvious one is the distinction between *anuloma* and *pratiloma*; also, the fact that *caṇḍāla* and *niṣāda/pāraśava* occupy the two extremes. *Sūta* as P^1k is a very special and intriguing type of invariable. Finally, all nine versions make it a point to provide names for all twelve possible combinations of *anuloma* and *pratiloma*: this is no longer true when it comes to secondary mixed castes.

§27. The question that remains to be answered is that of the nine different versions of primary mixed castes. The obvious answer is that they reflect differing situations in real life, both in time and space. Although this argument cannot be *a priori* discarded, there are a number of reasons which make it difficult to accept without qualifications.

§28. Here as elsewhere in Dharmaśāstra, Manu seems to have had a greater impact than any other text. Except for the three cases of A^1, Manu's distribution of caste names is followed invariably by Yājñavalkya and Kauṭilya. Therefore, the argument of differing local situations no longer applies for them. On the other hand, there is no pattern to Manu's agreement or disagreement with the —earlier— Dharmasūtras. Manu follows either Gautama or Baudhāyana or Viṣṇu or Vasiṣṭha or a combination of them. But no term appears in Manu for the first time. Hence it looks as if Manu's contribution primarily consisted in systematizing the varied data of earlier texts, using some of them for primary mixed castes, others for its own secondary mixed castes.

§29. Also, there is the problem of the two texts that exhibit not one but two passages on mixed castes. As indicated earlier, B^1 and B^2 seem to describe identical situations. Hence the question there is one of textual criticism rather than of content. Gautama, on the contrary, first gives his own sets of six *anulomas* and *pratilomas*, followed by the twelve primary mixed castes "according to others." G^1 and G^2 are so differently arranged (see Table 2) that G^2 has to be more than Gautama's providing us information on "another" system of mixed castes; it is a direct quotation from some unknown source. Yet, the author again does not assign G^2 to any specific part of the country different from his own. We are left, once more, with the impression that the names of specific primary mixed castes and their respective places in Table 1 were less important to the classical authors than their desire to present complete and coherent systems.

It is possible that, for mixed castes as for other topics of Dharmaśāstra, we shall never know the exact roles played by real life at the time and in the part of India the treatises were written in on the one hand, and the systematizing influence of the authors on the other. This article wants to show that the latter too, is important, and that it should not be overlooked in our reconstruction of classical Indian society.

15

Inheritance and Śrāddha*: The Principle of "Spiritual Benefit"*

In 1870 the Full Bench of the Calcutta High Court was called on to determine "whether under the Hindu Law current in the Bengal School, the son of a paternal uncle's daughter is entitled to succeed to the estate of a deceased Hindu, if no nearer heirs are forthcoming."[275] If he was, the property should be his; if not, the property should revert to the Crown.

The answer to this question depended on whether or not Jīmūtavāhana's *Dāyabhāga*, the highest authority on inheritance in Bengal (see Rocher 1972: 167–176), recognized the paternal uncle's daughter's son as an heir. It was clear that it did not do so explicitly. A further question was then raised, namely whether the order of succession discussed in the *Dāyabhāga* was meant to be exhaustive, or whether the text merely provided general principles to be applied in the light of specific circumstances. The Court, in a judgment delivered by Mr. Justice D.N. (Dwarkanath) Mitter, decided in favor of the latter alternative: the paternal uncle's daughter's son qualifies as an heir, for he ranks among the *sapiṇḍa*s as defined by Jīmūtavāhana (on the uncertainty of the law prior to 1870, see Mitra 1881: 77–78).

There is absolute agreement in the texts on Hindu law that a deceased person's inheritance first goes to his *sapiṇḍa*s, and, among these, to whoever happens to be the closest surviving *sapiṇḍa*:

> *anantaraḥ sapiṇḍād yas tasya tasya dhanaṃ bhavet.*

[275] *Guru Gobind Shaha Mondal* v. *Anand Lal Ghose*, 5 Beng. L.R. 15 (1870); Reprinted in Banerjea 1893: 137–149.

> Property always goes to the one who is closest to the deceased *sapiṇḍa*.[276] (MDh 9.187ab)

There is less agreement, however, on the meaning of the term *piṇḍa*, and, hence, on the definition of *sapiṇḍa* relationship.

Vijñāneśvara's *Mitākṣarā*, the most authoritative text on inheritance in India outside Bengal, discusses the meaning of *piṇḍa* at length, in connection with the rule of the *Yājñavalkyasmṛti* (1.52) to the effect that a man should not marry a woman who is his *sapiṇḍa*:

> He should marry a girl, who is a non-Sapinda (with himself). She is called his Sapinda who has (particles of) the body (of some ancestor, &c.) in common (with him). Non-Sapinda means not his Sapinda. Such a one (he should marry). Sapinda-relationship arises between two people through their being connected by particles of one body. Thus the son stands in Sapinda-relationship to his father because of particles of his father's body having entered (his). In like (manner stands the grandson in Sapinda-relationship) to his paternal grandfather and the rest, because through his father particles of his (grandfather's) body have entered into (his own). Just so is (the son of a Sapinda-relation) of his mother, because particles of his mother's body have entered (into his). Likewise (the grandson stands in Sapinda-relationship) to his maternal grandfather and the rest through his mother. So also (is the nephew) a Sapinda-relation to his maternal aunts and uncles, and the rest, because particles of the same body (the paternal grandfather) have entered into (his and theirs); likewise (does he stand in Sapinda-relationship) with paternal uncles and aunts, and the rest. So also the wife and the husband (are Sapinda-relation to each other), because they together beget one body (the son). In like manner brothers' wives also are (Sapinda-relations to each other), because they produce one body (the son), with those (severally) who have sprung from one body (i.e. because they bring forth sons by their union with the offspring of one person, and thus their husbands' father is the common bond which connects them). Therefore one ought to know that wherever the word Sapinda is used, there exists (between the persons to whom it is applied) a connection with one body, either immediately or by descent. (Tr. West and Bühler 1919: 112–113)

It is clear from this that Vijñāneśvara adopted the position that *sapiṇḍa* relationship "is based upon community of corporal particles, or, in other words, upon consanguinity."[277]

Jīmūtavāhana (11.6.17) quotes Manu 9.187ab. He does not

[276] My translation agrees with Bühler's rather than with any of the various interpretations adopted by the commentators on the *Manusmṛti*. On these, see Bühler's note (1886: 366–368).

[277] *Lallubhai Bhapubhai* v. *Makuvarbhai*, 2 Born. L.R. 388, 424 (1878), after quoting the entire *Mitākṣarā* passage.

discuss the meaning of *piṇḍa*, and tacitly takes it in its ordinary sense: *piṇḍa* is the ball or cake, mostly made of rice, which a person offers to his ancestors when he performs *śrāddha* (Kane 1930–1961: 2.472). He points to the fact that the immediately preceding verse (Manu 9.186) ordains that one should offer *piṇḍa*s to three generations of ancestors:

> Three generations shall be given water, three generations must be offered *piṇḍa*s. It is the fourth generation that offers these. The fifth generation plays no role.

There is more to this verse, Jīmūtavāhana adds, than the obligation to offer *śrāddha*s. Since it occurs in the middle of the chapter of inheritance, it also means to say that offering *piṇḍa* plays a role in inheritance. Accordingly, the purpose of the immediately following verse (9.187ab) is to specify how this is so: the inheritance always goes to the person who is closest to the deceased as far as his *piṇḍa* offerings are concerned.

Jīmūtavāhana obviously also knew the other point of view, for he concludes:

> It would be wrong to say (*na ca... iti vācyam*) that being closest in Manu 9.187ab is meant to be understood in terms of birth rather than in terms of offering *piṇḍa*s. Nothing in the wording of this text hints at the order of birth. On the contrary, Manu introduces the term 'closeness' after having said that *piṇḍa*s and water shall be offered to three generations, that the fourth at the lower end offers the *piṇḍa*s, and that neither the fifth at the top receives *piṇḍa*s nor does the fifth at the lower end offer them. In doing so he makes it known that the criterion for being closest is being superior as far as offering *piṇḍa*s is concerned. (11. 6.18)

There is no doubt that here and elsewhere in the *Dāyabhāga* Jīmūtavāhana repeatedly and explicitly invokes the criterion of being *upakārika* "of service" to the deceased by offering *piṇḍa*s, for someone to qualify as an heir. There is also no doubt that here and elsewhere in the text he often and specifically calls on the concept of *upakārātiśaya* "being of greater service" to the deceased, for someone to be closer to him (*ānantarya*) and to inherit prior to someone else (the principal passages are summarized in Kane 1930–1962: 3.736–738). As I indicated earlier, Justice Mitter held that all these instances were merely illustrative of Jīmūtavāhana's attitude to inheritance generally, and that the underlying principle ought to be applied in cases not explicitly discussed in the *Dāyabhāga* as well.[278]

[278] "Every one who has gone through the Dayabhaga must have perceived that the specific enumeration of each individual heir was not the object which

He defended his thesis in a lengthy opinion in the case brought before the Court in 1870, to which I referred earlier.

If Mitter's thesis is correct, Jīmūtavāhana's view of *sapiṇḍa* and *sapiṇḍa* relationship can be summarized as follows. Once the *ekoddiṣṭa śrāddhas*, which are intended for a single recently deceased ancestor, are completed, he is elevated to the rank of a *pitṛ* and united with the ancestors generally by means of the *sapiṇḍīkāraṇa* (or *sapiṇḍana*) (on the symbolism used to express this "unification," see, e.g., Padfield 1908: 217–219). From then onward he shares in the "undivided" (*avibhakta*) *piṇḍas* which the descendant offers at his *pārvaṇa śrāddhas*, to three generations of ancestors on his father's side (father, father's father, father's father's father) as well as to three generations of his mother's ancestors (mother's father, mother's father's father, mother's father's father's father). All of them, together with the person who offers the *pārvaṇa śrāddha*, are *sapiṇḍa*.

At this stage Jīmūtavāhana goes one important step further. Since the deceased shares in the *piṇḍas* offered to his ancestors, he also shares in any *piṇḍa* that is offered to any one of them, irrespective of the identity of the person who offers it. In other words, in addition to survivors who offer *piṇḍas* to the deceased personally, the *sapiṇḍas* of the deceased also include any person who offers one or more *piṇḍas* to any ancestor to whom he himself would have offered *piṇḍas* had he been living.

In 1870 Mitter applied these principles to the case before him. In addition to the *piṇḍas* which a father's brother's daughter's son (FBDS) offers to three generations of ancestors on his father's side, he also offers *piṇḍas* to three generations of ancestors on his mother's side. These are: his maternal grandfather, i.e. the deceased man's paternal uncle (FB), and his maternal grandfather's father and paternal grandfather, i.e. the deceased man's paternal grandfather (FF) and great-grandfather (FFF). Although the deceased himself does not enjoy any of the *piṇḍas* which his FBDS offers at his *pārvaṇa śrāddhas*, the *piṇḍas* offered there to his FF and his FFF are *piṇḍas* which he himself would have offered had he been living. A FBDS, therefore, is a *sapiṇḍa*, and he qualifies as an heir.

Mitter's thesis that "the principle of spiritual benefit... constitutes the fundamental basis of the law of inheritance propounded in the Dayabhaga" (145) has not been universally accepted.

the author had in view. It is perfectly true that a few of the heirs have been mentioned by name here and there; but the great majority of them have been left to be determined by the application of the principle of spiritual benefit" (See note 275 at p.145).

In the background of the opposition to Mitter's approach lies the fact that most scholars, often tacitly, seem to assume that the *Dāyabhāga* is more recent than the *Mitākṣarā*.[279] A few of them, even Bengalis, went as far as to believe that, prior to the time when Jīmūtavāhana wrote the *Dāyabhāga*, inheritance in Bengal was indeed governed by the law of the *Mitākṣarā* (such was the opinion even of D.N. Mitter 1913: 138; cf. also Mitra 1881: 60–61). In their opinion Jīmūtavāhana's purpose was not to void the existing law of inheritance and establish a new law based on totally different principles, but to alter it only on some specific points,[280] namely by slightly changing the order of succession, "specially by recognising some dear and near cognates as heirs in preference to remoter agnates" (Sarkar 1904: v–vi; Sen 1918: 161–162). To do so he reinterpreted the ancient texts, using a variety of arguments "of which the capacity to confer spiritual benefit by the performance of the Párvana Sráddha is most prominent and conspicuous" (Sarkar 1904: vi). However, since Jīmūtavāhana only intended to amend specific aspects of *Mitākṣarā* law, his text must be construed strictly. On any point of law on which the *Dāyabhāga* is silent, *Mitākṣarā* law applies, even in Bengal (Sarkar 1927: 498).[281] The fact that Jīmūtavāhana resorted to spiritual benefit in a number of cases does not imply that he accepted it as a general and absolute principle to be applied in each and every decision on the order of succession (Sarkar 1904: xii–xiii). As far as the case under consideration is concerned, that means that, since Jīmūtavāhana does not explicitly make a father's brother's daughter's son an heir on the basis of spiritual benefit, *Mitākṣarā* law applies, and he does not qualify as an heir.

I do not want to focus in this article on the question whether Jīmūtavāhana intended the principle of spiritual benefit to be applicable in general or restricted terms (for relevant law cases, see Mayne 1950: 681–682). The fact is that he relies on it repeatedly, and that, in the Courts of British and Independent India, it made *Dāyabhāga* law, i.e. the law of inheritance in Bengal different from the law in the rest of India:

[279] E.g., Kane mentions in passing: "...Jīmūtavāhana who also is certainly a little later than the Mit[ākṣarā] ..." (1930–1962: 1.709). For a detailed analysis of the relation between both texts, see Derrett 1952: 9–14.

[280] "The Dáyabhága bears the distant analogy of being as it were an amending Statute of the Mitákshará as far as Bengal is concerned" (Sarkar 1904: viii).

[281] Again, even according to Dwarkanath Mitter, "of all the commentaries, that by Vijaneswara known as the Mitakshara has the widest range of influence... Its authority is denied in Bengal in so far that it yields to the Dayabhaga in points where they differ" (1913: 43–44).

> The Dayabhaga lays down the principle of religious efficacy as the ruling canon in determining the order of succession; consequently it rejects the preference of agnates to cognates, which distinguishes the other system, and arranges and limits the cognates upon principles peculiar to itself. (Mayne 1950: 55; Gharpure 1931: 31)

When it comes to explaining why the *Dāyabhāga*, followed by all later treatises on inheritance in Bengal, is different from the *Mitākṣarā* and all other texts used and applied in the law courts elsewhere in India, there are two premises which surface again and again in the scholarly literature.

The first premise notes that all *dharma* commentaries and digests basically present interpretations of the same body of ancient *smṛti* literature. If these interpretations are different, as they indeed are, this must be due to the fact that their authors made conscious efforts to interpret the same ancient texts in such a way as to bring them into harmony with different local usages: "closer investigation into the systems of law prevailing in the different provinces of India with the aid of the history of their peoples seem to me to lead to the discovery of the true causes of their uniformity and differences" (Mitra 1905: 382).[282]

In the case of inheritance this premise has led to a vast scholarly literature. I must mention, though, that these investigations have centered nearly universally around another principle on which the *Dāyabhāga* differs from the law in the rest of India, and which I will therefore only mention in passing. Again to quote Mayne's *Treatise*:

> [The *Dāyabhāga*] wholly denies the doctrine that property is by birth, which is the corner-stone of the joint family system under the Mitakshara. Hence, it treats the father as the absolute owner of the property, and authorises him to dispose of it at his pleasure. It also refuses to recognize any right in the son to a partition during his father's life-time. (1950: 55; Gharpure 1931: 31–32)

In other words, to *janmasvatvavāda* "the theory that one becomes owner by birth," which Vijñāneśvara defends at length at the beginning of his chapter on inheritance, Bengal opposes the theory of *uparamasvatvavāda* "the theory that someone's ownership comes into being by and not before the death of the previous owner" (cf. Rocher 1971: 1–13). Arguments which scholars invoke to explain why Bengal was different in this respect from

[282] According to S. Śrinivāsa Setlur, "no Hindu writer could hope to impose his treatise on his community or province without taking good care to bring it into harmony with their legal consciousness as expressed in their customs" (1907: 204).

the rest of India range from the fact that Bengal was a center of trade and the heads of families therefore needed free and easy access to family property, to the fact that for a long time Buddhism and Tantrism were stronger in Bengal than elsewhere,[283] and even to influence of Islam (e.g. Bose 1917: xviii).

To test the validity of this premise as far as the principle of spiritual benefit is concerned, it would be helpful if it could be shown that performing *pārvaṇaśrāddha* and offering *piṇḍa*s to the ancestors was more prominent in Bengal than elsewhere. Unfortunately, even the data on present day performance of *śrāddha* in various parts of India are confusing, and extensive field work would be required to determine whether, at least today, it is given more importance in Bengal than elsewhere. To be sure, there are descriptions of lavish *śrāddha* ceremonies performed in Bengal (e.g. Ghose 1901: 180–183). Yet, there are also voices, from within Bengal, to the effect that the *pārvaṇaśrāddha* "has become obsolete among the Hindus and is not generally celebrated at all at the present day."[284]

The second premise involves an element which I already referred to, namely that, starting from the —as yet unproven— belief that the *Mitākṣarā* is older than the *Dāyabhāga*, some scholars, even within Bengal, go as far as to say that, prior to the time when Jīmūtavāhana wrote the *Dāyabhāga*, inheritance in Bengal was governed by *Mitākṣarā* law. But even among those who refrain from making as specific a statement as this, there is the general notion that, if the law of inheritance is different in Bengal from what it is elsewhere, this was the work of Jīmūtavāhana, "the founder of the Bengal school."[285]

Yet, at least as far as the theory of *maraṇasvatvavāda* is concerned, the fact that it is older than the *Mitākṣarā* is beyond dispute. In the introduction to the chapter on inheritance, which I referred to earlier, Vijñāneśvara refutes it at great length, in

[283] Mitra 1905 for example, uses the *Mahāparinirvāṇatantra* to explain certain traits of *Dāyabhāga* inheritance law. Meanwhile, see Derrett 1968: 138–181.

[284] Sarkar 1904: xiv. Sarkar 1910: 335–336. It should be noted that Sarkar also objects to the principle of spiritual benefit itself, at least as far as *piṇḍa*s offered by collateral relatives and *piṇḍa*s offered to maternal ancestors by a maternal uncle etc., are concerned (1904: xxiv–xxv). Using the principle of *apūrva*, he maintains that a *pārvaṇaśrāddha* cannot be of use to the deceased; it is solely for the benefit of the performer (1910: 337). According to Kane too, "several objections can be raised against the theory of Jīmūtavāhana" (1930–1962: 2.473).

[285] E.g., Sarvadhikari 1922: 307. According to Sarvadhikari, "the doctrines of Vijnanesvara and those of the teachers of the Mithila School must have been widely prevalent in Bengal, when Jīmūtavāhana undertook to refute their doctrines, and conclusively proved that the principles laid down by the teachers of Benares and Mithila were not applicable in Bengal."

favor of his own theory of *janmasvatvavāda*. It is interesting to note, on the other hand, that Jīmūtavāhana does not insist on defending his own view on the origin of proprietary rights. The single expression of his opinion on that point appears, almost casually, in his interpretation of the term *pitrya* (1.3.). According to the *Nāradasmṛti* one speaks of *dāyabhāga* (or *dāyavibhāga*) when sons proceed to a partition of *pitryaṃ dhanam*.[286] Alluding to the *Aṣṭādhyāyī* (4.3.74 and 79), Jīmūtavāhana interprets *pitryaṃ* as *pitṛta āgatam*; it therefore means, he says, *pitṛmaraṇopajātasvatvam*. In fact, more than a century ago Julius Jolly recognized that the theory of *maraṇasvatvavāda* was accepted by the author of the *Smṛtisaṃgraha* (8–10th century, quoted by Vijñāneśvara) and by Dhāreśvara Bhojadeva (ca. 1005–ca. 1054, quoted by Vijñāneśvara and Jīmūtavāhana) (Jolly 1885: 109; on the *Smṛtisaṃgraha*, see Kane 1930–1962: 1.538).

The premise that Jīmūtavāhana was the founder of the Bengal school has been applied to the principle of spiritual benefit as well. Even though it has been said by as great an authority as P.V. Kane that Jīmūtavāhana's system, based on a close connection between inheritance and *śrāddha*, may be closer to the ancient texts than Vijñāneśvara's:

> Many of the passages from the Dharmasūtras are capable of being explained away on the theory of Vijñāneśvara, but one cannot help feeling on a careful study of the Dharmasūtra that the ancient sūtra writers saw an intimate connection between taking the inheritance and the offering of *Piṇḍa*s and laid little emphasis on mere relationship by blood (1921–23:79),[287]

the view is still widely held that "the doctrine of spiritual benefit [was] introduced for the first time, by the founder of the Bengal school" (Sarkar 1927: 498). In Derrett's words,

> Jīmūtavāhana discovered a principle, the famous principle of "spiritual benefit," which he could use, like a knife, to cut his way through the jungle of texts, and to discover harmony amongst

[286] *vibhāgo 'rthasya pitryasya putrair yatra prakalpyate / dāyabhāga iti proktaṃ tad vivādapadaṃ budhaiḥ* (13.1 in both Jolly's 1885 and Lariviere's 1989 editions).

[287] Cf., in more general terms, Derrett 1978: "It seems that the *Dāyabhāga* outlook, if we may so call it, was more true to the Hindu tradition than the much more sophisticated and difficult conceptions developed for the Peninsula by Vijñāneśvara in his *Mitākṣarā*, which never became a basis authority in Bengal" (Foreword to *Dāyabhāga*, ed. Heramba Caṭṭopādhyāya Śāstrī. Part. I. Howrah: Howrah Saṃskṛta Sāhitya Samāja, 1978). On the other hand, Jogendra Chunder Bose: "[The *smṛtis*] leave absolutely no room for doubt that the theory of spiritual benefit as understood by the Bengal lawyers, was absolutely unknown to the Hindu Lawgivers" (1917: 31).

> authorities which had previously been discrepant. In order to achieve his effect he was obliged to make many obvious exceptions to his theory, and to pass with a discreet silence over some unexplained anomalies. But the idea was so simple and congenial, so easily remembered and so attractive, that pandits adopted his principles in what would appear to be a short time, and he eclipsed his predecessors. (Derrett 1978)

What this means is that, according to general scholarly consensus, the principle of spiritual benefit was "invented" by Jīmūtavāhana, i.e. in the 11th century according to some or as late as the 15th century according to others.

As to the question whether, in reality, the principle of spiritual benefit too, might be older than Jīmūtavāhana, I must refer to the fact that Jīmūtavāhana (11.6.32) explicitly attributes it to *niravadyavidyodyota*. Unfortunately, no writer by the name of Vidyodyota or Udyota is known from other sources. The commentators on the *Dāyabhāga* interpret the term either as a reference to one of Jīmūtavāhana's predecessors or as a reference to himself.

It has also been suggested that Śrīkara, whom Jīmūtavāhana quotes not only in the *Dāyabhāga* but also in the *Vyavahāramātṛkā*, and hence one of Jīmūtavāhana's undisputed predecessors, "seems to have propounded the view of spiritual benefit as the criterion for judging superior rights of succession." This suggestion, made by Kane, was based on a passage from Śrīkara quoted in Harinātha's *Smṛtisāra* (1930–1962: 1.572).[288] It is true that Śrīkara's text corresponds in some ways to a passage from the *Dāyabhāga* (11.6.8–9); yet, there is no reference whatever to *śrāddha*, the offering of *piṇḍa*s, or the heir being of service to the deceased. In fact, out of the seven occasions on which Jīmūtavāhana quotes Śrīkara, five are negative, some even strongly negative: Śrīkara's opinions are rejected *mandam* (6.1.41), *asaṃgatam* (11.5.16), and *atimandam* (11.5.31). Of the two cases in which Jīmūtavāhana agrees with Śrīkara, one (11.5.12) may or may not have a bearing on Śrīkara's subscribing to the principle of spiritual benefit. The passage refers to the fact that a half brother inherits after a brother german but before a brother german's son:

> *sāpatnasya ca*
> 1. *sodarāt mṛtadeyaṣāṭpauruṣikapiṇḍadātur mṛtabhogyamātrapitrādipiṇḍatrayadātṛtayā jaghanyatvāt*

[288] Kane quotes only the latter part of a longer citation from a *Śrīkaranibandhana*, as preserved in an India Office Library manuscript. I have checked the entire quotation; unfortunately, the earlier part is highly corrupt, and I hesitate to draw from it as specific a conclusion as Kane.

2. *bhrātṛputrāc ca mṛtabhogyapiṇḍadvayadātur mṛtabhogyapiṇḍatraya-dātṛtayā upakārakatvātirekeṇa balavattvāt, madhya evādhikāraḥ Śrīkara Viśvarūpokta evādaraṇīyaḥ.*

One thing this passage fails to make clear is whether only the fact that the half brother inherits in between a brother german and a brother german's son is an integral part of Śrīkara's opinion, or whether the two reasons why this is so are taken from Śrīkara's writings as well. The fact that Jīmūtavāhana attributes the same opinion to Viśvarūpa further complicates the issue. The arguments mentioned by Jīmūtavāhana definitely do not appear in the printed text of Viśvarūpa's commentary on the *Yājñavalkyasmṛti*, but this *argumentum ex silentio* loses much of its value, since, as far as this printed text is concerned, it is well established that "there are grounds to hold that it is corrupt and deficient" (Kane 1925: 204).

In comparison with Udyota, Śrīkara and Viśvarūpa, we are on much firmer ground with another commentator on the *Yājñavalkyasmṛti*, Aparāditya (or Aparārka, which may have been the title of his book). Jolly noted, in 1883, that "certain opinions, which have been viewed as peculiar to the Bengal School, may be traced to Aparārka's commentary" (Jolly 1885: 14). Kane not only reiterated this view, but pointed out, more specifically, that "Aparārka bases the right to take a deceased person's property on the superior spiritual benefit conferred by the claimant on the person deceased" (Kane 1930–1962: 1.719).

Commenting on *Yājñavalkya* 2.135, according to which, failing male offspring, a widow, daughters, and parents, the inheritance goes to the brothers, Aparāditya points out that only brothers german inherit, because they are closer (*pratyāsannatara*) to the deceased than half brothers. Indeed, he says, they offer *śrāddhas* to the same maternal ancestors as their deceased brother; half brothers do not (*te hi mṛtabhrātrapekṣayaikasyaiva mātṛvargasya śrāddhakāriṇo na tu sāpatnāḥ*). And, after quoting MDh 9.187ab and 186 —referred to earlier in this article—, he again insists that it is the brother german who is closer to the deceased "because he offers water etc. to the same beneficiaries" (*samānasampradānodakādidātṛtvāt*). The brother german's son is slightly removed (*īṣadvyavahitaḥ*) from the deceased, because the *piṇḍa* he offers to his father cancels one of the beneficiaries of the deceased. His grandson is even farther removed (*tato 'pi vyavahitaḥ*), because of the two *piṇḍas* he offers to his father and grandfather. Finally, his great-grandson is totally removed (*atyantavyavahitaḥ*), because the three *piṇḍas* to his ancestors exclude any *piṇḍas* for the benefit of the deceased's ancestors. Hence, Aparārka concludes, only the brother, his son, and his grandson are *sapiṇḍa*s of the deceased. The reference to *śrāddha* and the repeated references to *piṇḍa*s and their beneficiaries (*sampradāna*) leave no doubt that, according to Aparāditya, succession generally and the order of succession in particular were based on the principle of spiritual benefit.

Whether Aparāditya is older than Jīmūtavāhana, and whether the principle of spiritual benefit therefore antedated the author of the *Dāyabhāga*, is uncertain. Neither author quotes the other. If Kane is correct in saying that the *Dāyabhāga* was written between AD 1090 and 1130 and that Aparāditya wrote ca AD 1125 (Kane 1930–1962: 1.709, 723), Aparāditya may have been slightly older or younger than Jīmūtavāhana but, for all practical purposes, they may be considered contemporaries.

At least one important conclusion can be drawn from the fact that Aparāditya subscribed to the principle of spiritual benefit. In the colophons of his commentary he is described as follows:

> *śrīvidyādharavaṃśaprabhavaśrīśilāhāranarendrajīmūtavāhanānvaya prasūtaśrīmadaparādityadevaḥ.*

In other words, Aparāditya was a king, born in the family of Jīmūtavāhana, king of the Śilāhāras of the Vidyādhara race.[289]

Even if Aparāditya belonged to the most northern branch of the Śilāhāras (for details and references to studies on the Śilāharas, see Kane 1930–1962: 1.713–715), he reigned somewhere near India's west coast, in present-day Surat District and farther south. This means that the principle of spiritual benefit was upheld in an area far away from Bengal; to put it differently, it means that the principle of spiritual benefit was not, as has been claimed, typically Bengali. It is a recognized fact that "worship of the dead and inheritance appear everywhere in closest connexion with each other" (Schrader 1909: 11–57 at 28–29). Earlier in this paper I quoted Kane to the effect that this was also the case in the Dharmasūtras. Under these circumstances the choice was one of emphasis: either the fact that one inherited implied the duty of performing *śrāddha*, or the fact that one performed *śrāddha* meant that one became an heir. Jīmūtavāhana —and probably many others, not necessarily in Bengal— interpreted the ancient texts in favor of the latter alternative. It is only at the time when the *Dāyabhāga* became recognized as its standard authority, that Jīmūtavāhana's views on the role of the

[289] H.T. Colebrooke refers to the conjecture that the author of the *Dāyabhāga* is identical with Jīmūtavāhana, son of Jīmūtaketu and "a prince of the house of Silāra," but adds: "That, however, is not the opinion of the learned of Bengal" (1810: xii).

pārvaṇaśrāddha in determining the order of succession became one of the characteristic traits of, and limited to, the Bengal School and the law of inheritance in Bengal. It was left to Mr. Justice Dwarkanath Mitter to draw the logical conclusion, and to formulate, in detail, the implications of the principle of spiritual benefit.

16

The Theory of Matrimonial Causes According to the Dharmaśāstra

Introduction

Before dealing with the subject of matrimonial causes according to the Dharmaśāstra a few comments on the title of this paper may not be out of place. These comments will be mainly of a methodological nature.

A first comment is that the Dharmaśāstra does not have a Matrimonial Causes Act, as is the case in England since 1857. In other words, in the whole of ancient Hindu law one would look in vain for a treatise, or even for a separate chapter, dealing exhaustively with what we call matrimonial causes. The result is that the data which I shall present to you as a more or less coherent whole are really drawn from various unrelated chapters of Dharmaśāstra literature.

This first comment leads me on to my second preliminary remark. The fact that no Sanskrit text deals with matrimonial causes as such should not make you think that the data upon which I shall have to work are few in number. In reality they are numerous, far too numerous to be dealt with at all completely in a short paper. Moreover, they are not only numerous; as is the case with most other topics of ancient Hindu law, here, too, the various sources often seem to contradict or even to be repugnant to each other.

It is true that in Roman law, too, the law of marriage and matrimonial causes is far from being uniform. However, in Rome we are usually able to ascribe a date to the various changes, and we are well equipped to place them in their historical perspective. We know, for instance, that from being very strict in early periods, marriage gradually developed into a *liberum matrimonium* at the time of the Republic, to become much more strict again with Justinian who, here as elsewhere, made a conscious effort to return to ancient purity (Buckland 1939: 70–71). The problem is that in India this broad historical background is missing. Here we find the varying legal prescriptions simply juxtaposed; and if we consider that Indian history is much longer than that of Rome, and that the territory encompassed by ancient Hindu law is much vaster than that of Roman law, it will be evident that the number of varying situations in India must have been immensely greater than was the case in Rome.

If I mention all this as a preliminary remark, it is mainly to tell you that, in this state of affairs, various attitudes are possible, and to explain to you the attitude which I have myself adopted while preparing this paper.

It is, of course, possible for the historian of ancient Hindu law to try to emulate the historian of Roman law, and to search for the historical background of the changes in Hindu law too. But I have two objections against such a procedure. In the first place, I cannot regard the efforts which have been made in that direction so far particularly convincing: far too often they lead to a vicious circle, in which the Dharmaśāstra texts are used to reconstruct historical situations which are, then, in their turn employed to explain the changing data in the *smṛtis*. And my second objection is that such historical reconstructions go straight against the very spirit of the ancient Hindu law texts. Differently from us —and this includes a number of modern Indian authors— the ancient *dharmaśāstrīs* firmly believed in a single and unchangeable *dharma*. If their works display differences, it is not because they wanted them to do so. On the contrary, whenever possible they tried very hard harmoniously to integrate the variants into one single system. To give only one example: the various forms of marriage existing in ancient India have not only been integrated into the classical Dharmaśāstras, but have been worked out into a wonderful system of eight forms methodically arranged in a series proceeding from the most respectable to the most detestable.

If I, therefore, reject the approach of those who try to explain the rules of Dharmaśāstra against their historical background, this does not imply that I want to be blind to the changes which undoubtedly manifested themselves in the long history of Hindu law generally and Hindu matrimonial causes in particular. This, then, is the reason why you will hear me quote far more often from the old *śāstras* than from the more recent commentaries. The commentaries are characteristic of one period of ancient Hindu law, no doubt: namely, of the later period. And, once Sir William Jones had stated that "nothing could be more obviously just than to determine private contests according to those laws which the parties themselves had ever considered as the rules of their conduct and engagements in civil life" (qtd. in the preface to Colebrooke 1786–1797), it was completely justified, at the end of the eighteenth century, to have Jagannātha Tarkapañcānana compile a digest based on the commentaries. On the other hand, the commentators are not representative of the whole history of Dharmaśāstra. Their reconstruction of the theory of matrimonial causes is based on the axiom of a perfectly static corpus of Dharmasūtras and Dharmaśāstras, a concept which is as unacceptable as the steady search for the historical background which I referred to before. Like the commentators, we, too, shall have to reconstruct the theory of matrimonial causes on the basis of the several Dharmasūtras and Dharmaśāstras — not to speak of Arthaśāstra— which, although theoretically uniform, in reality display a wide range of variety. I can only hope that my precautions, some of which I have just mentioned, will allow me to reach a certain degree of historical precision. I apologize for these theoretical speculations. But I thought that, in a series of papers touching upon different legal systems, it was my duty to indicate briefly the difficulties and the restrictions which research on matrimonial causes in ancient Hindu law is confronted with. But I shall now come to the study of matrimonial causes themselves.

Since the treatises on Dharmaśāstra do not provide us with an intrinsically binding scheme, I had to establish one myself. I propose to divide this paper into three parts. In the first place I should like to examine the Dharmaśāstra theories on matrimonial rights. Next, I shall try to answer the question whether and, if so, how far ancient Hindu law recognizes the dissolution of marriage. And, finally, I shall venture to give you my opinion on the vexed problem as to how the theory of matrimonial causes was worked out in practice.

Matrimonial Rights

There is no doubt that the Dharmaśāstra pays much attention to the mutual rights of husband and wife, at least indirectly. I shall immediately explain my restriction: "at least indirectly." As is well known, the Dharmaśāstra primarily establishes not "rights" but "duties," duties to be performed by human beings in all situations of life. Hence, as far as married persons are concerned, too, the ancient Indian law texts enumerate their various duties, not their rights. However, inasmuch as a duty of one spouse coincides with a right of the other, I shall conform to modern usage, and speak of matrimonial "rights" in ancient Hindu law.

The mutual rights of husband and wife in a Hindu marriage cannot, I think, be fully appreciated without a short reference to one aspect of the Hindu marriage itself.

Far be it from me to desire to open the file of Hindu marriage as such; although I must confess that, when trying to understand the Hindu theory of matrimonial causes, I often had a feeling that a clearer insight to the nature of the Hindu marriage itself would have been extremely useful. Unfortunately here, too, the data are not such as easily to allow a clear and neat picture.

Whether we agree with Westermarck or not when he holds that among the Indo-European peoples generally there has been a stage when, as a rule, the woman was sold to the man (Westermarck's *History of Human Marriage*, chapter 23, as quoted in Corbett 1930: 1), it cannot be denied that the element of "sale" is not completely absent from the Hindu marriage.[290] I am the more inclined to say so because the authors of the lawbooks vigorously react against this conception. My impression is that the non-legal texts represent a widely spread "popular" view which was unacceptable to the *dharmaśāstrīs* who not only had a more technical notion of sale but also, as we shall see, a more idealistic view of marriage.[291]

On the other hand, if the Dharmaśāstra thus rejects the identification of marriage and sale, it definitely discloses another characteristic which for our purpose is no less interesting. One has only to read the definitions of at least four of the eight forms of marriage —the most respectable ones— to be convinced of the constant presence in the minds of the authors of the idea of a gift, a gift of the maiden by the father to the husband.[292]

However, as I said before, I do not want to discuss here the nature of the Hindu marriage. My only purpose was to point out the

[290] E.g. *Maitrāyaṇīyasaṃhitā* 1.10.11: "she indeed commits falsehood (or sin) who being purchased [*krītā*] by her husband roams about with other males." Cf. Kane 1930–1962: 2.503–7.

[291] E.g. MDh 3.51: "No father who knows (the law) must take even the smallest gratuity for his daughter; for a man who, through avarice, takes a gratuity, is a seller of his offspring." For other references, cf. Kane, *ubi cit.*

[292] Thus MDh 3.27–30: "*The gift of a daughter* after decking her (with costly garments) and honouring (her by presents of jewels), to a man learned in the Veda and of good conduct, whom (the father) himself invites, is called the Brahma rite.

"*The gift of a daughter* who has been decked with ornaments, to a priest who duly officiates at a sacrifice, during the course of its performance, they call the Daiva rite.

"When (the father) *gives away his daughter* according to the rule, after receiving from the bridegroom, for (the fulfillment of) the sacred law, a cow and a bull or two pairs, this is named the Ârsha rite.

"*The gift of a daughter* (by her father) after he has addressed (the couple) with the text, 'May both of you perform together your duties,' and has shown honour (to the bridegroom), is called in the *Smṛti* the Prâjâpatya rite."

existence —consciously or unconsciously— of the view according to which the future husband participated to some extent in the characteristics of a buyer or a donee. In other words, through marriage the husband acquired some kind of ownership over his wife.

If, after all this, I say that according to the Dharmaśāstra both spouses had a right to each other's affection and society, it will be clear from the outset that, if such a right existed on both sides, it was given a completely different content when applied to the husband and wife, respectively.

As far as the wife is concerned, not only does she have to share her husband's life, but she has to do so under any circumstances, even if the husband is wholely vicious. Manu (5. 154) holds:

> Though destitute of virtue, or seeking pleasure (elsewhere), or devoid of good qualities, (yet) a husband must be constantly worshipped as a god by a faithful wife.[293]

The same idea has been expressed again and again in the Dharmaśāstra texts, and equally numerous are the other literary sources illustrating in practice the theoretical rule of the *smṛti*. When, in the *Śatapathabrāhmaṇa*, the young princess Sukanyā has been given in marriage to the old sage Cyavana who had been wronged by her brothers, the Aśvins come by, and they desire to win the young wife's favor:

> They said, "Sukanyā, what a decrepit, ghostlike man is that whom thou liest with; come and follow us!" She said, "To whom my father has given me, him will I not abandon, as long as he lives!" But the Rishi was aware of this. (4.1.5.9)

The highest rewards have been promised to a wife who thus behaves as a *pativratā*, "one faithful to her husband":

> She, who, controlling her thoughts, speech, and acts, violates not her duty towards her lord, dwells with him (after death) in heaven, and in this world is called by the virtuous a faithful (wife, *sādhvī*). (MDh 5.165 = 9.29)

But if a wife cannot tolerate the presence of her vicious husband, a sanction follows automatically:

> She who shows disrespect to (a husband) who is addicted to (some evil) passion, is a drunkard, or diseased, shall be deserted for

[293] Here as elsewhere, rather than translating ourselves —which would involve repeated discussions and justifications— we quote from the existing classical translations of the ancient Hindu lawbooks.

> three months (and be) deprived of her ornaments and furniture. (MDh 9.80)

Whereas the husband thus has a quasi-absolute right to the wife's affection, the same can hardly be said about the wife's right to the husband's affection. For instance:

> She who drinks spirituous liquor, is of bad conduct, rebellious, diseased, mischievous, or wasteful, may at any time be superseded (by another wife). (MDh 8.90)

It is true that supersession by another woman did not leave the superseded wife without means of existence —I shall come to that later— nevertheless it could be a severe punishment from which the husband in similar circumstances remained exempt.

Another eloquent example opposing the husband's absolute and the wife's relative rights to the other's loyalty may be quoted from Kauṭilya (3.2.46–47). It refers to the case in which either spouse is suffering from an incurable disease:

> And the man, if unwilling, need not approach a (wife) who is leprous or insane.
> A woman, however, shall approach a (husband) even of this type, for bearing a son.

Here the element "for bearing a son" is fundamental; I shall have to mention it again very soon.

In connection with the purely sexual aspect of the spouses' rights to each other, too, the difference between the rights —or the duties— of husband and wife is considerable. About the wife who shuns this type of marital duty Baudhāyana (4.1.20) has the following *sūtra*:

> Let him [i.e. the husband] proclaim in the village a wife who, being obdurate against her husband, makes herself sterile, as one who destroys embryos, and drive her from his house.

The husband, under the same circumstances, is, of course, guilty of the same offense:

> He who does not approach, during three years, a wife who is marriageable, incurs, without doubt, a guilt equal to that of destroying an embryo (4.1.17),

but the sanction could hardly have been more different:

> But for the transgression of that husband who does not approach a wife who bathed after temporary uncleanness, (the performance of) one hundred suppressions of breath is prescribed (as a penance). (4.1.21)

A right which undoubtedly belonged to the wife is that of maintenance by the husband. One of the basic principles of Dharmaśāstra in connection with women is that they must be constantly protected. Manu (9.3) says:

> Her father protects her in childhood, her husband protects (her) in youth, and her sons protect (her) in old age; a woman is never fit for independence.

Even though this protection has in a number of cases been interpreted as a kind of custody —"Woman must particularly be guarded against evil inclinations"— the fact remains that it also implied that, as far as married life is concerned, the wife has a right to be maintained by her husband.

Moreover, even if some texts seem to suggest that the husband's duty to maintain his wife applies only as long as she is faithful to him:

> The husband receives his wife from the gods, (he does not wed her) according to his own will; doing what is agreeable to the gods, he must always support her (while she is) faithful (MDh 9.95),

there are other texts which suggest that maintenance should be continued even after the wife has, for some reason or other, been superseded (YDh 1.74; cf. below).[294]

A factor which must have profoundly influenced the matrimonial rights —especially as enjoyed by the wife— was the birth of a son. When reading the texts I often wondered whether the procreation of a son was one of the main results of marriage, or whether it was the very purpose of marriage for a man.[295] But even if I am unable clearly to answer the question —it is one of those questions about the nature of marriage about which I feel I should like to come to a better understanding— the very fact that the question can be raised whether marriage was not contracted with a view to the husband's having a son is a sufficient indication that everything in marriage, i.e. also the matrimonial rights of the wife, depend to a large extent upon whether she gives birth to a son or not.

I cannot refer here to all the rules in which the matrimonial rights of the wife are influenced by her having a son or not, but

[294] The texts about maintenance have been discussed in detail *per* Chandavarkar, J., in *Parami* v. *Mahadevi*, I.L.R. 34 Bom. 282, 285 (1909).

[295] Kauṭilya (3.2.42), when treating the possibility for a man to supersede his wife by one or more others if she does not give birth to a son, adds: "For wives are (necessary) for having sons."

I must at least mention the most remarkable one, namely that a wife who fails to give birth to a son may be superseded by another woman. Thus Kauṭilya (3.2.38–9; cf. MDh 9.81):

> The (husband) shall wait for eight years if the wife does not bear offspring or does not bear a son or is barren, for ten if she bears dead offspring, for twelve is she bears only daughters. After that he may marry a second wife with the object of getting a son.

I shall come back to the legal consequences of supersession later, but it is clear that the status of a sonless woman changed considerably when superseded by another woman who was capable of giving her husband a son.

The high esteem which the ancient Indian sources display for the mother of a son —as against women generally— is well known. For our subject, it might, however, be not without interest first to quote a rule from VaDh (13.47) dealing with the relations between a son and his parents:

> A father who has committed a crime causing loss of caste must be cast off. But a mother does not become an outcast for her son.

Indeed, this *sūtra* helps us to understand another rule, from Śaṅkha-Likhita's Dharmaśāstra (quoted by Kane 1930–62: 2.580), concerning the attitude to be taken by the son in a dispute —the text is so vague that we must assume it includes matrimonial causes— between his parents:

> The son should not take sides between his father and mother: indeed he may, if he so chooses, speak in favour of his mother alone, since the mother bore him (in her womb) and nourished him.

Dissolution of Marriage

It is a well-known fact that the peoples of ancient India had a very high conception of marriage as such. Says Kane: "This is the most important of all saṃskāras. Throughout the ages for which literary tradition is available in India marriage has been highly thought of" (1930–62: 2.427).

The aura of sanctity with which the Hindu marriage has ever been surrounded is so real that it has even influenced the recent developments of Indian marriage law. To quote Derrett: "In fact, in no other respect are the feelings of Hindus so acutely sensitive as when their concept of and beliefs in the importance of marriage as an institution are questioned or attacked. This is largely the work of the Dharmaśāstra, which, after more than two millennia of relentless propaganda, has produced an effect which the West would unhesitatingly label 'puritanical.' Nor is there any trace of conscious hypocrisy in the attitude which is characteristic of caste Hindus: profession and practice keep good company with each other. Such a fact is not to be ignored when considering the proposed alterations in the law" (Derrett 1957: 82).

In principle the Hindu marriage is indissoluble; the basis for this principle has been found in passages like this, from the *Nāradasmṛti* (12.27–8):

> Therefore a father must give his daughter in marriage once (for all), as soon as the signs of maturity become apparent. (By acting) otherwise he would commit a heavy crime. Such is the rule settled among the virtuous.
>
> Once is the (family) property divided, once is a maiden given in marriage, and once does a man say, "I will give"; each of these three acts is done a single time only among the virtuous.

Add to this that one of the traditional duties of husband and wife has been the common performance of religious acts:

> ...from the time of marriage, they are united in religious ceremonies. Likewise also as regards the rewards for works by which spiritual merit is acquired... (ĀpDh 2.6.14.16–17),

and it will be clear that as far as its sanctity and indissolubility are concerned, the ideal Hindu marriage corresponds to the old view of Roman law as expressed in the definition given at the end of the classical period by Modestinus —and accepted by Justinian: *nuptiae sunt coniunctio maris et feminae et consortium omnis vitae divini et humani iuris communicatio* (Buckland 1939: 70).

However, even though marriage in ancient India —in theory and in practice— was so highly thought of, we may state without hesitation that marriage has never been completely indissoluble. I promised to speak about matrimonial causes "according to the Dharmaśāstra"; so I should not go beyond this restriction. Otherwise it would not be difficult at all to produce evidence of the fact that the ideal of the Dharmaśāstra has not been adhered to by the whole population of India.

I shall restrict myself to quoting one single example from a report on the customary law of the Punjab: "It is well known that according to the strict principles of Hindu law, which in this respect is entirely different to the Muhammadan, marriage is regarded as a sacrament, which, when once solemnized, becomes indissoluble....But amongst the Jat population of the province these sacerdotal notions of marriage have obtained but little if any countenance; and thus nothing is more common than to find a deserted wife, or one who has been set aside by her husband, marrying another man in the lifetime of the first husband, and succeeding to his property as a wife" (Boulnois and Rattigan 1876: 95–96).

But I shall come back to the Dharmaśāstra, and quote two stanzas from Manu (9.101–2):

> "Let mutual fidelity continue until death," this may be considered as the summary of the highest law for husband and wife.
>
> Let man and woman, united in marriage, constantly exert themselves, that (they may not be) disunited (and) may not violate their mutual fidelity.

It is clear from these verses that, although in the ideal situation marriage should be for life, this ideal was not always fulfilled. The fact husband and wife are encouraged to make an effort in order to avoid separation implies that separation was not always avoidable.

We shall now try to establish how far separation of spouses existed in the Dharmaśāstra, and which were the forms it assumed.

A first question which I shall try to answer is whether or not ancient Hindu law draws a distinction between what we call void and voidable marriages.

Remarkably enough the distinction has not only been made, but marriages have been declared null and void for a reason which today, in English law and elsewhere, continues to be a ground for nullity: namely, relationship within the prohibited degrees.

This is not the place to examine the exact extent of the prohibited degree in ancient Hindu law —which would mean to define the terms *gotra*, *pravara*, and *sapiṇḍa*; the main point is that such prohibited degrees exist from the Dharmaśāstra onward. Medhātithi, when commenting on MDh (3.11), appeals to a basic principle of Mīmāṃsā to say that when a rule forbidding some action has a "visible," worldly purpose (*dṛṣṭārtha*), it is meant only to express a recommendation; but when such a rule has an "invisible," transcendental purpose, it is a mandatory injunction. The practical difference is that in the former case the act committed is valid and remains so; in the latter case, on the contrary, the act itself is to be considered as not having taken place. When applied to marriage, this means that the purpose of rules forbidding a man to marry, e.g. a diseased girl, is patent, with the result that he who does marry such a girl commits an offense but the marriage as such remains valid; the rules forbidding him to marry a girl who is a *sagotra*, *sapravara*, or a *sapiṇḍa*, on the other hand, have no immediately patent purpose, so that those who marry such girls not only commit an offense but such marriages are also null and void.

Whatever the practical value of these Mīmāṃsā speculations may have been, and even if another commentator on Manu, Nārāyaṇa, rejects the distinction established by Medhātithi, the fact remains that the ancient Hindu commentators, too, have at least conceived the distinction between void and voidable marriages (cf. Das 1962: 144–5).

It seems to me that the concept of a void marriage as against a voidable one also found expression in another way; namely, through the channel of the well-known distinction between two stages in marriage. It is true that the later one goes in the history of Dharmaśāstra, the more it is the second stage only which has been considered as marriage *stricto sensu*; the first stage more and more becomes a preparatory one which finally —I suspect, under Western influence— is spoken of as "betrothal."[296]

Personally, however, I am convinced that this is a later evolution only, and that, according to the Dharmaśāstra, both the so-called betrothal and the actual marriage were but two successive stages of the same *saṃskāra*, "sacrament," marriage. Let me quote the following *śloka* from Nārada (12.2):

> When a woman and man are to unite (as wife and husband), the choice of the bride must take place first of all. The choice of the bride is succeeded by the (ceremony of) joining the bride and bridegroom's hand. Thus the ceremony (of marriage) is twofold (*saṃskāro dvilakṣaṇaḥ*).

But Nārada (12.3) goes on:

> Of these two parts (of the marriage ceremony) the choice of the bride is declared to lose its binding force, when a blemish is (subsequently) discovered (in either of the two parties). The Mantra (prayer), which is recited during the ceremony of joining the bride and bridegroom's hands, is the permanent token of marriage.

In other words: although the *saṃskāra* did actually start with the so-called betrothal, even after this the marriage can be considered null and void; but it can no longer be so once the second stage of the ceremony has taken place. At that moment marriage becomes, in principle, indissoluble, provided that in a number of cases, which we shall come to immediately, it can become voidable.

To be complete I must add that, in the lower forms of marriage especially, nullity during the period separating the two stages of the ceremony seems to have been easily accepted. In connection

[296] E.g. "Marriage is not to be confounded with betrothal. The one is a completed transaction; the other is only a contract" (Mayne 1950: 136).

with the uniqueness of the father's giving his daughter in marriage, Nārada (12.29–30) adds:

> This rule applies to the five (first) marriage forms only, beginning with the Brâhma (form of marriage). In the three (others), beginning with the Âsura form, the (irrevocable) gift (of a maiden to a particular suitor) depends on the qualities (of the suitor).
>
> Should a more respectable suitor (who appears), eligible in point of religious merit, fortune, and amiability, present himself, when the nuptial gift has already been presented (to the parents by the first suitor), the verbal engagement (previously made) shall be annulled.

One of the reasons which most surely render marriage insecure is the husband's prolonged absence from the house. What is meant by absence from the house is clear from a stanza in MDh (9.76); differently from Roman law, where absence includes such situations as captivity and military enlistment (Corbett 1930: 211), ancient Hindu law conceives mainly of three forms of absence:

> If the husband went abroad for some sacred duty (she) must wait for him eight years, if (he went) to (acquire) learning or fame six (years), if (he went) for pleasure three years.

Nārada (12.98–100), without mentioning other forms of absence, takes into account several other factors in order to determine the length of the period during which the wife has to wait for her husband: caste, the fact whether or not there are children, and the fact whether or not any news is received from the absent husband:

> Eight years shall a Brahman woman wait for the return of her absent husband; or four years if she has no issue; ...A Kshatriya woman shall wait six years; or three years if she has no issue; a Vaiśya woman shall wait four (years) if she has issue; any other Vaiśya woman (i.e. one who has no issue), two years.
>
> No such (definite) period is prescribed for a Śûdra woman, whose husband is gone on a journey. Twice the above period is ordained, when the (absent) husband is alive and tidings are received from him.

Manu (9.74–5) seems to see no ground for dissolution of the marriage in cases where the husband duly provided for maintenance for his abandoned wife:

> A man who has business (abroad) may depart after securing a maintenance for his wife; for a wife, even though virtuous, may be corrupted if she be distressed by want of subsistence. If (the husband) went on a journey after providing (for her) the wife shall subject

herself to restraints in her daily life; but if he departed without providing (for her), she may subsist by blameless manual work.

As a matter of fact, Manu never states what the wife shall or may do after having waited for the said periods of eight years, six years, etc. Nārada (12.101), however, leaves no doubt:

> The above series of rules has been laid down by the Creator of the world for those cases where a man has disappeared. No offense is imputed to a woman if she goes to live with another man after (the fixed period has elapsed).

In connection with the absent husband I found one interesting case in which the marriage is capable of termination because of the husband's connivance. Kauṭilya, who of course does not profess to lay down the requirements of righteousness (*dharma*), states (4.12.30–2):

> The husband's kinsmen or his servant should keep under guard the wife who misbehaves when the husband is away on a journey. Kept under guard, she should wait for the husband. If the husband were to tolerate, both should be set free (*nisṛjyetobhayam*).

The same *śloka* of Nārada (12.97) which allows the wife to take another husband when her first husband has been absent for a long time, also allows her to do so "when he has been expelled from caste." According to Kauṭilya (3.2.48), too:

> A husband who... is... an outcast... may be abandoned (*tyājyaḥ*).

The fact that a husband may thus be abandoned because he has been excluded from his caste is, in my opinion, extremely important. I shall not insist upon it here, but I shall not omit using it as an argument in discussion later.

In order to exhaust the *śloka* of Nārada (12.97) I must add that a wife is also entitled to take another husband if the first husband proves to be impotent (cf. AŚ 3.2.48; for further details, see NS 12.15–18).

At first glance impotence is just another ground which makes a marriage voidable. The question of impotence is, however, complicated by another stanza of Nārada (12.8):

> The man must undergo an examination with regard to his virility, when the fact of his virility has been placed beyond doubt, he shall obtain the maiden (but not otherwise).

This prescribed physical examination of the husband must have taken place after the girl had been verbally promised to him but before their hands had been ceremoniously joined together, i.e. between the so-called betrothal and marriage proper. Thus impotence fits in with the whole theory of blemishes attaching to either spouse; compare Manu (9.72–3):

> Though (a man) may have accepted a damsel in due form, he may abandon her (if she be) blemished, diseased, or deflowered, and (if she have been) given with fraud. If anybody gives away a maiden possessing blemishes without declaring them, (the bridegroom) may annul that (contract) with the evil-minded giver.

Although the texts are not very clear on this point, my impression is that all blemishes,[297] whether detected before or after the final marriage ceremony —most of these blemishes could hardly have been detected before— having a bearing not upon the "marriage" but upon the "betrothal." The result is that, if my reasoning is correct, impotence and the other blemishes, instead of being grounds for dissolution of marriage, actually rendered the ancient Hindu marriage null and void from the beginning, or at least voidable.

A number of passages from the Dharmaśāstras deal with situations which we would normally qualify as cases of cruelty. After what I said before, I need no longer insist that cruelty is to be understood as cruelty committed by the wife; for we saw that the wife has to endure her husband, however mischievous he may be.

I shall merely remind you of the verse of Manu (9.80) quoted above:

> She who drinks spirituous liquor, is of bad conduct, rebellious, diseased, mischievous, or wasteful, may at any time be superseded (by another wife);

to which is added in the next verse that she who is quarrelsome may be superseded without delay.

Nārada (12.93) has a slightly different sanction:

> One who shows malice to him, or who makes unkind speeches, or eats before her husband, he shall quickly expel from his house.

According to whether the commentators are more or less favourably disposed towards such wives, Nārada's "banishment from the house" has been extended to "banishment from the

[297] For an enumeration of such blemishes, see NS 12.36–37: "Affliction with a chronic or hateful disease, deformity, the loss of her virginity, a blemish, and proved intercourse with another man: these are declared to be the faults of a maiden. Madness, loss of caste, impotency, misery, to have forsaken his relatives, and the two first faults of a maiden (in the above text): these are the faults of a suitor."

village" in the *Nāradabhāṣya* or reduced to "banishing her from the principal habitation, let him assign to her a *separate* dwelling within his close" in Colebrooke's *Digest* (4.1.63).

Kauṭilya's *Arthaśāstra* has still another ground for dissolution of marriage, a ground which, I think, we may interpret as mutual agreement. In the section on *dveṣa* "hatred, disaffection" the following passage occurs (3.3.15.16):

> A disaffected wife is not to be granted divorce from the husband who is unwilling, nor the husband from the wife. But mutual disaffection (*parasparaṃ dveṣāt*) (alone) a divorce shall be granted.

The only restriction would be that such a dissolution of marriage would be possible in the four lower forms of marriage only.[298]

I suppose the reader must have been struck by the fact that, in a discussion about terminating marriages, I have not so far mentioned adultery. Adultery, which even in the Ecclesiastical Courts in England before 1857 was a ground for a divorce *a mensa et thoro*, is certainly not unknown to the authors of the Dharmaśāstra. On the contrary, the ancient Hindu lawbooks contain numerous rules about adultery; even more so, adultery with other similar offenses appeared as one of the eighteen *vivādapada*s "titles of law" into which ancient Hindu substantive law has been traditionally divided.

In the MDh alone about thirty-five stanzas have been devoted to the subject of adultery. As far as the details of the prescriptions are concerned I admit that it is extremely difficult to detect a system underlying these rules. If it is true that the laws of Manu as we have them are the result of several revisions, revisions which severely undermined its unity, this certainly is the case in the portion dealing with adultery. For the later commentators such portions were a special treat: on them they could display all their skill in harmonizing rules which at first sight were not very harmonious. However, these details are of less importance to us today. I shall rather stress a few basic characteristics of adultery as far as its place within the theory of matrimonial causes is concerned.

A first remark must be that adultery, according to Nārada (14.2) and others (BS 22.1, tr. Jolly) is one of the four types of "heinous offenses" (*sāhasa*):

> Manslaughter, robbery, an indecent assault on another man's wife, and the two species of insult, such are the four kinds of Heinous Offenses (*sâhasa*).

[298] NS 12.90, on the contrary, states: "When husband and wife leave one another, from mutual dislike, it is a sin,..."

This is extremely important, as it locates adultery within the framework of ancient Hindu substantive law, with far-reaching consequences upon adjective law as well —but I shall come to that later.

Moreover, not only is adultery a *sāhasa*, but, *sāhasa* being divided in the usual way into *sāhasa* of the first degree, the middlemost degree, and the highest degree, Nārada (14.6) adds:

> Taking human life through poison, weapons or other (means of destruction), indecent assault on another man's wife, and whatever other (offenses) encompassing life (may be imagined), is called Sâhasa of the highest degree.

With the result that he who commits adultery is liable to the punishment normally prescribed for this highest degree of *sāhasa*:

> For Sâhasa of the highest degree, a fine amounting to no less than 1,000 (Paṇas) is ordained. (Moreover) corporal punishment, confiscation of the entire property, banishment from the town and branding, as well as amputation of that limb (with which the crime has been committed), is declared to be the punishment for Sâhasa of the highest degree. (NS 14.8)

To be complete I must add that, according to a general rule of ancient Hindu criminal law, in the case of a Brāhmaṇa offender, corporal punishment is replaced by some other type of punishment. Thus Nārada (14.9–10) continues:

> This gradation of punishments is ordained for every (caste) indiscriminately, excepting only corporal punishment in the case of a Brahman. A Brahman must not be subjected to corporal punishment.
>
> Shaving his head, banishing him from the town, branding him on the forehead with a mark of the crime of which he has been convicted, and parading him on an ass, shall be his punishment.

Much more important, however, and far more characteristic of the degree to which the adulterer was resented, is his actual exclusion from society:

> Those who have committed Sâhasa of either of the two first degrees are allowed to mix in society, after having been punished, but if a man has committed Sâhasa of the highest degree, no one is allowed to speak to him, even if he has received punishment. (NS 14.11)

It only rarely —too rarely— happens that the ancient Hindu lawbooks explicitly inform us about the justification for their rules.

With regard to the extremely severe treatment of adultery, however, we are lucky to possess the following passage in Manu (8.352–3):

> Men who commit adultery with the wives of others, the king shall cause to be marked by punishments which cause terror, and afterwards banish.
>
> For by (adultery) is caused a mixture of the castes (*varṇa*) among men; thence (follows) sin, which cuts up even the roots and causes the destruction of everything.

My next remark in connection with adultery is that adultery is a very comprehensive term, I mean that it includes acts which, in our opinion, are still relatively innocent. In Halhed's *Code*[299] (1777) it has been described as follows:

> *First* Species is, when, in a Place where there are no Men, a Person, with intent to commit Adultery, holds any Conversation with a Woman, and Winks, and Gallantries, and Smiles pass on both Sides; or the Man and Woman hold Conversation together in the Morning, or in the Evening, or at Night, or any such improper Times; or the Man dallies with the Womans' Cloaths, or sends a Pimp to her; or the Man and Woman are together in a Garden, or an unfrequented Spot, or such other secret Place, and bathe together in the same Pool, or other Water; or the Man and Woman meet together in One visiting Place: This is called the First or most trifling Species.
>
> *Second* Species is, when a Man sends Sandal Wood, or a String of Beads, or Victuals and Drinks, or Cloaths, or Gold, or Jewels to a Woman: This is called the Second, or middle Species.
>
> *Third* Species is, when the Man and Woman Sleep and Dally upon the same Carpet, or in some retired Place kiss and embrace, and play with each others Hair; or when the Man carries the Woman into a retired Place, and the Woman says Nothing: This is called the Third, or worst Species of Adultery.

But not only does adultery cover a large range of acts, it even applies to intercourse with women who are not really married to another man. Nārada (12.7), after enumerating the women with whom intercourse is allowed —prostitutes, female slaves, etc.— adds:

> When, however, such a woman is the kept mistress (of another man), intercourse with her is as criminal as (intercourse) with

[299] Chapter XIX (*Of Adultery*), Sect. I (*Of the several Species of Adultery, which are of Three Sorts*). The work as printed is an English translation of a Persian version of the Sanskrit original.

> another man's wife. Such women, though intercourse with them is not (in general) forbidden, must not be approached because they belong to another man.

Finally there is a last remark about adultery which, I think, is also the most important one as far as this paper is concerned. What I have so far briefly called "adultery" really corresponds to a much longer term in Sanskrit which may be translated literally as "connection with another man's wife." That means that the whole chapter on adultery deals with the crimes committed by and the punishments prescribed for the man who has intercourse with the wife of another person. In other words: if in the Dharmaśāstra texts the king is called upon to inflict punishment for adultery upon a male, he never does so because the said male committed adultery *as a husband.*

As to the adulteress, a number of texts are very severe with her too. The punishment which in the GDh (23.14) is still reserved to the woman who commits adultery with a man of lower caste, seems to have been generalized with Viṣṇu (5.9) and Manu (8.371):

> If a wife, proud of the greatness of her relatives or (her own) excellence, violates the duty which she owes to her lord, the king shall cause her to be devoured by dogs in a place frequented by many.

But there is another text which propounds a completely different view:

> When a married woman commits adultery, her hair shall be shaved, she shall have to lie on a low couch, receive bad food and bad clothing, and the removal of the sweepings shall be assigned to her as her occupation. (NS 12.91)

This is the text which has been quoted repeatedly by later commentators, such as Mitramiśra in his *Vīramitrodaya*, in order to show the humane character of ancient Hindu law which, even for such a serious offense as adultery, far from casting off the adulteress, upholds her claim to maintenance. And the framers of the Indian Penal Code could not have been more in agreement with Nārada than they were when they declared, in regard to section 497 where the other man's wife is said not to be punishable as an abettor in case of adultery: "There are some peculiarities in the state of society in this country which may well lead a humane man to pause before he determines to punish the infidelity of wives. They are married while still children: they are often neglected. They share the attention of a husband with several rivals" (Raju 1957: 1335).

After this long discussion about dissolution of marriage, you must have noticed that I have avoided using the term divorce.

And I have done so on purpose: instead of asking the question immediately whether or not ancient Hindu law knew the concept of divorce, I have preferred to deal with the various aspects of the problem first, and only then to introduce the word divorce.

I suppose that the answer to the question whether or not ancient Hindu Law knew divorce depends on what one exactly understands by "divorce." I consulted the Oxford English Dictionary in order to compare the Indian situation with what I hoped would be the standard definition but nothing could be more vague than:

> Legal dissolution of marriage by a court or other competent body, or according to forms recognized in the country, nation or tribe. [In small type]: Formerly and still often (e.g. historically or anthropologically) used in the widest sense; hence, including the formal putting away of, or separation from, a spouse by a heathen or a barbarian;...

Certainly the situation in which the wife is superseded by another woman can hardly be identified with divorce. Although the husband actually contracts another marriage during the lifetime of his first wife,[300] the superseded woman is supposed to stay on in the house, as may be inferred from Manu (9.83):

> A wife who, being superseded, in anger departs from (her husband's) house, must either be instantly confined or cast off in the presence of the family.

A verse from Yājñavalkya (1.74) even suggests that the husband should maintain his wife in the same way before and after the supersession.[301]

Moreover, as I said before, according to certain authors at least, it seems as if even adultery was not a sufficient reason to expel the wife from the house; and although some older Dharmaśāstras do prescribe expulsion from the house for apparently minor offenses, the later commentators are found prepared to interpret these passages in such a way that they merely refer to expulsion from the main body of the house.

It has been said by a modern Indian author that "*Tyāga* in Kauṭilya is a technical term denoting 'separation from conjugal

[300] Colebrooke, *Digest* IV.1.67: "A *second* marriage, *or one* subsequent to her's, contracted by the husband, is supersession."

[301] Even then her situation cannot have been a highly appreciated one; she seems to have become a symbol with Nārada (1.203): "A perjured witness shall spend his nights in the same manner as a wife who has been superseded (by another)..."

intercourse' as opposed to *moksha* ('freedom'), the technical divorce" (Jayaswal 1930: 230). Even *a priori* I feel suspicious about such applications of modern Western concepts to the ancient Indian situation; moreover, I am unable to find confirmation for this distinction in the texts.

My own impression is that a husband could not obtain a decree of divorce against his wife according to any rule of Dharmaśāstra. But the Dharmaśāstra alludes to and actually permits a situation which, in practice, came very close to divorce, for the husband at least. And even though the Dharmaśāstra does not say so, custom seems to have recognized what we would call the rights of a divorced wife. However, if complete dissolution of marriage —let us call it divorce— was not explicitly sanctioned by the Dharmaśāstra and by the public authorities recognized therein, the question remains to be answered, which authority did sanction the situation which so closely corresponded to divorce? In order to answer this question, I must now turn towards the last point which I wanted to treat here.

Procedure

As I said in my introduction, the last question I should like to pose is that of procedure: how were matrimonial causes dealt with in practice? Here my task becomes perhaps even more difficult than it has been so far. The point is that we do possess whole chapters and, later, complete treatises on the subject of ancient Hindu adjective law. In the Dharmaśāstras these rules have been expounded in the context of the first "title of law," namely, recovery of debts; later they become more or less independent. But in both cases they are cast in such general language that they do not teach us anything about matrimonial causes in particular.

The *prima facie* view would, then, be that we shall assume that matrimonial causes were treated along the same lines as the general theory of ancient Hindu procedure, which I shall outline briefly. However, from the very circumspection with which I introduce the topic it will be understood that this would not be completely correct.

Indeed, all our rules concerning procedure refer exclusively to the procedure as applied in the royal courts. Either *suo motu* or after a plaint has been introduced —that depends upon the nature of the offense— the king hears the plaintiffs and the defendant, examines the various kinds of evidence, and pronounces a judgment. As far as matrimonial causes are concerned, however, we have good reason to believe that they mainly lay outside the king's jurisdiction.

The case of adultery is clear enough. Adultery being a species of *sāhasa*, not only did it belong to the royal jurisdiction, but the king had a right to intervene on his own initiative. The perpetrator of adultery is brought into court not through a plaint introduced by a plaintiff, but by the action of the king's spies whose duty it is to find him out and arrest him (Rocher 1955: 31–2).

So much for adultery; but this is, as we saw before, not a regular matrimonial cause. In regard to the real matrimonial causes the situation is much more complex.

Both Nārada (Quotations 1.6, trans. Jolly 1889: 234) and Bṛhaspati as quoted in the *Vyavahāramātṛkā* (p. 285) have a most embarrassing *śloka*:

> A lawsuit cannot be instituted between a teacher and his pupil, or between father and son, or man and wife, or master and servant.

It is true that such a *śloka* should not *a priori* surprise us: other legal systems too have forbidden spouses to bring actions against each other.[302] However, against the *śloka* of Nārada and Bṛhaspati stands the undeniable fact that "duties of husband and wife" do form one of the eighteen classical "titles of law" or "grounds of judicial procedure." The result is that one would be entitled to infer with Kane: "As it was the husband's duty to provide residence and maintenance for his wife and as the wife was bound to stay with the husband, it follows that either party could after marriage enforce his or her rights in a court of law if the other party refused to perform his or her duties."[303]

The principle put forward by Kane has actually been applied in the Anglo-Indian Courts. Says the headnote of a leading case in which an exhaustive judgment was delivered by the celebrated

[302] "Husband and wife owe to each other a respect and a kindness which cannot indeed be directly enforced by action, but which have important legal consequences... So long as the marriage lasts, they may not institute penal or defaming actions against one another, and even after separation the *actio furti* for things appropriated in contemplation of divorce is replaced *in honorem matrimonii* by the less drastic *actio rerum amotarum*" (Corbett 1930: 125).

[303] It is certainly true that the modern courts often use ancient remedies, as Kane himself rightly points out: "where the courts make the husband pay maintenance, they are in principle following Yāj. I.76 and Nārada" (Kane 1930–1962: 2. 569); but the fact that modern courts do use these ancient remedies in no way justifies the conclusion that the ancient courts did so too. The Anglo-Indian courts may well have started to do so without there being any precedent. The situation is far more correctly presented by Derrett: "Each spouse has a right to the affection and society of the other, unless forfeited. The current law has developed various remedies which may be used to protect the interests of one spouse when they are threatened by the misconduct, neglect or spite of the other. Though the remedies are foreign in nomenclature they are in reality founded upon a *shastric* basis, and not upon justice, equity and good conscience, which would otherwise have supplied them" (1957: 100).

Mr. Justice Mahmood: "The texts of Hindu law relating to conjugal cohabitation and imposing restrictions upon the liberty of the wife, and placing her under the control of her husband, are not merely moral precepts, but rules of law. The rights and duties which they create may be enforced by either party against the other and not exclusively by the husband against the wife. The Civil Courts of British India, as occupying the position in respect of judicial functions formerly occupied in the system of Hindu law by the king, have undoubtedly jurisdiction in respect of the enforcement of such rights and duties. The Civil Courts of British India can therefore properly entertain a suit between Hindoos for the restitution of conjugal rights, or for the recovery of a wife who has deserted her husband."[304]

Various solutions have been proposed in order to reconcile both points of view, none of them, however, being such as to satisfy me completely.

In the typical commentator-like fashion Jīmūtavāhana in his *Vyavahāramātṛkā* (p. 285) refers the texts of Nārada and Bṛhaspati to minor matrimonial matters; only when they are more important do they constitute "titles of law."

A little more sophisticated but equally unsatisfactory is Caṇḍeśvara's explanation in the *Vivādaratnākara* (p. 409):

> Though the appearance of Husband and Wife as Plaintiff and Respondent at the Royal Court has been forbidden —yet it is quite possible that the King may have to hear indirectly of their dereliction of duty towards each other; and in that case it becomes his duty to bring them to the path of righteousness; or otherwise, to punish them. This is the reason why this subject has been brought in as a *Head of Dispute.*[305]

Much more helpful is a modern proposal by N.C. Sen-Gupta. According to Sen-Gupta disputes between husband and wife are not *vyavahāra* because "*vyavahāra* means litigation before the King's Court while these disputes were matters for domestic tribunals" (Sen-Gupta 1953: 46). In his opinion matrimonial causes only gradually came within the range of royal justice; thus a number of topics which do not appear in such old Dharmasūtras as Gautama's do appear later with Manu, Nārada and Bṛhaspati.[306]

[304] *Binda v. Kaunsilia*, I.L.R. 13 All. 126, 127 (1891).

[305] According to G.N. Jha, in his translation of the *Vivādacintāmaṇi*,165.

[306] "This indicates a course of development of King's justice not dissimilar to developments elsewhere. As we shall find more fully later, originally people's tribunals were the authorities for deciding all disputes. The King's justice was first confined to punishment of crimes and more serious social offences. Gradually the King began to deal with a few matters of a civil nature not involving

I cannot agree with the latter part of Sen-Gupta's theory, viz. the suggestion that matrimonial causes gradually passed from the jurisdiction of inferior courts to the royal court. If his reasoning were correct, the evolution should have come to an end by the time of Manu, when matrimonial causes have been dealt with in detail. I fail to see, then, how still later authors like Nārada and Bṛhaspati, who also have a detailed treatment of matrimonial causes, would again declare them not to belong to the royal jurisdiction.

But I do agree with Sen-Gupta that matrimonial causes normally were dealt with by lower courts. My only contention is that this has always been the case, irrespective of whether rules about matrimonial causes are found in the contemporary Dharmaśāstras or not. In short, I think that we have a right to say that caste and, therefore, the caste council, was very important in matters of matrimonial disputes.

Here I should like to come back to the fact that a husband may be abandoned by his wife when he is excluded from his caste. If such could be the case —whereas normally a wife must bear any vice, physical as well as moral, of her husband— or, in other words, if caste could prevail over marriage, it seems to me that marriage must primarily have been a caste affair.

Moreover, not only are there indications of the importance of caste in matrimonial causes in the Dharmaśāstras; the same conclusion is also borne out by the evidence provided by customary law. There are numerous cases, in early Anglo-Indian law, where the judges intervened in matrimonial causes which had already been dealt with by the caste *panchayat* according to the customs prevailing in that particular caste.[307]

In *Reg. v. Sambhu Raghu*, e.g. it has been held that "Courts of law will not recognize the authority of a caste to declare a marriage void, or to give permission to a woman to remarry. Bona fide belief that the consent of the caste made the second marriage valid does not constitute a defence to a charge." The point which interests us most in all this is, in the words of H. Batty, Assistant Sessions

punishment. For some reason or other, administration of justice by the King became popular and people began to flock to King's Courts for redress of their grievances which were previously adjudicated by popular tribunals, with the result that topics of law which, being matters for domestic tribunals, were kept by early law outside the King's justice were absorbed under Vyavahāra step by step" (Sen-Gupta 1953: 46–47).

[307] *Reg. v. Karsan Goja* and *Reg. v. Bai Rupa*, 2 Bom. H.C.R. 124 (1864); *Uji v. Hathi Lalu*, 7 Bom. H.C.R. 133 (1870); *Rahi v. Govinda*, I.L.R. 1 Bom. 97 (1875); *Reg. v. Sambhu Raghu*, I.L.R. 1 Bom. 347 (1876); *Narayan Bharthi v. Laving Bharthi*, I.L.R. 2 Bom. 140 (1877); *Jukni v. Queen Empress*, I.L.R. 19 Cal. 627 (1892); *Sankaralingam Chetti v. Subhan Chetti*, I.L.R. 17 Mad. 479 (1894); etc. See also Derrett 1963: 161ff.

Judge of Khandesh: "Among the lower classes of the Hindus it was a widespread, if not a correct, belief, that where *pharkut, sod chitty* or letter of divorce has been given by the husband, and a *Panchayat* has decided that the marriage has been dissolved, the party so divorced is at liberty to marry again on repayment of the marriage expenses incurred by the first husband."[308]

However, even if caste has been very important, to say simply that matrimonial causes were a matter of caste is not sufficient. The king does in certain cases have to intervene, as, for example in this case cited by Nārada (12.95):

> If a man leaves a wife who is obedient, pleasant-spoken, skilful, virtuous, and the mother of (male) issue, the king shall make him mindful of his duty by (inflicting) severe punishment (on him).

Even more instructive is a passage from Viṣṇu (5.9.18):

> Let the king put to death...a woman who violates the duty which she owes to her lord, the latter being unable to restrain her.

This passage says in so many words that the king does not intervene as long as the husband himself is capable of restraining his wife; he merely does so when the husband fails. And this notwithstanding the means at his disposal, which go as far as permission to beat his wife with a rope or a split bamboo.[309]

My general impression about the Dharmaśāstra theory of matrimonial causes would be this. Ancient Hindu law, whatever be its fluctuations in detail, is, as far as marriage and matrimonial causes are concerned, subject to two tendencies which, if taken strictly, point in opposite directions.

The first of these two tendencies is the idea that marriage is something more than a contract between the two persons directly concerned. The ancient Hindu lawyers understood, as well as Mr. Justice Scrutton in *Hyman v. Hyman*, that "the stability of the marriage tie, and the terms in which it should be dissolved, involve far wider considerations than the will or consent of the parties to the marriage."[310] Marriage also concerns the family; perhaps we might even say that it concerns the Hindu joint family far more than it normally concerns any other family. It also

[308] *Reg. v. Sambhu Raghu*, I.L.R. 1 Bom. 350 (1876).

[309] Thus MDh 8.299–300: "A wife, a son, a slave, a pupil, and a (younger) brother of the full blood, who have committed faults, may be beaten with a rope or a split bamboo. But on the back part of the body (only), never on a nobler part; he who strikes them otherwise will incur the same guilt as a thief."

[310] *Hyman v. Hyman*, P. 1,30, (1929). Qtd. in *Latey on Divorce*, 11th ed., 135.

concerns the caste, and here Manu was explicit: if matrimonial causes are not properly dealt with, the order and the purity of the castes will be upset. Finally marriage also concerns the State: in ancient Hindu law, too, it would be true to say that "the State is too deeply concerned with the sanctity of family life…to leave marriage to the caprice of the individual spouses, to be made a mere temporary union and relaxed or dissolved at will."[311]

At the same time, however, there was also a secondary tendency at work. Section 199 of the Criminal Procedure Code (Act V of 1898) says that "no court shall take cognizance of an offense under section 497 [i.e. adultery] or section 498 [i.e. the offense of enticing or taking away or detaining with a criminal intent a married woman] of the Indian Penal Code, except upon a complaint made by the husband of the woman, or in his absence, made with the leave of the Court by some person who had care of such woman on his behalf at the time when such offense was committed." More than the section of the Criminal Procedure Code itself I want to quote a comment made on it by Mr. Justice Pigot and Mr. Justice Hill: "The intention of the law is to prevent Magistrates inquiring, of their own motion, into cases connected with marriage unless the husband or other person authorized moves them to do so."[312]

In other words, marriage also is —perhaps, essentially is— a private affair, where, as far as possible, disputes must be settled *intra muros* without any public authority intervening. I am convinced that this second general principle, too, is strongly present in ancient Hindu law. And here I should like to come back to the text of Nārada and Bṛhaspati according to which, in Jolly's translation, "a lawsuit cannot be instituted between man and wife." In reality this text does not mean that a lawsuit must not or may not be instituted between husband and wife; the Sanskrit expression *vyavahāro na sidhyati* simply means that a lawsuit between spouses is "not accepted," i.e. "not acceptable," i.e. "not to be recommended." In other words, the stanza of Nārada and Bṛhaspati implies that such lawsuits could exist, that they did exist, but that they should be avoided as much as possible.

Moreover, the interpretation which I propose here is not only in agreement with the Sanskrit text; it is also confirmed by legal practice. In his book, *Hindu Law of Marriage and Stridhan*, Sir Gooroodass Banerjee says that, although his subject is a difficult one, at least "it is free from one source of complication which often perplexes the student of law. It has not to be disentangled out of a mass of unconnected precedents." And, after this state-

[311] *Nachimson v. Nachimson*, P.85, 217 C.A. (1930).
[312] *Jatra Shekh v. Reazat Shekh* (1892), I.L.R. 20 Cal. 483 (headnote).

ment, he offers an explanation which, I think, is a most interesting one: "One cause of this scantiness of case-law is, I believe, the sacramental character of marriage in Hindu law. Owing to this, the Hindus are so careful to observe the rules concerning marriage and to avoid error, unless it be on the safe side, and so strong is their disinclination to question the validity of marriage in any case, that disputes concerning this topic seldom arise for judicial determination" (Banerjee 5th ed. 1923: 33–4).

Indeed, marriage and matrimonial causes being considered highly private affairs, it is but natural that, rather than the royal court, caste and caste customs were allowed to play an important part. These customs were very much closer to the spouses than the general rules of Dharmaśāstra.

I gladly confess that my understanding of this difficult problem of legal procedure in ancient Hindu law has been helped very much by another modern judgment. It is by Mr. Justice Sankaran Nair of Madras who, when having to decide about the validity of a particular marriage, said: "Where... the religious and legal consciousness of a community recognizes the validity of a certain marriage, it follows that it cannot be discarded on account of its repugnance to that system of law [i.e. the Dharmaśāstra]. Whether the marriage is valid or not, according to the caste rules, it is for the caste itself to decide. So far as ancient history and modern usages go, marriage questions have always been settled by the caste itself and the validity of a marriage between members of a caste who recognize it as binding has not been questioned by outsiders though the caste itself may be lowered in their estimation when such marriages are repugnant to their notion of morality. When, therefore, a caste accept a marriage as valid and treat the parties as members of the caste, it would be, it appears to me, an unjustifiable interference for the courts to declare those marriages null and void."[313]

The ancient Hindu law texts have perhaps less eloquently worded these principles than the modern authors and judges. However, the principles are there, be it with variations and fluctuations. On the one hand, marriage and matrimonial causes are private affairs, to be dealt with, if not by the spouses themselves, by their family and their caste, according to the caste customs. Only if and when this is insufficient do the public authorities intervene, and then in so far as possible according to local customs, and otherwise according to the general principles of Dharmaśāstra. Either tendency may prevail with a particular author, or even in different parts of the works of the same author, but I think that these variations are of less importance than the general principles underlying them.

[313] *Mushusami Mudaliar v. Masilamani*, I.L.R. 33 Mad. 342, 355 (1910).

17

Jīmūtavāhana's Dāyabhāga *and the Maxim* Factum Valet

For a number of years I have been working on a new translation, to be followed by a first critical edition, of Jīmūtavāhana's *Dāyabhāga*, the twelfth-century[314] *nibandha* which the British authorities in Calcutta heralded as the principal Sanskrit text on inheritance for the Bengal School of Hindu Law. The *Dāyabhāga* has been translated only once, in 1810 (together with the section on inheritance of Vijñāneśvara's commentary on the YDh, the *Mitākṣarā*), by Henry Thomas Colebrooke. Colebrooke's translation has been often reprinted but has never been replaced.

The new translation has been close to completion for some time, except, first, for a few specific and well circumscribed passages in which Jīmūtavāhana's reasoning is not yet sufficiently clear,[315] and, second, on account of some general problems which make me wonder whether anyone so far has understood Jīmūtavāhana as he wished to be understood. It is one of these general problems which I want to address in the following pages.

One important way in which Jīmūtavāhana and, as a result, the Bengal School of Hindu law under British rule and in Independent India until 1956[316] differed from Hindu law elsewhere

[314] The date of Jīmūtavāhana has been debated for a long time. A discussion of the various views on the subject, and the arguments in favor of the twelfth century will be found in the introduction to my forthcoming *Dāyabhāga* translation [Ed.: See now Rocher 2002].

[315] E.g., when Jīmūtavāhana uses words such as *tathā* or *kiṃca* it is not always obvious to what they correlate. Occasionally equally uncertain is the implication of terms such as *ataḥ* or *ata eva*.

[316] The Hindu Succession Act, 1956, Sec. 4(1) abrogated "any text, rule or interpretation of Hindu law or any custom or usage as part of that law in force

in India, was that, for the author of the *Dāyabhāga*, the head of the joint family has absolute power over joint family property. No one else, not even his sons, has any right of ownership as long as he is alive. They cannot sell it, gift it, or dispose of it in any form, without their father's permission.

Jīmūtavāhana had no problem demonstrating that the head of the joint family has absolute power over property acquired by himself during his tenure. Even with regard to movable ancestral property, i.e., movable property that came to the family head from his own father, Jīmūtavāhana could find *smṛti* texts that supported his view that the head of the family, and he alone, owns it, i.e. can do with it anything he likes.

An often quoted verse[317] says so explicitly, but, at the same time, as far as immovable ancestral property is concerned, it seems to say exactly the opposite:

> *maṇimuktāpravālānāṃ sarvasyaiva pitā prabhuḥ;*
> *sthāvarasya tu sarvasya na pitā na pitāmahaḥ.*

> The father is master of gems, pearls, and corals, all of it; but neither the father nor the grandfather is master of immovable property, all of it.

By means of arguments too long to go into here, and not relevant to the thesis of this paper, Jīmūtavāhana proves that even the latter half of this verse allows the head of the family to dispose of immovable ancestral property by gift or otherwise, the sole proviso being that his actions are *kuṭumbavartanāvirodhin* "provided they do not interfere with the sustenance of the family," for the family must be sustained by all means (*kuṭumbasyāvaśyaṃ bharaṇīyatvāt*).

After these introductory remarks I propose to look more closely at the immediately following passage in the *Dāyabhāga*. At 2.27 Jīmūtavāhana introduces a *pūrvapakṣa* to the effect that, based on two Vyāsa verses, no single individual member whosoever of a joint family is entitled to dispose of any joint immoveable property.

> *sthāvarasya samastasya gotrasādhāraṇasya ca*
> *naikaḥ kuryāt krayaṃ dānaṃ parasparamataṃ vinā.*

immediately before the commencement of this Act...with respect to any matter for which provision is made in this Act"; it declared that "any other law in force immediately before the commencement of this Act shall cease to apply to Hindus in so far as it is inconsistent with any of the provisions contained in this Act."

[317] Jīmūtavāhana attributes the verse to Yājñavalkya, though it is not part of the YDh. Most often (DhK, *Vyavahārakāṇḍa*: 1219) it is attributed to Nārada, even though it does not appear in the NS either.

vibhaktā avibhaktā vā sapiṇḍāḥ sthāvare samāḥ;
eko hy anīśaḥ sarvatra dānādhamanavikraye.

No single individual shall,[318] without the consent of the others, trade or gift any immovables that are common to his *gotra.*

Whether separated or not, *sapiṇḍa*s are equal with regard to immovable property; each of them individually is powerless to gift, pledge, or sell any of it.

Jīmūtavāhana comments:

na ca…etad Vyāsavacanadvayena ekasya vikrayādyanadhikāra iti vācyam

It is not so that these two Vyāsa verses deny a single person the right to sell, etc.

Indeed, he continues, denying that right would amount to a contradiction in terms with the definition of ownership:

yatheṣṭaviniyogārthatvalakṣaṇasya svatvasya dravyāntara ivātrāpy aviśeṣāt

Owning something means that one can use it at one's own discretion; that definition applies to immovable property as well as to any other property.

The correct interpretation of Vyāsa, Jīmūtavāhana says, is as follows:

Vyāsavacanaṃ tu svāmitvena durvṛttapuruṣagocaravikrayādinā kuṭumbavirodhād adharmabhāgitājñāpanārthaṃ niṣedharūpaṃ na tu vikrayādyaniṣpattyartham,

i.e., an evil person who disposes of property, and thereby makes the family suffer, incurs *adharma*; the text does not mean to say, however, that the sale and so on are null and void.

Obviously, some predecessor stated that the optative form *na kuryāt* in the first Vyāsa verse must be interpreted "*shall* not make";[319] we know that Jīmūtavāhana's successors too, generally were of the same opinion.[320] In fact, Jīmūtavāhana, and with him the Bengal

[318] On the translation of the Sanskrit optative as "shall," see below.
[319] Hence my translation "shall" in the context of the *pūrvapakṣa* above.
[320] Śrīkṛṣṇatarkālaṅkāra, the most important commentator on the *Dāyabhāga*, maintains that Jīmūtavāhana's purpose here was *Caṇḍeśvaramatam apākartum.* In fact, Caṇḍeśvara is more recent than Jīmūtavāhana; yet such anachronisms are common in the *Dāyabhāga* commentaries.

School of Hindu law, stand alone with the interpretation to the effect that *na kuryāt* here merely means "*ought* not to make."

At least, in this specific case Jīmūtavāhana makes it clear that, in his opinion, the optative does not mean "shall," and, as a result, that the verse does not imply that the transaction is null and void. For the translator of the *Dāyabhāga*, however, the question arises as to the extent to which Jīmūtavāhana wished to interpret other optatives, gerundives, etc. in the same way. To answer that question it may be helpful to look at the next passage in the *Dāyabhāga* (2.29).

Apropos of another Vyāsa verse,

sthāvaraṃ dvipadam caiva yady api svayam arjitam
asambhūya sutān sarvān na dānaṃ na ca vikrayaḥ

No gift or sale of immovables or slaves without calling all his sons together, even if he acquired them on his own,

Jīmūtavāhana says:

evaṃ ca...ityevamādikam; tad apy evam eva varṇanīyam; tathāhi kartavyapadam avaśyam atrādhyāhāryam,

i.e., what is true for the earlier two Vyāsa verses is also true for this verse and other verses to the same effect; they too must be interpreted in the same way. Indeed it is necessary to supplement them with the word *kartavya*.

In other words, the latter Vyāsa verse as it stands may seem to suggest that the transactions it refers to are null and void; however, the verbal form to be supplemented here is the gerundive *kartavya*, with the result that this verse too, says that the transactions may be morally reprehensible, but they are not null and void.

After this Jīmūtavāhana concludes. And he introduces his conclusion with *tena*, which means that this is not a conclusion pertaining only to the immediately preceding *smṛti* text; it is his conclusion concerning the entire discussion of the father's right to dispose of immovable ancestral property:

tena dānavikrayakartavyatāniṣedhāt tatkaraṇād vidhivyatikramo bhavati na tu dānādyaniṣpattiḥ,

i.e., as a result, on account of the negative injunction to the effect that the gift or sale ought not to be made, if one gifts or sells immovable property nevertheless, one defies an injunction, but the gift or sale is not null and void.

Immediately thereafter follows a sentence that serves as the overall justification of the entire discussion:

> *vacanaśatenāpi vastuno 'nyathākaraṇāśakteḥ*
>
> Because no deed once done can be changed even by a hundred texts.

This sentence, with potentially far-reaching consequences, appears only once in the *Dāyabhāga*. Also, as far as I know, it is unique in Sanskrit legal literature.[321]

In other legal systems, of course, such a principle is well known. Jīmūtavāhana's statement comes close to the maxim in Roman law, *factum valet*, or, more completely, *quod fieri non debuit factum valet* "what ought not to be done is valid when done." More important for the impact of the maxim on Anglo-Hindu law and even Hindu law after Independence is the fact that *factum valet* also has a long history in British jurisprudence (Derrett 1958: 280–302; reprinted in Derrett 1977: 3.1–24).

There are two possible interpretations of Jīmūtavāhana's single reference to *vacanaśatenāpi vastuno 'nyathākaraṇāśaktiḥ*. Either he mentions it only once because he considered disposition of immovable property to be an exceptional situation, or else, the fact that he does mention the principle suggests that he also considers it applicable to other injunctions as well.

Before returning to the *Dāyabhāga*, I will mention only briefly that the British jurists working in India leaned in both directions (For details on relevant case law, see Derrett 1958). Right from the first edition of *A Treatise on Hindu Law and Usage* John D. Mayne wrote, with a reference to the problem discussed in this article:

> It is usual to speak of the doctrine *factum valet* as one of universal application in the Bengal school. But this is a mistake. When it suits Jimuta Vahana, he uses it as a means of getting over a distinct prohibition against alienation by a father without permission of his sons (II.30). I am not aware of his applying the doctrine in any other case. (1950:28)[322]

[321] My colleague Wilhelm Halbfass kindly draws my attention to a number of Mīmāṃsā texts using the formula *na vacanaśatenāpi*, be it in a slightly different context (if something is impossible, not even a hundred texts can enjoin it). E.g., Śabara on PMS 3.1.12: *na hi vacanaśatenāpy anārabhyo 'rthaḥ śakyo vidhātum. yo hi brūyād udakena dagdhavyam agninā kledayitavyam iti, kiṃ sa vacanaprayojanasāmañjasyam aśnīta?* Similarly, both Śabara and Kumārila on *sūtra* 3.2.4. Cf. also Śaṅkara's use of the phrase *na hi śrutiśatam api*... (e.g., *Gītābhāṣya* 1866; *Bṛhadāraṇyakopaniṣadbhāṣya* 3.3 intro.). [Ed. note: Medhātithi's commentary on MDh 8.3 has a similar statement, namely "*na smṛtivirodhād vastusthitir āhantum śakyate.*"]

[322] Mayne went on to say: "No Bengal lawyer would admit of any such subterfuge as sanctioning, for instance, the right of an undivided brother to dispose

On the other hand, in one of the most recent editions of Mulla's *Principles of Hindu Law*, edited by Sunderlal T. Desai (1970: 467), *factum valet* is described as a "doctrine of the Hindu law enunciated by the author of the *Dayabhaga* and recognized by the *Mitakshara* school."

To be sure, the advocates of a broader application of the *vacanaśatena* rule immediately add a caveat: "The 'texts' referred to…are texts that are directory as distinguished from those that are mandatory... It is different where an act is done in contravention of texts which are in their nature *mandatory*" (ibid.: 467–468). Yet, the responsibility to decide which *smṛti* rules belong to the former category and which belong to the latter lay entirely with British judges and British magistrates. They elaborated different criteria at different times and in different places, but they never reached a general agreement.[323] Horace H. Wilson went as far as to blame the British for the ensuing confusion: "We are confident, that the question between illegality and validity would never have been agitated under a Hindu administration."[324]

Finally I would like to return to the text of the *Dāyabhāga*, to investigate whether or not Jīmūtavāhana himself gives us other indications than the single *vacanaśatenāpi* passage on those *smṛti* rules the transgression of which he considers as legal wrongs and on those *smṛti* rules which, if transgressed, entail a moral wrong only. I am inclined to think that on many occasions —I would dare to say on all occasions where the distinction is important— he did, and he did so in various ways.

First, it is quite common for Jīmūtavāhana, in order to prove a point, initially to quote one or more *smṛti* texts, but, subsequently, to add *yuktaṃ caitat* or a similar expression to that effect, followed by reasons why the *smṛti* is not only a *vidhi* but a matter of common sense as well. Even though he never says so explicitly, the implication is that transgressing that kind of *smṛti* text would be wrong, both legally and morally.

of more than his own share in the family property for his own private benefit, or as authorizing a widow to adopt without the husband's consent, or a boy to be adopted after *upanayana* or marriage. The principle is only applied where a legal precept has been already reduced by independent reasoning to a moral suggestion."

[323] Derrett introduced his own solution as follows: "Before passing to consider the present condition in India, the writer would like, with great diffidence (seeing the acknowledged intricacy of the subject), to suggest the way out" (1958: 298).

[324] In a review of Francis Workman Macnaghten's *Consideration of the Hindoo Law, As It is Current in Bengal* (1824). The review was published originally in the *Quarterly Oriental Magazine* 3 (1825): 171–240, and reprinted in Wilson (1865: 5.1–98). See p. 74.

At 11.2.4–5, for instance, Jīmūtavāhana quotes two *smṛti* texts in support of the fact that, when daughters are next in line to inherit, and when there are different kinds of daughters at that time, the unmarried daughters alone inherit first. At 11.2.6 he continues:

> *yuktaṃ caitat dhanam antareṇāpariṇītāyaḥ kanyāyā ṛtudarśane pitrādīnāṃ narakapātaśruteḥ.*

The evil consequences for a father whose daughter reaches womanhood before she is married are then substantiated by texts of Vasiṣṭha and Paiṭhīnasi.

On the basis of ViDh 17.5–7, failing daughters and daughter's sons, the inheritance goes to the father, then to the mother (11.3.1). Jīmūtavāhana goes on (11.3.3): *nyāyāgataṃ caitat.* In this case the argument of common sense is drawn from the theory of spiritual benefit: the father is of less service to the deceased than a daughter's son, but of greater service than the mother.[325]

Again, at 11.4.1–2, ViDh 17.7 (in conjunction with ViDh 17.8 at 11.5.1) is quoted to establish that the mother inherits prior to the brothers, *yuktaṃ caitat.*

The difference between legal wrongs and moral wrongs is made even more clearly in a different way, namely when Jīmūtavāhana observes that the transgression of a *smṛti* rule is "not *dharmya.*"

At 3.1 Jīmūtavāhana refers —*pratīkena*— to MDh 9.104 which he quoted earlier (1.14):

> *ūrdhvaṃ pituś ca mātuś ca sametya bhrātaraḥ samam bhajeran paitṛkaṃ riktham anīśās te hi jīvatoḥ,*

and he comments:

> *uparate pitari bhrātṛṇāṃ vibhāgaḥ...mātari jīvantyāṃ saty api pitruparamād dhanasvāmitve dharmyo na...bhavati.*

i.e., when the father dies his sons become the owners of his property. Yet, MDh 9.104 says that they *bhajeran* the paternal property only after their mother is deceased as well. That means, according to Jīmūtavāhana, that a partition of paternal property before the mother's death is not *dharmya.*

Jīmūtavāhana subsequently (3.4–11) quotes four other texts to the same effect as MDh 9.104, but from 3.12 onward he goes on

[325] Being of greater or lesser service to the deceased depends on a combination of the number of *piṇḍa*s any survivor offers to the deceased himself and/or to other ancestors to whom the deceased would have to offer *piṇḍa*s if he were living. Cf. Rocher (1992: 637–49).

to describe at length what happens when the sons do proceed to a partition prior to the mother's death, notwithstanding all the texts to the contrary. First, in such partition the mother plays a pivotal role:

ata eva jīvantyāṃ mātari mātṛpradhānakaṃ vibhāgam nirdiśati Vyāsaḥ;

in fact, without the mother's consent the partition is again said to be not *dharmya* (3.13). Second, at 3.29 Jīmūtavāhana lays down that in such cases the mother is entitled to a share equal to that of her sons:

pitari coparate sodarabhrātṛbhir vibhāge kriyamāṇe mātre 'pi putrasamāṃśo dātavyaḥ,

based on NS 13.12c: *samāṃśahāriṇī mātā.*

All this clearly shows that, for Jīmūtavāhana, the verb *bhajeran* at MDh 9.104 only means "ought to," i.e., that a partition of paternal property by sons prior to the mother's death is morally wrong, but that the partition stands nevertheless.[326]

On the other hand, in connection with partition of ancestral property Jīmūtavāhana quotes two texts allowing the father to take two shares, i.e., twice as much as he gives to each son:

jīvadvibhāge tu pitā gṛhṇītāṃśadvayam svayam (BS 26.16),

and,

dvāv aṃśau pratipadyeta vibhajann ātmanaḥ pitā (NS 13.12ab).

In this case he does not say that, if the father takes more than two shares for himself, the partition is merely "not *dharmya*," i.e., that it is morally wrong but that it stands nevertheless. That such was indeed not his intention is made explicit only much later in the *Dāyabhāga* when, after a lengthy excursus, he returns to the texts quoted at 2.35, and concludes:

kramāgatadhanād...bhāgadvayaṃ pitā svayaṃ gṛhṇīyāt; ato 'dhikam icchann api nārhatīti vacanārthaḥ (2.73),

i.e., even if the father feels inclined to take more of the ancestral property than a double share, the BS and NS texts prevent him from doing so.

[326] Cf. Śrīkṛṣṇa's commentary: "*dharmyo na*" *iti. tathā ca vibhāgaḥ sidhyaty eva kiṃtu sa dharmyo neti bhāvaḥ. ata evoktaṃ* "*saty api*" *ityādī vibhāgādhikārajñāpanārtham.*

In other words, transgressing these texts is not only morally wrong but legally wrong as well: in this case *factum valet* does not apply, and the partition would be null and void.

It is too early to decide whether and, if so, to what extent, Jīmūtavāhana differs from other commentators and *nibandhakāras* in applying to the Indian *smṛtis* a principle corresponding to the Latin maxim *factum valet*. In other areas too, Jīmūtavāhana "has been sometimes regarded in the light of a bold reformer" (Jolly 1885: 108); *factum valet* may well prove to be a case in point.

18

The Divinity of Royal Power in Ancient India according to Dharmaśāstra

I

In order to avoid any misunderstanding about the bearing of the remarks contained in the present paper, I feel obliged to draw the reader's attention to its very distinct limitations. As expressed in the title, the present paper deals with the divinity of royal power in ancient India *according to the texts on* Dharmaśāstra.

I do not propose to deal with and to make pertinent statements about the problem of the divinity of royal power in ancient India generally. There are several reasons for my imposing the restriction *according to the* Dharmaśāstras.

The main reason is that I am aware of the limitations of my knowledge. There are so many aspects to the problem of the divinity of royal power, that I have not been able yet to closely examine *all* sources dealing with the problem.

To quote just a few examples:

1. A complete survey of the problem should start with a thorough survey of the situation in Vedic times (cf. Schlerath 1960).
2. Next it should turn its attention to the period of the Brāhmaṇas. I think, for instance, of the numerous data that could be drawn from a close examination of the *rājasūya* the royal consecration ceremony as described in the Brāhmaṇas belonging to the various Vedic schools. However, in order to show the difficulties involved in only this single aspect, I shall refer to the fact that a Dutch scholar spent several years studying the *rājasūya* according to the Yajus school of the Veda alone (cf. Heesterman 1957).

3. After that, a complete survey of the divinity of royal power should draw its data from the whole epic literature: *Mahābhārata*, *Rāmāyaṇa* and the Purāṇas. It should examine the various branches of classical Sanskrit literature, and should not neglect the references occurring in inscriptions, etc.
4. But this is not all. An examination of all these sources which I just enumerated would give an acceptable historical perspective of the problem as a whole. However, there are also a number of side problems which are perhaps not wholly and directly related to our subject but which have a definite bearing upon it. And the sources to be examined here often go far beyond purely written documents. I shall merely refer to one such study which has been undertaken by Jeannine Auboyer, first in a short article: "The Symbolism of Sovereignty in India according to Iconography (Parasols-Thrones)" (1938: 26–36) and later in a book, i.e., *Le trône et son symbolisme dans l'Inde ancienne* (1949).

I hope that this brief enumeration will constitute an adequate apology for the fact that I do not deal here with the problem of the divinity of royal power in ancient India generally.

One more reason is that a general survey has been offered recently, viz. by Gonda (1956–57). With a remarkable sense of synthesis, a brilliant Sanskritist at the height of his career, Gonda brought together everything which is known about the religious aspects of ancient Indian kingdoms. If I were to give a general idea of the problem under consideration, I would merely summarize the points dealt with by Gonda. But there would be nothing original and there would certainly be no merit to it.

All these reasons were at the basis of my restricting the subject to one particular series of sources. As to the reason why it had to be the Dharmasūstra, I shall first of all admit that this is the type of literature which I know better than any other. But there also is a more valid reason: I hope to be able in this way to present some personal and new views. And I also hope that these views drawn from the Dharmaśāstra texts will throw some important light upon the problem as a whole.

II

A first and preliminary fact which deserves our attention is the extreme divergence of the opinions that have been voiced about the divinity of royal power in India.

As a representative of one extreme I shall quote Monier-Williams. In his book *Religious Thought and Life in India* (1883: 259) he defends the thesis that "In India every King is regarded as little short of a present God." And this point of view, according to which royal power was indeed sacred, will be found expressed again and again in later works.

To quote one example. In his note on "Hindu Theories of the Origin of Kingship and Mr. K.P. Jayaswal," the anonymous "G" analyzes a passage of Viśvarūpa, a commentator on Yājñavalkya, ca. 9th century AD, and derives from it the conclusion that this passage "expresses in the clearest terms the divine creation of the human king" (1925: 577).

But there are other opinions too. Not merely opinions which differ from the one held by Monier-Williams and others, but actually diametrically opposed to it.

Prof. A.S. Altekar in an article on "Divinity of King in Hindu Polity," quotes a number of examples to prove his thesis that "the conception of the divinity of the king was never taken by anybody very seriously. No one was prepared to concede infallibility to the king on the strength of that theory as was done in the West" (1939: 155).

It is true that Altekar's article may appear to be biased to a certain extent: it was meant to demonstrate that the Indian thinkers had been less naive than their Western counterparts, and that they never went so far as to deify their kings. But even then I am convinced that Altekar was perfectly honest when he uttered the opinion that the Sanskrit texts do not testify to the sacrality of royal power in India.

As a matter of fact, the same opinion has been voiced by Westerners as well. For instance, Louis Gray in his article "King (Indian)," explicitly states that "anything even approximating to a priest-king is unknown in Aryan India" (1914: 720).

Thus, a number of very honest and serious scholars, although working upon one and the same set of sources, have come to contradictory conclusions. According to some, all ancient Indian kings were considered to be regular deities; according to others, the royal power of the ancient Indian kings has never assumed a sacred character.

Moreover, all these contradictory conclusions seem to have been based upon a sound and unobjectionable analysis of certain Sanskrit texts, which lead us to the embarrassing conclusion that the sources themselves must be mutually contradictory, with the result that, according to whether one bases one's conclusions upon certain texts rather than upon others, these conclusions are bound to be completely different.

The main goal which I have set myself is to show how one should deal with such contradictory texts. I shall try to demonstrate which texts should be interpreted literally and which should not. Or to put it more clearly and more correctly, I shall try to show what were the author's intentions behind these apparently contradictory texts. The contradictions are, indeed, only apparent; we should do away with them in order to come to the true picture as it was intended by the authors of the Dharmaśāstras themselves.

III

On examining the most reputed of the Dharmaśāstras, the *Mānava-Dharmaśāstra* or *Manusmṛti*, it seems as if the divine character of the king's personality has been expressed in the clearest possible terms: "Even an infant king must not be despised, (thinking) that he is a (mere) mortal; for he is a great deity in human form" (7.8).

Actually, the verse from Manu is the conclusion of a much more detailed passage (7.3–5) where the author dwells upon the origin and the constituent parts of the king:

> For, when these creatures, being without a king, through fear dispersed in all directions, the lord created a king for the protection of this whole (creation) taking (for that purpose) eternal particles of Indra, of the wind, of Yama, of the sun, of fire, of Varuṇa, of the moon and the lord of wealth (Kubera). Because a king has been formed of particles of those lords of the gods, he therefore surpasses all created beings in luster.

And about the exact relationship between the king and these various gods, the text goes on as follows: "Through his (supernatural) power he (is) fire and wind, the sun and moon, he the lord of jusfice (Yama), he Kubera, he Varuṇa, he great Indra" (7.7).

I am perfectly aware that, at this stage, some of the specialists on Dharmaśāstra would raise an objection: all texts quoted so far, they will say, have been borrowed from the *Manusmṛti*—similar texts in the *Mahābhārata* might originate from the same quarters. Now, the fact that the situation is such with Manu does not prove anything for the Dharmaśāstras as a whole. On the contrary, the *Manusmṛti* is representative of very special historical circumstances only.

For instance, U.N. Ghoshal in his book, *A History of Hindu Political Theories*, holds that the *Manusmṛti* essentially is a reaction against Buddhism. Within the framework of this general thesis, the special point of Manu's recognizing the divinity of royal power would constitute a reaction towards the Buddhist conception of royal power as a kind of contract. "It was, therefore, necessary that new theories of the king's origin should be propounded involving a higher basis for the king's office than mere agreement of the people. Of such a nature, in our view, are the theories of the *Mahābhārata* and the *Manusaṃhitā*" (Ghoshal 1927: 125).

The point of view according to which the various Dharmaśāstras reflect changing political situations raises a basic problem of Dharmaśāstra interpretation which I cannot possibly deal with in this paper. Several years ago I expressed my own opinion on this matter (cf. Rocher 1957: 472–95). My researches at that time led me to the conclusion that the different texts may perhaps reflect some political differences, but, if they do so, they do so unconsciously and certainly not on purpose. The main purpose of the Dharmaśāstra is to describe one eternal and unchanging system of *dharma*. In my opinion they have been successful in this undertaking. There are differences, no doubt, but in texts separated by hundreds of miles and hundreds of years, it is not the differences in detail but the overall unity which is of the greatest importance.

To come back now to the divinity of royal power, the situation described by Manu is not at all peculiar to that text. Here, too, Manu does not describe an exceptional situation such as prevailed at the time of the composition of the *Manusmṛti* only.

I can easily prove this thesis by quoting a few other Dharmaśāstra texts which present a picture which is identical with the one presented by Manu.

In the first place I shall quote from a text which is generally accepted to be older than the *Manusmṛti*. I mean: the *Vasiṣṭha-Dharmasūstra*: "And with reference to this (matter) they quote a verse proclaimed by Yama, 'No taint of impurity, forsooth, falls on kings...; for they are seated on the throne of Indra...'" (19.48).

In the second place, I want to refer to a text which undoubtedly is more recent than Manu. *Nāradasmṛti* reads as follows: "In this world there are eight auspicious things: the brahmin, the cow, fire, gold, ghee, the sun, the waters, and, the king as the eighth" (18.54).

There is even more: the idea of the divine character of kingship also occurs in Kauṭilya's *Arthaśāstra*: "The king occupies the place of Indra and Yama."

This fact is indeed very significant, if we consider the very nature of the Arthaśāstra. It is a well known fact that after the recent discovery of Kauṭilya's *Arthaśāstra*, a number of authors have expressed their happiness. After having had to draw our knowledge about ancient Indian society and polity from nothing but the Dharmaśāstra —which gave us a distorted picture resulting merely from the Brahmin's wishful thinking—, finally, we have at our disposal a de-mystified, un-sacerdotal and matter-of-fact description of ancient Indian society. From now onwards we can dispose of the data of the Dharmaśāstra; we shall rather rely on the data contained in the Arthaśāstra.

Personally, I cannot believe in the sharp distinction which has been drawn between the Dharmaśāstra on the one hand and the Arthaśāstra on the other. In the article which I already referred to,

I have tried to prove that there may be some differences between Arthaśāstra and Dharmaśāstra —such as there are differences between the Dharmaśāstras themselves—, but these few differences should not prevent us from seeing the more essential fact, i.e. the basic unity that exists amongst all our sources about ancient Indian society, be they called Dharmaśāstra or Arthaśāstra.

To come back to our subject, the point which I wanted to call attention to is that the sacrality of ancient Indian royal power also occurs in the *Arthaśāstra*.

I am not even the first one to say so. E.W. Hopkins in "The Divinity of Kings," states: "Kauṭilya also uses the same argument as Vasiṣṭha. Kings occupy the position of gods and hence should be honoured and obeyed" (Hopkins 1931: 310).[327]

If one says that Kauṭilya adopted the current idea of the king's divine nature, it affords proof for my thesis that Arthaśāstra and Dharmaśāstra are not as different as some scholars pretend them to be. If, on the contrary, one holds the opinion that the Arthaśāstra is a de-mystified form of Dharmaśāstra, it is the more remarkable that the king is described there as a divine being.

This is the very conclusion which I would like to stress once again before proceeding farther: in all the texts dealing with ancient Indian institutions —be they called Dharmaśāstra or Arthaśāstra— the king has been presented as a divine being, in a number of cases even as the sum total of several divinities incorporated in one single human being.

IV

I should now like to investigate the role which the same texts ascribe to the king within the framework of the social and administrative organization of the kingdom. And I shall state straightaway that we will soon discover a number of indications and features of ancient Indian kingship which only with difficulty fit in with the divine character which has been expressed in such elaborate and unequivocal terms.

In the first place, there is the well-known fact that the king belongs to the *varṇa* of the Kṣatriyas. I am perfectly aware of the objection that will be raised against such a statement: there have indeed been kings who were not Kṣatriyas. We know of kings who belonged to the Śūdra class. But, we should never forget that these are the exceptions, and that the vast majority of kings —I would say the normal type of kings— always were Kṣatriyas. In order to demonstrate

[327] Cf. also U.N. Ghoshal: "...Kauṭilya...[adopted] the familiar idea of the king's divine nature..." (1927: 113).

this fact, I shall again return to the *Manusmṛti* (4.84–86):

> Let him (i.e., the Veda-student) not accept presents from a king who is not descended from the Kṣatriya race, nor from butchers, oil-manufacturers, and publicans, nor from who subsist on the gain of prostitutes. One oil-press is as (bad) as ten slaughter-houses, one tavern as (bad as) ten oil-presses, one brothel as (bad as) ten taverns, one king as (bad as) ten brothels. A king is declared to be equal (in wickedness) to a butcher who keeps a hundred thousand slaughter-houses; to accept presents from him is a terrible (crime).

Consequently, the king normally belongs to the Kṣatriya-*varṇa*, that means to the second class. This inevitably raises the problem of the relations of the king with some of his subjects who happen to belong to the first class, I mean the Brahmins.

I need not repeat here that, from the oldest times onwards, a certain relationship between the Brahmins and the Kṣatriyas has been established. One only has to refer to the *Puruṣasūkta* of the *Ṛgveda* where it is said about the Puruṣa: "His mouth gave birth to the Brahmins, his arms to the Rājanya, his thighs to the Vaiśya, and from his feet sprang the Śūdra" (10.90).

The same conception, even more strongly, has been perpetuated in the Dharmaśāstras. Thus, the *Manusmṛti* says (1.93–96):

> As a Brāhmaṇa sprang from (Brahman's) mouth, as he was the first-born, and as he possesses the Veda, he is by right the lord of this whole creation. For the self-existent (Svayambhū), having performed austerities, produced him first from his own mouth, in order that the offerings might be conveyed to the gods and manes and that this universe might be preserved. What created beings can surpass him, through whose mouth the gods continually consume the sacrificial viands and the manes the offerings to dead? Of created beings the most excellent are said to be those which are animated; of the animated, those which subsist by intelligence; of the intelligent, mankind; and of men, the Brāhmaṇas.

Moreover, if we look somewhat more closely at some of the attributes of the Brahmins in the Dharmaśāstras one of them at least has a direct bearing upon the subject which concerns us at this stage.

To quote again from the *Manusmṛti* (9.317–319):

> A Brāhmaṇa, be he ignorant or learned, is a great divinity, just as the fire, whether carried forth (for the performance of a burnt oblation) or not carried forth, is a great divinity. The brilliant fire is not contaminated even in burial-places, and, when presented with oblations (of butter) at sacrifices, it again increases mightily. Thus, though Brāhmaṇas employ themselves in all (sorts of) mean occupations, they must be honoured in every way; for (each of) them is a very great deity.

The important fact to be noticed here is that we have discovered in ancient Indian society not just one divine person, but two kinds of divine individuals: the king on the one hand, the Brahmins on the other.

Faced with such a situation, and in view of a correct appraisal of the king's divine status, a comparison of both types of so-called divinities may be expected to procure some useful indications.

A text which I should like to quote first establishes a comparison, not between the Brahmins and the king, but between the Brahmins and the Kṣatriyas generally. However, it will not be without interest to quote it, not only because it clearly indicates the general relations between both *varṇas*, but also because, as is clear from the context, the *śloka* more particularly aims at the first among the Kṣatriyas, i.e., the king.

> When the Kṣatriyas become in any way over-bearing towards the Brāhmaṇas, the Brāhmaṇas shall duly restrain them; for the Kṣatriyas sprang from the Brāhmaṇas. Fire sprang from water, Kṣatriyas from Brāhmaṇas, iron from stone: the all-penetrating force of those (three) has no effect on that whence they were produced. (MDh 9.320–21)

Now, coming to the texts about the Brahmins and the king in particular, I shall refer to the *Gautamadharmasūtra*: "The King is master of all, with the exception of the Brāhmaṇas" (11.1).

A direct result of this situation is that the king who normally upholds the *dharma* as far as the other *varṇas* are concerned —we shall come back to this point— is advised not to interfere in a discussion between Brahmins on such matters. As is clear from Manu, "If twice-born men dispute among each other concerning the duty of the orders, a king who desires his own welfare should not (hastily) decide (what is) the law" (8.390).

It is true that certain other judicial cases have been withdrawn from the king's authority. I think of cases between merchants, military people, etc.

> For those who stay in the forests the session should be held in the forest, for the soldiers in the army, and for the merchants in the caravans. (BS I.73)

However, it is clear that the purpose behind such prescriptions was the creation of special courts of justice, of courts *ad hoc*, the members of which were considered to be more familiar with the customs of their own groups.

In the case of the Brahmins, on the other hand, the motive was completely different. It will suffice to quote the following solemn warning addressed to the king by Manu (9.313–16):

> Let him (i.e. the king) not, though fallen into the deepest distress, provoke Brāhmaṇas to anger; for they, when angered, could instantly destroy him together with his army and his vehicles. Who could escape destruction, when he provokes to anger those (men), by whom the fire was made to consume all things, by whom the (water of the) ocean was made undrinkable, and by whom the moon was made to wane and increase again? Who could prosper, while he injures those (men) who provoked to anger, could create other worlds and other guardians of the world, and deprive the gods of their divine station? What man, desirous of life, would injure them to whose support the (three) worlds and the gods ever owe their existence, and whose wealth is the Veda?

The relative status of the king and the Brahmins is also evidenced by the elevation of the seat they are supposed to occupy. To quote GDh: "All, excepting Brāhmaṇas, shall worship him who is seated on a higher seat, (while they themselves sit on a) lower (one)" (11.7).

In other words, the Brahmin is the only person of the assembly who should occupy a seat more elevated than the king's.

More evidence in the same direction is provided by the rules concerning priority on the roads. Gautama, for instance, after quoting the general rule: "Way must be made for a man seated in a carriage, for one who is in his tenth (decade), for one requiring consideration, for a woman, for a *snātaka*, and for a king" (6.24); adds that "But a king (must make way) for a *śrotriya*" (6.25). It is as if Āpastamba, after having stated that:

> And (way must be made), by the other castes, for those men who are superior by caste. (2.5.11.8)

fears that this general rule will not be sufficient and, therefore, specifically adds:

> The road belongs to the king except if he meets a Brāhmaṇa. But if he meets a Brāhmaṇa, the road belongs to the latter. (2.5.11.5–6)

Vasiṣṭha, finally, simply states: "If a king and a *snātaka* meet, the king must make (way) for the *snātaka*s" (13.59).

As a last example which is apt to illustrate the relations between the king and the Brahmins, I should like briefly to refer to the person of the *purohita*, who is more or less the king's assistant in religious matters. Gautama (11.12–14), e.g., says:

> And he shall select as his domestic priest a Brāhmaṇa who is learned (in the Vedas), of noble family, eloquent, handsome, of (a suitable) age, and of a virtuous disposition, who lives righ-

> teously and who is austere. With his assistance he shall fulfill his religious duties. For it is declared (in the Veda): "Kṣatriyas, who are assisted by Brāhmaṇas, prosper and do not fall into distress."

We shall not deal here with the origin of the office of the *purohita*: this topic belongs to the sphere of the Brāhmaṇas, rather than to the Dharmaśāstras. Those interested may be referred to Gonda's article on the same (1955: 107–24).

As far as the functions of the *purohita* are concerned, there is one especially interesting text which states that the gods refuse to accept the food which is offered to them without the intermediary of a *purohita*. Therefore, before proceeding to any sacrifice, the king should appoint a *purohita*, who should be a Brahmin, and on this occasion pronounce the formula: "May the gods accept the food which I offer to them" (*Aitareyabrāhmaṇa* 8.24.2).

I believe this text does not leave any doubt. The so called divine king does not, by himself, find any audience with the gods; the gods would actually refuse to hear the message which he would personally address to them. The real ambassador to the gods is not the king but the Brahmin, and it will even depend upon the latter whether the gods will be favorable towards the king or not.

V

Before proceeding I should like to recall the two facts which have been established so far with regard to the Dharmaśāstras:

1. The king is, without any doubt, described as a deity, or even as the incarnation of several deities.
2. However, there is in the Dharmaśāstras another great deity: the Brahmin. Moreover, the latter is certainly more divine than the former.

I now propose to examine the practical implications of this situation and, thus, the positive restrictions imposed upon the divine character of the king.

It may not be out of place here to refer to the twofold meaning of the Sanskrit term *dharma*. It means:

1. the duties which every element of the universe has to fulfill, and
2. as a result thereof, collectively, a kind of cosmic balance, dependent upon the fulfillment of their duties by all the elements.

If one or more elements do not fulfill their duties, the result is *adharma*, i.e., a disturbance of the general cosmic balance, with all the evil results thereof.

Now, in order to understand the position of the king in ancient Indian society, it is essential to keep in mind that he, too, forms part of this all-embracing system of *dharma*. In other words: that there is a *rājadharma* which is essential in order to keep up the general cosmic balance.

Consequently, the king's office, far from being a right —a divine right— basically consists of an extensive set of duties.

There is even more: the recognition of the fact that the king's office mainly consists of duties leads us towards a better appreciation of his so-called divinity. However strange it may seem, there is an intimate relationship between the royal duties on the one hand and his divine right on the other. A few examples will make clear what I mean.

The first of the the royal duties is *prajāpālanam* or *rājyapālanam*, "the protection of his subjects" or "the protection of his kingdom." Now, "protection of the kingdom" means: protection of the frontiers of the country, all around, against foreign invasions.

At this stage I should like to refer again to the few verses from Manu which I quoted before in order to show that the king embodies not just one but several —I shall add now: eight— gods. Or I shall quote another verse from Manu in which the same idea has been expressed again, even more clearly as far as the point under consideration is concerned. The verse says: "A king is an incarnation of the eight guardian deities of the world, the Moon, the Fire, the Sun, the Wind, Indra, the lords of wealth and water (Kubera and Varuṇa) and Yama" (5.96).

After this verse, I suppose the actual meaning of the identification of the king with the said eight deities is clear. The king is said to incarnate these deities because they symbolize one of his main duties.

We even can go one step farther in establishing the connection between *rājadharma* and the king's divine nature and in order to show the dependence of the latter on the former. In the *Mahābhārata* it is said: "If the king follows his *dharma*, he attains the dignity of a god; if not, he goes to hell" (12.90.30).

In the *Rāmāyaṇa* (2.102.4) too, Bharata tells Rāma that, whereas the king is normally considered as a man, he considers him as a god, on the condition that his conduct is in accordance with his *dharma* and, therefore, superhuman. On the contrary the *Rāmāyaṇa* (7.53.6) says, if the king does not every day fulfill his duties with regard to his subjects, he will go to hell.

In other words, the king's divine status depends on the condition that he upholds his *rājadharma*. As soon as he goes astray, the divine status, too, is lost.

It has not been said anywhere *who* decides whether the king upholds his *dharma* or not; in other words, whether he still is a divine being or not. But even if it has not been explicitly stated, there are a number of hints which leave little doubt about the question. I shall at least refer to some of them.

We know that the king who does not follow his *dharma* should be dethroned and even put to death. The king should be dethroned, according to *some* texts, by the people (MBh 8.61.33; Rām 3.33.16). According to other texts, the king should be dethroned by the Brahmins (*Śukranītisāra* 4.7.332). Taken together, these texts strongly create the impression that it is the Brahmin's privilege to decide —and to allow the people— that the king should be dethroned.

There is one more indication which points in the same direction. It has been said that the king is the protector of *dharma*; one of his obligations which derives therefrom is the duty to preside over the law courts. The king is indeed the presider of the court of law operating in his state. Thus the impression is created that it is the king who decides what is each subject's *dharma*, who decides when this *dharma* has been deviated from, and who assigns punishment accordingly. But if we look more closely at the composition of the law courts, we find that the king is assisted by a committee of Brahmin assessors. They are the actual interpreters of dubious points of *dharma* and; what is even more interesting, they should not withhold from saying *apriya* "unfriendly things" whenever they consider the king to deviate from his *dharma*. To quote *Kātyāyanasmṛti*: "When the judge knows that the mind of the king has deviated from the path of equity he should not speak merely to please him; when he does so, he is guilty" (76).

To sum up this latest point: the king's divine character, according to the Dharmaśāstras, is far from absolute. On the contrary, it is purely dependent upon his fulfilling his royal duty, his *rājadharma*. If he does not fulfill it, his divinity is irreparably lost. And those who decide in these matters are precisely the other group who equally have been described as gods, I mean the Brahmins.

VI

Finally, before concluding, I feel obliged to provide an answer to one more question.

If I point more and more strongly into the direction that the ancient Indian king according to the Dharmaśāstras was actually not a divine being, I have in some way or other to account for the explicit statements which I quoted before and according to which he *is* such a divine being. In other words, what shall be done with the equation king = god which seems totally to contradict the actual situation? Have we a right to disregard the meaning which they verbally convey?

However strange this may seem at a first glance, we are indeed entitled *not* to take these texts strictly and verbally. Those who are familiar with the rules of interpretation contained in the Mīmāṃsā are aware that beyond the *vidhi*s "the strictly prescriptive rules" there is another category of texts called *arthavāda*, i.e., texts which, if taken strictly, would lead to serious inconsistencies.

With regard to these *arthavāda*s, Kisori Lal Sarkar, in his book on *The Mimansa Rules of Interpretation as applied to Hindu Law*, states: "There is another way of effecting conciliation between apparently conflicting texts. It is by taking one of the texts to be an *Arthavāda*" (1909: 92).

In other words, if the authors of the Dharmaśāstras have inserted in their works statements which are too laudatory to fit in with the real situation described by them elsewhere in their works, these texts should be interpreted as purely laudatory statements, as statements saying much more than they actually wanted to say. The authors of the Dharmaśāstras, and of other works too, were aware of the fact that they had the liberty every now and then to resort to such exuberant statements, and they often availed themselves of this liberty.

In order to show, in the special case of the description of certain categories of beings as divinities or even the highest divinity, how a literal interpretation would lead to absurdities, I shall quote a few statements from ancient Sanskrit literature where individuals other than Brahmins as well as the king are described as divine:

1. For a wife, the husband is a divine being (Rām 7.48.117);
2. The ancient sages all together form "the highest divinity" (*Kādambarī* 62.5.6);
3. And the title "the highest divinity" has not even been reserved to persons only. Thus, "science is the highest divinity" (Bhartṛhari).

The necessity to interpret the text saying that the king *is* a divinity as pure *arthavāda* is the more incumbent, since we have other texts where his divine status has been represented quite differently. Thus, Manu (9.304–11)

> Let the king emulate the energetic action of Indra, of the Sun, of the Wind, of Yama, of Varuṇa, of the Moon of the Fire, and of the Earth. As Indra sends copious rain during the four months of the

> rainy season, even so let the king, taking upon himself the office of Indra, shower benefits on his kingdom. As the sun during eight months (imperceptibly) draws up the water with his rays, even so let him gradually draw his taxes from the kingdom; for that is the office in which he resembles the Sun. As the Wind moves (everywhere), entering (in the shape of the vital air) all created beings, even so let him penetrate (everywhere) through his spies; that is the office in which he resembles the Wind. As Yama at the appointed time subjects to his rule both friends and foes, even so all subjects must be controlled by the king; that is the office in which he resembles Yama. As (a sinner) is seen bound with ropes by Varuṇa, even so let him punish the wicked; that is his office in which he resembles Varuṇa. He is a king, taking upon himself the office of the Moon, whose (appearance) his subjects (great with as great joy) as men feel on seeing the full moon. (If) he is ardent in wrath against criminals and endowed with brilliant energy, and destroys wicked vassals, then his character is said (to resemble) that of Fire. As the Earth supports all created beings equally, thus (a king) who supports all his subjects (takes upon himself) the office of the Earth.

It would not have been possible to state more clearly that such expressions as "he assumes the form of" (Agni, Indra, etc.) do not mean anything more than that one expects the king to be ardent, courageous, mild, severe, liberal, etc., respectively. It also means that the verses saying that the king *is* Indra, Agni, etc., are to be interpreted in exactly the same way as those declaring the king *to be* the father, the mother, the guru, etc., of his subjects (MBh 12.139.103).

The conclusion we thus arrive at is very similar to the point of view defended by Altekar according to whom the sources "emphasise upon *the functional resemblance* between the king and some gods and not upon his divine origin, either in the real or in the metaphorical sense" (1939: 154).

Although I am extremely happy to see my own conclusion corroborated by an eminent scholar like Altekar, I may not neglect to draw attention towards the different bearings of this common point of view. For Altekar, the said point of view holds for ancient India in general, without any restriction. Personally, I do not pretend to have demonstrated anything beyond the very limited sphere of the Dharmaśāstras, perhaps not even beyond the very restricted quarters where these texts originated from.

There is no doubt that other conceptions of royalty have equally well been held in India.

As far as the period preceding the Dharmaśāstras is concerned, the belief in the king's divine character seems to have spread rather widely. Heesterman who has more especially examined the Vedic texts, came to the conclusion that every student of Indian culture "perforce must be" aware of the divinity of the ancient Indian king (1957: 5).

Gonda goes one step further, and defends the opinion that "in India the divinity of kings, however small their domain, has always been accepted *by the masses*" (1956–57: 36).

I am also convinced that even in modern India several examples could be quoted which witness to the divine character of the king's royal power. The Rāja of Puri, for instance, has until very recently been considered as an incarnation of Viṣṇu.

And when plague broke out in Bombay just after Queen Victoria's statue had been damaged by a number of unruly subjects, voices were raised according to which the plague was nothing but the revenge of the outraged queen-goddess (Hopkins 1931: 314).

Now, it is true that if the divine nature of royal power did exist before the creation of the Dharmaśāstras, and if it is true that the same conception continued, even up to the present day, we must ask the question where we should insert the Dharmaśāstra point of view into the picture; we must ask how it came about, etc.

It would be too easy an answer to say that the restricted royal power as seen in the Dharmaśāstra came about with Dharmaśāstra literature itself. In reality, there are several hints in earlier literature pointing to the existence of similar ideas at that early time.

In a passage of the *Aitareyabrāhmaṇa* (1.15), the human king is presented as definitely inferior as compared to the king Soma.

In the description of the *Rājasūya* in the *Śatapathabrāhmaṇa*, the Brahmin as it were apologizes because he has to assign to the king a position inferior to his own:

> A Brāhmaṇa then hands to him the sacrificial (wooden) sword —either the *Adhvaryu*, or he who is (the king's) domestic chaplain— with, "Indra's thunderbolt thou art: therewith serve me" —the sacrificial sword being a thunderbolt, that Brāhmaṇa, by means of that thunderbolt, makes the king to be weaker than himself; for indeed the king who is weaker than a Brāhmaṇa is stronger than his enemies: thus he thereby makes him stronger than his enemies. (5.4.415)

Some scholars have spoken of a gradual desacralization of royal power in India. The gradual strengthening of the caste system, bringing the Brahmins to the top of the social ladder, led to a situation in which the king lost his divine power in order to be subjected to the Brahmins. For instance, Démètre Makrydimas, in his book *La royauté hindoue d'après les codes brahmaniques*: "Ainsi le pouvoir brahmanique aurait peu a peu mis indirectement sous sa tutelle le pouvoir royal qui parait avoir été le plus ancien" (1923: 90).

Personally, I am convinced that the situation is not as simple as that. It is not just a question of one conception of royal power at a certain moment being replaced by another. Several conceptions may have existed simultaneously. The *arthavādas* in the Dharmaśāstra, preaching the divine character of royal power, may well reflect the more popular point of view as against the more learned view expressed elsewhere in the same texts. This, however, must remain a pure hypothesis, until the moment it will have been supported by decisive evidence.

19

A Few Considerations on Monocracy in Ancient India

A. Preliminary Remarks

1. As indicated by the title, this paper does not pretend to offer an exhaustive survey of monocracy in ancient India.[328] The limitations which had to be imposed are twofold:

a) It would not be possible to take into account *all* the sources from which data can be drawn on the subject. The situation is such that all types of Indian literature happen to casually refer to the subject. It would be a preliminary task that all these passages be duly collected and interpreted. To this should be added references from inscriptions and all available historical data (to be collected from works of foreign visitors to India, etc.). The present paper will draw its material from the classical sources of Hindu law and institutions only, i.e., from the treatises on Dharmaśāstra and Arthaśāstra and from the parallel passages of the epics dealing with these subjects.

b) Even within this limited range of sources, it will not be possible to enter into a discussion of all aspects of monocra-

[328] For a more exhaustive discussion of ancient Indian kingship we strongly recommend J.W. Spellman 1964. Apart from the treatment of the material as such, we especially refer to Spellman's *Glossary* (244–63) which will prove very useful for those who are less familiar with Sanskrit terminology, and to the *Bibliography* (264–74). Amongst recent studies which do not figure in the latter, we shall mention Saletore 1963 and Drekmeier 1962.

cy raised by the authors.[329] On principle we shall not pay much attention to those aspects which are not directly relative to the comparative history of institutions;[330] and amongst those that are, a selection will be made so as to lay emphasis mainly upon the great principles which underlie the whole theory of Indian monocracy.

2. Notwithstanding the twofold limitations referred to in the preceding paragraph, the amount of material to be examined remains considerable. Moreover, it comprehends Sanskrit texts which have been composed over a period of several centuries and which have been written in various parts of the extensive Indian subcontinent. Needless to say that the texts, therefore, to a certain extent reflect varying historical situations and that they display a number of differences.[331]

These divergences present a serious danger: according to one's paying attention to a particular set of texts to the exclusion of others, the image becomes completely different. In the special case of monocracy this has allowed a lot of speculation on the side of modern interpreters. Not to speak of those who were less favorably inclined towards the Indian system, even those who could not be accused of such feelings have drawn fantastic pictures of the Indian theory of government which are in no way warranted by the texts at our disposal.[332]

Especially in a paper meant for comparatists we shall abstain from any form of such speculation and merely try to make the texts speak for themselves. We rather prefer to leave it to the reader to assign to the Indian system the place which it deserves

[329] The best guide through the source materials is still the encyclopedic work of the dean of all students of Hindu law, P.V. Kane, *History of Dharmaśāstra (Ancient and Mediaeval Religious and Civil Law).* Except when explicitly stated, we refer to vol. 3. For Indian kingship according to the Dharmaśāstras, cfr. also D. Makrydimas 1932.

[330] As far as the various *religious* aspects of ancient Indian kingship are concerned, cf. Gonda 1956–57. In this connection we shall also mention Schlerath 1960.

[331] Cf. Kane: "…it has to be borne in mind that the works referred to cover a period of several centuries and further that India is not one country but a continent which Northern India formed one more or less homogeneous unit, while the Deccan formed another and South India formed a third unit" (1930–62: 3.14, n. 19).

[332] We fully agree with the statement of Kane: "Nor is it possible to enter here into formal and lengthy refutations of the several views propounded by Western and Indian writers about the forms and functions of Government and the state of society in Ancient India. Most of the modern works referred to in note 16 above are more or less based on the same material in Sanskrit and Pali, but the emotional or subjective element is different in each case" (1930–62: 3.15).

amongst the parallel systems in other parts of the world and at other moments of history.

3. The fact that this paper addresses itself to comparatists is equally responsible for other features which would be different if the text had been written for the sake Indologists. We shall as far as possible avoid quotations from Sanskrit texts, and whenever they have to be referred to translations will be added.

For the same reason references will be added mainly to those Sanskrit texts for which reliable translations are available. A list of them is added in the notes.[333]

4. It might not be out of place to draw the reader's attention to the complete lack of historical perspective which he may vainly look for in this paper. As has been said before, the texts undoubtedly reflect actual historic circumstances. But if they do, this is practically of no avail since the circumstances themselves are not known to us. Moreover, the authors of the texts essentially make an effort to describe the *dharma* which is beyond time and beyond change.[334]

B. Importance of Monocracy

1. The main general fact to be derived from all the sources which have been examined is the omnipresence of monocracy. All texts without discussion accept the existence at the head of the state of a king.

This does not imply that there have been no other types of government at all. On the contrary, at the time of Buddha and a few centuries after him —according to the evidence contained in epic poetry (cf. Hopkins 1889: 57–376)— there are traces of a type of government which has been indicated with the terms *gaṇa* or *saṃgha* which have been translated either as republics or as oligarchies.

The texts on *dharma* and *artha* are practically silent about them; only very casually do they intimate that this type of government was not completely unknown to them either.[335]

[333] In the first place, we refer to five volumes published in the SBE (2, 7, 14, 25, 33). Moreover, the notes will refer to: *Yājñavalkya's Gesetzbuch.* Sanskrit und Deutch herausgegeben (Stenzler 1849); *Kātyāyanasmṛti on Vyavahāra (Law and Procedure)* by Kane (1933); *The Kauṭilīya Arthaśāstra,* part II: An English Translation with Critical and Explanatory Notes (Kangle 1963);

[334] This circumstance affords another justification for a study which "is restricted to the conception of kingship as distinct from its actualities" (Dumont 1962: 48–77).

[335] AŚ 1.17.53: "Or, the kingdom should belong to the (royal) family; for, a family oligarchy is difficult to conquer, and remains on earth for ever without (having to face) the danger of a calamity befalling the king" (tr. Kangle).

In a paper which is primarily concerned with monocracy the study of these *gaṇas* or *saṃghas*, be they republics or oligarchies, would be out of place. We shall restrict ourselves to raising a few points which at the same time have a direct bearing upon the mutual relationship between *gaṇas* and monocracy.

(a) The nature of *gaṇas* or *saṃghas* interests us in so far as they were definitely different from monocracy. In one of the grammatical texts, in which much importance is attached to terminology, the *ekarāja* the "single king" is explicitly opposed to the *saṃgha*.[336]

(b) The sources referring to *gaṇas* clearly create the impression that in the minds of their authors this type of government suffered considerably from the disadvantage of creating little surety; above all it is very difficult to maintain unity amongst the members of the *gaṇa* (cf. the passages from the *Śāntiparvan* of MBh, as quoted and translated by Kane 1930–62: 3.87–88). This remark is the more important since care for surety and stability has been one of the incentives for the creation of the king: the gods created the king in order that he establish law and order in the chaotic state (cf. infra, E 1). In other words: as far as the authors of the law books are concerned, the ancient Indian republic or oligarchy was considered as markedly inferior to the ideal monarchic system.

(c) The quasi complete silence of the law books might be an indication that the republics or oligarchies disappeared from the Indian soil from an early moment onward.[337] This is, however, a mere hypothesis, and the answer might have to be sought in many other reasons. It is possible that the law books happened to originate in monarchic states so that there was no reason also to deal with the republics.[338] But it is equally well possible that the *gaṇas* have not been described in detail simply because they were not considered as the most excellent type of state organization.

[336] Pāṇini's grammatical rule 4.1.168 prescribes the addition of the suffix –*a* in the sense of a descendant after a word which denotes a country and indicates a Kṣatriya *monarch* (*ekarāja*), and this to exclude the Kṣatriya *saṃghas*.

[337] Thus, e.g., Kane: "From about the 5th or 6th Century AD the oligarchic States or Republics became rare and gradually disappeared" (3.89).

[338] Thus, e.g., W. Foy: "Zum Schluss sei noch auf die Möglichkeit einer weiteren Verfassungsart aufmerksam gemacht, die zur Zeit der epischen Litteratur in einzelnen Ländern oder Städten existiert zu haben scheint (vgl. Hopkins, Ruling Caste, S. 135f). Ich meine die Republik. In unsern Rechtsbüchern ist von einer solchen nicht die Rede. Doch ist dies für ihr Nichtvorhandensein in Indien zur Zeit der Rechtsbücher durchaus nicht beweisend, da diese sehr wohl nur in Ländern entstanden sein können, die eine monarchische Verfassung hatten, und infolgedessen Vorschriften für die Republik aus praktischen Gründen ausser Betracht bleiben mussten" (1895: 13).

2. Within the monarchic type of government, the place of honor and importance goes to the king. He is the most basic element of the state upon whom everything else depends: he has been compared to the root of the tree which is composed of his subjects; if one wants the tree to prosper, care should first be taken of the root.[339]

According to classical Hindu theory, the state is composed of a number of elements (*prakṛtis* or *aṅgas*) which are normally seven in number.[340] They are: *svāmin* the ruler, *amātya* the ministers, *janapada* or *rāṣṭra* the territory and the people, *durga* the fortified capital, *kośa* the wealth of the treasury, *daṇḍa* the armed forces, and *mitra* the allies. Not only is the king invariably mentioned first,[341] but in a text which —according to a well established Indian tradition[342]— compares the state (*rājya*) and its *aṅgas* with a human body and its parts, the king is compared to the head.[343] Kauṭilya[344] leaves no doubt when he says that these seven *prakṛtis* might be summarized in the single formula: "the state is the king."[345]

[339] *Matsyapurāṇa* 219.34: "The king was the root and the subjects were the tree; in saving the king from dangers the whole kingdom was on the road to prosperity and therefore all were to make effort to guard the king" (tr. Kane 3.87).

[340] MDh 9.294: "The king and his minister, his capital, his realm, his treasury, his army, and his ally are the seven constituent parts (of a kingdom); hence a kingdom is said to have seven limbs" (tr. Bühler). See also YDh 1.352, ViDh 3.33, AŚ 6.1.1, etc. (for other sources, cf. Kane 3.37, n. 20).

[341] This fact has its importance. Manu, after verse 9.294 quoted above; in the next verse (9.295) goes on as follows: "But let him know (that) among these seven constituent parts of a kingdom (which have been enumerated) in due order, each earlier (named) is more important and (its destruction) the greater calamity" (tr. Bühler). Cf. also AŚ 8.1.5.

[342] We refer to the often used simile in which the elements of an enumeration are compared to the various parts of the body. The simile is invariably worked out in such a way that the relative importance of the elements of the original enumeration is indicated through the particular parts of the body they are compared with.

[343] *Śukranītisāra* 1.61–62, quoted by Kane 3.18, n. 21. The comparison is as follows: the king = the head, the army = the mind, the capital = the hands, the territory = the feet.

[344] AŚ 8.2.1. We hesitate to accept Kangle's translation: "The king and (his) rule, this is the sum-total of the constituents" (cf. Meyer 1925–26: 497, n. 2).

[345] It goes without saying that a statement of this kind has led to comparisons with the other famous statement: "*L'État c'est moi.*" Thus K. Hoffmann (1953: 334): "In gewisser Hinsicht scheint Indien der klassiche Anwendungsbereich für den legendären Ausspruch des französischen Sonnenkönigs 'l'État c'est moi,' steht doch der König (*Rājā* auch *Mahārāja* = 'Grosskönig.' Die von der fremdstämmigen Kushan-Dynastie gefürthen Titel *rājātiraja* = 'König der Könige,' und *devaputra* = 'Göttersohn,' weisen auf iranische bzw. chinesische Vorbilder) im Mittelpunkt alles staatsrechtlichen Denkens und haben Begriffe wie Volk, Staat, Reich (*vijita* = 'das Eroberte,' *rāshtra* = 'Königreich'), Macht und Gewalt

To a similar concept according to which the *rājadharma* "the royal duties" imply the *dharma* of everybody else in the state we shall come back below (cf. infra, G 3).

C. Designation of the King

1. As a rule, Indian kingship is hereditary. Succession is by male primogeniture. It is true that we know of cases in which women sat on the royal thrones. In a text bearing upon the occupation of a throne which had been conquered by another king, the enthronement of the subjected king's daughter has been prescribed in the absence of a male successor (the former king's brother, son or grandson).[346]

However, this case seems to be a very exceptional one, bearing no prejudice on the general situation in which the king was succeeded by his eldest son. Kauṭilya is very clear when he states that "in normal circumstances kingship befalls on the eldest son."[347] Both the *Nirukta* and the *Bṛhaddevatā* tell a story in which the younger brother had been crowned, with the result however that there was no rain for twelve years.[348]

The younger son comes into consideration only in the case where his elder brother is physically or mentally unfit to be enthroned.[349] Among the reasons for such disqualification the *Śukranītisāra* enumerates deafness, leprosy, dumbness, blindness, and impotence (1.343–44; for examples from the epics, see Kane 3.43).

Whether it be the eldest son or, in his absence, his younger brother, the rule is that the successor should be single.[350] In

(*bala*, *daṇḍa*, das letzte besonders 'Strafgewalt') Geltung nur in direktem Bezug auf den König. Eine Betrachtung des Wessens indischer Staatlichkeit muss sich also auf den Fürsten konzentrieren." For a relevant warning against too hasty comparisons, see Kane 3.18.

[346] According to the *Śāntiparvan* of the MBh (33.43–46). The normal procedure for the conquering king is to place on the throne the defeated king's brother, son or grandson. If there happens to be no male candidate, he may also crown the king's daughter. For instances of Indian queens, cf. Kane 3.40–41.

[347] AŚ 1.17.52: "Of many (sons, who are undisciplined) confinement in one place (is best); (however), the father should be beneficently disposed towards the sons. Except in case of a calamity, sovereignty passing on to the eldest son is praised" (tr. Kangle). A number of examples from the epics have been related by Kane 3.42–43.

[348] It is the story of Śantanu who was crowned although Devāpi was older. See *Nirukta* 2.10, and, especially, *Bṛhaddevatā* 7.156–57; 8.1–9. Cf. Macdonell 1904: 292–95.

[349] In the story of Śantanu and Devāpi too, the latter had been affected by a skin-disease. Even then succession by the younger one was considered defective.

[350] We do have a few vague references to a system of dual kingship (*dvairājya*), in which either father and son or two brothers simultaneously held the office of the king. Cf. Kane 3.102–103.

no case should the kingdom be divided among more than one prince. By doing so the kingdom would be weakened and easily fall prey to the enemies. The text adds that younger brothers should rather be appointed governors of the provinces or superintendents of the royal stables, the treasury, etc. (*Śukranītisāra* 1.346–48, quoted by Kane 3.43).

In very exceptional cases only do the texts indicate a larger range of successors to the king. One such instance has the following sequence: a son, a full brother, a half brother, a paternal uncle, a member of the family, a daughter's son, and a stranger (thus the *Nītivākyāmṛta* [sect. 29: 249] of Somadevasūri quoted by Kane 3.43).

It is, however, clear that succession by a person who is not the king's son should by all means be avoided; Kauṭilya goes to the extent of allowing the king who has no male descendant to have a third person procreate in his stead.[351]

The crown prince who was thus to succeed his father was to be subjected to a very special training. We shall come back to this point below (cf. infra, C 5).

The ideal situation seems to be that the young crown prince succeeds to the throne during his father's lifetime.[352] As to the behavior of the latter after handing over kingship to his son, Manu prefers him to seek death in battle.[353] The epics on the other hand have several references to a more peaceful solution: the king should withdraw into the forest and end his life as a *rājarṣi* "a royal sage."[354]

2. The general rule of hereditary kingship does not prevent us from finding occasional references to an election of a king. Several Vedic passages have been quoted to prove the occurrence of elected kings (e.g., *Ṛgveda* 6.8.4, 10.124.8; *Atharvaveda* 3.4.2;

[351] AŚ 1.17.50: "An old or a diseased king, however, should get a child begotten on his wife by one of the following, (viz.) his mother's kinsman, a member of his own family, and a virtuous neighboring prince" (tr. Kangle).

[352] Although, on the other hand, "He should guard against princes right from their birth. For, princes devour their begetters, being of the nature of crabs" (AŚ 1.17.4–5, tr. Kangle). Cf. the whole chapter 1.17 on "Guarding against Princes."

[353] MDh 9.323: "But (a king) who feels his end drawing nigh shall bestow all his wealth, accumulated from fines, on Brāhmaṇas, make over his kingdom to his son, and then seek death in battle" (tr. Bühler). Cf. also Bühler's note to this verse: "Medhātithi adds that, if the king cannot die in battle, he may burn or drown himself. Kullūka says that he may kill himself by starvation."

[354] Kane (1930–1962: 3.101) quotes several examples from both epics, MBh and Rām, and also from *Raghuvaṃśa*. In *Vanaparvan* 202.8, Bṛhadaśva is said to have crowned his son Kuvalāśva; in *Āśramavāsiparvan* 3.38 Dhṛtarāṣṭra tells Yudhiṣṭhira that "in their family it was customary for kings to transfer the sovereignty to their sons and resort to a forest towards the close of their lives."

etc.; cf. Zimmer 1879: 162–65). In some of them the election is made by *rājakṛts* "king makers,"[355] a term which also occurs in the descriptions of the royal coronation.

3. In order to be complete we should also refer to another group of texts which bear testimony to a designation of the king by means of a simultaneous application of the two methods referred to above. In the *Rāmāyaṇa*, for instance, king Daśaratha, at the moment when he wants to proceed to the coronation of his son Rāma, assembles his allies and the representatives of the people; he informs them about his intention and asks for their authorization which is readily granted (Rām 2.1–2; cf. Kane 3.29, Foy 1895: 7, etc.).

4. When comparing the above mentioned texts about the various ways of designating the king, the distribution is as follows: (a) according to a number of Vedic texts, the king was elected; (b) according to an epic story, the election bears upon a very distinct person, the king's son; (c) according to numerous references in the texts on *dharma* and *artha* monarchy is strictly hereditary. One might, then, be tempted to discover behind these data a rectilineal historical evolution: monarchy, from originally being elective,[356] gradually becomes hereditary, partly first, completely later on. This evolution has been accepted by several scholars. Personally we would not dare to defend such a simple situation. One often forgets that our data are extremely fragmentary and that they do not cover the whole picture at every moment of history. It is very probable that the different ways of designating the king have at all times been applied simultaneously in the numerous kingdoms which existed in the different parts of the country.[357]

As a matter of fact, the above threefold enumeration may be far from exhaustive. Perfectly orthodox though isolated *dharma* texts preach a revolutionary theory in that they prescribe the king's coming to power by means of violent usurpation.[358]

5. Independently of the way in which he was designated, the future king had to respond to a number of conditions. In the first place he had to have gone through a thorough and broad educa-

[355] Cf. Kane: 29, who refers to *Atharvaveda* 3.5.6–7. For more ample information about the *rājakṛts* and *ratnins*, cf. Kane 1930–62: 2.1215–16 and Spellman 1964: 69, 72.

[356] The gods too, when they had no king, elected one; cf. *Aitareyabhrāhmaṇa* 1.14.

[357] From a number of historical examples of elected kings quoted by Kane: 30–31, it is clear that election has been resorted to at different moments all over ancient Indian history.

[358] Cf. Parāśara 1.68: "Royalty depends not on a hereditary right; nor can it be transmitted by written deeds. It should be enjoyed after acquisition by means of the sword; the earth is enjoyed by heroes."

tion, both morally and intellectually. The various texts go into detail about the different branches of learning and the kind of moral training that were judged indispensable (for the education of the king, cf. Kane 3.46–55). Moreover, they are equally eloquent with regard to a number of qualities which must be united in the future king (for the qualities required in the king, cf. Kane 3.44–46). Since these endless enumerations are not directly relevant to the study of monarchy in ancient India, we shall not go beyond mentioning the very existence of such requirements.

6. Finally, before assuming office the king must undergo the ceremony of the *rājasūya* "the royal consecration." The *rājasūya* is an extremely complicated rite which has to be administered to the king by a Brāhmaṇa priest,[359] but the details of which largely vary from one treatise to the other according to the Vedic schools to which they belong. Its description[360] belongs to the field of ritual rather than to the comparative study of institutions.

D. The Basis of Royal Power

1. A thorough understanding of the nature and basis of royal power in ancient India may best be obtained from a reference to the etymology of the most important Indian word for "king," i.e., *rājan* (nominative: *rājā*).[361]

For the scientific etymologist the Sanskrit word *rājan* corresponds to Latin *rex, regis*, to Celtic *rīg*, to Gothic *reiki*, etc. In other words: the nominal stem *rājan* corresponds to the Sanskrit verbal root *rāj-* (this interpretation also occurs in *Nirukta* 2.3: *rājā rājateḥ*). We are not concerned here with the linguistic discussion whether Sanskrit originally possessed one or two roots *rāj-*; the main point is that this root —or these roots— conveys the meanings: (a) to be illustrious or resplendent, shine, glitter, and (b) to rule, direct, govern, be chief or king.

The Hindu law books, on the contrary, usually propose a completely different etymology. According to them, *rājan* corresponds the verbal root *rañj-*. *Rañj-*, and especially its causative form *rañjayati* which is always referred to, means: (a) to dye, color, paint, redden, illuminate (it is probably related the Greek *rezō*, to

[359] This fact provoked the following remark by Foy: "Die Brahmanen hatten durch dieses Recht der Königsweihe eine gewisse Macht in Händen, etwa eine solche wie die Päpste des Mittelalters gegenüber den deutschen Kaisern" (1895: 7).

[360] Among the extensive literature on the ancient Indian coronation ceremony, we shall refer to Weber 1893, and Heesterman 1957.

[361] For all other names of kings, cf. Kane 3.63–71. Several indications point to the fact that these terms more or less corresponded, from Vedic times onward, to a certain hierarchy among the ancient Indian kings. Cf. infra, F 4.

dye), and (b) to rejoice, charm, gratify, conciliate. It is the latter set of meanings which is thought of in connection with the word *rājan*: the king is the one who "charms, gratifies" his subjects.

Needless to say, the linguist will not be found prepared to accept this type of etymology: it does not comply with the phonetic rules and should, therefore, be rejected. For the historian of Hindu Law, on the contrary, this "popular" etymology is of the utmost importance. To him it reveals in eloquent terms the very idea which to the Indian mind the *rājan* "the king" stood for.[362]

The derivation of *rājan* from *rañj* seems to have been universally accepted: it is to be found not only in the technical texts on *dharma* and *artha* but in literature generally as well. Therefore, there is no reason not to believe that it was not accepted in practice too, by the kings as well as by their subjects.

Among the technical texts we might quote the example of Kauṭilya: "in the happiness of the subjects lies the happiness of the king and in what is beneficial to the subjects his own benefit. What is dear to himself is not beneficial to the king, but what is dear to the subjects is beneficial (to him)."[363]

The general acceptance of the concept may be illustrated by means of a verse of India's greatest poet Kālidāsa, who says with regard to Rāma that "he was a *king* worth this name, since he *rejoiced* his subjects."[364]

2. The etymological interpretation of *rājan* as the person who "charms, rejoices" his subjects has, then, been translated into more practical terms: the basic task of the king, the very reason for his existence, about which all texts unanimously agree, is *prajāpālana*, i.e., the protection of his subjects.

The *Mahābhārata*, after enumerating seven expounders of the theory of kings, states that all of them prescribe protection of the subjects as the highest obligation of the king.[365] And the same idea has been reiterated again and again all over the cor-

[362] Many examples could be given of similar popular etymologies which, for being unscientific, nonetheless marvelously illustrate the connotations attributed to certain technical legal terms. To give only one other example: the complete background of the importance attached to a son shines forth from the etymology according to which a son is called *putra* because he saves (*trāyate*) his father from the hell called Put (MDh 9.132; ViDh 15.44).

[363] AŚ 1.19.34 (tr. Kangle). For other examples of this high ideal set before the king, cf. Kane 3.61–62.

[364] The entire verse has been translated as follows: "Si la lune s'appelle lune, c'est qu'elle provoque l'allégresse; le soleil, c'est qu'il brûle avec splendeur; lui aussi était roi au vrai sens: 'celui qui charme ses sujets'" (Renou 1928: 33).

[365] *Śāntiparvan* 68.1–4 "notes that all the seven expounders of polity (*rājaśāstrapraṇetāraḥ*) named by it extol protection as the highest dharma of the king" (Kane 3.56).

pus of texts on *dharma* and *artha*. For Viṣṇu, for instance, "Now the duties of a king are: to protect his people,..." (ViDh 3.1–2, tr. Jolly), and Manu too, after the initial announcement: "I will declare the duties of kings," continues: "A Kṣatriya,[366] who has received according to the rule the sacrament prescribed by the Veda,[367] must duly protect this whole (world)."[368]

We purposely used the expression that protection of his subjects was the very reason of the king's existence. We shall come back to this point below (cf. infra, E 1); at this stage we shall merely indicate that the gods decided to create the office of the king at the very moment when men on earth needed protection very urgently: "For, when these creatures, being without a king, through fear dispersed in all directions, the lord created a king for a protection of this whole creation."[369]

3. In connection with the king's obligation to protect his subjects, it might not be out of place to point out that this protection has been conceived as comparable to the protection of his children on the part of the father. Several texts refer to protection of the subjects *putravat*, i.e., as if they were the king's children.[370] The hypothesis may be formulated that the equation of the king with the head of the family is also responsible for the double meaning of the Sanskrit term *prajā*: within the family and according to its normal derivation it means "the descendants, the children"; in the context of the king, it indicates his "subjects."

4. The protection of the subjects manifests itself at a twofold level: the king is to protect his subjects within the boundaries of

[366] For the interchange of terms "king" and "Kṣatriya," cf. infra, F 2 and note 75.

[367] The sacrament alluded to in this sentence has been variously interpreted by the commentators. Some propose the "initiation" (*upanayana*) which is common to all persons of the three highest classes. Personally we rather agree with the commentator Nandapaṇḍita who thinks of "the sacrament of the coronation," i.e., the *rājasūya* mentioned above (C 6).

[368] MDh 7.1–2 (tr. Bühler). Cf. also MDh 7.144: "The highest duty of a Kṣatriya is to protect his subjects, for the king who enjoys the rewards, just mentioned, is bound to (discharge that) duty"; MDh 5.93–94: "The taint of impurity does not fall on kings...For a king, on the throne of magnanimity, immediate purification is prescribed, and the reason for that is that he is seated (there) for protection of (his) subjects"; NS 18.33: "His duties are, the protection of his subjects,..." (tr. Jolly); etc.

[369] MDh 7.3 (tr. Bühler). The story about the origin of the king has been integrated into the Indian theory of the *yuga*s, cf. Kane 3.33–34.

[370] This concept is met with on numerous occasions and in various kinds of literature. It occurs in the texts on *dharma* and *artha*: YDh 1.333; AŚ 2.1.18. The epics have repeatedly referred to it: MBh 12.139.105; Rām 2.2.28–47, 3.6.11, 5.35.9–14. In classical literature too (*Śakuntalā*, *Raghuvaṃśa*, *Harṣacarita*), the idea has found admission: instances with Kane 3.62–63. Finally, its acceptance by the kings themselves is evident from Aśoka's first separate Jaugadh Edict.

the state and outside the boundaries as well.[371] We accordingly propose to successively examine the power of the king at the national and at the international level.

E. National Power

1. To protect his subjects within the boundaries of the state means that the king should protect them from one another, i.e., protect the weaker ones against the abuses on the part of the stronger ones.

As already noticed above, here too, the protection of the subjects one against the other is a theme which has been repeatedly referred to in connection with the origin of kingship. A country which is without a king (*arājaka*) falls victim to chaos.[372] The simile which has found general recognition in this context is that of the fish (*matsya*): in a country without a king the stronger ones devour the weaker ones, as is the case with fish in water. It has, therefore, been said that a country without a king is subject to *mātsyanyāya* "the rule of the fish."[373]

2. In the more technical language of Hindu social organization the obligation to protect the subjects one against the other has been formulated as follows: the king should act in such a way that his subjects keep to their respective *dharma*'s "obliga-

[371] A verse attributed to Bṛhaspati (1.39 of K.V. Rangaswami Aiyangar's edition, unknown to Jolly) says that the so-called protection of the subjects is threefold: against the army of the enemy, against the danger of robbers, and against the one who does not abide by the rules. The two latter items referring to inland protection are opposed to the former one which relates to protection against a neighboring country.

[372] We fully agree with Kane who objects to a statement of K.P. Jayaswal: "The *Arājaka* or 'non-ruler' was an idealistic constitution which came to be the object of derision of political writers of Hindu India. The ideal of this constitution was that Law was to be taken as the ruler and there should be no man-ruler. The basis of the state was considered to be mutual agreement or social contract between the citizens. This was an extreme democracy almost Tolstoyian in ideal" (1943: 86–87). Indeed, "a perusal of these (= a number of epic texts referring to *arājaka*) will convince anyone not carried away by the over-patriotic desire to find the latest European thought in our ancient books that *arājaka* was viewed as a state of chaos and the negation of any constitution; that when a country was without a ruler, no private property in anything existed or was respected and people preyed upon each other like fishes and that no Tolstoyian ideals were present before the eyes of the writers that drew such a harrowing picture of a State without a ruler" (Kane 3.30). This is an excellent example of the speculation against which we warned, above A 2.

[373] E.g., AŚ 1.13.5: "People, overwhelmed by the law of the fishes, made Manu, the son of Vivasvat, their king"; Rām 2.67.31: "like fish the people will devour each other." For other references to *mātsyanyāya*, cf. Kane 3.21, n. 22, and Spellman 1964: 4–8.

tions." In other words: the king should force everybody in the state to follow his own specific *svadharma* and to prevent that any of them deviate therefrom and commit *adharma*.[374] Now, since the *svadharmas* essentially differ according to one's pertaining to one of the four social classes (*varṇa*)[375] and to one of the traditional four stages of life (*āśrama*),[376] the king's obligation within the state is to safeguard the integrity of *varnāśramadharma*. Viṣṇu, after the above quoted text (cf. ViDh 3.1–2) continues: "And to keep the four castes and the four orders in the practice of their several duties" (ViDh 3.3, tr. Jolly). Similarly, according to Gautama, "He shall protect the castes and orders in accordance with justice."[377]

Apart from these general references to the social classes and the stages of life a number of texts have enumerated particular groups of subjects which are weaker than the others and which, therefore, deserve to be made the object of a special protection on the part of the king. There is no point in giving exhaustive enumerations;[378] we shall only quote a few selected cases which illustrate the sections of the population which were considered especially helpless. On the one hand, the king's protection had to make up for physical (the diseased, aged people, pregnant women), social (widows, orphans) or mental (lunatics) disabilities.[379] On the other hand, the king had to assure safety to those who were responsible for the spiritual benefit of the community and who, therefore, should not be burdened with the task

[374] GDh 11.10: "And those who leave (the path of) duty, he shall lead back (to it)" (tr. Bühler).

[375] i.e., Brāhmaṇas, Kṣatriyas, Vaiśyas, and Śūdras.

[376] i.e., the *brahmacārin*, the *gṛhastha*, the *vānaprastha*, and the *saṃnyāsin*.

[377] GDh 11.9 (tr. Bühler). Cf. also VaDh 19.7: "Let the king, paying attention to all the laws of countries, (subdivisions of) castes (*jāti*) and families, make the four castes (*varṇa*) fulfill their (respective) particular duties" (tr. Bühler); MDh 7.35: "The king has been created (to be) the protector of the castes (*varṇa*) and orders, who, all according to their rank, discharge their several duties" (tr. Bühler); MDh 7.144; NS 18.5–7, 33. This idea too, has spread beyond the sphere of technical Dharmaśāstra texts: *Raghuvaṃśa* 14.67, in the message which Sītā addresses to Rāma through Lakṣmaṇa, has the following words: "Protection of the castes and stages of life, that is the very duty which has been prescribed for a king by Manu."

[378] For an enumeration of the series of people who had to be specially protected, see Kane 3.58–60.

[379] Thus MDh 8.27–28: "The king shall protect the inherited (and other) property of a minor, until he has returned (from the teacher's house) or until he has passed his minority. In like manner care must be taken of barren women, of those who have no sons, of those whose family is extinct, of wives and widows faithful to their lords, and of women with diseases" (tr. Bühler). Similar prescriptions also with GDh 10.48, VaDh 16.8, ViDh 3.65, and several epic and Purāṇic texts.

of taking care of themselves: students, sacrificers, and learned Brāhmaṇas.[380]

3. The ideal situation would, of course, be that the king succeeds in preventing all breaches of *dharma*, i.e., that his kingdom remains absolutely free from injustice amongst the subjects. A king who realizes this ideal participates in the spiritual merit of all,[381] and after death he is promised the world of Indra.[382]

However, it is well understood that this situation cannot normally be maintained. It so happens that people are by nature inclined towards committing sinful acts.[383] They will find ample opportunity to give vent to this tendency, and the *adharma* will come to the notice of the king only after it has been committed. In such cases it is the king's duty to make up for the *adharma* committed and to restore the *dharma*.

It is a matter of dispute whether in such cases the king may act *suo motu*. We believe that, in a number of specifically listed items, the king has indeed the power and the obligation to take the initiative to restore the *dharma*.[384]

In the vast majority of cases, however, it is the party who has become a victim of the *adharma* committed by another person, who is supposed to take the initiative and to inform the king. In the rigidly established daily timetable of the king's activities,[385] every day a certain amount of time has been reserved to hear-

[380] E.g., ViDh 3.79–80: "And he must not suffer any Brāhmaṇa in his realm to perish with want; nor any other man leading a pious life" (tr. Jolly). Cf. also MDh 7.82, 134–35; GDh 10.9–12, 18.31; ĀpDh 2.10.25.11; YDh 1.314,338; AŚ 2.1.7, etc.

[381] Cf. YDh 1.334: "Den sechsten theil der tugend empfängt er, wenn er den gehörigen schutz ertheilt, denn die beschützung der unterthanen steht höher als alle gaben." Also MDh 8.304. For the king's participation in his subjects' demerit, see note 420 below.

[382] ViDh 5.196: "A king in whose dominion there exists neither thief, nor adulterer, nor calumniator, nor robber, nor murderer, attains the world of Indra" (tr. Jolly).

[383] The Dharmaśāstras assume that we are actually living in the worst of all ages, the *Kaliyuga*. In this age people are inclined towards abandoning their dharma. For the theory of *yugas* generally, cf. Kane 3.885–902.

[384] It has been said that such was the case with Kauṭilya's *Kaṇṭakaśodhana* (= Book 4: The Suppression of Criminals), as against his *Dharmasthīya* (= Book 3: Concerning Judges). However, the matter is a highly disputed one, and raises a great number of problems. Thus, it is true that "Manu after dealing with the 18 *vyavahārapadas* (in 8.1 to 9.251) requires the king (in 9.252–53) to make efforts to destroy *kaṇṭakas* (thorns, harmful persons) and dilates upon many aspects of his activities in this respect" (Kane 3.251); we dare not pretend to have found a completely satisfying solution, but we have a feeling that a correct insight into the growth and composition of books 8 and 9 of MDh will help us understand the transitional verses 9.252–53.

[385] The whole of the king's daily occupations have been strictly codified. Cf. infra, G 3 and note 418.

ing the complaints of the persons who have been submitted to *adharma*.[386]

Once the plaint was entered with the king, it is up to him to make a full investigation. Practically speaking this means that the king has been appointed as the presider of the law court in the state.[387]

At this stage we should deal with the ancient Indian judicial organization as a part of the king's responsibilities. However, the actual development of the judicial proceeding is beyond the scope of a study on monocracy; moreover, as far as the theory of proof is concerned, judicial proceeding has been made the object of a former meeting of the *Société Jean Bodin*, and the essential points of the Indian theory of proof have been dealt with in a preceding volume in this series (cf. Rocher 1963). Be it sufficient here to say that the king is supposed to preside over the whole course of the procedure, from hearing the statements of both parties to receiving and evaluating the various means of proof offered by them.

4. The point which is of much more direct importance with regard to the king as the president of the law court is that he is also to *decide* the law cases.[388] That means that he is to fix the punishment to be inflicted on the party who has been found guilty.[389] Much stress has been laid in the texts upon this obligation of the king to impart just and equitable punishments.[390]

[386] MDh 8.1–3: "A king, desirous of investigating law cases, must enter the court of justice, preserving a dignified demeanor, together with Brāhmaṇas and with experienced councilors. There, either seated or standing, raising his right arm, without ostentation in his dress and ornaments, let him examine the business of suitors, daily (deciding) one after another (all cases) which fall under the eighteen titles (of the law) according to the principles drawn from local usages and from the Institutes of the sacred law" (tr. Bühler).

[387] NS 18.33: "His duties are...the trial of lawsuits" (tr. Jolly).

[388] "When the evidence has been pled, the king (or chief justice) should with the help of *sabhyas* decide upon the success or failure of the plaintiff" (Kane 3.379). Against this opinion, which reflects the generally accepted situation, we personally raise the question of the actual interference of the king in deciding right or wrong. We shall come back to this question below. At present we shall merely quote Nārada *Mātṛkā* 2.42: "When the (false) assertions have been removed, the judges shall pass a decree" (tr. Jolly). The king being the presider over the judges, he is among those who pass the decree; nevertheless, the text does not say that the decree is passed by the king but by the judges who are his assessors.

[389] Here we may again quote Nārada *Mātṛkā* 2.43: "One condemned by the judges shall be punished by the king according to law" (tr. Jolly).

[390] MDh 8.126–28: "Let the (king), having fully ascertained the motive, the time and place (of the offence), and having considered the ability (of the criminal to suffer) and the (nature of the) crime, cause punishment to fall on those who deserve it. Unjust punishment destroys reputation among men, and fame

The extremely close connection which has been established between the king and punishment, and the extreme attention which has been paid to it, testify to the importance which the ancient lawgivers attached to this aspect of the king's activities.

For this reason one of the classical appellations of the Indian king has been *daṇḍadhara* which applies to him in two different ways: he is the carrier (*dhara*) of the scepter (*daṇḍa*), but his is also the upholder (*dhara*) of punishment (*daṇḍa*).[391]

Some texts even go to the extent of identifying the king and punishment and practically using the two terms as synonyms.[392]

Finally, it is again the importance attached to the king as the punisher which is responsible for the science of government to have been indicated, among many terms, by *daṇḍanīti*.[393]

5. Once the decision of the law suit has been taken, the king is again responsible for the next step: the execution of the decision.

In order to facilitate this obligation, the king has been designated as the head of the armed forces, i.e., of the police and the army. As far as the police are concerned the situation of the king is clear from terminology itself: the technical term for the police is *rājapuruṣa* "the king's men" (about this term, cf. Meyer 1925–26: 745–46). The intimate relation of the king with the army will become clear below in connection with the constant obligation of the king to make wars of defence and aggression (cf. infra, F1 and 3).

6. It has become a habit also to raise the problem whether the Indian king had any legislative power. And it has become equally customary to propose highly different solutions. Apart from the purely positive and unconditionally negative answers, we must refer to an intermediate answer according to which the king does have legislative power with regard to secular matters, whereas he

(after death), and causes even in the next world the loss of heaven; let him, therefore, beware of (inflicting) it. A king who punishes those who do not deserve it, and punishes not those who deserve it, brings great infamy on himself and (after death) sinks into hell" (tr. Bühler). Cf. YDh 1.355–56, etc.

[391] Cf. MDh 9.245: "Varuṇa is the lord of punishment, for *he holds the scepter* even over kings" (tr. Bühler); Nārada *Mātṛkā* 1.2: "and the king has been appointed to decide lawsuits, because *he has authority to punish*" (tr. Jolly). In reality both meanings hold good in either case.

[392] MDh 7.17: "Punishment is (in reality) the king (and) the male, that the manager of affairs, that the ruler, and that is called the surety for the four orders' obedience to law" (tr. Bühler).

[393] AŚ 1.4.3: "The means of ensuring the pursuit of philosophy, the three Vedas and economics is the Rod (wielded by the king) (*daṇḍa*); its administration constitutes the science of politics (*daṇḍanīti*), having for its purpose the acquisition of (things) not possessed, the preservation of (things) possessed, the augmentation of (things) preserved and the bestowal of (things) augmented on a worthy recipient" (tr. Kangle). Other references, cf. Kane 3.5–6.

does not as far as religious topics are concerned.[394] Here too, the defendants of this thesis refer to an authoritative text which, in their opinion, does draw such a distinction.[395]

Personally we believe that the main error in all this consists in the very desire to raise the question and provide for an answer to it. It is an excellent example of the mistaken zeal to force matters Indian into the framework of western categories. In reality the problem of legislative power in the state, whether it be with the king or with any other established body, never occurred to the Indian mind. The king has his *dharma*, based upon the obligation of *prajāpālana*; this basic obligation presented numerous aspects, but it has never been thought of as being threefold according to the western subdivision of power into executive, judicial and legislative. If we do not accept the existence of legislative power generally, this implies that we *a fortiori* reject the above distinction that the king would have such power in secular matters only. Once again the opposition between secular and religious is a Western subdivision completely foreign to the Indian mind.

The king would have exercised his so-called legislative power through *rājaśāsanas*. It would be very difficult to delimitate their sphere of application;[396] it is, however, certain that *rājaśāsana* has never figured among the sources of law to be followed in legal proceedings.[397]

[394] E.g., Foy: Über die weltliche Gesetzgebung verfügte der König allein, zum grössten Teile wohl nach einer Beratung mit seinen Ministern" (1895: 14); "Die religiöse Gesetzgebung ruht nach unsern Rechtsbüchern in den Händen der Brahmanen, speziell der Pariṣad" (16).

[395] This distinction is based upon Medhātithi on MDh 7.13. Cf. Kane: "In his gloss on this verse Medātithi carefully points out what orders the king can issue and on what subject he cannot issue orders. He gives the following instances of orders of both kinds: 'Today all should observe a festival in the capital; all should attend a marriage ceremony at the house of the minister; animals should not be killed today by the butchers and birds should not be caught; debtors should not be harassed by creditors on these days (to be specified); no one should associate with such a man (an undesirable person); no one should allow a certain (undesirable) person to enter the house.' Medhātithi adds that the king is not authorized to interfere with the *śāstric rules* governing the *varṇas* and *āśramas* such as the performance of *agnihotra*" (3.98–99).

[396] *Śukranītisāra* 1.292–311 gives examples of the content of *rājaśāsanas*; cf. Kane 3.99–100.

[397] To quote only one example in which the sources of law have been exhaustively enumerated, GDh 11.19–25: "His administration of justice (shall be regulated by) the Veda, the Institutes of the Sacred Law, the Aṅgas, and the Purāṇa. The laws of countries, castes, and families, which are not opposed to the (sacred) records, (have) also authority. Cultivators, traders, herdsmen, money-lenders, and artizans (have authority to lay down rules) for their respective classes. Having learned the (state of) affairs from those who (in each class) have authority (to speak he shall give) the legal decision. Reasoning is a means for arriving

F. International Power

1. The basic obligation of the king, i.e., to protect his subjects, is not restricted to protecting them one against the other. The king was also under the obligation to protect his subjects as a whole against the assaults of neighboring countries. That means that the king had to be ready to fight in defence of his own subjects against the attacks made on them by other kings. This obligation explains the insistence upon the fact that the king should maintain a strong army and the extensive treatment of things military even in the texts on *dharma* and *artha*.[398]

In many texts we meet with exhortations to battle. The highest rewards are promised to the king who fights courageously and, better even, to the king who seeks death in battle.[399]

2. These exhortations to battle, however fierce they may look at first glance, should not surprise us if we take into consideration that, normally speaking, the king at the same time is the first among the Kṣatriyas, i.e., the warrior class, whose very reason of existence is the defence of the country.[400]

at the truth. Coming to a conclusion through that, he shall decide properly. If (the evidence) is conflicting, he shall learn (the truth) from (Brāhmaṇas) who are well versed in the threefold sacred lore, and give his decision (accordingly)" (tr. Bühler). It would not be possible here to raise the problem of the "four feet" of legal procedure in which the royal decree figures in the fourth place, after *dharma*, *vyavahāra*, and *caritra*, but in such a way that it is said to overrule the former ones. The problem is a highly disputed one. Personally we think that the royal decree is appealed to when neither the rules of Dharmaśāstra nor the evidence produced during the trial, nor customs lead to a decision.

[398] Thus, the whole of book 10 in the AŚ is "Concerning war." We already quoted *daṇḍa* or *bala* "the armed forces" amongst the seven constituent elements of the state (*supra*, B 2). Cf. also Kane 3: 200–215.

[399] E.g., MDh 7.87–89: "A king who, while he protects his people, is defied by (foes), be they equal in strength, or stronger, or weaker, must not shrink from battle, remembering the duty of Kṣatriyas. Not to turn back in battle, to protect the people, to honor the Brāhmaṇas, is the best means for a king to secure happiness. Those kings who, seeing to slay each other in battle, fight with the utmost exertion and do not turn back, go to heaven" (tr. Bühler). Cf. also ViDh 3.44: "There is no duty for kings equal to losing one's life in battle" (tr. Jolly).

[400] Even in a purely metaphysical —not to say religious— poem such as the *Bhagavadgītā* one of the reasons for god Kṛṣṇa to exhort Arjuna to battle is his belonging to the Kṣatriya class. Cf. *Bhagavadgītā* 2.31–37: "Likewise having regard for thine own (caste) duty Thou shouldst not tremble; For another, better thing than a fight required of duty Exists not for a warrior. Presented by mere luck, an open door of heaven —Happy the warriors, son of Pṛthā, That get such a fight! Now, if thou this duty-required Conflict wilt not perform, Then thine own duty and glory Abandoning, thou shalt get thee evil. Disgrace, too, will creatures Speak of thee, without end; And for one that has been esteemed, disgrace Is worse than death. That thou has abstained from battle thru fear The (warriors) of great chariots will think of thee; And of whom thou wast highly

We shall not enter here into discussing the class to which the Indian kings belonged (on the *varṇa* of the king, cf. Kane 3: 37–40, and Spellman 1964: 47–50): we prudently said that, "normally speaking," the king belonged to the Kṣatriya class. It is certain that there have been kings who belonged to other classes; even the *dharma* texts contain a number of indications to that effect.[401]

The idea behind such allusions is, however, uniformly patent: countries governed by non-Kṣatriyas suffer from a number of anomalies; the only ideal situation is the one in which the throne is occupied by a member of the Kṣatriya class.

The unconscious interchanges of the terms *rājan* and Kṣatriya in passages where the class of the king is not directly at stake also bear evidence to the conception of the authors of the law books.[402]

A very important result of the king's belonging to the Kṣatriya class will be dealt with below (cf. infra, G 6).

3. An examination of the above mentioned text in which the kings are exhorted to battle reveals another important aspect of the king's power at the international level. It is clear that the goal set before the king actually goes beyond the sole protection of the subjects. In reality the king should not restrict his efforts to purely defensive battles; he should also undertake regular wars of aggression. In other words: the king should constantly try his utmost to extend the limits of his own kingdom at the cost of the neighboring kings.

Accordingly, the texts have elaborated a complete theory of aggression;[403] they go into ample detail about the offices of the

regarded, Thou shalt come to be held lightly. And many sayings that should not be said Thy ill-wishers will say of thee, Speaking ill of thy capacity: What, pray, is more grievous than that? Either slain thou shalt gain heaven, Or conquering thou shalt enjoy the earth. Therefore arise, son of Kuntī, Unto battle, making a firm resolve" (tr. F. Edgerton 1952).

[401] In the chapter on the Vedic student (*brahmacārin*), MDh 4.84 has the following reference to a king who does not belong to the Kṣatriya race, nor from butchers, oil-manufacturers, and publicans, nor from those who subsist by the gain of prostitutes" (tr. Bühler). GDh 9.65 is less explicit: "He (= *Snātaka*) shall seek to dwell in a place...which is governed by a righteous (ruler)" (tr. Bühler), but ViDh 71.64 makes it very clear who is to be considered a "righteous ruler": "He (=*Snātaka*) must not dwell in a kingdom governed by a *śūdra* king" (tr. Jolly). Speaking about the way in which the conquering king should deal with the defeated monarch, ViDh 3.48–49 has the following rule: "Let him not extirpate the royal race; unless the royal race be of ignoble descent" (tr. Jolly).

[402] E.g., MDh 7.1,3: "I will declare the duties of *kings*,...A *Kshatriya*...the lord created *a king*" (tr. Bühler). Cf. *supra*, D 2.

[403] We refer to the famous theory of *maṇḍala*. It is true that this theory mainly consists in making allies, but it should not be forgotten that these allies are selected in such a way that the common enemy is more easily defeated. At that moment the previous ally in his turn becomes an enemy and a new ally is looked

spy (*cara* or *cāra*) and the ambassador (*dūta*) and the role they have to play in neighboring countries;[404] they distinguish different types of conquest;[405] and they work out a detailed deontology to be observed by the conqueror with regard to the conquered regard to the conquered country and its ruler.[406]

4. The various degrees to which the kings succeeded in enlarging their own countries led to the elaboration of a complicated hierarchy of monarchs.[407] The various intermediary grades may be less important, but the general idea which is in the background of the scheme definitely deserves our attention. The theory of aggression indeed culminates in the ideal of the *cakravartin*; the composition of the term is not clear, but its sense is: "the conqueror of the world."[408] The Indian king is convinced that he potentially is a *cakravartin*, and that he must make an effort to

for to defeat him. The earliest source for this theory is AŚ 7.2 and 7, but it has been adopted in many other texts. For complete references and details, cf. Kane 3: 217–22. Spellman (1964: 157) has ventured a hypothetical but highly illuminating illustration.

[404] Although the Sanskrit terms for spies and ambassadors are different, it is often difficult to neatly draw the distinction. The dictum that a *dūta* is an overt spy, whereas a *cara* is a secret spy can only confirm this opinion. The main source is again Kauṭilīya, with no less than five chapters on the subject (1.11–14 and 16). Cf. Kane 3: 127–31, and Spellman: 137–44.

[405] E.g., AŚ 12.1.10–16: "There are three kings who attack: the righteous conqueror, the greedy conqueror and the demoniacal conqueror. Of them, the righteous conqueror is satisfied with submission. He should submit to him, also when there is danger from others. The greedy conqueror is satisfied with the seizure of land and goods. He should yield money to him. The demoniacal conqueror (is satisfied only) with the seizure of land, goods, sons, wives and life. By yielding land to him and goods to him, he should take counter-steps, remaining out of reach himself" (tr. Kangle).

[406] For a survey of the conqueror's duties, cf. Kane 3: 71–72. We shall merely stress here the obligation of the victorious king to protect the conquered country like his own and to respect the local customs. E.g., YDh 1.341–42: "Dasselbe verdienst, welches für einen herrscher in der beschützung seines reiches liegt, erwirbt er ganz, wenn er ein fremdes reich in seine gewalt bringt. Welches herkommen, rechtspflege und verhältniss der Stämme in einem lande ist, nach eben denselben soll er das land regieren, wenn es in seine gewalt gekommen" (tr. Stenzler).

[407] Thus, *Śukranītisāra* 1.183–87 (quoted by Kane 3: 67–68) distinguishes a *sāmanta* (yearly revenue: from 100,000 to 300,000 silver *karṣas*) a *maṇḍalika* (from 400,000 to 1,000,000), a *rājan* (from 1,100,000 to 2,000,000), a *mahārāja* (from 2,100,000 to 5,000,000), a *svarāṭ* (from 5,100,000 to 10,000,000) a *vīrāṭ* (up to 100,000,000), and a *sārvabhauma* (up to 500,000,000). As pointed out by Kane, the amounts are of less importance; they might even be discarded as "scholastic and too rigid to have been practically followed." However, the far reaching hierarchy cannot be denied.

[408] On the *cakravartin*, cf. Spellman 1964: 173–74, Kane 3: 66–67, and H. Jacobi 1910: 336–37.

conquer the whole earth[409] or at least as large a portion of it as possible.[410]

Very few ancient Indian kings have realized the ideal of the *cakravartin*, and even then their unified states disappeared immediately after their death. Ancient Indian history, thus, creates the impression of a continuous struggle between numerous local dynasties; periods of peace seem to have been almost nonexistent.[411] The apparent reason for this political instability is the ideal of the *cakravartin* as described above.

G. Appreciation of Indian Kingship

1. The description of royal power as contained in the latter two sections (E, F) should not be considered exhaustive; on the contrary, there are several aspects of the king's power which had to be passed over in silence.

To quote only a few examples, we have not been able to mention the fact that the king levies the various taxes and contributions, nor the interesting theory according to which these taxes are the king's remuneration in exchange for the protection he offers his subjects.[412] No reference has been made to the king's responsibility in supervising weights and measures (cf. Kane 3: 166). We also had to pass over in silence the role the king has to play in the agricultural and economic matters of the state (cf. Kane 3: 191), etc. (for various other charges of the king, cf. Kane 3: 161–68).

As a result of the extensive character of royal power a number of scholars have drawn the conclusion that ancient Indian kingship was a form of absolute monocracy (cf. Foy 1895: 10). In the next few paragraphs we want to examine whether or not such a conclusion can be accepted.

2. It must be said that, apart from the texts directly enumerating the king's numerous activities, there are others which, at a more general level, do create the impression that royal power was

[409] It would be more correct to say: the whole of Bhāratavarṣa, i.e., the whole of India. Within these limitations we may say that the ideal of the Indian texts on government was an ideal monocracy for the whole of India (Hoffmann 1953: 337–39).

[410] Cf. AŚ 9.1.17–18: "Place means the earth. In that, the region of the sovereign ruler extends northwards between the Himavat and the sea, one thousand *yojanas* in extent across" (tr. Kangle).

[411] "This ideal of *cakravartin* was set before them by all ambitious and energetic Indian rulers from ancient times. The result was that constant wars took place" (Kane 3: 67).

[412] NS 18.48: "Both the other customary receipts of a king and what is called the sixth of the produce of the soil, form the royal revenue, the reward (of a king) for the protection of his subjects" (tr. Jolly).

simply absolute. We think of a number of epic passages in which it is said that the king is the maker of his age, that the king makes or destroys the other beings, etc.[413] But we think especially of the texts which proclaim that the subjects should not react against a king however bad he may be: "When an evil-minded man assails *a wicked king even*, he shall be (fastened) on a stake and burnt in fire; (for he is) more criminal than one who has committed a hundred times the crime of killing a Brāhmaṇa."[414]

A *prima facie* interpretation of this latter text especially must lead to the conclusion that the king was indeed beyond criticism and that his power was really absolute. However, there are other arguments which forbid us to read into such texts the meaning they apparently express. Actually these passages are not meant to be understood literally; their authors themselves did not conceive them as such.

For those who are less familiar with the rules of interpretation which are applicable to Indian law texts, the above statement undoubtedly requires some elucidation. It is a problem which we cannot deal with here in detail (Sarkar 1909); however, since the correct interpretation of a number of texts we are concerned with is at stake, we shall at least set forth the general principle. Texts such as the Dharmaśāstras contain verses which should not be reckoned amongst the regular prescriptions (*vidhis*) but which should be interpreted as *arthavādas*, i.e., exaltations, exaggerated statements whose only purpose is to emphatically praise certain persons or objects, and which, therefore, are given a verbal expression which goes far beyond the actual meaning they want to convey. The *arthavāda* character of a particular verse is to be derived from the circumstance that, if not taken as an *arthavāda*, it contradicts other well established facts. In the case under consideration, for instance, it would not be possible to commit a crime more serious than the murder of a Brāhmaṇa which is, by itself, the most serious possible wrong.[415]

In short, those texts which verbally extol royal power as being absolute are not such as to convince us of the reality of absolute

[413] A number of such epic passages have been collected by Kane 3, n. 5.

[414] NS 15–16.31 (tr. Jolly). This verse serves as a climax after the preceding one in which it has been said that: "If a man censures a king devoted to the discharge of his duties, he shall have his tongue cut out or his entire property confiscated, as an atonement for such crime" (tr. Jolly).

[415] MDh 8.381: "No greater crime is known on earth than slaying a Brāhmaṇa" (tr. Bühler). It might, of course, be argued that this verse too, is an *arthavāda*. However, even if killing a Brāhmaṇa is not the very highest crime, it has on several other occasions been referred to as the first one among the *mahāpātakas* "the great sins" (e.g. MDh 9.235, 11.55).

monocracy. But there is more: there are other arguments which directly demonstrate that royal power cannot have been absolute.

3. The office of the king has never been presented as a *right*, but has invariably been held as a *duty*. Whenever we used the expression "royal power," we actually translated the Sanskrit term *rājadharma*, i.e., the *dharma* of the king. As such, *rājadharma* ranks with the numerous other forms of *dharma* which pertain to all human beings or, for that matter, to all elements in the universe. Now, *dharma* means: one's way of behaving; further, the right way in which to behave, and, finally, the way in which one should behave, i.e., one's duty.[416]

In other words: the king, like anybody else or perhaps more than anybody else,[417] is supposed to obey a rigorous set of rules. Add to this that *dharma* always pretends to be *sarvavyāpaka* "all pervading," i.e., complete and exhaustive, and it is understood that for the king, too, each and every act is supposed to have been codified by his *dharma*; each and every activity of his should be in accordance with this pre-existing *dharma*. Even if the exhaustive character of the *dharma* is partly theoretical, the fact remains that the king, too, enjoys very little freedom of action.

An excellent example of this situation is the degree up to which the king's daily time table has been codified, a fact which we already alluded to above.[418]

[416] With regard to the specific case of *rājadharma* in MDh 7.1, the commentator Medhātithi says that the word *dharma* indicates *kartavyatā*, i.e., necessity, obligation, task.

[417] "*Rājadharma* is said to be the root or the quintessence of all dharmas" (Kane 3). The same author quotes two passages from the *Śāntiparvan* of the MBh in which it has been explicitly stated that *rājadharma* embraces the *dharmas* of all other beings.

[418] Cf. *supra*, E 3. Numerous texts deal with this subject (cf. Kane: 60–61, also 1930–62: 2.805–806), and although they vary on details, the rigidness of the subdivision is apparent in all of them. Due to the length of the text itself, we shall summarize AŚ 1.19.6–24 as follows. During the eight parts of the day the king's activities should be, respectively: (1) listen to measures taken for defence and (accounts of) income and expenditure; (2) look into the affairs of the citizens and the country people; (3) take his bath and meals and devote himself to study; (4) receive revenue in cash and assign tasks to heads of departments; (5) consult the council of ministers by sending letters, and acquaint himself with secret information brought in by spies; (6) engage in recreation at his pleasure or hold consultations; (7) review elephants, horses, chariots and troops; (8) deliberate on military plans with his commander-in-chief and worship twilight. For the eight parts of the night the subdivision is this: (1) interview secret agents; (2) take a bath and meals and engage in study; (3) go to bed; (4) (5) sleep; (6) awaken and ponder over the science (of politics) and the work to be done; (7) sit in consultation (with councilors) and dispatch secret agents; (8) receive blessings from priests, preceptors and chaplain, and see his physician, chief cook and astrologer.

4. Differently from the text quoted above (NS 15–16.31, G 2) which created the impression that the king was beyond all criticism, a great number of passages speak about the sanctions to be imparted to the king in case he deviates from his *dharma*. Here too, the king is not different from any other person in the country.

In the first place, one provides for sanctions of a purely religious nature. We shall only briefly refer to the popular concept that a king who fails to do his duty will have to pass a considerable lapse of time in hell in order to expiate his sins.[419] But there is one type of religious sanction which is much more important, so much so that it has been called "a rather striking feature of the Indian kingship" (Gray 1914: 720). The sanction relates to the case in which the king neglects to duly punish *adharma* committed by his subjects: the criminal, whether he be punished or not, is freed from guilt; however, if he had been unjustly pardoned, his guilt passes on to the king.[420]

Besides the religious sanctions there are others which have a strictly legal character. Not only do the texts provide for real punishments for the king,[421] but they provide for a much heavier punishment when a particular wrong is perpetrated by the king than when it is committed by a common subject.[422]

5. Next, the power of the king could hardly be called absolute in a system which provides for overt insurrection against a king who falls short of his duties. Not only does such a king lose his fame, but he is also turned out of the kingdom.[423] Other texts go

[419] Nārada *Quotations* 5.10: "Perjured witnesses, as well as those who rob others of their property, and wicked kings, shall have to reside (hereafter) in a very dreadful hell for the time of a *kalpa*" (tr. Jolly); *Kātyāyana* 10: "That king, who gives way to sudden wrath without proper thought, no doubt would reside in an horrible hell for half a *kalpa*" (tr. Kane).

[420] MDh 8.316: "Whether he be punished or pardoned, the thief is freed from (guilt of) theft; but the king, if he punishes not, takes upon himself the guilt of the thief" (tr. Bühler). Cf. also ĀpDh 1.6.19.16, 1.9.25.5; GDh 12.43–45. Besides these rules which deal with the special case of a thief, we also possess more general prescriptions such as ĀpDh 2.11.28.13: "If a king does not punish a punishable offence, the guilt falls upon him" (tr. Bühler). For the king's participation in his subjects' merits, see note 381 above.

[421] MDh 7.28: "Punishment (possesses) a very bright luster, and is hard to be administered by men with unimproved minds; it strikes down the king who swerves from his duty, together with his relatives" (tr. Bühler). About the special case of unduly imposing a fine, YDh 2.307: "Wenn der könig unrechtmässig eine geldstrafe erhoben hat, so soll er selbst das dreissigfache derselben, indem er es dem Varuṇa weihet, den Brāhmaṇas geben" (tr. Stenzler); cf. also AŚ 4.13.42–43.

[422] MDh 8.336: "Where another common man would be fined one *kārṣāpaṇa*, the king should be fined one thousand; that is the settled rule" (tr. Bühler).

[423] MDh 7.111: "That king who through folly rashly oppresses his kingdom, (will), together with his relatives, ere long be deprived of his life and his kingdom" (tr. Bühler). The fact that the sanction sometimes consisted in merely

one step further and allow the wicked king to be killed, either by his subjects generally or by the Brāhmaṇas in particular.[424]

6. The latter intervention of the Brāhmaṇas leads us to another factor, perhaps the most fundamental of all, which prevents royal power from being absolute. We refer to the above mentioned fact (cf. *supra*, F 2) that the king normally belongs to the Kṣatriya class, which means that he too, participates in the Kṣatriyas' inferiority with regard to the members of the first class, i.e., the Brāhmaṇas.

The singular situation in which the head of the state occupies an inferior position as compared to the class of the Brāhmaṇas as a whole manifests itself on numerous occasions.[425] It is said in general that the king rules everybody except the Brāhmaṇas.[426] Every morning the king is supposed to attend upon Brāhmaṇas and to take their advice.[427] In a meeting hall the king's seat should be more elevated than anybody else's except for the seat of the Brāhmaṇas which should be higher than his.[428] On the roads the king is to accord priority to nobody but the Brāhmaṇas.[429]

having to leave the kingdom is corroborated by the prescriptions providing for the *sautrāmaṇi iṣṭi* as a rite enabling the king to regain his country (Kane 3.26; also 2.1227).

[424] It seems as if even MDh 7.112 thought of the possibility of the king being killed: "As the lives of living creatures are destroyed by tormenting their bodies, even so the lives of kings are destroyed by their oppressing their kingdoms" (tr. Bühler). As to who is supposed to kill the king, we refer to AŚ 8.3.7: "And mostly kings under influence of anger are known to have been killed by risings among the subjects" (tr. Kangle). Kane (3.26–27) quotes other instances to the same effect from the MBh and *Yaśastilaka*. Other passages, however, from the MBh and especially from the *Śukranītisāra* clearly leave the initiative to the Brāhmaṇas (see again Kane: 26–27). On the right of revolution in ancient India, its justification and methods, see Spellman (1964: 225–243), who devotes a whole chapter to the subject.

[425] *vide* Kane 1930–62: 2.138–145, for the peculiar sanctity attaching to the person of a Brāhmaṇa and the superior position of Brāhmaṇas as a class *vis-à-vis* the king" (Kane 3.97).

[426] GDh 11.1: "The king is master of all, with the exception of Brāhmaṇas" (tr. Bühler). Cf. MDh 9.313–322.

[427] MDh 7.37–39: "Let the king, after rising early in the morning, worship Brāhmaṇas who are well versed in the threefold sacred science and learned (in polity), and follow their advice. Let him daily worship aged Brāhmaṇas who know the Veda and the pure; for he who always worships aged men, is honored even by *Rākṣasas*. Let him, though he may already be modest, constantly learn modesty from them; for a king who is modest never perishes" (tr. Bühler). Cf. also MDh 7.145, and AŚ, book 10.

[428] GDh 11.7: "All, excepting Brāhmaṇas, shall worship him who is seated on a higher seat, (while they themselves sit on a) lower (one)" (tr. Bühler).

[429] GDh 6.24–25: "Way must be made for a man seated in a carriage, for one who is in his tenth (decade), for one requiring consideration, for a woman, for a *Snātaka*, and for a king. But a king (must make way) for a *Śrotiya*" (tr. Bühler);

Moreover, the entire system of dharmic organization of society is such that the Brāhmaṇas continually exercise control over the king. There is no doubt that the brahmanic authors of the texts of Dharmaśāstra have accorded enormous powers to the king. The king is one of the most important pawns on the chess-board of *dharma*, but he nevertheless remains a pawn in a game the rules of which have been laid down by the Brāhmaṇas. To take the example of the organization of law courts. As we have said above (cf. *supra*, E 3), it is the king who presides over the daily sessions of the court. However, he is not the only authority present there; on the contrary, he is surrounded by a committee of *sabhyas*, and these *sabhyas* are Brāhmaṇas.[430] It has become a habit to translate the term *sabhya* as "assessor." Actually their task goes far beyond merely assisting the royal president: judging from a number of texts which all the *sabhyas* to go against the opinion of the king[431] one cannot but feel inclined towards considering the *sabhyas* the real judges and the king the assessor.

7. The way in which the king is thus surrounded in the law courts is only illustrative of a much more general situation. For his other activities too, the king is assisted by a council of persons who have been called by various names: *amātya*, *saciva*, or *mantrin*, all of which are generally translated as "ministers."[432] Their number and activities greatly vary in the different texts.

ĀpDh 2.5.11.5–6: "The road belongs to a king except if he meets a Brāhmaṇa. But if he meets a Brāhmaṇa, the road belongs to the latter" (tr. Bühler). Cf. also VaDh 13.59.

[430] BS 1.11: "That judicial assembly is equal (in sanctity) to a sacrificial meeting in which there sit seven or five or three Brāhmaṇas, who are acquainted with the world, with (the contents of) the Veda, and with law" (tr. Jolly). Cf. MDh 8.1: "A king, desirous of investigating law cases, must enter his court of justice, preserving a dignified demeanor, together with Brāhmaṇas and with experienced councilors" (tr. Bühler); VaDh 2.1; KS 57.

[431] KS 74–75: "The members of the court should not connive at the king when he begins to act unjustly; if they do so, they along with the king fall headlong into hell. Those members of the court, who follow (approve of) the king who proceeds in an unjust manner, also become participators therein (i.e. in the sin due to unjust decision); therefore the king should be awakened by them (to the right course)" (tr. Kane). We cannot agree with Kane's translation of KS 76: "Coming to know that the mind of the king is straying from the path of justice, a member of the court should then say what is agreeable (to the king); (by so doing) the *sabhya* would not incur sin"; it is in contradiction with the previous verse. Moreover there exists another reading (cf. Rocher, *Vyavahāracintāmaṇi*, 44) which does away with this contradiction: "But when the judge knows that the mind of the king has deviated from the path of equity, he should not speak merely to please him; when he does so, he is guilty" (tr. Rocher). See also KS 77–78.

[432] For a detailed study of the ministers, cf. Kane 3.104–131; Spellman 1964: 69–92.

It is also true that they are not invariably Brāhmaṇas: Kṣatriyas and Vaiśyas too could be members of the council of ministers (thus, *Śukranītisāra* and *Nītivākyāmṛta* as quoted by Kane 3.108). However, some of them necessarily were —we think of the *purohita*, the minister of religious affairs—, and they did not fail to play the most important part. To quote Manu: "Let him (i.e., the king) daily consider with them the ordinary (business, referring to) peace and war, (the four subjects called) *sthāna*, the revenue, the manner of protecting (himself and his kingdom), and the sanctification of his gains (by pious gifts). Having (first) ascertained the opinions of each (minister) separately and (then the views) of all together, let him do what is (most) beneficial for him in his affairs, but with the most distinguished among them all, a learned Brāhmaṇa let the king deliberate on the most important affairs which relate to the six measures of royal polity. Let him, full of confidence, always entrust to that (official) all business; having taken his final resolution with him, let him afterwards begin to act" (MDh 7.56–59; about the *purohita* generally, cf. Gonda 1955: 107–24).

8. A highly controversial problem in connection with the nature of royal power is whether it is vested with a sacred character or not. We recently had an opportunity to deal with this problem elsewhere (Rocher 1962: 123–37). Here too, we had to conclude to the existence of a number of *arthavāda*s which proclaim the king to incorporate one or more gods. But here too, we met with a category of much more profoundly divine beings on earth: the Brāhmaṇas.

9. In order to situate ancient Indian kingship, we would be inclined to regard it as a form of very strong monocracy which, however, never attained the stage of an autocracy. Its most peculiar aspect probably consists in the fact of limitations being imposed on it by a corpus of written customary law. This corpus which is vested with a sacred and revealed character and which claims to be eternal and unchangeable, is the work of a section of the population which through it has assured itself a situation superior to that of the otherwise very powerful king.

Part Three

Hindu Legal Procedure

20

The Theory of Proof in Ancient Hindu Law

1. The Sources

The main sources for our knowledge of the theory of proof in Hindu law are the numerous treatises on *dharma*.[436] We could not possibly go into details here of the exact sense of the technical term *dharma*; we merely want to remind the reader of the important fact that *dharma* and law are not at all synonyms. As a matter of fact, law constitutes but a very small portion of the much wider concept of *dharma*; we are not even sure whether, at the outset, the treatises of *dharma* actually intended also to deal with the matter which we habitually group under the title law.

As a result, we should not be surprised if the data about law in general and about procedure and proof in particular are rather scarce in the oldest texts: the Dharmasūtras, i.e. the treatises written in prose. It would not be possible to reconstruct a coherent system of proof when appealing to no other sources than these Dharmasūtras.

From the beginning of the period of the Dharmaśāstras, all of a sudden the data become much more numerous and complete. In the following pages, we shall have ample opportunity to draw

[436] Since this paper is meant for comparative jurists who are not supposed to read the original Sanskrit texts, we shall, as a rule, only quote from and refer to those texts for which translations are available. In the first place, we may refer to five volumes published in *The Sacred Books of the East* (Oxford, Clarendon Press); they are:

- Vol. II and XIV: *The Sacred Laws of the Aryas as taught in the Schools of Āpastamba, Gautama, Vāsiṣṭha, and Baudhāyana*, translated by Georg Bühler (1879; 1882).

materials even from the older Dharmaśāstras, those of Manu and Yājñavalkya. However, it is not before the Dharmaśāstra of Nārada that we are provided with a more or less comprehensive and systematic survey of the theory of proof. Like its predecessors, the *Nāradasmṛti* too, has been subdivided according to the eighteen so-called "titles of law" (*vivādapadas*): still, the treatment of substantive law as a whole is preceded by a triple introduction containing several details on procedure. Moreover, on the occasion[437] of the first title of law —Non-payment of Debts— the author has inserted a substantial passage dealing with proof.

The data contained in later Dharmaśāstras, those of Bṛhaspati, Kātyāyana, Vyāsa, Pitāmaha, etc., definitely confirm and even supplement those given by Nārada. The only disadvantage with these texts is that they have not been preserved except for numerous isolated fragments to be found in later legal literature; thus, we neither know how these works had been arranged, nor do we have any idea as to how each single rule fitted into the whole.

It can hardly be denied that the rules contained in all these ancient texts, from the oldest Dharmasūtras down to the most recent Dharmaśāstras, show a good deal of variants and differences. On the other hand, however, they provide us with a system the basic unity of which should not be underestimated. It was left to the commentators to further work out this system and to propose explanations for the apparent discrepancies.

For various reasons[438] this paper will be based mainly upon the Dharmasūtras and the Dharmaśāstras; in very exceptional cases

- Vol. VII: *The Institutes of Vishnu*, translated by Julius Jolly (1880).

- Vol. XXV: *The Laws of Manu*, translated with Extracts from Seven Commentaries by Georg Bühler (1886).

- Vol. XXXIII: *The Minor Law-Books*, translated by Julius Jolly. Part. I: Nārada, Bṛhaspati (1889). With regard to Bṛhaspati we want to draw attention to the fact that references are to Jolly's translation and not to K.V. Rangaswami Aiyangar's edition (Baroda 1941); the reference to the latter may easily be obtained by consulting Rangaswami Aiyangar's "Comparative statement of verses" at the end of his edition.

Other reliable translations are:

- *Yājnavalkya's Gesetzbuch*, Sanskrit und Deutsch, herausgegeben von A.F. Stenzler (1849): the second volume contains the translation.

- *Kātyāyanasmṛti on Vyavahāra (Law and Procedure)*. Text (reconstructed), Translations, Notes and Introduction, by P.V. Kane (n.d.).

- *Die Fragmente des Pītamaha*, Text und Übersetzung, von Karl Scriba (1902).

[437] To a certain extent the same situation is already found with Manu; we fail to see how Jolly came to the opinion, according to which it was the first *vivādapada* which was treated on the occasion of the rules on legal procedure. Cf. Jolly 1878.

[438] These reasons are indeed multifarious:

(a) First ranks an argument which is inherent to the very nature of the texts on *dharma*. The only actual basis of Hindu law, up to the latest *nibandhas*, is the

only shall we quote the opinions of the commentators. We shall try to present the main facts as we find them in the ancient texts, without attempting to minimize the divergences, and without concerning ourselves with interpretations which may not have occurred to the authors themselves.[439]

As is generally known, the sources which we are thus forced to base these pages upon, have raised a number of problems which should at least be briefly referred to here. In the first place, the non-appearance of a particular rule before a particular text, say, Manu or Nārada, does not necessarily imply the non-existence of the prescription prior to these texts. We already pointed out that the original scope of the treatises on *dharma* may not have been to give a complete survey of legal rules. Without therefore going as far as the orthodox Hindu interpreters who assume all rules of *dharma* "to have a Vedic base," i.e., to have existed from time immemorial, the historian of Hindu law must never exclude the possibility of his not possessing the exact *terminus a quo* for the appearance of any prescription whatsoever.[440]

Secondly, in a study meant for comparative jurists we shall not neglect to refer to a certain point of view which holds that the theo-

whole of the Dharmasūtras and Dharmaśāstras. It would, of course, be wrong to say that the commentaries and the *nibandhas* did not create anything new; however, their contribution is of a secondary nature, to be compared with the contribution of continental "jurisprudence" to the texts of law.

(b) It goes without saying that the study of the works of the commentators should not be absent from a complete survey of proof in Hindu law. Still, the present paper can in no way claim to be such a complete survey, since the limitations of space do not allow us to enter into detail about the numerous and intricate discussions contained in the commentaries and the *nibandhas*. Rather than to quote some of the commentaries to the exclusion of others and, thus, to create a false image, we prefer to completely abstain from treating the commentaries, reserving this treatment for another occasion.

(c) Unlike the Dharmasūtras and the Dharmaśāstras, very few commentaries and *nibandhas* on legal procedure are available in reliable translations to be efficiently used by non-sanskritists. The reader excuse us if we occasionally make an exception for our translation of one of the important *nibandhas*: Vācaspatimiśra's *Vyavahāracintāmaṇi* (1956).

[439] We do not think here of the interpretations proposed by the Sanskrit commentators, but of the modern works of certain Indian authors. Being —rightly— proud of their ancient system of law, they too often are inclined to motivate ancient Indian rules by means of modern legal principles. Such considerations are, of course, meant to prove that some of these modern principles "already" existed in ancient Hindu law. Even though we too, are convinced of the truth of many of these assertions, we prefer to leave it to comparative jurists to draw the adequate conclusions from the facts presented here on the basis of the Sanskrit texts.

[440] Examples of the problems raised by this state of affairs will be found below: the various modes of proof, the number of ordeals known to ancient Hindu law, etc.

ries developed in the treatises on *dharma* do not at all correspond to the rules observed in legal practice. Personally, however, we are convinced that, at least as far as the period of the Dharmasūtras and the Dharmaśāstras is concerned, this point of view cannot be supported by any valid arguments. On the contrary, a summary of the prescriptions of the books on *dharma* may be assumed to provide us with a fairly correct picture of ancient Hindu law, no more but also no less than in any other system of law, ancient or modern.

After these preliminary remarks about the sources which the data for this paper shall be drawn from, we propose to examine the place occupied by the passages on proof within the general framework of the texts on legal procedure as a whole.

At least from Bṛhaspati onward, *vyavahāra* in its sense of legal procedure, is divided into four parts.[441] First comes the plaint (*bhāṣā*, literally: "statement") to be produced by the plaintiff; next follows the "reply" (*uttara*) to be produced by the defendant; the third place is occupied by the trial (*kriyā*, literally "action"); finally, the cause is concluded by the "decision" (*nirṇaya*). Apart from minor discrepancies, this fourfold subdivision has been adhered to by most later authors and has constituted the general framework all *nibandhas* built upon. Among these four major parts it is the chapter called *kriyā* which contains the rules on proof to be discussed below.

Although the passages on proof, thus, constitute only one quarter of the texts on legal procedure, which, in their turn, are but a small portion of the legal sections contained in the, again, much larger books on *dharma*, still the field they cover is enormous, and we can only hope to point out some of the main points which are likely to interest the comparative jurist.[442]

[441] BS 3.1: "The part called the declaration; the part called the answer; the part called the trial; and the part called the deliberation of the judges regarding the *onus probandi*: these are the four parts of a judicial proceeding." The term "declaration" refers to the plaint: the technical term used in the Sanskrit text is identical with the one used by logicians for one of the statements in the syllogism. By means of "the deliberation of the judges regarding the *onus probandi*," Jolly translates a term which has been variously interpreted by the commentators and whose sense is not at all sure; later on, it is replaced by *nirṇaya*, the technical term for "judgment."

[442] We may abstain here from giving a complete bibliography on the subject of legal procedure in general and proof in particular: the essential works will be found in our bibliographical note on Hindu law to be published shortly by the Centre d'Ethnologie Juridique of the Institut de Sociologie in the University of Brussels. Nevertheless, we want to single out two volumes which had been used continually: P.V. Kane: *History of Dharmasāstra*, vol. 3 (1930–62) and A. Thakur: *Hindu Law of Evidence According to the Smṛtis* (1933). The main sources, however, have been the texts of the Dharmasūtras and Dharmaśāstras enumerated above eventually supplemented by data drawn from the Vyci.

2. *The Burden of Proof*

Before examining the various modes of proof recognized by ancient Hindu law, it is important to know by which party the evidence should be produced. In this respect the texts have elaborated a system which may look complicated at a first glance but which actually is nothing but the rigorous application to the various cases of one and the same principle.

We would not dare decide whether it was the principle or its applications that have been formulated first. Even if we have to wait for the commentators to find the principle worded explicitly, it evidently has been the underlying element of the several special rules found in the Dharmaśāstras.

Hindu law assumes that evidence cannot be produced but for a positive statement:[443] it would not be possible to produce evidence for one's not owing a certain amount of money or for one's not having committed a certain crime. For all practical purposes this principle implies that the burden of proof will be assigned differently according to the affirmative or negative character of the reply which the defendant opposes to the plaint. Since Hindu law distinguishes four kinds of reply, the burden of proof shall in each case be allotted accordingly, as follows:[444]

a) In case of confession the problem of the burden of proof should not even be raised. It goes without saying that a reply in the form: "Yes, I do owe you this amount," or "Yes, I did commit this crime," at once brings the trial to an end. It is held that through a reply of this kind the four parts of *vyavahāra* are reduced to two only: the third part (*kriyā*) is missing and the reply itself implies the decision.[445]

[443] The principle has been very clearly stated in Vijñāneśvara's *Mitākṣarā* on YDh 2.7: "An *arthī* is one who alleges the facts to be established. The adverse party denying the allegation is *pratyarthī*. The issue is to be proved by the *arthī* because he states an affirmative and not by the *pratyarthī* simply on the ground that he states a negative. The proof of a negative depends upon the presumption of its corresponding affirmative and that of an affirmative does not require its corresponding negative to be proved as existing. Witnesses and other means of proof cannot establish a negative and thus a negative is incapable of proof. Therefore the *arthī* (one who states an affirmative) is the party on whom the burden of proof should lie" (quoted in Thakur 1933: 42). For an exception to this rule in the case of ordeals, cf. note 554 below.

[444] The most complete account is found with Vyāsa 1.29 (quoted *Vyavahāracintāmaṇi* 178): In the case of a former judgement or a reply by way of exception the burden of proof is upon the defendant; in the case of a denial, upon the plaintiff; in the case of a confession, there is no burden of proof." —For similar verses, cf. Nārada *Introduction* 2.26; BS 5.3 and 5.20.

[445] In the commentaries this case has given rise to endless discussions in

b) In case of denial the reply is, of course, negative: "No, I do not owe you this amount," or "No, I did not commit this crime." If we apply the principle quoted above, the burden of proof is to lie with the plaintiff. It should be added that in some cases the latter enjoys a particularly favorable situation: as soon as he succeeds in proving only part of the plaint, judgment should be passed in his favor for the whole of it.[446]
c) The situation is different in case of a reply by way of exception. Here the defendant is supposed to say: "Yes, I did owe you this amount, but I have paid it back." The defendant's statement thus contains a positive element, and it is left to him to afford proof for it. In other words: the exception is to be proved by the defendant.
d) Finally, the reply by way of former judgment is not essentially different from the reply by way of exception. As a matter of fact, the reference to a former judgment is nothing but a special case of the reference to an exception. If the defendant replies: "Yes, I did owe you this amount, but a judgment has been pronounced about it," it is again left to him to produce evidence for this former judgment. In order to do so, he shall have to produce a *jayapattra* ("document of victory") which we shall come back to below in the chapter dealing with documents.

Besides these simple cases, the Hindu authors have also examined the more intricate problem of the burden of proof in case of the so-called "mixed reply".[447] Suppose a plaint in the form: "You owe me a hundred coins," the reply to which is worded as follows: "I did owe you seventy-five coins, twenty-five of which have been repaid and another twenty-five of which have been the object of a former judgment." In this statement the four types of reply have been combined simultaneously, and accordingly the question has been asked who should bear the burden of proof. The Dharmaśāstras do not provide us with a solution

order to know whether there are only parts, or whether there actually are four parts some of which have coincided.

[446] ViDh 6.22: "If the whole demand has been contested by the debtor, and even a part of it only has been proved against him, he must pay the whole." Cf. also YDh 2.20.

[447] We have dealt with this problem elsewhere; cf. Rocher 1960. In this paper we examined the problems of the mixed reply inasmuch as "it demonstrates in the clearest terms the way in which Hindu law has been capable of gradually pasing on from a stage of strict absolute formalism to a basically realistic system where equity and good sense became more and more preponderant."

for this problem; the commentators, on their side, have thought it a problem which was particularly fit to be made the object of their learned and ingenious speculations. The solutions they propose vary from a split burden of proof —caused by a rigorous application of the general principle to the various parts of the plaint— on the one hand, to various other systems in which, for instance, the burden of proof for one part prevails so as to make proof of the other parts superfluous, etc.

Another problem connected with the application of the general principle was raised in case of both statements, the plaintiff's and the defendant's, being positive.[448] Take the example of both parties pretending: "This inheritance is mine." Even though in later centuries a number of ancient verses have been interpreted as if they referred to this point, personally we are under the impression that this problem has not been envisaged before the period of the commentators. Anyhow, the burden of proof is said to lie with the *pūrvavādin*, literally: the "first, former" party, i.e., either the party who introduced the plaint, or the party whose claim had arisen first.[449]

After the burden of proof has, thus, been assigned either to the plaintiff or to the defendant, it is his duty to produce his evidence.[450] This duty shall have been particularly heavy in the case of the plaintiff; indeed, as far as the defendant is concerned, his position is a privileged one in that he enjoys the benefit of the doubt: from the most ancient times onward it has been said that nobody should be punished on mere suspicion only.[451]

[448] The following verses are said to refer to this case: —YDh 2.17: "Wenn Zeugen auf beiden Seiten sind, so sollen zuerst die Zeugen desjenigen befragt werden *welcher die früheren Ansprüche macht*; ..."; —ViDh 8.10: "In a dispute between two litigants the witnesses of that party have to be examined *from which the plaint has proceeded*"; —NS 1.163: "If two persons quarrel with one another, and if both have witnesses, the witnesses of that party shall be heard *which was the first to go to law*. —The words printed in italics in each case translate the Sanskrit term *pūrvavādin*.

[449] We have to leave aside a further complication arising when the *pūrvavādin's* evidence is or becomes *adhara*, literally: "lower, weaker." In that case the other party's evidence is to be examined. The commentators themselves apparently have had some difficulty explaining this case; in the present state of our knowledge we prefer to abstain from entering into a detailed discussion.

[450] YDh 2.7–8: "Die Antwort des Verklagten, wenn er die Sache gehört, ist niederzuschreiben in Gegenwart des Klägers welcher zuerst gesprochen, und dann soll der Kläger sogleich den Beweis seiner Behauptung niederschreiben lassen. Beweist er sie, so gewinnt er, sonst verliert er...". The word "Kläger," stands for the more vague Sanskrit term who actually means that party with whom lies the burden of proof.

[451] ĀpDh 2.5.11.2: "And the king shall not punish on suspicion." "Modern Indian authors are very proud of this rule; cf. Kane 1930–62: 3.360: "The ben-

3. The Modes of Proof

As soon as we try to establish the history of the modes of proof in Hindu law, we are faced with a problem already referred to above. The number of the modes of proof indeed varies from a single one with Gautama up to at least five with Nārada and Bṛhaspati.[452] Shall we interpret the appearance of an ever-increasing number of modes of proof in the texts as corresponding to an actual augmentation in fact? Is Gautama's reference to witnesses only really meant to be exhaustive? In the present state of our knowledge we prefer to abstain from giving a definite answer to all these questions; we even doubt whether a definite answer will ever be possible.

From the time of Nārada and Bṛhaspati onward, and throughout the whole period of the commentators, the classification of the various means of proof is more or less uniformly established as follows:

Human Evidence:

a) witnesses
b) documents
c) possession

Divine Evidence:

a) oath
b) ordeals

The main distinction of two groups: human evidence on the one hand and divine evidence on the other, is not without importance; on the contrary, especially with regard to India, which has been traditionally regarded as the country where the spiritual overrules anything material, we may not fail to refer to the mutual relationship between both groups of modes of proof.

All texts unanimously hold that human means of proof are more valid than divine means of proof. One never appeals to divine means of proof unless no human means of proof are available at all.[453] In

efit of doubt is to be given, accoding to modern ideas on the administration of justice, to the accused. This principle was put forward several centuries before Christ by Āpastamba...".

[452] For a statistical survey of the gradual appearance of the various modes of proof, cf. Thakur 1933: 9.

[453] YDh 2.22: "Als Beweis gilt eine Schrift, der Genuss und Zeugen; *wenn eins von diesen fehlt*, so gilt eins von den Gottesurtheilen." KS 217 speaks of the absence of witnesses only, but there is no reason to reject the unanimous interpre-

cases where both human and divine means of proof are produced, the former only should be allowed to be examined.[454] Moreover, even if the divine evidence covers the whole matter under dispute, whereas conflicting human evidence only covers part of it, it is still the latter which prevails to the exclusion of the former.[455]

4. First Mode of Proof: Witnesses

The Sanskrit technical term for a witness, *sākṣin* (nominative: *sākṣī*), has been the object of an etymological explanation with Indian grammarians: it is formed with the suffix *-in* added to the stem of the adverb *sākṣāt* "with one's own eyes"; so, *sākṣin* is the person who sees something with his own eyes.[456] Indian legal texts too, refer to and adopt this etymological explanation; in order to be a valid witness one has to have seen the facts with one's own eyes or, by an analogical extension, one has to have heard the facts with one's own ears.[457] The same texts also have not neglected to rigidly apply the definition in practice so as to exclude all witnesses who do not fulfill these requirements. There is but one exception to this rules: if a witness has died or gone abroad, one may accept in his place the deposition of the person to whom the former has communicated the evidence he would have given himself.[458]

tation of the commentators according to which "witnesses" is merely illustrative for all kinds of human evidence. Nārada *Introduction* 2.29–30 is worded quite differently; it is, however, clear that here too, the examples are such as to allow divine evidence in the only cases where human evidence could not possibly by obtained.

[454] KS 218: "If one (party to the litigation) puts forth human (means of proof) while the other (party) puts forth divine means, then the king should accept human means of proof and not divine."

[455] KS 219: "When men dispute, if there is human means of proof though only reaching a portion (of the allegations in the plaint), then the human means should be accepted and not divine means, though they may be complete (i.e. completely cover all the allegations)."

[456] Thus Pāṇini: *Aṣṭādhyāyī* 5.2.91.

[457] NS 1.148: "He should be considered as a witness who has witnessed a deed with his own ears or eyes: with his ears, if he has heard another man speaking; with his eyes, if he has seen something himself." —For similar verses, cf. BDh 1.10.7; MDh 8.74; ViDh 8.13; KS 346.

[458] NS 1.166: "If a witness dies or goes abroad after having been appointed, those who have heard his deposition may give evidence; for indirect proof (through a second-hand statement) makes evidence (as well as direct proof)." Cf. also ViDh 8.12. What is meant here is the *uttarasākṣin* "the indirect witness," one of the six *kṛta* witnesses to be referred to below. Cf. BS 7.10: "That witness who communicates what he has heard to another man at the time when he is about to go abroad, or lying on his deathbed, should be considered as an indirect witness." (Notice the error in Jolly's translation: it is not the person who informs the other who is the indirect witness, but the one who has been

After some other less elaborate subdivisions,[459] from Nārada and Bṛhaspati onward witnesses have been divided into two main groups each of them again being sixfold.[460]

Among the first group rank all the *kṛta* witnesses, i.e. those who have been "made," "appointed" witnesses. They are persons who have witnessed the facts and who haw been requested by the party eventually to appear before the court in order to produce their evidence. To this category of witnesses belongs the person whose name has been inscribed on the contract, the one who has been invited to secretly attend the facts, the above mentioned person who has heard the deposition of a direct witness, etc.

Among the second group rank the various *akṛta* witnesses, i.e. those who have "not been made, appointed" witnesses. There are indeed persons who, without having been invited by the party to come and depose, still are in a position to provide useful information in the course of the trial. They are: the party's kinsmen or co-villagers, the king or the chief judge concerning former trials, etc.

One has, of course, a right to ask whether this subdivision has or has not a deeper meaning and, more particularly, whether witnesses are treated differently on the basis of their belonging to one or the other of the said categories. In fact, no prescription to this effect is to be found anywhere in the Dharmaśāstras; on the contrary, the twelvefold subdivision seems to respond to no other motive than the Hindus' general tendency towards harmonious subdivisions, the number twelve being considered as particularly fitting for this purpose.[461]

Several rules in the Dharmaśāstras deal with the number of witnesses to be produced by the party who bears the burden of proof. They essentially refer to two points: the witnesses should

informed in order to appear as a witness at the moment when the trial comes up before the court.)

[459] Manu, for instance, distinguishes between two kinds of witness: *nibaddha* and *anibaddha*. Since this subdivision has not met with much success, we do not treat it here. For its relation to the classical subdivision into *kṛta* and *akṛta* witnesses, cf. Thakur 1933: 20–22.

[460] Cf. NS 1.149–152; Nārada actually distinguishes eleven kinds of witnesses only; cf. below; —BS 7.1–15, with elaborate definitions of the twelve species of witnsses; equally so KS 371–376, 356–357, etc.

[461] To support this view we merely want to refer to the fact that the number twelve was reached by Bṛhaspati and, especially, to the fact that it was reached by splitting up Nārada's *likhita* witness into both *likhita* and *lekhita*. No doubt, Bṛhaspati has different definitions for both of them but they are worded in such a way as to clearly indicate the artificial character of the distinction. Moreover, the commentators, who normally try their utmost in order to interpret —and often to rationalize— the data of the ancient texts, in this case acknowledge the purely speculative character of the twelvefold subdivision.

be many, and their number should be uneven. All texts seem to attach a great importance to the exclusion of the single witness.[462] As early as Gautama, it has been said that witnesses should be many;[463] later on, from Manu onward, it becomes clear that "many," should be interpreted as "a minimum of three."[464] Nevertheless, most of the treatises do contain a number of exceptions to this rule, however important it may be. Generally speaking, these exceptions either cover cases in which a plurality of witnesses is not obtainable, or they refer to a witness who might be supposed to speak the truth without the necessity of his statements being checked by means of other witnesses:

a) A single witness is admitted by common consent of both parties.[465]
b) A single witness is also admitted if he is known to be particularly virtuous or learned.[466] The king and the chief judge apparently also belong to this category,[467] and equally so a number of experts on particular matters.[468]
c) Finally, a single witness is admitted in a number of special cases which, by their very nature, are not likely to have been attended by many witnesses. The examples illustrating this latter motive being often of a criminal nature,

[462] ViDh 8.5: "Nor can one man alone be made a witness" —The single person also figures among incompetent witnesses with MDh 8.66; NS 1.179.

[463] GDh 13.2: "The (latter) shall be many ...".

[464] Thus MDh 8.60 and, similarly, YDh 2.69; NS 1.153. More explicitly even BS 7.16: "There should be nine, seven, five. four, or three witnesses; or two only, if they are learned Brahmins, are proper (to be examined); but let him never examine a single witness." This text also allows two witnesses, but in very special circumstances only.

[465] NS 1.192: "By consent of both parties, one man alone even may become a witness in a suit. He must be examined in public as a witness, though (he has been mentioned as) an incompetent witness"; cf. also YDh 2.72.

[466] Especially ViDh 8.8–9: "Descendants of a noble race, who are virtuous and wealthy, sacrificers, zealous in the practice of religious austerities, having male issue, well versed in the holy law, studious, veracious. aquatinted with the three Vedas, and aged (shall be witness). If he is endowed with the qualities just mentioned, one man alone can also be made a witness"; cf. MDh 8.77.

[467] Cf. BS 7.13–14: "The king in person having heard the speeches of plaintiff and defendant, may act as witness if both should quarrel with one another. If after the division of a suit a fresh trial should take place, the chief judge, together with the assessors, may act as witnesses there, but not in any other case." —Cf. also BS 7.18; KS 355.

[468] A number of texts mention messengers, accountants, etc. (BS 7.18; KS 353), but we especially want to refer to KS 354: "(In disputes about manufactured articles such as ear-rings) one should establish (identity of) that thing by (the evidence of) that man who produced the finished article; in such disputes he, though alone, is declared to be the means of proof."

> deposition by a single witness may be said to constitute a point of difference between civil procedure on the one hand and criminal procedure on the other.[469]

As to the requirement of an uneven number of witnesses, its scope will be clear when we discuss the cast of contradictory evidence below: since the quantitative majority plays an important role in this case, it is but natural that an uneven number only is liable to bring about this required majority.

Long passages in the Dharmaśāstras have been devoted to enumerations of people who may be accepted as competent witnesses and to those who should be refused as such.[470] In view of the authors' special preoccupation in any case to arrive at a decision corresponding to truth —we shall come back to this element below—, we understand the extreme care with which competent witnesses have been selected.

First of all, witnesses must be impartial towards both parties; as soon as there is the slightest fear that they might be favorably disposed towards one party or unfavorably towards another, they must be excluded.[471]

Next, witnesses must possess the necessary moral qualities: their acts and thoughts must be as many guarantees for their straightforwardness.[472]

There are several other requirements which witnesses must fulfill before they can be allowed to depose before the court, all of which cannot possibly be mentioned here. In order to give at least an idea as to the degree of minute analysis which has been reached in this matter, we shall quote the example of witnesses being allowed to depose if their position in society is such as to compel them to speak the truth. Not only persons belonging to more or less closed groups such as caste, occupation or even sex, are supposed to be more likely to speak truth in cases where both

[469] YDh 2.72: "Jeder gilt als zeuge bei unzucht, raub, beleidigung und gewaltthat." —Actually the problem whether Hindu law distinguished between civil and criminal procedure is a very complicated one, which in its turn depends upon whether Hindu law made a distinction between civil and criminal law as such. We have dealt with the various aspects of these problems in Rocher 1955.

[470] In view of the great member of texts dealing with this point, a few examples of which only can be quoted below, we give the following list of references: GDh 13.14; ĀpDh 2.11.29.7; VaDh 16.28–30; BDh 1.10.19.13; MDh 8.61–72; YDh 2.68–72; ViDh 8.7–9; NS 1.152–162; BS 7.27–30; KS 361–364.

[471] GDh 13.2: "The (latter) should be... free from affection for, or hatred against either (party)"; cf. MDh 8.64.

[472] NS 3.153: "They shall be of honorable family, straightforward, and unexceptionable as to their descent, their actions and their fortune. The witness shall... be... unimpeachable, honest, and pure-minded"; cf. MDh 8.63.

parties also belong to the same groups,[473] but the texts have even envisaged such very special cases as that of a householder whose sense of responsibility with regard to his family is likely to make him fear the evil consequences of a false deposition.[474]

More numerous even are the ancient texts enumerating all those who should be considered as incompetent witnesses. A complete analysis of all these categories of people and of the various motives underlying their incompetence lies beyond the scope of this paper. One of the texts themselves has already undertaken a certain classification[475] which, without being exhaustive, still has the advantage to bring to the fore a number of important aspects of the theory of witnesses in Hindu law.

a) In the first place, some persons are said to be incompetent witnesses *vacanāt*, i.e., "on the basis of an authoritative text." Learned Brāhmaṇas, devotees, ascetics, and aged people should not be summoned to act as witnesses for no other reason than their figuring in an authoritative text.[476] The underlying reason in this case seems to be the authors' concern that people of this kind should not be disturbed by a summons to appear before the court.

b) People are also considered incompetent witnesses *doṣāt* i.e. "on account of depravity."[477] Here we need not go into detail, for the depravity which is meant in this text is nothing else than the lack of the very moral qualities which were required for a person to be accepted as a competent witness.

c) A much more interesting case is the one in which witnesses are incompetent *bhedāt*, i.e., "on account of contradiction."[478]

[473] NS 1.154–156: "They shall be Brahmins, Vaiśyas, or Kṣatriyas, or irreproachable Śūdras. Each of these shall be (witness) for persons of his own order, or all of them may be (witness) for all (orders). Among companies (of artizans, or guilds or merchants, other) artizans or guilds or merchants shall be witnesses; and members of an associalion among other members of the same associations; persons living outside among those living outside; and women among women. And if in a company (of artizans or guild of merchants) or in any other association any one falls out (with his associates), they must not bear witness against him for they all are his enemies" —Similar prescriptions: MDh 8.68; YDh 2.69; VaDh 16.29–30; KS 349–351.

[474] BDh 1.10.19.13: "(Men of) the four castes who have sons may be witnesses..." —Cf. also MDh 8.62. We already referred to a man having a male issue even as a single witness.

[475] NS 1.157: "The incompetent witnesses, too, have in this law book been declared by the learned to be of five sorts: under a text of law and on account of depravity, of contradiction, of uncalled-for deposition and of intervening decease."

[476] NS 1.158: "Learned Brahmanas, devotees, aged persons, and ascetics, are those incapacitated under a text of law; there is no (special) reason given for it."

[477] NS 1.159: "Thieves, robbers, dangerous characters, gamblers, assassins, are incompetent on account of their depravity; there is no truth to be found in them."

[478] NS 1.160: "If the statements of witnesses, who have all been summoned

Although there are indeed several texts stating that witnesses pronouncing contradictory statements should be considered incompetent, there also are other texts which prescribe several other criteria to be taken into consideration in case of contradiction. They are, in this order: the quantitative majority, referred to above; the moral qualifications; the firmness of the witnesses' memory. Witnesses actually become incompetent only in the case where neither of these arguments permit a decision in favor of either deposition.[479] The commentators, being faced with these two tendencies, have tried to reconcile them, but not without coming to very different conclusions.

d) Witnesses are also styled incompetent if they depose *svayamukti* i.e. "a declaration *suo motu.*" In other words: witnesses cannot be competent unless they have been summoned to depose.[480]

e) Finally, a witness is incompetent if he is *mṛtāntara,* i.e., "if there is a dead person meanwhile," i.e., if the party for whom the witness was to depose has died in between the facts and the trial.[481]

In view of the extreme attention which has, thus, been paid to the distinction between competent and incompetent witnesses, it is interesting to notice a few rules saying that in some cases witnesses should not be examined too strictly with regard to their competence. These cases are: theft, violence, abuse and assault, and adultery,[482] i.e., all those *vivādapadas* which rank among criminal law. In other words: the requirements which witnesses have to fulfill are different in civil and in criminal procedure.

Let us now turn towards another set of rules dealing with the deposition of witnesses.

by the king for the decision of the same cause, do not agree, they are rendered incompetent by contradiction. —Cf. also KS 359.

[479] NS 1.229–230: "Where there is conflicting evidence, the plurality of witnesses decides the matter. If the number of witnesses is equal (on both sides), the testimony of those must be accepted as correct, whose veracity is not liable to suspicion. If the number of such witnesses is equal (on both sides) (the testimony of these must be accepted), who are possessed of superior memory. Where, however, an equal number of witnesses possessed of a good memory is found on both sides, the evidence of the witnesses is entirely valueless, on account of the subtle nature of the law of evidence. —Cf. also MDh 8.73; YDh 2.78; ViDh 8.39.

[480] NS 1.161: "He who, without having been appointed to be a witness, comes of his own accord to make a deposition, is termed a spy in the lawbooks; he is unworthy to bear testimony. —Cf. ViDh 8.4.

[481] NS 1.162: "Where can (any person) bear testimony if the claimant is no longer in existence, whose claim should have been heard? Such a person is an incompetent witness by reason of intervening decease."

[482] MDh 8.72: "In all cases of violence, of theft and adultery, of defamation and assault, he must not examine the (competence of) witnesses (too strictly)." —Exactly the same idea also occurs: GDh 13.9; YDh 2.72; ViDh 8.6.

A first point to be noticed is the obligatory character of the summons: if a witness when being summoned before the court refuses to appear within the lapse of a fortnight —except in cases of *vis maior*: illness, etc.—, he is liable to be fined, either in proportion to the amount involved, or with a fixed amendment when no amount is involved, or even with both.[483]

Moreover, when making his appearance before the court, a witness is obliged to say anything he knows. Here again he incurs a punishment if he refuses to do so.[484] As to his deposition, it should, of course, be relevant to the cause.[485]

As a general rule, the witnesses should be questioned inside the hall of justice. Apart from a few exceptional cases in which an examination of witnesses outside the hall of justice was required —about which below[486]—, the latter seems to have been the most adequate place to create a sufficiently solemn atmosphere to make witnesses speak nothing but the truth.

In the first place, this solemn character was obtained through the various people by whom the witness found himself surrounded: not only the members of the court (judges, assessors, and officials), but also both parties,[487] and eventually the public at large. All texts, indeed, insist upon the necessity of the trial being held in public.[488]

Next, in front of all these people the witness is invited to take an oath. As far as the content of the oath is concerned, it is in no way different from the oath imposed on the parties themselves; we shall come back to this point below.[489] It is but natural that the witnesses are invited and that they consequently swear to speak the truth and nothing but the truth. But is it very characteristic of Hindu law that, in most texts, these rules have given rise to exten-

[483] MDh 9.107: "A man who, without being ill, does not give evidence in (cases of) loans and the like within three fortnights (after the summons), shall be responsible for the whole debt and (pay) a tenth part of the whole (as a fine to the king). —Cf. also YDh 2.76–77; BS 7.31; KS 405.

[484] KS 1.107: "He who conceals his knowledge (at the time of trial), although he has previously related (what he knows) to others. deserves specially heavy punishment, for he is more criminal than a false witness even."

[485] NS 1.232: "Where, the time for giving testimony having arrived, a witness does not make a consistent statement with reference to the questions under notice, his testimony is as good as ungiven." —The commentators have elaborated various theories on *ekadeśa* proof, i.e., the case in which the evidence covers part of the subject-matter only; cf. Thakur 1933: 126–133.

[486] Cf. note 491 below.

[487] Cf. MDh 8.79: "The witnesses being assembled in the court in the presence of the plaintiff and of the defendant, let the judge examine them...". —Similarly, YDh 2.73; Kātyāyana 342 and 388.

[488] NS Appendix 10: "...when they do not give evidence in public...".

[489] Cf. § 9 Fifth mode of proof: oaths.

sive dithyrambs on truth as such, which should be recited in front of the witnesses by the king or the chief judge.[490]

The fact of the hall of justice thus being the most adequate spot to make witnesses speak the truth has, however, not prevented the ancient authors from providing for examinations elsewhere, whenever the necessities of the case required to do so: we know of examinations being held on an immovable property, etc.[491]

The Hindu legal treatises not only tried their best to avoid false depositions *a priori*, they also did the utmost in order to detect and punish them *a posteriori*. In the first place, the authors have worked out long lists of indications which create many presumptions of the falseness of the witnesses' depositions. Apparently these considerations are based on the assumption that inward tensions and emotions cannot fail to exteriorize themselves through the outward demeanor. It therefore is the witnesses' outward behavior which should attract the judge's attention, for several elements in a person's behavior at the same time reflect the untruthfulness of his deposition.[492] In certain cases the outward indications might even manifest themselves a long time after the actual deposition.[493] In this case, too, they should make the deposition un-done. There is no need here to go into details about the punishments which have been prescribed for false witnesses; they vary according to the different authors, some of these even having gone so far as to prescribe different punishments according

[490] These exhortations to the witnesses are too long to be quoted here; we refer to BDh 1.10.19.10–12; VaDh 16.32–34; MDh 8.80–101; YDh 2.73–75; ViDh 8.24–37; NS 1.200 and 210–220.

[491] Cf. especially KS 387–389: "Witnesses should give their deposition inside the hall of justice and not anywhere else; this is the rule as regards all oral evidence; but it is otherwise as regards immovable property. Witnesses should depose in the presence of the plaintiff and the defendant and near the matter to be established (in the suit) and never behind the back (of the parties). Depositions should be taken down near (*lit.* over) the matter (in dispute) and in some cases even in places other than these two; this is the rule in (disputes about) quadrupeds and about bipeds and immovable property."

[492] NS 1.193–196: "One who, weighed down by the consciousness of his guilt looks as if he was ill, is constantly shifting his position, and runs after everybody; One who walks irresolutely and without reason, and draws repeated sighs; one who, scratches the ground with his feet, and who shakes his arm and clothes; Whose countenance changes colour, whose forehead sweats, whose lips become dry, and who looks above and about him; Who makes long speeches which are not to the purpose as if he were in a hurry, and without being asked: such a person may be recognized as a false witness, and the king should punish that sinful man. —Cf. also MDh 8.25–26; YDh 2.13–15; ViDh 8.18.

[493] MDh 8.108: "The witness to whom within several days after he has given evidence, happens (a misfortune through) sickness, a fire, or the death of a relative, shall be made to pay the debt and a fine. —Cf. also KS 410.

to the varying motives which gave rise to the false deposition.[494] In the system of *dharma* which inseparably comprehends legal and religious prescriptions as well, it is no wonder that false witnesses are said also to suffer some evil consequences after death.[495]

In view of all these data converging towards a regular cult of truth, it is the more remarkable that in some exceptional cases untruth is said to be excusable.[496] For instance, if a true declaration would occasion the death of a man, it is preferable to depose falsely rather than to speak the truth. Still, even if such a false declaration is not punished, the witness nevertheless does incur sin, and he consequently is not exempt from an adequate expiation.[497]

5. Second Mode of Proof: Documents

The length at which we had to deal with witnesses sufficiently indicates the importance the ancient authors attached to that mode of proof; it can hardly be doubted that witnesses actually were the most usual form of evidence and that most of the trials were treated with the help of witnesses only.

[494] Thus MDh 8.120–123: "(He who commits perjury) through covetousness shall be fined one thousand (*paṇa*s), (he who does it) through distraction, in the lowest amercement; (if a man does it) through fear, two middling amercements shall be paid as a fine, (if he does it) through friendship, four times the amount of the lowest (amercement). (He who does it) through lust, (shall pay) ten times the lowest amercement, but (he who does it) through wrath, three times the next (or second amercement); (he who does it) through ignorance, two full hundreds, but (he who does it) through childishness, one hundred (*paṇa*s). They declare that the wise have prescribed these fines for perjury, in order to prevent a failure of justice, and in order to restrain injustice. But a just king shall fine and banish (men of) the three (lower) castes (*varṇa*) who have give false evidence, but a Brāhmana he shall (only) banish." —Cf. also ĀpDh 2.11.29.8; GDh 13.23; YDh 2.81; BS 7.22.

[495] From ĀpDh 2.11.29.9 and GDh 13.7 onward, false witnesses are said to go to hell; the punishments to be expected in hell as well as the other sins attributed to false witnesses have been described in detail by MDh 8.89–101; YDh 8.25–26: NS 1.201–225.

[496] GDh 13.24–25: "No guilt is incurred by giving false evidence, in case the life (of a man) depends thereon. But (this rule does) not (hold good) if the life of a very wicked (man depends on the evidence of a witness)." —Other texts specifiy that it may be the life of a man of any of the four castes: MDh 8.104; YDh 2.83; ViDh 8.15.— MDh 8.103 still adds another case: "In (some) cases a man who, though knowing (the facts to be) different, gives such (false evidence) from a pious motive does not loose heaven; such (evidence) they call the speech of the gods."

[497] In view of the highly technical character of the various penances that have been prescribed and the extensive ritual explanations which their descriptions would require, we merely refer to BDh 1.10.19.16; MDh 8.105–106; YDh 2.83; ViDh 8.16–17.

However, this does not at all imply that witnesses were also regarded as the most reliable mode of proof. On the contrary, the ancient authors have been fully aware of the extreme weakness of human memory: if made after a certain lapse of time, the deposition of witnesses loses its validity because they are likely to have forgotten many an important detail.[498] A number of texts also warn against taking witnesses only as evidence during a deed for another reason: witnesses may decease in between the facts and the trial and, thus, deprive the party of all evidence in a cause where the burden of proof comes to rest with him.[499] Since none of these blemishes attach to written evidence, documents are claimed to be a more reliable mode of proof than witnesses.[500]

As was the case with witnesses, documents too, have been subjected to several subdivisions.[501] The subdivisions which finally prevailed in most texts are private documents on the one hand and public documents on the other. Among the public or official documents[502] we shall only mention the most important ones. First ranks the *rājaśāsana*, being an official grant of land or the like, executed on a copperplate or on a piece of cloth. Another important official document is the *jayapattra* "the document of success" delivered by the king to the victorious party in a lawsuit, and which should be produced by the defendant in case he appeals to a reply by way of denial. This case has already been referred to above.

[498] BS 8.2: "Within a sixmonth's time even, doubts will arise among men (regarding a transaction). Therefore the letters occurring in a writing were invented of yore by the Creator." —Nārada, after having enumerated various periods of validity for the depositions according as they have been made by the various types of witnesses (1.167–169), also comes to the conclusion that the duration of the validity, in fact, only depends upon the relative strength of the witness' memory (1.170–171).

[499] This argument is to be found NS 1.73 and 75. Since these verses not only describe documents as a more valid means of proof than witnesses, but at the same time proclaim possession as an even more valid mode of proof than documents, they will be quoted below, notes 518 and 519.

[500] As a result, the texts at this stage contain regular eulogies written as such. E.g., NS 1.70–71: "If the Creator had not created writing as an excellent eye (as it were), the affairs of this whole world would not lake their proper course. Writing is an excellent eye (as it were), because it solves all doubts which may have arisen in regard to place, time, profit, matter, quantity, or stipulated period."

[501] Just to quote a few examples: for NS 1.135 documents are of two sorts: the first, in the handwriting of the party himself; the second in that of another party (we shall come back to this distinction below); for ViDh 7.1–5 documents are of three kinds: attested by the king, or by witnesses, or simply unattested; BS 8.3, although equally distinguishing three kinds of documents, enumerates them in a different way: those written by the king, those written in a particular place, and those written by a person with his own hand.

[502] Cf. especially BS 8.12–19, with elaborate definitions of "the royal edict, *the writing containing a mark or royal favour*, and the document of success."

The private documents are much more numerous than the public ones. They refer to the principal civil transactions: partition, gift, purchase, mortgage, debt, etc.[503] The authors who deal with documents most exhaustively have also paid great attention to the requirements the documents must fulfill in order to be considered valid evidence. These requirements are multifarious according to the form of the document, its contents, the persons by whom they should be executed, etc.

The criteria applied to the examination of official documents are, of course, less severe than those applied to private documents. It goes without saying that the presence of the royal seal on a document constitutes by itself a sufficient reason for accepting its genuineness[504] whatever be the defects it might display otherwise. The mere presence of the royal seal is a sufficient condition for the validity of the document even if all the other persons whose signatures are inscribed on the document are dead, a circumstance which normally leads to the non-validity of any private document.[505]

Private documents, on the other hand, must fulfill a great number of conditions, and they are subject to several defects that might lead to their not being accepted as valid evidence. Some of these defects bear upon the capacity of the person who executed the document: he should not have been intoxicated, under fear or misfortune; he should not be a lunatic or a child, etc.[506] Other defects affect the contents of the document: it must clearly indicate the nature of the subject, it must be free from confusion in the arrangement of the subject-matter, etc.[507] Other defects again relate to the

[503] Cf. especially BS 8.4–11, defining "a deed of partition, of gift of purchase, of mortgage, of agreement, of bondage, of debt, and other (such deeds)."

[504] Cf. KS 296: "A (royal) edict becomes valid when it is free from defects as to the seal (thereon), as to the mode of writing it, as to its enjoyment (or custody), when it has the proper characteristics (of an edict) and when it bear the genuine signature of the king."

[505] About the royal document, cf. KS 278: "Even when all these (viz. writer, witnesses and executant) whose signatures are made on the document which bears the royal seal are dead, that document is still held valid even though they are all dead." —The general case of the private document has been treated by NS 1.138: "A bond ceases to be valid in that case also, if the witnesses, creditor, debitor, and scribe be dead, unless its validity can be established by the existence of a pledge."— Other texts are less severe, and prescribe only a careful examination of the document: ViDh 7.13; KS 285–286.

[506] NS 1.137: "That document is invalid which has been executed by a person intoxicated, by one charged (with a crime), by a woman, or by a child, and that which has been caused to be written by forcible means, by intimidation or by deception. —Cf. also MDh 8.163, 168; YDh 2.89; ViDh 7.6–10: BS 8.23; KS 271.

[507] ViDh 7.1: "(That instrument is termed) proof which is not adverse to peculiar local usages, which defines clearly the nature of the pledge given, and is free

form in which the document has been drafted: it should mention certain particulars about all persons involved; it should bear the exact date of the transaction; at the end it should bear certain handwritten formula of the parties, the witnesses and the scribe; etc.[508]

Several authors further stress the difference between handwritten documents and documents written by another person; documents executed in the debtor's own handwriting constitute valid evidence without there being mentioned any witnesses, whereas a bond of debt not executed by the debtor personally cannot be accepted as valid evidence unless it also bears the names of witnesses.[509]

Another requirement for the validity of a document is its not having been kept secret for a long time; on the contrary, a document in order to be accepted as genuine, should have been repeatedly urged and publicly proclaimed.[510]

The persons who are to point out all these defects are different according to the latter being either latent or patent. The former should be pointed out by the party who wants to impugn them, whereas the latter should be pointed out automatically by the members of the court.[511] Anyhow, the defects should be brought

from confusion in the arrangement of the subject matter and (in the succession of) the syllables. —Cf. NS 1.136; KS 252.

[508] YDh 2.84–88: "Wenn über irgend eine Sache mit gegenseitiger Beistimmung eine Übereinkunft getroffen ist, so ist darüber eine Schrift aufzusetzen mit Zuziehung van Zeugen, in welcher der Name des Gläubigers vorausteht. Dieselbe muss bezeichnet sein mit dem Jahr, Monate. Halb-monate, Tag, dem Namen, der Kaste und Familie, mit der Benennung der Veda Studien, und den Namen der Väter der Personen, u.s.w. Wenn die Verhandlung vollendet ist, soll der Schuldner seinen Namen mit eigener Hand darunter schreiben: 'was hier oben geschrieben ist, dem stimm ich, der Sohn von N.N. bei.' Und die Zeugen sollen allesammt mit eigener Hand nebst dem Namen ihres Vaters schreiben: 'hierin bin ich N.N. Zeuge.' Darauf soll der Schreiber am Ende schreiben: 'dies ist auf bitten beider Parteien geschrieben von mir N.N., den Sohn des N.N.'" (trans. Stenzler).

[509] Thus NS 1.135 already referred to above: "Documents should be known to be of two sorts: (the first), in the handwriting of the party himself; (the second), in that of another person, (the former being valid) without subscribing witnesses, the latter requiring to be attested... —Cf. also YDh 2.89: "Auch ohne Zeugen soll jede Scrift, welche van der eigenen Hand (des Schuldners) geschrieben ist, als Beweis gelten, ausser wenn sie mit Gewalt oder durch Betrug erlangt ist."

[510] BS 8.26: "Let a man show (a document) on every occasion to (meetings of) families, associations (of traders), assemblies (of cohabitants), and other (bodies of persons), and read it out to them, and remind them of it, in order to establish its validity." —Cf. NS 1.140–141.

[511] KS 275: "The defects of the means of proof (such as documents and witnesses), when they are latent, must be declared (pointed out) by the litigant, (who wants to impugn them) at the proper time (viz. when they are adduced in the trial), but the patent defects must be declared by the members of the court at the time (of the considerations of the evidence) by reference to the (rules of) Smritis." —Patent defects can however, no longer be objected to after twenty years: KS 298–299, 301.

to the fore in the course of the trial; if one neglects to do so at the right moment, documents become unobjectionable.[512]

As soon as documents thus are objected to, it is the duty of the party who produced them to remove these objections.[513] The texts have elaborated a complete system of rules to be applied by the court in these circumstances in order to establish the authenticity or the non-authenticity of the document: there are rules about the examination of the party's handwriting, about the examination of the witnesses, the tenor of the document, the way in which the party got hold of it, etc.[514] It is not until all objection have been removed that the party is allowed to make all effective use of the document and to hope for a favorable judgment to be based upon it.

The numerous rules dealing with the careful examination of the validity of documents seem to respond to an actual necessity: forgery of documents must have been common practice in ancient India, for private and for official documents as well.[515] It should, however, be noticed that the attempts to detect forgery of documents were also dictated by the anxiety to protect the numerous people who were unacquainted with the art of writing and who were, therefore, apt to fall victim to those who profited off their ignorance.[516]

This extreme care taken against forgery of documents finds its logical counterpart in the severe punishments that have been prescribed against it: forgers of royal documents according to some texts, and forgers of both public and private documents according to other texts, should be put to death or at least severely punished.[517]

[512] BS 7.25: "Whatever faults there may be in a document or in witnesses, they should be exposed at the time of the trial; those cannot be used as valid objections which are declared afterwards."

[513] BS 7.26: "He whose documents or witnesses are objected to in a suit, cannot gain his cause till he has removed the objections raised against it."

[514] NS 1.143: "If a doubt should subsist, as to whether a certain document be authentic or fabricated, its authenticity has to be established by examining the handwriting (of the party), the tenour of the document, peculiar marks, circumstantial evidence, and the probabilities of the case. —Cf. YDh 2.92; ViDh 7.12; KS 284.

[515] BS 8.20: "Clever forgers acquainted with place and time will make a writing similar (to the original documents). Such (writings) should be examined with great care. —Cf. KS 306.

[516] BS 8.21: "Women, infants, the suffering, and persons unacquainted with the art of writing, are deceived by their own relations fabricating documents signed with their names. Such (forgery) may be found out by means of internal evidence and legitimate titles."

[517] MDh 9.232: "Forgers of royal edicts, those who corrupt his ministers, those who slay women, infants, or Brāhmaṇas, and those who serve his enemies, the

6. *Third Mode of Proof: Possession*

The third mode of proof is variously called *bhukti* or *bhoga*, both terms being derived from the verbal root *bhuj*, literally "to enjoy," whence "to possess." Hindu law, indeed, clearly distinguishes between *svatva* "ownership," being a legal right, on the one hand, and *bhukti* or *bhoga* "possession," being a mere fact, on the other hand. There are, however, a number of cases in which *bhukti* may be accepted by the courts as valid evidence of ownership.

Before examining these cases, we must refer to the place which the Indian authors have attributed to possession as compared to witnesses and documents. Extending the comparison of witnesses and documents already referred to above, the texts hold that possession has the advantage of being a much surer means of proof than the two others,[518] whereas on the other hand it has the disadvantage of taking effect only after a long lapse of time.[519]

In order that it might serve as valid evidence of ownership possession must fulfill a number of requirements which have been enumerated as follows: it must be supported by a title, it must be of long standing, uninterrupted, not claimed by others, and held in the presence of the other party.[520] We propose to use this fivefold subdivision as a basis for discussing at least some of the numerous texts dealing with possession as a mode of proof in legal procedure.

a) Possession may be of two kinds: either it is supported by a title (*sāgama*), or it is not (*anāgama*). This distinction is extremely important, for in the former case only possession may be held valid evidence of ownership. The texts are worded in such a way that it is not always very clear which of both elements, possession or title, is considered to be the more important one; in any case, in order to be accepted as a valid mode of proof, possession and

king shall put to death"; —YDh 2.295: "Wer ein vom Könige ausgestelltes Schenkungsedikt auf weniger schreibt, so wie wer den Rauber den Frau frei lässt, soll die höchste Geldstrafe zahlen"; —ViDh 5.9–10: "Let the king put to death those who forge royal edicts; And those who forge (private) documents."

[518] NS 1.73: "A document is subject to many blemishes; witnesses are neither exempt from old age nor from death; possession, which has been continually held, is the only sure mode of proof, as it is not connected with any material object (liable to decay)."

[519] NS 1.75: "A document is valid at all times; witnesses (may give valid evidence) as long as they live; possession acquires legal validity through the lapse of a certain period. This is a legal maxim."

[520] Vyāsa (quoted *Vyavahāracintāmaṇi* 452): "Possession is acceptable if it fulfills the following five requirements: if it is (1) supported by a title, (2) of long standing, (3) uninterrupted, (4) not claimed by other, and (5) in the presence of the defendant."

title must be produced simultaneously.[521] It is for the same reason that possession as such never figures amongst the classical ways of acquiring ownership as enumerated by various ancient texts (see GDh 10.3941; MDh 10.115; VaDh 16.16; BS 9.2.)

b) The only circumstance which is capable of making up for the absence of a title is the fact that the possession is of long standing.

Very exceptionally it has been held that possession, whatever be its duration, never leads to regular ownership.[522] However, the purpose of such texts is clear: they only want to extol the principle quoted just above, according to which title is a necessary supplement without which possession can never lead to any valid conclusions.[523]

Most of the texts agree that possession held for a certain lapse of time does constitute a sufficient proof for the possessor also to be held as the owner. The periods of prescription —for this is what really happens— however vary according to the different authors.

In the first place, these periods are different according as they refer to movable or immovable property: the oldest texts provide for a period of prescription of twenty years with regard to immovables and ten years for movable property.[524]

Another period which is to be found in later texts especially refers to three generations,[525] one of the texts specifying that each generation is to be counted as lasting twenty years.[526]

[521] NS 1.84–86: "Where there is enjoyment, but no title of any sort, there a title is required in order to produce proprietary right. Possession is not sufficient to create proprietary right in that case. A clear title having been produced possession acquires validity. Possession without a clear title does not make evidence (of ownership). He who can only plead possession, without being able to adduce any title, has to be considered as a thief, in consequence of his pleading such illegitimate possession. —Cf. also MDh 8.200; YDh 2.27.

[522] NS 1.87: "He who enjoys without a title for ever so many hundred years, the ruler of the land should inflict on that sinful man the punishment ordained for a thief."

[523] Not only such rules extolling a certain idea without actually meaning what they literally say are common procedure in Hindu law texts —the so called *arthavādas*—, but our statement will be clear to anyone who reads NS 1.87 immediately after NS 1.86.

[524] YDh 2.24: "Ein Stück Land welches von einem Fremden benutzt wird. geht in zwanzig Jahren verloren, wenn der Eigenthümer es sieht und nichts dazu sagt; anderes Eigenthüm in zehn Jahren. —Cf. also GDh 12.37; VaDh 16.16–17; MDh 8.147; NS 1.79.

[525] KS 317: "Possession is declared to be of two sorts: viz. with title and without title. Possession which continues for three generations is independent means of proof of ownership without actual proof of title), but if it is less (than for three generations), then it (is proof of ownership) if accompanied with title. —Cf. also ViDh 5.187; BS 9.26–28.

[526] KS 318: "Possession from the grandfather is superior, possession from

Finally the same texts also introduce another criterion: the period falling within the memory of man (*smārtakāla*). Accordingly possession lasting for a period extending beyond the memory of man entails ownership; possession for a period falling within the memory of man should be supported by a title.[527]

The principle of possession of long standing leading towards legal ownership has, however, suffered a number of exceptions. On the one hand, objects owned by certain categories of people could never be lost to them through adverse possession: thus objects belonging to children, women, learned Brahmins, or the king. On the other hand, in a number of cases the nature of the objects determined their not changing owners even after possession of long standing: pledges, deposits, etc.[528]

c) The three other requirements for possession to be considered valid proof of ownership being intimately connected, they may be treated here under one and the same heading.

In the first place, possession should have been uninterrupted; if interrupted, possession alone would not be sufficient but it should have to be substantiated by other means of proof such as documents or witnesses.[529]

Next, both the absence of any claim on the side of the original owner and his allowing his property to be used by others before his own eyes, are indicative of his indifference and carelessness against which the law refuses to protect him. In this case adverse possession is even more valid than a written title produced by the original owner.[530] Moreover, even the objects enumerated

father also is approved; unbroken (possession) for these three generations (viz. grandfather, father and the man himself), extending over sixty years, becomes firm (i.e. independent means of proof as to ownership)." —BS 9.23–24 takes one generation to be equal to thirty years.

[527] NS 1.89: "In cases falling within the memory of man, possession with a title creates ownership. In cases extending beyond the memory of man, and on failure of documents, the hereditary succession of three ancestors (has the same effect). —Cf. also KS 321.

[528] NS 1.81: "A pledge; a boundary, the property of a child; an open deposit, an Upanidhi deposit; women; and what belongs to the king or to a learned Brahman, none (of these descriptions of property) is lost (to the owner) by adverse possession. —Cf. GDh 12.39; NS 1.83; MDh 8.145–146, 149; YDh 2.25; VaDh 16.1–8; BS 9.21; KS 330, 331–334.

[529] BS 9.15: "If a doubt should arise in regard to a house or field, of which its occupant has not held possession uninterruptedly, he should undertake to prove (his enjoyment of it) by means of documents, (the depositions of) persons knowing him as possessor, and witnesses. —Cf. also KS 318.

[530] BS 9.9: "He who does not raise a protest when a stranger is giving away (his) landed property in his sight, cannot again recover that estate, even though he be possessed of a written title to it."

above[531] as escaping prescription are lost to their owners if the possession has taken place openly before their eyes.[532]

In the period of the Dharmaśāstras the loss of property through neglect has been explained by some very simple similes such as that of a cow being lost because of the cowherd's carelessness;[533] however, in the period of the commentaries and the *nibandhas* it has been elaborated into exhaustive and deeply philosophical considerations and solutions which, unfortunately, are not suificiently known yet since they are buried in a great number of texts which still remain to be edited, but which shed a sharp light on the way in which Hindu lawyers tackled such intricate juridical problems as the relation of possession and ownership.[534]

7. A Subsidiary Means of Proof: Circumstance

Hindu law also recognizes certain forms of evidence which, without therefore being less important,[535] difficultly fit into the general scheme of human and divine evidence as indicated above. On the one hand, they have certain characteristics in common with human evidence and especially with possession —namely, to create a presumption—; on the other hand, however, although essentially remaining human, they strongly resemble divine evidence. For these reasons they have generally been treated in between both extreme forms of evidence. While discussing them at this stage, we therefore respect the order adopted by most Indian authors themselves.[536]

The various forms of evidence we are referring to at present, although showing a good number of differences between them, nevertheless have sufficient elements in common in order to be treated under one and the same title. The general terminology

[531] Cf. note 528 above.

[532] NS 1.82: "Pledges and the rest, excepting the property of a woman and of the king, are however lost to the owner if they have been enjoyed in his presence for twenty years."

[533] Vyāsa (quoted *Vyavahāracintāmaṇi* 508): "Just as a cow disappears when it is neglected and left without a cowherd, in the same way in the course of time land is lost when it is used by others under the eyes (of the owner)."

[534] Cf., for instance, *Vyavahāracintāmaṇi* 463, and the various solutions proposed by Vācaspatimiśra and his predecessors.

[535] On the contrary, "No sentence should be passed merely according to the letter of the law. If a decision is arrived at without considering the circumstances of the case, violation of justice will be the result" (BS 2.12).

[536] The place occupied by circumstance (here called "reasoning") has been clearly indicated by KS 214: "Documents, witnesses, enjoyment (or possession) —these three are known as means of proof. Reasoning is the consideration of certain characteristics which cannot be explained otherwise (than on the hypothesis propounded), and there are ordeals of poison and the like."

adopted by the Sanskrit texts on *dharma* is not uniform; without diverging into this problem which is one of mere terminology, we shall translate it with the usual term "circumstantial evidence."

The most important form of circumstantial evidence is called *yukti*. The term *yukti* by itself, when used in Sanskrit literature as a whole, is rather vague and has highly divergent meanings, going from the general sense of "means," especially "magic means," up to the more precise meaning "reasoning, argumentation." The same phenomenon manifests itself within the scope of *dharma* literature: *yukti* has been used with various meanings —sometimes even covering possession—, but especially with the more restricted sense of "reasoning, argumentation."

This particular sense is the more interesting, because it bears witness to the intimate contact existing between the several branches of learning in India, *in casu*: between *dharma* and logic (*nyāya*). As soon as we find evidence for the identity *yukti* = *liṅga*,[537] we may be sure that in the minds of the authors on *dharma* there has been a connection between the trial before the court and the inference in Hindu logic, *yukta* and *liṅga* both indicating the middle term of the syllogism. As a matter of fact, in a number of texts *anumāna*, i.e., the very technical term used for inference by the authors on Indian logic, figures among the modes of proof in legal procedure.[538]

Under the heading "circumstantial evidence" also figure a number of cases where certain indications are strong enough to adequately replace witnesses and other human means of proof. If a person is caught carrying a firebrand in his hand, he may be supposed to be the incendiary; one found carrying a weapon may be supposed to be the murderer; etc.[539] However, the authors have

[537] Notice that the identification *yukti* = *liṅga* was the more easily obtained because *liṅga* had already been recognized as a mode of proof by ĀpDh 2.11.3.6: "In doubtful cases (they shall give their decision) after having ascertained (the truth) by inference, ordeals, and the like (means)."

[538] The appearance of this term in a few isolated texts has not failed to create serious problems of interpretation for the commentators. They definitely have tried their best to integrate *anumāna* into the classical system of the modes of proof, but, by doing so, they have made it extremely difficult for us to ascertain its original meaning, the more so because the main text in which the term appears, i.e., BS, is only known to us through fragments which do not allow us to locate the term in its original context. [Ed. note: On *anumāṇa*, see chapter 24 in this volume.]

[539] NS 1.171–175: "However, six different kinds of proceedings have been indicated in which witnesses are not required. (Other) indications of the crime committed are substituted for the evidence of witnesses in these cases by the learned. It should be known that one carrying a firebrand in his hand is an incendiary; that one taken with a weapon in his hand is a murderer and that, where a man and the wife of another man seize one another by the hair, the man

been fully aware of the unavoidable limitations adhering to such evidence; they repeatedly point out that these indications can only create presumptions, which should carefully be examined as to their actual value.[540] To stress the necessity of such examination they refer to a famous example in the epics, where Māṇḍavya was condemned as a thief whereas he actually was not.[541]

Finally, a great number of texts distinguish a category of people as *avasanna* and *hīna*, literally: "lost, inferior, deficient." They are people whose behavior either on being summoned to appear before the court or during the trial is such as to create a presumption against them: the one who hides himself after receiving the summons, the one who refuses to appear, the one who fails to produce a reply, the one who continually alters his statements, etc.[542]

8. *The Divine Modes of Proof*

The place occupied by divine evidence within the general scheme of the modes of proof and its relation toward human evidence have been outlined above. It has also been indicated that in classical Hindu law divine evidence is said to be twofold: the oath and ordeals.

At present, before entering into descriptions of both forms of divine evidence, we must add that the distinction between oaths and ordeals has not always been a very neat one. On the contrary,

must be an adulterer. One who goes about with a hatchet in his hand and makes his approach may be recognized as a destroyer of bridges (and embankments); one carrying an axe is declared a destroyer of trees. One whose looks are suspicious is likely to have committed an assault. In all these cases witnesses may be dispensed with...".

[540] To continue the text of NS (1.175–176): "...only in the (last-mentioned case of assault careful investigation is required. Some one might make marks upon his person through hatred, to injure an enemy. In such cases it is necessary to resort to inductive reasoning, (ascertaining) the fact of the matter, and stratagems, in order to get a (reliable) test."

[541] E.g., BS 2.13–14: "The issue of a lawsuit may convert a a thief into a honest man, and an honourable man into an offender. Māṇḍavya acquired the reputation of a thief in consequence of a decision passed without considering the circumstances of the case. Dishonest men may seem honest, and honest men dishonest, so that wrong notions may be easily created; therefore sentences should be passed after due consideration of the circumstances only."

[542] NS *Introduction* 2.32–33: "One who takes to flight after having received the summons; one who remains silent; one who is convicted (of untruth) by (the deposition of) the witnesses; and one who makes a confession himself: these are the four kinds of Avasannas (losers of their suit). One who alters his former statements; one who shuns the judicial investigation; one who does not make his appearance (before the tribunal); one who makes no reply; and one who absconds after receiving the summons: these five kinds of persons are called Hīna (cast in their present suit)."

the oldest texts have a tendency to indicate the modes of divine proof as a whole either by means of *divya*, which as an adjective will always continue to indicate divine evidence generally side by side with the neutre substantive *divya* indicating ordeals, or even by means of *śapatha*[543] which at a later stage will be exclusively reserved to oaths.

The final distinction seems, as a matter of fact, to have passed through an intermediary one based merely on a matter of degree: the oath should be administered in small causes, ordeals being reserved for heavier crimes.[544] It is not before the time of the commentaries, that one has tried to find out basic differences between both forms of divine evidence.[545]

9. Fifth Mode of Proof: Oaths

The information we possess about oaths is very scarce and uncertain. Several passages dealing with oaths have been variously interpreted, both as referring to oaths imposed upon witnesses and as oaths imposed upon the parties as well. Actually, the situation seems to be such that several rules originally dealing with oaths sworn by witnesses have been taken out of their contexts by the commentators in order to fill the gaps existing in the rules about oaths sworn by the parties.[546]

Although the texts do not explicitly say so, we may assume that Hindu law only knew the oath imposed by the judge: in the absence of human modes of proof, he invites the party to swear an oath which will constitute sufficient evidence for the case to be decided upon.[547]

[543] E.g., MDh 1.109; even more clearly, NS 1.239: "If arguments are of no avail, let him cause the defendant to undergo one of the *śapatha*, by fire, water, proof of virtue, and so forth...," and this notwithstanding NS 1.247: "If no witness is forthcoming for either of the two litigant parties, he must test him through ordeals and oaths of every sort."

[544] NS 1.249–250: "Where a heavy crime has been committed, the ruler shall administer one of the ordeals. In light cases, on the other hand; a virtuous king shall swear a man with (various) oaths. Thus have these oaths been proclaimed by Manu for trifling cases. In a suit concerning a heavy crime, divine test should be resorted to. —Cf. BS 10.2 and 7; especially ViDh 9.5–14.

[545] For the arguments produced by the *Mitākṣarā* and other commentaries, cf. Kane 3.358.

[546] Take, for instance, GDh 13.12–13. The commentators on Gautama: Haradatta and Maskari —and even Thakur 1933: 142— interpret these *sūtras* as referring to oaths to be sworn by the parties. Actually, the context of GDh 13 does not leave any doubt: they refer to oaths to be taken from witnesses (thus, e.g., *Vyavahāracintāmaṇi* 359).

[547] MDh 8.109: "If two (parties) dispute about matters for which no witnesses are available, and the (judge) is unable to really ascertain the truth, he may

The formula of the oath and, more particularly, the object by which the party has to swear, differs according to the caste which he happens to belong to: the Brahmin should simply swear by truth, the Kṣatriya by his horse or his weapons, the Vaiśya by his worldly possessions, and the Śūdra should call upon himself the results of all grievous offenses.[548] Alternatively, the party may be invited to swear by the head of his wife or children,[549] or even by certain objects such as *dūrvā* grass, a blade of gold or silver, etc. (see ViDh 9.5–9)

Finally, the texts have provided sanctions for swearing false oaths, to be undergone in this world and after death as well,[550] except, however, for a number of cases where false oaths were considered excusable.[551]

10. Sixth Mode of Proof: Ordeals

Differently from oaths, we possess ample information about the other form of divine evidence: ordeals. As a matter of fact, ordeals seem to be a very ancient institution for whose existence we possess a lot of information relating to periods anterior to those of the books on *dharma*.[552]

A rule holding good for all forms of ordeals to be enumerated below is the one saying that ordeals should be made to be undergone by the defendant only.[553] In only one case may the plaintiff also be subjected to ordeals, namely when both parties decide so by common understanding and on the condition that they agree

cause it to be discovered even by an oath. —Cf. also NS 1.247— Both texts subsequently refer to an oath taken by the sage Vasiṣṭha, according to ṚV 7.104.15.

[548] MDh 8.113: "Let the (judge) cause a Brāhmana to swear by his veracity, a Kshatriya by his chariot or the animal he rides on and by his weapons, a Vaiśya his kine, grain, and gold, and a Śūdra by (implicating on his own head the guilt) of all grievous offences. —Cf. also NS 1.248.— NS 1.199, which exactly corresponds to MDh 8.113, refers to oaths to be taken by witnesses.

[549] MDh 8.114: "Or the (judge) may cause the (party)... severally to touch the heads of his wives and children."

[550] MDh 8.111: "Let no wise man swear an oath falsely, even in a trifling matter; for he who swears an oath falsely is lost in this (world) and after death. —Cf. YDh 2.235.

[551] MDh 8.111: "No crime, causing loss of caste, is committed by swearing (falsely) to women, the objects of one's desire, at marriages, for the sake of fodder for a cow, or of fuel, and in (order to show) favour to a Brāhmana. —Cf. GDh 23.29. This text at least partly refers to oaths taken outside the court of justice.

[552] For a number of references to ordeals in Vedic literature, cf. Kane 3.361–362. The strongly religious character of ordeals continues to manifest itself in the Dharmaśāstras; see, for instance, the elaborate rules about the preliminary ceremonies common to all ordeals, as described by Pitāmaha 51–80.

[553] ViDh 9.21: "And the defendant must go through the ordeals. —Cf. KS 411.

to act according to the outcome of the ordeal and, especially, that the other party agrees to eventually undergo punishment.[554]

The number of ordeals recognized by the various texts is highly different: apart from a number of authors who do not mention ordeals at all, it varies from two only with Manu up to nine with Bṛhaspati and Pitāmaha.[555] Moreover, there are several reasons to believe that many other forms of ordeals, not mentioned in the texts on *dharma*, have been applied in India: not only do we have references to other ordeals in literary texts, but some treatises of *dharma* themselves accept that within certain categories of people ordeals should be administered which are peculiar to their group.[556]

The descriptions of the various forms of ordeal have been repeated so often, that we may restrict ourselves to giving some brief references only.

The ordeal of the balance consists in the party being weighed twice again at a very short interval —the time needed for the person to address the balance as the abode of truth and to hear some exhortations about untruth; if he weighs less the second time, he is considered innocent; if he weighs more or even equally much, he is declared guilty.[557]

In the ordeal of fire, the party has to cover a certain distance carrying a red-hot iron ball in his hand, the latter however being protected with seven *aśvattha* leaves, grains of rice and curds. If he does not show an injury on his hand either at the very moment or at the end of the day, he is considered innocent.[558]

The ordeal of water requires the party to dive into water for the time needed for a man to go and bring back an arrow shot from the spot where he is standing in the water. If the runner who brings back the arrow does not perceive the man at all or at the

[554] YDh 2.96 (as quoted *Vyavahāracintāmaṇi* 589): "Or at their pleasure one of them may undergo the ordeal and the other one should be willing to undergo punishment...". The author of the *Vyavahāracintāmaṇi* rightly points out that the prescription contained in this verse holds good irrespectively of the party's statement being positive or negative; it, thus. constitutes an exception to the principle according to which evidence should be produced for positive assertions only.

[555] For statistical data about the number of ordeals known to the different texts, cf. Kane 3.362.

[556] KS 433: "But in the case of the untouchables, the lowest castes, slaves, mlecchas and those who are the offsprings of mixed unions in the reverse order of castes when guilty of sins the determination (by the above named ordeals) should not be done by the king. He should indicate such ordeals as are well-known among them in case of doubt (about their guilt)."

[557] YDh 2.100–102; ViDh 10.1–13; NS 1.260–284; BS 10.19–20; Pitāmaha 81–108.

[558] YDh 2.103–107; ViDh 11.1–12; NS 1.285–303; KS 441; Pitāmaha 109–131.

most the back of his head, the latter is innocent; otherwise, he is considered guilty.[559]

With the ordeal of poison the decision depends upon whether the person who has been made to drink it, shows any signs of the effect produced by the poison within a certain lapse of time.[560]

The ordeal of the holy water consists in drinking water that has been used to bathe the images of certain deities. The person will be declared guilty if, within a rather long waiting period, he suffers any kind of calamity: an illness of himself or a near relative, loss of property, etc.[561]

In the ordeal of the grains of rice, the person is made thrice to swallow and, consequently, spit out grains of rice which have undergone a special treatment the previous day. He is considered guilty if, on his spitting out the grains, blood is mixed with his saliva.[562]

The ordeal of the hot piece of gold consists in making the party take out a differently described piece of metal from a vessel filled with boiling ghee or oil. He should not be injured in order to be declared innocent.[563]

Similarly, in the ordeal of the ploughshare the party should be able, within being hurt, to lick with his tongue a redhot ploughshare.[564]

In the ordeal of Dharma the party is faced with a vessel containing images of Dharma and Adharma; if he takes out Dharma he is innocent, if he takes out Adharma he is guilty.[565]

The choice of a particular ordeal in each case is determined by a number of factors of highly different order. Generally speaking, the ordeal to be administered in a particular case is selected according to the nature of the crime, according to the status of the individual who is to undergo it, and according to the time when the ordeal is to be administered.

a) We already referred to the rule according to which ordeals were restricted to heavy crimes only, smaller items on the contrary being decided by means of oaths.[566] However, within the

[559] YDh 2.108–109; ViDh 12.1–8; NS 1.304–317; BS 10.21; KS 442–445; Pitāmaha 132–148.

[560] YDh 2.110–111; ViDh 13.1–7; NS 1.318–326; BS 10.22; KS 446–451; Pitāmaha 149–156.

[561] YDh 2.112–113; ViDh 14.1–5; NS 1.327–336; BS 10.23–24; KS 452; Pitāmaha 157–162.

[562] NS 1.337–342; BS 10.25; KS 453–461; Pitāmaha 163–168.

[563] NS 1.343–348; BS 10.26–27; Pitāmaha 169–180.

[564] BS 10.28–29.

[565] BS 10.30–33; Pitāmaha 181–189.

[566] It should, however, be noticed that Kātyāyana 427–431 prefers great criminals and sinners not to undergo the ordeals themselves but prescribes that they should rather be replaced by representatives.

sphere of cases to be decided by means of ordeals, the particular form of ordeal to be resorted to is again determined by the respective value of the object involved in the lawsuit.[567] Moreover, we even know of some prescriptions requiring particular ordeals to be administered in trials about certain well-defined crimes.

b) The status of the individual who is to undergo the ordeal gives rise to even much more complex prescriptions. The choice of the ordeal is, indeed, dependent upon his age, sex, caste, occupation, physical strength, moral qualifications, etc. Even if, considered in detail, these rules may not be free from contradictions, we shall at least quote a few examples to enable the reader to evaluate the highly humanitarian considerations underlying these minute rules of Hindu law.

In the first place, some people are exempt from any ordeal whatsoever. For example, men engaged in religious occupations, the diseased, women, etc.[568]

According to a much more important set of rules some particular forms of ordeals either are prohibited for certain people, or they are explicitly reserved for them. According to the criteria enumerated above —which, however, in the texts themselves are not neatly separated at all— we list the following examples:

1. according to age: children and aged people should be subjected to the ordeal of the balance (YDh 2.98; ViDh 9.23);
2. according to sex: for women —whom some texts have declared exempt from any ordeal— other sources prescribe the ordeal of balance, too (ViDh 9.23);
3. according to the occupation: blacksmiths should not be made to undergo the ordeal of fire (ViDh 9.25; KS 424), whereas all those who gain their subsistence from water, i.e., fishermen and the like, should not be subjected to the ordeal of water (YDh 2.98; NS 1.334–335; ViDh 9.23 and 27; KS 422);

[567] The general principle has been announced by BS 10.8: "When a quarrel between two litigants has arisen regarding a debt or other charge, that ordeal must be administered which corresponds to the amount (of the sum in dispute)...". BS 10.9–11 apply this principle to the special case of theft; coming down from the highest to the lowest amount, the ordeals are, in this order: poison, fire, hot piece of gold, grains of rice, holy water, and Dharma —the ploughshare is reserved tor thieves of cows. However, here too, the "caste" element intervenes: "These figures are applicable in the case of low persons; for persons of a middling kind, double is ordained; and for persons of highest rank, the amount has to be fixed four times as high by persons entrusted with judicial affairs." —For similar rules, cf. KS 417 together with three other verses quoted *Vyavahāracintāmaṇi* 681–683; ViDh 9.4–19.

[568] NS 1.256: "An ordeal should never be administered to persons engaged in performing a vow, to those afflirtd with a heavy calamity to the diseased, to ascetics, or to women, if the dictates of justice are listened to. —Cf. also Pitāmaha 44.

4. according to caste: Brahmins should be subjected to the ordeal of the balance but be free from the ordeal of poison, Kṣatriyas deserve the ordeal of fire but not that of the hot piece of gold, Vaiśyas that of water only, and Śūdras those of fire, water, or the grains of rice (YDh 2.98; NS 1.334–335; ViDh 9.23 and 27; KS 422);
5. according to physical strength: the ordeal of the balance should be reserved for those who are lame or blind; the ordeal of fire is excluded for those afflicted with white leprosy, blindness or bad nails; the ordeal of water is not administered to those afflicted with phlegm nor to the asthmatic or those who suffer from difficulty in breathing generally; the ordeal of poison is prohibited for the bilious; the ordeal of grains of rice should not be ordained for those suffering from a mouth disease; etc. (YDh 2.98; NS 1.255; ViDh 9.25, 27 and 29; KS 424–425).
6. according to moral qualifications: the ordeal of the holy water is forbidden for all those who have committed serious crimes and especially to all irreligious people (NS 1.332; ViDh 9.31; KS 426).

c) Finally, the choice of a particular form of ordeal is determined by circumstances of time: the ordeal of balance is the only one that may administered in any season, but on condition that the wind is not blowing (NS 1.260; ViDh 9.24); the ordeal of fire should be avoided in autumn or in summer whereas it should be preferred during the rains; the ordeal of water should not be administered in the cold season, but it should be applied in summer; on the contrary, the ordeal of poison should be avoided in the rainy season and should rather be reserved for the cold weather; etc.[569]

Numerous other prescriptions about ordeals: the time[570] and place[571] where all of them or some only should be administered, etc., cannot be mentioned here. Whatever has been the attitude of the commentators and however skeptical some of them have been,[572] the extremely rich information about ordeals bears witness to the importance which the ancient authors attributed to this form of evidence.

[569] NS 1.254 and 259; ViDh 9.26, 28 and 30.

[570] NS 1.268: "It is ordained that all ordeals should be administered in the forenoon, the person (to be tested) having fasted for a day and night, taken a bath, and wearing his wet dress." And about the ordeal of poison in particular, NS 1.320: "A man acquainted with law, must not (administer this ordeal) in the afternoon, nor in the twilight, nor at noon...". —Similarly, YDh 2.97.

[571] NS 1.265: "...the balance, (which should be erected) either in the midst of a public assembly, or before the gates of the royal palace, or in sight of a temple, or in a cross-road."

[572] Cf. Medhātithi on MDh 8.116, quoted by Kane 3.363.

21

The Problem of the Mixed Reply in Ancient Hindu Law

The Fourfold Subdivision of the Reply

It is a well known fact, that in all sources dealing with ancient Hindu adjective law four different types of legal reply have been neatly distinguished (Kane 1930–62: 3.300–301). This fourfold subdivision of the reply might perhaps even be said to be one of the more stable and constant factors among the endless series of enumerations and subdivisions to be found in the ancient Indian law books.

Inasmuch as a clear insight into the said four types of reply will prove necessary in order to fully appreciate the intricacies called forth by the mixed reply, at first the main types of reply shall be briefly defined and illustrated here.

In the first place, confession (*satya, saṃpratipatti*) is the statement in which the defendant acknowledges the truth of the facts mentioned in the plaint (Vyāsa 1.24).

Secondly, at least as far as the age of the Dharmaśāstras is concerned, a reply is said to be a reply by way of denial (*mithyā, mithyottara*) when the defendant contradicts the facts referred to in the plaint (KS 167).

Later on, at the time when Dharmaśātra literature —and all other branches of learning as well— becomes deeply influenced by the concepts of Indian logic (Nyāya) a much more subtle definition comes to the fore.

The plaint itself is, then, moulded in the form of the traditional Indian syllogism:

a) You owe me a hundred coins,
b) since you had borrowed them from me,

in which (a), i.e., "to owe me a hundred coins," is the *sādhya*, the *probandum*, or major term, whereas (b), i.e., "their having been borrowed from me," is the *hetu*, the *probans*, or middle term (See Rocher 1956: 1–19, esp. 5).

In the light of this, only the reply by way of denial has been worded as follows:

a) I do not owe you a hundred coins,
b) since I had not borrowed them from you.

In other words: the defendant denies the *probandum* of the plaint, indeed, but the essential element in the reply by way of denial is the fact that the *probans* of the plaint too, is being rejected (Vyci 136, 139).

We cannot possibly dwell here upon the several interesting considerations that have been devoted by various authors to the reply by way of exception (*kāraṇottara*, *pratyavaskandana*). A mere translation of the relevant texts in the ancient Dharmaśāstra would not be of much help;[433] we rather prefer at once to avail ourselves of the material contained in the *nibandhas* and the commentaries.

If we again consider the plaint referred to above:

a) You owe me a hundred coins,
b) since you had borrowed them from me,

the reply by way of exception —or by way of a special plea, as it has been translated by others— may be represented as follows:

b) I did borrow a hundred coins from you indeed,
c) but I already paid them back to you;
c) I, therefore do not owe you a hundred coins.

In other words: once again the defendant denies (a1) the *probandum* of the plaint (a); still, unlike the reply by way of denial, he does not reject (b1) the *probans* referred to by the plaintiff (b). In his turn he adduces a new element (c), *viz.*, *a cause* (*kāraṇa*) or a *special plea*, which is such as to delete the validity of the *probandum* notwithstanding the acceptance of the *probans*.

Finally, the reply by way of former judgment (*prāṅnyāya*, *pūrvanyāya*) is sufficiently known from other systems of law, too: the party who had been defeated again produces a similar plaint, but the defendant turns it down by referring to the judgement previously passed in the matter (BS 3.21).

Differently from so many other subtle and ingenious but equally unnecessary distinctions introduced by the learned au-

[433] E.g., Vyāsa 1.24; Bṛhaspati (ed. Rangaswami Aiyangar) 5.14, 19; etc.

thors of Sanskrit literature, the above fourfold subdivision of the reply has never been a mere intellectual game; on the contrary, from the very beginning it also had a highly practical meaning, in that it was a decisive factor as far as the assignment of the burden of proof was concerned.

The rules applied here may be summarized as follows:

1. In the case of a confession, the very question of the proof does not even come up for consideration;
2. In case of a denial, the burden of proof is with the plaintiff;
3. When there is a reply by way of exception or by way of denial, the burden of proof is upon the defendant.[434]

The Mixed Reply

So far, no serious objection can be raised against the theory of the reply as it has been elaborated by the authors of the texts on Dharmaśāstra. Still, the subject was not, thereby, completely exhausted. The Indian *dharmaśāstrins* have very well been aware of the fact that it might not in all cases be possible to assign a particular reply to any of the four groups which we have been discussing so far, with exclusion of all others. It might equally well happen, that a reply, as produced by the defendant, ranks among various groups of reply simultaneously. This case, then, poses the problem of the so-called 'mixed reply' (*saṃkīrṇottara*), for which various solutions have been proposed in the course of the centuries. In the following pages we shall try to draft a brief survey of the solutions proposed, and, at the same time, attempt to draw therefrom some definite conclusions of a much wider bearing.

1

The first author to deal with the matter at some length, is Kātyāyana:

> If a reply contains a confession with regard to one part of the plaint, an exception with regard another part, and a denial with regard to still another part, on account of its mixed nature the reply is invalid (*anuttara*). (KS 189)

The text of Kātyāyana leaves little doubt as to the interpreta-

[434] E.g. Hārīta (ed. Jolly) 1.29. For a more subtle distinction with regard to the reply by way of exception —according to the latter being stronger, equally strong, or weaker than the *probans* of the plaint—, Vyci nos. 145–146.

tion which should be given to it. As soon as the defendant simultaneously appeals to various types of reply, his reply is no longer considered to be an *uttara*, i.e., a *valid* reply, but it becomes an *anuttara*, i.e., an *invalid reply*.

After the above remarks on the burden of proof, the reason behind this statement should not strike us as particularly astonishing:

> In one and the same case the burden or proof should not be upon both parties, nor is it possible for both parties to establish their claims, nor can there be a double burden of proof upon a single person. (KS 190)

In other words: the reason for the inadmissibility a mixed reply is the very requirement that, in any particular lawsuit, the burden of proof should be single and undivided.

As a matter of fact, we are faced here with an instance of a phenomenon which is most characteristic of the ancient period of Hindu law: in general —as of many other ancient systems of law, too— once a particular basic rule has been adopted, it is carried out logically and strictly, whatever its consequences may be. *In casu*: as a rule, the burden of proof should be undivided; consequently, any reply involving a combined burden of proof, i.e., any reply of a mixed character, should, therefore, not even be examined, but it should in all cases be rejected *a priori*.

2

However, Hindu lawyers seem to have abandoned this conception of strict formalism at a very early stage. During the very period of the Dharmaśāstras, we already meet with the following question occurring in the Dharmaśāstra attributed to Hārīta:

> If in one and the same case there are both a reply by way of denial and by way of exception and also a confession with it, which type of reply should be admitted in this case? (1.23)[435]

The change is no less than remarkable. From now onward, any rejection *a priori* of a mixed reply is no longer possible; on the contrary, it is silently understood that any reply, however mixed it may be, shall be equally well received by the court. The problem which is raised instead is a completely different one,

[435] If the reply by way of former judgment has not found a place in this text, this omission should not be attributed to any other reason than the restrictions imposed by metre only.

viz. which one among the various types of reply is the more important one and should, therefore, be admitted with exclusion of all others.

The answer to this question has been given by Hārīta himself, as follows:

> That reply which refers to the richest content or in which the trial is likely to yield an appropriate result should be considered to be unmixed; the reply is mixed as far as the other parts are concerned.
>
> In case of a mixture of denial and exception, one should admit the reply by way of exception. (1.24)

We must hasten to add here, that the Sanskrit terms used in the first half of the latter quotation are by themselves rather vague and allowing of various interpretation. Still, apart from this point which is relatively irrelevant for our purpose, the two important conclusions to be derived from the text of Hārīta are rather as follows:

1. The mixed reply as such is no longer to be rejected;
2. On the other hand, the basic principle of the unity of the burden of proof has not, therefore, been abandoned.

If several of the four possible types of reply are joined together, all except one should be rejected. In other words: the absolute and unqualified rejection of Kātyāyana has now been replaced by a partial rejection only.

3

Such was the situation by the end of the age of the Dharmaśāstras, at the outset of the period of the *nibandhas* and commentaries. Needless to say, that, as in so many other cases, here too, the authors of the latter group of works have found themselves in the presence of a set of texts which, though all of them were supposed to enjoy the same degree of authority, apparently could not fail to impress them as representing two totally different points of view. It would be interesting to pursue the matter in detail and to collect all the various ways in which the numerous commentators have tried to reconcile these discrepancies. An inquiry of this kind would, however, vastly exceed the space allotted to the present paper. We shall, therefore, prefer to draw our data essentially from two sources which not only have devoted much attention to the problem but which, at the same time, will again be quite representative for the further evolution of the problem in later times.

In Vijñāneśvara's *Mitākṣarā* the problem comes up for discussion under YDh 2.7. After having quoted two *ślokas* from an anonymous *smṛtyantara*, "another Dharmaśāstra" —unless he actually wants to refer to the text of Yājñavalkya himself, where the same word also occurs— the author draws attention to the fact that again and again "the valid reply" has been indicated through the singular number *uttaram*. Hence he derives the conclusion that a reply, in order to be valid, should indeed be single, i.e., un-mixed. In support of this statement he, then, quotes the two verses from Kātyāyana referred to above, thereby indicating that the interdiction of a mixed reply is, indeed, based upon the necessity of the burden of proof being single and undivided. Subsequently, a number of very specific examples are quoted to illustrate the rules expounded by Kātyāyana.

However, the learned author of the *Mitākṣarā* was equally well aware of the existence of the verses of Hārīta; moreover, he even most cleverly used them, not only so as to avoid their apparent inconsistency with the verses of Kātyāyana, but at the same time so as again to put a step forward in turning Hindu law away from an ancient stage of mere formalism.

First of all, Vijñāneśvara avails himself of the well know fact that that the terms *vivāda* and *vyavahāra* repeatedly have been interchanged. Whereas Kātyāyana actually says that the burden of proof should be a single one *ekasmin vivāde*, thereby implementing that the burden of proof should be undivided "in one and the same lawsuit," according to Vijñāneśvara the meaning should be this: the burden of proof is to be a single one *ekasmin vyavahāre*, i.e., "in one and the same legal procedure."

Secondly, when Hārīta puts the question which particular type of reply should be "admitted" (*grāhya*) in case of a mixed reply, in Vijñāneśvara's opinion the word *grāhya* stands for "should be given preference to," "should be admitted first."

Thus, not only is there no longer any contradiction between the two sets of texts, but they even admirably supplement each other. On the one hand, Kātyāyana states that, whenever a mixed reply is produced, the case should be split up into as many parts as there are different types of reply; each part should thus be tried separately, so as to involve only one burden of proof at a time. On the other hand, so Vijñāneśvara says, the sequence of the individual trials should not be an arbitrary one; on the contrary, the sequence in which the various parts should be tried has been clearly delimited in the texts of Hārīta.

In other words: a lawsuit involving a mixed reply should no longer be rejected, neither wholly (Kātyāyana) nor even partially (Hārīta); it should be admitted *as a whole*, but the different parts of it should be taken up in as many separate trials.

4

The second of the *nibandha*s and commentaries to be referred to in this connection is Vācaspati Miśra's *Vyavahāracintāmaṇi*. As was the case when the *Mitākṣarā* was chosen as a source to illustrate the preceding stage of the solution, equally so by referring to the Vyci we by no means want to create the impression as if both texts should have been the first ones to reach these two stages, respectively. If we, finally, have decided to quote from the *Mitākṣarā* and from the Vyci only, this has been done for the only reason that both texts were considered to afford the most representative specimens of the two stages involved. In the case of Vācaspati Miśra, e.g., we have been unequivocally informed that the views held by him already had been those of Bhavadeva, the *Pradīpa*, and others (Vyci 155.3).

There can be no doubt that the Vyci to a large extent continues the views held by the *Mitākṣarā*. Vācaspati even explicitly argues against those who proclaim that, on the basis of the two verses of Kātyāyana, any mixed reply should be rejected. He also agrees with Vijñāneśvara in that the texts of Hārīta actually are meant to indicate the sequence in which the different parts of the mixed case should be tried.

Moreover, Vācaspati has some most sensible remarks which clearly prove that he too, had totally turned away from any formalism whatsoever. First, it is perfectly possible that the mixed reply produced by the defendant is, indeed, in accordance with reality; it would, then, be most inequitable to prevent a defendant from delivering his reply in accordance with the facts (Vyci 151.6–7). Next, the authoritative texts of the Dharmaśāstras cannot but be based upon equitable motives; consequently, they could never be supposed to require that the court should refuse to try a case for the mere reason that it has given rise to a mixed reply (Vyci 154.18) Both arguments had, of course, already been implicitly adopted by the author of the *Mitākṣarā*, too. The only thing which Vācaspati has added to his predecessor, is to state the underlying principles more clearly and in more explicit manner.

In other respects, however, Vācaspati has gone much farther than Vijñāneśvara. Although he does not actually criticize the latter's point of view as if a mixed reply should inevitably lead towards a number of separate trials, with him even the necessity of splitting up the case no longer comes up, as will be clear from the following quotation:

> The investigation should be carried out on all topics in which the doubt that has given rise to the dispute subsists, and on which decisive evidence can be gathered. (Vyci 155.2)

Elsewhere, he quotes the following example:

> Take a claim for a hundred coins, to which one replies like this: "Fifty have been cleared off, twenty five are due, and twenty five have not been appropriated at all." First one should investigate the part of the exception. After that, the twenty five that are denied either should be proved with the evidence of the plaintiff, or they should be opposed with the evidence of the defendant. (Vyci 154.8–9)

It goes without saying, that Vācaspati's theory of the mixed reply can hardly be held to agree with the first text of Kātyāyana as translated above. Without going so far as to maintain that Vācaspati had to force the text into the particular sense he wanted it to convey, we shall merely say that the meaning he gave to it was not the normal one, though not impossible either. As a matter of fact, the passages which we translated in three different ways, *viz.* "with regard to one part," "with regard to another part," and "with regard to still another part," quite validly reproduce the same Sanskrit word *ekadeśe*, "with regard to one part," which has been repeated thrice in the same text.

According to Vācaspati's interpretation, however, the text should be translated quite differently:

> If a reply with regard *to one and the same part* (sc. simultaneously) contains a confession, an exception, and a denial, on account of this mixture the reply is invalid.

On the basis of this interpretation, Vācaspati concludes in the following terms:

> A reply is invalid when it is mixed *ekadeśe*, i.e., "with regard to one part," the other two expressions "with regard to one part" being meaningless supplementary repetitions. Example: "A hundred coins either have been appropriated or they have not"; "either they have been cleared off, or I still owe them." On the other hand, a reply is valid when it touches upon various types of reply in connection with different parts of the claims; in this case there is no actual mixture. (Vyci 152.12–15)

Conclusion

To sum up, in the above analysis we have seen the problem of the mixed reply pass through four different stages successively:

1. Kātyāyana: the mixed reply should be rejected as a whole.
2. Hārīta: the mixed reply should be entirely rejected except for one of its parts.

3. Vijñāneśvara: the mixed reply should be admitted, but it causes the case to be split up into as many separate trials.
4. Vācaspati Misra: the mixed reply should be admitted, and the various parts should be investigated by the same court one after the other.

The former two stages had been reached in the age of the Dharmaśāstras themselves. The latter two have been elaborated in the period of the commentaries; as such they definitely provide us with an excellent example of the commentators' strenuous attempts to reconcile into a single harmonious structure the various authoritative texts they found at their disposal, contradictory as they may seem to be at a first glance.

Apart from this, the history of the problem of the mixed reply at the same time teaches us another far more important lesson. It demonstrates in the clearest terms the way in which Hindu law has been capable of gradually passing on from a stage of strict and absolute formalism to a basically realistic system where equity and good sense became more and more preponderant. On the other hand, we should not fail to notice the important fact that Hindu lawyers have succeeded in bringing about this radical change without in any way detracting from their fundamental conception of the eternal and unalterable *dharma*. Of this remarkable though often overlooked phenomenon the mixed reply is only one out of numerous possible examples.

22

The Reply in Hindu Legal Procedure: Mitra Miśra's Criticism of the Vyavahāra-Cintāmaṇi

The *Vyavahāra-prakāśa* (Vpra) of Mitra Miśra's *Vīramitrodaya* appears to be one of the largest digests on *vyavahāra* (judicial procedure). And not only is it one of the largest texts of its kind, but, through its numerous references to predecessors, it also serves as a most valuable source of information about earlier works on this subject, many of which have been lost in the course of time. One such work frequently referred to is Vācaspati Miśra's *Vyavahāra-cintāmaṇi* (Vyci). A complete list of these references will be found in the author's forthcoming edition of this text, together with the data to be derived from them with regard to the critical constitution of the text of both the Vyci and the Vpra.

The present paper is intended to discuss more extensively a limited number of Mitra Miśra's references to the work of Vācaspati. It is hoped not only to further a correct understanding of both texts, but also to provide a contribution to the history of Hindu legal procedure.

The treatment of the reply ranks among the most remarkable chapters of the Vyci. This fact must also have been recognized by Mitra Miśra when dealing with the same subject as he frequently refers to Vācaspati's point of view and, wherever necessary, refutes it at great length. In the following pages this controversy will be arranged under four headings corresponding to the four types of reply recognized by the authors of Dharmaśāstra:

1. Confession (*saṃpratipattiḥ*).
2. Reply by way of denial (*mithyottaram*).
3. Reply by way of exception (*kāraṇottaram*).
4. Reply by way of former judgment (*prāṅnyāyaḥ*).

1. Confession

Very little is to be said about the first type of reply, for though Mitra Miśra refers to Vācaspati, he does not really criticize his predecessor's point of view.

The problem is as follows: Both Vācaspati and Mitra Miśra agree that, when the plaint, "You owe me a hundred coins" is replied to with the words, "Yes, I do," the plaintiff actually offers to prove a thesis which is accepted to be true by the defendant. Such a proof is pointless, or, as the Naiyāyikas (Logicians) say, the plaintiff's statement suffers from the defect of *siddha-sādhana* (proving what is proved).

Vācaspati (Vyci 138.4.7) does not accept the fact that for this reason a confession would make the plaint invalid. His argument is based upon the practical ground that the only purpose of a judicial investigation is the establishment of truth, and this purpose is served by the case where a plaint is replied to by means of a confession as well as otherwise.

But he also says that in case of a confession there is no *nigraha* for the plaintiff. From the mere text of the Vyci it is not possible to be sure whether this term was intended to have the technical meaning used by the Logicians or not; there are, however, two arguments which seem to point towards the former alternative.

(1) The defect of *siddha-sādhana*, though originally included among the *hetvābhāsas* (fallacies) is considered as a *nigraha-sthāna* (an occasion for reproof) in the Modern School of Logic (cf. Keith 1921: 147). If further we know that the entire Vyci has been composed against the background of Indian logic (other examples will be found below), we may assume the term *nigraha* also to have been conceived in its technical sense.

(2) The fact that in the Vpra (56.33–57.1) Vācaspati's interpretation has been opposed to that of Mitra Miśra by means of the expression, "Vācaspati, *however*, says..." The interpretation of the corresponding passage in the Vpra will thus serve as an *argumentum e contrario* for the understanding of the text of the Vyci.

As far as this interpretation is concerned (Vpra 56.31–33), Mitra Miśra agrees with Vācaspati that the plaint cannot be invalidated by means of a confession, and he also says that the plaint is not for that reason a *nigraha-sthāna*. But in this case the sense of the term *nigraha* is made clear by the following explanatory note:

parājaye'pi pūrvavādino daṇḍaḥ paraṃ na bhavati, aparādhābhāvāt |

This means that even when the plaintiff is put in the wrong, he is not given punishment (*daṇḍa*) on that account, for even then he has not committed an offense. *A fortiori*, he should not be *punished* (*nigraha*) in the case of a confession where he is put in the right. In other words, Mitra Miśra uses the words *daṇḍa* and *nigraha* as synonyms.

2. Reply by Way of Denial

In a text from *Vyāsa-smṛti* three kinds of reply are described as follows:

> *sādhyasya satyavacanaṃ pratipattir udāhṛtā* |
> *kāraṇaṃ syād avaskando mithyā syāt sādhyanihnutiḥ* || (VySm 1.24 (DhK 1.187)

The present paragraph will be concerned with the last quarter of this verse, where the reply by way of denial has been defined as: "a denial of the *probandum* of the plaint."

It should be noticed beforehand that in the works on Dharmaśāstra the plaint and the reply have often been treated as inferences of the type:

> There is fire on the mountain because there is smoke;

or more literally:

> The mountain is having fire because of smoke.

In this inference,

> "mountain" is the *pakṣa* or minor term (p),
> "fire" is the *sādhya*, *probandum*, or major term (s), and
> "smoke" is the *hetu*, *probans*, or middle term (h).

In the same way the plaint is generally worded as follows:

> You owe me a hundred coins, because you have borrowed them from me;

or more literally:

> A hundred coins are being owed by you, because they have been borrowed.

In the latter inference,

> p = a hundred coins,
> s = they are being owed, and
> h = they have been borrowed.

If we now apply the definition of VySm 1.24, the reply by way of denial corresponding to the above plaint will be as follows:

> I do not owe a hundred coins.

Vācaspati Miśra (Vyci 136.1–2) raises an objection to this definition. To put it in Nyāya terminology, he maintains that the definition suffers from the defect of *ativyāpti*, i.e., the definition is too wide inasmuch as it also covers a number of replies which are not replies by way of denial. The two kinds of reply falsely covered by the definition are, the reply by way of exception, and the reply by way of former judgment.

A reply by way of exception to the above plaint would be as follows:

> I do not owe a hundred coins, since I paid them back.

And the reply by way of former judgment would be:

> I do not owe a hundred coins, since this matter has been decided in the court before.

To understand the real nature of these types of reply they must be further analyzed as follows:

1. The reply by way of exception actually says:

a) I had borrowed a hundred coins,
b) but I have paid them back;
c) therefore, I do not owe them.

In other words: (a) the defendant agrees with the *h* of the plaint, but (b) he raises an exception to the effect that (c) he denies the *s*.

2. The reply by way of former judgment reflects the following reasoning:

a) I had borrowed a hundred coins,
b) but this matter has been decided in the court before;
c) therefore, I do not owe a hundred coins.

Again, (a) the defendant accepts *h* of the plaint, but (b) due to the intervening fact of the earlier decision (c) he denies the *s*.

The reply by way of denial, on the other hand, means:

> I do not owe a hundred coins, since I did not borrow them.

Here the defendant denies both the *h* and the *s* of the plaint.

Vācaspati concludes that in order that the definitions of the reply by way of denial should not also cover the other two types of reply where the *s* of the plaint is denied as well, it should be worded as follows:

a denial of the *probandum* of the plaint *together with its probans.*

Mitra Miśra again objects to this modified definition of Vācaspati Miśra. According to him (Vpra 57.13–14) even the insertion of "together with its *probans*" cannot absolve the definition of the same defect of *atiyāpti* referred to by Vācaspati. Even the definition "a denial of the *probandum* of the plaint together with its *probans*" is also so wide as to cover the other two types of reply.

Examples

1. Vācaspati's definition applies to the following reply by way of exception:

I do not owe a hundred coins, since I received them as a gift.

That means:

a) I have not borrowed a hundred coins,
b) but I received them as a gift;
c) therefore I do not owe them.

2. It also applies to the following reply by way of former judgment:

I do not owe a hundred coins, since this matter has been decided in the court before,

when this reply stands for the following argumentation:

a) I have not borrowed a hundred coins,
b) thus it has been decided in the court before,
c) therefore I do not owe them.

In both examples the defendant not only denies the *s* of the plaint but the *h* as well.

In order to avoid the latter *ativyāpti*, Mitra Miśra (Vpra 57.14–15) proposes the following distinction between the denial on the one hand and the exception and the former judgment on the other:

1. A reply by the way of denial is a pure denial of the *s* of the plaint without anything else being added:

I do not owe a hundred coins.

2. In both other cases the *s* of the plaint is also denied, but in addition this denial is further supported

a) either by an exception:

I do not owe a hundred coins, since I have paid them back,

or:

since I received them as a gift;

b) or by a former judgment:

I do not owe a hundred coins, since this matter has been decided in the court before.

3. Reply by Way of Exception

The definition of the reply by way of exception will be discussed below, in connection with the definition of the reply by way of former judgment. The present section will be concerned only with its subdivision. The Vyci (141.34–145) draws a distinction between three possible kinds of reply by way of exception:

1. The exception may be stronger than the *h* of the plaint.

Example

Plaint: You owe me a hundred coins, since you have borrowed them.
Reply: I do not owe you a hundred coins, since I paid them back.

This type of reply is illustrated by means of the following texts: BS 3.19 (DhK 1.166):

arthinābhihito yo 'rthaḥ pratyarthī yadi taṃ tathā |
prapadya kāraṇaṃ brūyāt pratyavaskandanaṃ hi tat ||

When the defendant replies to the content set forth by the plaintiff by adducing an exception, this is a case of *pratyavaskandana.*

KS 170 (DhK 1.176):

arthinābhihito yo 'rthaḥ pratyarthī yadi taṃ tathā |
prapadya kāraṇaṃ brūyād ādharyaṃ bhṛgur abravīt ||

When the defendant replies to the content set forth by the plaintiff by adducing an exception, Bhṛgu calls this weakness (of the plaint).

It should be understood that even before Vācaspati's time these verses had been the subject of various interpretations which would require as many different translations; the above rendering is intended to reproduce Vācaspati's way of understanding the texts.

2. The exception may be equally as strong as the *h* of the plaint.

Example

Plaint: This land is mine, since I obtained it by inheritance.
Reply: It is mine, since I obtained it by inheritance.

3. The exception may also be less strong than the *h* of the plaint.

Example

Plaint: This land has been mine for twenty years by way of a pledge, since for such a time it has been pledged to me by the owner.
Reply: It has been mine for five years by way of a pledge, since for such a time he has pledged it to me.

The latter *h* is less strong than the *h* of the plaint in accordance with the text YDh 2.23cd (DhK 1.723) where it has been laid down that in the case of a pledge the first transaction only is valid.

According to Vācaspati Miśra (Vyci 145.1–147.2) this threefold subdivision of the reply by way of exception also bears upon the assignment of the burden of proof: when the exception is stronger than the *h* of the plaint, the *onus probandi* is upon the defendant; in the other two cases it is upon the plaintiff.

Mitra Miśra first reproduces Vācaspati's point of view (Vpra 58.33–60.5), but he then rejects it for two main reasons: neither has this subdivision been prescribed in any text of the ancient Dharmaśāstras nor is there a reasonable ground to call for it. His argument is as follows (Vpra 60.5–61.14):

There is no valid reason to restrict the field of application of the text BS 3.19 (in the Vpra this text is ascribed to Nārada) to the case where the exception is stronger than the *h* of the plaint.

On the contrary, not only is there no reason in favor of this restriction, but there are actual arguments against it. Indeed, if BS 3.19 refers to the said case only, there is no ancient text left to serve as a definition for the reply by way of exception in general. In any case, whether it refers to the reply by way of exception in general or to its first species only, there are no texts to define the latter two species of the threefold subdivision.

Subsequently, Mitra Miśra removes two objections which might be raised (or even may have been raised) against his point of view.

In the first place, the following argument might be proposed in support of Vācaspati's theory that BS 3.19 should be restricted to the case where the exception is stronger than the *h* of the plaint. (It may be under the influence of this objector that in the Vpra too, BS 3.19 is called "a text of Nārada.")

KS 170 clearly cannot apply to the case where the exception is equally strong or less strong than the *h* of the plaint. Nor can this be the case with the text NS 1.64 (DhK 1.220) where it is said:

> *ādharyaṃ pūrvapakṣasya yasminn arthavaśād bhavet* |
> *vivāde sākṣiṇas tatra pṛṣṭavyāḥ pūrvavādinaḥ* ||

> When in a law-suit the content of the plaint is such that it is less strong (than the reply), the witnesses of the defendant should be questioned.

There are, thus, two verses of Nārada referring to the reply by way of exception, namely, NS 1.164 and NS (= BS 3.19); inasmuch as there can be no doubt about the interpretation of NS 1.164, in accordance with the principle of *ekavākyatā* the other one, too, should be considered applicable under the same circumstances. In other words, NS (= BS 3.19) too, should be restricted to the case where the exception is stronger than the *h* of the plaint.

Mitra Miśra refutes this objection as follows:

If NS actually contained two *śloka*s on the same subject, one of them would be pointless. Such a defect cannot, however, be accepted in an authoritative text like Nārada's. Consequently, even when NS 1.164 is taken to refer to the special case mentioned by the objector, the application of the rules of interpretation of authoritative texts requires the other verse of Nārada to have another field of application. The most obvious solution then, would be that NS (= BS 3.19) refers to the reply by way of exception in general.

Conclusion: Even when applying NS 1.164 and KS 170 to a single species of the genus *kāraṇottara*, the objector has to accept Mitra Miśra's point of view that BS 3.19 refers to the reply by way of exception in general.

Another objector is, then, supposed to have proposed the following solution.

The reference of BS 3.19 to the reply by way of exception in general offers a considerable advantage inasmuch as it remedies the above-mentioned lack of a general definition of *kāraṇottara*. But even then it is inconsistent to suppose that the *smṛti* texts have described the general case and one special case only, without at the same time alluding to the other special cases. Why not solve the problem by means of the following distinction: KS 170 and NS 1.164 apply to an exception which is less strong than the *h* of the plaint, whereas BS 3.19 refers to the case where the exception is stronger or equally strong?

It has been noticed that both objections were based upon the assumption that the expression *ādharyaṃ pūrvapakṣasya* in KS 170 and NS 1.164 covers the specific case where the exception is such that it causes the "weakness of the plaint," i.e., where the *h* of the plaint is less strong than the exception.

Mitra Miśra says this very basis of both objections is wrong. When the texts state that an exception "causes the weakness of the plaint," or that it "destroys or annuls the plaint," that means that when the plaintiff accepts the *h* of the plaint but raises an exception whereby the *s* of the plaint is rejected, it is the exception *which is allowed to be proved* whereas no evidence is accepted for the *h* or the *s* of the plaint. In support of the latter interpretation Mitra Miśra quotes the *Vyavahārakalpataru* 69 (Ed. Aiyangar 1953), where the "weakness of the plaint" has been explained as "not deserving to be established by means of evidence."

Mitra Miśra's interpretation of the term *ādharya* has another important consequence with regard to the *onus probandi*. Instead of its being upon the defendant or upon the plaintiff according to the exception being stronger or not, respectively (thus Vācaspati Miśra, cf. above), in the Vpra it is said to be invariably upon the defendant.

This rule about the *onus probandi* requires the removal of one more objection.

There is, indeed, an anonymous *smṛti* text (DhK 1.236) which strongly leans towards the opposite point of view; as a matter of fact, it is this very text which has been quoted by Vācaspati in support of his theory of differentiation in the assignment of the burden of proof:

gurāv abhihite hetau prativādikriyā bhavet |
durbale vādinaḥ proktā tulye pūrvakriyaiva ca ||

According to Vācaspati this *śloka* should be understood as follows:

> When he produces a stronger exception, the burden of proof is upon the defendant; when it is less strong, upon the plaintiff; when it is equally strong, upon the plaintiff.

The peculiarities to be noticed in this translation are: (a) *hetu* = exception, and (b) *pūrvakriyā* (*pāda* d) = *pūrvavādikriyā* (cf. *pāda* b) = the *onus probandi* is upon the plaintiff.

The interpretation of Mitra Miśra is completely different:

> When he produces a stronger reply, the burden of proof is upon the defendant; when it is less strong, upon the plaintiff; when it is equally strong, upon the party who offers evidence first.

In other words:

1. When the defendant produces a reply by way of exception or by way of former judgment, it is that reply of his which is considered worthy of being established by means of evidence.
2. When the defendant produces a weaker reply, i.e., a reply by way of denial, it cannot be made the object of a valid proof, inasmuch as no real evidence can be offered for a negative statement. Here the burden of proof is upon the plaintiff.
3. When both parties rely upon equally strong facts, the *onus probandi* is upon him who comes first to prove that the object in dispute is his.

Note: Actually, this third case is redundant, since all types of reply have been exhausted by the first two cases; it is nothing but a special case of denial.

4. Reply by Way of Former Judgment

In the Vyci (141.32–33) the reply by way of exception and the reply by way of former judgment have been distinguished as follows. The former contains an exception (literally, a cause) which *deletes* the *s* of the plaint.

> *Example*
>
> Plaint: You owed me a hundred coins, since you have borrowed them.
> Reply: I do not owe you a hundred coins, since I paid them back.

In other words, the defendant accepts the truth of the fact mentioned in the *h* of the plaint: it is true that he borrowed a hundred coins from the plaintiff. But in the *h* of the reply the defendant states another fact by which the fact mentioned in the *s* of the plaint has been deleted: the hundred coins have been paid back.

There can be little doubt as to the idea underlying this definition. Indeed, one of the forms of "absence" or "negation" recognized in the doctrine of Nyāya is termed *dhvaṃsābhāva* or *pradhvaṃsābhāva*, i.e., "absence through (or, after) destruction."

Example

> When a pot which has once existed has been destroyed, afterwards one can speak of the *dhvaṃsābhāva* of the pot.

In the same way, when the *h* and the *s* of the plaint were true at a certain time before they were deleted by the *h* of the reply, afterwards one can speak of the *dhvaṃsābhāva* of the former.

On the other hand, the reply by way of former judgment is said to indicate the *sāmānyābhāva* (literally, the absolute absence) of the *s* of the plaint. This statement of Vācaspati Miśra should be interpreted as follows: inasmuch as the same case has already been treated and previously decided by the court, the question whether or not a hundred coins are due cannot even be raised and, consequently, it cannot come up for consideration again.

Mitra Miśra (Vpra 58.32–33 and 61.21–25) does not accept the distinction made by Vācaspati. His thesis is as follows: it is not right to say that the reply by way of former judgment indicates *sāmānyābhāva* only, since it sometimes also states *dhvaṃsābhāva.*

The rejection of Vācaspati's theory in the Vpra is due to the fact that Mitra Miśra's interpretation of the term *sāmānyabhāva* used by Vācaspati, is different from the one proposed above. According to the author of the Vpra, *sāmānyābhāva* was intended to mean that the *s* of the plaint has not been true at any time. Upon this assumption he argues as follows:

> In a reply by way of former judgment the defendant says, "I do not owe a hundred coins, since the plaintiff has been defeated by me in this matter in a former judgment."

In other words, in the past the plaintiff has already claimed the same amount, but on that occasion the court has decided that the amount was not due by the defendant.

The defendant's reaction against this former plaint may have been twofold: either he has denied the claim, or he has adduced an exception. And when the defendant at the present moment succeeds in proving the former judgment, that means that his former denial (or his former exception too), is accepted to have been true.

In other words, when the defendant succeeds in proving his plea of former judgment, there are two possibilities:

1. If the former judgment was based upon a successful reply by way of denial, it can be said that the *s* of the plaint has never been true (*sāmānyābhāva*).
2. But the *sāmānyābhāva* of the *s* of the plaint is not true when the former judgment was based upon a reply by way of exception. In this case the reply by way of former judgment mediately indicates *dhvaṃsābhāva.*

Mitra Miśra's conclusion is that Vācaspati's definition of the reply by way of former judgment suffers from the defect of *avyāpti* inasmuch as it is too narrow to cover the second case above.

According to Mitra Miśra it is better to draw the distinction between the reply by way of denial and the reply by way of exception on the one hand and the reply by way of former judgment on the other as follows:

1. The reply by way of denial and the reply by way of exception indicate the absolute negation (*sāmānyābhāva*) of the *s* of the plaint and its absence through destruction (*dhvaṃsābhāva*), respectively.
2. The reply by way of former judgment can indicate either.

Note: As said above, Mitra Miśra's interpretation of the term *sāmānyābhāva* in the Vyci is different from the one which we originally proposed. Though Mitra Miśra's interpretation is based upon the more common meaning of the word, the other is the only one to give Vācaspati's text a good sense, and, vice versa, the term is perfectly adequate to express the idea behind it. According to Mitra Miśra's explanation Vācaspati would have overlooked the alternative of the former judgment's being the result of a reply by way of exception. However, this case is too obvious to have escaped the attention of a subtle Naiyāyika of the standing of Vācaspati. Even if the origin of Mitra Miśra's interpretation can thus be easily traced, it cannot be denied that the misunderstanding of a statement of Vācaspati has induced him unduly to object to it.

23

"Lawyers" in Classical Hindu Law

There can be no doubt that parties to a lawsuit in ancient Hindu law had a right to be represented by other persons. The question arises whether or not the representative referred to in the ancient texts correspond to the pleaders, advocates, vakils or attorneys of modern India. In other words, did ancient Hindu law have the kind of legal procedure in which the rights of the parties were safeguarded through the services of a class of experts, as is the case in present day India and in most other modern legal systems?

Looking at Hindu law as it became known to the West in the latter half of the eighteenth century, it did indeed seem as if the question was to be answered in the affirmative. Halhed's *Code of Gentoo Laws* (1777), his translation of the *Vivādārṇavasetu*, did have a section (Ch. 111 § 11) explicitly called "Of appointing a vakeel (or attorney)." Its contents are as follows:

> If the plaintiff or defendant have any excuse for not attending the court, or for not pleading their own cause, or, on any other account, excuse themselves, they shall, at their own option, appoint a person as their *vakeel*; if the *vakeel* gains the suit, his principal also gains; if the *vakeel* is cast, his principal is cast also.

> In a cause where the accusation is for murder, for a robbery, for adultery. for eating prohibited food, for false abuse, for thrusting a finger into the *pudendum* of an unmarried virgin, for false witness, or for destroying any thing, the property of a magistrate, a *vakeel* must not be appointed to plead and answer in such cases; the principals shall plead and answer in person; but a woman, a minor, an ideot [sic], and he who cannot distinguish between good and evil for himself, may, even in such causes as these, constitute a *vakeel*.

> Except the brother, father and son of the plaintiff and defendant, if any other person, at the time of trial, should abet, and speak for either party, the magistrate shall exact a fine from him: if a brother, a father, a son, or a *vakeel*, should assist, and speak for either party, it is allowed (Halhed 1777: 93).

As we shall see below, this passage comprises most of the ancient rules connected with representation in court. If the English version gave a faithful rendering of the original Sanskrit, little doubt would remain that the present day vakil had his counterpart in ancient India. The answer to this question must, however, be left open at the moment. The only point we want to stress here is this: from the first translated Sanskrit text onward, scholars were confronted with a picture according to which ancient Hindu law had a system of pleaders similar to the one they were so familiar with in contemporary India.

Such an eminent authority as Julius Jolly went one step further, and drew a conclusion which under the circumstances was perfectly logical: "Instead of appearing in person, each party has a right to be represented at the trial; thus, even today the vakils, i.e., advocates, constitute an unusually numerous professional group in India" (1890: 346). In other words, Jolly interpreted the particular attraction on the part of contemporary Indians to the legal profession as the natural outcome of a factor that had its root deep in ancient Indian tradition. In his opinion the legal profession in ancient India was an important one, and one that attracted many recruits. In his classic treatise *Hindu Law and Custom*, Jolly does not refer to lawyers explicitly. But at least one passage of the book (1928: 299), and several statements elsewhere (especially in his translations quoted below) clearly suggest that Jolly firmly believed in the existence of a legal profession in ancient India.

Nothing was more natural than that the ideas of the greatest European specialist on Hindu law were drawn upon by other legal historians who had no direct access to the Sanskrit sources and who used Jolly as their main authority. As a result, Jolly's opinion found its way into other Western publications dealing with Hindu law (Kohler 1891: 20).

The existence of legal practitioners in ancient India has also been maintained, quite independently of Jolly, by Indian scholars. According to K.P. Jayaswal, for instance, professional lawyers existed at least from the time of the MDh and perhaps even earlier:

> Manu, VIII. 169, shows that professional lawyers were already in existence in the time of the Manava Code. The verse says that the people who suffer for the sake of others are witnesses, sureties and the judges, but that those who are benefited by legislation, are the king ("who gets court-fees"), the creditor ("who gets his decree"),

> the merchant ("the speculator who supplies money for defence to the defendant and acquires his property in return"), and the Brahmin. This Brahmin is the Brahmin who advised each party on law... The definition of *vidya-dhana*, with its history going back to the Dharmasūtras, presupposes the existence of the profession much earlier. (1931: 88–89)

The viewpoint of the Indian dean of Dharmaśāstra is completely different. Concerning the legal profession in ancient times, P.V. Kane says:

> An interesting question arises whether lawyers as an institution existed in ancient India. The answer must be that so far as the smṛtis are concerned, there is nothing to show that any class of persons whose profession was the same as that of modern counsel, solicitors or legal practitioners and who were regulated by the State existed. (Kane 1930–62: 3.288)

However, Kane too admits that, "This does not preclude the idea that persons well-versed in the law of the smṛtis and the procedure of the courts were appointed (*niyukta*) to represent a party and place his case before the court." His reasons for this restriction are mainly three. First, from a story narrated in Asahāya's commentary on the NS (1.4) "it appears that persons who had studied the smṛtis helped parties in return for a monetary consideration to raise contentions before the court." Next, there are "some important rules" in the *Śukranītisāra.* And, to these two arguments directly derived from the texts, is then added a general consideration: "The procedure prescribed by Nārada, Bṛhaspati and Kātyāyana reaches a very high level of technicalities and skilled help must often have been required in litigation."

An equally cautious opinion has been voiced by U.C. Sarkar:

> There is no sufficient indication that at the time of the Smritis there was any legal profession in the modern sense of the term. Persons versed in the science of law could give their opinion for the consideration of the king and his councillors. The system was perhaps most analogous to the Responsa Prudentium of the early Romans. The opinions of the legal experts also were not binding on the king. They had no other part to play except giving their opinion. (Sarkar 1958: 37)

Others were even much more outspoken. Thus, in P. Varadachariar's opinion: "It is not possible to say anything as to the existence of a legal profession in Ancient India" (1946: 156). The same author makes it a point to reject Jayaswal's above mentioned statement according to which the Brahmin referred to in MDh 8.169 is "the Brahmin who advised each party on law":

> Mr. Jayaswal thinks that professional lawyers ought to have existed from the days of Manu or at least from the first century A.D. I find it difficult to interpret the reference to Vipra in Manu VIII, 169, as a reference to a "Lawyer Brahmin." The commentaries on this verse lend no support to such a reading.

We have quoted opinions about the legal profession in ancient India at some length, mainly to show the degree of confusion to which the problem has led. Various authors working on an identical set of data have been able to draw from them a number of apparently contradictory conclusions. Nothing could be more characteristic in this respect than two passages from an issue of the Madras Law journal. At the yearly "Vakils' Gathering," held in Madras on April 17, 1909, the Advocate-General had this to say:

> The origin of the English Bar is shrouded in the remotest antiquity. It has been traced as far back as Edward I. Turning to the History of India, whether ancient or medieval, you find no glimpses of the existence of the legal profession. For the sake of curiosity, I looked into some of our sacred books. While you find an abundance of rules about causes of action, pleadings, plaints, written statements, burden of proof, rules of trial and judgment, you find no mention whatever of arguments of Counsel.[573]

However, in a discussion of the Advocate-General's address, an anonymous author makes the following statement:

> In this the learned Advocate-General would seem to have fallen into an error, and notwithstanding his statement that he had looked into the Sanskrit-books and arrived at that conclusion, we should think there is express authority in the Sanskrit-books the other way. The following passages from the Sukranitisara would clearly show that the Vakils were not unknown in ancient or medieval India as the Advocate-General would seem to think.[574]

And he adds an English translation of a number of verses from the *Śukranītisāra*, to which we shall return below.

We shall now examine the original data. It is hoped that the mere presentation of these data will demonstrate how the opinions cited above could come to be held. We apologize to those readers who are not familiar with Sanskrit. In each case we shall have to start from the original Sanskrit text, to show how these texts lend themselves to different interpretations according to the general context in which one is willing to place them. Fi-

[573] Madras L.J. 201 (1909).
[574] Ibid.: 153.

nally we shall add a few general remarks and draw conclusions which, it is hoped, will help to place the problem in its correct perspective.

The Textual Data

Nārada

A first point to be noted is that representation in a law court is not referred to before the NS. Truly enough, the earlier texts on Dharmaśāstra are not very explicit with regard to law in general and legal procedure in particular. This absence of explicit data allows of a twofold interpretation. Either representation did exist from an earlier time, but Nārada was the first one to mention the institution explicitly, or representation did not exist before Nārada. We prefer not to go beyond presenting the alternatives. Tentatively, in view of the silence of Manu (like Varadachariar, we cannot follow Jayaswal's interpretation of MDh 8.169) and of Yājñavalkya we lean slightly toward the latter alternative.

In the NS we are faced with two stanzas which definitely refer to representation in the court. The first verse (Introduction 2.22) is as follows:

arthinā saṃniyukto vā pratyarthiprahito 'pi vā
yo yasyārthe vivadate tayor jayaparājayau

In Jolly's translation this means:

If one deputed by the claimant, or chosen as his representative by the defendant, speaks for his client in court, the victory or defeat concerns the party [himself and not the representative] (Jolly 1889: 29).

This is another piece of evidence for Jolly's belief in the existence of a class of lawyers. The words "for his client" are nowhere present in the Sanskrit text; literally the latter says: "for somebody" or "for him," referring thereby to the claimant and the defendant. On the other hand, it is clear that reference is made in the text to two persons who carry on litigation for two other persons, the decision binding the latter and not the former: (1) one who is *saṃniyukta* by the plaintiff, and (2) one who is *prahita* by the defendant. Both terms are clear without being precise; they refer to persons "appointed," "proposed" by either party.

The second stanza of NS (Introduction 2.23) is this:

yo na bhratā na ca pitā na putro na niyogakṛt
parārthavādī daṇḍyaḥ syād vyavahāreṣu vibruvan.

Jolly translates:

> He deserves punishment who speaks in behalf of another, without being either the brother, the father, the son, or the appointed agent; and so does he who contradicts himself at the trial (Jolly 1889, 29).

As in the preceding verse —*yo yasyārthe vivadate*— here too, reference is made to "somebody stating the affair of another" or "somebody speaking for another" (*parārthavādin*). Moreover, among the eventual *parārthavādins* figure: the father, the son, the brother, and the *niyogakṛt*. The latter especially is important for our purpose. Jolly, in the light of his idea referred to above, translates: "the appointed agent." We do not dare to go so far, but we do notice that *niyogakṛt* ("he who performs *niyoga*") derives from the same verbal root preceded by the same preverb which we already met with in the preceding stanza: there it was *saṃniyukta*, here it is *niyogakṛt*. The only, but important conclusion to be drawn from this is that, according to Nārada, a party could give to another person a *niyoga* ("appointment") to speak for him in the court.

Unfortunately, nothing allows us to draw any more specific conclusions. Both verses apparently go together and deal with the same topic, but they have no contextual relation either with the preceding or with the following stanzas. We would venture to say, with S. Varadachariar, about the first verse: "Such a declaration would be uncalled for if the passages were to refer to a professional class whose profession itself was to represent others" (1946: 157).

Before proceeding we must raise an objection to Jolly's translation of the second stanza, especially to his final words: "and so does he who contradicts himself at the trial." There is nothing in the Sanskrit text to warrant the inclusion of the conjunction "and"; on the contrary, the grammatical subject of *vyavahāreṣu vibruvan* is the same as that of *parārthavādin*. However, it is not easy to propose a more correct translation than Jolly's; the point is that *vibruvan* can have two different meanings which give equally different meanings to the verse as a whole. And since no argument can be drawn from the context, the only valid treatment of the passage is to mention both interpretations. Both have found their adherents among the later commentators, but it is not, and never will be, possible to know with certainty, which interpretation was the original one. In the first place, it is possible that the preverb *vi* radically changes the meaning of *bruvan* ("speaking"), so that *vibruvan* means: "speaking wrongly, speaking untruthfully, lying." We ourselves have been tempted by this interpretation, and, when the verse occurred in the *Vyavahāracintāmaṇi* (78), we translated: "He who makes false statements in legal procedures while pleading the cause of another person, should be punished, except when he is [the party's] brother, father, son, or express deputy" (Rocher 1956:168).

We still hold that this is a valid interpretation. However, after examining the materials which serve as a basis for the present paper, we would prefer terms that are less precise than "pleading the cause" and "express deputy." In any case the verse then indicates that there are two classes of "persons speaking for somebody else," those explicitly enumerated and all others; the former may make false statements in the court without being punished, the others may not. In the second place, it is also possible that the preverb *vi* does not change the meaning of *bruvan*; *vibruvan* then simply means "speaking." In that case the verse prescribes punishment for anybody who speaks in lieu of a party to a lawsuit, except for the brother, father, son, and *niyogakṛt*.

Bṛhaspati

The BS (1.142) in its turn contains at least one stanza connected with representation (Aiyangar 1941: 23, v. 142).

apragalbhajaḍonmattavṛddhastrībālarogiṇām
purvottaraṃ vaded bandhur niyukto 'nyo 'thavā naraḥ

Jolly translates:

> For one timorous, or idiotic, or mad, or overaged, and for women, boys, and sick persons, a kinsman or appointed agent should proffer the plaint or answer [as his representative]. (Jolly 1889: 288)

Again Jolly uses the term "appointed agent," this time to render the Sanskrit term *niyukta*. For the present argument, we merely notice the use of *niyukta*, a variant form for Nārada's *saṃniyukta* and *niyogakṛt*.

Bṛhaspati's stanza raises, however, a number of questions which are important if one wants to understand what he meant by *niyukta*. First, Jolly's translation omits one word from the Sanskrit text: *anya* ("other"). Since we no longer have access to the original context, we cannot *a priori* reject either of the following interpretations: (1) a kinsman, or another man who is *niyukta*, i.e., either a kinsman or somebody who is not a kinsman but a *niyukta*; (2) a kinsman or another *niyukta*, i.e., anybody who had been *niyukta* by the party. In the former alternative, *niyukta* might eventually refer to a specific class of representatives; in the latter alternative, it could mean no more than "designated" generally.

A second problem raised by Bṛhaspati's text is connected with a variant reading found in the *Vyavahāracintāmaṇi* (no. 74 of our edition) and in the *Vīramitrodaya* on YS 2.6. Here the second line reads: *purvottaraṃ vadet tadvad aniyukto.* That means: "In the same way even a person who has not been deputed may speak first or last for...". In this case too, *aniyukta* —and, for that matter, *niyukta*— comes closer to the general "designated" than to the technical meaning of an "appointed agent."

Kātyāyana

Of all Dharmaśāstras, the KS seems to have been most prolific in connection with representation. P.V. Kane (1933: 14–15) collected no less than seven stanzas on the subject; in his translation (1933: 133–34) he arranged them under the title "Substitutes or recognised agents of parties."

The first two distichs (KS 89–90) are as follows:

samarpito 'rthinā yo 'nyah paro dharmādhikāriṇi
prativādī sa vijñeyaḥ pratipannaś ca yaḥ svayam ||
adhikāro 'bhiyuktasya netarasyāsty asaṃgateḥ
itaro 'py abhiyuktena pratirodhīkṛto mataḥ ||

Kane translates:

> A person though other [than the defendant,] if put forward by the defendant before the judge [as defendant] should be regarded as the defendant and he also who is accepted [by the plaintiff] himself [as the defendant]. It is the right of the person charged [to give a reply] and not of another person, since the latter is unconnected [with the dispute]; [but] even a stranger may be allowed [to have the right to defend] if he is put forward [as the defendant] by the person charged [by the plaintiff].

These verses, the original of which is lost, present a number of variant readings in the later commentaries in which they have been quoted. Several Sanskrit words are problematic and might be given different translations from those proposed by Kane. A detailed discussion of all these problems is not relevant here. We must, however, remark that the words "a stranger" used by Kane are definitely too precise and too strong; the Sanskrit words *itaro 'pi* say nothing more than "even another person" without any further specification.

KS 91 does not present any new problem: it corresponds word for word with NS (Introduction 2.22). In view of Varadachariar's remarks quoted above, we can hardly agree with Kane's statement that "this verse contains the germs of the modern profession of pleaders" (Kane 1933: 135).

KS 92 reads as follows:

dāsāḥ karmakarāḥ śiṣyā niyuktā bāndhavās tathā
vādino na ca daṇḍyāḥ syuḥ yas tv ato 'nyaḥ sa daṇḍabhak

i.e., in Kane's translation:

> Slaves, menials, pupils, persons deputed, and relatives, these should not be punished when they speak [on behalf of another, their master, etc.]; any one other than these [if meddling in litigation] deserves punishment.

Here we have a clear enumeration of those who may represent a party: (1) *dāsāḥ*, (2) *karmakarāḥ*, (3) *śiṣyāh*, (4) *niyuktāḥ*, and (5) *bāndhavāḥ*. Thus, a *niyukta* is a specific kind of representative (*vādin* or *prativādin*), along with slaves, menials, pupils, and relatives; all others are excluded.

KS 93–95 deal with the same subject:

brahmahatyāsurāpānasteyagurvaṅganāgame
anyeśu cātipāpeṣu prativādī na dīyate ||
manuṣyamāraṇe steye paradārābhimarśane
abhakṣyabhakṣane caiva kanyāharaṇadūṣaṇe ||
pāruṣye kūṭakaraṇe nṛpadrohe tathaiva ca
prativādi na dātavyaḥ kartā tu vivadet svayam ||

Kane's translation is as follows:

> A representative [of plaintiff or defendant] is not allowed in [charges of] brahmana murder, drinking wine, theft, sexual intercourse with the wife of an elder [incest] and in other grave sins. A representative should not be given in man slaughter, theft, indecent assault on another's wife, eating forbidden food, kidnapping of a maiden and intercourse with her, harshness..., counterfeiting coins and measures, and also in sedition; but the man himself [the plaintiff or defendant] should engage in the dispute.

The interesting point here is that all representatives (*prativādin*), i.e., including the *niyukta*, are excluded in a number of specific lawsuits. The nature of these lawsuits may have its importance for our conclusions; we shall return to it below.

Vyāsa

One of Vyāsa's stanzas (DhK 1.134) comes very close to the one by Bṛhaspati quoted above:

kulastrībālakonmattajaḍārtānāṃ ca bāndhavāḥ
pūrvapakṣottare brūyur niyukto bhṛtakas tathā

Although this stanza does not seem to have been particularly popular with the commentators (it occurs only in few medieval compilations), it provides us with a new element: the payment of the representative. Unfortunately, again two interpretations are possible. The representatives "who may speak up for women of good family, children, madmen, idiots, and disturbed persons, concerning the plaint and the defense," are either *bāndhava* ("a relative"), *niyukta* whom we have met with above, and *bhṛtaka* ("a person receiving a remuneration"), or *bāndhava* ("a relative"), and *niyukta bhṛtaka* ("an appointed person who receives a remuneration"). In the latter case the relative, who is unpaid, is opposed to the *niyukta* who earns a salary. In our view the more faithful interpretation is: a relative, a *niyukta*, and a *bhṛtaka*. In that case we do not learn anything new about the *niyukta*, and about the term *bhṛtaka* we can merely say that it is connected with *bhṛti* ("salary").

Finally, we must mention two verses by Pitāmaha (DhK 1.133):

pitā mātā suhṛd vāpi bandhuḥ saṃbandhino 'pi vā
yadi kuryur upasthānaṃ vādaṃ tatra pravartayet ||
yaḥ kaścit kārayet kiṃcid niyogād yena kenacit
tat tenaiva kṛtaṃ jñeyam anivartyaṃ hi tat smṛtam ||

which were thus interpreted by Scriba (1902):

The king should conduct a lawsuit when the father, the mother, a friend, relative, or a servant appear [as representatives].

Whenever somebody appoints another person to act in his behalf, it is as if the act was done by himself, and it cannot be annulled.

The first stanza is unambiguous: the king should allow a party to be represented by his father, mother, friend, or relative. But the second stanza, following after the first, again allows various interpretations. Either it means that any one of those referred to before, when acting through *niyoga*, acts in the other person's name. Or it indicates that anybody speaking for anybody else through *niyoga* is his real representative. In that case, *niyoga* does not refer to an "appointment" given to a specific class of representatives, but it suggests that anybody can be anybody's *niyukta*.

Commentaries and Nibandhas

Pitāmaha's verses conclude our survey of the available materials on representation as far as the ancient Dharmaśāstras are concerned. To these we might now add the medieval materials drawn from the commentaries and *nibandhas*. However, after a careful examination of the Sanskrit texts, we decided not to include these materials, since they do not add any really new data to those already discussed. None of the commentaries or *nibandhas* quotes all relevant passages from the older treatises. Even those that cite most of them try to adapt them into a coherent system, a task that was not easy and that led to highly varied results. Inasmuch as we have tried to provide all possible interpretations for the Dharmaśāstra passages we are confident that we have included all interpretations proposed by the commentators. The latter would be important for our purpose only if they showed a definite development in one direction or another, e.g., in the direction of gradual recognition of real lawyers. This is not the case; here as elsewhere the commentators did not aim at introducing any novelties. Their sole purpose was a correct interpretation of the ancient texts as such.

Arthaśāstra

Instead of quoting from the commentaries and *nibandhas*, we shall briefly refer to two *Arthaśāstra* passages. Kauṭilya has no reference at all to the representation in the court. The only text which is partly relevant is (3.20.22):

devabrāhmaṇatapasvistrībālavṛddhavyādhitānām anāthānām
anabhisaratām dharmasthāḥ kāryāṇi kuryuḥ,

i.e. in R.P. Kangle's translation:

> The judges themselves shall look in to the affairs of gods, Brahmins, ascetics, women, minors, old persons, sick persons, who are helpless, when these do not approach [the court]. (1963: 2.293)

This faithful rendering makes it clear the Sternbach went too far when, in connection with this text, he spoke of the judges as "official legal advisors" (1965: 1.324–25).

The situation is completely different in the *Śukranītisāra*. Here we are provided with a long passage dealing with the representation in the court. In G. Oppert's edition (Madras 1882) the text runs as follows:

vyavahārānabhijñena hy anyakāryākulena ca
pratyarthinārthinā tajjñaḥ kāryaḥ pratinidhis tadā (4.5.108)
apragalbhajaḍonmattavṛddhastrībālaroginām
purvottaraṃ vaded bandhur niyukto 'thavā naraḥ (109)
pitā mātā suhṛd bandhur bhrātā saṃbandhino 'pi vā

yadi kuryur upasthānaṃ vādaṃ tatra pravartayet (110)
yaḥ kaścit kārayet kiṃcin niyogād yena kenacit
tat tenaiva kṛtaṃ jñeyam anivartyaṃ hi tat smṛtam (111)
niyogitasyāpi bhṛtiṃ vivādāt ṣoḍaśāṃśikīm
viṃśatyaṃśaṃ tadardhaṃ vā tadardhaṃ ca tadardhikam (112)
yathā dravyādhikaṃ kāryaṃ hīna hīna bhṛtis tathā
yadi bahuniyogī syād anyathā tasya poṣaṇam (113)
dharmajño vyavahārajño niyoktavyo 'nyathā na hi
anyathā bhṛtigṛhṇantaṃ daṇḍayec ca niyoginam (114)
kāryo nityo niyogī na nṛpena svamanīṣayā
lobhena tv anyathā kurvan niyogī daṇḍam arhati (115)
yo na bhrātā na ca pitā na putro na niyogakṛt
parārthavādī daṇḍyas syād vyavahāreṣu vibruvan (116)
manuṣyamāraṇe steye paradārābhimarśane
abhakṣyabhakṣane caiva kanyāharaṇadūṣaṇe (119)
pāruṣye kūṭakaraṇe nṛpadrohe ca sāhase
pratinidhir na dātavyah kartā tu vivadet svayam (120)

B.K. Sarkar's translation of verse 108 reads (1914):

> Representatives have to be appointed by the plaintiff and defendant who do not know the legal procedure or who are busy with other affairs.

One important word in the text remains untranslated; the representative should be *tajjña* ("knowing it"). It is tempting to have *taj* ("it") refer to *vyavahāra* ("legal procedure") in the first line, and to say that whenever a party is not an expert on such matters. If this is the case, the verse comes very close to describing a class of professional lawyers. Sarkar himself must have had this in mind when he added the following note to his translation: "Pleaders and lawyers are to represent such persons and state their cases as their own." However, we cannot accept that *taj* refers to *vyavahāra*. From verse 118, in which a son is to be accepted as a representative of his father on the condition that he is *tajjña* ("knowing it"), it is clear that *tajjña* means "knowing the circumstances of the case." In other words, the representative, to be acceptable, must have known the party whom he represents intimately enough to be fully aware of the circumstances in which the contested activities took place. This element will be an important one in our conclusions below.

Verses 109, 110, and 111 bring nothing new; apart from a few insignificant variant readings they are identical with the passages from Bṛhaspati and Pitāmaha quoted above.

Much more important are the following four verses (112–115). This is Sarkar's translation:

> The lawyer's fee is one-sixteenth of the interests involved (i.e., the value defended or realised). Or the fee is one-twentieth or

> one-fortieth, or one-eightieth or one hundred and sixtieth portion, etc. Fees ought to be small in proportion as the amount of value or interest under trial increases. If there be many men who are appointed as pleaders in combination they are to be paid according to some other way. Only the man who knows the law and knows the Dharma should be appointed [as pleader]. The king should punish the pleader who receives fees otherwise. The pleader is to be appointed not at the will of the king. If the pleader acts otherwise through greed he deserves punishment.

The only problem in these verses is the expression "who receives fees otherwise" in 114. Sarkar duly states the two possibilities in a note to this translation: "He may be punished if he takes exorbitantly or if he practices without knowing the law, etc." After what has been said in the former half of the stanza, we would be inclined toward the second alternative, with Kane: "if the representative takes wages without knowing these" (1930–62: 3.158–59). However, the first alternative should not be excluded either: if 112cd–114ab are a more recent insertion into the text (we shall return to this in our conclusions), the latter part of 114 originally belonged together with the former part of 112. In that case "otherwise" means: 'otherwise than one sixtieth part."

Verse 116 is identical with NS Introduction 2.23, and verses 119 and 120 correspond to KS 94–95.

Besides the points which we had become familiar with from the Dharmaśāstras, we do find in the *Śukranītisāra* a number of new and interesting elements: (1) representatives are appointed by parties who are *vyavahārānabhijña* ("who do not know the rules of legal procedure"); (2) the payment of the *niyojita* or *niyogin* is dealt with in great detail; (3) the *niyogin* is to be appointed by the party, not by the king. It hardly needs to be recalled that these elements played an important part in some of the opinions of modern scholars, quoted in our introductory remarks.

Interpretation

As indicated at the outset, the principal reason for raising the question of the existence of lawyers in ancient India was the awareness of the existence of such a professional class in modern Indian law, and in Western law as well. Consciously or unconsciously, the general background of the investigations on ancient Hindu lawyers —as of many other aspects of research on Hindu law— has been one of defensiveness. Was it possible that such a wonderful legal system as the one depicted by Dharmaśāstra did not include the institution of legal practitioners?

An excellent example of this tendency to look for "the germs of the modern profession of pleaders" is Kane who, notwithstanding his admirably sound approach, when translating KS 91, could not withhold from adding the note cited above. Even Judge S. Varadachariar, who completely denies the existence of a legal profession in ancient India, unwittingly takes up the defense of Hindu law. He cites examples of various other ancient legal systems that did not know a legal profession either. The underlying idea is that we should not really be surprised if ancient Hindu law had no lawyers, since contemporary systems were not more advanced. Characteristically, the enumeration of the other legal systems ends with the following statement: "In England there was no definite legal profession till more than a century after the Norman conquest" (Varadachariar 1946: 158–159).

Our approach to the problem is completely different. We maintain that such an apologetic attitude is not at all necessary. In our opinion, the ancient Hindu legal system was such that a legal profession not only did not exist, but that it was not called for and hardly could have existed. The reasons that led us to assume that a legal profession did not exist in ancient India are at least three in number.

First, the only term which might eventually have referred to professional lawyers was *niyogin*, *niyukta*, or *niyogakṛt*. We are not much concerned about the fact that there is no uniformity of nomenclature. There are other examples of well established institutions in ancient Hindu law which did not enjoy a uniform terminology. But we are concerned about the fact that not a single text on *dharma* pays any special attention to the *niyukta* as such. If he had been an important and constant element of the law court, we may be assured that some Dharmaśāstra would have elaborated on the qualifications to become a *niyukta* —e.g., under the heading *niyuktaguṇa*— and on the disqualifications which would have prevented a person from entering the profession. All participants in a lawsuit have been duly enumerated and described in the texts; the authors of the Dharmaśāstras would have fallen short of their duty if they had not paid attention to one of these participants, the "lawyer."

Secondly, if the main purpose of *niyoga* had been a more effective presentation of the party's interests than he could normally provide himself, we do not see why *niyoga* was so fiercely opposed in what we may call major criminal cases (see Rocher 1955). Kātyāyana's three stanzas (93–95) which deal with this aspect of the problem seem to indicate that, when it came to really serious cases, *niyoga* was prohibited. From this we must infer that *niyoga* was allowed only as long as the case was a less serious one. Whenever a party was unable or unwilling to appear in person, he was allowed to be represented by another person in minor cases; but he had to appear personally in major issues. Such a criterion is hardly compatible with the role of a professional legal adviser as we conceive it today.

This second argument leads us to a third, namely, that the existence of a class of professional representatives was not called for in Hindu law. This argument is undoubtedly the most important and most basic one. Administration of justice in ancient India was the concern of the king; it was part of *rājadharma*. Several rules in the Dharmaśāstra lay down that the king is responsible for punishing those who deserve to be punished. But it is added that the king is also responsible for the innocent not to be punished. Thus, e.g., MDh 8.126–128, in Bühler's translation:

> Let the [king], having fully ascertained the motive, the time and place [of the offense], and having considered the ability [of the criminal to suffer] and the [nature of the] crime, cause punishment to fall on those who deserve it.
>
> Unjust punishment destroys reputation among men, and fame [after death], and causes even in the next world the loss of heaven; let him, therefore, beware of [inflicting] it.
>
> A king who punishes those who do not deserve it, brings great infamy on himself and [after death] sinks into hell.

That means that the only person in the court who is responsible for the party's interests being safeguarded is the king, or, in practice, the king's representative: the chief judge. The fact that the parties might not be *vyavahārajña* ("acquainted with legal procedure") and hence unable to defend themselves properly, was no reason why they should be assisted by professional lawyers. The person responsible for the correct course of the case and for safeguarding the parties' interests was the king himself or whoever presided over the court in his name. It is in the light of these considerations that we must also understand the passage from Kauṭilya quoted above: parties who are unable to appear in person need not, therefore, be represented; the king himself is responsible for their interests.

So, as we see it, professional lawyers did not exist and could hardly have existed. To this we now want to add a restriction. As it so often happens in ancient Hindu law and in Hindu civilization generally, in the case of legal representation too, a certain degree of development must have taken place in the course of the centuries. We are not among those who believe that the more recent Dharmaśāstras were composed with the intention to innovate and depart from what had been said by the older ones. On the contrary, we are convinced that the more recent authors tried their very best to maintain the general scheme laid out by their predecessors. But in the meanwhile the actual situation did change, and every now and then authors of more recent Dharmaśāstras could not prevent themselves from reflecting some of these changes.

Thus, we believe that at an early date —let us roughly say at the time of the Dharmaśāstras— professional lawyers or, to be more precise, specialized *dharmaśāstrins* could not exist. The Indian sage in those days was a specialist in all of the texts related to a particular Vedic school. His specialized knowledge concentrated on a specific version of the Vedic *saṃhitā* and all its related texts: *brāhmaṇa, āraṇyaka, upaniṣad, śrautasūtra, gṛhyasūtra, dharmasūtra,* etc. There were no specialists on Dharmaśāstra, and, *a fortiori,* no specialists on laws that were part of it.

But the situation changed. The texts on *dharma* grew away from the Vedic schools. Gradually there may have come into being a specialized group of learned men whose main interest was *dharma,* and the various Dharmaśāstras as such.

Finally, as the amount of textual material increased, we may assume that certain experts, without detaching themselves from other aspects of Dharmaśāstra and from Hindu learning generally, accumulated a very specialized knowledge of one aspect of *dharma*: *vivāda* and *vyavahāra,* or, in modern terminology, law. It is very possible that at this stage the nature of legal representation (*niyoga)* also underwent a certain change. We do not want to exclude the possibility that, at that moment, in a number of cases legal competence played a role in the choice of representative. We are even willing to accept that Vyāsa refers to the very special circumstances in which the representative was paid for his services. However, no legal matters ever developed in to a professional group whose regular activities consisted in representing parties in court. The impression which we gather from the texts is that, even in cases where the representative was chosen because of his special competence on legal matters, and, *a fortiori,* in all other cases, the necessary condition for a person to represent a party was the existence, between the former and the latter, of a certain form of close personal relationship.

In this connection we want again to refer to the categories of *niyukta* enumerated by Nārada (Introduction 2.23): brother, father, son; and by Kātyāyana (92): slaves, menials, pupils, etc. Some of these terms were vague enough to be interpreted very broadly, and we can very well see how a party who wanted to be represented in the court may have tried to fit into these categories a person who knew the *dharma* rather than one who did not. But the main requisite was the personal relationship stresses by the Dharmaśāstras, not the representative's legal competence.

Moreover, our point of view offers an adequate explanation for the passage from Asahāya quoted by Kane and referred to above (cf. Sahay 1931: 4–6). Here again, it is true that the representative is said to be an expert on *dharma*, but nothing points to him as a professional lawyer. On the contrary, he is a friend of the family, and, as such, serves as their adviser. He does represent the party in court, but only after having assured the judge that he is entitled to do so because "he and his ancestors were friends of the family." In other words, he does not act as a professional expert (*vyavahārajña*) but as a person friend (*suhṛd*); the fact that the *suhṛd* is *vyavahārajña* is purely coincidental.

Finally, our interpretation is also confirmed by the above quoted passage from the *Śukranītisāra*, about which we want to add a few words here. There is no doubt that, of all sources examined in this paper, the *Śukranītisāra* is the one which most strongly reminds us of the modern legal profession. While commenting on it, Kane went as far as to say:

> The rule of Śukra made a near approach to the modern institution of the Bar and the fees prescribed by Śukra are similar to those allowed by the Bombay Regulation II of 1827 and by Schedule III to the Bombay Pleaders' Act (Bombay Act XVII of 1920). (1930–62: 3.290)

The main support for this statement is the detailed description of the representative's remuneration (verses 112–114). However, it has been so far overlooked that at least part of these verses (112cd–114ab), although reproduced in Oppert's edition, actually occurred in only one manuscript; they were missing in all four other manuscripts and in the printed version used by Oppert. We would not hesitate to consider them as a very recent addition to the original text. As a matter of fact, the entire *Śukranītisāra*, as we have it today, is of recent origin (Winternitz 1920: 3.531). It seems to us that it is a recent compilation, based upon a number of ancient rules —some of the verses identical with those quoted from the Dharmaśāstras— but into which were inserted certain very modern ideas, even ideas belonging to the colonial period. We would not be surprised if the rules about the representative's remuneration belonged to this latter category.

Under the circumstances it is all the more noteworthy, as Varadachariar puts it, "that it provides for the appointment of a 'representative' not only on the ground of the party's ignorance of Vyavahara but also on the ground of his being otherwise busy" (1946: 157.) Thus, even such a very recent text as the *Śukranītisāra*, which seems to have known a real professional class of lawyers and does not hesitate to incorporate it into the classical system of Dharmaśāstra, does not exclude the idea that the legal representative and the person represented by him should be linked by a personal tie of blood relationship, friendship, etc.

This, more that anything else, shows that this traditional element was a very important one, probably the most important of all in legal representation according to classical Hindu law.

24

Anumāna in the Bṛhaspatismṛti

There are instances in the Dharmaśāstras in which the term *anumāna* has the classical, technical meaning: "inference." For instance, in the KS:

ākāreṅgitaceṣṭābhis tasya bhāvaṃ vibhāvayet,
prativādī bhaved dhīnaḥ so 'numānena lakṣyate.

kampaḥ svedo 'tha vaikalyam oṣṭhaśoṣābhimarśane,
bhūlekhanaṃ sthānahānis tiryagūrdhvanirīkṣaṇam,
svarabhedaś ca duṣṭasya cihnāny āhur manīṣiṇaḥ. (385–86)

Kane translates the first stanza as follows: "(The judge) should discern the (real) intention (or mental state) from the outward manifestations (such as sweat, horripilation), the gestures (looking down at the ground, etc.) and physical movements; the litigant becomes a losing party and he is found out (to be so) by inference (from the signs mentioned above)." The possibility for the judge to derive conclusions from certain indications in the behavior of the parties to a lawsuit was known long before Kātyāyana: examples of *duṣṭalakṣaṇāni* are found in Manu, Yājñavalkya (2.13–15), Nārada (1.193–96), Viṣṇu (8.18), and others. The relevant passage from Manu is as follows:

bāhyair vibhāvayel liṅgair bhāvam antargataṃ nṛṇām,
svaravarṇeṅgitākārais cakṣuṣā ceṣṭitena ca;

ākārair iṅgitair gatyā ceṣṭayā bhāṣitena ca,
netravaktravikārais ca gṛhyate 'ntargataṃ manaḥ. (8.25–26)

This is Bühler's translation of the first stanza: "By external signs let him discover the internal disposition of men, by their voice, their colour, their motions, their aspect, their eyes, and their gestures." Manu merely mentions the term *liṅga*. It is clear, however, that the text envisages a process in which the observation of a *liṅga* leads to the establishment of a *sādhya*, to which the *liṅga* is related by *vyāpti*. In fact elsewhere Manu explicitly uses the term *anumāna* for a similar process:

yathā nayaty asṛkpātair mṛgasya mṛgayuḥ padam,
nayet tathānumānena dharmasya nṛpatiḥ padam. (8.44)

Bühler translates: "As a hunter traces the lair of a (wounded) deer by the drops of blood, even so the king shall discover on which side the right lies, by inference (from the facts)."

This paper concentrates on a few occurrences of *anumāna* in the BS where the term is used with a different meaning —which has not always been recognized. As is well known, the Hindu "lawbooks" distinguish various kinds of evidence that can be accepted in a law court. These types of evidence gradually developed into the following classical system:

		sākṣin
	mānuṣī {	*likhita, lekha, lekhya*
kriyā {		*bhukti, bhoga*
	daivikī {	*śapatha*
		divya

The only text that introduces a different term within the category of human evidence is BS:

sākṣilekhyānumānaṃ ca mānuṣī trividhā kriyā;
sākṣī dvādaśabhedas tu likhitaṃ tv aṣṭadhā smṛtam. (4.8; Jolly 5.18)

Assuredly, K.V. Rangaswami Aiyangar's reconstruction of the BS also quotes a stanza containing the three classical types of human evidence:

sākṣiṇo likhitaṃ bhuktir mānuṣaṃ trividhaṃ smṛtam,
dhaṭādyā dharmajāntā tu daivī navavidhā kriyā. (4.7)

Yet, there is no doubt that at least the first half of this stanza is an interpolation.[575] On the other hand, Bṛhaspati's inclusion

[575] I have not been able to trace the origin of this verse in the *nibandhas*. See also Renou 1963: 42.

of *anumāna* in the *mānuṣī kriyā* is no accident; it is confirmed by another well attested stanza:

likhite sākṣivāde ca saṃdigdhir jāyate yadi,
anumāne ca sambhrānte tatra divyaṃ viśodhayet. (4.17; Jolly 10.17)

The commentators have tried their best to bring Bṛhaspati's *anumāna* in line with the classical subdivision of human evidence. Two tendencies manifest themselves. First, Bṛhaspati's *anumāna* is said to be equivalent with *bhukti* in the other texts. Thus the *Nṛsiṃhaprasāda* (39): *anumānaṃ bhuktiḥ.* Second, and far more frequently, *anumāna* is given the technical meaning "inference"; it replaces *bhukti* because inference and possession have certain elements in common. Some commentators hold that *anumāna* is a generic term, and *bhukti* one of its species. Thus in the *Vyavahāratattva* (211): *anumānaṃ tu bhuktyādi*; in the *Smṛticandrikā* (3.121): *anumānaṃ bhuktir ulkāhastatvādiyuktiś ca*; and in the *Madanaratnapradīpa* (31): *atra bhukteḥ pṛthaganirdeśo 'numāne 'ntarbhāvāt.* The reason why *bhukti* is implied by *anumāna* is that possession is the *probans* from which the *probandum* ownership can be inferred. Thus, in the *Smṛticandrikā* (3.114): *anumānaṃ bhuktiḥ svatvānurūpakatvāt.* Even more clearly, Aparārka on YDh (2.22): *anumānaṃ bhuktis tayā bhoktur bhogye svāmyam anumīyate*; in the *Vyavahāraśiromaṇi* (14): *bhuktiḥ svatvahetubhūtakriyānumānam*; in the *Vyavahāranirṇaya* (73): *bhuktiḥ kaiścid viśeṣaṇair viśiṣṭā svatvahetuḥ sā tu krayasākṣilekhyādikam avyabhicārād anumāpayati.* Jolly follows the general trend in his translation of BS 4.8 (his 5.18): "Human evidence is threefold, as it consists of witnesses, writings, and inference…" and in that of 4.17 (his 10.17): "When a doubt arises with regard to a document or oral evidence, and when ratiocination also fails…"

I shall first show that *anumāna* in the BS is not a mere substitute for *bhukti* as a separate type of evidence, as is shown by the large number of stanzas —seventy in Rangaswami Aiyangar's collection— which the BS devoted to this subject. Even though the loss of the original text makes it impossible for us accurately to reconstruct its treatment of *bhukti*, we have proof that Bṛhaspati devoted a separate chapter to it, after the chapters on witnesses and written documents:

etadvidhānam ākhyātaṃ sākṣiṇāṃ likhitasya ca;
samprati sthāvare prāpte bhukteś ca vidhir ucyate. (7.22; Jolly 9.1)

Some of the oldest *nibandhas* (*Kṛtyakalpataru* 177, *Vyavahāramātṛkā* 341), the authors of which are most likely to have known the BS, open their discussions of *bhukti* with this stanza.

Moreover, unless the following stanza originally belonged to the KS (identical with KS 315, see also note 576 below), Bṛhaspati uses both terms in one and the same stanza. They occupy the extreme positions in a scale of four types of evidence, and are separated by witnesses and written documents:

anumānād guruḥ sākṣī sākṣibhyo likhitaṃ guru,
avyāhatā tripuruṣī bhuktir ebhyo garīyasī. (7.34; Jolly 9.32)

Jolly translates: "A witness prevails over inference; a writing prevails over witnesses; undisturbed possession which has passed through three lives prevails over both."

The fact remains that, if my interpretation is correct, BS 4.8 omits *bhukti* in the enumeration of human types of evidence. The obvious reason is that enumerations in Sanskrit texts are not necessarily exhaustive; they can be merely illustrative. A case in point is a similar situation in the NS. On one occasion the text lists two kinds of human evidence:

kriyā tu dvividhā proktā mānuṣī daivikī tathā:
mānuṣī lekhyasākṣibhyāṃ dhaṭādir daivikī smṛtā. (Mātṛkā 2.28)

Yet, elsewhere it exhibits the classical threefold division:

likhitaṃ sākṣiṇo bhuktiḥ pramāṇaṃ trividhaṃ smṛtam;
dhanasvīkaraṇaṃ yena dhanī dhanam avāpnuyāt. (1.69)

The commentators explained this discrepancy without difficulty. The *Smṛticandrikā* (3.114), for example, notes: *lekhyasākṣibhyāṃ bhuktyā ca proktā mānuṣīty arthaḥ bhukter api manuṣyasambandhitvāt*; similarly the *Sarasvatīvilāsa* (105): *lekhyasākṣigrahaṇaṃ bhukter apy upalakṣaṇaṃ tasyā api mānuṣasambandhitvāviśeṣāt.*

Next I shall show that *anumāna* in the BS does not have the usual technical meaning "inference." The term also occurs in the enumeration of the various sources of law on which a judge bases his decision:

dharmeṇa vyavahāreṇa caritreṇa nṛpājñayā:
catuṣprakāro 'bhihitaḥ saṃdigdhe 'rthe vinirṇayaḥ.

ekaiko dvividhaḥ proktaḥ kriyābhedān manīṣibhiḥ;
aparādhānurūpaṃ tu daṇḍaṃ ca parikalpayet.

samyag vicārya kāryaṃ tu yuktyā samparikalpitam,
parīkṣitaṃ tu śapathaiḥ sa jñeyo dharmanirṇayaḥ.

pramāṇaniścito yas tu vyavahāraḥ sa ucyate;
vākchalānuttaratvena dvitīyaḥ parikīrtitaḥ.

anumānena nirṇītaṃ caritram iti kathyate;
deśasthityā dvitīyaṃ tu śāstravidbhir udāhṛtam.

pramāṇarahito yas tu rājājñā nirṇayas tu saḥ,
śāstrasabhyavirodhe ca tathānyaḥ parikīrtitaḥ. (9.1–7; Jolly 2.18–24)

This passage distinguishes four different sources of law, each of which is again divided into two sub-groups:

1.	*dharma*	{	a.	*yukti, śapatha*
			b.	*pratipatti, divya*
2.	*vyavahāra*	{	a.	*pramāṇaniścita*
			b.	*vākchala, anuttaratva*
3.	*caritra*	{	a.	*ANUMĀNA*
			b.	*deśasthiti*
4.	*nṛpājñā*	{	a.	*pramāṇarahita*
			b.	*śāstrasabhyavirodha*

Another passage form the BS establishes the relative value of these four sources of law:

kevalaṃ śāstram āśritya kriyate yatra nirṇayaḥ,
vyavahāraḥ sa vijñeyo; dharmas tenāvahīyate.

deśasthityanumānena naigamānumatena ca
kriyate nirṇayas; tatra vyavahāras tu bādhyate.

vihāya caritācāraṃ yatra kuryāt punar nṛpaḥ
nirṇayaṃ, sā tu rājājñā; caritraṃ bādhyate tayā. (1.19–21; Jolly 2.25–27)

A combined interpretation of these two passages will, I hope, solve some of the controversies which they have raised (most recently Lingat 1962), and contribute to a better understanding of the term *anumāna* used in them. Stanza 1.19 gives a clear definition of the second source of law: *vyavahāra* (9.5). In this case the judge bases his decision on nothing but the written rules contained in the *śāstras*. Evidence gathered on this basis overrules evidence based on the first source of law: *dharma.* Even though I cannot enter here into a detailed discussion of all the four elements that constitute *dharma*, it clearly refers to cases in which the decision is based on some indications given by a supernatural power. For instance, if a party swears an oath and does not, within a certain number of days, become the victim of a calamity —inflicted by a supernatural power— it follows that he has spoken the truth. There are numerous rules in the texts stating that one should not resort to this kind of "divine evidence," if and when more earthly means of proof, such as witnesses, are available (e.g., YDh 2.22; KS 217–19). At the other end of the list, *nṛpājñā* "a royal decree" overrules the third source of law, and, *a fortiori*, the second and the first. The king —or his representative: the chief justice— shall use his own judgment in cases where the texts or the judges are at variance, and in cases in which no *pramāṇas* "valid means of proof" are available. The nature of the third source of law is clear from the terminology: *caritra* (9.6), *caritācāra* (1.21). It refers to accepted behavior which is not codified in the *śāstras*; in other words, valid custom. Here again, many rules in the Dharmaśāstras could be cited to show that unwritten custom overrules the written texts.

Anumāna belongs to the third type of source of law, and should be interpreted accordingly, irrespective of its regular meaning "inference." The fact that BS 9.6 is not clear in itself does not justify Jolly's translation: "When a sentence is passed according to the inference (to be drawn from circumstantial evidence), it is termed (a decision based on) custom. When it is passed according to local usages, it is termed another sort (of a decision based on custom) by the learned in law." Nor can I agree with his translation of BS 1.20: "When a decision is passed in accordance with local custom, logic, or the opinion of the traders (living in that town), the issue of the case is overruled by it."

In reality, the juxtaposition of °*anumānena* and °*anumatena* in BS 1.20 shows that we are dealing with "an agreement, that which has been agreed upon." In other words, *anumāna* in this passage derives from the root *anu* √*man* rather than *anu* √*mā*, and refers to unwritten custom which "has been agreed upon, has been accepted, is acceptable" by a certain category of citizens.[576] Hence its listing together with *deśasthiti* "regional custom" in BS 9.6.

[576] The only problem with this interpretation is BS 7.34, quoted earlier. Whereas according to 1.20 *anumāna* overrules witnesses, documents, and possession, 7.34 makes it less valid than these. Several hypotheses can be envisaged. Either Bṛhaspati did once use anumāna with the meaning pointed out at the beginning of this paper; or 7.34 is a pure arthavāda the sole purpose of which is to praise possession held for three generations. It is also possible that 7.34, which is identical with KS 315, originally belonged to the KS rather than the BS, and was erroneously attributed to the latter by the commentators. The same is true for BS 7.35 which, after having been quoted separately —perhaps anonymously— by some commentator, was later added immediately after 7.34 (see, e.g., *Kṛtyakalpataru* 181).

The constant interpretation of *anumāna* as "inference" even in cases where this interpretation is not warranted is an interesting phenomenon in itself. It shows that two identical nominal derivatives (*anumāna*) from two different roots (*anu* √*man*, *anu* √*mā*) can, ultimately, be connected by usage with one of the two roots only. *Anumāna* from *anu* √*mā* became so well established, that commentators and interpreters no longer thought of *anumāna* from *anu* √*man*, even when this meaning was as clearly suggested as in the BS.

The Hoshiarpur Vedic indexes seem to suggest that *anumāna* from *anu* √*man* is older than *anumāna* from *anu* √*mā*. The former occurs twice in the *Maitrāyaṇīyasaṃhitā*[577] and once in the *Kāṭhaka*,[578] whereas the latter is not attested in the Saṃhitās. The Brāhmaṇa volume again exhibits no occurrences of the latter, whereas the former is attested in the *Taittirīyabrāhmaṇa*[579] and *Taittirīyāraṇyaka*.[580] On the contrary, in the Upaniṣads and Vedāṅgas there is no longer any *anumāna* from *anu* √*man*, whereas *anumāna* from *anu* √*mā* becomes more and more prominent. Perhaps some of these cases, and others in later literature, ought to be reexamined in the light of the experience gained from the BS.

577 3.9.6 *adbhyo hy eṣa oṣadhībhyo juṣṭaṃ prokṣāmīti. yasyā eva devatāyai paśur ālabhyate tasyā enaṃ juṣṭam akar. anu tvā mātā manyatām anu pitety. anumata evainaṃ mātrā pitrā bhrātrā sakhyālabhate 'numānāvaha devān devāyate yajamānāyeti devatābhya evainaṃ nirdiśaty...* Cf. also 1.2.15.

578 37.2 *indro vai vṛtrāya vajram udayacchata taṃ dyāvāpṛthivī nānvamanyetāṃ tam etena bhāgadheyenānvamanyetāṃ vajrasya vā eṣo anumāno 'numatavajras suyātā iti.*

579 2.7.3.2–3 = *Kāṭhaka* 37.2, with minor variants, among which: *anumānāya* instead of *anumāno.*

580 1.2.1: *smṛtiḥ pratyakṣam aitihyam anumānaṃ catuṣṭayam etair; ādityamaṇḍalaṃ sarvair eva vidhāsyate.* Sāyana's commentary is characyeristic: *anumānaḥ śiṣṭācāraḥ; tena hi mūlabhūtaṃ śrutismṛtilakṣaṇam pramāṇam annmīyate.* He correctly interprets *anumāna* as 'valid custom', but derives it nevertheless —from *anu* √*mā.*

Part Four

Technical Studies of Hindu Law

25

Possession Held for Three Generations by Persons Related to the Owner

While a critical edition of the *vyavahāra* section of Gaṅgāditya's *Smṛticintāmaṇi* was being prepared, the following quotation of Bṛhaspati was found in the manuscripts:

bhuktis tripuruṣāt sidhyet pareṣāṃ nātra saṃśayaḥ |
anivṛtte sakulyatve sapiṇḍānāṃ na sidhyati ||

A comparison of the variant readings given in both K.V. Rangaswami Aiyangar's edition of the BS (75) and the first volume of the *Dharmakośa* (414) shows that the *Smṛticintāmaṇi* is the only *nibandha* having the readings underlined above. The second half of the *śloka* generally runs as follows:

anivṛtte sapiṇḍatve sakulyānāṃ na sidhyati ||

Thus, the question arose whether it was possible to preserve the reading found in the manuscripts of the *Smṛticintāmaṇi* or not. Since the general principle which we have adopted for selecting readings provides that variant readings in the manuscripts should be preserved if they afford good sense, even if they differ from the readings found in all other sources, the problem was reduced to an enquiry into the sense of the reading of the manuscripts and at the same time, by way of comparison, into the meaning of the reading found in the other *dharmanibandhas*. In view of this principle, the reading of the manuscripts had to be rejected in favor of the generally accepted version; the meaning of the latter, however, presents some difficulties, and it is the purpose of this paper to seek to explain them.

Jolly (1889: 310), who collected this *śloka* from Jīvānanda's edition of the *Vīramitrodaya* (221), translates it as follows:

> Possession held by three generations produces ownership for strangers, no doubt, when they are related to one another in the degree of a Sapiṇḍa; it does not stand good in the case of Sakulyas.

Jolly, then, makes the following distinction:

1. Possession held by three generations does not create ownership when held by strangers related to the owner in the degree of *sapiṇḍa*.

2. Possession held by three generations does create ownership when held by people who belong to the owner's *sakulya*s.

To his translation Dr. Jolly adds the following footnote:

> Sapiṇḍaship in this rule includes four generations; the term Sakulya is used to denote more remote relations.

Jolly is undoubtedly right in saying that *sakulyatva* indicates a more remote relationship than *sapiṇḍatva* which includes only those direct descendants who offer the *piṇḍa*s. But it is very difficult to understand how in his translation strangers can be related in the degree of *sapiṇḍa*. Furthermore, people who are in the degree of *sapiṇḍa*, i.e., more closely related people, would obtain ownership after three generations, whereas more remote relatives would not.

The following quotations are at variance with this interpretation:

1. KS 335 (ed. P.V. Kane):

sanābhibhir bāndhavaiś ca yad bhuktaṃ svajanais tathā |
bhogāt tatra na siddhiḥ syād bhogam anyatra kalpayet ||

In the above the following distinction is made:

(a) Possession (held for three generations) does not create ownership for a *sanābhi*, *bāndhava* and *svajana*.
(b) It does create ownership for other people.

2. A verse of Pitāmaha:

bhuktir balavatī tatra bhoktā yatra paro bhavet |
svagotre bhoginām bhuktir na śaktā śāśvatī nṛṇām ||

The distinction made here is:

(a) Possession held for three generations does not create ownership in *svagotra* (cf. *Smṛticandrikā* 2.158: *svagotre svamātāpitṛbandhuṣu*).
(b) It does create ownership for other people.

3. BS 7.44, which is generally quoted together with the verse under consideration:

asvāminā tu yad bhuktaṃ gṛhakṣetrāpaṇādikam |
suhṛdbandhusakulyasya na tadbhogena hīyate ||

This verse makes the following distinction:

(a) Possession held for three generations does not create ownership for a *suhṛd*, *bandhu*, and *sakulya*:
(b) [It does create ownership for other people.]

Therefore, the persons for whom possession held for three generations does not create ownership according to the above verses may be summarized as follows:

KS 335	: *sanābhi, bāndhava, svajana;*
Pitāmaha	: *svagotra;*
BS 7.44	: *suhṛd, bandhu, sakulya.*

As to the reason underlying these distinctions, the following explanations are found in the commentaries:

1) In the *Vyavahāramātṛkā* (351), BS 7.43, 44, 46, is introduced as follows:

yatra hetvantarād eva saṃnihitasyāpy upekṣā saṃbhavati na tatra puruṣabhuktiḥ pramāṇam ityāha bṛhaspatir eva —

2) The *Smṛticandrikā* (2.158) comments as follows on KS 335 (quoted here under the name of Vyāsa):

tatra sanābhyādibhoge saṃbandhitvenopekṣāsaṃbhavāt.

3) Medhātithi (962, ed. Mandlik) on MDh 8.147:

yat kiṃcid daśavarṣāṇi saṃnidhau prekṣate dhanī |
bhujyamānaṃ parais tūṣṇīṃ na sa tal labdhum arhati ||

makes the following remark: *paraiḥ* cannot be interpreted as "except for *jñātisaṃbandhinaḥ*" as some people do, since this would make the rule uncertain, because of the difficult question *ke jñātayaḥ ke vā saṃbandhinaḥ*? On the other hand, *paraiḥ* cannot mean "all other people," because then it would serve no purpose. Consequently, *paraiḥ* must mean "except between husband and wife and between father and son, since one's wife, father, and son are all called oneself (*tatra hy ātmany api vyapadeśo 'sti*)."

Besides these commentaries, there is also the following verse to the same effect, generally ascribed to Vyāsa (exceptionally also to Bṛhaspati) and quoted in the *nibandhas* with a few variant readings which are, however, irrelevant here:

> *dharmakṣayaḥ śrotriye syād bhayaṃ syād rājapuruṣe* |
> *snehaḥ suhṛdbāndhaveṣu bhuktam etair na hīyate* ||

From these four quotations the reason why some persons are an exception to the general rule according to which possession held for three generations should make them the owners of the things possessed, has been made clear: because these persons have some relation to the real owner, out of affection the latter is likely to overlook the fact that they are possessing his property. In other words, there is a presumption that during the whole time the objects have actually been possessed by the owner himself.

We now return to Jolly's translation of BS 7.43 to which we took exception above. The owner is bound to have less affection for a *sakulya* than for a *sapiṇḍa*. Consequently, he is less likely to overlook possession held by a *sakulya* than possession held by a *sapiṇḍa*, a *sakulya* never being considered to be the self of the owner. We must, therefore, expect that the idea to be expressed in BS 7.43 is that possession held for three generations does not create ownership for a *sapiṇḍa*, whereas it does for a *sakulya* and all other people. And not only should this idea be expected, but a faithful and literal interpretation of the verse under consideration actually conveys this idea. The commentary of the *Kṛtyakalpataru* (189), which perhaps could not make the point clear without the preceding analysis, may be introduced now to support this: *anivṛtte sapiṇḍatve iti. sapiṇḍatve vidyamāne saty api tripuruṣabhuktau sakulyānāṃ bhujyamānaṃ svaṃ na bhavatīty arthaḥ.*

As a matter of fact, BS 7.43 distinguishes two categories of possessors:

1. *sakulyas*, and
2. all other people.

The former are again subdivided:
1a) *sapiṇḍas*, and
1b) all other *sakulyas*.

Altogether there are three groups of people which can be indicated by three areas (see chart below):

A: *sapiṇḍāḥ*;
B (including A): *sakulyāḥ*;
the whole remaining area C: *pare*.

For persons belonging to area A possession held for three generations does not create ownership; for persons belonging to areas B and C it does.

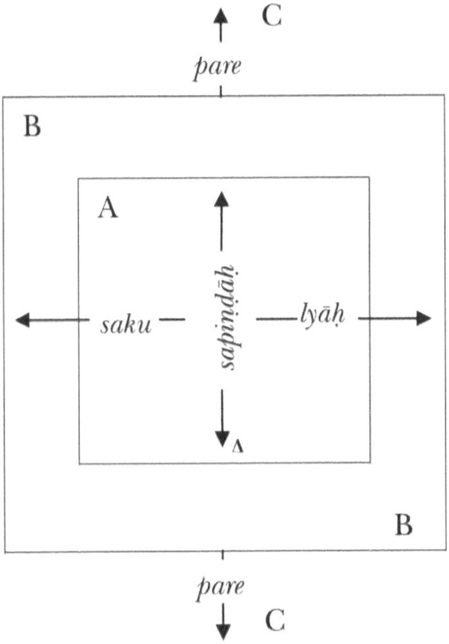

The *śloka* for Bṛhaspati should, then, be translated as follows: "Possession held for three generations creates ownership for other people, no doubt; it does not for those *sakulyas* who are not beyond the degree of *sapiṇḍa*." In connection with this a short note should be added with regard to the following statement of Dr. P.V. Kane:

> BS (SBE vol. 33 p. 310 v. 11) and KS 335 (both quoted by Aparārka p. 637, V.P. p. 166) state that what is enjoyed by a man's agnates and cognates and his own people does not pass to their ownership by their mere possession: one should regard possession (as leading to ownership) in cases other than these. (Kane 1930–1962: 3.326–27)

As far as the verse of Bṛhaspati is concerned (i.e., BS 7.44 quoted above) a minor restriction should be made to this assertion. It should be borne in mind that this verse does not constitute the general rule as might be inferred from the unqualified words "what is enjoyed." As a matter of fact, it constitutes an exception to the general rule contained in the verse discussed in this paper (BS 7.43). Whereas, in general, possession held for three generations does not create ownership for *sapiṇḍas* only, with regard to possession of certain specific objects enumerated in BS 7.44, viz. *gṛhakṣetrāpaṇādikam*, the category of people for whom possession does not create ownership is broadened so as to include also *suhṛd*, *bandhu*, and *sakulya* (in general).

26

The Vīramitrodaya *on the Right of Private Defence*

Aan Prof. Dr. B. Faddegon bij zijn 80e verjaardag

After a chapter "On Punishments," in which all kinds of general principles about punishments are set out, the Indian Penal Code sets forth another chapter to "General Exceptions" to criminal liability. The commentators of the Code arrange the 31 sections of this chapter IV under seven headings: judicial acts (ss. 77.78), mistake of fact (ss. 76.79), accident (s. 79), absence of criminal intent (ss. 81–86.92–94), consent (ss. 87–90), trifling acts (s. 95), and private defence (ss. 96–106).[581]

The treatment of the last item in this enumeration starts as follows (s. 96):

> Nothing is an offense which is done in the exercise of the right of private defence.

And in the following sections the extent and the limitations of this exception to criminal liability are dealt with in detail.

This is the situation as created under British influence by the Indian Penal Code, i.e., Act XLV of 1860. But the Indian people did not await the interference of British jurists to recognize the right of private defence. Anybody who has studied criminal law in the ancient and medieval texts of Hindu law will have met this principle adopted unreservedly.

Nevertheless there are two other provisions of modern Indian law, which we want to refer to in this respect:

[581] I used the 16th ed. of the Indian Penal Code (Rancchodas and Thakore 1939: 53).

(a) Section 2 of the Indian Penal Code states that

> *Every person* shall be liable to punishment under this Code and not otherwise for every act of omission contrary to the provisions thereof of which he shall be guilty within India.

(b) Recently in the Constitution itself among the Fundamental Rights article 14 has been inserted as follows:

> The State shall not deny to any person equality before the law or the equal protection of the laws within the territory of India.

By applying the latter regulations to the above mentioned s. 96 of the Penal Code, we may draw the conclusion, that nowadays no exception to the right of private defence can be introduced on the mere ground of an individual's distinctive quality, such as rank, creed, or caste, adhering to the persons to whom s. 96 would eventually be applicable.

And so we touch upon a point, in which ancient Hindu criminal law is at variance with modern Indian law. Indeed, though Hindu law recognizes the right of private defence in general, the authors of digests have always been troubled about the question, whether the said principle was to prevail or not when it came into conflict with another great principle of Hindu law, according to which no corporal pain may be caused to a Brāhmaṇa.

Formulated more concretely, the problem is as follows: does the murder of an assassin cause criminal liability or not in the special case in which the latter is a Brāhmaṇa?

We do not want to summarize here the different views which have been held about the question; the reader may find this exposition elsewhere.[582] We just want to translate and explain the treatment of the subject in one *nibandha*, viz., in the *Vyavahāraprakāśa* of Mitramiśra's *Vīramitrodaya*,[583] not only because it deals with the problem most exhaustively by quoting the views of the authors whose works have been lost themselves, but also because it contains a few very complicated pages of Dharmaśāstra literature, of which an analysis may be useful to students of Hindu law.

[582] See, e.g., Kane 1930–1962: 2.150–51, and 2.517–18. With regard to *Vīramitrodaya* the author says: "The *Vīramitrodaya* has a long disquisition on this subject but space forbids us from giving even a brief summary of it." Kane has also treated the matter in notes to his edition of the *Vyavahāramayūkha* of Bhaṭṭa Nīlakaṇṭha (1926: 416–22).

[583] The edition used for the translation is: *Vīramitrodaya* by MM. Pandit Mitra Miśra, edited by Pant and Bhandari, 1906–1932, and especially *fasc, lasc*, 385 (14–21). Incidentally, for other readings, we refer to *Vira Mitrodaya, a treatise on Hindu Law*, by Mitra Mishra (ed. Vidyasagara 1875).

Generally the point is referred to on the occasion of the treatment of the conflict between texts of Arthaśāstra and Dharmaśāstra. And so also does Mitramiśra. But in his opinion, the right to kill a Brāhmaṇa acting as an assassin is not a good example of this conflict. So, at first he gives another instance, which is really fit to be quoted for the purpose. It may be rendered as follows:

An example, however, of the contradiction (between Arthaśāstra and Dharmaśāstra) is this:

(a) Arthaśāstra:[584]

Since it is better to gain a friend than to acquire gold or land, one shall apply oneself on getting the former. (YDh 1.351)

(b) Dharmaśāstra:

(Let the king examine procedure) according to Dharmaśāstra, free from anger or lust. (YDh 2.1)

And sometimes, when a *catuṣpāt*-procedure[585] is going on, a contradiction between both (teachings) arises. If for fraud etc. the victory is adjusted to the one who, by whatever means of proof,[586] merits to be defeated, the (king), being highly qualified for friendliness, gains a friend; if this (victory) is adjudged to the other (party), he obtains *dharma* and he is free from *adharma*, because he speaks truth.

In this case only the *dharma* is to be looked for, without taking account of the acquisition of a friend: because (a) although both authoritative texts[587] have the same value while originating from the same author,[588] of both directives, viz., *artha* and *dharma*, the *dharma* is the most valid one; (b) even if the comparative power

[584] By Arthaśāstra the author understands not a rule taken from the very works on politics (*arthaśāstra, nītiśāstra*); but certain texts from authentic works on *dharma* (see the text of *Vīramitrodaya*, 14, lines 6–7). This was also the case in *Mitākṣarā* on YDh 2.21.

[585] For procedure being *catuṣpāt*, i.e., "having four feet," see Kane 1930–1962: 3.259–61.

[586] Here the word "*pramāṇa*" has its juridical meaning of "a means of proof" before a court. Otherwise, see next note.

[587] Contrary to the foregoing note, here "*pramāṇa*" means a particular concrete text of Dharmaśāstra or Arthaśāstra, whereas "*prameya*" refers to Dharmaśāstra or Arthaśāstra in general and *in abstracto*. This distinction may relate to the analogous use of both terms in the Nyāya-system, as "means of cognition" and "objects of cognition" respectively.

[588] In the case under consideration, e.g., both texts are taken form the YDh.

of the authoritative texts is inverted,[589] in the *śiṣṭākopa*-rule[590] this (inversion) is settled to be annulled according to the comparative strength of the directives; how much more if the comparative power is the same!

Therefore, for taking *artha*, which is contrary to *dharma*, Āpastamba prescribes the twelve years' penance, which (in the following text) is hinted at by the word "this":[591]

> This very (twelve years' penance is ordained) for him who, when *dharma* and *artha* come into conflict, chooses the latter. (ĀpDh 1.9.24.23)

After this example the author proceeds to reject another instance, which was given for the same purpose by one or more predecessors who are not called by name. The only thing we can say about it, is, that the theory referred to was anterior to Viśvarūpa and Vijñāneśvara also. Indeed, in these authors' commentaries on YDh, too, its propriety as an example of the conflict between Dharmaśāstra and Arthaśāstra had been disapproved.

The headings, which the reader will find for the different parts of the text, are not Mitramiśra's. They are added for the sake of introducing some clearness into the long digression.

Translation

A. Circumscription of the problem

Yet, some people give the following example of the contradiction between Arthaśāstra and Dharmaśāstra:

(a) Arthaśāstra:

> One may slay without hesitation an assassin who approaches (with murderous intent), whether (*vā*) (he be one's) spiritual teacher, a

[589] Although the authors of *nibandhas* generally hold that any rule of Dharmaśāstra is equally authoritative, here Mitramiśra inclines to the view according to which the authoritativeness of the textbooks on *dharma* is different. As early as Aparārka on YDh 2.21 (628) we meet with the statement, that in a conflict between MDh and another *smṛti* the former prevails. For a modern application of the principle, see, e.g., *Balusu* v. *Balusu*, 26 I.A. 129,130 (1899).

[590] Mitramiśra refers to PMS 1.3.5–7, which are differently interpreted by the commentators. Our author seems to read in them the intention, that the value of a particular precept does not depend on its own intrinsic value, but on the principles which it is derived from. For an analogous interpretation, see Kumārila *ad locum*.

[591] The word *etat* indeed refers to the twelve years' penance, which had been mentioned before in ĀpDh 1.9.24.20.

> child or (*vā*) an aged man, or (*vā*) a Brāhmaṇa deeply versed in the Vedas. By killing an assassin the slayer incurs no guilt, whether (he does so) publicly or secretly; in this case fury (*manyuḥ*) recoils upon fury (*manyum*). (MDh 8.350–51)

Fury (*manyuḥ*) kills fury (*manyum*), but not a man another man: this is an explanatory text (*arthavāda*).
Also:

> In a fight one may slay (*jighāṃsīyāt*) an assassin who knows the whole Veda, though (*api*) he approaches with murderous intent; by that (act) one (does) not (incur the guilt of) a slayer of a Brāhmaṇa.[592]

"One may slay" (*jighāṃsīyāt*) means: one may approach (*iyāt*), desirous of killing (*jighāṃsin*). Etc.

> An incendiary, a poisoner, the one having a weapon in his hand, a thief of goods, a thief of a field or of a wife: these are the six[593] (kinds of) assassins. (VaDh 3.16)

The separate mention[594] of the theft of a field, though it be included in the theft of goods, must be understood as follows: (a) the thief even of a small field obtained by a royal grant, and (b) (the thief) of larger goods (the theft of which) causes deprivation of the means of livelihood —the thief of such (goods) is an assassin.
Also:[595]

> The one who has raised a sword, poison or fire, the one who has raised his hand for an imprecation, the one who kills by an incantation contained in the *Atharvaveda*,[596] and the one who acts as a traitor towards the king. (KS 802)

[592] This *śloka*, corresponding to VaDh 3.17, is ascribed to KS by Vma (241), and to VySm by Aparārka (1042) who also quotes the reading *bhrūṇahā* for *brahmahā*.

[593] With regard to the limitative word "six," Sca (which ascribes this *śloka* to VaDh) remarks: "The number six is used here because the most notorious kinds of assassins, who serve as examples, are six in number; its intention is not to be exhaustive, because in this world other kinds of assassins are known" (3.731). And to support the latter statement he quotes the two *śloka*s which immediately follow in our text.

[594] The author wants to reply to the objection, that the presence in the same text of both words "the thief of goods" and "the thief of a field" might cause the defect of *pauṇaruktya* (repetition).

[595] This *śloka* and the next are quoted as KS by both Sca III (731) and Vma (241).

[596] In his edition of Vma (416) Kane noted, that "there are numerous hymns in the *Atharvaveda* which are employed against enemies, e.g., 1.19; II.19; III.1–2 (which hymns are styled *mohanāni* in the *Kauśikasūtra*); 8.108; etc."

"A traitor": the one who notifies the king of backbiting the carrying over of which necessarily causes danger to the life (of another person).

> The one who violates (another man's) wife, the one who is occupied in finding out vulnerable points: all those and the like without any exception (*sarvān eva*) one has to consider as assassins. (KS 803)

"Those and the like": by these words is meant: those inflicting upon their (victims) pain equal to death.[597]

As (the other kinds of assassins) are mentioned together with the words "the one who has raised a sword," only those persons are assassins who are engaged in the act, but not those whose acts are finished or (those whose acts) have not yet begun.

The (foregoing) group of texts, which prescribe absence of guilt for killing these persons if they act as assassins, are Arthaśāstra, their purpose being self-defence.

(b) Dharmaśāstra:

> This expiation has been prescribed for unintentionally killing a Brāhmaṇa; but for intentionally slaying a Brāhmaṇa no atonement is ordained. (MDh 11.90)

This is Dharmaśāstra, because it has no visible object.

When, notwithstanding the patent contradiction between these (two teachings), one fails to decide which of both is to be avoided and which is avoiding (the other one) according to the (respective) general and particular character as relating to assassins and non-assassins respectively, only the general teaching has force, because of its being Dharmaśāstra. But the prescription of the absence of guilt in case of the murder of an assassin, which only relates to the absence of a punishment by the king —because no mischief is committed by the one who, self-defence in any other way being impossible, commits the murder of an assassin with the intention of self-defence— is without force, because of its being Arthaśāstra.

B. The theory of Vijñāneśvara

On this point Vijñāneśvara:[598]

(a) Because the words "*guruṃ vā*, etc." (i.e., MDh 8.350–51),

[597] Contrary to the next *śloka*, the verses prescribing absence of guilt are *dṛṣṭārtha*, their "visible object" being self-defence.

[598] According to YMtā on YDh 2.21 it is not suitable to quote MDh 11.90 and MDh 8.350–51 as examples of a contradiction between Dharmaśāstra and Arthaśāstra

which prescribe absence of guilt for killing an assassin, are supplementary to other injunctions, and (b) because it is known that the word *api*, the word *vā*, etc.,[599] undermine (their having) the power of an injunction —these (texts) do not have an independent meaning.

On the contrary, having started as follows:

> Twice-born men may take up arms when (they are) hindered (in the fulfillment of) their duties. (MDh 8.343ab)

(Manu continues:)

> In their own defence, in a strife for the fees of officiating priests, and in order to protect women and Brāhmaṇas; he who (under such circumstances) kills in the cause of right, commits no sin. (MDh 8.349)

(In this way Manu) prescribes absence of punishment, because no guilt occurs in him who kills an assassin by means of a non-malicious weapon (under the following circumstances:) in self-defence, in his protection of fees, etc., and the implements of sacrifices, etc., and in a contest caused[600] by helping women and Brāhmaṇas.

And as an *arthavāda* hereof he says: *guruṃ vā*, etc. (i.e., MDh 8.350–51).[601] It is evident, that by the rule (of reasoning) "*a fortiori*," viz., "although they may not be killed at all, no guilt occurs in him who kills spiritual teachers, etc., if they act as assassins; how much more in him who (under the same circumstances) kills other persons than these!" only a eulogy is meant; so one may not derive (from it) the permission to kill spiritual teachers, etc.

And if those texts are explained as having an independent meaning, there is also a contradiction with the text of Sumantu:

respectively. As a matter of fact, there is no contradiction: because both cannot have the same object, any reflection on their comparative strength is in vain.

[599] Such words as *api* and *vā* lay down a syntactical connection with a preceding injunction (*vidhi*); the sentence containing them is a mere eulogy (*arthavāda*). Śabarasvāmin on PMS 1.2.7 says: "There is syntactical connection between the injunction and the eulogy, because the words (of the two sentences) are interdependent" (trans. Jhā: 55). The instance from the *Taittirīyasaṃhitā*, given by Śabara, is also mentioned by Kane (Vma 418), who also quotes a similar example from the *Subodhinī*.

[600] We seriously suspect the accusative °*nimittam*; YMtā itself has the locative *strībrāhmaṇahiṃsāyām*. So we prefer to read °*nimitte*.

[601] Vijñāneśvara was not the first author to hold this theory. Before him, Medhātithi on MDh 8.350, too, had done so.

> One does not incur guilt by killing an assassin, except (if the latter is) a cow or a Brāhmaṇa.

And as to the text of Manu:

> Let him never offend the teacher who initiated him, nor him who explained the Veda, nor his father and mother, nor (any other) guru, nor cows, nor Brāhmaṇas, nor any men performing austerities (MDh 4.162) —

if the murder of spiritual teachers, etc., who act as assassins, would not give rise to guilt, this (text), too, would be contradictory to it (i.e., to MDh 8.350–51), because this (text), too, has a good sense only if its meaning is as follows: the murder of Brāhmaṇas, etc., being also forbidden by other texts,[602] these persons may not be killed even if they act as assassins.

C. Objections to Vijñāneśvara's theory

One can object (to Vijñāneśvara): because in your opinion MDh 8.350, etc., being intended as a eulogy, does not prescribe[603] absence of guilt for (killing Brāhmaṇas acting as) assassins, the counter-exception (*pratiprasava*),[604] according to which the absence of guilt does not attach (to this case), is meaningless. So (in order that MDh 4.162 shall have a good sense) its real meaning is to state that the guilt is greater when one kills them, if they are not assassins (than if they are assassins). (In this way) there is no contradiction between both (as you pretended above).

(To this objection we reply:) not so. Vijñāneśvara's intention is, to bring about that (texts such as MDh 8.350–51, etc.) intend a counter-exception, and this against him in whose opinion these texts lay down (an exception to the general rule forbidding murder, viz.,) absence of guilt in case of a murder of an assassin.

Now one may object (again): in this opinion, too, in like manner there is some contradiction,[605] because in your opinion MDh 4.162 necessarily implies greater guilt.

[602] Kane (Vma 417): "In the Vedic passage *na hiṃsyāt sarvāṇi bhūtāni* there is a general prohibition against killing any being."

[603] *°pratipādakatvāt*. Read: *°apratipādakatvāt* (so does the Jibananda-edition).

[604] This refers to MDh 4.162. If MDh 8.350 intends to prescribe guilt in case of killing a Brāhmaṇa behaving as an assassin, the express statement of the *pratiprasava*, i.e., of the reestablishment of guilt in the particular case in which the assassin is a Brāhmaṇa, to this end is useless.

[605] Although the first objector says that all contradiction disappears if the texts are understood according to his opinion, the second objector pretends that even so there is still some contradiction.

(To this objection we reply:) you are wrong, because, spiritual teachers, etc., being mentioned in both (texts),[606] the attachment of a contradiction is unavoidable.

In the opinion of Vijñāneśvara, however, there is no failure. (He correctly reasons as follows:) with respect to spiritual teachers, etc., the text of Manu (i.e., MDh 4.162) means an exception to the absence of punishment by the king and to the small penance, which according to the *arthavāda* (i.e., MDh 8.350–51) are both to be allotted in the case of the slaughter of any assassin but spiritual teachers, etc., behaving so, which (slaughter) was committed unintentionally and in self-defence by a person who did not intend to hurt (and who acted in this way) because any other way to escape failed.

In reality, however, (one should explain as follows:) (a) with regard to teachers, etc., the text of Manu (i.e., MDh 4.162) means an exception to the absence of guilt and to the absence of penance and punishment by the king in case of the murder of an assassin, as prescribed by the text "Twice-born men may take up arms" (MDh 8.348); (b) and the absence of guilt in case of the murder of an (ordinary) assassin must be considered applicable to cases wherein it is impossible to save oneself by any other means such as flight, etc.

Otherwise two things arise which are both equally illogical: (a) the text (i.e., MDh 4.162) has no visible object;[607] (b) the (general) rule which prescribes guilt in case of violence is eliminated (by exception) too widely with respect to the guilt of (killing) an assassin.[608]

And the idea which underlies the *arthavāda* (i.e., MDh 8.350–51), prescribing absence of guilt with regard to spiritual teachers, etc., i.e., for killing them if they act as assassins; lesser guilt and a smaller penance than for killing them if non-assassins; and no punishment by the king —this is a *guṇavāda*[609] contributing to eulogy.

[606] This word is not to be understood "in both opinions," i.e., "in my opinion and in Vijñāneśvara's" (so does the footnote to the text, p. 16), but "in both texts," i.e., in MDh 4.162 and MDh 8.350–51. The author wants to say: since in these texts both punishment and non-punishment are prescribed for the murder of a spiritual teacher, etc., a contradiction is unavoidable.

[607] Here the word *adṛṣṭārthatvam* can only be a synonym of *ānarthakya* on *vaiyarthya* (text p.16, 11) and is to be considered as a defect, whereas on p. 15, 17 it means a good quality which makes a text belong to Dharmaśāstra.

[608] Argument (b) above taught, that even a common assassin may not be killed on the mere ground that he attacks his victim. This would be too wide an extension of the exception to the general rule which forbids any corporal hurt. Exceptions are to be construed strictly: so an assassin may be killed only if another means of escaping is impossible.

[609] The *guṇavāda* is defined as follows by the *Śabarabhāṣya* on PMS 1.210: "It is

D. The theory of Bhavadevabhaṭṭa

On this point Bhavadeva says the following.
From the text of Vasiṣṭha:

He who slays an assassin learned in the Veda and belonging to a noble family, does not incur by that act the guilt of the murderer of a learned Brāhmaṇa; (in) that (case) fury recoils upon fury (VaDh 3.18),

it is evident, that the texts about spiritual teachers, etc. (i.e., MDh 8.350–51), because of their consistency in meaning with this (VaDh quotation), though the words *vā*, etc., are explicitly mentioned, are real *pratiprasava*-rules,[610] but not mere *arthavādas* (as YMtā says).

And (against the other argument of Vijñāneśvara) there is no contradiction between (MDh 8.350–51 being a *pratiprasava*-rule and) the text of Sumantu:

ātatāyivadhe na doṣo'nyatra gobrāhmaṇāt[611]

because (the author of YMtā is wrong, since) he did not recognize the (adequate) division of (this) *sūtra*.

For (the said words of Sumantu are not one *sūtra*, but) they are three *sūtras*:

(a) firstly:

In case of the murder of an assassin no (guilt);

(b) secondly:

Guilt elsewhere;

(c) thirdly:

One shall perform a penance by bathing from a cow or a Brāhmaṇa.

an indirect or figurative way of saying things when, for the purpose of eulogizing a certain thing, we praise another thing related to it" (trans. Jhā: 58).

[610] According to Bhavadeva, MDh 8.350–51 are no mere eulogies having another meaning than that which they verbally express; they really mean, that even spiritual teachers, acting as assassins, may be killed without any punishment or even guilt being incurred. The *pratiprasava* is an exception to the general prohibition of killing living beings.

[611] This text of Sumantu is read differently in Sca (3.729): *ātatāyivadhe na doṣo'nyatra gobrāhmaṇād yadā hataḥ prāyaścittaṃ syāt.* Vma (240) has the same reading as our text, p. 16, 3–4.

In this respect Sumantu proceeds as follows:

(a) He lays down the penance for the murder of a Brāhmaṇa, and prescribes that this very penance is also to be performed by him who is related to the (murderer).

(b) Then he says:

In case of the murder of an assassin no (guilt).

The meaning of (this) first *sūtra* is: if the murder of a Brāhmaṇa is effectuated when he is acting as an assassin, no penance.

(c) (The meaning) of the second (*sūtra*),

Guilt elsewhere,

is: (the slayer incurs) guilt in all cases wherein the victim did not act as an assassin.

(d) (The meaning) of the third one is as follows:

(The words) "One shall perform a penance by bathing from a cow or a Brāhmaṇa" prescribe bathing as a part of the penance. (Of the two cases mentioned) herein, Vyāsa determines the bathing from a cow in this way:

The anointment with the water from the horns of cows equals (bathing in) all holy places which are heard of in the three worlds.

There is no text to prescribe (a particular bathing) with respect to the word Brāhmaṇa. The bathing caused by it is accompanied by the muttering, etc., of the *aghamarṣaṇa*,[612] etc. And (the *dvandva*-compound) "*gobrāhmaṇāt*" is a singular.[613] Therefore one administers the penance (only) by means of bathing caused by a cow or caused by a Brāhmaṇa, and not by means of whatever bathing in general.

Also as to the text of the *Bhaviṣyapurāṇa*:

[612] By this name the hymn *Ṛgveda* 10.190 is indicated. By reciting it one obtains the same result as by bathing in all holy places (see BDh 3.5.7). For a detailed description, see Gampert 1939: 57–58.

[613] Mitramiśra refers to the "*ekavadbhāvaprakaraṇa*" of the *Mahābhāṣya*, which comprises the commentary to Pā 2.4.1–16. That *gobrāhmaṇāt* belongs hereto, shall be inferred from Pā 2.4.11: (*ekavacanaṃ*) *gavāśvaprabhṛtīni ca*."

The one who, even intentionally, has killed a Brāhmaṇa deeply versed in the Vedas who attacked him, shall perform the highest penance called the twelve years' (penance), o hero!

This (text), too, does not relate to killing an assassin, because the word "attack" does not indicate "death." So the sense is this: although he even intentionally kills the one who is especially occupied in taking away limbs such as eyes, etc.,[614] (the murderer) shall perform only a twelve years' penance.

E. Objections to the theory of Bhavadeva

This is not right for the following reasons.

(a) Refutation of Bhavadeva's interpretation of Sumantu.

If we want to save the suitableness of the dictum,[615] the text of Manu (i.e., MDh 4.162) is established to mean the abolishment of the absence of guilt (which is prescribed for slaying other assassins) in (the particular) case of killing teachers, etc., who act as assassins.

The text of Sumantu, while having the same basis as this (text of MDh), is to be explained only according to the division (accepted) by the YMtā. If the division is made according to your proposal, it results that the words "guilt elsewhere" are meaningless.

Arguments:

a') In explaining "from a cow or a Brāhmaṇa" as "the ablative (*gobrāhmaṇāt*) means that (the cow and the Brāhmaṇa) are the causes[616] of bathing," the word "cow" which is to indicate a part (of a cow) results in a metaphor (*lakṣaṇā*)[617] indicated by means

[614] Bhavadeva resorts to the etymological explanation of the verb *praharati* as *prakarṣeṇa harati*. This etymological analysis (*yoga*) will be rejected by Mitramiśra in favor of the popular meaning (*rūḍhi*).

[615] Bhavadeva does not take in account MDh 4.162 as relating to teachers, etc., acting as assassins. To this conception Mitramiśra objects, that, if MDh 4.162 was to forbid to kill Brāhmaṇas in general, i.e., when they are not assassins, this text might have been omitted as well. As long as the victim is not an assassin, one may not kill anybody at all: this prohibition is not restricted to teachers, etc. Consequently MDh 4.162 suffers from the defect of *vaiyarthya*, from a lack of *yukti*. Now, a dictum of MDh is to be presumed to be free from these faults: under the influence (the power °*balāt*) of these considerations, another explanation is to be accepted.

[616] According to Vārtika 1499 and the *Mahābhāṣya* on Pā 2.3.23: *hetau*, the cause may be expressed by any case.

[617] For a definition of *lakṣaṇā*, see, e.g., *Kāvyaprakāśa* (BS 60: 25–26).

of the horn which is part (of it),[618] because it is not the cow (itself) which is the cause of bathing.

b') (The foregoing explanation of the ablative) would give rise to the error of diffuseness, because the Brāhmaṇa being a *jñāpaka*-cause, it is an inconsistency to take the cow to be a *kāraka*-cause.[619]

(b) Refutation of Bhavadeva's interpretation of *Bhaviṣyapurāṇa*.

As to (Bhavadeva's) explanation of the *Bhaviṣyapurāṇa*, this is also highly outside the real meaning, because it is opposite to the *rathakāra*-rule[620] to use the etymological meaning, i.e., "especially taking away limbs such as eyes, etc.," for the root "*praharati*," which popularly means corporal pain beginning with beating and ending with killing.

Besides, the only reason for the smallness of the guilt which gives rise to a diminution of penance, which (smallness) is referred to by this and other similar texts, (and which, according to Bhavadeva, is to be explained as follows):

> in the case of killing a Brāhmaṇa who is occupied in tearing off limbs such as eyes, etc., even intentionally, the penance for killing a Brāhmaṇa is only the twelve years' one, but neither double compared with the penance for a Brāhmaṇa-murder committed non-intentionally, nor the penance ending with death,

[618] The accumulation of the words *lakṣaṇā* and *lakṣita* is highly subject to suspicion the more the Jibananda-edition omits *tadudakalakṣaṇāyām*.

[619] A *jñāpaka*-cause and a *kāraka*-cause are two different figures of speech. Says the commentary on *Kāvyaprakāśa* 114 (BS 60: 408): *yatra hetuḥ kārakarūpas tat kāvyaliṅgaḥ* (trans. Jhā: "poetical reason"), *jñāpakahetau tv anumānālaṃkāraḥ* ("inference").

[620] This refers to PMS 6.1.44–50 (= *adhikaraṇa* 12). With regard to the text: "The *Rathakāra* should install the fire during the rains," the question arises as to who is meant by the word *Rathakāra*: is he to be a member of the three higher castes, or is he distant from these?

The trouble is caused by two foregoing statements:

(a) the fire is to be installed by the Brāhmaṇa, Kṣatriya and Vaiśya in spring, summer and autumn respectively;

(b) the Śūdra is completely excluded from the installation of the fire.

The *pūrvapakṣin* argues: from statement (b) it is evident, that the *Rathakāra* shall belong to one of the three higher castes. But the members of these castes in general having to install the fire in other seasons than the *Rathakāra*, the latter is to be understood in its etymological meaning: the author means those members of the three higher castes who exercise the profession of chariot-makers, i.e., *ye ratham kurvanti*. The *siddhānta*-view rejects this etymological explanation in behalf of the common use of the word in the *smṛti*-literature, i.e., the son of a *māhiṣya* and a *karaṇī*, who in their turn are the offspring of a Kṣatriya and a Vaiśyā and of a Vaiśya and a Śūdrā respectively.

is the killed person's being an assassin, because (a') there is no other (reason), and (b') when a person has a sword in his hand, his status as an assassin is real.

And in the same way the assertion "this (text) does not relate to (killing) an assassin" is absurd:

a') because, (if so,) the contradiction with the texts of Saṃvarta and the *Bhaviṣya*, viz.,

> In the case of an assassin no guilt, excepted (if the latter is) a cow or a Brāhmaṇa; if one kills a cow or a Brāhmaṇa, one shall perform a penance,

and

> One should never slay a cow or a Brāhmaṇa, even if they are intent upon killing,

is difficult to be eliminated in any way;

b') and because it cannot be granted, that the text about spiritual teachers, etc., (i.e., MDh 8.350–51), which is supplementary to another injunction and which contains the words "*api*," etc., opposing to the power of an injunction, would be a *pratiprasava*-rule.

(c) Refutation of Bhavadeva's interpretation of MDh 8.350–51 as a *pratiprasava* rule.

And one may not speak as follows:

a') because it is impossible that the words of Vasiṣṭha, etc., which are not supplementary to (other) injunctions, are *arthavādas*, the texts "*guruṃ vā*, etc." (i.e., MDh 8.350–51), too, are not *arthavādas* for the (mere) reason that they are supplementary to other rules;

b') or, admitting these (texts) to be *arthavādas*, this is no harm, because the realization of the meaning aimed at by us is accepted by other texts which are (equally) dependent.

For (against this we might set up another equally) far-fetched explanation as these (texts) on which you found your conclusion of the absence of guilt too are contrary to a greater number of other texts which lay down guilt for killing assassins such as cows and Brāhmaṇas, in order to assume that they have the same origin with the latter, it is suitable to say that they prescribe a small fault: because otherwise the contradiction is not to be eliminated.

F. The theory of Śūlapāṇi

Śūlapāṇi, however,

(a) describes the text of Bṛhaspati,

> In case of the murder of an assassin the murderer does not incur sin at all; the one who kills another, who approaches with murderous intent, does not commit a mischief. (BS 23.17)

as being the authority for asserting that killing an assassin does not give rise to any guilt;

(b) explains that absence of guilt means prohibition of penance, whereas absence of mischief means prohibition of punishment;

(c) minutely observes that, because it is based on the *śruti*-precept "one shall defend oneself against any (assailant)," its real meaning is, that it relates to cases in which it is impossible to save oneself also by flight, etc.;

(d) also points to the texts of Manu: "*guruṃ vā*, etc." (i.e., MDh 8.350–51), as supporting it;

(e) suspects the above texts of Saṃvarta: "*ātatāyiny adoṣaḥ*, etc.," and the text of the *Bhaviṣya*: "*kṣiṇvānam*, etc.,"[621] as being contradictory to it.

(And after all this) he puts forward a distinction as follows: an assassin who, in comparison with his murderer, is superior in asceticism, knowledge, caste and family, such a Brāhmaṇa, a spiritual teacher, etc., may not be killed; an equal while an inferior one may be so killed.

In this way Kātyāyana:

> In case of an assassin superior (to his victim) in asceticism, knowledge and birth, it is not proper to kill him; but it is no sin to kill him, if he is inferior in this respect. (KS 801)

Therefore it is said in the *Gītā*:

> Really sin would accrue to us, if we killed these assassins. (1.36cd)

"These" means: by killing Bhīṣma, etc., who are highly superior to us, then if they be assassins, sin would indeed accrue to us.

In abstaining from killing superior assassins Bṛhaspati even prescribes a reward:

[621] These texts have been quoted above, in the refutation of Bhavadeva's interpretation of *Bhaviṣyapurāṇa*.

> If one does not kill a superior assassin who possesses good conduct and knowledge, who has murderous intents, one obtains the reward of an *aśvamedha*-sacrifice. (BS 23.18)

Consequently, when abstaining from killing a superior assassin, (two results are equally possible: a compulsory result, viz.,) avoiding the sin which accrues to slaying him, and (an optional result, viz.,) the reward of an *aśvamedha*-sacrifice, because of the rule of connection and disconnection.[622]

Although there is an explicit precept: "one may slay a spiritual teacher deeply versed in the Vedas,"[623] and although in this case the said distinctive statement[624] (*vyavasthā*) is difficult to be held, because the spiritual teacher is no doubt superior to his student —nevertheless even in this case this distinctive statement is really well-founded, because compared with his spiritual teacher himself, the student, too, may be more elevated with regard to good qualities such as family, knowledge, asceticism, etc.

A cow, however, though acting as an assassin, may not be killed anyhow, because there is no contradictory text.[625]

And although these assassins (as described above) may be killed, the absence of sin refers to the murder of those (among them) who are at the very moment occupied in the performance of the act which is essential to the state of an assassin,[626] but not also to (the murder of) those who have abstained form the act, (this) according to the text of Kātyāyana:

> No sin attaches to him who kills wicked men that are ready (to kill

[622] This is the title of PMS 4.3.5–7 (= *adhikaraṇa* 3), as translated by Jhā. With regard to the *Agnihotra* in general, which is performed without any particular purpose, one shall offer curds. Then again we read, that one shall offer curds for the very limited purpose of obtaining efficient sense-organs. The conception of the *pūrvapakṣin*, according to which both cases refer to different curds, is rejected: in fact both sacrifices are to be performed by means of identical curds. So, it appears, that it is the same material (*dravya*), that is used for the essential, compulsory (*nitya*), as well as for the nonessential, contingent (*kāmya*) act. The same theory holds good in our case. Abstention from killing a superior Brāhmaṇa (this corresponds to the "*dravya*" in the sacrifice) has both an essential result (i.e., absence of guilt), and a non-essential result (i.e., the reward of an *aśvamedha*-sacrfice).

[623] This refers to texts such as MDh 8.350.

[624] i.e., the distinction, that an inferior assassin may be killed, but not a superior one.

[625] Such as there are contradictory texts with regard to Brāhmaṇa-assassins, e.g., MDh 350–51, etc.

[626] This is a second restriction to the permission to kill an assassin. As a first restriction it was said, that the assassin shall be inferior to his slayer; now another limitation is added: even if the assassin is inferior, he is to be killed only at the very moment of his attack.

another); but when they have abstained from their attempt, they should be captured and not killed. (KS 800)

G. Objections to the theory of Śūlapāṇi

This explanation, too, is not capable of standing a test. For, (on the one hand,)

(a) an exception to the guilt ascertained by the prohibition "one shall not kill" is settled in case of assassins by means of the words *śastraṃ dvijātibhiḥ*, etc. (i.e., MDh 8.348);
(b) by way of an *arthavāda* of it, it is said: *guruṃ vā*, etc. (i.e., MDh 8.350–51);
(c) with respect to cows and Brāhmaṇas this (guilt) is reestablished by the texts of Manu, Sumantu, Saṃvarta, and the *Bhaviṣya.*

(Now, on the other hand,) because all texts have their good meanings, (one shall reason as follows:) taking in account the high rank of the state of a teacher, a Brāhmaṇa, etc., (which terms are) used by the texts of Manu, etc., it is suitable that the text of Kātyāyana: *ātatāyini cotkṛṣṭe*, etc. (i.e., KS 801), too, has nothing but the same meaning with them, but it is not restricted as if relating to the most elevated teachers, etc., among these: because the elevation procured by the state of a Brāhmaṇa, etc., is implied also by the words "as to asceticism, knowledge, and birth" (in KS 801).

Besides,[627] when you say that an assassin of a higher caste may not be killed by a man of a lower caste, the word "these" occurring in the *Gītā*[628] supporting it, the exception to the absence of

[627] The criterion for the admissibility or the inadmissibility of killing an assassin is, that the latter should be inferior or superior to his slayer respectively. Consequently a Brāhmaṇa, who occupies the highest rank among all castes, may never be killed: his slayer cannot but be inferior to him. (This is the general statement: *sāmānya*).

On the other hand you say, that Brāhmaṇa-assassins may not be killed only if they excel through asceticism, etc. (This is the special statement: *viśeṣa*).

The case in which the *viśeṣa* does not annul (this would be *paryudāsa*), but only restricts the *sāmānya*, is called *upasaṃhāra*. Both statements retain their full validity. So much for the abstract reasoning. Now, there are certain texts which prescribe absence of guilt for killing Brāhmaṇa-assassins in general. Conclusion: Śūlapāṇi's explanation is wrong! It causes the latter group of texts to suffer from *ānarthakya*. For the distinction between *paryudāsa* and *upasaṃhāra*, see, e.g., *Arthasaṃgraha*, section 88: *upasaṃhāro hi tanmātrasaṃkocārthaḥ…paryudāsas tu tadanyamātrasaṃkocārtha iti bhedāt.*

[628] *gīta°*. With the Jibananda-edition we shall read *gītā°*, because it refers to the verse of the *Bhagavadgītā* quoted above.

guilt in case of the murder of an assassin is accepted by you only according to the comparative elevation (of both parties).

Now, because the state of a Brāhmaṇa, etc., in general is placed in front (of the scale of castes), (by reasoning) in that way (set out in the foregoing paragraph) the texts which make exception to it[629] would be meaningless:

(a) because we have to do with a restriction —for, where both have a good meaning, such as in the case of the Mitravindā sacrifice,[630] there the special case is assumed to be a restriction of the general statement—;

(b) because you acknowledge the very absence of guilt in case of the murder of this (Brāhmaṇa) who does not occupy the highest position[631] (among the members of his caste).

The fact, that on the ground of the only text of Kātyāyana the many texts such as "*guruṃ vā*, etc." (i.e., MDh 8.350–51), which you approve to be *pratiprasava*-rules,[632] imply only (Brāhmaṇas) of inferior rank, is nothing but another proceeding resulting in their being meaningless.

Or, if (you maintain that in your theory) it is possible that all texts are consistent (by explaining them as follows): "after a *pratiprasava* has been made based on the state of a cow, a Brāhmaṇa, etc., the text of Kātyāyana teaches a higher degree of fault in accordance with their elevated rank —" (you shall also accept the logical conclusion of this statement, viz.,) the acceptance of a split of the power of the texts corresponds to the acceptance of an object of that split.

(In this case) there should also be a higher degree of reward, if one abstains from killing a more elevated person, because of the connection and disconnection.

[629] i.e., those texts in which it is said, that the slayer of a Brāhmaṇa-assassin does not incur sin.

[630] Mitravindā is an ectypical sacrifice, which is mentioned by the commentators on PMS 10.8.17–19 (= *adhikaraṇa* 9). There is a general statement, without reference to any sacrifice: "One should recite seventeen Sāmadhenīs." Again, with regard to certain ectypical sacrifices such as Mitravindā, etc., the same precept occurs. The question arises: what is the meaning of the reiteration of the number seventeen with regard to these particular ectypes? The right solution is, that the declaration relating to the Mitravindā, etc., is supplementary to and to be taken along with the previous isolated injunction. (See *Śabarabhāṣya*, trans. Jhā: 2048–49.)

[631] *utkṛṣṭa°*. Read: *anutkṛṣṭa°*. According to Śūlapāṇi the texts such as MDh 8.350–51, which prescribe absence of guilt, refer to assassins who are inferior to their slayers.

[632] In this respect Śūlapāṇi agrees with Bhavadeva: both hold, that MDh 8.350–51 are to be taken in their literal meaning, and not as having their intention contrary to the meaning they verbally express (so did YMtā).

In this case, too, the word *aśvamedha* does not have its literal meaning: because (if so,) the (texts relating to) other (cases) would have no object.

Or (it should be that, because of the identity with the non-arising of the guilt caused by it, the overcoming of the Brāhmaṇa-murder is used figuratively with the meaning of the abstaining from the murder consisting merely in a fault smaller than the fault caused by it.

But in this hypothesis the word "reward" is out of place. Because, if anything forbidden is abstained from, non-arising of guilt is not a reward. So the foregoing explanation is better.

Or one shall consider it so, that the (texts relating to) other (cases) are not deprived of an object, because here, too, the reward of the *aśvamedha* is partly present.

Besides —because in the texts of Kātyāyana, Devala, etc., which you considered as prescribing absence of guilt for the murder of Brāhmaṇas, etc., who act as assassins, the words "although he knows the whole Veda," "even if he is a Brāhmaṇa," etc., illustrate their elevation of rank— how can the text of Kātyāyana: *ātatāyini cotkṛṣṭe,* etc. (i.e. KS 801), which relates to the fault for (killing a Brāhmaṇa of) an elevated rank, be proper for cleaning up the contradiction?

And as to the text of Devala, which you quote as an instance:

> The one who kills an assassin who approaches with his weapon raised, even if he is a Brāhmaṇa (*bhrūṇaḥ*), would not be a Brāhmaṇa-murderer; if he did not kill him, he would be a Brāhmaṇa-murderer,

and as to its interpretation: *bhrūṇaḥ*:[633] especially the most elevated Brāhmaṇa; the prescription of guilt has the intention of a restrictive injunction (*niyama*)[634] —this is highly absurd: because nobody at all is considered to be guilty when he does not kill a Brāhmaṇa; on the contrary, there is simply absence of guilt when he kills him. Consequently one must explain (the text of De-

[633] Kane (Vma 419) notes that the word *bhrūṇa* ordinarily means "a child in the womb, embryo"; but Sca takes it to mean Brāhmaṇa, and Vma explains it as *uttamabrāhmaṇaviśeṣa* (in fact it was not Mitramiśra, but Śūlapāṇi who did so!).

[634] Mr. Jhā defines a *niyama*-injunction as follows: "The Niyama-vidhi or Restrictive Injunction, which lays down the doing of a certain act for a certain result, in preference to other acts leading to the same result; e.g., 'The corn should be threshed,' this threshing being the one method selected out of a number of the methods of removing the chaff from the grains" (1942: 197). See, e.g., the same definition in the *Arthasaṃgraha,* section 74. Śūlapāṇi says, that if a Brāhmaṇa approaches with murderous intent, two alternatives are possible: either to kill him, or not to do so. Because in the latter case one incurs the guilt of a Brāhmaṇa-murder, it is preferable to kill him.

vala as follows): this is only an explanatory text (*anuvāda*) based on the injunction of protecting the own (body), viz., if self-protection is impossible otherwise, the (guilt for the) murder of a Brāhmaṇa (which is said to) attach to not killing him is really (the guilt of) suicide.

So, in the general line of our explanation, the text of Kātyāyana: *ātatāyini cotkṛṣṭe*, etc. (i.e. KS 801), must be considered either as having the same object as the texts of Sumantu, Saṃvarta, etc., or as aiming at a higher degree of guilt in accordance with their elevated rank, but not as a distinctive assignment (*vyavasthā*)[635] in a contradiction.

This may suffice: we already went too far.

H. Conclusion

For me, however, it is obvious, that, even if the texts "*guruṃ vā*, etc." i.e. MDh 8.350–51, really are *pratiprasava*-rules, they are not Arthaśāstra:[636]

(a) because, even the absence of an invisible fault being invisible, they have no visible object;

(b) and because, in these circumstances, the object merely being self-defence, no penance would be possible. And this is not a desirable conclusion (*iṣṭāpatti*),[637] because in the texts[638] "By that (act) one (does) not (incur the guilt of) a Brāhmaṇa-slayer," "In case of an assassin no guilt, excepted (if the latter is) a cow or a Brāhmaṇa; if one kills a cow or a Brāhmaṇa, one shall perform a penance," "Really sin would accrue to us," etc., both guilt and absence of it are clearly understood.

[635] The process of *vyavasthā* consists in explaining apparently contradictory texts as referring to different cases. With regard to killing a Brāhmaṇa who behaves as an assassin the texts are conflicting, in so far as part of them allows such an assassin to be killed, whereas another part forbids to do so. The process of *vyavasthā* explains this contradiction away by distinguishing Brāhmaṇas of a lower and of a higher rank respectively.

[636] Sense: even if texts such as MDh 8.350–51 state that one may kill Brāhmaṇa-assassins without being punished, this is not a sufficient reason to call them *arthaśāstra*.

[637] Another example of an *iṣṭāpatti* is mentioned in the *Arthasaṃgraha*, section 91. An *arthavāda* has a real meaning if one understands it to intend praise or blame; if understood in its primary meaning, it would be meaningless. And this meaninglessness is not an *iṣṭāpatti*, i.e., not a desirable conclusion, because the whole Veda necessarily has a good sense.

[638] For the texts referred to, see in the text of *Vīramitrodaya* (14, 29; 18, 7–8; 19, 6).

So, because in any opinion it is inconsistent to take this as an instance of the contradiction between Arthaśāstra and Dharmaśāstra, enough with the diffuseness of the considerations continuously connected with it. We return to our subject.

27

The Technical Term Anubandha *in Sanskrit Legal Literature*

In his book *Manu and Yājñavalkya* (1930: 83–84), when treating the term *anubandha* in its technical sense, K.P. Jayaswal proposes the meaning: "cause, motive" of an offense. He draws this conclusion from two sources: a passage from the *Mānava-Dharmaśāstra* and one from a pillar edict of Aśoka.

Nevertheless, in our experience, not only does the learned author's opinion not agree with a great number of sources other than those used by him, but in the said sources themselves the recorded meaning is open to serious objections.

We are not sufficiently acquainted with the language of Aśoka's edicts so as to be inclined to draw conclusions from them. Yet, below we shall venture an interpretation which is different from Jayaswal's. Before that, however, we want to make a few annotations on the meaning of *anubandha* in the legal texts.

We shall not maintain that this short note fixes the meaning of *anubandha* definitively; for this purpose all the texts on *vyavahāra* would have to be exhausted. The only thing we want to do is to deliver a limited contribution to circumscribing the meaning of the term.

The text on which Jayaswal has founded the meaning of *anubandha* is MDh 8.126: when inflicting punishment the king shall take into consideration:

(1) *anubandha*,
(2) *deśa* = place,
(3) *kāla* = time,
(4) *sāra* = the power or ability of the wrongdoer,
(5) *aparādha* = the offense.

The first thing we notice is that from this mere text of MDh no conclusion can be drawn about the meaning of the first factor *anubandha*. So, for an explanation we cannot but have recourse to the commentaries on MDh. Jayaswal refers to the *bhāṣya* of Medhātithi which, as printed in Mandlik editions, runs as follows:

> *tatra paunaḥpuṇyena pravṛttir anubandhaḥ pravṛttikaraṇaṃ vā anubadhyate prayujyate yena tasmin karmaṇi taṃ parijñāya kim ayam ātmakuṭumbakṣudravasā yena dharma uta saṃgena vā atha madyadyūtādiśauṇḍatayā tathā pramādād buddhipūrvaṃ vā paraprayuktasvecchayā vetyādir anubandhaḥ* |

We completely agree with Jayaswal in saying that Medhātithi mentions two quite different meanings:

(1) repetition of the offense,
(2) cause or motive of the offense.

Now, this distinction is all the more important because of the different or even opposite effects obtained in both cases. (1) If the term means "repetition," an offense attached by *anubandha* shall be punished more severely than if it was not; (2) if it means "cause, motive," the defendant may refer to the *anubandha* in order that his punishment may be lighter.

Against all this, however, when reading legal texts we were struck by another fact: as far as we know, Medhātithi is the only commentator to give this double meaning, whereas the other commentators unanimously have only one. And what is most remarkable in it is the fact that this only given meaning is the very one which was rejected by Jayaswal.

The other commentators on MDh 8.126 explain as follows:

(1) Sarvajñanārāyaṇa: *anubandhaṃ punaḥpunaḥkaraṇam*,
(2) Kullūkabhaṭṭa: *punaḥ punar icchāto 'parādhakaraṇam*,
(3) Rāghavānanda: *anubandhaṃ sakṛdasakṛdādyaparādhakaraṇam*,
(4) Govindarāja: *punaḥ punar icchāto 'parādhakaraṇam*.

We might even go further and compare a few *nibandhas*:

(1) *Vivādaratnākara* 634: *anubandho mandakriyāvṛttiḥ*,
(2) *Daṇḍaviveka* 65: *anubandho mandakriyānuvṛttiḥ*.[639]

For another argument for *anubandha* as "motive," Jayaswal draws on MDh 7.16. According to this text elements to be taken

[639] Compare also *Daṇḍaviveka* 36 about *aparādhaḥ sa dvividhaḥ anubandho 'nanubandhaś ca* | *tatrānubandho nāma punaḥ punar icchayā mandakriyākaraṇam* |

into consideration when inflicting punishment are:

(1) *deśa*,
(2) *kāla*,
(3) *śakti* = *sāra* above,
(4) *vidyā*.

On the basis of this text Jayaswal notes: "*vidyā* = knowledge or consciousness. The last element corresponds to *anubandha*. It thus undoubtedly refers to mentality."

If again we look up the commentators on MDh, we read what follows:

(1) Medhātithi: *vidyā vedārthaviṣayā*,
(2) Saravajñanārāyaṇa: *vidyām iti vedādipāṭhaśīlatayā daṇḍālpatārtham*,
(3) Nandana: *vidyā vedavittvam ityādirūpā*,
(4) Govindarāja: *vedādhyayanādi*.

From these quotations we may draw the conclusion that all interpretations unanimously understood *vidyā* as the accused party's versedness in the Veda and similar kinds of learning. *Vidyā* is "knowledge" indeed, but "knowledge" in the sense of "learning," not in the sense of "consciousness."

There is just one point in these quotations which is open to discussion, viz., the influence of *vidyā* on punishment. Yet, this point being irrelevant for the meaning of *anubandha*, we shall just mention it without solving the problem here. Although according to Sarvajñanārāyaṇa the presence of *vidyā* is a cause of the punishment being lighter, we rather suppose it to be a cause of punishment being severer, by comparing it with such texts as MDh 8.337–38.

Anyhow, the commentaries on *anubandha* (MDh 8.126) and *vidyā* (MDh 7.16) sufficiently prove that even with Medhātithi both terms covered quite different things.

As Jayaswal points out, the list in YDh 1.367 (or 368) does not contain *anubandha*. To the factors enumerated there, the *Mitākṣarā* makes the following addition:

tathā buddhipūrvābuddhipūrvasakṛdasakṛdāvṛttyanusāreṇa ca |

Unfortunately, Vijñāneśvara does not indicate whether it is *anubandha* he wants to be added here or not, nor does he say whether, if so, *anubandha* refers to the offense being committed intentionally or repeatedly. In Rāghavānanda's opinion, at least, the latter meaning was meant: see above.

Jayaswal also refers to GDh 12.51. But the same remark as above holds good here: from the mere text of GDh the meaning of *anubandha* cannot be determined at all. And if we again appeal to the commentary, viz., Haradatta's *Mitākṣarā* (ed. Gokhale 1931: 101), once more we read: *anubandho'bhyāsaḥ*.

The last source Jayaswal refers to is AŚ 226.7 (2nd ed.: 228.7; ed. Shamasastry 1st ed. 1906, 2nd ed. 1919; Kangle 4.10.17) where the same problem is treated again.

If to all sources mentioned thus far we add ViDh 3.91 and VaDh 19.9, we obtain the scheme presented in Table 1 below.

First of all we shall remark that, in the presence of so great a number of various elements, there is no need to equate *anubandha* (MDh 8.126) and *vidyā* (MDh 7.16) merely because they are quoted along with a series of other elements which correspond in both lists. Even if we were allowed to treat both lists mathematically, we should not apply to them the principle: "when from two equal quantities two other equal quantities are subtracted, the remainders are also equal," because the minuends themselves are not necessarily intended to be equal.

Besides, with regard to AŚ particularly, we note *anubandha* and *kāraṇa* mentioned in the same list. If one of these terms is to mean the "motive" of the offense, this is certainly *kāraṇa*. And if we want to save *anubandha* from the fault of *vaiyarthya*, its meaning shall be different at least.

Table 1

MDh 8.126	MDh 7.16	YDh 1.367	AŚ 226	GDh 12.51	ViDh 3.91	VaDh 19.9
1 *anubandha*			5 *anubandha*	4 *anubandha*		
2 *deśa*	1 *deśa*	2 *deśa*	7 *deśa*			1 *deśa*
3 *kāla*	2 *kāla*	3 *kāla*	8 *kāla*			2 *kāla*
4 *sāra*	3 *śakti*	4 *bala*		2 *śakti*		
5 *aparādha*		1 *aparādha*	2 *aparādha*	3 *aparādha*	1 *aparādha*	
	4 *vidyā*					5 *vidyā*
		5 *vayaḥ*				4 *vayaḥ*
		6 *karma*				
		7 *vitta*				
			1 *puruṣa*	1 *puruṣa*		
			3 *kāraṇa*			
			4 *gurulāghava*			
			6 *tadātva*			
						3 *dharma*
						6 *sthāna*

Let us go further, and examine the meaning of *anubandha* elsewhere in AŚ. If by means of the *Index Verborum* we go through all passages where the word is used, most of them cannot help us much farther for the meaning we want to fix here. Nevertheless the similarity of two passages is obvious, viz., the passage under consideration *anubandhaṃ tadātvaṃ ca* (2nd ed.: 228.7, Kangle 4.10.17), and *tadātvānubandhau* (2nd ed.: 351.4, Kangle 9.4.24), the latter *dvandva*-compound being meant to indicate a couple of factors to be taken into consideration when a choice is to be made between equal profits.

If we look up Shamasastry's translation, we find: (1) 228.7: "the antecedent and present circumstances," (2) 351.4: "the present and future effects."

Is the mere fact of both terms being interchanged a sufficient argument for translating *anubandha* differently? We are inclined to deny this; at least we should prefer to take *anubandha* in both cases as a synonym for *āyatti*, which is generally opposed to *tadātva*. Now *āyatti* means (according to the dictionary of Monier-Williams): "stretching, extending; following or future time." So, with regard to profit one shall consider, whether a particular kind of profit entails or not any particular consequence in future; with regard to an offense one shall take into consideration, whether it "extends" or not because of an obstinacy towards it in the wrongdoer.

Only one other example can we draw from a *smṛti*, in which *anubandha* is used in another context. On BS 26.140[640]: "If a man makes a partition with his own consent but afterwards contests it, the king shall compel him to be content with his own share; the one who makes *anubandha* shall be punished," the commentators are unanimous in giving as synonyms for *anubandha*, "*nirbandha* or *āgraha*," which both mean "pertinacy, obstinacy."[641] Jolly, too, rightly translates: "if he should persist in contention" (SBE 33: 384).

This survey of the meaning of *anubandha* in legal literature may be closed by means of a few examples taken from the commentaries and *nibandhas*.

1. When MDh 9.287 for the same offense prescribes different punishment, viz., the lowest and the middlemost amercements, according to Kullūkabhaṭṭa this gradation corresponds to a gradation of *anubandha*.
2. A text of Nārada and one of Bṛhaspati treat the same act: the former prescribes a punishment; the latter does not consider the act to be an offense. *Vivādaratnākara* 274–75 removes this *virodha* by making the following distinction: the former refers to *anubandha*, whereas the latter does not.

[640] Ed. K.V. Rangaswami Aiyangar, 1941: *svecchākṛtavibhāgo yaḥ punar eva visaṃvadet | sa rājñāṃśe svake sthāpyaḥ śāsanīyo'nubandhakṛt ||*

[641] Thus, e.g., *Madanaratnapradīpa* (ed. Kane) 335, *Vyavahāramayūkha* (ed. Kane) 137 (and notes, p. 233). In Sca (ed. Srinivasacharya) III, 717 we shall probably correct *nirbandha* for *nibandha*.

The following examples are taken from *Daṇḍaviveka*:

1. 20.10–11. The amount of the amercement is higher: *aparādhānubandhādinā*.
2. 53.14–16. Punishment is severer: *aparādhānubandhagauravādinā*.
3. 54.13–14. In case of *anubandha* certain punishments are to be multiplied by four.
4. 83.2. A severe punishment is to be explained *anubandhagauravāt*.
5. 106.13. In texts of MDh and YDh referring to the same offense the punishment is severer or lighter respectively: *anubandhagauravāgauravābhyām*.
6. 133.22–23. Different kinds of punishment may not be inflicted simultaneously if there is no explicit text to the effect and *anubandhagauravābhāve*.
7. 219.13. The three degrees of punishment for attack in NS 15.5 correspond to as many degrees in the action itself: *praharaṇasya prārambho niṣpattiḥ phalānubandhaḥ*.
8. 261.5–6. The punishment shall be as severe as to detain wrongdoers from offense. If no punishment is adequate to this effect, the person is to be punished. About the latter case it is said: *etadanubandhātiśayaviṣayam*.

We do not want to amplify this by means of examples from classical Sanskrit literature. But that this would also be possible is obvious from such cases as this. In the second act of *Ratnāvalī* the king says to the princes:

> *ayi | prasīda | na khalu sakhījane yuktam evaṃvidhaṃ kopānubandhaṃ kartum* (Böhtlingk 1909: 345.1), i.e., "It is not proper for you to persist in your anger."

Let us now for a moment turn to the lexicographers. With three of them we find the following synonyms for *anubandha*:

> *Amarakośa*: *doṣotpāde* (Nirṇaya Sāgara Press edition: 414),
> *Medinikośa*: *doṣotpāde* (Kashi Sanskrit Series, 41: 81–82),
> *Anekārthsaṃgraha*: *doṣāpādane* (Kashi Sanskrit Series, 68: 121).

In Böhtlingk's Dictionary these three sources are also quoted. And the following note is added: "Colebrooke erklärt dies durch 'offense or guilt'...Es ist vielleicht das Motiv des Vergehens gemeint."

If we compare these synonyms of the lexica to the texts quoted above, our conclusion about the meaning of *anubandha* as a technical term is as follows. *Anubandha* is *doṣotpāda* or *doṣāpādana* indeed, i.e., *anubandha* is a factor which gives rise to an offense. But as such it is not the cause or the motive of the offense; actually it is the wrongdoer's inclination or his propensity to committing offenses. *Anubandha* is the internal mental condition of a man, which continually puts him up to criminal activity.

This mental condition of the criminal is a factor, which in modern jurisdiction the judge is to take into consideration indeed. But we may not omit stressing the fact the term *anubandha* in such texts as MDh 8.126 depicts that wonderful and exciting system of ancient Hindu criminal law as it was established in the centuries about the beginning of the Christian era.

After all this, as a mere appendix we shall take up again Aśoka's Rock-Edict V, which in Jayaswal's opinion is another argument for the meaning "motive." Jayaswal writes as follows: "Aśoka uses the term in connection with remission of punishment. His officers of the *dharma* department were to examine and reduce punishment awarded to prisoners on the consideration of: (1) *anubandha*, (2) the children of the prisoner (to be supported), (3) absence of free agency, and (4) old age."

As stated above we are not sufficiently acquainted with Aśoka's language for deciding the question from this point of view. Nevertheless we ask ourselves, whether the variant readings may correspond to such a Sanskrit equivalent as *anubaddhapraja*, being a *bahuvrīhi*-compound meaning "one who has an extended offspring," i.e., one who has many children. Such a person is characterized by *prajānubandha*, by "obstinacy towards having offspring."

If this may be possible linguistically, a person's being *anubaddhapraja* would be a ground for a lighter punishment indeed: the more children one has to support, the lighter shall be the punishment!

28

The Kāmasūtra*: Vātsyāyana's Attitude toward* Dharma *and Dharmaśāstra*

The first *sūtra* of Vātsyāyana's *Kāmasūtra*[642] pays homage, not only to *kāma*, but to all three components of the *trivarga*:

dharmārthakāmebhyo namaḥ. (1.1.1)

The reason for this initial statement is provided in the next *sūtra*:

śāstre prakṛtatvāt. (1.1.2)

Neither Schmidt's ("Weil sie in dem Lehrbuche immer wiederkehren") nor Upadhyaya's ("The three Aims of Life that are dealt with in this Shastra") translations adequately express the meaning of this *sūtra*. What Vātsyāyana claims is that he pays homage to *dharma*, *artha*, and *kāma*, because they are the three topics which are "genuine, relevant" (*prakṛta*) to *a śāstra*, i.e., to any *śāstra*.

The fact that all three elements of the *trivarga* are interconnected has been stressed elsewhere in the *Kāmasūtra*. In a sequence of *sūtras* which will be discussed later in this article, and in which Vātsyāyana suggests that different aspects of the *trivarga* shall be the primary ones in different periods of a person's life (*kālaṃ vibhajya*), at the same time he emphasizes that, throughout life,

[642] References to the text of the *Kāmasūtra* are according to the edition, with Yaśodhara's commentary, *Jayamaṅgalā*, Kashi Sanskrit Series 29, 1929. I will occasionally quote the translations by Richard Burton and F.F. Arbuthnoth (1863; I use the Panther Book ed., London 1963), Richard Schmidt (1907), and S.C. Upadhyaya (1961).

anyonyānubaddhaṃ parasparasyānupaghātakaṃ trivargaṃ seveta. (1.2.1)

That means that in any period of life in which one of the elements of the *trivarga* is the primary one, the other two should be natural adjuncts of it, and that, under no circumstances, any one of the *trivarga* should be detrimental to the other two.[643] Again, later in the same chapter:

trivargasādhakaṃ yat syād dvayor vaikasya vā punaḥ |
kāryaṃ tad api kurvīta na tv ekārthaṃ dvibādhakam || (1.2.51)[644]

To be sure, a similar statement also appears in the Dharmaśāstra. Says Manu:

dharmārthāv ucyate śreyaḥ kāmārthau dharma eva ca |
artha eveha vā śreyas trivarga iti tu sthitiḥ || (2.224)

There is a difference, though. Whereas the passages dealing with the *trivarga* in the *Kāmasūtra* quite naturally fit into the general contexts, the verse from the *Manusmṛti* stands all alone. It has no connection whatever with the preceding or following verses. Also, it is one of the few verses for which the footnotes in Bühler's translation fail to refer to similar statements in other Dharmaśāstra texts.

Not only is *dharma* —and *artha*— referred to in the *Kāmasūtra*. Vātsyāyana also establishes a relative hierarchy among the three elements of the *trivarga*. Commenting on the initial *sūtra* mentioned earlier Yaśodhara points out that in the compound *dharmārthakāmebhyaḥ* Vātsyāyana intentionally fails to comply with a rule of the *Aṣṭādhyāyī* (2.2.33: *ajādyantam*), according to which *artha* should have been mentioned first in the *dvandva* compound. Whether or not the author was conscious of violating

[643] *Anyonyānubaddha* is more than "in such a manner that they harmonize together" (Burton), "eins an das andere anknüpfend" (Schmidt), or "in such a way as to harmonize with each other" (Upadhyaya). *Anubaddha* clearly suggest that one element is primary and the other one or two subordinate to it. Cf. Rocher 1955. The commentator provides examples for the following combinations: *dharma°* *°arthānubaddha, °kāmānubaddha, °arthakāmānubaddha*; *artha°* *°dharmānubaddha*; *°kāmānubaddha, °dharmakāmānubaddha*; *kāma°* *°dharmānubaddha, °arthānubaddha, °dharmārthānubaddha.*

[644] With 1.2.51 —and 1.2.1 mentioned earlier— compare, with reference to the king, AŚ 1.7.3–5 (also 15.1.29–30): *dharmārthāvirodhena kāmaṃ seveta na niḥsukhaḥ syāt. samaṃ vā trivargam anyonyānubaddham. eko hy atyāsevito dharmārthakāmānām ātmānam itarau ca pīḍayati.* The relation between the *Kāmasūtra* and Kauṭilya's AŚ has received much attention in the scholarly literature; it will only occasionally be referred to in this article. Cf., especially, Jolly 1914: 351–354; Wilhelm 1966.

a rule of Pāṇini's grammar, the fact remains that the *Kāmasūtra*, i.e., a text on *kāma*, opens with the word *dharma*.[645] Elsewhere in the text (1, ch. 2) Vātsyāyana defines *dharma* first, *artha* second, and *kāma* last. The definitions are then followed by the unequivocal statement:

> *teṣāṃ samavāye pūrvaḥ pūrvo garīyān.* (1.2.14)[646]

The important point here is, first, that the *Kāmasūtra* operates within the framework of the *trivarga*, and, second, that even the *Kāmasūtra* places *kāma* at a lower level than *artha* and considers *dharma* to be the highest of the three goals in life.

This impression is further confirmed by the fact that Vātsyāyana is clearly on the defensive, both for the pursuit of *kāma* generally, and for his writing a treatise on it in particular. Differently from the discussions —each time with a negative *pūrvapakṣa* and a positive *siddhānta*— on the necessity to practice *dharma* and *artha*, in which the other two elements of the *trivarga* are not even alluded to, in the case of the pursuit of *kāma* both the objection and its refutation contain explicit —and comparative— references to the other two. The objection (1.2.40–45), attributed to the *Arthacintakāḥ*,[647] maintains that acts of *kāma* are contrary to (*pratyanīka*) the two *principal* goals in life: *dharma* and *artha* (*dharmārthayoḥ pradhānayoḥ*). They therefore lead to all kinds of undesirable results: contact with wicked people, unworthy enterprises, defilement, forfeiture of one's future, negligence, rashness, distrust, etc. Many individuals attached to acts of *kāma* are known to have met with disaster.[648] Following the argument that acts of *kāma* are like food —both *kāma* and food are necessary to sustain the body—, Vātsyāyana subsequently claims that acts of *kāma*, far from being contrary to *dharma* and *artha*, actually are their natural outcome (1.2.47: *phalabhūtāś ca dharmārthayoḥ*). Moreover, unlike the unqualified *siddhānta*s on *dharma* and *artha*, at this point Vātsyāyana admits (1.2.48) that

[645] Cf. 4.1.55, on faithful wives (*nāryaḥ sadvṛttam āśritāḥ*): *dharmam arthaṃ tathā kāmaṃ labhante...* See also 7.2.53, 58, below.

[646] More specifically with regard to the *Kāmasūtra*, Vātsyāyana insists that its study, and the study of its *aṅgas*, be undertaken without interfering with the time reserved for the study of *dharma* and *artha*, and their *aṅgas*: *dharmārthāṅgavidyākālān anuparodhayan kāmaśāstraṃ tadaṅgavidyāś ca puruṣo 'dhīyīta* (1.3.1).

[647] Burton: "those who think that Artha is the chief object to be obtained"; Schmidt: "die Opportunisten"; Upadhyaya: "the champions of Artha"; Wilhelm (1966: 299): "Politologen."

[648] Notice that the first example of individuals who were ruined by *kāma* (1.2.44) corresponds literally to AŚ 1.6.5: *yathā Dāṇḍakyo nāma Bhojaḥ kāmād brāhmaṇakanyām abhimanyamānaḥ sabandhurāṣṭro vinanāśa.*

the pursuit of *kāma*, even as certain other activities, does involve risks which one ought to be alert to. One does not refrain from cooking food simply because that might attract beggars, nor does one refuse to sow barley just because wild animals might eat a part of it.

In the discussion on the appropriateness of composing a treatise on *kāma* Vātsyāyana introduces the opinion of Ācāryas (1.2.18–21) that, of course, *dharma* requires a *śāstra* because it is *alaukika*, and so does *artha*, because its success depends on the mastery of the proper means (*upāyapratipatti*). On the contrary *kāma* which, even among animals, comes naturally and instinctively, does not require a *śāstra*. In this case Vātsyāyana's answer (1.2.22–24) does not introduce the concepts of *dharma* and *artha* but he does claim that there is a difference between *kāma* of animals and humans: here too, humans have to acquire the proper means of success and, therefore, need a *śāstra*.

Far more revealing for Vātsyāyana's views on the *trivarga* and the place of *kāma* within it are the final *ślokas* of the *Kāmasūtra*. Not less than four times (7.2.53, 54, 57, 59) Vātsyāyana makes it a point to dispel the notion that the main purpose of the *Kāmasūtra* is to promote *rāga*. On the contrary, he composed his book

> *brahmacaryeṇa pareṇa ca samādhinā*. (7.2.57)

A person who truly understands the message of the *Kāmasūtra* knows how to control his senses:

> *asya śāstrasya tattvajño bhavaty eva jitendriyaḥ*. (58)

Twice he insists that the *Kāmasūtra* promotes not one but all three elements of the *trivarga*:

> *dharmam arthaṃ ca kāmaṃ ca … paśyaty etasya tattvajñaḥ* (53);
> *rakṣan dharmārthakāmānāṃ sthitiṃ svāṃ lokavartinīm asya śāstrasya tattvajñaḥ*. (58)

And, even as *dharma* —and *artha*— figure in the very first *sūtra* of the text they are given a place in its final stanza:

> *tad etat kuśalo vidvān dharmārthāv avalokayan* |
> *nātirāgātmakaḥ kāmī prayuñjānaḥ prasidhyati* || (59)

Notwithstanding all this there are, in the *Kāmasūtra*, exceptions to the rule that *dharma* is the highest and most important element of the *trivarga*. Two of these are introduced immediately after the general statement: *teṣāṃ samavāye pūrvaḥ pūrvo garīyān* (1.2.14). These exceptions concern kings and courtesans:

arthaś ca rājñaḥ. tanmūlakatvāl lokayātrāyāḥ. veśyāyāś ca. (1.2.15–17)

The first *sūtra* unambiguously states that, when it comes to the king, the most important element of the *trivarga* is *artha.* In connection with the second *sūtra* the commentator reasons as follows: *lokayātrā* is the correct behavior of the *varṇas* and *āśramas*; this can be maintained only by means of protection provided by the king; to provide protection the king has to be strong; to be strong the king needs an adequate treasury, army, etc.; these are elements of *artha*; therefore *lokayātrā* is founded in *artha.*[649]

Strictly speaking the last *sūtra* states that, "also when it comes to a courtesan, (scil., the most important element of the *trivarga* is *artha*)." This is the interpretation of the commentary, followed by Schmidt. On the other hand, since *sūtras* 1.2.15–17 are meant to provide exceptions —different exceptions— to *sūtra* 1.2.14 in the cases of kings and courtesans, one might be tempted to consider Burton's interpretation (followed by Upadhyaya): "Again, Kama being the occupation of public women, they should prefer it to the other two" (cf. 6.1.1–3, below).

There is even a more far-reaching exception to the superiority of *dharma* —and *artha*— vis-à-vis *kāma* in the *Kāmasūtra.* I referred earlier to a sequence of *sūtras* in which Vātsyāyana advises his readers to pay special attention to different elements of the *trivarga* in different periods (*kālaṃ vibhajya*)[650] of an individual's —ideal— life span of one hundred years. Even though these rules are prefixed with the proviso *anyonyānubaddhaṃ parasparasyānupaghātakam* (1.2.1), the text continues:

bālye vidyāgrahaṇādīn arthān kāmaṃ ca yauvane sthāvire dharmaṃ mokṣaṃ ca. (1.2.2–4)

I intentionally print the text without dividing it into separate *sūtras*. According to Burton: "He should acquire learning in his childhood, in his youth and middle age he should attend to Artha and Kama, and in his old age he should perform Dharma, and thus seek to gain Moksha." Upadhyaya follows Burton to a certain extent but totally neglects the term *arthān*: "In childhood, he should devote himself to acquiring knowledge; in youth, he should engage in worldly pleasures, and in his old age, he should aspire to salvation through the practice of Dharma." The only cor-

[649] Cf. AŚ 1.7.6–7 (immediately after 1.7.3–5 quoted earlier): *artha eva pradhāna iti Kauṭilyaḥ. arthamūlau hi dharmakāmāv iti.*

[650] Cf. *Mahābhārata* 12.69.68ab (CE): *dharmaś cārthaś ca kāmaś ca sevitavyo 'tha kālataḥ.* For the discussions on the priorities of the different elements of the *trivarga* in the *Śāntiparvan*, see Hillebrandt 1923: 16–20.

rect interpretation, based on a proper separation of the *sūtras*, is Schmidt's: "In der Kindheit beschäftige man sich mit der Erlangung des Wissens und ähnlichen Gegenständen des Artha. Und in der Jugend mit der Liebe.[651] Im reifen Alter mit Dharma und Erlösung."

It is indeed clear that, syntactically, *vidyāgrahaṇādīn arthān* belong together, all the more so because of the definition of *artha* elsewhere in the *Kāmasūtra*:

> *vidyābhūmihiraṇyapaśudhānyabhāṇḍopaskaramitrādīnām arjanam arjitasya vivardhanam arthaḥ.* (1.2.9)

However unusual it may be to have *vidyā* or *vidyāgrahaṇa* included under *artha*, the first period of life as envisaged by Vātsyāyana encompasses the time of *brahmacarya*. Elsewhere in the text (1.4.1) Vātsyāyana again makes it clear that his treatise on *kāma* addresses itself to a man who is *gṛhītavidya* "having acquired the necessary learning" (cf. 3.1.2: *śrutavān*) and *gārhapatyam adhigamya* "having advanced to the stage of a householder." Finally, since a man does not necessarily live the ideal life span of one hundred years (1.2.1: *śatāyur vai puruṣaḥ*), Vātsyāyana is willing to relax the strict repartition of the three goals of life, however with one exception:

> *anityatvād āyuṣo yathopapādaṃ vā seveta. brahmacaryam eva tv ā vidyāgrahaṇāt.* (1.2.5–6)

In other words, even though Vātsyāyana deviates from a basic principle of Dharmaśāstra in that he assigns different elements of the *trivarga* as the primary ones at different stages of life, he does so plainly within the framework of the *āśramas* established by the *dharma* texts. The *yuvan* he has in mind is one who has completed his period of *brahmacarya* on the one hand (see below for the time for women to study the *Kāmasūtra*), and who is not yet *sthāvire*, i.e., *vānaprasthye*, on the other.

In the *sūtra* mentioned earlier (1.4.1), in which Vātsyāyana lays down that he addresses himself to individuals who have reached the status of householders, he also enumerates the means by which they should assure their livelihood:

> *pratigrahajayakrayanirveśādhigatair arthair anvayāgatair ubhayair vā.*

The second means of acquiring wealth is a universal one: inheritance. The first alternative is more interesting in that it lists four

[651] Unless *ca* after *kāmam* implies *anuvṛtti* of *arthān*: *kāmaṃ* [*arthāñ*] *ca yauvane.*

distinctive activities which are recognized in the Dharmaśāstras as the lawful occupations for the Brāhmaṇa, Kṣatriya, Vaiśya, and Śūdra, respectively.[652] I have described elsewhere how, except in cases of emergency, in the Dharmaśāstras the occupations (*vṛtti*) and rules of behavior generally are strictly associated with —and different for— the several *varṇa*s (see Rocher 1975). Here again, while explicitly (cf. 3.2.1: *sārvavarṇikam*) operating within the framework of the four *varṇa*s, the *Kāmasūtra* goes against the grain of the Dharmaśāstras insofar as it lays down uniform rules for all householders, irrespective of their *varṇa*s. It even includes in its audience the householder of the Śūdra class, leaving unanswered the question how a Śūdra can have completed his *brahmacarya* and become *gṛhītavidya* prior to engaging in the activities prescribed by the *Kāmasūtra*.

Even though Vātsyāyana means to lay down uniform rules for householders for all *varṇa*s,[653] he introduces restrictions of his own. In the first place, he addresses himself solely to those householders who are *nāgaraka*s. Burton translated *nāgaraka* as "citizen"; Schmidt: "der Elegant"; Upadhyaya, incorporating a passage from the commentary: "a refined and educated gentleman (a poor man cannot adopt the role of a refined and educated gentleman)." Recognizing the well-to-do and urbane *nāgaraka*s as a separate class of people and prescribing special rules for their behavior is, of course, totally foreign to the Dharmaśāstras. The term is, however, well known in other branches of Sanskrit literature. Pāṇini even devotes a separate rule to it:

(*vuñ*) *nagarāt kutsanaprāvīṇyayoḥ*. (4.2.128)[654]

Śrīśa Chandra Vasu rightly points out that *nāgaraka* "always denotes a person having the vices or virtues of a town, such as a thief or an artist" (Vasu 1962: 746). In the case of the *Kāmasūtra*

[652] The term *nirveśa* is rare in the Dharmaśāstras. It occurs in a verse attributed to Bṛhaspati (13.34): artisans who work cooperatively shall take their *nirveśa* proportionately to their individual labor. An identical verse appears in the *Śukranītisāra* (4.794). The variant form *nirviṣṭa* occurs —only— in the GDh (10.40–42), in connection with specific ways of acquiring wealth for the four *varṇa*s, in addition to the general one, inheritance: *brāhmaṇasyādhikaṃ labdhaṃ kṣatriyasya vijitaṃ nirviṣṭaṃ vaiśyaśūdrayoḥ*. Even though the correspondence is not verbatim, the close verbal relationship of the *Kāmasūtra*, not with MDh —Vātsyāyana refers to Manu as the composer of the Dharmaśāstra (1.1.6)— but with GDh, is intriguing.

[653] Cf. *Jayamaṅgalā* ad 1.4.1: *cāturvarṇyaṃ gṛhastham adhikṛtya idaṃ śāstram*.

[654] This rule seems to indicate that the reading *nāgarika*, which often appears in *Kāmasūtra* editions instead of *nāgaraka*, is wrong. A *nāgarika* is a person who "protects" the city, as in the AŚ (2, ch. 36 and elsewhere); he is the "City-Superintendent" (Kangle). Cf. Pāṇini 4.4.33: (*ṣṭhanṣṭhacau*) *rakṣati*.

I would slightly alter Vasu's formulation: Vātsyāyana's *nāgaraka* is the kind of person who has both all the virtues and all the vices inherent in urban living.

Vātsyāyana introduces yet another restriction in the subject matter of the *Kāmasūtra*. Not only does he address himself to those householders who are *nāgarakas*. He is, moreover, concerned with their activities in the one area only: *kāma*.

Even though it is not always clear what the Dharmaśāstras mean when they use the term *kāma* —whether in its technical sense as one of the elements of the *trivarga*, or in its more general meaning of "wish, desire"—, at least one thing is beyond doubt: *kāma*, in the Dharmaśāstras, always has a negative, pejorative connotation.[655] An offense committed *kāmatas* is invariably more serious —and deserves a more severe punishment— than the same offense committed *akāmatas*. *Kāmatas* and *akāmatas* correspond to the distinction between "intentional" and "unintentional" offenses.

For Vātsyāyana, on the contrary, *kāma* is a positive concept. He formulates a definition of it which, if not actually borrowed from some *Nyāya-Vaiśeṣika* text, at least operates with the terminology of these *darśanas*:[656]

> *śrotratvakcakṣurjihvāghrāṇām ātmasaṃyuktena manasā adhiṣṭhitānāṃ sveṣu sveṣu viṣayeṣv ānukūlyataḥ pravṛttiḥ kāmaḥ.* (1.2.11)

This general definition of *kāma* is followed by a more specific one:

> *sparśaviśeṣaviṣaye tv asya ābhimānikasukhānuviddhā phalavaty arthapratītiḥ prādhānyāt kāmaḥ.* (1.2.12)

This specific type of *kāma* is the one which the *Kāmasūtra* is concerned with:

> *taṃ kāmasūtrān nāgarakajanasamavāyāc ca pratipadyate.* (1.2.13)

For his activities in the area of *kāma* the *nāgaraka* is given a special name: *nāyaka*, a term which is known to the *Alaṃkāra* literature, from the *Bhāratīyanāṭyaśāstra* onward, and which is the

[655] E.g., MDh 2.2ab: *kāmātmatā na praśastā na caivehāsty akāmatā*; ibid. 2.13ab: *arthakāmeṣv asaktānāṃ dharmajñānaṃ vidhīyate* (variously explained by the commentators).

[656] Cf., e.g., *Vaiśeṣikasūtra* 5.2.15: *ātmendriyamano 'rthasaṃnikarṣāt sukhaduḥkhe*; *Tarkasaṃgrahadīpikā* §43: *ātmā manasā saṃyujyate mana indriyeṇa indriyam arthena; tataḥ pratyakṣaṃ jñānam utpadyate.*

usual term for the "hero" in Sanskrit plays (for the qualities required in a *nāyaka*, see 6.1.12).

Vātsyāyana's treatment of women, when looked upon against the background of *dharma* and Dharmaśāstra, is far more complex than his treatment of men. I can only touch on a few aspects of this problem in the present article.

According to Vātsyāyana women too, are supposed to study the *Kāmasūtra* and its *aṅgas*. Since there is no period of *brahmacarya* for women as there is for men, they ought to study the *śāstra* even before they reach the time of *yauvana*:

prāg yauvanāt strī (kāmasūtraṃ tadaṅgavidyāś ca adhīyīta). (1.3.2)

They may also continue to do so after marriage, but this depends on the intentions of their husbands:

prattā patyur abhiprāyāt. (1.3.3)[657]

These positive statements are, however, followed by an objection attributed to Ācāryas: instructing women in the *kāmaśāstra* is futile,

yoṣitāṃ śāstragrahaṇasyābhāvāt (1.3.4),

which seems to imply both that women are not entitled to study a *śāstra* (comm.: *tāsāṃ śāstrānadhikārāt*) and that they are not intellectually capable of doing so (cf. 1.3.12). Even though Vātsyāyana goes on to defend his original position —women are familiar with the practice (*prayoga*) of *kāma*, and practice is based on the *śāstra* (1.3.5)—, the ensuing discussion is, at best, ambivalent, and ends up stressing women's knowledge of the sixty-four subsidiary *vidyās* rather than the *śāstra* itself.

In any case, Vātsyāyana does provide the *nāyaka* with a female counterpart: *nāyikā*. Differently from the single[658] *nāyaka* the *Kāmasūtra* distinguishes three types of *nāyikās*, using a terminology which is well known to the Dharmaśāstras:

tatra nāyikās tisraḥ kanyā punarbhūr veśyā ca. (1.5.4)

[657] The rules of behavior for a married woman in the *Kāmasūtra* are very similar to those of the Dharmaśāstras. E.g., the section on the *ekacāriṇī* "the single wife" (4.1.1–42), opens with the statement: *bhāryā ekacāriṇī gūḍhaviśrambhā devavat patim ānukūlyena varteta.*

[658] Except for the threefold distinction *liṅgatas* (2.1.1). For subdivisions of the *nāyaka*, in a variety of texts on *alaṃkāra* and *kāma*, see Schmidt 1922: 108–148.

The term *kanyā* is pivotal in marriage as conceived by the *dharma* texts. It appears explicitly in six of Manu's eight definitions of different types of marriage (3.27–34), it is understood in one, and replaced by *sutā* in another. Irrespective of whether the maiden is given away (*kanyādāna*), or whether she goes away on her own as in the *gāndharva* marriage, or whether she is abducted (*kanyāharaṇa*), the bride of the Dharmaśāstras is invariably a *kanyā* (cf. Rocher 1979: 207–14). The entire third *adhikaraṇa* of the *Kāmasūtra* is devoted to *Kanyāsamprayuktakam*; for Vātsyāyana, even as for the Dharmaśāstras, a *kanyā* is not only unmarried (3.1.1: *ananyapūrvā*) but also a virgin.[659]

The status of Vātsyāyana's second type of *nāyikā*, the *punarbhū*, is more complex in the Dharmaśāstras. Definitions (for definitions of *punarbhū*, see, e.g., Schmidt 1922: 148–50) vary in detail —whether a widow or one who abandoned her husband, whether still a virgin or not, etc.— but they all agree that the *punarbhū* is *parapūrvā* "one who previously belonged to another man." Many *dharma* texts treat her very much at the same level with the *svairiṇī* "the independent, wanton woman." Most explicit is the *Nāradasmṛti* (12.45–53): it divides women who are *parapūrvā* into seven kinds, three of which are *punarbhū*, four *svairiṇī*, the latter being considered more respectable than the former. Even though the Dharmaśāstras recognize the *paunarbhava* "the son of a *punarbhū*" as one of the —normally eight— kinds of sons, the *punarbhū* is obviously in violation of other principles of Dharmaśāstra, such as eternal faithfulness to her previous husband (e.g., MDh 5.160–61), etc.; she is therefore a far less desirable wife than the *kanyā*. Vātsyāyana simply defines the *punarbhū* (for *punarbhūvṛtta*, see 1.2.39–59) as a widow who seeks remarriage:

> *vidhavā tv indriyadaurbalyād āturā bhoginaṃ guṇasampannaṃ ca yā punar vindet sā punarbhūḥ.* (4.2.39)

The status of the courtesan is, in a way, rather uncomplicated in the Dharmaśāstras. The courtesan, whether she be called *veśyā*, *gaṇikā*, *paṇyastrī*, etc., is hardly mentioned in these texts (hence the paucity of *dharma* texts used in Sternbach 1953). On the other hand, the few references that do occur are invariably pejorative. There are no statements on courtesans in particular; the term always appears as one item in long series of individuals upon whom the Dharmaśāstras do not look favorably. On a

[659] *Kanyāvisrambhaṇa* —the topic of 3, ch. 2— results in the girl being *vimuktakanyābhāvā* (3.2.38).

few occasions the courtesan is listed among those individuals from whom no one, especially not a Brahmin, should accept any food (MDh 4.209, 219; cf. ViDh 51.7, VaDh 14.10, etc.). More often than not *veśyās* are mentioned in one breath with thieves (e.g., ViDh 51.7); "clever harlots" (*nipuṇāḥ paṇyastriyaḥ*), even as thieves and the like, are "public thorns (in the side of the king's subjects)" (MDh 9.259). As such, the king should provoke them, by means of "spies wearing various disguises" (MDh 9.260), to commit their crimes, and, subsequently, inflict on them the punishment they deserve (MDh 9.261). Brothels (e.g., MDh 9.264) are one in a long list of places which should be guarded by "companies of soldiers, stationary or patrolling," this time not because they themselves are places of evil, but because a variety of scoundrels are likely to hang out around them. Notwithstanding all this the courtesan is one of the main characters of the *Kāmasūtra*. One of its seven *adhikaraṇas* —the sixth— is entirely devoted to her: *Vaiśikam*. The chapter opens with the matter-of-fact statement:

> *veśyānāṃ puruṣādhigame ratir vṛttiś ca sargāt. ratitaḥ pravartanaṃ svābhāvikaṃ kṛtrimam arthārtham. tad api svābhāvikavad rūpayet.* (6.1.1–3)

It is clear that Vātsyāyana ranks at the same level three types of women who are, in the eyes of the Dharmaśāstras, very different. Even though the *Kāmasūtra*, like the Dharmaśāstras, praises most highly *kāma* with an *ananyapūrvā* (1.5.1), and even though *kāma* with a *punarbhū* is attributed to her being *indriyadaurbalyād āturā* (4.2.39), the overriding, common criterion for Vātsyāyana's list of three *nāyikās* is that these women, at the time of their relationship with the *nāyaka*, are not attached to another man. *Kāma* with married women raises, even for Vātsyāyana, a different set of problems.

Adultery is, of course, strongly censured by the Dharmaśāstras (e.g., MDh 4.133–34; 8.352 sqq.). The same idea is reflected in the *Kāmasūtra*:

> *(kāmaḥ)...paraparigṛhītāsu...pratiṣiddhaḥ.* (1.5.2)

Yet, Vātsyāyana devotes far more attention —the entire fourth *adhikaraṇa* is called *Pārakārikam*— to the opinion of his predecessor Goṇikāputra, who is said to have been the author of a book on the subject (1.1.16). Immediately after the *sūtra* enumerating the three types of *nāyikās* the *Kāmasūtra* continues:

> *anyakāraṇavaśāt paraparigṛhītāpi pākṣikī caturthīti Goṇikāputraḥ.* (1.5.5)

The existing translations[660] fail to do justice to Goṇikāputra's statement, in particular to the term *pākṣikī* used in it. The *sūtra* means that, even according to the author of *Pāradārikam*, the fourth type of *nāyikā* is *pākṣikī* "optional, allowable only under certain specific conditions." Even (*api*; repeated 1.5.20: *parastriyam api*) a married woman can be a *nāyikā*, but there have to be different reasons for it (*anyakāraṇavaśāt*) than those that prevail in the case of the other three types: offspring or pleasure.[661]

In other words, even in the *kāmaśāstra* adultery is placed at a different level than *kāma* with the other three kinds of *nāyikās*, Vātsyāyana devotes not less than fifteen *sūtras* (1.5.6–20) to enumerating the reasons (*kāraṇa*) for which a man is allowed to seduce a married woman. This list of reasons, which is too long and detailed to reproduce here, appropriately concludes with the *sūtra*:

> *iti sāhasikyaṃ na kevalaṃ rāgād eva iti paraparigrahagamanakāraṇāni.* (1.5.21)

It is one of the best specimens to illustrate the extent to which the *Kāmasūtra* occasionally emulates the "Machiavellian" tendencies of the AŚ;[662] more than most other passages in the *Kāmasūtra* it justifies Winternitz's description of Vātsyāyana as "the Indian Machiavelli of love" (Winternitz 3, 1920: 537; trans. Jhā 1967: 621).

The Dharmaśāstras make it very clear that the only true union in marriage is the one between two members of the same *varṇa*.[663] Here again the *Kāmasūtra* operates within the categories of the *dharma* texts:

> *kāmaś caturṣu varṇeṣu savarṇataḥ śāstrataś ca ananyapūrvāyāṃ prayujyamānaḥ putriyo yaśasyo laukikaś ca bhavati* (1.5.1);

[660] Burton: "Gonikaputra has expressed an opinion that there is a fourth kind of Nayika, viz., a woman who is resorted to on some special occasion even though she be previously married to another"; Schmidt: "Aus anderen Gründen wird selbst eine von einem anderen geheiratete Frau zu einer Vierten, die man besuchen darf, sagt Goṇikāputra"; Upadhyaya: "According to Gonikaputra, however there is yet a fourth type of Nayika: one who is already married to another, but who is resorted to for some special reason (i.e., other than the reasons of procreation or pleasure)."

[661] Cf. *Jayamaṅgalā*: *putrāt sukhāc ca yad anyat kāraṇaṃ tadvaśāt.*

[662] Even the way in which the arguments are presented: *sa yadā manyeta... vā...vā...*etc. (1.5.6 sqq.), is reminiscent of certain passages of Kauṭilya. Cf. AŚ: *yadi vā paśyet...*(7.1.32, 33); *yadi vā manyeta...* (7.1.34–37; 7.4.5–19; 7.6.8–10); etc.

[663] E.g., MDh 3.43ab: *pāṇigrahaṇasaṃskāraḥ savarṇāsūpadiśyate.* Cf. YDh 1.62a; ViDh 24.5; etc.

also:

savarṇāyām ananyapūrvāyāṃ śāstrato 'dhigatāyāṃ dharmo 'rthaḥ putrāḥ sambandhaḥ pakṣavṛddhir anupaskṛtā ratiś ca. (3.1.1)[664]

Among marriages the partners of which belong to different *varṇa*s the Dharmaśāstras censure most severely the one in which the wife is of a higher *varṇa* than the husband.[665] Yet, they acknowledge its existence and describe in great detail the offspring of all possible types of *pratiloma* marriages. On the subject of *kāma* "against the grain" the *Kāmasūtra* is as clear and even less tolerant than the Dharmaśāstras; even as *kāma* with a married woman (see above) *kāma* "against the grain" is forbidden. After praising *kāma* among members of the same *varṇa* the text continues:

tadviparīta uttamavarṇāsu paraparigṛhītāś ca pratiṣiddhaḥ. (1.5.2)

Finally, the Dharmaśāstras, while not recommending *anuloma* marriages, at least consider them less objectionable than the *pratiloma* type. Here too, they describe in detail the offspring of the different possible combinations. Even though Vātsyāyana is aware that an *anuloma* relationship is undesirable,[666] he assimilates love with women of a lower *varṇa* with love with *punarbhū*s, *veśyā*s, and others:

avaravarṇāsv aniravasitāsu veśyāsu punarbhūṣu ca na śiṣṭo na pratiṣiddhaḥ sukhārthatvāt. (1.5.3)

The *Kāmasūtra* gave no reason why love "against the grain" is forbidden; only the commentator did:

ekāntena dharmavirodhitvāt.

Vātsyāyana himself, however, provides a reason for his statement concerning love "with the grain":

sukhārthatvāt.

Under influence of the commentary on this term: *tadānīṃ sukhārthaiva pravṛtthiḥ na putrārthā*, Burton translates: "The object

[664] Cf. the more general statement: *samasyādyāḥ sahakrīḍā vivāhāḥ saṃgatāni ca | tādṛśair eva kāryāṇi nottamair nāpi vādhamaiḥ* || (3.1.22)

[665] See Rocher 1980–1981: 132–46 at 140. On mixed castes generally, see Kane 1930–1962: 2.69–104; more recently, Brinkhaus 1978.

[666] Cf. 3.1.24cd: *aślāghyo hīnasambandhaḥ so 'pi sadbhir vinindyate*; 3.1.26cd: *na tv eva hīnasambandhaṃ kuryāt sadbhir vininditam.*

of practicing Kama with such women is pleasure only"; similarly Schmidt: "da sie nur zum Vergnügen dient"; even more explicitly, Upadhyaya: "Since this relation is entered into for mere pleasure."

Translating *sukhārthaiva pravṛtthiḥ* as "a relation entered into *for mere pleasure*," is misleading. It creates the wrong impression that, ideally, *sukha* ought to be subordinated to, if not replaced by, something far more valuable. In reality *sukha* is a positive concept in its own right, not a negative concept, in the *Kāmasūtra*. It figures prominently throughout Vātsyāyana's text. As we saw earlier, *sukha* appears in the definition of the special kind of *kāma* (*prādhānyāt kāmaḥ*) which is the subject matter of the *Kāmasūtra* (1.2.12, above). Differently from relationships with women of higher or lower rank (see note 666), only the meeting of equals assures mutual *sukha*:

parasparasukhāsvādā krīḍā yatra prayujyate |
viśeṣayantī cānyonyaṃ sambandhaḥ sa vidhīyate || (3.1.25)

Sukha is also the reason why the *Kāmasūtra* advocates one particular form of marriage: the *gāndharva* marriage. In the lists of eight types of marriage mentioned, in declining order of respectability, in the Dharmaśāstras (see Rocher 1979), the *gāndharva* marriage occupies the sixth place. It is not the worst type of marriage; *rākṣasa* and *paiśāca* rank even lower. Yet, it is the only form of marriage the definition of which refers to *kāma*. For instance, Manu:

icchayānyonyasaṃyogaḥ kanyāyāś ca varasya ca |
gāndharvaḥ sa tu vijñeyo maithunyaḥ kāmasambhavaḥ || (3.32)

The author of the *Kāmasūtra* is obviously aware of the eight forms of marriage of the Dharmaśāstras. At one point (3.1.21) he even prescribes the four superior forms: *brāhmaṇa*, *prājāpatya*, *ārṣa*, and *daiva*, "depending on local customs" (*deśavṛttisātmyāt*). He also alludes (3.5.29) to the fact that the *gāndharva* form is *madhyama* "middlemost, average." Yet, the text (3, ch. 5) only deals at length with the *gāndharva* marriage, then (3.5.24–27) briefly describes —without mentioning their names— the *paiśāca* and *rākṣasa* forms, and concludes:

pūrvaḥ pūrvaḥ pradhānaṃ syād vivāho dharmasaṃsthiteḥ |[667]
pūrvābhāve tataḥ kāryo yo ya uttara uttaraḥ || (3.5.28)

[667] Notice the expression *dharma-saṃsthiteḥ*.

Literally speaking this verse might apply only to the three —lower— types of marriage discussed immediately before the *śloka*. Yet, it clearly aims at all eight forms of marriage recognized by the Dharmaśāstras, since the following verse (3.5.29) adds that the *gāndharva* marriage, even though it is only a "middlemost" one, nevertheless should be considered to be *the* right kind of union (*sadyoga...pūjitaḥ*). Also, the last verse of the chapter (3.5.30) unequivocally proclaims the *gāndharva* marriage as the best possible form (*gāndharvaḥ pravaro mataḥ*). Four reasons are given for Vātsyāyana's preference for the *gāndharva* marriage: besides *abahukleśāt* "because it does not create excessive anguish," *avaraṇāt* "because it avoids the cumbersome procedure of courtship,"[668] and *anurāgāmakatvāt* "because it is based on affection,"[669] the very first reason is *sukhatvāt* "because it leads to happiness" (comm.: *sukhahetutvāt*).

Sukha may well be the basic concept which sets the *Kāmasūtra* apart from the texts on *dharma*. The Dharmaśāstras lay down positive and negative rules; not performing activities prescribed by the former as well as doing what is forbidden by the latter entails unpleasant consequences both in the present and in future existences. The *Kāmasūtra* operates, as far as possible, within the concepts and guidelines of the Dharmaśāstras, but it also has a purpose of its own: it aims at providing *sukha*.[670] Perhaps the *Jayamaṅgalā*, commenting on the *sūtra* (1.5.3) which "neither prescribes nor forbids" *kāma* with women of a lower *varṇa* —and *punarbhūs*, *veśyās*, etc.— captures best the true meaning of the *Kāmasūtra*'s *sukha*. Yaśodhara points out that *kāma* with these women leads to *sukha*, here and now, because if a man decides to abstain from it, it is not forced upon him by any *śāstra*, and, if he chooses to engage in it, there is no *śāstra* to censure his actions.

668 *Varaṇavidhānam* is the title of the twenty-third *prakaraṇa* (3.1.1–21), at the end of which Vātsyāyana recommends the four superior forms of marriage (see above).

669 Cf. 3.5.29ab: *vyūḍhānāṃ hi vivāhānām anurāgaḥ phalaṃ yataḥ*. This notwithstanding the fact that the main purpose of the *Kāmasūtra* is not to promote *rāga* (see above).

670 Notice that *Vaiśeṣikasūtra* 5.2.15 (see note 656), the terminology of which I compared with Vātsyāyana's definition of *kāma*, is a definition of *sukhaduḥkhe*.

29

In Defense of Jīmūtavāhana

Every student of Dharmaśāstra knows that Jīmūtavāhana's *Dāyabhāga*, which "is of paramount authority in modern British Indian courts in Bengal" (Kane 1930–1962: 1.322), defends the view that the head of the family is the sole owner of the joint family property. The other members do not acquire any proprietary rights, for instance by birth, as is the case in other Hindu "legal texts." They only become owners at the time when the right of the present owner ceases to exist, by his death or otherwise.

Jīmūtavāhana himself (1.13) introduces a possible objection to this theory. The opponent states that in order to become the owner of an object, there has to be acquisition (*arjana*). And *arjana* is an activity (*vyāpāra*) on the part of the acquirer (*arjayitṛ*). Therefore, the acquirer acquires the status of an owner contingent upon his activity of acquisition. For instance, birth is an activity of the son (*putravyāpāra*); it constitutes acquisition of a proprietary right in the joint property. Consequently, the son acquires this right while his father is still alive, not after his father's death.

Jīmūtavāhana (1.21) refutes this objection. The activity of the acquirer does not make him the owner. A person's proprietary right can very well come into being by an act on the part of someone else:

anyavyāpāreṇānyasya svatvam aviruddham.

Consequently, the death of the father —literally, the father's act of dying— can create his son's proprietary right, without any activity on the part of the son. The parallel situation which

Jīmūtavāhana refers to in support of his thesis is that of a gift (*dāna*); Colebrooke translates this passage as follows:

> Since, in the case of donation, the donee's right to the thing arises from the act of the giver; namely from his relinquishment in favour of the donee who is a sentient being.

This passage from the *Dāyabhāga* has been quoted in a recent Supreme Court case.[671] The question was whether a testator could bequeath property to an unborn person in an area of India where, at the time the succession opened, the unamended Hindu law rule was in force. In the course of the proceedings one of the Supreme Court judges, V. Ramaswami J., was led to reexamine *Dāyabhāga* 1.21. He formulated "the correct translation" of the passage as follows:

> Since in a gift the donee's ownership in a thing (given) arises from the very act of the donor, consisting of the relinquishment of his ownership with the intention of passing the same to a sentient being.

From this the judge drew the conclusion that "a gift is completed by the donor's act alone, the acceptance of the donee being not necessary."

This conclusion and, as a result, the sentence from the *Dāyabhāga* on which it was based, have been severely criticized by Derrett (1971): "The *Dayabhaga* position, to the effect that gift is the work of the donor, is a 'rogue' and excentric position...It is, shortly, nonsense." I want to examine in this article whether Derrett's dissatisfaction with Jīmūtavāhana's statement on gifts is justified and, if not, why. The Sanskrit text is as follows:

> *dāne hi cetanoddeśaviśiṣṭatyāgād eva*
> *dātṛvyāpārāt sampradānasya dravye svāmitvam.*

The basic element of my argument is that first Colebrooke, later Ramaswami, and finally Derrett have failed to give two terms in Jīmūtavāhana's statement the technical meaning the author intended them to convey: *dātṛ*° and *sampradānasya.* The latter is far more than "the donee" (Colebrooke, Ramaswami). It is not a legal but a grammatical term. According to Pāṇini 1.4.32:

> *karmaṇā yam abhipraiti sa sampradānam.*

[671] *Raman Nadar Viswanathan Nadar* v. *Snehappoo Rasalamma* , 2 S.C.J. 738 (1970): A.I.R. (1970) S.C. 1759.

Freely translated this means: "the *sampradāna* of an act is he whom the agent (*kartṛ*) of the act approaches —whom he has in view— with the object (*karman*) of the act." The *karman* with which the *sampradāna* is approached is, in the case of a gift, *dāna*. Again, in Pāṇinian (1.4.49) terms:

kartur īpsitatamaṃ karma,

"the *karman* of an act is that which the agent (*kartṛ*) wants to achieve more than anything else." Finally, the agent of the activity of giving (*dātṛ*), which is the other term used in the text, implies more than "the giver" (Colebrooke) or "the donor" (Ramaswami). The form *datṛ* inevitably reminds Jīmūtavāhana of Pāṇini 1.4.54:

svatantraḥ kartā.

The agent (*kartṛ*), in this case the *dātṛ*, is the one and only element that, in the action of *dā* "giving," acts independently and autonomously.

Jīmūtavāhana's reasoning, in purely grammatical terms, can be formulated as follows. In a gift the activity is *dā*; the only person who initiates and accomplishes this activity is the *dātṛ*; his activity consists in relinquishing the object of which he is the owner; he directs this object and the ownership toward a beneficiary (*sampradāna*); therefore the latter's ownership arises from the activity of the *dātṛ*.

This grammatical rather than legal interpretation also accounts for the beginning of the following paragraph (1.22) —which is the logical continuation of 1.21 and should not have been separated from it:

na ca svīkaraṇāt svatvam svīkartur eva dātṛtvāpatteḥ.

That means that the proprietary right of the donee does not come into being as a result of an activity of his, namely: his appropriation. If it were, the donee —again in grammatical terms: the agent of the activity of appropriation (*svīkartṛ*)— would be the independent agent of the action of *dā*, not the *dātṛ*. This is a contradiction in terms.

My next point is that Ramaswami erroneously concluded from the preceding passage that acceptance by the donee is not necessary. In paragraph 1.23 Jīmūtavāhana again introduces an opponent who, once more on grammatical grounds, draws attention to the subsequent acceptance, which is an activity on the part of the donee:

nanu grahaṇaṃ svīkāraḥ abhūtatadbhāve cviprayogād asvaṃ svaṃ kurvan vyāpāraḥ svīkāro bhavati; kathaṃ tatprāg eva svatvam.

This sentence has to be interpreted rather than translated. Appropriation, "making something one's own," is called *svīkāra*, not *sva-kāra*. It is, therefore, a *cvi* compound. According to Pāṇini (5.4.50) *cvi* —*ī* instead of *a*— means that something becomes what it was not previously. Therefore *svīkāra* by the donee indicates an activity on his part: he becomes the owner of something of which he was not the owner prior to his activity. "Hence how could he be the owner before it?"

Jīmūtavāhana does not deny that the donee performs an activity of his own. In 1.24 he actually speaks of *sampradānavyāpāra*, but he gives it a different content than the opponent:

ucyate: utpannam api svataṃ samprādanavyāpāreṇa 'mamedam' iti jñānena yatheṣṭavyavahārārham iti svīkāraśabdārthaḥ.

Whereas the opponent referred to the *cvi* compound *svīkāra* to show that acceptance of a gift creates the proprietary right which did not exist earlier, Jīmūtavāhana interprets the activity in which the *sampradāna* is the autonomous agent —which has nothing to do with the act of the *dātṛ*— as the recognition by the donee that the object is his and that he can transact it at will.

This description of the donee's activity should in turn be read in conjunction with one element of Jīmūtavāhana's definition of the activity of the donor in 1.21:

cetanoddeśaviśiṣṭatyāgāt.

The donor relinquishes his own proprietary right, but not without qualification. The relinquishment is neither "in favour of the donee who is a sentient being" (Colebrooke) nor "with the intention of passing the same to a sentient being" (Ramaswami); it is "qualified by the stipulation of a donee who is *cetana*." And *cetana* is clearly defined in 1.24: someone who is mentally capable of realizing that the object is his and that he can use it at will.

If we take all these elements together, Jīmūtavāhana undoubtedly presents a coherent theory on the acceptance of gifts. By this I do not mean to say that he was right and his critics —e.g., Mitramiśra in the *Vyavahāraprakāśa* (Chowkhamba edition: 426–427)— wrong. They both interpreted the terms *dāna* and *pratigraha* (or *arjana*, *svīkāra*). In doing so they both looked for and emphasized those arguments which proved their respective points, and which made the theories on gifts fit in the framework of their larger ideas on ownership in joint family property.

All along they demonstrated that they were good commentators, nothing more, nothing less.

As a result, I have to disagree with Ramaswami's interpretation that, according to *Dāyabhāga* 1.21, a bequest can be made in favor of an unborn child; Jīmūtavāhana never thought of that kind of situation when he wrote this passage. At the same time, I cannot subscribe to Kane's evaluation (1930–1962: 3.475, quoted Derrett 1971: 43b) that Jīmutavāhana more than fellow commentators "indulges in casuistical reasoning." Nor is there any necessity to dismiss the *Dāyabhāga* and rather look "at what the jurists, that excentric Jīmūtavāhana apart, say about *danam*, gift" (Derrett 1971: 44a).

The misunderstandings to which Jīmūtavāhana's remarks on gifts have led underscore a problem which I have repeatedly tried to point out in other publications. The *Dāyabhāga* —and other *nibandhas* and commentaries on Dharmaśāstras— were not meant to be read as law books. Their authors were *paṇḍits* who commented on *smṛti* texts against the vast background of their śāstric learning; they were only incidentally concerned with law as we understand it. Jīmūtavāhana explained *dāna* logically and consistently from the *paṇḍit*'s point of view. As indicated earlier, he did not think of judges or lawyers applying his statement to justify a bequest in favor of an unborn child. He may or may not have thought of "what is to happen if the intended donee refuses the gift" (Kane, quoted Derrett 1971: 43b); the basic element for him was the term *dāna*, which has an independent agent who is the *dātṛ* on the one hand and, on the other hand, a beneficiary who is the *sampradāna* and, therefore, not the determining factor in the act of giving. Finally, if Jīmūtavāhana happened to be called upon to solve the —real— case cited by Derrett (43b–44a): "if acceptance is not requisite a Chandala could make a ritual gift to a Brahmin and thus cause him to be outcasted," I imagine that, once he recovered from his surprise, he would point to his paragraph on *svīkāra* without any concern for the *Cāṇḍāla* who had lost part of his property.

30

Dāsadāsī

Introduction

The Dharmaśāstras do not encourage *anuloma* marriages.[672] Yet they are concerned about the inheritance of sons born of marriages in which the wife's *varṇa* is lower than that of her husband.[673] To be sure, the higher the *varṇa* of the wife, the larger the share of the son, but all legitimate *anuloma* sons, including the son of a Brahmin and a Śūdra wife, are entitled to fixed shares.[674] Just as sons of legally wedded wives of twice-born *varṇa*s are, the son of a Śūdra wife is *rikthabhāk*: he is entitled to a share of the estate in his own right. And, since a son by a Śūdra wife is the only possible legitimate son for a Śūdra husband,[675] he inherits the entire estate of his father.[676]

[672] E.g., MDh 3.12–13: *savarṇāgre dvijātīnāṃ praśastā dārakarmaṇi; kāmatas tu pravṛttānām imāḥ syuḥ kramaśo 'varāḥ* (or *varāḥ*): *śūdraiva bhāryā śūdrasya, sā ca svā ca viśaḥ smṛte, te ca svā caiva rājñaś ca, tāś ca svā cāgrajanmanaḥ.*

[673] MDh 9.149–53 prescribes two different ways of dividing the inheritance, in case there are sons by wives of equal and of all lower *varṇa*s: 3, 2, 1 ½, 1 shares, or 4, 3, 2, 1 shares. YDh 2.125 and, especially, ViDh 18.1–33 go into great detail on how to divide the property when not every kind of *anuloma* sons shares in the partition or inheritance.

[674] The respective shares of the sons vary from text to text. Yet the basic idea seems to be that the share of the son of a twice-born husband and a Śūdra wife should not exceed one tenth of the estate. Cf. MDh 9.154cd: *nādhikaṃ daśamād aṃśāc chūdrāputrāya dharmataḥ.*

[675] MDh 3.13a (see note 672), and, again, 9.157ab: *śūdrasya tu savarṇaiva nānyā bhāryā vidhiyate.*

[676] ViDh 18.28–31: *athaikaputrāḥ...sarvaharāḥ... śūdraḥ śūdrasya*, on which ViNpa comments: *śūdrasya śūdra evaikaḥ putraś ced asau sarvam eva haret.*

The *śāstras* are less favorably disposed toward sons born out of wedlock. As a rule, illegitimate sons of twice-born fathers may be given maintenance, but they cannot claim a share in the inheritance: they are not *rikthabhāk*. For sons of twice-born males and Śūdra females in particular, there are a number of rules that either prescribe maintenance or say that they are not *rikthabhāk*; these texts are most often interpreted as referring to illegitimate sons.

First, Gautama:

śūdrāputro 'py anapatyasya śuśrūṣuś cel labheta vṛttimūlam[677] *antevāsividhinā.*[678] (28.39)

Following the Vra,[679] Colebrooke (1798: 5.169) translated *anapatya* as "a man who leaves no *legitimate* offspring."[680]

Second, a verse from Bṛhaspati agrees perfectly with Gautama:

anapatyasya śuśrūṣur guṇavāñ chūdrayonijaḥ
labhetājivanaṃ; śeṣaṃ sapiṇḍāḥ samavāpnuyuḥ.[681] (26.125/tr. 25.31)

Third, Śaṅkha and Likhita:

na śūdrāputro 'rthabhāgī; yad evāsya pitā dadyāt sa evāsya bhāgaḥ.[682] (277)

Fourth, Manu:

brāhmaṇakṣatriyaviśāṃ śūdrāputro[683] *na rikthabhāk;*
yad evāsya pitā dadyāt tad evāsya dhanaṃ bhavet. (9.155)

This last text created a problem for commentators, since they

[677] GHda explains *vṛttimūla* as follows: *yāvatā kṛṣyādikarmasamartho bhavati, tāval labheta*; similarly, GMka 28.40, Vra 1509, etc.

[678] Even though GHda introduces 28.39: *brāhmaṇasyeti vartate* (from 28.35), he wants it to apply to sons of all twice-born classes: *evaṃ kṣatriyavaiśyayor api śūdrāputro vṛttimūlaṃ labhate.*

[679] Vra 1509: *anūḍhaśūdrāputraḥ*. Hence, Bühler (GDh) and Olivelle (GDh) "a Śūdra wife" are misleading.

[680] Throughout this article italics and parentheses in translations are those of the translators.

[681] Jolly (BS) translates *anapatya* as "a man having no male offspring." Colebrooke (1798: 5.168), again from Vra 1509, as "a man who leaves no *legitimate* offspring." Cf. Vci 223: *idaṃ cānūḍhaśūdrāputraparam*; etc.

[682] Colebrooke (1798: 5.170): "Chandeśwara also expounds this text as in effect relating to the son of an unmarried Śūdra."

[683] For Śūdrā, Jones (MDh), Haughton (MDh), Colebrooke (1798: 5.166): "a woman of the servile class"; Loiseleur Deslongchamps (MDh): "une femme Soûdrâ"; Burnell (MDh): "a Çūdra woman"; Bühler (MDh): "a Sûdra (wife)"; Derrett (MBhru): "a śūdrā wife"; Doniger (MDh): "a servant woman."

had to reconcile it with the immediately preceding verse, by which the father is allowed to give the *śūdrāputra* a share, be it no more than one tenth of the total assets (*nādhikaṃ daśamād aṃśāt*).[684] Some commentators consider two possible solutions: either MDh 9.154 refers to a *śūdrāputra* who is *śuśrūṣu* and *guṇavant* (from Gautama and Bṛhaspati) and MDh 9.155 to a *śūdrāputra* who cannot claim these virtues, or MDh 9.154 pertains to the son of a wedded Śūdrā and MDh 9.155 to the son of a Śūdrā who is not wedded to the twice-born father.[685] Most commentators, however, restrict themselves to a single interpretation: the son of an unwedded twice-born father and a Śūdra woman is excluded from the inheritance.[686]

These four texts led to Jones' heavily italicized translation of MDh 9.155: "The son of a brahmana, a ksatriya, or a vaisya, by a woman of the servile class, shall inherit no part of the estate, *unless he be virtuous*; *nor jointly with other sons, unless his mother was lawfully married*; whatever his father may give him, let that be his own."[687] Anglo-Hindu law followed suit: "Illegitimate sons of the three higher classes are entitled to nothing but maintenance" (Mayne 1950: 525).

The Problem

Having established that an illegitimate son of a twice-born father and a Śūdra mother is not entitled to a share of the inheritance, I now wish to introduce two Dharmaśāstra passages which are the main concern of this article.

First, Manu:

dāsyāṃ vā dāsadāsyāṃ vā yaḥ śūdrasya suto bhavet,
so'nujñāto hared aṃśam iti dharmo vyavasthitaḥ. (9.179)

Second, Yājñavalkya:

jāto 'pi dāsyāṃ śūdreṇa kāmato 'ṃśaharo bhavet.

[684] Cf. note 675.

[685] MMdhā: *anye tv anūḍhāyāḥ śūdrāyāḥ putrasyemaṃ vidhim icchanti. na hi vivāhaliṅgaṃ kiṃcid astīti....yathā gautamaḥ śūdrāputraprakaraṇa evāha.* MMdhā objects to this: *teṣāṃ mate kṣatriyavaiśyayor anūḍhayor jātā rikthaharāḥ prāpnuvanti. tatra ca kiyān aṃśa iti na jñāyate.* MKlū: *evaṃ ca pūrvoktavibhāganiṣedhād vikalpaḥ. sa ca guṇavadaguṇāpekṣaḥ. athavā anūḍhaśūdrāputraniṣedho 'yaṃ daśamabhāganiṣedhaḥ.* Similarly, MBhru.

[686] Vma 103 introduces MDh 9.155 as follows: *apariṇītaśūdrāputras tu dravyāṃśam api na labheta.* Cf. Vra 1508: *anūḍhāputraviṣayam etat.*

[687] Also Colebrooke (1798: 5.166) and Haughton (MDh); Loiseleur Deslongchamps: "à moins qu'il ne soit vertueux, ou que sa mère n'ait été légitimement mariée."

mṛte pitari kuryus taṃ bhrātaras tv ardhabhāgikam;
abhrātṛko haret sarvaṃ duhitṛṇāṃ sutād ṛte. (2.133cd–34)

Thus, according to Manu and Yājñavalkya, the son of a Śūdra[688] by a *dāsī*[689] or by a *dāsī* or a *dāsadāsī*, at will,[690] inherits a share. After their father's death, his brothers must give him half a share,[691] and, if there are no brothers, he inherits everything, unless there is a daughter's son. Most important, if the father is a Śūdra, the son of a *dāsī*/ *dāsadāsī* is recognized as a full-fledged son (*suta eva*) of his father, and, even if there is a daughter's son, he inherits equally with him (*sati tasminn aurasavat kalpanā*).[692]

As Jolly pointed out, "[t]hese two verses contain everything that is to be found in the Smṛtis on the subject, but the various constructions put on, and important rules derived from, them

[688] YMtā underscores that, on account of the word *śūdreṇa*, the rule applies to Śūdras only, not to members of the higher *varṇas*: *atra ca śūdragrahaṇād dvijātinā dāsyām utpannaḥ pitur icchayāpy aṃśaṃ na labhate, nāpy ardhaṃ, dūrato eva kṛtsnam. kiṃtv anukūlaś cej jīvanamātraṃ labhate.* Similarly, Mbhru, Vma 104, Svi 395, YApa, Vtā 379, Mra 337, Vpra 488, Pmā 523. MMdhā 9.179, too, agrees, but offers different reasons: *dauhitrasyānyāsyāśrutatvāt tasya ca prakṛtatvena buddhau saṃniveśād brāhmaṇādīnāṃ tu dāsīsutāḥ prajīvanamātrabhojanarikthabhāja iti sthitiḥ.*

[689] The term *dāsyāḥ putraḥ* occurs early. At *Aitareya Brāhmaṇa* 2.2.19 = 8.1, Kavaṣa Ailūṣa is the son of a Brahmin and a *dāsī*, and is berated for it by the *ṛṣis*: *ṛṣayo vai sarasvatyāṃ sattram āsata. te kavaṣam ailūṣaṃ somād anayan: dāsyāḥ putraḥ kitavo 'Brāhmaṇaḥ kathaṃ no madhye 'dīkṣiṣṭeti.* Cf. *Kauśītakibrāhmaṇa* 12.3, etc. Chanana: "On s'en sert parfois pour injurier quelqu'un, comme en témoigne le *Setaketu Jâtaka*" (Chanana 1957: 75). Cf. Pāṇini 6.3.21–22: *ṣaṣṭhyā ākrośe. putre 'nyatarasyām,* and the standard example: *dāsyāḥ putraḥ* or *dāsīputraḥ*.

[690] For the interpretation of the ambiguous phrase "at will," see below.

[691] YBā 2.138 merely states that the illegitimate son should get less than his legitimate brothers: *ardhapadaṃ ca nyūnāṃśapratipattyartham.* Some commentators make it clear that the illegitimate son should be given one half of the share of the legitimate son: YApa *ekasya yāvān bhāgo bhavati tadardham*; Vci 224 *ūḍhāputrasya bhāgāpekṣayā.* Vpra 487 takes pain to justify the use of the plural *bhrātaraḥ* with the maxim *vyaktyabhiprāyeṇa jātyabhiprāyeṇa ca bahuvacanaikavacane,* and concludes: *ekaputrasya yāvān bhāgas tadardhabhāgaṃ śūdrāputrā labhante.* Other commentators are of the same opinion, but their use of the reflexive *sva-* may be ambiguous: YMtā *svabhāgād ardham*; MMdhā *svāṃśāpekṣayā ātmanā dvau dvau parigṛhṇīyur bhāgau tasyaikaṃ dadyuḥ*; Vra 1513, Mra 337 *svabhāgāpekṣayā*; Pmā 523 *svabhāgād ardhabhāginaṃ kuryuḥ*; YMtāSbo *svāṃśāpekṣayā ardhaṃ samuditadravyād dadyuḥ*; similarly, YMtāBbha. As a result, Colebrooke (1798: 5.174) translated: "half a share; that is half of such share as would have been assigned had his mother been legally married." After some hesitation between these two alternatives, the Privy Council decided that the illegitimate son is to take one half of what he would have taken if he were a legitimate son, cf. *Kamulammal* v. *Vishwanathaswami*, 50 I.A. 32 (1923).

[692] MMdhā. Cf. Dbhā 9.31: *sati tu dauhitre samaṃ vibhajya gṛhṇīyād viśeṣāśravaṇāt,* explained by DbhāKta: *samaṃ syād aśrutatvād viśesasyeti nvāyāt.* Dta 169 *sati tu dauhitre tasyaiva svīyasaṃtānatvāt tayos tulyāṃśitvaṃ yuktam* (quoted Colebrooke 1798: 5.175).

in modern works have given rise to several interesting controversies" (1885: 186). In Anglo-Hindu law, the two verses have, indeed, been quoted and commented on in numerous cases in courts of law all over India. In Derrett's words, "[t]his interesting set of rules has bedeviled the development of the Anglo-Hindu law on the subject of illegitimates" (1961: 255). I intend to deal in a separate article with the motivations for the varying interpretations put on the Manu and Yājñavalkya verses by the Anglo-Hindu courts of law. The problem which I wish to address in this essay is the identity, in the two Sanskrit texts, of the *dāsī* and the *dāsadāsī*, whose sons with a Śūdra male are entitled to a share in the inheritance.

Before doing so I must briefly refer to a problem that affects the understanding of the Manu and Yājñavalkya verses: at whose "will" (MDh *anujñātaḥ*, YDh *kāmataḥ*) does the son of a Śūdra and a *dāsī*/ *dāsadāsī* receive a share? Except for some early neutral translations: "if permitted" (Colebrooke 1798: 5.176) and "einen beliebigen erbtheil" (Stenzler YDh),[693] most translators follow Jones: "if permitted *by the other sons.*"[694] Yet, the more cogent interpretation, adopted by most commentators,[695] is "at the father's pleasure."[696] Even though this is not evident from MDh 1.179, it is from YDh 2.133cd.[697] This half verse obviously refers to the time prior to the father's death, as opposed to 2.134 which lays down what the sons must do when the father has not expressed his desire, i.e., after his death.

At this point we can address the main question: what is the meaning of the terms *dāsī* and *dāsadāsī* in Manu and Yājñavalkya? I intend to show (1) that Yājñavalkya refers to a Śūdra woman, i.e., any Śūdra woman, who is not married to her son's Śūdra father, and (2) that, within that range, Manu distinguishes between a Śūdra woman who is not married to anyone, and a Śūdra woman who is married to another Śūdra. Both points have been

[693] Also, recently, Derrett (MBhru): "by permission"; Doniger (MDh): "if he is permitted."

[694] E.g., Haughton (MDh); Loiseleur Deslongchamps (MDh): "s'il est autorisé *par les fils légitimes*"; Tagore (Vci 274).

[695] Including MKlū, even though Jones supposedly translated MDh "according to the gloss of Cullūca." Cf. MMdhā: *anujñātaḥ pitrā...*; *yadā tu pitā nānujānāti*; Dbhā 2.29: *pitur anumatyā*; YApa, YDka, Dkra 48, Dta 169: *pitur icchātaḥ* (YApa adds: *abhrātṛkas tu pitṛpariṇītotpannabhrātṛrahitaḥ*); Vma 104; *kāmaḥ pitur icchā*; YBā 2.137, Vci 224, Vsā 249, Mra 337, Pmā 523, Vpra 487, Dkra 47: *pitur icchayā*.

[696] Burnell (MDh): "if permitted," with a footnote: "'Permitted' means permitted by the father"; Bühler (MDh): "if permitted (by his father)."

[697] Colebrooke noted the difference. He translates: "if permitted (Dbhā 9.29) for MDh, but "by the choice of the father" (Dbhā 9.30) and "by the father's choice" (Colebrooke 1798: 5.174, and YMtā I.xii, 1) for YDh.

hinted at in the *śāstras* and in the commentaries, but these hints have been overlooked in translations into European languages and, as a result, in the decisions proffered in the Anglo-Hindu courts of law.

The Dāsī and Dāsadāsī Are Not Wedded to the Śūdra

The fact that we are dealing with illegitimate sons, i.e., sons of a Śūdra father not married to the *dāsī/ dāsadāsī* mother,[698] is obvious.[699] According to Yājñavalkya, after the father's death "the brothers," i.e., the sons of the Śūdra and his Śūdra wife, must give half a share to his son by a *dāsī.* The YMtā refers to these "brothers" as *pariṇītāputrāḥ,*[700] and comments: *pitur ūrdhvaṃ yadi pariṇītāputrāḥ santi, tadā te bhrātaras taṃ dāsīputram ardhabhāginaṃ kuryuḥ...atha yadā pariṇītāputrā na santi...* Medhātithi describes the "brothers" as their father's *aurasa* sons.[701] According to the Vci (224, on YDh 2.134cd): *śūdrasya ūḍhāputradauhitrayor abhāve sakalam eva dhanam anūḍhāputro haret.*[702] In any case, the son of a Śūdra and his Śūdra wife is a *pariṇītāputra,* the son of a Śūdra and a *dāsī* is an *apariṇītāputra.*

Dāsa and Dāsadāsī Do Not Refer to Slaves

The recurring translation of *dāsa* as a "male slave" and of *dāsī* as a "female slave" in both Manu and Yājñavalkya goes back to Jones' 1794 rendition of Manu: "a son, begotten by a man of the servile class on his female slave, or on the female slave of his male slave."[703]

[698] Dbhā 9.31. To justify equal partition with a daughter's son, Dbhā 9.31 says: *tathā hy apariṇītājātatve 'py asya putratvāt.* Cf. Dta 169: *dāsīputrasyāpariṇītājātatvād aparasya tu pariṇītāsaṃtānatve 'pi dauhitratvāt tulyāṃśastyaiva yuktatvāt.*

[699] Hence the translation "concubine" in Anglo-Hindu jurisprudence.

[700] Cf. YDka: *pitṛpariṇītāputrāḥ*; Mra 337: *pariṇītāyāḥ putrāḥ*; Pmā 523: *pariṇītāputrāḥ*; Dkra 47: *pariṇītastrījātaputreṇa saha*; Vpra 487: *pariṇītaśūdrāputraḥ*; Vra 1513: *yadi pitur ūrdhvaṃ pariṇītāputrāḥ santi.*

[701] Colebrooke (1798): "the brethren, born of a wife legally married."

[702] Kane, who is strongly influenced by legal practice on the subject of illegitimate sons, states that "[a]n illegitimate son may be the son of a concubine who is a *dāsī* (i.e., who is in exclusive or continuous keeping) or he may be the son of a woman who is not a *dāsī.* The first is called *dāsīputra* and the second is hardly dealt with in the dharmaśāstra works" (1930–62: 3. 600).

[703] Colebrooke (1798: 5.176, but slightly different at Colebrooke 1810: "a son begotten by a Çúdra on a female slave"); Haughton (MDh); Loiseleur Deslonchamps (MDh): "Le fils engendré par un Soudra et par une femme, son esclave, ou par l'esclave femelle de son esclave mâle"; Stenzler (YDh): "Ein sohn der ein Śūdra mit einer Sklavin hat"; Burnell (MDh): "If a son is born to a Çūdra by a slave woman (or dāsī), or by a slave's slave-woman (dāsadāsī)"; Bühler (MDh):

The existence in classical India of a distinct social class called *dāsa* is well documented in Sanskrit and Pāli literatures. It is described in detail in the Dharmaśāstras and in Kauṭilya's *Arthaśāstra* (III.13; Cf. Kane 1930–1962: 2.180–87; Chanana 1957; Bongert 1963). Yet scholars have noted that the term *dāsa* is not always used in the technical meaning "slave," but that it occasionally stands as a synonym for Śūdra: "The word 'slave' may itself mean Çūdra" (Burnell, MDh); or, "[i]t is quite certain...that the Commentators and Çāstris have persistently explained the term Dāsī as including any unmarried female of the Çūdra caste" (Jolly 1885: 187).

As far as the *śāstras* are concerned, I wish to draw attention to the verse in which Manu defines the last of the twelve kinds of sons (called *śaudra* in the list at MDh 9.159–60):

> *yaṃ brāhmaṇas tu śūdrāyāṃ kāmād utpādayet sutam,*
> *taṃ pārayann eva śavas; tasmāt pāraśavaḥ smṛtaḥ.* (9.178)

To be sure, the sequence of verses in the MDh is not necessarily a logical one. Yet, verse 9.178 unambiguously refers to the son of a Brahmin male and a Śūdra female. Their son should, for all practical purposes, be considered legally dead: "though yet alive, he is a corpse." This being the case, I am inclined to read the immediately following verse (9.179) as referring to the son of a Śūdra male and a Śūdra female: "on the other hand, when it is not a Brahmin but a Śūdra male who has a son with a Śūdra female, that son does inherit."[704]

In another passage Manu (8.411–14) instructs Brahmins on what to do when members of the lower *varṇas* become

"A son who is (begotten) by a Sûdra on a female slave, or on the female slave of his slave"; Derrett (1956: 182): "That son of a Śūdra father who is begotten on a female slave or the female slave of his male slave"; Derrett (MBhru): "Where a Śūdra is born to a man on his female slave (or kept mistress) or the female slave (or kept mistress) of his slave"; Doniger (MDh): "A son whom a servant man begets in his slave girl, or in the slave girl of his male slave." Jones' translation is also cited in treatises on modern Hindu law, e.g., Mayne 1950: 633.

[704] The phrase *kāmād utpādayet* is ambiguous. It can refer either to a husband who desires offspring even though he is the father of a son —only the first son is *dharmaja*, all others are *kāmaja* (MDh 9.107)— or to a man who seeks intercourse out of wedlock. As a result, like GDh 28.39, BS 26.125/25.31, ŚL 277, and MDh 9.155 quoted earlier, MDh 9.178, too, has been variously interpreted by the commentators. MMdhā is neutral: *kāmād iti śūdrābhigamasya kāmamātraparatvād uktam.* MKlū explains *śūdrāyāṃ* as *pariṇītāyām eva śūdrāyām*, and so does MRvā: *śūdrāyāṃ yathāvidhyūḍhāyām.* On the other hand, according to Dbhā 9.28, *tad apariṇītaśūdrāputrābhiprāyam.* None of the translators is specific: Jones (MDh), Haughton (MDh), Burnell (MDh), Bühler (MDh), Derrett (MBhru): "through lust," Doniger (MDh): "out of lust," Loiseleur Deslongchamps (MDh): "par luxure."

vṛttikarśita.[705] They should compassionately support Kṣatriyas and Vaiśyas, and make it possible for them to continue living by the activities that are appropriate for their *varṇas*;[706] under no circumstances should they subject Kṣatriyas or Vaiśyas to *dāsya*. The status of and the activities connected with *dāsya* must be reserved for the Śūdra, because

dāsyāyaiva hi sṛṣṭo 'sau brāhmaṇasya svayambhuvā. (8.413cd)

And again, about *dāsya*, in the next verse:

nisargajaṃ hi tat tasya; kas tasmāt tad apohati.[707] (8.414cd)

These verses show that, even in the *śāstras*, the status of a *dāsa* was associated with Śūdras.

As is to be expected, the commentators most often interpret *dāsī* in the context of Manu's sevenfold division of *dāsas*:

dhvajāhṛto bhaktadāso gṛhajaḥ krītadattrimau
paitriko daṇḍadāsaś ca saptaite dāsayonayaḥ. (8.415)[708]

Hence, Kullūkabhaṭṭa comments on *dāsyām* at MDh 9.179: *dhvajāhṛtādyuktalakṣaṇāyām* (Similarly, MRvā, Vra 1512).

Yet, at least one commentator on Manu, Rāmacandra, identifies *dāsī* in this verse with *śūdrā*: *dāsyāṃ śūdrāyām anūḍhāyāṃ vā dāsadāsyāṃ vā śūdrasya yo dāsas tasya yā dāsī tasyām*. After establishing that the illegitimate son of a twice-born male and a Śūdra female does not inherit (Sci quotes BS 26.125 and ŚL 277 (see above)), the Sci (87) introduces MDh 9.179 and YDh 2.133cd–34 as follows: *atra śūdrasyāpariṇītaśūdrāputro 'pi dhanabhāg bhavati*; and so does the Vtā (378): *śūdrasyānūḍhaśūdrāputre sa eva*.

More clearly and unambiguously than any other commentary or *nibandha*, Nīlakaṇṭha's *Vyavahāramayūkha* (103–4) places Yājñavalkya's son of a *dāsī* in the context of sons of Śūdra women, as follows:

[705] MKlū: *vṛttikarśitau bhṛtyabhāvena pīḍitau*.

[706] MDh 8.411cd: *bibhṛyād ānṛśaṃsyena svāni karmāṇi kārayan*.

[707] MKlū comments: *adṛṣṭārtham apy avaśyaṃ śūdreṇa brāhmaṇādidvijaśuśrūṣā kartevyeti evaṃparam etat*.

[708] According to MMdhā: *dāsyām utpanno garbhadāsaḥ*. More often (MBhru, MSnā, MKlū, MRvā, MNda) *gṛhaja* is the kind of slave identified with *dāsīputra*. Hence Jones (MDh), Haughton (MDh): "one born of a female slave in the house"; more cautiously, Colebrooke (1798: 3.33): "one born *of a female slave* in the house"; Loiseleur Deslongchamps (MDh): "le serf né *d'une femme esclave* dans la demeure du maître."

(1) The son of a Śūdra female wedded to a *dvijāti* male gets a share in movable property, but not in land. Nīlkaṇṭha quotes: *śūdryāṃ dvijātibhir jāto na bhūmer bhāgam arhati* (D 1592ab), and comments: *dravyasya tu labhata eva.*

(2) The son of a Śūdra female,

(a) who is not wedded to a *dvijāti* male, does not get a share even in movable property: *apariṇītaśūdrāputras tu dravyāṃśam api na labhate,* but only what his father gives him. Nīlakaṇṭha quotes MDh 9.155, BS 26.125, GDh 28.39 (see above). After the father's death, and provided there is no other offspring, he gets maintenance (BS *labhetājīvanam*, GDh *labhate vṛttimūlam*);

(b) who is not wedded to a Śūdra male, gets a share on the basis of YDh 2.133cd–34.[709]

In his notes on the *Vyavahāramayūkha* edition (152–53), Kane rightly observes: "the word *dāsī* has a somewhat vague import. It does not necessarily mean 'a female slave.' Very often *śūdra* and *dāsa* were synonymous."[710]

The Meaning of Dāsadāsī

The commentators vary a great deal in their interpretation of *dāsadāsī* as distinct from *dāsī.*[711] The Vci (224) quotes both Manu and Yājñavalkya, and nonetheless comments, without regard to Manu: *śūdrasyānūḍhaśūdrāputraḥ...*[712] Lakṣmīdhara probably stands alone with the interpretation *dāsadāsī paricārikadāsī.*[713] Some analyze the compound *dāsadāsī* as *dāsasya dāsī,* without further comment. Thus Sarvajñanārāyaṇa: *dāsyāṃ śūdrasyānūḍhāyāṃ tathā śūdrasya yo dāsas tasya dāsyāṃ.*[714]

The Dbhā (9.29) introduces MDh 9.179 as follows: *śūdrasya punar apariṇītādāsyādiśūdraputraḥ...,* which, in Colebrooke's translation, reads: "But the son of a Śūdra, by a female slave

[709] Vma does not quote MDh 9.179, and, hence, does not distinguish between *dāsī* and *dāsadāsī.*

[710] Yet, seven years later, he translates: "a son begotten by a śūdra on a dāsī (concubine)" (Vma tr. 94). Cf. my remark at note 702.

[711] MMdhā's text is obviously corrupt: *śūdrasyānūḍhāyām aniyuktāyām api.* Jha (MMdhā tr.): "In the case of a Shūdra, the child from an unmarried woman, or from an unauthorised woman" (repeated by Mayne 1950: 634).

[712] Similarly, after quoting MDh 9.179 and YDh 2.133cd–34, Vni 432: *sarvatra dāsīputrasya dhanagrahaṇam.*

[713] Kta 704. Quoted Vra 1512, yet Colebrooke (1897: 5.176): "on the female slave of his servant. The *Calpataru.*"

[714] Cf. Vra 1512: *dāsyāṃ...dāsadāsyāṃ tathāvidhalakṣaṇadāsadāsyāṃ vā.*

or other unmarried Śūdra woman...." Even though this translation was accepted as correct by a Full Bench of the Calcutta High Court,[715] Jīmūtavāhana actually intended to say: "the son of a Śūdra by an *unmarried dāsī* or by *other dāsīs*." Medhātithi clearly distinguishes between a *dāsī* and a *dāsī* "connected with a *dāsa*" (*dāsyāṃ dāsasambandinyāṃ vā dāsyām*). Some commentators go further, but in two different directions: two commentators on the *Dāyabhāga* interpret *dāsadāsī* as a *dāsī* "belonging to but not wedded to a *dāsa*": *dāsasyāpariṇītarakṣitā* (DbhāRca and DbhāKta), whereas another commentator on the *Dāyabhāga* and one commentator on MDh take the ultimate step: a *dāsadāsī* is a *dāsī* "married to a *dāsa*": *dāsasya bhāryā dāsī* (DbhāŚnā) and *tathāvidhadāsasya bhāryā dāsī* (MRvā).

It has been suggested that, as far as Śūdras are concerned, "the Hindu regarded...their marriages as little better than concubinage."[716] If that was the case, it makes little difference whether the term *dāsadāsī* refers to a Śūdra female "belonging to" or "married to" another Śūdra. Others, however, recognized that Śūdras do distinguish between marriage and concubinage,[717] in fact, that marriage is the only *saṃskāra* which a Śūdra can look forward to.[718] Keeping in mind the clear distinction which YDh 2.133cd–34 draws between the rights of the son of a Śūdra by a *dāsī* on the one hand, and his brothers, i.e., his Śūdra father's legitimate sons, on the other, I submit that Manu's *dāsadāsī*, differently from the unmarried *dāsī* in the same *śloka*, refers to a Śūdra woman married to a Śūdra other than her son's father.

[715] *Rajani Nath v. Nitai Chandra*, 48 I.L.R. Calcutta 643 at 683 (1921).

[716] Mr. Justice Raymond West at 3 I.L.R. Bombay 273 at 289 (1879).

[717] *Ranoji* v. *Kandoji*, 8 I.L.R. Madras 557 (1885).

[718] Mr. Justice Krishnaswami Ayyar, in *Kameswara Sastri* v. *Veeracharlu*, 34 I.L.R. Madras 422 at 427 (1911).

31

The Definition of Vākpāruṣya

Although we originally intended this paper to be a comprehensive study on *vākpāruṣya* as a whole, we had to abandon that project and limit ourselves to one point among many. Even for such a title of law as *vākpāruṣya*, which may be called one of the least extensively treated ones, a thorough study of the ancient and medieval works on *dharma* has to deal with so large a mass of materials, that the whole subject cannot be treated here at once.

Unfortunately not all texts are available in print, and even a number of those which have been edited we could not compare in the place where we are to work now. Yet, if we decided to publish these pages, it was on the ground of the following consideration. For the definite history of Dharmaśāstra we shall have to wait until all texts have been critically edited. Nevertheless, for attaining this final result there shall be some continual interaction between editing texts and writing a history of Hindu law: may this contribution, however incomplete it may be, contain some useful data for future editors of texts, which in their turn will be helpful for a more complete historical survey subsequently.

The problem, we want to treat here, is the definition of *vākpāruṣya* as the Indian authors themselves formulated it.

The oldest Dharmasūtras are not largely concerned with abuse.

1. BDh does not mention it at all.
2. In ĀpDh we do not find the generic terms *vākpāruṣyam* or *daṇḍapāruṣyam*, but a few cases of *ākrośaḥ* = "reviling" occur (ĀpDh 1.9.26.3–5; 2.10.27.4).
3. VaDh 19.9 opposes *ahiṃsā* = "assault" to *ākrośaḥ* "reviling," an antithesis which later on shall become the one between *daṇḍapāruṣyam* and *vākpāruṣyam*. Besides, in the chapters on pen-

ances the author quotes a verse, which we shall find back in NS's chapter on abuses (VaDh 20.30 = NS 15.21), and falsely charging another person with an offense causing expulsion from caste is a mere isolated case, which from NS onward will be connected up into a complete system (VaDh 23.39–40).

4. A rather extensive treatment of abuse for the first time occurs in GDh. Not only do we meet with the general term *vākpāruṣyam* as opposed to *daṇḍapāruṣyam*, but a certain number of *sūtras* are devoted to as many special cases of *ākrośaḥ*, etc. (GDh 11.32.; 12.8–14; 21.17–18; 23.27–28).

In the Dharmaśāstras, from MDh onward, *vākpāruṣya* definitely ranks among the *vivāda* or *vyavahārapadas*, the "titles of Law" (see the comparative table in Kane 1930–1962: 3.249).

ViDh (5.23–39), too, although not having a list of *vivādapadas* of its own, contains an exhaustive treatment of abuse, and so does YDh (YDh 2.204–211).

Before inquiring into the definition of *vākpāruṣya*, a general remark should be made. From the isolated cases mentioned in the oldest Dharmasūtras and Dharmaśāstras up to NS, the treatment of *vākpāruṣya* exhibits a wonderful casuistry of all species of abuse without even an attempt being made to circumscribe what *vākpāruṣya* as a genus actually is. We hope to point out elsewhere, how the texts before NS and even Nārada himself prescribe most variable punishments for *vākpāruṣya*, to such an extent that the *nibandhakāras* had to appeal to all their ingenuity in order to make them agree with each other.

In this respect NS means a turning-point in the treatment of *vākpāruṣya* Besides taking over a great number of verses from MDh,[719] the chapter on *vākpāruṣya*, (which treats of *daṇḍapāruṣya* at the same time) opens with a general definition and a subdivision of the subject-matter.

Unhappily the two greatest *smṛtis* after NS, viz. BS and KS, are known to us only through collections of quotations from the *dharmanibandhas*. Consequently the notion we may form to ourselves of the contents of BS and KS always runs the risk of being incomplete and false. Nevertheless we may not neglect to notice, that the said *smṛtis*, in as far as we know them, have proceeded further on the way shown by NS: the verses of BS and KS, which have been preserved nearly exclusively contain general notions on *vākpāruṣya*, whereas the old casuistry of punishments has disappeared as well.

Apart from the *dharma*-literature we shall mention the very short definition given by AŚ 193.8 (Kangle 3.18.1):

[719] NS 15.15 = MDh 8.267; 16 = 268; 17 = 269; 18 = 274; 22 = 270; 23 = 271; 24 = 272.

vākpāruṣyam upavādaḥ kutsanam abhibhartsanam iti,

which Shama Sastry translated as follows: "Calumny, contemptuous talk, or intimidation constitutes defamation." This, however, cannot teach us very much: the terms used are too vague and of no accurate circumscription.

The earliest text, which may be considered as a real definition of *vākpāruṣya*, is NS 15.1. This *śloka*, however, poses so many questions of its own, that it does not allow of a mere immediate translation, but it requires us to enter into a short discussion of it. In Jolly's edition the verse runs as follows:

deśajātikulādīnām ākrośanyaṅgasaṃyutam |
yad vacaḥ pratikūlārtham vākpāruṣyaṃ tad ucyate[720] ||

This text not only is the earliest definition of *vākpāruṣya*, but it has also remained so in the largest number of *nibandha*s. Nevertheless, its interpretation is not uniform everywhere.

1. YMtā 257 opens the chapter on *vākpāruṣya* by quoting NS 15.1. As to the text itself, it corresponds to Jolly's edition, but it takes *ākrośam* separately as noted in the variant readings. The interpretation is as follows: *ākrośaḥ* = "speaking aloud," *nyaṅgam* = "blame, censure." A speech, which is accompanied by both these elements, and which is uttered with an inimical intention *pratikūlārtham*, i.e., in order to provoke agitation or anxiety, this is *vākpāruṣya*.[721]

This way of interpreting NS 15.1 seems to have enjoyed a great authority. It was often followed in later centuries.

Thus, e.g., Pmā 428–9 and Vmi 379, which, however, accordingly read *ākrośanyaṅgasaṃyutam*. Vmi 379 differs from YMtā only by explaining *ākrośa* as *ākṣepaḥ* or *bhartsanam* (see below).

Analogously to YMtā, NMSBha 15.1 also enumerates three requirements, but they are grouped differently: "A speech, which (1) is accompanied by both *ākrośaḥ* + *nyaṅgam*, (2) refers to one's country etc., (3) has an inimical intention, this is *vākpāruṣya*."

[720] A few variant readings shall be noticed:

(a) *ākrośa*: sometimes taken separately as *ākrośam*. Thus 2 Mss. used by Jolly, Svi 476, etc. Or *krośanam* YApa 805.

(b) °*Nyaṅga*: °*nyaṅku* Vci 69, Dvi 196; *vyaṅga*° Svi 476, Kdhe (Dvi 198).

(c) °*saṃyutam*: °*saṃjñitam* YApa 805, Vra 240, SSā (Dvi 197), Vci 69, Dvi 196, etc.: *saṃhitam* NMS.

[721] This interpretation, which wants to refer °*saṃyutam* to both *ākrośa*° and *nyaṅga*, requires both words to be taken together as a *dvandva*, forming one *tatpuruṣa*-compound with °*saṃyutam*. *Ākrośam* cannot be put separately as, e.g., the NSP-edition does. To the same result points Vra 240 when quoting YMtā.

Less complete, but certainly influenced by YMtā, is Rkau 488: "*nyaṅgam* = blame, *ākrośaḥ* = speaking aloud; he who utters both these things, his speech is *vākpāruṣya.*"

Very loosely connected with YMtā is the interpretation of Sca 12: "*Vākpāruṣya* is that speech, which contains a purport of scolding one's country etc., and which is intended to provoke an excessive pain."

Vci 69, reading *nyaṅkusaṃjñitam*, explicitly follows YMtā, and even rejects all other interpretations as being improper, because they overlook NS 15.1 to be a generic definition. This detail is highly interesting: (1) as will be proved below, another interpretation was current in Vci's time indeed; (2) whereas this variant interpretation will be shown to have been accepted by the authors of the school of Mithilā (Vra, Dvi), Vācaspatimiśra is a sufficiently independent personality so as to defend the view of YMtā against his fellow countrymen, viz., his predecessor Caṇḍeśvara and his contemporary (pupil?) Vardhamāna.

2. Before quoting the interpretation of YMtā, Vra 240 gives an explanation of its own. *Ākrośaḥ* is circumscribed as "scolding (*ākṣepaḥ*) one's country, caste, family, etc.," and *nyaṅgasaṃjñitam* as "that which contains (*vat*) the name of a detested (*nikṛṣṭa*) limb (*aṅga*)."

This interpretation would scarcely justify the quotation from YMtā being introduced by the particle *tu*, "but," if we did not dispose of Dvi to make Vra's intention clear.

Dvi 196, too, opposes another interpretation to YMtā, which is said to go back to Gaṇeśvaramiśra's *Vyavahārataraṅga.* The objection raised against YMtā is this. In the latter's opinion NS 15.1 as a whole comprises nothing but the generic definition (*sāmānyalakṣaṇam*) of *vākpāruṣya* In other words: any *vākpāruṣya* is a speech, which necessarily requires the simultaneous[722] presence of three elements: (1) speaking aloud, (2) a blame, and (3) an inimical intention. This is not right, Dvi 197 says, because this definition would fail to cover such cases of *vākpāruṣya* as imitating the sound *hūm* (cf. KS 768, see below).

Now Gaṇeśvaramiśra, who should be placed before the 14th century (cf. Chakravarti 1915), has stated, that NS 15.1 actually is not a generic definition in as far as in each case of *vākpāruṣya* the said three elements are necessary, but its real intention is to dis-

[722] This simultaneity is stressed by YMtāBbha 882: "Because what is meant is not, that the inimical intention should be accompanied by speaking aloud and blame separately, YMtā says: "accompanied by both these elements at the same times."

tinguish three different kinds of *vākpāruṣya*, viz., (1) *ākrośaḥ*, (2) *nyaṅkusaṃjñitam* (this is the reading printed in Dvi 196), and (3) *pratikūlārtham.*

Dvi does not expressly quote Vra's opinion to have been the same as Gaṇeśvara's,[723] but its adhering to this point of view without mentioning Vra's being different, may be considered a sufficient argument to hold, that the author of Dvi thought himself to be in accordance with his great predecessor Caṇḍeśvara (cf. Rocher 1951–1952: 214–224).

And the same note we find back in Svi 476, where after quoting NS 15.1 it is said: "*pāruṣyam* is making rough (*rūkṣīkaraṇam*); making rough the mind by means of speech is *vākpāruṣyam.*"

With regard to the Vra, however, there is a difficulty. After the quotation of NS 15.3 the following note is added:

> *evaṃ ca nyaṅgasaṃjñitatvasya vibhāgopādhitvāt sāmānyalakṣaṇaṃ vīvakṣitaṃ prāk.*

We translate as follows: "And because in this way (i.e., from the way in which the term *nyaṅgasaṃjñitam* is used in NS 15.3) the fact of containing the name of a detested limb (which also occurs in NS 15.1) is in close connection with the subdivision (of *vākpāruṣya*), above (*prāk*) it was the generic definition which was meant."

A first difficulty is the vagueness of the reference *prāk*, "above." Nevertheless we suppose, this cannot but refer to NS 15.1 quoted and interpreted on the preceding page (Vra 240). Now, if so, Vra's interpretation, which Dvi opposes to YMtā's in order to establish that NS 15.1 is not the generic definition of *vākpāruṣya*, would by its author himself be intended to be so. This is highly improbable at least.

We shall confess, for the moment we are not able to solve this problem sufficiently. We can only risk a conjecture: shall we read in Vra 241 on 15.3 *avivakṣitam* instead of *vivakṣitam*, i.e., "NS 15.1 quoted above *was not* intended to be the generic definition (as YMtā etc., maintain)?" This, however, shall remain a conjecture, unless some other evidence for it is brought out elsewhere.

This second way of interpreting NS 15.1 is based on reading this *śloka* as a whole with the two verses which immediately follow (NS 15.2–3):

> *Vākpāruṣya*, too, is of three sorts, according to its being either *niṣṭhura*, or *aślīla*, or *tīvra*. The abuse thus being gradually more

[723] Consequently, opposite to note 721 above, in Vra 240 we should prefer to read *ākrośam* separately, instead of printing it as a part of the compound *ākrośanyaṅgasaṃjñitam* as the BI-edition does.

> and more serious, the punishment, too, gradually becomes more and more severe.
> Know *niṣṭhura* to be *vākpāruṣya* accompanied by scolding, *aślīla* to be *vākpāruṣya* connected with *nyaṅga*; *tīvra* people call *vākpāruṣya* charging the offended person with an offense which causes expulsion from caste.[724]

Personally we are convinced that NS 15.1 was intended as a generic definition indeed, whereas NS 15.2–3 are to contain the subdivision: "This *vākpāruṣya*, as generally defined before, too (*api*), i.e., like many other titles of law mentioned above, is threefold..."

Accordingly in a great number of *nibandhas* the following scheme is adopted:

1. NS 15.1: generic definition of *vākpāruṣya*,
2. NS 15.2: three kinds of *vākpāruṣya*,
3. NS 15.3: definitions of these three kinds.[725]

Nevertheless we perfectly understand how NS 15.1, too, has come to be interpreted as a subdividing verse: as soon as the second element required for *vākpāruṣya* in NS 15.1, viz., *nyaṅga* or *nyaṅku* returns as a synonym for the second kind of *vākpāruṣya* in NS 15.3, why should the other two elements not be assimilated to the remaining two kinds of *vākpāruṣya*?

Even the commentators on YMtā felt inclined to do so, and in order to apologize for Vijñāneśvara, for the second *nyaṅga* in NS 15.3, YMtāBbha 883 had to appeal to an interpretation as follows: "Above (i.e., with regard to NS 15.1) YMtā declared *nyaṅga* to be a blame. And because, there, this being blameful is common to the three kinds of *vākpāruṣya*, viz., *niṣṭhura*, etc., it might appear as if giving accompanied by *nyaṅga* as a definition for one kind of *vākpāruṣya*, viz. *aślīla*, is wrong here. Therefore YMtā says: 'here (it is so),' which accordingly means: the meaning of the word *nyaṅga* is a particular kind of blame, viz., a vulgar one."

Along with the general definition itself, the threefold subdivision of *vākpāruṣya* for the first time occurs in NS. And like the definition the subdivision, too, has been generally accepted by all authors of *nibandhas*, even such commentaries as YMtā and YAP, which actually may be called *nibandhas* rather than commentaries, did so. On the other hand, commentaries like YBā,

[724] NS 15.2–3 *niṣṭhurāślīlatīvratvāt tad api trividham smṛtam |*
gauravānukramāt tasya daṇḍo'pyatra kramād guruḥ ||
ākṣepaṃ niṣṭhuraṃ jñeyam aślīlaṃ nyaṅgasaṃyutam |
pātanīyair upakrośais tīvram āhur manīṣiṇaḥ ||

[725] More or less explicitly this scheme occurs in YMtā 257, Sca 12, Mra 280, *Vīramitrodaya* 379, Rkau 488, Dnī 30, etc.

which closely follows the original text, do not mention it. And so does, e.g., Mklū, but at the same time he cannot conceal his being familiar with NS's subdivision, as is evident from the following three points:

1. MDh 8.267, 268, 269ab are said to be cases of *ākrośaḥ* or *ākṣepaḥ*;
2. In MDh 8.269cd, the words *vādeṣv avacanīyeṣu* are explained as *mātṛbhaginyādyaślīlarūpeṣu*;
3. MDh 8.270 is said to apply to a case, in which a Śūdra reviles twice-born men *pātakābhiyoginyā vācā*.

Let us now enter into a more detailed analysis of the several terms used by NS.

1. *ākrośaḥ* has always been *the* form of *vākpāruṣya par excellence.* Not only did we meet with it as early as ĀpDh and VaDh, when the general term *vākpāruṣyam* itself was not used yet, but that it has remained so later on is obvious from such examples as follow:

(a) Mklū 8.6 about *vākpāruṣya* simply says: *vākpāruṣyam ākrośanādi*
(b) MRvā 8.6: *vākpāruṣyam ākrośādi*;
(c) Even if more extensive, MNda 8.6, too, does not go beyond *ākrośaḥ: jātikulācārādīnām ākrośo vākpāruṣyam*;
(d) On the other hand MMdhā 8.267 explains *ākrośaḥ* by *paruṣavacanam*.

As to the synonyms given for *ākrośaḥ* according to the above distinction between the interpretations of YMtā and Vra, two currents are to be mentioned:

(a) *ākrośaḥ* = *uccair bhāṣaṇam*, "speaking aloud" (YMtā 257, PMā 429, Rkau 488, Dnī 29).
(b) *ākrośaḥ* = *ākṣepaḥ bhartsanam*, "scolding" (YApa 805, Vra 240, Mra 280, Vmi 379).

In general the commentators agree as to the different kinds of *ākrośaḥ*.[726] NS 15.1 *deśajātikulādīnām ākrośam* is explained as follows:

(a) *deśākrośaḥ*: "reviling one's country." e.g., the Gauḍas are quarrelsome.
(b) *jātyākrośaḥ*: "reviling one's caste." e.g., the Brāhmaṇas are very covetous.

[726] These examples are given even by YMtā 257, although —as said above— there *ākrośaḥ* is merely "speaking aloud." In YApa 805 they are given as examples of *deśākṣepaḥ*, etc.

(c) *kulākrośaḥ*: "reviling one's family." e.g., the Vaiśvāmitras are of cruel practices.[727]
(d) *ādyākrośaḥ*: "reviling similar things." These "similar things" are said to cover one's knowledge, handicraft, etc.[728]

2. For *sākṣepam*, "scolding," which in NS 15.3 is the synonym for the first kind of *vākpāruṣya*, viz., *niṣṭhuram*, the examples are uniform again: "fie! you silly man! you wretch!" etc. (YMtā 257, Sca 12, Mra 280, Vmi 379, Dnī 29).

3. The third kind of *vākpāruṣya*, *tīvram*, is the abuse charging another person with one of the five great sins (*mahāpātakam*) causing expulsion from caste. E.g., you are drinker of spirituous liquors (YMtā 257, Sca 12, Mra 281, Vmi 379, Dnī 29).

4. There is less uniformity in the interpretation of the terms *aślīlam* and its synonym *nyaṅgasaṃyutam* (for the variant readings, see above).

(a) A first series of texts explains *nyaṅgam* as *avadyam*, i.e., "something blamable,"[729] or as *asabhyam*, i.e., "not fit for an assembly, vile" (YApa 805, YMtā 257 (with regard to NS 15.3; for the note of YMtāBbha on this point, see above). This *avadyam* is even further limited as referring to intercourse with one's sister, etc. (YMtā 257, Sca 12, Mra 280–1, Vmi 379 (read *avadyam* for *avadya*°), Dnī 29).
(b) As said above, Vra 240 explains *nyaṅgasaṃjñitam* as "containing the name of a detested limb." This kind of etymological interpretation is quoted by Dvi 197, and, in accordance with KS 770 (see below), explained as "scolding by truly or falsely disclosing one's having a detested limb." By doing so Vardhamāna undoubtedly thought of Vci 70, which interprets *nyaṅgasaṃjñitam* as "containing the name of the penis and the like."
(c) In both preceding explanations this kind of *vākpāruṣya* was supposed to contain something immoral. This was not the case with Kdhe (quoted Dvi 198): reading *vyaṅga*, the author refers this case to reproaching a cripple and the like with their being deficient in limb (*vyaṅgatvena*).

[727] YMtā 257, YApa 805, Vra 240, PMā 428, Dvi 197, Vmi 379. Somewhat differently formulized is Sca 476: (a) *hiṃsakāḥ prācyāḥ*, (b) *viprās tv anācārāḥ*, (c) *maitrīśūnyā vaiśvāmitrāḥ*.

[728] YMtā 257 *svavidyāśilpādi*, Vra 240 *buddhyāder upādānam*, Svi 476 *svarūpākṣepaḥ*, Rkau 488 *svavidyotkarṣādi*.

[729] YMtā 257 (with regard to NS 15.1), PMā 429, Mra 280, Vmi 379, Rkau 488, Dnī 29. For *avadyam* YMiBbha 882 gives as a synonym: *garhyam* = "contemptible."

(d) Quite apart from these interpretations is Halāyudha (quoted Dvi 197): the terms under consideration mean "threatening somebody with the hand etc."

So much for the text of NS.

We also possess a general definition (BS 20.1) and a three-fold subdivision (BS 20.2–4), ascribed to Bṛhaspati.

The general definition is very simple: *vākpāruṣya*, is said to be a synonym of *apriyoktiḥ*: "speaking unkindly or harshly." Thus it is opposed to *daṇḍapāruṣyam*, which is explained by *tāḍanam* "beating, striking."

With BS, too, *vākpāruṣya* is three-fold, but analogously to many other threefold subdivisions, viz., first or lowest, middlemost, and highest, *vāk-pāruṣya* is subdivided into *prathamam*, *madhyamam*, and *uttamam*.[730] NS's terms *aślīlam* and *niṣṭhuram* have disappeared; *tīvram* only has remained as a synonym for *vākpāruṣya* of the highest degree. Besides, another three-fold gradation has been put along with it: the three kinds of *vākpāruṣya* correspond to charging with a *pāpam*, *upapātakam* and *mahāpātakam* respectively.

1. *vākpāruṣya* of the first degree: scolding one's country, village,[731] family, etc., charging with a sin (*pāpam*). And this is to happen *dravyaṃ vinā* (see below).
2. *vākpāruṣya* of the middlemost degree: charging with a minor sin *upapātakam* with regard to one's sister or one's mother (Kane, Vma 401: speaking of one's (the abuser's) connection with the sister or mother (of the abused)).
3. *vākpāruṣya* of the highest degree: charging with using forbidden food or drinks; charging with a mortal sin *mahāpātakam*; maliciously exposing one's weakest points."[732]

About these verses the commentators are very concise. We may restrict ourselves to the following notes:

[730] BS 20.2: *deśagrāmakulādīnāṃ kṣepaḥ pāpena yojanam* |
dravyaṃ vinā tu prathamaṃ vākpāruṣyaṃ tad ucyate ||
bhaginīmātṛsaṃbaddham upapātakaśaṃsanam |
pāruṣyaṃ madhyamaṃ proktam vācikaṃ śāstravedibhiḥ ||
abhakṣyāpeyakathanaṃ mahāpātakadūṣaṇam |
pāruṣyam uttamaṃ proktaṃ tīvraṃ marmābhighaṭṭanam ||

[731] As to this word the following variant readings shall be mentioned: *grāma* Sca 13, Vra 242, PMā 429, Mra 281, Vma 227, Vmi 380; *dharma* YApa 806; *jāti* Vni 358 (mentioned by Aiyangar); *kāla* Vci 70, YMtāVmi 681.

[732] Thus Jolly (355) translates the reading *marmābhighaṭṭanam*; YApa 806 however, has *marmātipātanam*. *Abhighaṭṭanam* is explained as *udghāṭanam* (Mra 281, Vma 227) or *utpāṭanam* (Vmi 380).

1. The expression *dravyaṃ vinā* (BS 20.2) is explained differently:

(a) According to some of the oldest texts the word *dravyaṃ* here means "that which is to be expressed" (*abhidheyam*) i.e., "the meaning, signification." Consequently, *dravyaṃ vinā* means: "such words as have another meaning than the one expressed" (YApa 806) or "even without the meaning to be expressed by them" (Vra 242).
(b) Elsewhere *dravyaṃ vinā* is explained as "without referring to any particular object" (Sca 13, Mra 281); to this very explanation Vma 227 adds: "made by mere words."[733]
(c) Vmi 380 quotes both a. and b. as Kta's and Mra's respectively.
(d) Vci 70 and YMtāVmi 681 both say what follows: *padārthaṃ vinā tenāsatyam* (YMtāVmi *asatyam iti yāvat*). In this way they reconcile both a. and b. above: *padārtham* may be understood as "the meaning of the words," i.e., *abhidheyam,* and as "object," i.e., *dravyam* as well.

2. The clause "with regard to one's sister or one's mother" (BS 30.3), Vra 242 explains: "addressing somebody in this way: I may have intercourse with your sister or with your mother," and the same interpretation is also ascribed to Halāyudha (quoted Dvi 198).

Dvi adds a restriction: "one's mother" does not mean one's own mother, but the mother's fellow-wives. Because, if taken literally, the sin committed would not be a minor sin (*upapātakam*) but —we may add— a mortal sin (*mahāpātakam*).

The third author, generally quoted for defining *vākpāruṣya,* is Kātyāyana.

Under Kātyāyana's name we know a verse (KS 769), which literally corresponds to NS 15.2ab+3 indeed (in YApa 805 it is quoted in one quotation after KS 768 and before KS 770–772).

Although in this way the three kinds of *vākpāruṣya* have been defined, viz.

1. *niṣṭhuram*	= *ākṣepaḥ*
2. *aślīlam*	= *nyaṅgasaṃjñitam*
3. *tīvram*	= *patanīyair upakrośaiḥ*

[733] Cf. Jolly (trans.: 355): "without (mentioning an (individual ignominious) act"; Kane, Vma 401: "without specifying any definite act or object."

In three other verses K again starts defining the subdivisions separately.[734]

1. *niṣṭhura*-word: scolding somebody with accessories (or limbs?) (*aṅga*), which are termed bad, either existing or not.
2. *aślīla*-word: humiliating one's conduct, country, family, etc., by word through wrath.
3. *tīvra*-word: a word charging with a mortal sin, causing affection or hatred, causing expulsion from caste.

On this text we notice:

1. By "humiliating" (KS 771) we translate the word *nyagbhāvakaraṇam* (Sca 13, Pmā 429, Vmi 379, and mentioned there as occurring in Mādhava, etc.), but much more frequently we meet with the reading *nyaṅgāvagūraṇam*, which is explained as "despising by displaying a detested limb."[735]

2. In KS 772 a few *nibandhas* read *rājadveṣa*,° "the king's hatred," for *rāgadveṣa*,° "affection and hatred" (Kta [according to Vmi 379], YApa 806, Vra 241).

The three groups of texts mentioned thus far have always been considered as not excluding each other, and in the *nibandhas* they are quoted one after the other without either any *virodha* being mentioned or any attempt being made to bring into accordance the mutual discrepancies.

Sometimes they are quoted without any connecting link whatever, e.g. YApa 805–6: NS 15.1 + KS 768–772 + BS 20.1–4, Vra 240–2: NS 15.1–3 + KātŚr 770–772 + BS 20.1–4.

More generally, NS and KS are connected by a mere particle (*api* Pmā 429, Vmi 379; *tathā ca* Sca 12), and BS is introduced somewhat like this: "Bṛhaspati, however (*tu*), distinguishes three kinds of *vākpāruṣya* according to its being of the fist, the middlemost, or the highest degree" (Sca 12–13, Pmā 428–30, Mra 280–1, Vmi 379–80).

The relation between NS and KS is felt to be as near as to enable the author of Dvi 197–198 to illustrate the several technical terms of NS by the three corresponding verses of KS.

[734] KS 770. *yat tvasatyasaṃjñitair aṅgaiḥ param ākṣipati kvacit |*
abhūtair vātha bhūtair vā niṣṭhurā vāk smṛtā budhaiḥ ||
771. *nyagbhāvakaraṇam vācā krodhāt tu kurute yadā |*
vṛttadeśakulādīnām aślīlā sā budhaiḥ smṛtā ||
772. *mahāpātakayoktrī ca rāgadveṣakarī ca yā |*
jātibhraṃśakarī vātha tīvrā sā prathitā tu vāk ||

[735] YApa 805, Vra 241, Dvi 198 (read *avagūraṇam* for *avapūraṇam*). And so did Kta (according to Vmi 379), whereas Kdhe (according to Dvi 198) read *aṅgāvagūraṇam*.

Now there is another verse of KS, which no doubt also wants to be a definition of *vākpāruṣya*, but about whose position in the whole system *nibandhakāras* disagree.[736]

Kane translates as follows: "that is said to be harshness of words (i.e. abuse) when one makes the sound 'hum' (before another), coughs (before him) or imitates or utters (before another) whatever is censurable according to popular notions."

If Kane puts this verse at the top of the chapter on *vākpāruṣya*, he has a good reason for doing so: he follows the order of verses as found in YApa 805–6.

Besides, Vra 240 also points to the same order. Although there KS 768 is quoted (falsely as being Manu's) without either any introductory note or any commentary, from the very place which it occupies, viz., immediately after NS 15.1 but before the subdividing *ślokas* NS 15.2–3, KS 770–2, and BS 20.2–4, we may assume Cāṇḍeśvara to have considered KS 768 as a general definition of *vākpāruṣya.*

Nevertheless we shall notice, not all *nibandhhas* have treated this verse in the same way. Sca 13 quotes the verse after and separately from the classical three-fold subdivisions of NS, KS and BS. According to this author, KS 768 together with KS 773 is said to contain "other kinds of *vākpāruṣya.*"

When writing his chapter on *vākpāruṣya*, Dvi 197 undoubtedly made use of Vra. Nevertheless he disagrees with his model as to the interpretation of KS 768. Vardhamāna again considers the latter verse as a mere species of *vākpāruṣya*, and even such a species which may serve as an objection against YMtā's interpretation of NS 15.1. It proves *uccair bhāṣaṇam*, i.e, "speaking aloud," is not a requisite for all kinds of *vākpāruṣya.*

At last for KS we shall mention two other verses (KS 773–774), which are also merely concerned with defining *vākpāruṣya*, without troubling about the punishments to be inflicted.[737]

They enumerate a few cases of a person's being *vāgduṣṭaḥ*, "abusive in speech." Such is a man, who "through wrath" (KS 773) or "for the sake of mere fault-finding" (KS 774) acts in one of the following ways:

1. if he discloses faults, —to be understood as follows: in a person who is free from such faults (Vra 243, Dvi 199);

[736] KS 768. *huṃkāraḥ kāsanaṃ caiva loke yacca vigarhitam |*
anukuryād anubrūyād vākpāruṣyam tad ucyate ||

[737] KS 773. *yo 'guṇān kīrtayet krodhānnirguṇe vā guṇajñatām |*
anyasaṃjñānuyogī vā vāgduṣṭaṃ taṃ naraṃ viduḥ ||

774. *aduṣṭasyaiva yo doṣān kīrtayed doṣakāraṇāt |*
anyāpadeśavādī ca vāgduṣṭaṃ taṃ naraṃ viduḥ ||

2. if he says a man without good qualities to know good qualities;
3. if he designates a man by another name —which according to Vra 243 means: designating a man by a blamable names (Vra 242 and Dvi 199 read: *anyasaṃjñāniyojī*);
4. if he discloses faults in a man who really is untainted by them. This translation presupposes the reading *aduṣṭasyaiva*. A few *nibandhas*, however, have *duṣṭasyaiva tu* for it. Hence we find such commentaries as follow: "the word *doṣakāraṇāt* is intended to exclude the fault of disclosing the faults of relatives for the sake of judicial investigation" (Dvi 199), or "because of *doṣakāraṇāt* there is no fault in disclosing a fault for the sake of contact with wicked people being avoided" (Sca 760 (quoting the verse under N's name), Vmi 380–81);
5. if he points out the faults of one man while referring to another.

As stated above, Sca 13 quotes the first of these verses together with KS 768: they contain "other kinds of *vākpāruṣya*" In Vra 242–3, from the mere place both verses occupy, we may conclude to the same result.

In Dvi 199, too, they close the paragraph, we should like to call *vākpāruṣyamātṛkā*, "the introductory chapter on *vākpāruṣya*" *atrāpyevam evāstu.*

32

Janmasvatvavāda *and* Uparamasvatvavāda: *The First Chapters on Inheritance in the* Mitākṣarā *and* Dāyabhāga

"An...important question is whether Jīmūtavāhana who is certainly a little later than the *Mitākṣarā* criticizes it...All that one can advance is that it is quite within the bounds of possibility that Jīmūtavāhana criticizes the *Mitākṣarā*" (Kane 1930–1962: 1.326–27). Here —as on many other occasions— Kane has replaced wild speculation with sober reasoning. The fact that he places Jīmūtavāhana's activity between AD 1090 and 1130 makes the Dbhā practically contemporaneous with Vijñāneśvara's YMtā. The problem whether or not Vijñāneśvara influenced Jīmūtavāhana, and whether or not the Dbhā criticized the chapter on inheritance in the YMtā, therefore, becomes all the more important. This paper intends to contribute to solving this problem through an analysis and comparison of the introductory chapters[738] of the Dbhā and the YMtā (section on *dāyavibhāga*).

1. One cannot help being struck by the unusual length of Vijñāneśvara's introductory remarks to the chapter on *dāyavibhāga*.[739] In the Nirṇayasāgara Press edition this introduction covers 123 lines, as against 38 lines for *abhyupetyaśuśrūṣā*, 27 for *daṇḍapāruṣya*, 23 for *sākṣin*, 19 for *prakīrṇaka*, 13 for *dattāpradānika* and *vākpāruṣya*, 11 for *aśauca*, and 10 to 1 for the other 35 chapters. It is clear that Vijñāneśvara wanted to make an important point before actually commenting on Yājñavalkya's *ślokas* on inheritance. The argument develops as follows:

[738] i.e., the first chapters of Colebrooke's translations. All references to the YMtā and Dbhā in this paper are according to Colebrooke's paragraphs.

[739] [Ed. note: See now the full translation of this introduction to inheritance in the YMtā by Ludo and Rosane Rocher (2001)].

- definition of *dāya* (1.2–3);
- definition of *vibhāga* (1.4–5);
- the specific problem to be examined in the introduction is: *kasya vibhāgaḥ?* (1.6).[740] That means: *vibhāgāt svatvam?* or *svasya mato vibhāgaḥ?* (1.7)
- preliminary problem: *kiṃ śāstraikasamadhigamyaṃ svatvam uta pramāṇāntarasamadhigamyam?*
- *pūrvapakṣa*: *śāstraikasamadhigamyam* (1.8);
- *siddhāntapakṣa*: *laukikam eva svatvam* (1.9–16);
- Vijñāneśvara returns to the main problem raised in 1.7 (1.17):
- *pūrvapakṣa*: *vibhāgāt svatvam* (1.18–22);
- *siddhāntapakṣa*: *janmanaiva svatvam* (1.23–33).

Jīmūtavāhana (Dbhā 1.1) also refers to the fact that the subject of *dāyabhāga* has led to difference of opinion among the learned:

manvādivākyānyavim śya yeṣāṃ
yasmin vivādo bahudhā budhānām |
teṣāṃ prabodhāya sa dāyabhāgo
nirūpaṇīyaḥ sudhiyaḥ śṛṇudhvam ||[741]

Yet, Jīmūtavāhana does not make *uparamasvatvavāda* the main point of the discussion. Right from the beginning (Dbhā 1.3), Jīmūtavāhana interprets the term *pitryam* in NS 13.1 (Dbhā 1.2; YMtā 1.4; DhK 1132)[742] as *pitṛmaraṇopajātasvatvam*, without further comment or justification. Again, when explaining *dāya* as a derivative form of the root *dā* with secondary meaning (Dbhā 1.4) Jīmūtavāhana states: *mṛtapravrajitādisvatvanivṛttipūrvakaparasvatvotpattiphalasāmyāt* and he repeats in Dbhā 1.5: *tatsvāmyoparame.*

2. In connection with the definition of *dāya* in Dbhā 1.5: *pūrvasvāmisambandhādhīnaṃ tatsvāmyoparame yatra dravye svatvaṃ tatra nirūḍho dāyaśabdaḥ*,[743] I want to point out a detail in

[740] This is one of four questions asked by Vijñāneśvara (YMtā 1.6): *kasminkāle kasya kathaṃ kaiś ca vibhāgaḥ kartavyaḥ*. Cf. Saṃgrahakāra:

yasmin kāle yayā bhangayā yair eva kriyate 'pi ca |
yāddṛśasya ca dāyasya yathāśāstraṃ pradarśyate ||

(quoted Sca, *Vyavahārakāṇḍa* (1916: 598.13–14; and elsewhere).

[741] Cf. *Vīramitrodaya*, *Vyavahāraprakāśa*, ChSS, 1932, 411.3–4:

yatra manvādivacanavyākhyāsu bahudhā budhāḥ |
vivadante dāyabhāgaḥ sa prabandhena varṇyate ||

Notice that Mitramiśra, who rejects most of Jīm's opinions, is often strongly influenced by Dbhā.

[742] For easy reference the quotations from *smṛti* texts are followed by their page numbers in the DhK, *Vyavahārakāṇḍa* (mainly vol. 1.2, 1938).

[743] Cf. *Vīramitrodaya* 411.8. While rejecting Jīm's etymological explanation of *dāya* (*Vīramitrodaya* 411.25–412.9), Mitramiśra introduces a quotation from the *Nighaṇṭukāra*, as follows: *dāyaśabdaścartthaṃ svāmisambandhamātrādy atra dravye*

Vijñāneśvara's definition of *dāya* (YMtā 1.2): *tatra dāyaśabdena yad dhanaṃ svāmisambandhāde va nimittādanyasya svaṃ bhavati tad ucyate.* The addition of *eva* after *svāmisambandhād* becomes meaningful only if we accept that Vijñāneśvara intends to avoid a restriction which *is* mentioned in Dbhā, namely: *tatsvāmyoparame.* Mitramiśra saw this very clearly, when he objected to Jīmūtavāhana's definition that *tatsvāmyoparama iti janmanāpi svatvasyopapādayiṣyamāṇa tvādavyāpakam* (*Vīramitrodaya* 412.8–9). If the information in the *Sarasvatīvilāsa* (1927: 347.1–3) is correct, the definition of *dāya* in YMtā 1.2 is older than Vijñāneśvara; it is attributed there to "Asahāya, Vijñānayogin, etc." (Kane 1925: 195).

3. It is normal that Jīmūtavāhana does not introduce the distinction between *apratibandhadāya* and *sapratibandhadāya*, which is basic in YMtā (1.3). Yet, it is worth noticing that Jīmūtavāhana also does not refute the necessity of such a distinction.

4. Jīmūtavāhana argues for the first time in connection with the definition of *vibhāga.* He quotes and rejects (Dbhā 1.6) the following two definitions: (a) *dāyasya vibhāgo vibhaktāvayavatvam*, which is refuted: *dāyavināśāpatteḥ*; (b) *dāyena saha vibhāgo 'saṃyuktatvam*, which is refuted: *saṃyukto 'pi na mamedaṃ vibhaktaṃ svaṃ bhrātur idam iti prayogāt.*

Neither definition is referred to in YMtā.

5. Jīmūtavāhana then quotes and rejects a third definition of *vibhāga* (Dbhā 1.7): *sambandhaviśeṣāt sarveṣāṃ sambandhotpannasya svatvasya dravyaviśeṣe vyavasthāpanaṃ vibhāgaḥ.* This definition has been interpreted[744] as a reference to the sole definition of *vibhāga* in YMtā (1.4): *vibhāgo nāma dravyasamudāyaviṣayāṇām anekasvāmyānāṃ tadekadeśeṣu vyavasthāpanam.*[745] In reality, Jīmūtavāhana does not refute Vijñāneśvara. He does not refer to property which was held in common during the father's lifetime, and which is divided after the father's death. Jīmūtavāhana refutes the opinion that at the time of the father's death the heirs become undivided co-owners, and that partition puts an end to this situation. It is enough to read his refutation to understand that the period he has in mind is the one between the father's death and partition: *sambandhyantarasadbhāvapratipakṣa*

svatvaṃ tadrūḍhayā vadati. The quotation itself: *vibhaktavyaṃ pitṛdravyaṃ dāyam āhur manīṣiṇaḥ* (*Vīramitrodaya* 411.21; DhK 1142), occurs neither in YMtā nor in Dbhā (although *pitṛdravyam* would have been a valuable argument for Jīm). Cf. also Dhāreśvara (Sca 597.14–15) and Saṃgrahakāra (Sca 598.4–5).

[744] See Colebrooke's note on Dbhā 1.7, referring to Raghunandana ("The author here censures the doctrine of the Mitākṣarā"), and Maheśvara ("He canvasses the doctrine of the Maithilas"). Notice, however, the silence of Śrīkṛṣṇa.

[745] The same definition is repeated in *Vīramitrodaya* 412.10–11; it was rejected by Bhāruci (*Sarasvatīvilāsa* 347.11).

sya sambandhasyāvayaveṣv eva vibhāgavyaṅgyasvatvāpādakatvāt kṛtsnapitṛdhanagatasvatvotpādavināśakalpanāgauravād yatheṣṭaviniyogaphalābhāvenānupayogāc ca.

6. In Dbhā 1.8–10, Jīmūtavāhana gives two other definitions of *vibhāga*:

(a) *ekadeśopāttasyaiva bhūhiraṇyādāv utpannasya svatvasya vinigamanāpramāṇābhāvena vaiśeṣikavyavahārān arhatayā avyavasthitasya guṭikāpātādinā vyañjanaṃ vibhāgaḥ*, a definition which is described as *prācyoktam* in the *Bālambhaṭṭī* (ChSS 1912: 419.12–13);

(b) *viśeṣeṇa bhajanaṃ svatvajñāpanaṃ vā vibhāgaḥ*

He also quotes three verses by Bṛhaspati relative to the special case in which the inheritance consists of a single slave girl, a single cow, etc.

This entire section is again unconnected with YMtā.

7. After the discussion of *vibhāga*, Jīmūtavāhana points out that the heir becomes the owner of inherited property at the time of his father's death. This excludes two other possible moments: the time of partition (Dbhā 1.11–12), and the time of birth (Dbhā 1.13–21). At this stage only does Jīmūtavāhana finally refer to *janmasvatvavāda*.

I shall now examine the discussion of *janmasvatvavāda* versus *uparamasvatvavāda* through the *pūrvapakṣa* and *siddhāntapakṣa* views in YMtā and Dbhā. I shall first list the *pūrvapakṣa* arguments in YMtā, together with Vijñāneśvara's refutation; wherever possible they will be compared with Jīmūtavāhana's *siddhānta* and *pūrva* views, respectively. This list will be followed by the arguments in Dbhā for which there are no corresponding statements in YMtā.

As indicated above, YMtā (1.8–16) first deals with a preliminary problem, which is not raised independently in Dbhā: can property be acquired by means of restricted ways enumerated in the *śāstra* only, or is it a mere *laukika* concept?[746]

8. Vijñāneśvara's *pūrvapakṣin* (YMtā 1.8) quotes GDh 10.39–42 (DhK 1122–24): *svāmī rikthakrayasaṃvibhāgarigrahādhigameṣu | brāhmaṇasyādhikaṃ labdham | kṣatriyasya vijitam | nirviṣṭaṃ vaiśyaśūdrayoḥ*, and he argues: if ownership could be acquired through other means (such as birth), Gautama's restrictive enumeration would be meaningless (*na…arthavat syāt*).

Vijñāneśvara (YMtā 1.12–14) rejects this argument. Gautama's *sūtras* are not prescriptive *vidhis*; they are mere *niyamas*. That

[746] Vijñāneśvara justifies this discussion in YMtā 1.16. Cf. Bālambhaṭṭa's introduction (431.24–25) to it: *nanu svatvasya tattvanirūpaṇam atra prakaraṇe nopayuktaṃ tadgatalaukikatvālaukitvayor vibhāgādyaprayojakatvād ata āha…*

means: Gautama's *sūtra*s did not establish ownership, which existed before and without them; they only lay down preferential ways of acquiring ownership, without therefore excluding other ways, such as birth.

It is at least strange, and probably significant, that Jīmūtavāhana does not quote GDh 10.39–42, a literal interpretation of which definitely supports his point of view.[747]

9. Vijñāneśvara's *pūrvapakṣin* (YMtā 1.8) also quotes MDh 8.340 (DhK 1697), according to which a Brāhmaṇa should be considered a thief, if he seeks to acquire property from a person who has taken the goods without their having been given him, even if the Brāhmaṇa obtains the property in return for typically brahmanical services such as a sacrifice or instruction. The *pūrvapakṣin* argues that rules prescribing punishment for such acquisition of property would be out of place (*anupapannaṃ syāt*) if property were *laukika.*

Jīmūtavāhana does not quote MDh 8.340.

10. YMtā 1.8 contains a third argument by the *pūrvapakṣin* in favor of the śāstric nature of property: *laukikaṃ cet svatvaṃ mama svam anenāpahṛtam iti na brūyāt | apahartur eva svatvāt | anyathānyasya svaṃ tenāpahṛtam iti nāpahartuḥ svam | evaṃ tarhi suvarṇarajatādisvarūpavad asya vā svam anyasya vā svam iti saṃśayo na syāt.* Notice the objection raised and refuted within the *pūrvapakṣa* view.

Vijñāneśvara (YMtā 1.15) says that this statement is untrue (*tad apy asat*), because: *svatvahetubhūtakrayādisaṃdehāt svatvasaṃdehopapatteḥ.* Besides this direct refutation, Vijñāneśvara clearly refers to a similar objection when he says elsewhere (YMtā 1.11): *na caitāvatā cauryādiprāptasyāpi svatvaṃ syād iti mantavyam | loke tatra svatvaprasiddhyabhāvāt vyavahāravisaṃvādāc ca.*

Dbhā is silent on the whole argument.

The real source of the argument refuted by Vijñāneśvara has probably been preserved by Mitramiśra (*Vīramitrodaya* 422.10–16): *etena coryādiprāptasyāpi svatvaṃ syād iti saṃgrahakāradhāreśvarābhyāṃ svatvasya laukikatve dūṣaṇam abhihitaṃ tad api parāstam*, etc. Besides, *Vīramitrodaya* 416.12–16 (and a few other sources; see DhK 1142) has preserved the relevant passage from the *Saṃgraha*:

> *vartate yasya yad dhaste tasya svāmī sa eva na |*
> *anyasvam anyahasteṣu cauryodyaiḥ kiṃ na dṛśyate ||*
> *tasmāc chāstrata eva syāt svāmyaṃ nānubhavād api |*
> *asyāpahṛtam etena na yuktaṃ vaktum anyathā |*
> *vidito'rthāgamaḥ śāstre tathāvarṇi pṛthak pṛthak ||*

[747] The only possible reference is in Dbhā 1.19: *arjanarūpatayā janmanaḥ smṛtāv anadhigamāt.*

Finally, Mitramiśra's remark (*Vīramitrodaya* 417.1–2): *idam evābhisaṃdhāya dhāreśvareṇāpi śāstraikādhigamyam eva svatvam iti siddhāntitam*, suggests Dhāreśvara's conclusion too was the result of a refutation of a *pūrvapakṣa* view defending the *laukikatva* of property.[748]

11. Between the enumeration of the *pūrvapakṣa* views (YMtā 1.8) and their refutations (YMtā 1.11–16), Vijñāneśvara adds three arguments in favor of the *laukikatva* of property, for which no *pūrvapakṣa*s have been mentioned.

Property is *laukika*, in the first place (YMtā 1.9), *laukikārthakriyāsādhanatvād vrīhyādivat.* Vijñāneśvara deviates from the pattern set by YMtā 1.8, and introduces at this stage only an objection to his own view: *āhavanīyādīnām api pākādisādhanatvam asty eva*, which he immediately rejects. There are two aspects to the sacrificial fire: it is both fire as such and sacrificial fire, whereas *svatva* has but one function: *na hi yasya svatvaṃ na bhavati tat tasya krayādyarthakriyāṃ sādhayati.*

Property is also *laukika* (YMtā 1.9), because *pratyantavāsinām apy adṛṣṭaśāstravyavahārāṇāṃ svatvavyavahāro dṛśyate krayavikrayādidarśanāt.*

In the third place, Vijñāneśvara (YMtā 1.10) draws an argument from Prabhākara's discussion of the *lipsāsūtra* (PMS 4.1.2): if a sacrifice is performed with goods which have not been acquired in the prescribed ways, a blame is cast on the acquirer, but the religious ceremony remains valid. Hence, property can be acquired in other ways than the ones prescribed by the *śāstra*s.

Dbhā does not refer to any of these three arguments.

12. Beginning at YMtā 1.17, Vijñāneśvara's *pūrvapakṣin* enumerates a number of arguments directly in favor of *uparamasvatvavāda.*

The first argument (YMtā 1.18) is this: *jātaputrasyādhānavidhānāt | yadi janmanaiva svatvaṃ syāt tadotpannasya putrasyāpi tat svaṃ sādhāraṇam iti dravyasādhyeṣv ādhānādiṣu pitur anadhikāraḥ syāt.*

Vijñāneśvara's refutation follows in YMtā 1.26: *yady apy arthasādhyeṣu vaidikeṣu karmasv anadhikāra iti tatra tadvidhānabalād evādhikāro gamyate.*

The duty to perform Vedic sacrifices and, therefore, the necessity to be the unrestricted owner of one's property, involving the right to use it, is referred to in Dbhā 1.17: *svopātte'pi teṣām asvāmitve svadhanasādhyavaidikakarmocchedāc chrutivirodhaḥ syāt.* The context is, however, different. Jīmūtavāhana wants to show that the expression *anīśāste hi jīvatoḥ* in MDh 9.104 (DhK 1149;

[748] Cf. "It is probably due to Dhāreśvara's position that M. enters into an elaborate discussion on this point" (Kane 1925: 223).

Dbhā 1.14; not quoted in YMtā) really means absence of ownership, as against MDh 8.146 (DhK 822) where the right of ownership of wives, sons and servants is recognized with regard to self-acquired property; otherwise, they are "dependent."

Vijñāneśvara's *pūrvapakṣa* is already mentioned in Viśvarūpa's *Bālakrīḍā* (on YDh 1.124 [TSS 74, 1922: 244.19–20]) as follows: *anyathā jātaputrasyādhānādismṛtir dravyasādhāraṇyāt svatyāgāsaṃbhavād virudhyate.* Besides, Viśvarūpa seems to indicate, more generally, that the discussion about the moment when ownership originates existed well before his time. His statement: *atha kiṃ vibhāgāt svatvam uta svatve sati vibhāga iti*, may have been the source of Vijñāneśvara's (YMtā 1.17): *idānīm idaṃ saṃdihyate kiṃ vibhāgāt svatvam uta svatvasya sato vibhāga iti.*

13. The second argument of Vijñāneśvara's *pūrvapakṣin* in favor of *uparamasvatvavāda* (YMtā 1.19) is based on a quotation from Nārada (13.6; DhK 1220; quoted anonymously):

śauryabhāryādhane cobhe yac ca vidyādhanaṃ bhavet |
trīṇyetānyavibhājyāni prasādo yaś ca paitṛkaḥ ||

A text excluding from partition a gift made by the father out of affection before partition would not make sense (*nopapadyate*), if property was held from birth onward: the goods would have been given by general consensus and, therefore, there would be no question of excluding them from the partition.

Jīmūtavāhana refers twice to this text (Dbhā 6.1.12; 6.1.33), but in a totally different context, and without making use of Vijñāneśvara's *pūrvapakṣa.*

14. Similarly, says the *pūrvapakṣin* (YMtā 1.20), if property was acquired by birth, another text of Nārada (1.28; DhK 1448; quoted anonymously) would also not make sense (*nopapadyate*):

bhartrā prītena yad dattaṃ striyai tasmin mṛte'pi tat |
sa yathākāmam aśnīyād dadhād vā sthāvarād ṛte ||

The *pūrvapakṣin* again (cf. sect. 10 above) introduces an objection to his own thesis. The sentence should be construed: *sthāvarād ṛte yad dattam,* which limits the father's right to donate, and indicates the son's right by birth. But he discards the objection: it amounts to construing together disconnected parts of the sentence.

Vijñāneśvara's refutation follows in YMtā 1.25. His interpretation: *yat tu bhartrā prītena ityādiviṣṇuvacanaṃ sthāvarasya prītidānajñāpanaṃ tat svopārjiyasyāpi putrādyabhyanujñayaiveti vyākhyeyam,* has to be read in conjunction with YMtā 1.24, in which Vijñāneśvara's gives his own interpretation of the two stanzas which will be discussed in sect. 15. It would be interesting to know why NS 1.28 is here attributed to Viṣṇu.

Jīmūtavāhana (Dbhā 4.1.23) quotes NS 1.28 (*tad āha nāradaḥ*) in a different context.

15. The *pūrvapakṣin* (YMtā 1.21) quotes two stanzas (DhK 1219; quoted anonymously) which seem to support *janmasvatvavāda*:

(a) *maṇimuktāpravālānāṃ sarvasyaiva pitā prabhuḥ* |
sthāvarasya tu sarvasya na pitā na pitāmahaḥ ||
(b) *pitṛprasādād bhujyante vastrāṇyābharaṇāni ca* |
sthāvaraṃ tu na bhujyeta prasāde sati paitṛke ||

The limited right of the father to dispose of family property is not, according to the *pūrvapakṣin*, due to his son having a right of property by birth. Both texts refer to the special case of immoveable property inherited from the grandfather.

Vijñāneśvara rejects this interpretation in Ymtā 1.24: *maṇimuktāpravālānām ityādivacanaṃ ca janmanā svatvapakṣa evopapadyate | na ca pitāmahopāttasthāvaraviṣayam iti yuktaṃ na pitā na pitāmaha iti vacanāt.*

Dbhā (2.22) quotes the first stanza, and adds, without further discussion: *pitāmahaśrutestaddhanaviṣayakaṃ vacanam.* Although Jīmūtavāhana agrees with Vijñāneśvara's *pūrvapakṣin*, there is no reason to conclude, with Colebrooke (note on Dbhā 2.22), that Jīmūtavāhana "evidently" took the quotation from YMtā. If Jīmūtavāhana had borrowed the stanza from YMtā, he would not have attributed it to Yājñavalkya. He must have taken it from a *nibandha* in which it was either explicitly attributed to Yājñavalkya, or quoted anonymously but in such a way that a confusion with Yājñavalkya was possible. In the latter alternative, the same *nibandha* may also have been the source of YMtā.

16. After drawing his conclusion that *na janmanā svatvaṃ kiṃtu svāminaśād vibhāgād vā svatvam*, the *pūrvapakṣin* (YMtā 1.22) finally refers to a chicanery (*codya*) on the part of the *janmasvatvavādin*: if property is not by birth, it is possible for a third party to appropriate the goods between the time of the father's death and the moment of partition, the goods having no regular owner during that period. The *uparamasvatvavādin* says that this criticism is uncalled for (*anavakāśa*). In the case of several heirs, they become joint owners immediately after the father's death; partition will only specify the individual rights. In the case of an only son, he becomes the owner at the time of his father's death, and partition can be dispensed with.

Dbhā 1.11 mentions the same objection even more explicitly. Since NS 13.2 (DhK 1152) states that the sons should divide *pitur dhanam* one might conclude that sons have no right to the inheritance before partition. If strangers divide property before the sons do, the latter can no longer accede to it. Jīmūtavāhana answers (Dbhā 1.12) that the very death of a relative establishes the ownership of his heirs. First, it is well established that immediately after their father's death sons refer to his property as "theirs." Second, an only son accedes to his father's property without partition.

17. Vijñāneśvara (YMtā 1.23) bases the *janmasvatvavāda* on a text which he attributes to Gautama (DhK 1124): *utpattyaivārthasvāmitvaṃ labhetety ācāryā iti gautamavacanāt.*

This text, which does support Vijñāneśvara's point of view, is neither quoted nor referred to in Dbhā. It is possible that Jīmūtavāhana avoided it on purpose, but it is far more likely that he did not quote it because it was unknown to him. The text occurs neither in Gautama nor in any other *smṛti.* Mitramiśra (*Vīramitrodaya* 414.8–10) hesitatingly accepts it on the authority of Vijñāneśvara: *yat tu gautamavacanam…iti janmanaḥ svatvahetutve mitākṣarākṛtā pramāṇatvenopanyastam.* The commentators on Dbhā 1.19 reject its authority; Śrīkṛṣṇa, for example, says: *mitākṣarādhṛtagautamavacanam amūlam.* Besides, if Jīmūtavāhana had known the text and if he had wished to explain it in the light of *uparamasvatvavāda,* such an explanation could easily be found. See, for instance, Śrīkṛṣṇa (on Dbhā 1.19): *samūlatve vā…,* and *Dāyatattva* 162.20–23 (ed. Vidyāsāgara 1895, vol. II; referred to *Vīramitrodaya* 414.10–11; 418.23–24). For these reasons it is not possible to agree with Colebrooke (note on Dbhā 1.19): "The author apparently alludes to a passage of Gautama cited in the Mitákshará."

18. Jīmūtavāhana (Dbhā 1.13) quotes a *pūrvapakṣa* in favor of *janmasvatvavāda*: one becomes the owner of goods by acceptance, i.e., by an act of the acceptor. Birth is an act of the son; it can, therefore, be considered as acceptance, and a source of ownership. This view is supported by a dictum: *kvacij janmaiva* (probably understood: *arjanam*) *yathā pitrye dhane.* The dictum was obviously not a well known one. Śrīkṛṣṇa interprets: *kvacid iti granthāntare,* and calls the quotation: *laukikaṃ prāmāṇikavākyam.* Mitramiśra speaks of *prācīnagranthalikhanam* (*Vīramitrodaya* 417.9), and *prācīnalikhanam* (426.5).

Jīmūtavāhana (Dbhā 1.20) rejects the *pūrvapakṣa*: *kvacij janmaiveti ca janmanibandhanatvāt pitāputrasambandhasya pitṛmaraṇasya ca svatva-kāraṇatvāt paramparayā varṇanam.*

Vijñāneśvara neither uses Jīmūtavāhana's *pūrvapakṣa,* nor does he quote the "ancient text."

19. Jīmūtavāhana's main argument against *janmasvatvavāda* (Dbhā 1.14) is MDh 9.104 (DhK 1149):

ūrdhvaṃ pituś ca matuś ca sametya bhrātaraḥ samam |
bhajeran paitṛkaṃ riktham anīśāste hi jīvatoḥ ||

Vijñāneśvara does not quote this stanza. Here too (cf. sect. 17), one might be tempted to think that YMtā intentionally omitted a text which obviously supports *uparamasvatvavāda*. Yet, Jīmūtavāhana himself refers to a different interpretation: MDh 9.104, like MDh 8.146 (DhK 822; quoted YMtā 2.49), merely indicates that the sons are not independent (*asvatantra*) as long as their parents are alive. Jīmūtavāhana, of course, rejects this interpretation.

Again, Dbhā 1.29 states that, according to the *janmasvatvavāda*, MDh 9.104 means: although sons have a right to property during their father's lifetime, they cannot divide before his death. In Jīmūtavāhana's opinion, this interpretation is *anyāyyam asvārthaparatvāpatteḥ*.

Besides MDh 9.104, Jīmūtavāhana (Dbhā 1.18) quotes a stanza by Devala (DhK 1156), which is also not cited in YMtā :

pitary uparate putrā vibhajeyur dhanaṃ pituḥ |
asvāmyaṃ hi bhaved eṣāṃ nirdoṣe pitari sthite ||

Aparāditya, like Jīmūtavāhana, quotes both stanzas, and comments: *asvāmyam asvātantryam* (ĀnSS 46, 1904: 718.5; on YDh 2.114). Aparāditya, therefore, represents the type of interpretation to which Jīmūtavāhana objects, whereas YMtā does not.

I shall now return to the general questions asked at the beginning of this paper: did Vijñāneśvara influence Jīmūtavāhana and, if so, to what extent? did Jīmūtavāhana criticize YMtā and, if so, in what measure? It should be remembered that the conclusions which follow are based on a small portion of YMtā and Dbhā only. They will have to be confirmed or corrected after a careful comparison of *all* arguments put forth in both texts.

There are cases in which YMtā and Dbhā seem to cover the same ground. On three occasions (sects. 12–14), one might be tempted to identify Jīmūtavāhana's final views with Vijñāneśvara's *pūrvapakṣas*. Yet, in each case Jīmūtavāhana uses the argument in a different context, not to refute Vijñāneśvara. Similarly, when Jīmūtavāhana rejects a definition of *vibhāga* which resembles Vijñāneśvara's definition (sect. 5), he refers in reality to a different situation. In one case, in which Dbhā really agrees with Vijñāneśvara's *pūrvapakṣa* (sect. 15), a serious obstacle prevents us to accept direct influence. In another case of agreement between Jīmūtavāhana and Vijñāneśvara's *pūrvapakṣa* (sect. 16, the latter already quotes an argument which, by its very nature, has to be a criticism raised by a *janmasvatvavādin* against an earlier *uparamasvatvavāda*.

In all these cases the resemblance between Dbhā and YMtā is more apparent than real. Even though Colebrooke used two of these instances (sects. 5, 17) to show that Dbhā was influenced by YMtā and even though his statements were based on the Sanskrit commentators, we have to deny his conclusions all historical value.

The differences between YMtā and Dbhā are far more significant than their apparent similarities.

If Jīmūtavāhana wanted to criticize Vijñāneśvara, he would have discussed a number of arguments in YMtā, which are not mentioned in Dbhā. Jīmūtavāhana might have refuted the necessity to distinguish between *sapratibandhadāya* and *apratibandhadāya*, which is an important element in YMtā (sect. 3). He might have discussed the three arguments in favor of the *laukikatva* of property, which Vijñāneśvara adds without offering corresponding *pūrvapakṣa*s (sect. 11). Jīmūtavāhana might have questioned the authenticity of the text which Vijñāneśvara attributes to Gautama (sect. 17), or he might have offered his own interpretation. He might have elaborated on two *pūrvapakṣa*s quoted by YMtā (sects. 9–10). Finally, Jīmūtavāhana would have made full use of GDh 10.39–42 a literal interpretation of which supported the *janmasvatvavāda* (sect. 8).

Conversely, Dbhā does discuss arguments which do not appear in YMtā . Jīmūtavāhana refutes two definitions of *dāya* (sect. 4) and two definitions of *vibhāga* (sect. 6) unknown to Vijñāneśvara or at least not mentioned by him. He also introduces and rejects a *pūrvapakṣa* which does not correspond to any argument held forth in YMtā, even though it would have strengthened Vijñāneśvara's position (sect. 18). These are cases in which Jīmūtavāhana does not criticize YMtā, but some unknown predecessor or predecessors. In one case Aparāditya has preserved such an argument (sect. 19). This does not necessarily imply that Jīmūtavāhana argues against Aparāditya; it proves, however, that Jīmūtavāhana criticizes other authors than Vijñāneśvara.

The picture is made even more complex by the fact that Vijñāneśvara evidently argues more intensively and is on the defensive more often than Jīmūtavāhana. The theoretical introduction in YMtā is much longer than in Dbhā (sect. 1). Even the addition of an enclitic such as *eva* is evidence for Vijñāneśvara's aggressiveness (sect. 2). This, again, does not mean that Vijñāneśvara criticizes Jīmūtavāhana; but he does argue against authors whose views were similar to those of the author of Dbhā.

Even the short analysis contained in this paper provides sufficient indications for us to gain some insight into the true situation. The discussion of *janmasvatvavāda* versus *uparamasvatvavāda* is undoubtedly older than both YMtā and Dbhā. Vijñāneśvara has two long series of *pūrvapakṣa*s, some of which are in their turn interrupted by counterarguments (sect. 10). Jīmūtavāhana also refers to earlier differences of opinion (sect. 1), and quotes *pūrvapakṣas* (sect. 18). On one occasion, the text of YMtā almost literally corresponds to a sentence in the *Bālakriḍā* (sect. 12), and Vijñāneśvara's definition of *dāya* is said also to have been Asahāya's (sect. 2). We are told that one of YMtā's *pūrvapakṣas* reproduces the point of view of Dhāreśvara and the *Saṃgrahakāra*. If the information is correct that it represents Dhāreśvara's "final view," we are bound to conclude that the argument about the sources of ownership is older than Dhāreśvara (sect. 10).

Vijñāneśvara and Jīmūtavāhana knew the works —or at least some of the works— dealing with the theoretical aspects of ownership and inheritance. They found their predecessors already divided on whether ownership is acquired by birth or by inheritance. Vijñāneśvara and Jīmūtavāhana participated in the discussion. They criticized the views of their opponents, defended the opinions of their friends, and probably made their own original contributions to the debate. Since most of the older works have been lost, we cannot often be sure whom they criticize and whom they defend, nor is it possible to determine the extent of their respective contributions.

One thing is certain: Vijñāneśvara and Jīmūtavāhana never refer to each other, neither explicitly nor implicitly. If the dates which Kane assigns both works are correct, nothing could be more natural. The absence of mutual references may even be taken as an argument in support of Kane's proposal. Both authors probably did not know each other's works.

Even if Vijñāneśvara and Jīmūtavāhana were not contemporaries, there was no reason why Jīmūtavāhana should have singled out YMtā to make it the target of his criticism, and *vice versa*. YMtā and Dbhā were two texts among many dealing with property and inheritance; they did not yet have the unique importance which they were to acquire at a later stage, especially after Colebrooke's translation in 1810. The tendency to compare YMtā and Dbhā at the expense of all other *nibandhas* is a recent phenomenon, which we all too easily extend to earlier times when they had not yet become *the* authorities of two schools of law.

33

Karma and Rebirth in the Dharmaśāstras

The beginning of the twelfth book of the *Manusmṛti* is explicitly devoted to "the ultimate retribution for (their = the four castes') deeds" (MDh 12.1) or "the decision concerning this whole connection with actions" (MDh 12.2).[749] This topic is, again explicitly, concluded at 12.82ab: "All the results, proceeding from actions, have been thus pointed out." MDh 12.82cd introduces a related but different topic: "those acts which secure supreme bliss to a Brāhmaṇa," which is concluded at 12.107ab: "Thus the acts which secure supreme bliss have been exactly and fully described." I shall take the first of these passages in "the most important Dharmaśāstra" as the basis for the following discussion. I shall supplement it with data from other passages in Manu and compare these with similar passages from other texts, in order to reconstruct the theory of karma and rebirth as it appears in Dharmaśāstra literature. On the other hand, I shall exclude from this study all data from later commentaries. In addition to the fact that much of this literature, insofar as it relates to karma, remains unpublished, it is not possible at this point to present a balanced picture even of the printed commentaries in the field of *dharma*.

[749] Many citations in this article are from translations of Dharmaśāstras in *The Sacred Books of the East*. Even though these translations are often susceptible to improvement, they are, in general, reliable. Wherever I disagree with the existing translations, I shall either state so or replace them with my own. The following volumes of SBE will be referred to: vol. 2, Āpastamba, Gautama (Bühler); vol. 7, Viṣṇu (Jolly); vol.14, Vasiṣṭha, Baudhāyana (Bühler); vol 25 Manu (Bühler).

MDh 12.1–82 exhibits a strange mixture of general considerations on karma and *saṃsāra*, on the one hand, and different systems of reincarnation, on the other. One gets the impression that passages which originally belonged to a variety of sources —or were independent units— have been collected by the compiler of the *Manusmṛti* and put together in succession, often without the slightest transition. This procedure, which is not unknown elsewhere in Manu —and in other Dharmaśāstras— should be a warning to us when we try to describe *the* theory of karma and rebirth as it emerges from Dharmaśāstra literature. To be sure, there are a number of general underlying ideas and concepts. Yet these have been used to elaborate several very different systems, which are mutually independent but all equally within the range of *dharma*. I shall first describe the systems and then discuss some of the general ideas.

First System

As early as 12.3, Manu introduces a threefold origin of karma, corresponding to YDh 3.131:

mind (*manas*)
speech (*vāc*)
body (*deha* (MDh) = *kāya* (YDh))

"Action, which springs from the mind, from speech, and from the body." This threefold division of karma leads, both in MDh (12.5–9) and in YDh (3.134–36), to a first system of rebirth.[750] Both texts give the same examples for the three types of karma:

Mental action:

coveting the property of others
thinking in one's heart of what is undesirable
adherence to false (doctrines)

Verbal actions:

abusing (others)[751]
(speaking) untruth
detracting from the merits of all men
talking idly

[750] The five tables in this article provide the Sanskrit terminology on karma and rebirth in the Dharmaśāstras only. Translating many of the terms would require extensive notes. [Ed. note: Provisional translations of these terms were nevertheless provided by the original editor of this article, Wendy Doniger.]

[751] This is the only significant difference between MDh and YDh. MDh 12.6a

Bodily action:

taking what has not been given
injuring (creatures) without the sanction of the law
holding criminal intercourse with another man's wife

An important point in this system is that each of the three types of karma uniformly leads to a specific form of rebirth:

(sinful) mental action → a low caste
(evil) verbal action → a bird or a beast
(wicked) bodily action → something inanimate

Even though the "actions" are further subdivided into nine (YDh) or ten (MDh), the three types of rebirth are not. (See Tables 1 and 2.)

Manu (12.10–11) concludes his description of the first system in an equally straightforward fashion: he who has full control over his mind, his speech, and his body is called a Tridaṇḍin; such an individual attains *siddhi*, "complete success," which is normally interpreted as synonymous with *mokṣa*.

Table 1

act (karma)		
types	*subtypes*	*result (phalam)*
mental action	coveting the property of others thinking in one's heart of what is undesirable adherence to false (doctrines)	a low caste
verbal action	abusing (others) speaking (untruth) detracting from the merits of all men talking idly	a bird or a beast
bodily action	taking what has not been given injuring (creatures) without the sanction of the law committing adultery with another man's wife	something inanimate

has *pāruṣyam anṛtaṃ caiva* as two separate items of the —explicitly— fourfold "verbal action." YDh 3.135a, which does not say that this type of *karma* is fourfold, has *puruṣo 'nṛtavādī ca* as one item in a threefold subdivision.

Table 2

act (karma)		
types	*subtypes*	*result* (*phalam*)
mānasam	*paradravyeṣv abhidhyānam* (MDh) *paradravyāṇy abhidhyāyan* (YDh) *manasā aniṣṭacintanam* (MDh) *aniṣṭāni cintayan* (YDh) *vitathābhiniveśaḥ* (MDh) *vitathābhiniveśī* (YDh)	*yāty antyajātitām* (MDh) *jāyate ’ntyāsu yoniṣu* (YDh)
vāṅmayam	*pāruṣyam* (MDh) [YDh, see note 751] *anṛtam* (MDh) *puruṣo ’nṛtavādī* (YDh) *paiśunyam* (MDh) *piśunaḥ puruṣaḥ* (YDh) *asambaddhapralāpaḥ* (MDh) *anibaddhapralāpī* (YDh)	*yāti pakṣimṛgatām* (MDh) *mṛgapakṣiṣu jāyate* (YDh)
śārīram	*adattānām upādānam* (MDh) *adattādānaniratah* (YDh) *hiṃsā avidhānataḥ* (MDh) *hiṃsako ’vidhānena* (YDh) *paradāropasevā* (MDh) *paradāropasevakaḥ* (YDh)	*yāti sthāvaratām* (MDh) *sthāvareṣv abhijāyate* (YDh)

Second System

MDh 12.24 introduces the three *guṇa*s or inherent qualities of all matter: *sattva*, *rajas*, and *tamas* (goodness, passion, and darkness). After several stanzas dealing with aspects of the three *guṇa*s which are less relevant for our purpose, stanza 12.39 introduces the transmigrations (*saṃsārāḥ*) resulting from them. Before doing so, the text (MDh 12.41) further subdivides each of the three *guṇa*s into three levels, which have been used on numerous occasions in the Dharmaśāstras: "low, middling, and high." The following nine stanzas (MDh 12.42–50) list, within each of the nine subtypes, a number of possible forms of rebirth, starting from the low subtype of *tamas* up to the high subtype of *sattva*. Even as in the first system, each of the principal categories leads to a specific type of rebirth:

sattva → the state of gods
rajas → the state of men
tamas → the condition of beasts

Differently from the first system, each of the nine subtypes is associated with a variety of possible rebirths, ranging from four to seven. (See Tables 3 and 4.)

Table 3

Realm of Goodness		
First	*Second become Gods*	*Highest*
Ascetics	Sacrificers	Brahmās
Mendicants	Seers	All-creators
Priests	Gods	*Dharma*
Hosts in Heavenly	Vedas	The Great
Chariots	Lights	The Unmanifest
Constellations	Years	
Demons	Ancestors	
	Realized ones	
Realm of Passion		
Low	*Middle become Men*	*High*
Prize-fighters	Kings	Celestial musicians
Wrestlers	Nobles	Goblins
Dancers	Preceptors of kings	Spirits of fertility
Men who make their	Those Best in Wars	Followers of the Gods
living with weapons	of Words	Celestial Nymphs
Those addicted to gambling and drinking		
Realm of Darkness		
Low	*Middle become Beasts*	*High*
Immovable (beings)	Elephants	Actors
Worms and Insects	Horses	Birds
Fish	Servants	Men who Cheat
Snakes	Despised Foreigners	Murderous Demons
Tortoises	Lions	Flesh-eating Demons
Domestic Beasts	Tigers	
Wild Beasts	Boars	

Table 4

sāttvikī gatiḥ		
prathamā	*dvitīyā* *devatvaṃ yānti*	*uttamā*
tāpasāḥ	yajvānaḥ	brahmā
yatayaḥ	ṛṣayaḥ	viśvasṛjaḥ
viprāḥ	devāḥ	dharmaḥ
vaimānikā gaṇāh	vedāḥ	mahān
nakṣatrāṇi	jyotīṃṣi	avyaktaḥ
daityāḥ	vatsarāḥ	
	pitaraḥ	
	sādhyāḥ	
rājasī gatiḥ		
jaghanyā	*madhyamā* *manuṣyatvaṃ yānti*	*uttamā*
jhallāḥ	rājānaḥ	gandharvāḥ
mallāḥ	kṣatriyāḥ	guhyakāḥ
naṭāḥ	rājñāṃ purohitāḥ	yakṣāḥ
puruṣāḥ	vādayuddhapradhānāḥ	vibudhānucarāḥ
śastravṛttayaḥ		apsarasaḥ
dyūtapānaprasaktāḥ		
tāmasī gatiḥ		
jaghanyā	*madhyamā* *tiryaktvaṃ yānti*	*uttamā*
sthāvarāḥ	hastinaḥ	cāraṇāḥ
kṛmikīṭāḥ	turaṅgāḥ	suparṇāḥ
matsyāḥ	śūdrāḥ	puruṣā dāmbhikāḥ
sarpāḥ	mlecchā garhitāḥ	rākṣāṃsi
kacchapāḥ	siṃhāḥ	piśācāḥ
paśavaḥ	vyāghrāḥ	
mṛgāḥ	varāhāḥ	

Here again, YDh (3.137–39), immediately after its discussion of the first system, has a similar passage, but without the subdivision into nine subtypes. It connects directly the characteristics of *sattva, rajas,* and *tamas* —which are very similar to the ones mentioned at MDh 12.31–33— with rebirth as a god, a human, or an animal, respectively. Also, YDh (3.140) seems to suggest that only those who are subject to *rajas* and *tamas* enter into *saṃsāra.*

Third System

The sequence MDh 12.52–58 again opens with two stanzas which might have served as an introduction to any treatment of karma and rebirth:

> In consequence of attachment to (the objects of) the senses, and in consequence of the non-performance of their duties, fools, the lowest of men, reach the vilest births.
>
> What wombs this individual soul enters in this world and in consequence of what actions —learn the particulars of that at length and in due order.

However, what follows refers exclusively to the rebirth of "those who committed mortal sins" (*mahāpātaka*), which have been enumerated at MDh 11.55:

> killing a Brāhmaṇa
> drinking (the spirituous liquor called) Surā
> stealing (the gold of a Brāhmaṇa)
> adultery with a Guru's wife

The rules for these four shall, logically, also apply to those "associating with such (offenders)" (MDh 11.55), and to those guilty of offenses which are "equal to" each of the four mortal sins (MDh 11.56–59).

MDh 12.54 (cf. YDh 3.206) lays down the general rule: all those guilty of "mortal sins" will spend large numbers of years in dreadful hells and, at the end of that, enter into *saṃsāras* —hundreds (MDh 12.58), thousands (MDh 12.57). This rule is followed by four stanzas (MDh 12.55–58; cf. YDh 3.207–208), listing several forms of rebirth for each mortal sin. These include mainly animals, a few low types of human beings, and especially for the "violator of a Guru's bed," plants (Tables 5 and 6).

The third system is different from the two previous ones in several respects. First, it deals with a very small and well-circumscribed number of activities. Second, for each of the four activities there is a list of possible rebirths in which humans, animals, and plants appear side by side indiscriminately. Third, a comparison between Manu and Yājñavalkya shows that, although the system as such was well established, the specific forms of rebirth were not: some forms of rebirth which both texts have in common are related to one "mortal sin" in Manu and to a different one in Yājñavalkya.[752]

Table 5

Mortal sinners	*Rebirth*	
	Manu	*Yājñavalkya*
Brahmin-killer	Dog Pig Donkey Camel Cow Goat Sheep Deer Bird Untouchable Mixed-birth Tribal	Deer Dog Pig Camel
Wine-drinker	Worm Insect Moth Birds that eat excrement Vicious creatures	Donkey Mixed-birth tribal Musician/Magician
Thief	Spiders Snakes Lizards Aquatic animals Vicious flesh-eating Demons	Worm Insect Moth
Defiler of the Guru's bed (wife)	grass shrub creeper carnivores beast with fangs those doing cruel deeds	grass shrub creeper

[752] Three of the "low types of human beings," *caṇḍāla*, *paulkasa*, and *vaiṇa*,

Table 6

Mortal sinners	*Rebirth*	
	Manu	*Yājñavalkya*
brahmahā	śvā sūkaraḥ kharaḥ uṣṭraḥ gauḥ ajaḥ aviḥ mṛgaḥ pakṣī caṇḍālaḥ pukkasaḥ	mṛgaḥ śvā sūkaraḥ sūkaraḥ uṣṭraḥ
surāpaḥ	kṛmiḥ kīṭaḥ pataṅgaḥ viṅbhujaḥ pakṣiṇaḥ hiṃsrāḥ sattvāḥ	kharaḥ pulkasaḥ veṇaḥ
stenaḥ	lūtā ahiḥ saraṭaḥ tiryañco 'mbucāriṇaḥ hiṃsrāḥ piśācāḥ	kṛmiḥ kīṭaḥ pataṅgaḥ
gurutalpagaḥ	tṛṇam gulmaḥ latā kravyādaḥ daṃstriṇaḥ krūrakarmakṛtaḥ	tṛṇam gulmaḥ latā

Fourth System

The next set of stanzas in Manu (12.61–69) becomes even more specific; it deals, in great detail, with the rebirths of all kinds of thieves. There are corresponding passages in Yājñavalkya (3.213–15), and, even more closely, in Viṣṇu (44.14–43) (Tables 7 and 8).

also appear at ĀpDh 2.1.2.5, but as rebirths for "theft and Brāhmaṇa murder" (? *steno 'bhiśastaḥ*), by a Brāhmaṇa, a Kṣatriya, and a Vaiśya, respectively.

Table 7

	Rebirth		
Object stolen	*Manu*	*Yājñavalkya*	*Viṣṇu*
grain	rat	mouse	rat
yellow metal	goose	——	goose
water	aquatic bird	aquatic bird	water bird
honey	stinging insect	stinging insect	stinging insect
milk	crow	crow	crow
juice	dog	dog	dog
butter	ichneumon	——	ichneumon
meat	vulture		vulture
flesh		vulture	
fat	cormorant	——	
lard		——	cormorant
oil	"oil-eater" bird	——	"oil-eater" bird
salt	cricket	cricket	cricket
sour milk	crane	——	crane
silk	partridge	——	partridge
linen	frog	——	frog
cotton	heron	——	heron
cow	iguana	iguana	iguana
molasses	flying fox	——	flying fox
fine perfume	muskrat	muskrat	
perfume			muskrat
leafy vegetables	peacock	peacock	peacock
various cooked food	porcupine		
cooked food			hedgehog
uncooked food	porcupine	——	porcupine
fire	crane	crane	crane
household utensils	wasp	wasp	wasp
dyed cloth	partridge	——	partridge
deer or elephant	wolf	——	——
elephant	——	——	tortoise
horse	tiger	——	tiger
fruit and roots	monkey		
fruit		monkey	

fruit or flowers			monkey
woman	bear	——	bear
drinking water	b/w cuckoo	——	——
vehicles	camel	camel	camel
cattle	goat	——	goat (vulture)
garment	——	leper	——

Table 8

Rebirth			
Object stolen	*Manu*	*Yājñavalkya*	*Viṣṇu*
dhānyam	ākhuḥ	mūṣakaḥ	ākhuḥ
kāṃsyam	haṃsaḥ	——	haṃsaḥ
jalam	plavaḥ	plavaḥ	jalābhiplavaḥ
madhu	daṃśaḥ	daṃśaḥ	daṃśaḥ
payaḥ	kākaḥ	kākaḥ	kākaḥ
rasaḥ	śvā	śvā	śvā
ghṛtam	nakulaḥ	——	nakulaḥ
māṃsam	gṛdhraḥ		gṛdhraḥ
palam		gṛdhraḥ	
vapā	madguḥ	——	
vasā		——	madguḥ
tailam	tailapakaḥ khagaḥ	——	tailapāyikaḥ
lavaṇam	cīrīvākaḥ	cīrī	cīrivāk
dadhi	balākā śakuniḥ	——	balākā
kauśeyam	tittiriḥ	——	tittiriḥ
kṣaumam	darduraḥ	——	darduraḥ
karpāsatāntavam	krauñcaḥ	——	krauñcaḥ
gauḥ	godhā	godhā	godhā
guḍaḥ	vāggudaḥ	——	vālgudaḥ
śubhā gandhāḥ	chucchundariḥ	chucchundarī	
gandhāḥ			chucchundariḥ

patraśākaḥ	barhiṇaḥ	śikhī	barhī
kṛtānnaṃ vividham	śvāvit	——	
kṛtānnam		——	sedhā
akṛtānnam	śalyakaḥ	——	śalyakaḥ
agniḥ	bakaḥ	bakaḥ	bakaḥ
upaskaraḥ	gṛhakārī	gṛhakārī	gṛhakārī
raktāni vāsāṃsi	jīvajīvakaḥ	——	jīvajīvakaḥ
mṛgebhaḥ	vṛkaḥ	——	——
gajaḥ	——	——	kūrmaḥ
aśvaḥ	vyāghraḥ	——	vyāghraḥ
phalamūlam	markaṭaḥ		
phalam		kapiḥ	
phalaṃ puṣpaṃ vā			markaṭaḥ
strī	ṛkṣaḥ	——	ṛkṣaḥ
vāri	stokakaḥ	——	——
yānāni	uṣṭraḥ	uṣṭraḥ	uṣṭraḥ
paśavaḥ	ajaḥ	——	ajaḥ (gṛdhraḥ)
vastram	——	śvitrī	——

Again, the system is very different from the preceding ones. First, it confirms something we also know from other sources: classical India's preoccupation with theft; of all wrongdoings theft is, in this kind of text, invariably given the most exhaustive treatment. As a result, more than thirty types of theft are enumerated, each of them related to one single type of rebirth. Except for the fact that Yājñavalkya is less exhaustive than Manu and Viṣṇu, the three texts display far greater uniformity than Manu and Yājñavalkya did in the preceding system. Does this mean anything for the particular relation between stealing object A and being reborn as animal B? There is no easy answer to this question. We might understand why a thief of grain will be reborn as a rat, or someone who steals meat, as a vulture. We may be able to appreciate, for very different reasons, why the thief of a cow (*go*) is reborn as an iguana (*go-dhā*), or the thief of molasses (*guḍa*) as "a flying-fox" (*vāgguda*). We can even imagine why a thief of drinking water is reborn a "a black-white cuckoo," for this bird is said to subsist on raindrops. But, in general, names of animals in Sanskrit are often uncertain, and so is their relation to the objects stolen.

Of the two concluding stanzas in this sequence (MDh 12.68–69, ViDh 44.44–45), the first seems to summarize the whole section by stating that whoever steals something from someone else becomes an animal.[753] The second is interesting in that it specifically refers to the rebirth of women: women who are guilty of theft are reborn as the females of the animals listed in the preceding stanzas.

Fifth System

Finally, one sequence (MDh 12.70–72) approaches rebirth from the point of the specific duties of the four *varṇas*. In general, members of any *varṇa* who fall short of their specific duties, except in cases of emergency, "migrate into despicable bodies" and "will become the servants of the Dasyus." Next, more specific rules are laid down for the four *varṇas* separately:

Brāhmaṇa	→	*Ulkāmukha Preta* "who feeds on what has been vomited"
Kṣatriya	→	*Kaṭapūtana* (*Preta*) "who eats impure substances and corpses"
Vaiśya	→	*Maitrākṣajyotika Preta* "who feeds on pus"
Śūdra	→	*Cailāśaka* (*Preta*) "who feeds on moths" or "body-lice"

The criterion for rebirth in this fifth system is the lack of performance, by any member of a *varṇa*, of the specific duties assigned to that *varṇa*. The same criterion is also applied in other texts, but in very different ways. Āpastamba (2.5.11.10–11) lays down the general rule that members of any *varṇa*, "if they have fulfilled their duties," move up one *varṇa* in each future existence; on the contrary, "if they neglect their duties," they are each time reborn in the next lower *varṇa*. It is worth noticing that these two *sūtras* have no connection whatever with the context in which they occur. They obviously represent nothing more than floating aphorisms of a very general nature, which fail to inform us, for instance, what happens upward after the Brāhmaṇa or downward after the Śūdra.

[753] In reality, the stanza only partly refers to the subject of theft. It lists, together with the thief, "or (one) who has eaten sacrificial food (of) which (no portion) had been offered," which means that it had a different origin in a sacrificial context and was only secondarily inserted at this place.

Miscellaneous Rules

In addition to the five systems described so far, MDh —and other *dharma* texts— exhibit a number of isolated rules on karma and rebirth. Some of these rules are inserted in the sections on karma and rebirth generally; others appear in very different contexts.

For instance, in between Manu's third and fourth systems there are two stanzas (MDh 12.59–60) which not only have nothing in common with the surrounding systems, but also have no connection whatever with each other. The first stanza enumerates four activities and four resulting forms of rebirth:

men who delight in doing hurt	→	carnivorous (animals)
those who eat forbidden food	→	worms
thieves	→	creatures consuming their own kind
those who have intercourse with women of the lowest castes	→	*Pretas*

The second stanza (cf. YDh 3.212) is structured differently, listing three activities leading to the same result:

he who is associated with outcastes he who has approached the wives of other men he who has stolen the property of a Brāhmaṇa	} *Brahmarākṣasa*s

In the eleventh book Manu inserts, without any introduction, the following three stanzas on rebirth (MDh 11.24–26; cf. YDh 1.127, ViDh 59.11):

A Brāhmaṇa who begs from a Śūdra for a sacrifice	→	a *Caṇḍāla*
A Brāhmaṇa who, having begged any property for a sacrifice, does not use the whole (for that purpose)	→	for a hundred years a (vulture of the kind called) *Bhāsa*, or a crow
That sinful man, who, through covetousness, seizes the property of the gods, or the property of Brāhmaṇas	→	feeds…on the leavings of vultures

In the passage in Manu that deals with the duties of women, three stanzas (MDh 5.164–66) refer to their rebirth; the first two appear, identically but in reversed order, in the "legal" section on the duties of husband and wife (MDh 9.29–30). One stanza (MDh 5.164 = 9.30; cf. VaDh 21.14) is devoted to the fate of the unfaithful wife: she is "disgraced in this world, (after death) she enters the womb of a jackal, and is tormented by diseases, (the punishment for) her sins." Two stanzas (MDh 5.165 = 9.29, and 5.166) deal with the faithful wife "who controls her thoughts, speech, and body" —a formula reminiscent of the first system. Such a wife, besides gaining renown in this world, obtains "in the next (world) a place near her husband." This sequence, which forms a mini-system of its own, clearly illustrates the nature of Dharmaśāstra rules on rebirth—and on many other subjects. The stress in this case is definitely on the need for wives to be faithful to their husbands. Hence the opposition:

unfaithful wife → jackal
faithful wife → the world of (her) husband

The question whether the husband himself has lived the best of lives, and, therefore, whether he himself will move on to the best of worlds, is totally irrelevant. A similar stanza in Yājñavalkya (1.87) indicates the true meaning of Manu's "world of the husband"; it holds out, for the faithful wife, "the best possible destination."[754] Other isolated rules may very well have been part of similar mini-systems.

Theoretical Considerations

One cannot help being struck by the fact that, in the Dharmaśāstras, the construction and description of various systems outweigh by far the attention given to theoretical considerations and analyzing the technique of karma and rebirth.

The basic statement appears at the outset of Manu's twelfth book (MDh 12.3): *śubhāśubhaphalaṃ karma.* Bühler's translation: "Action…produces good or bad results," is misleading; the real meaning of the Sanskrit text is that actions produce "more or less" favorable results, that is, the entire gamut from very favorable to very unfavorable. Yet, the principal fact is that "action produces results."

There is no doubt that, for the typical Dharmaśāstra, the results of "sinful acts" are varied and complex. Manu (12.74–80; for a similar enumeration, see MDh 6.61–64) lists them in the following order:

[754] VaDh 21.11 threatens with non-access to the *patiloka* "that woman of the Brāhmaṇa caste who drinks spirituous liquour"; she will, instead, be "born again as a leech or a pearl-oyster."

pain here (below) in various births
(the torture of) being tossed about in dreadful hells, Tāmisra and the rest
(that of) the forest with sword-leaved trees and the like
(that of) being bound and mangled
various torments
the (pain of) being devoured by ravens and owls
the heat of scorching sand
the (torture of) being boiled in jars, which is hard to bear
births in the wombs (of) despicable (beings) which cause constant misery
afflictions from cold and heat
terrors of various kinds
the (pain of) repeatedly lying in various wombs
agonizing births
imprisonment in fetters hard to bear
the misery of being enslaved by others
separations from their relatives and dear ones
the (pain of) dwelling together with the wicked
(labor in) gaining wealth and its loss
(trouble in) making friends and (the appearance of) enemies
old age against which there is no remedy
the pangs of diseases
afflictions of many various kinds
and (finally) unconquerable death

Although rebirth, therefore, has to be viewed within a much larger framework, there is no doubt that, for the compilers of the Dharmaśāstras, it ranked as the first and most important result of action. After the long enumeration of possible consequences of "sinful acts," Manu's conclusion (MDh 12.81; cf. YDh 3.131–32) refers to rebirth and rebirth only:

> But with whatever disposition of mind (a man) performs any act, he reaps its result in a (future) body endowed with the same quality.

Manu (12.3) also immediately introduces another concept: *karmajā gatayo nṝṇām*, which means that a man's actions determine his *gati* —in the plural. Bühler translates: "the (various) conditions." But it is clear from several contexts in which the term occurs that *gati* has to be taken far more literally: "going, going away." YDh 3.131, which also corresponds with MDh 12.3 in other respects, makes this even more explicit by using the verbal form *prayāti* "goes forth."

The texts give only the most elementary indications on what exactly "goes forth." MDh 12.3 merely refers to "men," and so does MDh 6.61. Elsewhere the subject of "going" is "the inner self" (*antarātman*) (MDh 6.73) or "the individual soul" (*jīva*) (MDh 12.23, YDh 3.131).

Āpastamba (2.1.2.2) and Gautama (11.29–30) exhibit an interesting parallel passage on the nature of *gati*, even though they do not use the term. When a man who has duly fulfilled his own *dharma* dies, according to Āpastamba, he enjoys "supreme, unlimited happiness"; according to Gautama, "he experiences the results of his actions." Afterwards —both texts explicitly say *tataḥ*— "on his return" (ĀpDh: *parivṛttau*), he takes birth again under the best of circumstances —good family, beauty, wisdom, and so forth. Those who have not fulfilled their own *dharma* undergo a similar fate, but in the opposite direction.

Āpastamba compares the individual's movement from this world to a world of supreme happiness —or unhappiness— and back to this world, to a wheel (*cakravat*; *parivṛtti* also involves the idea of rolling). Although Āpastamba does not use the word *saṃsāra*, his text reminds us of MDh 12.124: the supreme being makes all created beings "revolve like the wheels (of a chariot)" (*saṃsārayati cakravat*).

Important in both texts is the statement that rebirth occurs, after the intermediate period in which "he enjoys happiness" —or its opposite— or in which "he experiences the results of his actions," *śeṣeṇa* (GDh) or *karmaphalaśeṣeṇa* (ĀpDh). Bühler translates: "by virtue of a remnant of their (merit)" (GDh), and "by virtue of a remainder of merit" (ĀpDh). These translations are acceptable only with the proviso that "remnant" and "remainder" not be understood to mean mere unimportant and incidental additions to that which they are the "remnant" or "remainder" of. The term *śeṣa* in Sanskrit always indicates an important and necessary complement to something which, without it, would remain incomplete and imperfect. Hence rebirth takes place "by way of a necessary supplement to the result of actions," or "in order to bring the result of actions to completion."

The passages from Āpastamba and Gautama are exceptional in that they actually describe the results of "good action," and, subsequently, conclude with a brief note: "from this you can also gather what happens to bad action." In most cases attention is paid primarily —often uniquely— to a person's *gati* as a result of "bad action" (*karmadoṣa*). This is obvious not only from most types of rebirth within the various systems described earlier, but also from the fact that the texts deal far more elaborately with the intervening "world of unhappiness" than they do with the "world of supreme happiness." Hells and suffering in hell are very prominent in Dharmaśāstra literature. Besides numerous shorter references in other texts, the most detailed treatment is exhibited by Viṣṇu. This text devotes an entire chapter (43) to the enumeration of twenty-one hells, to the periods of time to be spent there —one *kalpa*, one *manvantara*, one *caturyuga*, to a most graphic description of terrible pains and suffering.

The most revealing theoretical statement on the technique of transmigration is probably contained in MDh 12.12–13. Unfortunately, the text as we have it is susceptible to very different interpretations; the various explanations by the Sanskrit commentators are reflected in Bühler's unusually lengthy notes. The text clearly describes *ātman* or *bhūtātman* as the author of actions; the instigator of *ātman* is called *kṣetrajña*.[755] It also introduces, separately, *jīva* "through which (the *kṣetrajña*) becomes sensible of all pleasure and pain in (successive) births"; as was indicated earlier, this passage is one of those that attributes *gati* —in the plural— to *jīva*. Another concept which is clearly expressed is that, after death, another "strong body" is produced, "formed of particles (of the) five (elements)"; it is this body that is "destined to suffer the torments (in hell)," after which it is again dissolved into its elements. Any further interpretation at this point is likely to do injustice to the text.

We have seen earlier that, as a rule, action produces a result. In most cases this result is —upward or downward— *saṃsāra* or *saṃsāras*, for, like *gati*, this term is often used in the plural. There are, however, exceptions, such as the Tridaṇḍin, who has been referred to in the context of the first system. The distinction is made at a more general level at MDh 6.74, in connection with the ascetic:

> He who possesses true insight (into the nature of the world), is not fettered by his deeds; but he who is destitute of that insight, is drawn into the circle of births and deaths.

In other words, the distinction is between "being tied down by actions" and its opposite, which is not mentioned here, "being set free by actions."

The criterion for reaching the latter state is true insight. Thus, the ascetic is able (MDh 6.73), "by the practice of meditation," "to gain true insight"[756] in the *gati* of the Inner Self (*antarātman*).

The text adds (MDh 6.75) that ascetics can reach that level even during their lifetime:

> By not injuring any creatures, by detaching the senses (from objects of enjoyment), by the rites prescribed in the Veda, and by rigorously practicing austerities, (men) gain that state (even) in this (world).

[755] *Bhūtātmā = yaḥ karoti karmāṇi; kṣetrajñaḥ = yo 'syātmanaḥ kārayitā.* Compare MDh 12.119cd: *ātmā hi janayaty eṣāṃ karmayogaṃ śarīriṇām* "for the Self produces the connection of these embodied (spirits) with actions."

[756] There is no doubt a connection between *sam-paśyet* at MDh 6.73, and *samyagdarśana°* at MDh 6.74; the preverb *sam* is often interpreted as synonymous with the adverb *samyak*.

But, conversely, the state of being "released while still alive" (*jīvanmukta* —the text uses the term *mukta*) can again be lost (MDh 6.58):

> Let him disdain all (food) obtained in consequence of humble salutations, (for) even an ascetic who has attained final liberation, is bound (with the fetters of the *saṃṣāra*) by accepting (food given) in consequence of humble salutations.

The idea expressed at MDh 6.73–74 returns in the second section of the twelfth book (MDh 12.82–107), which, for Brāhmaṇas only, examines "those acts which secure supreme bliss." The list of these activities (MDh 12.83; cf. YDh 3.190) comes very close to that of the sixth book:

> Studying the Veda, (practicing) austerities, (the acquisition of true) knowledge, the subjugation of the organs, abstention from doing injury, and serving the Guru are the best means for attaining supreme bliss.

Two of these are then singled out as superior to the others and, in fact, encompassing them all: "knowledge of the soul" and "(the performance of) the acts taught in the Veda." The remainder of the section is primarily devoted to praising the Veda. Yet there are a few elements in it that touch on the subject of rebirth. The text (MDh 12.88–90) distinguishes two types of acts taught in the Veda:

1. *pravṛttaṃ karma*, "acts which secure (the fulfillment of) wishes in this world or in the next," and
2. *nivṛttaṃ karma*, "acts performed without any desire (for a reward), preceded by (the acquisition) of (true) knowledge."

The difference is that he who performs *pravṛttaṃ karma* "becomes equal to the gods," whereas he who performs *nivṛttaṃ karma* "passes beyond (the reach of) the five elements." Although the term is not used here, the tradition unanimously equates this state with *mokṣa.*

Irrespective of whether a person is "tied down" in *saṃsāra* or "set free" from it, in all cases discussed so far his fate is the result of his actions. I shall conclude this article by discussing a few situations in which the correlation "action → result" seems either to have been denied, or to have become the object of some theoretical discussion.

In the first place, certain activities have explicitly been labeled "without result." Thus, whereas the fifth system above lays down specific results for members of a *varṇa* who deviate from the duties of their *varṇa*, a short sequence in MDh (11.28–30) deals in a very different way with the fate of those who live, in normal times, according to the duties that shall apply to there *varṇa* in times of distress only.

> But a twice-born, who, without being in distress, performs his duties according to the law for times of distress, obtains no reward for them in the next world; that is the opinion (of the sages).
>
> By the Viśve-devas, by the Sādhyas, and by the great sages (of the) Bṛāhmaṇa (caste), who were afraid of perishing in times of distress, a substitute was made for the (principal) rule.
>
> That evil-minded man, who, being able (to fulfill) the original law, lives according to the secondary rule, reaps no reward for that after death.

Similarly, whereas the performance of the two types of Vedic action (*vaidikaṃ karma*) produces the most excellent results, performance of what might be called non-Vedic action (*avaidikaṃ karma* —a term not used in the text) produces, according to MDh 12.95, no result at all.

> All those traditions and all those despicable systems of philosophy, which are not based on the Veda, produce no reward after death; for they are declared to be founded on Darkness.

Bühler's "reward" (MDh 11.28, 30) translates Sanskrit *phalam*, and "produce no reward" (MDh 12.95) renders Sanskrit *niṣphalāḥ*. It is only normal that living by the wrong set of duties, or according to non-Vedic prescriptions, should not produce a "reward." What is more surprising is that the text actually denies such acts a "result."

In the second place, it is possible for individuals —exceptional individuals!— to counteract and eliminate, during their lifetime, the results of actions. One who knows the Veda is such a person. According to a simile used by Manu (12.101), he "burns down" the evil results of action.

> As a fire that has gained strength consumes even trees full of sap, even so he who knows the Veda burns out the taint of his soul which arises from (evil) acts.

It comes as no surprise that such an idea was widespread in Dharmaśāstra circles. VaDh (27.2) has an identical stanza, except that he replaces "he knows the Veda" (*vedajñaḥ*) by "the fire of the Veda" (*vedāgniḥ*). And "the fire of the Veda," or "the fire of knowledge" (MDh 11.247: *jñānāgninā*) also occurs elsewhere as the destroyer of the results of one's —sinful— actions.

The idea of "burning down" the results of actions during one's lifetime leads me to a final problem, which appears to have been of concern to the compilers of Dharmaśāstras: the relation between karma and rebirth on the one hand, and the performance of penances or expiations (*prāyaścitta*) on the other. The problem is raised in a passage which appears quasi-identically in three Dharmasūtras: GDh (19.2–6), VaDh (22.1–5), and BDh (3.10.2–5). This is Gautama's text:

> Now indeed, man (in) this (world) is polluted by a vile action, such as sacrificing for men unworthy to offer a sacrifice, eating forbidden food, speaking what ought not to be spoken, neglecting what is prescribed, practicing what is forbidden.
>
> They are in doubt if he shall perform a penance for such (a deed) or if he shallnot do it. (Some) declare that he shall not do it, because the deed does not perish. The most excellent (opinion is), that he shall perform (a penance).

In other words, the question was disputed whether expiation was at all a worthwhile enterprise, for, according to one opinion, "action does not pass, waste away, perish," understood: in this lifetime.

To be sure, the protagonists of penance prevailed: there are numerous texts stating that the sin incurred by such or such action is cleared by such or such penance. But the ambivalence remained, as in YDh (3.133):

> Some actions ripen (*vipāka*) after death, others ripen in this world, others again either here or there; the deciding factor is the disposition (*bhāva*).

Hence conflicting texts and, within the same texts, differing views, on whether to limit penance to sins committed unintentionally. For instance, according to MDh (11.45):

> (All) sages prescribe a penance for a sin unintentionally committed; some declare, on the evidence of the revealed texts, (that it may be performed) even for an intentional (offense).

More important for our present purpose is another type of uncertainty in the texts, namely with regard to a long list of physical deficiencies which are believed to be the results of wrongdoings. MDh (11.48) states that problem as follows:

> Some wicked men suffer a change of their (natural) appearance in consequence of crimes committed in this life, and some of those committed in a former (existence).

The whole passage is obviously meant to exhort people to undergo the required penances immediately. Compare Manu's concluding stanzas (MDh 11.53–54):

> Thus in consequence of a remnant[757] of (the guilt of former) crimes, are born idiots, dumb, blind, deaf, and deformed men, who are (all) despised by the virtuous.
>
> Penances, therefore, must always be performed for the sake of purification, because those whose sins have not been expiated, are born (again) with disgraceful marks.

The intervening four stanzas (MDh 11.49–52) exhibit sixteen specific cases of physical consequences of wrongdoings —according to the introductory stanza: in this life or in the preceding one. It is worth noticing that the first four offenses (MDh 11.49) are the four "mortal sins" (*mahāpātaka*) the rebirths for which are dealt with in Manu's twelfth book —and the third system above— and which will only be introduced at MDh 11.55, after the sequence we are now dealing with. The corresponding stanza in YDh (3.209), on the other hand, is an integral part of its sequence (YDh 3.206–208) on the rebirths of "mortal sinners." Vasiṣṭha (20.43–44) definitely relates the illnesses to "mortal sins" committed in a previous existence:

> Now they quote also (the following verses): "Hear, (how) the bodies of those who having committed various crimes died a long time ago, and were (afterwards) born again, are (marked)"; "A thief will have deformed nails, the murderer of a Brāhmaṇa will be afflicted with white leprosy, but he who has drunk spirituous liquour will have black teeth, and the violator of his Guru's bed will suffer from skin diseases."

Viṣṇu (45.1) also leaves no doubt that the physical defects for "mortal sinners" —and many others— obtain in future existences only. This text even establishes a time sequence for passage through hells, rebirths in animal form described in chapter 44 —see the fourth system above— and subsequent rebirths in human form:

> Now after having undergone the torments inflicted in the hells, and having passed through the animal bodies, the sinners are born as human beings with (the following) marks (indicating their crime).

But even then the chapter concludes with two stanzas (ViDh

[757] Bühler opts for the reading °*avaśeṣeṇa*, rather than °*viśeṣeṇa*. Either one is a variant, *metri causa*, for °*śeṣeṇa*.

45.32–33) very similar to MDh 11.52–53, exhorting people that "penances must be performed by all means."

The detailed list of offenses and resulting illnesses (MDh 11.49–52, YDh 3.209–11, ViDh 45.2–31; see Tables 9 and 10) contains at least a kernel that must have been widely accepted by the Hindu tradition. In many ways it is similar to the lists of rebirths in animal form in Table 7. For an unknown reason this type of "results of actions" was closely associated with exhortations to perform penances, so much so that at least one Dharmaśāstra, MDh, transferred it to its chapter on expiation. But everything seems to indicate that, in reality, we are dealing with yet another "system" of karma and rebirth.

Table 9

Deficiency			
Offender	*Manu*	*Yājñavalkya*	*Viṣṇu*
transgressor	——	——	leprosy
gold-thief	diseased nails		
gold-thief		bad nails	bad nails
wine-drinker	black teeth	black teeth	black teeth
Brahmin-killer	consumption	consumption	consumption
guru-wife-seducer	diseased skin	diseased skin	diseased skin
informer	foul-smelling nose	foul-smelling nose	foul-smelling nose
calumniator	foul-smelling breath	foul-smelling breath	foul-smelling breath
thief of grain	limb-deficiency	——	limb-deficiency
adulterator	limb-superfluity		
grain adulterator		limb superfluity	
grain adulterator/thief			limb-superfluity
thief of cooked food	dyspepsia	dyspepsia	dyspepsia
thief of the word (Veda)	dumbness	dumbness	dumbness
garment-thief	white leprosy		white leprosy
horse-thief	lameness	——	lameness
reviler of gods and Brahmins	——	——	dumbness
poisoner	——	——	rolling tongue

arsonist	——	——	madness
offender of guru	——	——	epilepsy
cow-slayer	——	——	blindness
lamp-thief	blindness	——	blindness
extinguisher	one eye	——	
lamp-extinguisher		——	one eye
injurer	general disease	——	——
non-injurer	freedom from disease	——	——
oil-thief	——	oil-drinking	——
seller of tin, yak-tail, & lead	——	——	washerman
seller of whole-hoofed (animals)	——	——	hunter
one supported by son of adulterous woman	——	——	fellatio (his mouth used as vulva)
thief	——	——	bell-ringer
usurer	——	——	vertigo
solitary eater of sweets	——	——	rheumatism
promise-breaker	——	——	severe cough
semen-spiller (chastity-vow-violator)	——	——	elephantiasis
ruiner of another's livelihood	——	——	poverty
oppressor	——	——	long illness

Table 10

Deficiency			
Offender	*Manu*	*Yājñavalkya*	*Viṣṇu*
atipātakī	——	——	kuṣṭhī
suvarṇacauraḥ	kaunakhyam		
hemahārī		kunakhī	
suvarṇahārī			kunakhī
surāpaḥ	śyāvadantatā	śyāvadantakaḥ	śyāvadantakaḥ

brahmahā	kṣayarogitvam	kṣayarogī	yakṣmī
gurutalpagaḥ	dauścarmyam	duścarmā	duścarmā
piśunaḥ	pautināsikyam	pūtināsikaḥ	pūtināsaḥ
sūcakaḥ	pūtivaktratā	pūtivaktraḥ	pūtivaktraḥ
dhānyacauraḥ	aṅgahīnatvam	——	aṅgahīnaḥ
miśrakaḥ	ātiraikyam		
dhānyamiśraḥ		atiriktāṅgaḥ	
miśracoraḥ			atiriktāṅgaḥ
annahartā	amayāvitam	amayāvī	
annāpahārakaḥ			amayāvī
vāgapahārakaḥ	maukyam	mūkaḥ	mūkaḥ
vastrāpahārakaḥ	śvaitryam	——	śvitrī
aśvahārakaḥ	paṅgutā	——	paṅguḥ
devabrāhmaṇā-krośakaḥ	——	——	mūkaḥ
garadaḥ	——	——	lolajihvaḥ
agnidaḥ	——	——	unmattaḥ
guroḥ pratikūlaḥ	——	——	apasmārī
goghnaḥ	——	——	andhaḥ
dīpahartā	andhaḥ	——	
dīpāpahārakaḥ		——	andhaḥ
nirvāpakaḥ	kāṇaḥ	——	
dīpanirvāpakaḥ		——	kāṇaḥ
hiṃsā	vyādhibhūyastvam	——	——
ahiṃsā	arogitvam	——	——
tailahṛt	——	tailapāyī	——
trapucāmara-sīsakavikrayī	——	——	rajakaḥ
ekaśaphavikrayī	——	——	mṛgavyādhaḥ
kuṇḍāśī	——	——	bhagāsyaḥ
stenaḥ	——	——	ghāṇṭikaḥ
vārdhuṣikaḥ	——	——	bhrāmarī
mṛṣṭāśy ekākī	——	——	vātagulmī
samayabhettā	——	——	khalvāṭaḥ
avakīrṇaḥ	——	——	ślīpadī
paravṛttighnaḥ	——	——	daridraḥ
parapīḍākaraḥ	——	——	dīrgharogī

34

Notes on the Technical Term Sāhasa: *"Fine, Pecuniary Penalty"*

Sāhasa is a well-known technical term in classical Hindu law. It has its regular place in the enumerations of *vivādapadas*, i.e., the —normally eighteen— "titles of law." For example in Manu's list of *vivādapadas* (8.4–7), the *śloka* containing titles ten to fifteen runs as follows:

sīmāvivādadharmaś ca pāruṣye daṇḍavācike |
steyaṃ ca sāhasaṃ caiva strīsaṃgrahaṇam eva ca ||

"(10) Disputes regarding boundaries, (11) assault and (12) defamation, (13) theft, (14) *robbery and violence*, (15) adultery" (trans. Bühler: 253).

There may be some doubt about the exact connotation of the term *sāhasa* even within a single text such as the *Manusmṛti* and Bühler's "robbery and violence" may only be partly valid. On the one hand, *sāhasa* seems to refer to "violent appropriation," different from *steya* only insofar as the latter indicates appropriation in the absence of the owner and, hence, without violence. Thus MDh 8.332:

syāt sāhasaṃ tv anvayavatprasabhaṃ karma yat kṛtam |
niranvayaṃ bhavet steyaṃ hṛtvāpavyayate ca yat ||

"An offense (of this description), which is committed in the presence (of the owner) and with violence, will be *robbery*; if (it is committed) in his absence, it will be theft; likewise if (the possession of) anything is denied after it has been taken" (trans. Bühler: 312). On the other hand, *sāhasa* is clearly distinguished from *steya*; says MDh 8.345:

vāgduṣṭāt taskarāc caiva daṇḍenaiva ca hiṃsataḥ |
sāhasasya naraḥ kartā vijñeyaḥ pāpakṛttamaḥ ||

"He who commits *violence* must be considered as the worst offender, (more wicked) than a defamer, than a thief, and than he who injures (another) with a staff" (trans. Bühler: 314). There is even a third meaning of *sāhasa,* which is much wider than the two preceding ones. Says NS 14.2:

manuṣyamāraṇaṃ steyaṃ paradārābhimarśanam |
pāruṣyaṃ dvividhaṃ jñeyaṃ sāhasaṃ syāc caturvidham ||

"Man-slaughter, robbery, an indecent assault on another man's wife, and the two species of insult, such are the four kinds of *Heinous Offenses*" (trans. Jolly: 202). In this and similar passages, *sāhasa,* in its broadest sense, comes very close to what we might call a "criminal case."

Notwithstanding the differences that exist between the three types of *sāhasa* referred to up till now, they have one important element in common: in each and every case *sāhasa* indicates a violent act which deserves to be punished. Although this kind of *sāhasa,* too, needs further investigation, we are less concerned here with *sāhasa* "violent act" than we are with a totally different meaning, namely: "fine, pecuniary penalty."

Let us first quote some of the relevant Dharmaśāstra passages:

1. MDh 8.138 = ViDh 4.14:

paṇānāṃ dve śate sārdhe prathamaḥ sāhasaḥ kṛtaḥ |
madhyamaḥ pañca vijñeyaḥ sahasraṃ tv eva cottamaḥ ||

"Two hundred and fifty paṇas are declared (to be) the first (or lowest) amercement, five (hundred) are considered as the mean (or middlemost), but one thousand as the highest" (trans. Bühler: 277);

2. YDh 1.365 (6):

sāśītipaṇasāhasro daṇḍa uttamasāhasaḥ |
tadardhaṃ madhyamaḥ proktas tadardham adhamaḥ smṛtaḥ ||

"One thousand and eighty paṇas are the highest amercement, one half of this is called the middlemost amercement, one half of that is said to be the lowest amercement."

3. NS Appendix 30, 31ab:

caturviṃśāvaraḥ pūrvaḥ paraḥ ṣaṇṇavatir bhavet |
śatāni pañca tu paro madhyamo dviśatāvaraḥ ||

sahasraṃ tūttamo jñeyaḥ paraḥ pañcaśatāvaraḥ |

"The first (or lowest) fine to be inflicted on a guilty person shall amount to neither more nor less than twenty-four (paṇas). The middlemost fine shall consist of not more than four hundred, and not less than two hundred (paṇas). The highest fine should be known to consist of not more than a thousand, and not less than five hundred (paṇas)" (trans. Jolly: 227);

4. BS 8.11 (K.V. Rangaswami Aiyangar):

kārṣāpaṇasahasraṃ tu daṇḍa uttamasāhasaḥ |
tadardhaṃ madhyamaḥ proktas tadardham adhamaḥ smṛtaḥ ||

"The punishment called highest amercement consists of a thousand *kārṣāpaṇa*s, half of this is called middlemost amercement, half of this the lowest amercement."

5. *Śaṅkhalikhita* 263 (Kane):

caturviṃśatir ekanavatiḥ prathamasāhasaḥ dviśataṃ pañcaśataṃ caiva madhyamasāhasaḥ ṣaṭśataṃ sahasraṃ cottamaḥ.

"The first amercement is (between) twenty-four and ninety-one (*paṇa*s), the middlemost amercement (between) two and five hundred, the highest amercement (between) six hundred and one thousand."

These texts clearly indicate that, besides "violent act," *sāhasa* also refers to a kind of punishment, and, more specifically a pecuniary penalty, a fine, of which there are three degrees:

1. *prathama, pūrva, adhama,*
2. *madhyama,*
3. *uttama.*

In other words: *sāhasa* belongs to *dhanadaṇḍa* or *arthadaṇḍa* "pecuniary penalty," a specific category of punishment which has been clearly distinguished by the ancient Dharmaśāstras. Compare the following texts:

1. MDh 8.129:

vāgdaṇḍaṃ prathamaṃ kuryād dhigdaṇḍaṃ tadanantaram |
tṛtīyaṃ dhanadaṇḍaṃ tu vadhadaṇḍam ataḥ param ||

"Let him punish first by (gentle) admonition, afterwards by (harsh) reproof, thirdly by a fine, after that by corporal chastisement." (Trans. Bühler: 276)

2. YDh 1.366 (7):

dhigdaṇḍas tv atha vāgdaṇḍo dhanadaṇḍo vadhas tathā |
yojyā vyastāḥ samastā vā hy aparādhavaśād ime ||

3. NS Appendix 53:

śārīraś cārthadaṇḍaś ca daṇḍas tu dvividhaḥ smṛtaḥ |
śārīro daśadhā prokto hy arthadaṇḍas tv anekadhā ||

"Punishment is pronounced to be twofold: corporal punishment and fines. Corporal punishment is again declared to be of ten sorts; fines are (also) of more than one kind." (Trans. Jolly: 231)

4. BS 29.2 (Rangaswami Aiyangar):

vāg dhig dhanaṃ vadham caiva caturdhā kalpitaṃ damam |
puruṣaṃ doṣavibhavaṃ jñātvā samparikalpayet ||

"When he finds out that a man has committed an offense, he should inflict upon him one of the four types of punishment: admonition, reproof, fine, or corporal punishment."

The problem to be examined in this paper is the origin of *sāhasa* "fine, pecuniary penalty." There can be little doubt about the origin of *sāhasa* "violent act." Nothing is easier and has been done more frequently than the derivation of the latter kind of *sāhasa* from *sahas*. For instance, KS 795:

sahasā yat kṛtaṃ karma tat sāhasam udāhṛtam |

"That is declared to be *sāhasa* which is an act done with force" (trans. Kane: 283) whereby *sahas* is a synonym of *bala*; says NS 14.1:

sahasā kriyate karma yat kiṃcid baladarpitaiḥ |
tat sāhasam iti proktaṃ saho balam ihocyate ||

"Whatever is performed by force (sahas) by persons inflamed with (the pride of) strength, is called Sāhasa (a heinous offense); sahas (force) means strength in this world." (Trans. Jolly: 202)

It is perhaps not surprising per se, that *sāhasa* also indicates a punishment, i.e., a violent act performed by the king. But, in view of the above-mentioned etymology, one would then expect the punishment indicated by *sāhasa* to be "violent" in nature, and, consequently, to refer to physical punishment. However, the texts are unanimous: *sāhasa* does not belong to *vadhadaṇḍa* or *śarīradaṇḍa*, but to *dhanadaṇḍa* or *arthadaṇḍa*. Why?

The most obvious solution is to establish a connection between the two meanings of *sāhasa*. This has been done by J.J. Meyer, in his commentary on AŚ 3.17.8: "*sāhasa* hiesses also ursprünglich Strafe für Gewalttat für eigenmächtige Besitznahme von einem Gegenstande." It seems also to have been the opinion of R.P. Kangle who, in 3.17.8–10 and elsewhere, translates:

pūrvaḥ sāhasadaṇḍaḥ: "the lowest fine for violence."
madhyamaḥ sāhasadaṇḍaḥ: "the middle fine for violence."
uttamaḥ sāhasadaṇḍaḥ: "the highest fine for violence."

As a matter of fact, this interpretation is probably correct as far as Kauṭilya is concerned; his definition of *sāhasa* "fine" occurs in the chapter on *sāhasa* "violence," "forcible seizure" (Kangle), and the terms *pūrvaḥ*, *madhyamaḥ* and *uttamaḥ sāhasadaṇḍaḥ* seem to be introduced quite naturally in the passage 3.17.8–10.

What has been said about Kauṭilya can also be applied to Bṛhaspati. Here (23.3 Rangaswami Aiyangar) *sāhasa* "fine" is even more closely associated with *sāhasa* "violence."

hīnamadhyottamatvena trividhaṃ tat prakīrtitam |
dravyāpekṣo damas tatra prathamo madhyamottamau ||

"It is declared to be threefold, as it may be (theft or violence) of the lowest, second, or highest kind; the punishment in each case should also be of the lowest, middling, or highest sort, according to the (nature of the) article (stolen or injured)" (trans. Jolly: 22.24, 363). That means: there are three degrees of fine, *because* there are three degrees of violence; the former are the respective punishments for the latter.

There are, however, a number of arguments, which prevent us from accepting the *prima facie* view of *sāhasa* "fine" being the punishment for *sāhasa* "violence," the latter having produced the former.

First, in the oldest text containing *sāhasa* "fine," i.e., the *Manusmṛti*, its definition (8.138) is not to be found in the chapter of *sāhasa* "violence," (8.344–351), but in the chapter of *ṛṇādāna* "non-payment of debts," i.e., under the first *vivādapada*; which harbors *all* general rules concerning legal procedure and punishment.

Second, *sāhasa* "fine" cannot have come into being as the punishment for *sāhasa* "violence," because, right from the beginning, it has been inflicted for many offenses which were never classified as *sāhasa* "violence," even in its widest sense. For instance:

1. MDh 8.120, about false witnesses: "(He who commits perjury) through covetousness shall be fined one thousand (*paṇas*), (he

who does it) through distraction, in the lowest amercement; (if a man does it) through fear, two middling amercements shall be paid as a fine, (if he does it) through friendship, four times the amount of the lowest (amercement)" (trans. Bühler: 275);

2. MDh 8.263, in the chapter on boundary disputes: "Should the neighbors give false evidence when men dispute about the boundary mark, the king shall make each of them pay the middlemost amercement as a fine." (Trans. Bühler: 300–301)

Third, the interpretation "the lowest fine for violence," etc., is acceptable only when the Sanskrit texts use compounds such as *prathamasāhasadaṇḍaḥ*, etc., or *pūrvaḥ sāhasadaṇḍaḥ*, etc. (AŚ). But it is no longer possible when the texts speak of *daṇḍaḥ prathamasāhasaḥ*, etc. (YDh, BS, ŚL), or *daṇḍaḥ prathamaḥ sāhasaḥ*, etc. (MDh, ViDh, NS). In the latter two cases the interpretation must be: "the punishment *is* the lowest *sāhasa*," etc.

Finally, it should be noticed that *sāhasa* "fine" is a masculine noun, whereas *sāhasa* "violence" is uniformly neuter.

For all these reasons we have to reject the explanations given by Kauṭilya and Bṛhaspati, and the modern interpretations based upon them (cf. Meyer, Kangle).

Perhaps rejecting explanations given as early and by such respected teachers as Kauṭilya and Bṛhaspati requires justification. Our impression is, that Kauṭilya and Bṛhaspati were as puzzled by *sāhasa* "fine" as we are. The fact is that *sāhasa* "fine" appears relatively late in Dharmaśāstra literature; it does not occur earlier than Manu. Moreover, it appears very suddenly without any effort at an etymological explanation on the part of the author of the MDh, and with a meaning which is very far away from the existing and easily understandable "violence." The origin of *sāhasa* "fine" has never been understood by the commentators either; whereas they are very eager to provide us with etymological explanations for all other technical legal terms, none of the frequent occurrences of *sāhasa* "fine" in the *smṛti* ever incited them to risk an etymological explanation. Even in recent dictionaries, such as *Vācaspatya*, 138 lines are devoted to *sāhasa* "violence," whereas only two lines deal with the meaning "fine": a mere quotation of Yājñavalkya's definition, without any kind of interpretation.

The starting point of our research on the origin of *sāhasa* "fine" was a brief remark by Kane (1930–1962: 3.515): "Probably the oldest reference to fines for assault in Sanskrit literature is contained in the TS II. 6.10.2."

The passage reads as follows:

yo apagurātai śatena yātayāt, yo nihanat sahasreṇa yātayāt, yo lohitaṃ karavad yāvat praskadya pāṃsūn saṃgṛhṇāt tāvataḥ saṃvatsarān pitṛlokaṃ na prajānād iti; tasmād brāhmaṇāya nāpa gureta na ni hanyān na lohitaṃ kuryād etāvatā hainasā bhavati

The text refers to the vow granted by the gods to the descendants of Bṛhaspati, i.e., to the Brāhmaṇas; whoever molests them shall be punished. It does not contain the term *sāhasa* or any form related to it, nor does it say what the "hundred" and "thousand" consist of. A careful examination of the text is, nevertheless, likely to be helpful for our investigation.

As indicated by Kane himself TS 2.6.10.2 has not always been understood to refer to a fine. At least two Dharmaśāstras have passages based upon it, and their interpretation is a completely different one:

1. GDh 21.20–22:

abhikruddhāv avagoraṇaṃ brāhmaṇasya varṣaśatam asvargyam, nighāte sahasram, lohitadarśane yāvatas tat praskandya pāṃsūn saṃgṛhṇīyāt,

"He who in anger raises (his hand or a weapon) against a Brāhmaṇa, will be banished from heaven for a hundred years. If he strikes, (he will lose heaven) for a thousand (years). If blood flows, (he will lose heaven) for a number of years equal to (that of the particles of) dust which the spilt (blood) binds together" (trans. Bühler: 279);

2. MDh 11.206–207 (207–208):

avagūrya tv abdaśataṃ sahasram abhihatya ca |
jighāṃsayā brāhmaṇasya narakaṃ pratipadyate ||
śoṇitaṃ yāvataḥ pāṃsūn saṃgṛhṇāti mahītale |
tāvanty abdasahasrāṇi tatkartā narake vaset ||

"But he who, intending to hurt a Brāhmaṇa, has threatened (him with a stick and the like) shall remain in hell during a hundred years as well as he who (actually) struck him, during one thousand years. As many particles of dust as the blood of a Brāhmaṇa causes to coagulate, for so many thousand years shall the shedder of that (blood) remain in hell." (Trans. Bühler: 473)

This interpretation by Gautama and Manu may seem most attractive; it supplements for "hundred" and "thousand" of the first two cases the "number of years" referred to in the last case. However, we fear that here too, we are faced with a rationalization *a posteriori*, introduced by Gautama, and taken over by Manu. Gautama overlooked the fact that the first two cases required a punishment for which the verb *yātayāt* is used, whereas the third cases only speaks of *pitṛlokaṃ na prajānāt*. Both expressions apparently refer to two different kinds of punishment.

Let us now come back to Kane's interpretation of the TS passage. His idea of a "fine" is clearly based upon Sāyaṇa's commentary on TS 2.6.10.2:

tato devā apagoraṇādikartur yātanā tvatputrādhīnā bhavatv iti varaṃ dattavantaḥ. apagoraṇaṃ tāḍanodyogaḥ. tam udyogaṃ brāhmaṇaviṣaye yaḥ karoti taṃ puruṣaṃ śataniṣkadaṇḍena yātayāt kleśayet. yo nihanat tāḍayet taṃ sahasraniṣkadaṇḍena kleśayet.

Sāyaṇa undoubtedly thinks of fines of one hundred *niṣkas* and one thousand *niṣkas*; *niṣka* is a well known pecuniary unit.

The idea of a fine also occurs in Keith's translation of the *Taittirīya* passage: "Him, who reviles him, he shall fine with a hundred; him, who strikes him, he shall fine with a thousand; he who draws blood from him, shall not behold the world of the Pitṛs for as many years as are grains of dust which the blood in its fall seizes upon. Therefore one should not revile a Brāhmaṇa, nor strike him, nor draw blood from him; for so great is his sin" (217). A similar translation is also to be found in Ganganatha Jha's rendering of *Śabarabhāṣya* 3.4.17 (1.506). Differently from Sāyaṇa's interpretation, this translation does not specify the nature of the fine: "he shall fine with a hundred," "...with a thousand." Whereas Kane hesitated: "a hundred (cows or niṣkas?)," Keith is categorical: "the unit is no doubt the cow, not *niṣkas* or other coins or measures." Thus we arrive at a third interpretation of TS 2.6.10.2: *yātayāt* refers to a fine, but the numbers "hundred" and "thousand" should be supplemented by "cows."

Although neither Kane nor Keith said so, it is evident that they were influenced by two other Dharmaśāstra passages:

1. ĀpDh 1.9.24.1–4:

kṣatriyaṃ hatvā gavāṃ sahasraṃ vairayātanārthaṃ dadyāt, śataṃ vaiśye, daśa śūdre; ṛṣabhas cātrādhikaḥ sarvatra prāyaścittārthaḥ,

"He who killed a Kṣatriya shall give a thousand cows (to Brāhmaṇas) for the expiation of his sin. (He shall give) a hundred cows for a Vaiśya, ten for a Śūdra. And in every one (of these cases) one bull (must be given) in excess (of the number of cows) for the sake of expiation" (trans. Bühler: 78–79);

2. BDh 1.10.19.1–2:

kṣatriyavadhe gosahasraṃ ṛṣabhaikādhikaṃ rājña utsṛjed vairaniryātanārtham, śataṃ vaiśye, daśa śūdre; ṛṣabhas cātrādhikaḥ,

"For slaying a Kṣatriya (the offender) shall give to the king one thousand cows and besides a bull in expiation of his sin. For (slaying) a Vaiśya one hundred cows, for (slaying) a Śūdra ten; and a bull (must be) added (in each case)." (Trans. Bühler: 210–212)

In these two texts we meet with the words *yātanā* and *niryātanā*, derived from the same root as *yātayāt* in TS 2.6.10.2, and we do have the amount of the fines expressed in a thousand, hundred and ten "cows."

In short, the "oldest reference to fines" in India is not a very conclusive piece of evidence; even if we discard the first interpretation followed by Gautama and Manu, we are left with the alternative of fines to be paid either in coins or in cattle. At this stage we shall compare the Indian situation with the early history of fines in Roman Law. We shall quote the translation of an important passage from Aulus Gellius' *Attic Nights* (*Noctes Atticae* 11.1.1–3):

> Timaeus, in the *History* which he composed in the Greek language about the affairs of the Roman people, and Marcus Varro in his *Human Antiquities*, wrote that the land of Italy derived its name from a Greek word, oxen in the old Greek tongue being called *italoi*; for in Italy there was a great abundance of cattle, and in that land pastures are numerous and grazing is a frequent employment. Furthermore, we may infer that it was for the same reason namely, since Italy at that time so abounded in cattle —that the fine was established which is called 'supreme,' consisting of two sheep and thirty oxen each day, obviously proportionate to the abundance of oxen and the scarcity of sheep. But when a fine of that sort, consisting of cattle and sheep, was pronounced by a magistrate, oxen and sheep were brought, now of small, again of greater value; and this made the penalty of the fine unequal. Therefore later, by the Aternian law, the value of a sheep was fixed at ten pieces of brass, of the cattle at a hundred a piece. Now the 'smallest' fine is that of one sheep. The 'supreme' fine is of that number which we have mentioned, beyond which it is not lawful to impose a fine for a period of successive days; and for that reason it is called 'supreme,' that is, greatest and heaviest. (Trans. Rolfe 1960: II, 299–301)

That means, that in ancient Rome, where "there was a great abundance of cattle," fines were originally imposed in the form of cattle. At a certain moment, by the *Lex Aternia*, i.e., a law passed under consul A. Atinius, in 454 BC, the fines were given corresponding pecuniary values. Would it be too much to assume that in ancient India too, where cattle was equally abundant and important, the older form of the "fine" to be paid by a convicted person was in cattle? Would it be too much to assume that in India too, at a certain moment which, differently from what happened in Rome, has not been recorded, fines in coins took the place of fines in cattle?

The Latin term used to indicate a fine —a fine in cattle first, a pecuniary fine later— was *multa*. Unfortunately, the origin of *multa* was not much clearer to the Romans than *sāhasa* to the Indians. According to Varro, quoted by Aulus Gellius (11.1.5), the word was of Sabine origin: "Furthermore, Marcus Varro, in the twenty-first book of his *Human Antiquities*, also says that the word for fine (*multa*) is itself not Latin, but Sabine, and he remarks that it endured even to within his own memory in the speech of the Samnites, who are sprung from the Sabines" (Rolfe 1960: II, 301). Other lexicographers refer to an Oscan origin.

The opinions of modern scholars too, are divided. We are tempted to follow Roland Kent, and derive *multa*, via ancient *mulcta* (Ernout and Meillet, *Etymological Dictionary of the Latin Language*, maintain that this form has been created by the grammarians), from the verb *mulcare*: "*Multa* 'fine' possibly taken from Sabine, but probably from the root in *mulcare* 'to beat'" (Varro 1958: I, 164n.). According to Lewis and Short (*Latin-English Dictionary*) *mulcare* means "to ill-treat, to injure, damage."

The etymology of *mulcare* is uncertain. According to Ernout-Meillet there is no equivalent outside Italic. Lewis-Short compare with Greek *marpto*, from *marp-io* ("to take hold of, seize, condemn"). The Sanskrit equivalent of Latin *mulc-* and Greek *marp-* is not *mṛś-*, as pointed out by Pokorny (*Indogermanisches Etymologisches Worterbuch*) and Frisk (*Griechisches Etymologisches Worterbuch*), but *mṛc* (*marcayati*) "to hurt, injure, annoy" (Monier-Williams). Comparative philology, thus, provides us with a third Sanskrit root, which is possibly connected with the early history of fines. In the following pages we shall examine, whether the early meanings of *mṛc-*, *yat-* and *sah-* can teach us anything about the reason why a fine came ultimately to be indicated by the term *sāhasa*.

Forms of *mṛc-* are rare in the Veda. In ṚV 5.3.7 *marcayati* is accompanied by the words *āgas*, *enas* and *abhiśasti*; in ṚV 2.23.7 *marcayāt* has as its direct object *anāgasaḥ*, but the subject refers to an inimical element rather than to a law-enforcing authority: *arātīvā martaḥ sānuko vṛkaḥ*. A similar subject occurs in ṚV 1.147.4: *ararivān aghāyur arātīvā*, and in ṚV 8.67.9 too, *mṛc-* (the substantive) belongs to *ripūṇāṃ vṛjinānām*. A striking feature is the combination *marcayati dvayena*, which occurs three times: ṚV 1.147.4, 5; 5.3.7. There is no consistency in Sāyaṇa's interpretations of *marcayati* and *marcayāt*: 1.147.4 *bhartsayati vidheyīkaroti vā*; 1.147.5 *vidheyīkaroti bhartsayati vā*; 2.23.7 *hiṃsyāt*; 5.3.7 *bādhate*.

In AV 13.1.40 it is said of the sun: *devo devān marcayasi*, and in AV 8.2.17 the present participle is applied to the razor: *kṣureṇa marcayatā sutejasā*, and means, according to Whitney, "*dangerous* (?)" (cf. however, Āśv. Gṛh, S. 1.17.16, where these words have been quoted: "wounding" Oldenberg, "purifying" Stenzler).

The root *yat-* has been the object of an exhaustive study by K.F. Geldner: *Wurzel yat* (Geldner 1901: 11–26), and the above-mentioned expressions *vairayātanā* and *vairaniryātanā* too, have, for a time, been discussed very fervently (by Bühler, Roth, Leist, Jolly, and von Schroeder). However, notwithstanding these investigations by a number of well-known Sanskritists, F. Sommer (1905: 157–158) came to the conclusion that "we are still far from really understanding the *oldest* meaning of the ancient Indian verb."

Not until the end of his paper does Geldner introduce "the technical use which the root *yat* has acquired in legal language" (Geldner 1901: 23), indicating thereby that the legal meaning is but a later development. His examples also belong to later texts:

1. *Tattirīya Āraṇyaka* 1.8.5:

pṛcchāmi tvā pāpakṛtaḥ yatra yātayate Yamaḥ |

"I ask you, where Yama *yātyate* ('zur Verantwortung zieht') the sinners";

2. MBh 13.102.16 (CE 13.105.16cd), in a dialogue between Gautama and Indra about an elephant which Indra had taken away from Gautama:

yatrābalā balinaṃ yātayanti |
tatra tvāhaṃ hastinaṃ yātayiṣye ||

"where the weak *yātayanti* (zur Rechenschaft ziehen, 'verklagen') the strong one [i.e., in the world of Yama], there I *yātayiṣye* ('belangen,' 'zurückfordern') you with regard to the elephant."

We fail to see why Geldner considers this technical meaning as a later development. In our opinion, both examples come very close to the very first meaning distinguished by Geldner himself: "einem oder einander *gleichkommen, ebenbürtig sein,*" and, hence, "nacheifern, wetteifern, gleichzukommen oder zu überbieten —es jemandem zuvorzuthun suchen," or, expressed negatively, "jemandem nicht nachstehen wollen." We could not agree more with Geldner than when he adds: "English 'to match' comes closest of all to Vedic yat" (Geldner 1901: 12). We shall do nothing more than paraphrase Geldner's Vedic meaning, to make it perfectly applicable to the passages from *Tattirīya Āraṇyaka* and MBh: *yat-* refers to somebody's reaction to somebody else; more specifically: a reaction which is strong enough to countervail the other person's previous action —which is normally a bad action—, and, thus, to restore what is right.

Tattirīya Āraṇyaka 1.8.5 is clear: "I ask you, where Yama restores the wrong done by sinners," or, to make our point as clear as possible: "I ask you, where Yama makes sinners pay for their sins."

In MBh 13.105.16cd the grammatical subjects of *yātayanti* and *yātayiṣye* are *abalāḥ* and *aham*, respectively. But Yama is again involved; cf. *pādas* ab:

vaivasvatī saṃyamanī janānām |
yatrānṛtaṃ nocyate yatra satyam ||

The real meaning of *pādas* cd is this: in the world of Yama, where the weak can appeal to Yama to make the strong pay for the wrong they did them, there I, Gautama, shall be able to appeal to Yama to make you, Indra, pay for having taken my elephant away.

An important occurrence of *yātayāse* in ṚV 5.3.9 will be discussed below.

A survey of all occurrences of *sah* —in the ṚV was not particularly enlightening; there is no reason to repeat it in this paper. In most cases Sāyaṇa interprets *sah-* as *abhibhū-* without any further explanation. Only occasionally did we meet with more precise and useful information. Thus, when commenting on ṚV 1.131.4ab:

viduṣṭe asya vīryasya pūravaḥ puro |
yad indra śāradīr avātiraḥ sāsahāno avātiraḥ ||

Sāyaṇa says: *sasahānas tatratyān abhibhavan dhanādyapahāreṇa pīḍayan,* thus establishing a connection between *sah-* and *dhanādyapahāra-* "taking away somebody's property, etc."

Another passage, ṚV 8.86.5c, has the usual object: "enemies," but deserves to be mentioned in view of the subject of *sah-*, namely: *ṛta-*, thus:

ṛtaṃ sāsāha mahi cit pṛtanyataḥ.

Even though the situation is different, we want to recall MBh 13.105.16c, according to which the action of *yat* —takes place *yatrānṛtaṃ nocyate yatra satyam.*

Since the verbal forms derived from *sah-* did not allow us to draw a sufficiently definite conclusion, we tried another approach: an examination of the substantive *sahas,* and, in particular, the expression *sūnuḥ sahasaḥ.*

From the numerous passages analyzed by Gonda (1957) we shall first select ṚV 6.4.4d:

rājeva jer avṛke kṣesy antaḥ.

Although the full stanza says only *sūno*, it is generally accepted that *sahasaḥ* is understood; compare Sāyaṇa: *he sūno sahasaḥ putra*. The important element in this stanza is that Agni, qua *sūnuḥ sahasaḥ*, is compared to the king.

If Gonda's theory about the relation between gods and powers is correct, i.e., if Agni is not only "the son of" *sahas* but at the same time "represents" the power *sahas*, we must assume that, in the mind of the Ṛgvedic poet, Agni was the one who *sāhayati*. The comparison with the king in ṚV 6.4.4, then, becomes very important for understanding the origin of *sāhasa* "fine."

Moreover, there is another element in *sūnuḥ sahasaḥ* that leads us to compare Agni with the Hindu king. Says Gonda: "What strikes us in perusing those Ṛgvedic passages in which it occurs is in the first place the comparatively frequent reference to the god's protective power, his victoriousness, his readiness to help and assist his worshippers, his ability to ward off influences and circumstances inimical to success and prosperity" (1957: 2). The main characteristic of the king too, is his protective power, the fact that he protects his subjects against their enemies, and, thus, safeguards their prosperity.

The element of protection also appears in ṚV 6.4.4, namely in *avṛke*. Sāyaṇa explains *avṛke* only in relation to Agni: *avṛke rāikṣasādibhir bādhakair viyukte 'smadīye 'gnyāgāre*. But the comparison *rājeva* forces us to look for a similar place which is *avṛka-* in relation to the king. The ṚV itself shows us the way, in another passage of *avṛka-*, not in connection with a place but with a person. The expressions *avṛkatamo narāṃ nṛpātā* (1.174.10b), and *avṛkāso… nṛpātāro janānām* (1.14.6ab) clearly indicate that the king too, can be considered as *avṛka-*. And the following arguments show that *avṛka-* can also be applied to the king's realm:

1. *Nighaṇṭu* 3.24 mentions *vṛka-* as one of the synonyms for "thief," *stena*;
2. In ṚV 2.34.9, *vṛkatāt* indicates a situation in which, according to Sāyaṇa, a *hananasādhanam āyudham* is used. Hence Petersburg Dictionary: "Mord- oder Raubanschlag";
3. ṚV 4.41.4 implores Indra's and Varuṇa's help against *durevo vṛkatir dabhītiḥ*. *Vṛkati-* is explained by Sāyaṇa as *atiśayenādātā*; PW has, accordingly, "Mörder, Räuber";
4. In *vṛkāyu-* (ṚV 10.133.4), *vṛka-* means, according to Sāyaṇa: *hiṃsako 'raṇyaśvā steno vā*. PW has: "mord-, raublustig."

In short, the comparison in ṚV 6.4.4 should be completed as follows: since Agni has the power of *sahas*, he resides in a fireplace from which Rākṣasas etc. have been removed, like a king who, through his power of *sahas*, rules over a kingdom from which thieves, murderers, etc. have been removed.

Even more interesting than ṚV 6.4.4 is ṚV 5.3.9:

ava-spṛdhi pitaraṃ yodhi vidvān
putro yas te sahasaḥ sūna ūhe;
kadā cikitvo abhi cakṣase no
'gne kadāñ ṛtacid yātayāse.

Agni is again appealed to in his capacity of *sūnuḥ sahasaḥ*, and he is asked: *kadāñ ṛtacid yātayāse.* The general background of the hymn is perhaps not very clear, but Geldner is right when he says that "the hymn alludes repeatedly to hidden enemies and plaintiffs, cf. stanzas 7, 9, 11" (trans. Geldner: 2.5). There is no doubt that the hymn appeals to Agni primarily as the representative of the power of *sahas*; *sūnuḥ sahasaḥ* is repeated in stanzas 1, 6 and 9, and *sahasā* occurs in stanza 10. The representative of *sahas* is requested to perform the act of *yātanā*, an activity which it is his duty to perform (*yātayāse*, subjunctive) since he is *ṛtacid* (Geldner: "als Rechtskundiger," is perhaps too specific, but cf. the role of *ṛta* above.).

The data which have been collected in the preceding pages do not exhaust the subject. We can only hope that, by scrutinizing more texts, the picture might become more complete. At present, we submit the following hypothesis about the origin of *sāhasa* "fine."

1. A comparison with the situation in Rome seems to indicate that a pecuniary penalty was a comparatively recent phenomenon. As indicated by the term "pecuniary" itself, it was preceded by an older stage, at which fines were not paid in coins, but in cattle. This stage is reflected in the passages from TS, ĀpDh, and BDh.

2. The terminology used in India was different from the one adopted in Rome; *mṛc-* the equivalent of Latin *mulc-* has nothing to do with punishment. The terms used for "imposing a fine" at this stage were forms derived from the root *yat-* (*yātayāt*, *yātanā*). There is no trace yet of *sāhasa.*

3. The term *sāhasa* "fine" appears for the first time in the MDh. However, *sāhasa* is never used as a generic term; this is *dhanadaṇḍa* or *arthadaṇḍa. Sāhasa* is used only for fines of fixed amounts (*pūrva-*, *madhyama-*, *uttama-*), i.e., for those fines which, at an unknown date in India, were fixed as equivalents for cattle. The situation is comparable with *minima* and *suprema multa* in Rome. The author of the MDh could have used *pūrvadhanadaṇḍa*, etc.; if he did not do so and preferred *pūrvasāhasa*, etc., we must assume that *sāhasa* was a readily available term that was capable of conveying that meaning. But, although *sāhasa* "violent act" occurs earlier (Cf. ĀpDh 2.6.13.7) than *sāhasa* "fine," there is no reason to conclude that the latter originated from the former.

4. In reality, *sah-* and its derivatives seem to have been associated, from a very early period, with *yat-* and its derivatives, not only in the sense of retaliatory action generally, but in the sense of "matching" punishment in particular.

We have no answer to the question, why Manu preferred *sāhasa* rather than *yātanā*. Either *sāhasa* was already a generally accepted synonym of *yātanā*; or *yātanā* (and *niryātanā*) had gradually acquired a different meaning: "acquittal (of debts)" and, through a well known semantic process, the vacuum thus created was filled by *sāhasa*, which, even though it had never been used for that purpose, was considered perfectly adequate.

35

Avyāvahārika *Debts and Kauṭilya 3.1.1–11*

The beginning of *Kauṭilīyārthaśāstra* 3.1 can be summarized as follows:

3.1.1 *dharmasthās... vyāvahārikān arthān kuryuḥ.*
3.1.2 *pratiṣedhayeyur vyavahārān*
(a) *tirohitān* [see Appendix]
3.1.6 ...*tirohitāḥ sidhyeyuḥ;*
(b) *antaragārakṛtān*
3.1.7 ...*antaragārakṛtāḥ sidhyeyuḥ;*
(c) *naktakṛtān*
3.1.8 ...*rātrikṛtāḥ sidhyeyuḥ;*
(d) *araṇyakṛtān*
3.1.9 ...*araṇyakṛtāḥ sidhyeyuḥ;*
(e) *upadhikṛtān*
3.1.10 ...*upadhikṛtāḥ sidhyeyuḥ;*
(f) *upahvarakṛtān*
3.1.11 ...*upahvarakṛtāḥ sidhyeyuḥ.*

The main sections of this passage have been translated by Shamasastry:

> ...three members acquainted with the Sacred Law...shall carry on the administration of justice. They shall hold as void agreements entered into...;

by Meyer:

> Drei Richter...sollen die bürgerlichen Gerichtssachen...entscheiden... abgeschlossene bürgerliche Handlugen sollen sie verbieten;

and by Kangle:

> Three judges...shall try cases arising out of transactions. They should declare as invalid transactions concluded....

AŚ 3.1.2 obviously provides a list of exceptions to 3.1.1. If 3.1.1 formulates the general rule for *vyāvahārikān arthān*, we may, then, conclude that 3.1.2: *tirohita°... °upahvarakṛtān vyavahārān*, refers to *avyāvahārikān arthān*.

To be sure, the term *avyāvahārika* does not occur in classical Sanskrit legal literature; but is has been used extensively in modern Hindu law of debts. The basis of the entire theory of *avyāvahārika* debts is a stanza attributed either to Vyāsa or Uśanas (DhK 1.714):

> *daṇḍo (°aṃ) vā daṇḍaśeṣo (°aṃ) vā*
> *śulkaṃ tac cheṣa (°aṃ) eva vā*
> *na dātavyaṃ tu putreṇa*
> *yac ca na vyāvhārikam.*

Kane rightly points out: "What is meant by 'debts that are not *vyāvahārika*' has presented the greatest difficulty to the medieval commentators and digests and also to modern courts" (1930–1962: 3.447). Colebrooke was the first one to propose a translation for *avyāvahārika* debts: "any debt for a cause repugnant to good morals" (Colebrooke 1798 1: 211). In *Durbar* v. *Khachar*,[758] Knight, J. spoke of "unusual or not sanctioned by law," of "debts attributable to his (father's) failings, follies or caprices," and of debts "which as a decent and respectable man the father ought not to have incurred." In *Chhakauri Mahton* v. *Ganga Prasad*,[759] Mookerji, J. used the expression: "not lawful, usual or customary." In *Venugopala* v. *Ramanadhan*,[760] Sadasiva Iyer, J. proposed a debt which is "not supportable as valid by legal arguments and on which no right could be established in a creditor's favour in a Court of Justice." In *Bal Rajaram* v. *Maneklal*,[761] the court discussed the various possible meanings of *avyāvahārika*, and in *Govind Prasad* v. *Raghunath Prasad*,[762] a Full Bench deliberated on it. In *Hemraj* v. *Kem Chand*,[763] the Privy Council decided that Colebrooke's interpretation came closest to the real meaning

[758] *Durbar* v. *Khachar*, 32 Bom. 348 (1908). Also at 351.
[759] *Chhakauri Mahton* v. *Ganga Prasad*, 39 Cal. 862 (1912). At 868–869.
[760] *Venugopala* v. *Ramanadhan*, 37 Mad. 458 (1914). At 460.
[761] *Bal Rajaram* v. *Maneklal*, 56 Bom. 36 (1932). At 50–53.
[762] *Govind Prasad* v. *Raghunath Prasad*, 63 Bom. 533 (1939).
[763] *Hemraj* v. *Kem Chand*, 70 I.A. 171 (1943).

of the word; the Supreme Court, in *Jakati* v. *Borkar*,[764] confirmed this opinion: the term did not admit of a more precise definition than the one proposed in Colebrooke's *Digest*. Most recently, Heramba Chatterjee reiterated that "the correct approach to the term *avyāvahārika* perhaps has been made by Colebrooke" (1971: 106).

Neither Colebrooke nor any of the judges or writers who came after him has made adequate use of the occurrence of *vyāvahārika* in AŚ 3.1.1. Yet, a combination of Vyāsa/Uśanas and Kauṭilya might well lead to a better understanding of both passages.

There is no doubt that, as stated in the DhK 1.1 (Index: 60), *vyāvahārika* indicates that which "relates to *vyavahāra*." However, *vyavahāra* has at least two distinct usages:

1. in a non-technical sense: any activity, practice, commerce, or intercourse between individuals;
2. in a technical sense: litigation, legal procedure, administration of justice.

Assuredly, both meanings theoretically fit AŚ 3.1.1: "the judges should perform those things that relate to legal procedures," and "they shall deal with those things that relate to commerce among men." Yet, the wording of 3.1.2:

> ... °*kṛtāṃś ca vyavahārān pratiṣedhayeyuḥ*,

makes it clear that *vyāvahārikān arthān* in 3.1.1 refers to the latter interpretation only. Shamasastry and Meyer failed to recognize this connection; Kangle is the only one who translates: "causes arising out of transactions."

At this stage I should like to draw attention to the following verbal terminology used by Kauṭilya:

3.1.1 General rule:
   ...*vyāhārikān arthān KURYUḤ*
3.1.2 Exceptions:
   ... °*kṛtāṃś ca vyavahārān PRATIṢEDHAYEYUḤ*
3.1.6–11 Counter-exceptions:
   ... *tirohitāḥ* (etc.) *SIDHYEYUḤ*

That means that, in certain well-defined circumstances, even though it suffers from the default of being *tirohita* etc., human commerce *sidhyati* "is successful, succeeds, holds good, is admissible, is valid"; or, in legal terminology, "is legally binding."

[764] *Jakati* v. *Borkar*, A.S.C. 282 (1959). At 286.

AŚ 3.1.2 uses the same verbal root *sidh*, with the preverb *prati*. This points to the fact that the author intends to express more than "to prevent, restrain, prohibit, interdict" (Monier-Williams), or "verbieten" in Meyer's translation. It seems that, in those cases of human commerce, the judges shall "make them unsuccessful; prevent them from succeeding, holding good, being admissible, being valid." The commerce has taken place and can no longer be "prevented, forbidden"; but it can be "made not legally binding," it can be "declared null and void."

Hence, if we formulate AŚ 3.1.2 as:

avyāvahārikān arthān pratiṣedhayeyuḥ,

the text states that the judges shall declare "not legally binding, null and void" those cases brought before them which relate to *avyavahāra* "commerce, activities which are defective," i.e., *vyavahāras* not done at the right time, in the right place, in the right form, etc.

Turning to AŚ 3.1.1, I propose to translate: "The judges shall examine those cases which relate to *vyavahāras* performed at the right time, in the right place, in the right form, etc."; in short, they shall examine in court those —and only those— activities or individuals which are valid and legally binding.

I shall go one step further, and remind the reader of the fourfold subdivision of Hindu legal procedure:

bhāṣā "plaint,"
uttara "reply,"
kriyā "examination,"
nirṇaya "decision."

In the light of this subdivision, the expression in AŚ 3.1.1:

dharmasthās … kuryuḥ,

means that in the case of valid transactions, and in these cases only, the judges should do more than hear the plaint and the defence; in these cases they shall proceed to an actual *kriyā* and, hence, to a *nirṇaya* based on it.

Finally, let us return to the stanza by Vyāsa or Uśanas, on debts. The statement that the son shall not be held liable for anything which is *na vyāvahārikam*, means that he is not responsible for anything done by his father that was not *vyavahāra*, i.e., a valid, legally binding transaction. Most commentators have restricted themselves to giving examples of *avyāvahārika*. Modern Hindu law —starting with Colebrooke— has looked at these examples only, and tried to find a common denominator for them. Hence their varied and involved interpretations of a concept which was, basically, very simple.

Appendix

Since AŚ 3.1.6–11 speak of *tirohitāḥ*, *antaragārakṛtāḥ*, *rātrikṛtāḥ*, *araṇyakṛtāḥ*, *upadhikṛtāḥ*, and *upahvarakṛtāḥ*, it is clear that in the compound in 3.1.2:

> *tirohitāntaragāranaktāraṇyopadhyupahvarakṛtān*,

°*kṛtān* is supposed to go, in the long *dvandva*, only with *antaragāra* and what follows.

This has not been recognized by Shamasastry:

> … entered into in seclusion, inside the houses, in the dead of night, in forests, in secret, or with fraud,

nor by Meyer:

> Ohne Beisein des Betreffenden, innerhalb des Hauses, bei Nacht, im Wald, mit Betrug oder im Geheimen abgeschlossene…

Although Kangle adds a note: "*kṛtān* is to be construed with *antaragāra* onwards," he too translates in the traditional way:

> … concluded in absence, inside the house, at night-time, in a forest, by fraud or in secret.

To safeguard the integrity of the text, I propose the following emendation:

> *tirohitā <na>ntaragār*° for *tirohitāntaragār*°,

which is not only paleographically justifiable, but also explains the presence of *ca* in °*kṛtāṃś ca*.

36

The Sūtras *and* Śāstras *on the Eight Types of Marriage*

This is not a study of the different types of marriage described in the classical Sanskrit texts; studies of this kind are available elsewhere in the scholarly literature. This article intends to examine the *sūtra* and *śāstra* texts dealing with the forms of marriage. A variety of texts —prose and verse; *dharma*, *artha*, and *gṛhya*— lay down rules for the same subject-matter. What are their individual characteristics? How do they relate to one another? No definitive answers will be obtained from a restricted analysis such as this. This is only a case study, leading to a number of general observations. But if the same type of analysis is repeated for various other topics, we may hope to come to a better understanding of the nature and scope of this branch —or, these branches— of Sanskrit literature.

Ten different texts will be drawn into the discussion: four prose Dharmasūtras, one Gṛhyasūtra, three versified Dharmaśāstras, one *dharma* text in which prose and verse alternate, and one text on *artha*. They are the following:

Āpastamba (Āp) 2.5.11.17–12.2
Gautama (G) 4.4–11
Baudhāyana (Bau) 1.11.20.2–9
Vasiṣṭha (Va) 1.30–35
Āśvalāyana (Āśv) 1.6.1–8
Manu (M) 3.27–34
Yājñavalkya (Y) 1.58–61
Nārada (N) 12.40–43
Viṣṇu (Vi) 24.19–26
Kauṭilya (Kau) 3.2.2–9

Eight of these ten texts agree in listing eight different types of marriage. The names are identical, but for one exception. Y alone includes a type called *kāya*, which obviously stands for the usual *prājāpatya*: *ka* is an accepted synonym for *prajāpati* (cf. also M 3.38). Two texts, both Dharmasūtras (Āp, Va), have only six types of marriage: they omit *prājāpatya* and *paiśāca*. Moreover, one of them (Va) replaces the *āsura* and *rākṣasa* types of all other texts by *mānuṣa* and *kṣātra*, respectively. Yet, even in these two cases the definitions, which will be examined later in this paper, make it clear that the difference is one of terminology only, not of substance.

Besides the names, we may also look at the order in which the types of marriage have been introduced in the individual texts. The order in which the texts are arranged in the following table, from left to right, is determined by the fact that they can clearly be divided into three groups.

	G	Bau	N	Kau	M	Y	Vi	Āśv	Āp	Va
brāhma	1	1	1	1	1	1	1	1	1	1
prājāpatya	2	2	2	2	4	4	4	3	—	—
						kāya				
ārṣa	3	3	3	3	3	3	3	4	2	3
daiva	4	4	4	4	2	2	2	2	3	2
gāndharva	5	5	5	5	6	6	5	5	4	4
āsura	6	6	6	6	5	5	6	6	5	6
										mānuṣa
rākṣasa	7	7	7	7	7	7	7	8	6	5
										kṣātra
paiśāca	8	8	8	8	8	8	8	7	—	—

Group I comprises G, Bau, N, and Kau. In these four texts the order is perfectly identical.

Group II, composed of M, Y, Vi, and Āśv, is less uniform. The most striking difference with group I is that, here, *prājāpatya* and *daiva* have been interchanged. Within the group we further notice that M and Y are more closely related with one another than they are with Vi or Āśv. In fact, their order is identical except for Y replacing *prājāpatya* by *kāya*. Vi differs from M and Y in that it interchanges *gāndharva* and *āsura* —in agreement with group I. Āśv does the same, and adds two more interchanges of its own: *prājāpatya/ārṣa*, and *rākṣasa/paiśāca*.

The remaining two texts (Āp, Va) make up group III, mainly because in them two items in the list of eight are missing. Except for this they are closer to group I than to group II. With *prājāpatya* missing in Āp, the next five types simply move up by one, in the order of group I. Va has two inversions vis-à-vis Āp, and, as stated earlier, it uses two different terms.

To sum up, the way in which the texts can be grouped does not necessarily correspond to their nature and composition. One identical group comprises two Dharmasūtras, one —relatively late— Dharmaśāstra, and the Arthaśāstra. M and Y, which are practically identical, form a group with the mixed Vi and a Gṛhyasūtra.

A look at the table horizontally, and moving from top to bottom, is revealing for a different reason. M, for example, states explicitly that the order in which the forms of marriage are introduced also indicates their relative importance and acceptability, from better to worse —*paiśāca* is *pāpiṣṭho vivāhānām.* Other texts make similar suggestions.

From this point of view we can distinguish four layers. Layer I consists of *brāhma* only. All texts —including Āp and Va— place it at the top: the best of all forms of marriage is the sole type to have the same position throughout.

The second layer is also the widest: *prājāpatya*, *ārṣa*, and *daiva.* Excluding Āp and Va, which are more difficult to include in this comparison, and with the exception of Āśv, *ārṣa* seems to be the pivot around which the other two revolve, more or less equally.

Gāndharva and *āsura* interchange within layer III, but less evenly than the items in layer II. M and Y alone go against the general trend represented by the other six "complete" texts, to which we may also add Āp.

Finally, layer IV —*rākṣasa* and *paiśāca*— shows even less variation. Here only one text (Āśv) reverses the order, against a majority of seven.

Again to sum up, the order in which eight —eventually six— items in a list are introduced in different texts displays variability, but only in a limited way. First, no item in the list is displaced by more than two digits —*prājāpatya* and *daiva.* Second, there is more variation at the center, and it diminishes towards the extremes. In fact, there is no variation at all at the top, and very little at the bottom. The surprising thing is that, in two texts, the normal bottom category is absent.

Finally, we can compare the form and wording of the definitions in the individual texts. In the three versified texts (M, Y, N) we notice that M alone formulates the definitions in such a way that they each occupy a complete *śloka.* N is equally uniform, but more succinct: each form of marriage is given half a *śloka* only. The internal uniformity of M and N is missing in Y. The first (*brāhma*) and fourth (*kāya*) definitions are extended to full *śloka*s; the second (*daiva*) and third (*ārṣa*) share one *anuṣṭubh* —Y immediately attaches to the definitions the respective benefits of the first four types, whereas M treats these separately at 3.37–38—; the last four types are combined within a single *śloka*, each occupying one *pāda*.

The prose definitions are of uneven length. In some of them, especially those of Āp, G, Bau, and Va, there is a tendency to be longer and more detailed for the highest types of marriage, and gradually become shorter for the lower types. Only Vi, and even more so Kau, reduce the definitions to a strict minimum throughout; in most cases there is not more than a single word.

I shall now reproduce the text of the definitions, eliminating every element which is not strictly part of the definitions —e.g., *brāhmo dharmaḥ prakīrtitaḥ* (M). This procedure will make it possible more clearly and in detail to see what the texts have in common, and where they differ. For each type of marriage the prose texts will be given first, followed by the versified *śāstra*s.

BRĀHMA	
Āp	*bandhuśīlaśrutārogyāṇi buddhvā prajāsahatvakarmabhyaḥ pratipādayec chaktiviṣayeṇa alaṅkṛtya.*
G	*vidyācāritrabandhuśīlasampannāya dadyād ācchādya alaṅkṛtām.*
Bau	*śrutiśīle vijñāya brahmacāriṇe 'rthine dīyate.*
Va	*icchata udakapūrvāṃ yāṃ dadyāt.*
Vi	*āhūya guṇavate kanyādānam.*
Āśv	*alaṅkṛtya kanyām udakapūrvāṃ dadyāt.*
Kau	*kanyādānaṃ kanyām alaṅkṛtya.*
M	*ācchādya cārcayitvā ca śrutiśīlavate svayam āhūya dānaṃ kanyāyāḥ.*
Y	*āhūya dīyate śaktyalaṅkṛtā.*
N	*satkṛtya āhūya kanyāṃ dadyād alaṅkṛtām.*

PRĀJĀPATYA	
Āp	—
G	*saṃyogamantraḥ saha dharmaś caryatām iti.*
Bau	*ācchādya alaṅkṛtya eṣā saha dharmaś caryatām iti.*

Va	—
Vi	*prārthitapradānena.*
Āśv	*saha dharmaṃ carata iti.*
Kau	*sahadharmacaryā.*
M	*sahabhau caratāṃ dharmam iti vācānubhāṣya kanyāpradānam abhyarc- ya.*
Y	*ity uktvā caratāṃ dharmaṃ saha yā dīyate 'rthine.*
N	*saha dharmaṃ carety uktvā.*
	ĀRṢA
Āp	*duhitṛmate mithunau gāvau deyau.*
G	*gomithunaṃ kanyāvate dadyāt.*
Bau	*pūrvāṃ lājāhutiṃ hutvā gomithunaṃ kanyāvate dattvā grahaṇam.*
Va	*gomithunena.*
Vi	*gomithunagrahaṇena.*
Āśv	*gomithunaṃ dattvā upayaccheta.*
Kau	*gomithunādānāt.*
M	*ekaṃ gomithunaṃ dve vā varād ādāya dharmataḥ kanyāpradānaṃ vidhivat.*
Y	*ādāya godvayam.*
N	*vastragomithunābhyām.*
	DAIVA
Āp	*yajñatantra ṛtvije pratipādayet.*
G	*antarvedy ṛtvije dānam alaṅkṛtya.*
Bau	*dakṣiṇāsu niyamānāsv antarvedy ṛtvije.*
Va	*yajñatantre vitata ṛtvije karma kurvate kanyāṃ dadyād alaṅkṛtya.*
Vi	*yajñasthaṛtvije.*
Āśv	*ṛtvije vitate karmaṇi dadyād alaṅkṛtya.*
Kau	*antarvedyām ṛtvije dānāt.*
M	*yajñe vitate saṃyog ṛtvije karma kurvate alaṅkṛtya sutādānam.*
Y	*yajñasthaṛtvije.*
N	*antarvedyām ṛtvije karma kurvate.*

	GĀNDHARVA
Āp	*mithaḥ kāmāt saṃvartete.*
G	*icchantyāḥ svayaṃ saṃyogaḥ.*
Bau	*sakāmena sakāmāyāṃ mithaḥ saṃyogaḥ.*
Va	*sakāmāṃ kāmayamānaḥ sadṛśīṃ yonim uhyāt.*
Vi	*dvayoḥ sakāmayor mātāpitṛrahito yogaḥ.*
Āśv	*mithaḥ samayaṃ kṛtvā upayaccheta.*
Kau	*mithaḥ samavāyāt.*
M	*icchayānyonyasaṃyogaḥ kanyāyāś ca varasya ca maithunyaḥ kāmasambhavaḥ.*
Y	*samayān mithaḥ.*
N	*icchantīm icchataḥ.*
	ĀSURA
Āp	*śaktiviṣayeṇa dravyāṇi dattvā vaheran.*
G	*vittenānatiḥ strīmatām.*
Bau	*dhanenopatoṣya.*
Va	[*paṇitvā dhanakritām.*]
Vi	*krayeṇa.*
Āśv	*dhanenopatoṣya upayaccheta.*
Kau	*śulkādānāt.*
M	*jñātibhyo draviṇaṃ dattvā kanyāyai caiva śaktitaḥ kanyāpradānaṃ svācchandyāt.*
Y	*draviṇādānāt.*
N	*śulkasaṃvyavahārataḥ.*
	RĀKṢASA
Āp	*duhitṛmataḥ prothayitvā vaheran.*
G	*prasahyādānāt.*
Bau	*prasahya haraṇāt.*
Va	*yāṃ* (*balena sahasā pramathya*) *haranti.*
Vi	*yuddhaharaṇena.*
Āśv	*hatvā bhittvā ca śirṣāṇi rudatīṃ rudadbhyo haret.*
Kau	*prasahyādānāt.*
M	*hatvā chittvā ca bhittvā ca krośantīṃ rudatīṃ gṛhāt prasahya kanyāharaṇam.*

Y	*yuddhaharaṇāt.*
N	*prasahya haraṇāt.*
	PAIŚĀCA
Āp	—
G	*asaṃvijñātopasaṃgamāt.*
Bau	*suptāṃ mattāṃ pramattāṃ vā upagacchet.*
Va	—
Vi	*suptapramattābhigamāt.*
Āśv	*suptānāṃ pramattānāṃ vā apaharet.*
Kau	*suptamattādānāt.*
M	*suptāṃ mattāṃ pramattāṃ vā raho yatra upagacchati.*
Y	*kanyakāchalāt.*
N	*suptapramattopagamāt.*

One cannot help being impressed by the amount of material which is common to several texts in the definitions of each type of marriage. In fact, cases in which one particular text exhibits formulas which are different from all other texts are rare.

Examples:

Vi *prārthitapradānena prājāpatyaḥ*;
N adds *vastra* to the common *gomithuna*, in *ārṣa*;
Y *paiśācaḥ kanyakāchalāt.*

In most cases the texts use a variety of synonyms, but the basic idea remains the same. For instance, in the case of the *āsura* marriage, we find:

śulka	N, Kau
dravya	Āp
draviṇa	M, Y
dhana	Bau, Āśv (both with *upatoṣya*)
vitta	G
kraya	Vi

One of the best examples to show how synonymous expressions can alternate concerns the *daiva* marriage. The dative *ṛtvije* appears in all the ten texts. To this, four texts add either *antarvedyām* (N, Kau) or *antarvedi* (G, Bau). The other additions display a most interesting variation:

Y and Vi add the same adjective, *yajñastha ṛtvije*;
Four texts have separate, but very similar locatives:

Āp	*yajñatantre*
Va	*yajñatantre vitate*
M	*yajñe (tu) vitate samyak*
Āśv	*vitate karmaṇi*

Three texts have the same formula: *ṛtvije karma kurvate*, i.e., a perfect even *pāda* of a *śloka*. This is to be expected in M and N, but it also occurs in the prose —Va.

Any effort to determine whether two or more individual texts are consistently more closely related to each other than they are to other texts seems, under these circumstances, futile. There are a few cases in which two or more texts contain elements by which they clearly distinguish themselves from the others; however, in each case the group of texts is a different one.

Examples:

Brāhma
āhūya Vi, M, Y, N
udakapūrvām Va, Āśv

Gāndharva
mithaḥ samayāt Āśv, Y (Kau *samavāyāt*)
emphasis on the root *iṣ* G, M, N
emphasis on *kāma* Āp, Bau, Va, Vi

Rākṣasa
striking correspondence Āśv (ca. a half *śloka*), M
yuddha° Vi, Y.

I have indicated earlier in this article that no final conclusions on the nature and interrelation of the texts can be derived from an analysis of so small a body of materials. Yet, it at least allows us to venture a few suggestions, which may be either confirmed or denied by similar analyses of other topics. First, no "one later text" can be shown to have derived its material directly from "one earlier text" or even "earlier texts." Second, even in the prose texts we meet with versified sections, which makes us wonder whether the generally accepted thesis that "the versified *śāstras* are more recent than the prose *sūtras*" has absolute validity. Third, perhaps too much stress has been laid on the differences between the texts. They rather tend to express the same or very similar ideas on each "point of law." If so, whenever the texts differ, the emphasis should be on reconciling the variants rather than looking for historical, geographical and other justifications. Fourth, even though I have restrained from doing so in this paper, word by word comparison of all sources on specific topics may help us establish better readings for a number of passages which, especially in the *sūtras*, are at present still very uncertain.

37

Caritraṃ Pustakaraṇe

The fact that litigation in classical Hindu law "rests on four feet" (*catuṣpād*) is well known. The texts enumerating and defining the four elements have been discussed repeatedly in recent scholarly literature.[765] Most of these writings center on the fact that, among *dharma*, *vyavahāra*, *caritra*, and *rājaśāsana*, each latter one *bādhate* "checks, prevents, sets aside," the preceding one(s). This leads to various —conflicting— theories on the relative role of the four "feet," and, especially, to efforts at explaining the obvious, but unexpected, importance given custom and royal decrees.

This article does not intend to deal with the relations between *dharma*, *vyavahāra*, *caritra*, and *rājaśāsana*. It will concentrate on *caritra*, and, more specifically, on one term which has been used —once(!)— in connection with it: *pustakaraṇa*.

The term *caritra* has been defined by most texts in which the "four feet" of *vyavahāra* have been enumerated. One of the simplest definitions appears in a verse attributed to Vyāsa (DhK 1.235):

> *deśasthitiḥ pūrvakṛtā caritraṃ samudāhṛtam.*[766]

Elsewhere in a stanza attributed to Bṛhaspati (9.6; DhK 1.99), *deśasthiti* occurs again, but as one of two types of *caritra*, the other one being based on *anumāna*:

[765] Especially Lingat 1962. For bibliography, see Derrett (1968).

[766] A discussion of the variant readings, with which this and other *smṛti* texts appear in commentaries and *nibandhas*, is beyond the scope of this article. Also, I uniformly adopt the reading *caritra*, even though *nibandhas* eventually use *carita*.

anumānena nirṇītam caritram iti kathyate;
deśasthityā dvitīyaṃ tu śāstravidbhir udāhṛtam.

Jolly (2.23) translates:

When a sentence is passed according to the inference (to be drawn from circumstantial evidence), it is termed (a decision based on) custom. When it is passed according to local usages, it is termed another sort (of a decision based on custom) by the learned in the law.

In another stanza on *caritra*, also attributed to Bṛhaspati (1.20; DhK 100) the two terms *deśasthiti* and *anumāna* appear again, in a different combination:

deśasthityanumānena naigamānumatena ca kriyate nirṇayas...

In Jolly's (2.26) translation:

When a decision is passed in accordance with local custom, logic, or the opinion of traders (living in that town)...

In the first Bṛhaspati stanza *anumāna* may indeed refer to "inference," namely the inference of guilt drawn from indications in the behavior of a certain individual. In the second Bṛhaspati quotation, however, as I have shown elsewhere (Rocher 1975), *anumāna* is not derived from the root *anu-mā-*, but rather from *anu-man-*; it does not mean "inference," but "acceptance of, agreement on certain forms of behavior within a group of individuals."

One thing is, therefore, clear from the preceding text: *caritra* invariably involves action, behavior, more often than not group behavior sanctioned by long standing; in other words: custom. I shall now quote another few *smṛti* texts to underscore that meaning.

First, a Bṛhaspati verse (1.21; DhK 100) which in most *nibandhas* follows immediately after the one just quoted:

vihāya caritācāraṃ yatra kuryāt punar nṛpaḥ nirṇayam...

The commentators are unanimous: *caritācāram pūrvapūrvācaritam ācāram.*[767] Jolly (2.27) translates accordingly: "Where a king, disregarding established usage, passes a sentence...".

Second, there is the following stanza attributed to Kātyāyana (37; DhK 103):

[767] E.g., *Kṛtyakalpataru, Vyavahārakāṇḍa*, p. 262; *Vīramitrodaya, Vyavahāraprakāśa*, p. 89.

yad yad ācaryate yena dharmyam vādharmyam eva vā deśasyācaraṇān nityaṃ caritraṃ tad dhi kīrtitam.

Kane translates:

Whatever a person practices, whether it be according to *dharma* (the letter of the law) or not, because it is the invariable usage in a country, is, declared to be *caritra* (usage).

Finally, a stanza of Pitāmaha (DhK 105) exhibits a variant on Kātyāyana's:

yad yad ācarati śreṣṭho dharmyam vādharmyam eva vā kulādideśācaraṇāc caritraṃ tat prakīrtitam.

Two other stanzas (DhK 105) add examples of cases in which *caritra* ought to be the deciding factor in litigation:

grāmagoṣṭhapuraśreṇisārthasenānivāsinām vyavahāraś
caritreṇa nirṇetavyo bṛhaspatiḥ;
deśapattanagoṣṭheṣu puragrāmeṣu vāsinām
teṣām svasamayair dharmaśāstrato 'nyeṣu taiḥ saha.

After all this we shall now turn to the definition of *caritra* as presented by Nārada (Mātṛkā 1.11c; DhK 92):

caritraṃ [sthitaṃ] pustakaraṇe.

This is Asahāya's commentary:

yac caritraṃ pustakaraṇa ity uktaṃ tac caritram iti pattrakabhūrjacīrakasaṃpuṭikādiṣu sākṣisvahastasunibaddhaṃ kṛtvā yo vyavahāraḥ pravartate sa caritram ity ucyate.

Jolly's translation follows Asahāya closely: "documentary evidence (rests) on declarations reduced to writing." In other words, in this case:

caritra = "documentary evidence."

Asahāya's interpretation also seems to be supported by other commentators. For instance, Bhavasvāmin, commenting on the *Nāradīyamanusaṃhitā* (1.11), says: *lekhyena nirṇīyate tac caritram.* The *Smṛticandrikā* (3.25) simply states: *pustakaraṇaṃ lekhyam.*

The reactions of modern scholars are most interesting. Lingat not only follows Jolly's translation: "*caritra* repose sur des documents écrits" (1962: 493); he actually defends it: "Le mot *pustakaraṇa* est partout glosé par *lekhya* ou *likhita*. Il désigne donc la preuve écrite, par opposition à *vyavahāra* qui désignerait exclusivement la preuve par témoins (*sākṣiṣu sthita*)" (ibid.: 496).[768]

Others are more cautious. Derrett (1968: 154) quotes Jolly's interpretation, but he inserts a question mark: "*Caritra* (documentary evidence[?]) is based on declarations reduced to writing." Renou (1963: 7) warns that it is at least "sujet à caution." Varadachariar (1946: 129–30) is even more negative: "Asahāya's commentary no doubt refers to some kinds of documents but is far from intelligible. I venture to doubt if on the strength of it Dr. Jolly was justified in rejecting the suggestion... made by other commentators that Charitra in this verse refers to 'usage.'"

Kane (1930–62: 3.261; quoted verbatim by Ayyar 1952: 83) exhibits a different approach: he maintains the traditional meaning of *caritra* "custom," but combines it with Asahāya's reference to written documents: "'Caritraṃ pustakaraṇe' means that... usages are valid means of decision if they have been written down by the king." Similarly, Rangaswami Aiyangar (1958: 7) interprets *pustakaraṇa* as "customary law, as recorded in books." The index to the Vyavahāramātṛkā volume of the DhK (39) also resorts to this type of combination: "*pustakaraṇa* = written document; book of traditional law."

In fact, this idea of "customs reduced to writing" also seems to go back to the time of the *nibandhakāra*s. For instance, the *Parāśaramādhavīya* (19) has the following note on *pustakaraṇa*:

> *karṇāṭakadeśe balān mātulasutāvivāho na doṣāya, keraladeśe kanyāyā ṛtumatītvaṃ na doṣāyetyevamādikas taddeśasamayas; tatra tatra pattrādiśāsane 'vatiṣṭhate.*

Mitramiśra's *Vyavahāraprakāśa* (7) attributes a similar interpretation to Caṇḍeśvara:

> *Caṇḍeśvareṇa tu caritram pustakaraṇam iti paṭhitvā pustaṃ pañjikety arthaḥ; tatkaraṇam adhikaraṇam yasyeti vyāhṛtam.* (Rocher 1956: 264)

At this point I would like to introduce two other texts, which define *caritra* in a different way, the only two texts also which, like Nārada, use the formula:

nominative + *sthita* + locative.

Both the *Agnipurāṇa* (253.5a) and Kauṭilya's *Arthaśāstra* (3.1.40c) state:

[768] Cf. p. 497: "... il n'est pas anormal que le mot *caritra* dans notre formule ait servi à désigner la preuve écrite, par une métonymie analogue à celle qui a fait de *vyavahāra* le synonyme de preuve testimoniale."

caritraṃ [sthitaṃ] saṃgrahe puṃsām.

There is no reason to doubt Kangle's translation:

customs [are based] on the commonly held view of men.[769]

Let us now return to Nārada, to notice that, besides the fact that *pustakaraṇe*—eventually *pustakaraṇam*— appears in no other text, it is also not the only reading attested for the NS. Jolly himself noted the variant *praśnakaraṇe* in three Nārada manuscripts. Bhavasvāmin, immediately after the interpretation mentioned earlier, takes notice of the reading of the *Agnipurāna* and the *Arthaśāstra* as a *varia lectio* for the *Nāradīyamanusaṃhitā*:

caritraṃ saṃgrahaḥ puṃsām iti pāṭhāntaram. pāramparyāvicchinnasmṛtideśādhiṣṭhānagaṇadharmaḥ satpuruṣaiḥ parigṛhītah; tasmin sthita iti sambandhaḥ.

Far more important is another variant reading, adopted in the *Vyavahāraprakāśa* of the *Vīramitrodaya*. Mitramiśra (7) explicitly rejects Caṇḍeśvara's reading *caritraṃ pustakaraṇam*, as follows:

tad rūḍhihīnatvād vacanāntarāsaṃvādāc ca heyam.

He prefers to follow the *Parāśaramādhavīya*:

atra Mādhavīye caritraṃ tu svīkaranam iti pāṭhaṃ likhitvā deśācāraś caritraṃ tatsvīkāre tu tad eva nirṇayahetur iti vyākhyātam.[770]

Taking Nārada, Kauṭilya, and the *Agnipurāna* together, we obtain the following variants for the definition of *caritra*:

pustakaraṇe
praśnakaraṇe
tu svīkaraṇe
saṃgrahe puṃsām

Faced with this situation we can adopt two different attitudes toward the text of Nārada. One can accept the fact that, from very

[769] Cf. Śrīmūla, *caritraṃ lokācāraḥ saṃgrahe grāmasamūhe daśagrāmyādau puṃsāṃ pratiṣṭhitam.*

[770] Cf. *Parāśaramādhavīya* 3.10, 17. Kane also seems to prefer this reading: "Nārada's text as read by Caṇḍeśvara: *caritraṃ pustakaraṇe*, means "documentary evidence," but Par. M. (111.10) reads *caritraṃ tu svīkaraṇe*" (*Kātyāyana*, 125 n.). Cf. Kane 1930–1962: 3.261: "'*caritraṃ tu svīkaraṇe*'... means 'usages become the rule of decision when they are accepted as valid by the people and by the courts.'"

early times, there have been variant readings —which however does not solve the problem of the strange and unique reading *pustakaraṇe*. Or one can go on the assumption that there was one original reading which has been corrupted in different ways.[771] If that be the case, I would like to propose *puṃsvakaraṇe*[772] or *puṃsvīkaraṇe*: "*caritra* (acceptable, recognized custom) rests on its being accepted by men."[773]

[771] There may have been other corruptions which have not been noticed in the editions. E.g., *Kṛtyakalpataru*, Vyavahārakāṇḍa, p. 260, notices *dusthakaraṇe*.

[772] Cf. Pāṇini 1.3.56: [ātmanepadam] *upād gamaḥ svakaraṇe*, however there with the meaning "to marry."

[773] After these materials had been collected, I noticed that at least one author (Meyer 1926: 241) has tried to emend *pustakaraṇe*. He proposes *puṃsakaraṇe* or *puṃsāṃ karaṇe*, but would prefer *puṃsacaraṇe or puṃsāṃ caraṇe*.

38

The Terms Niyukta, Aniyukta, *and* Niyoga *in Sanskrit Legal Literature*

I

Students of classical Hindu law usually distinguish two different kinds of judges in the law courts of the ancient Indian kingdoms: judges who are *niyukta* "appointed (by the king)," and judges who are *aniyukta* "not appointed (by the king)." For instance, the "Index of the important Sanskrit words" in the *Dharmakośa* interprets *niyukta* as "appointed" (1.1: 33), and, more explicitly, *aniyukta* as "not appointed, an assessor of a court who has not been formally appointed and is not entitled to vote" (1.1: 3–4; apparently from Monier-Williams' dictionary).

This distinction is based on information drawn from the Sanskrit commentaries. Thus, in his commentary on YDh 2.2, Vijñāneśvara quotes KS 56 (DhK 60a):

> *saprāḍvivākaḥ sāmātyaḥ sabrāhmaṇapurohitaḥ*
> *sasabhyaḥ prekṣako rājā svarge tiṣṭhati dharmataḥ;*

to account for the simultaneous presence in this stanza of the two terms *brāhmaṇa* and *sabhya*, he draws the following distinction: *tatra brāhmaṇā aniyuktāḥ sabhāsadas tu niyuktā iti bhedaḥ*. And, since different terminology presupposes different responsibilities, the author of the *Mitākṣarā* adds:

> *tatra niyuktānāṃ yathāvasthitārthakathane 'pi yadi rājānyathā karoti tadāsau nivāraṇīyo'nyathā doṣaḥ... aniyuktānām punar anyathābhidhāne 'nabhidhāne vā doṣo na tu rājño 'nivāraṇe.*

This and similar distinctions are perpetuated in modern scholarly literature. Says Kane (1930–1962: 3.274):

> The chief justice (*prāḍvivāka*) with the Sabhyas constituted the Court, being appointed (*niyukta*) by the king. It was stated above that the king was to enter the Hall of Justice with the chief justice, Sabhyas and Brāhmaṇas. The distinction is that sabhyas were appointed by the king as judges, while Brāhmaṇas were persons who were well-versed in Dharmaśāstra, who could attend the Court, though not appointed (*aniyukta*) and whose opinions on difficult points of law were respectfully received by the judges.

I shall show in this article that the distinction between *niyukta* and *aniyukta* drawn by the commentators and adopted by modern interpreters is a rationalization *a posteriori*, and that the terms *niyukta* and *aniyukta* originally referred to a basically different distinction.

KS 63 (DhK 57a) states:

> *yadā na kuryān nṛpatiḥ svayaṃ kāryavinirṇayam*
> *tadā tatra niyuñjīta brāhmaṇaṃ śāstrapāragam.*

Kane (KS: 129) translates in the traditional way:

> When the king cannot himself decide the causes (of litigants), then *he should appoint thereto* (in the court) a Brāhmaṇa learned in the various *śāstras*.

ViDh 3.72–73 (DhK 26a) evidently refers to the same situation:

> *svayam eva vyavahārān paśyed vidvadbhir brāhmaṇaiḥ*
> *sārdham; vyavahāradarśane brāhmaṇaṃ vā niyuñjyāt.*

Jolly (SBE 7: 20) does not use the expression "appoint" but the idea is the same:

> Let him try causes himself, accompanied by well-instructed Brāhmaṇas. Or *let him entrust* a Brāhmaṇa with the judicial business.

In reality, both texts clearly imply that the Brāhmaṇa is not just "appointed" by the king; the important element is that the Brāhmaṇa who is *niyukta* is designated by the king to act as his substitute. Reading YDh 2.3 (DhK 39a):

> *apaśyatā kāryavaśād vyavahārān nṛpeṇa tu*
> *sabhyaiḥ saha niyoktavyo brāhmaṇaḥ sarvadharmavit,*

in conjunction with 2.1ab (DhK 38a):

> *vyavahārān nṛpaḥ paśyed vidvadbhir brāhmaṇaiḥ saha,*

makes it clear that, under normal circumstances, the court is composed of:

the king + learned Brāhmaṇa assessors,

but that, when the king is unable to attend, he appoints a substitute, so that the court consists of:

the king's *niyukta* + the same learned Brāhmaṇa assessors.

Compare also *Agnipurāṇa* 253.32–33 (DhK 65a):

vyavahārān nṛpaḥ paśyet jñānaviprair akopanaḥ
śatrumitrasamāḥ sabhyā alobhāḥ śrutivedinaḥ
apaśyatā kāryavaśāt sabhyair vipraṃ niyojayet.

If more convincing evidence for the interpretation of *niyukta* as "substitute" is needed, it is provided by Manu. MDh 8.9 (DhK 31b) corresponds closely to KS 63 quoted earlier:

yadā svayaṃ na kuryāt tu nṛpatiḥ kāryadarśanam
tadā niyuñjyād vidvāṃsaṃ brāhmaṇaṃ kāryadarśane;

Bühler (SBE 25: 254) again follows the traditional interpretation:

But if the king does not personally investigate the suits, then *let him appoint* a learned Brāhmaṇa to try them.

However, MDh 8.10ab (DhK 31b) says about the *niyukta*:

so 'sya kāryāṇi saṃpaśyet sabhyair eva tribhir vṛtaḥ.

Bühler's translation (SBE 25: 254), "That (man) shall..., accompanied by three assessors, ...fully consider (all) causes (brought) before the (king)," is based on the commentators; for instance, Kullūka: *sa brāhmaṇo 'sya rājño draṣṭavyāni kāryāṇi... paśyet.* In reality, MDh 8.10 states that, in the king's absence, the three judges are the same (*sabhyair eva*) as those who normally assist the king according to MDh 8.1; the difference is that the king's substitute *asya kāryāṇi saṃpaśyet.* The genitive *asya* reminds us in certain ways of the Pāṇinian use of the genitive, according to *sūtra* 1.1.49: *ṣaṣṭhī sthāneyogā*: he (= the *niyukta*) examines cases in his (= the king's) stead. The same substitute for the king is again referred to in MDh 8.11 (DhK 32a), with a synonym for *niyukta* but with a similar use of the genitive:

yasmin deśe niṣīdanti viprā vedavidas trayaḥ
rājñaś cādhikṛto vidvān brāhmaṇas tāṃ sabhām viduḥ;

Bühler's translation (SBE 25: 254) again misses the point:

Where three Brāhmaṇas versed in the Vedas and the learned (judge) appointed by the king sits down, they call that the court of the (four-faced) Brahman.

Other cases in which the king's substitute is singled out by means of the term *niyukta* can only be briefly referred to. One such case is that of the *sūcaka*, as opposed to another type of informer: the *stobhaka*. Says KS 34 (DhK 123b):

nṛpeṇaiva niyukto yaḥ paradoṣam avekṣitum
nṛpāya sūcayej jñātvā sūcakaḥ sa udāhṛtaḥ;

Kane (KS 124) translates:

That man is declared to be a sūcaka *who is appointed* by the king himself for discovering the wrong-doing of others and who coming to know of it conveys it to the king.

II

The preceding interpretation of the texts on the king's substitutes agrees well with a different use of the term *niyukta* in legal literature: the substitution of a party to a lawsuit. Numerous texts deal with this particular topic; I shall only quote a few of them, and illustrate the implications of the *niyukta*'s activities.

The normal term for the substitute of a party to a lawsuit is again *niyukta*; for example, in BS 1.142 (not in SBE 33; DhK 122b):

apragalbhajaḍonmattavṛddhastrībālarogiṇām
pūrvottaraṃ vaded bandhur niyukto 'nyo 'thavā naraḥ.

Also, KS 92 (DhK 130a):

dāsāḥ karmakarāḥ śiṣyā niyuktā bāndhavās tathā
vādino na ca daṇḍyāḥ syuḥ yas tato 'nyaḥ sa daṇḍabhāk.

where Kane (KS 134) translates *niyuktāḥ* as "persons deputed," and a text by Vyāsa (DhK 134b):

kulastrībālakonmattajaḍārtānāṃ ca bāndhayāḥ
pūrvapakṣottare brūyur niyukto bhṛtakas tathā.

If a person is *aniyukta*, his word shall not be taken without additional evidence; thus BS 1.171 (not in SBE 33; DhK 123a):

yo 'dattavyavahāratvād aniyuktaḥ pravartate
vacanaṃ tasya na grāhyaṃ likhitapreṣitād ṛte.

Whereas the judge who replaces the king is practically always called *niyukta*, when it comes to representatives of parties to a lawsuit there is a tendency also to use synonymous forms built on the root *ni-yuj*. Nārada (Mātṛkā 2.33; DhK 116a) uses *niyogakṛt*, translated by Jolly (SBE 33: 29) as "the appointed agent":

yo na bhrātā na ca pitā putro na niyogakṛt
parārthavādī daṇḍyaḥ syād vyavahāreṣu vibruvan;

another stanza attributed to Nārada (DhK 402a) refers to *niyogasthāḥ*, whereas the *Śukranītisāra* (DhK 135b) has both *niyokita* (*niyojita*?) and *niyogin*.

In this kind of replacement too, it is clear that the *niyukta* does not act in his own name but rather as a substitute for the party he represents. Thus, Nārada (Mātṛkā 2.22; DhK 116a = KS 91; DhK 130a):

arthinā saṃniyukto vā pratyarthiprahito'pi vā
yo yasyārthe vivadate tayor jayaparājayau;

Jolly (SBE 33: 29) translates:

If *one deputed* by the claimant, or chosen as his representative by the defendant, speaks for his client in court, the victory or defeat concerns the party (himself and not the representative),

and, similarly, Kane (KS 133):

For whomsoever a man carries on a dispute (in a law court) whether the latter be *appointed* by the plaintiff or deputed by the defendant, the victory or defeat belongs to the former (and not the representative).

With a note: "This verse contains the germs of the modern profession of pleaders."

Equally characteristically, BS 1.138 (not in SBE 33; DhK 123a) compares the *niyukta* to the priest who performs a sacrifice in the name and for the benefit of the *yajamāna*:

ṛtvig vāde niyuktaś ca samau saṃparikīrtitau
yajñe svāmy āpnuyāt puṇyaṃ hānim vāde 'thavā jayam.

And Pitāmaha (Scriba 6; DhK 133a) lays down the general principle that any act performed by a *niyukta* is considered not performed by himself but by the person he represents:

> *yaḥ kaścit kārayet kiṃcin niyogād yena kenacit*
> *tat tenaiva kṛtaṃ jñeyam anivartyaṃ hi tat smṛtam;*

Scriba's translation: "*in seinem Auftrag,*" fails to do justice to the real meaning of the term *niyoga.*

Even as the king can eventually be replaced in other ways than as the judge in a law court, so can a private individual be represented in other ways than as a party to a lawsuit. The first of these cases is still connected with legal procedure: individuals can be replaced by substitutes in ordeals. KS 430 (DhK 460a) states in connection with certain kinds of accused:

> *etair eva niyuktānāṃ sādhūnāṃ divyam arhati*
> *necchanti sādhavo yatra tatra śodhyaḥ svakair naraiḥ;*

Kane (KS 200) translates:

> The king should offer ordeal (in the case of these men) to good men *appointed* by these (to undergo the ordeal); where good men do not desire (to undergo ordeal for them), the king should test their innocence by (offering ordeal) to their own men (i.e. relatives and friends).

Another text is also generally quoted in connection with the rules of legal procedure, but it "might also have been inserted in the chapter on Master and Servant" (Jolly SBE 33: 298, note). I refer to BS 9.29 (= SBE 33: 6.7; DhK 562b):

> *yaḥ svāminā niyuktas tu dhanāyavyayapālane*
> *kusīdakṛṣivāṇijye nisṛṣṭārthas tu sa smṛtaḥ;*

Jolly translates (SBE 33: 298):

> *One appointed* by his master to look after his expenses and to superintend (transactions regarding) tillage, loans, and trade, is called a manager.

BS 9.28 (= SBE 33: 6.8; DhK 562b–563a) at the same time clearly defines the impact of the acts of this kind of *niyukta:*

> *pramāṇaṃ tatkṛtaṃ sarvaṃ lābhālābhavyayodayam*
> *svadeśe vā videśe vā svāmī tan na visaṃvadet;*

according to Jolly's translation (SBE 33: 298):

> Whatever has been transacted by him is valid, whether relating to receipt, non-receipt, expenses or income, and whether it may have been transacted at home or abroad. The master must not annul such transactions as these.

Finally, the father is bound by debts contracted by his son, provided the latter acted as his *niyukta*. Says NS 1.11 (DhK 696a):

> *pitur eva niyogād vā kuṭumbhabharaṇāya vā*
> *kṛtam vā yad ṛṇam kṛcchre dadyāt putrasya tat pitā*;

once again Jolly (SBE 33: 45) reflects the traditional interpretation:

> Such debts of a son as have been contracted *by his father's order*, or for the maintenance of the family, or in a precarious situation, must be paid by the father.

III

A few words must also be added about a third type of substitution: the well known case of the deceased husband being replaced by his brother in the levirate. Among the many passages dealing with this institution a few will be selected to illustrate, first, the regular use of *niyukta* in this situation: the *devara* acts as a substitute for his deceased brother.

One of the clearest examples in MDh 9.60 (DhK 1065b):

> *vidhavāyām niyuktas tu ghṛtākto vāgyato niśi*
> *ekam utpādayet putram na dvitīyam kathaṃcana*:

In this case too Bühler (SBE 25: 338) uses the English term "appointed":

> He (*who is*) *appointed* to (cohabit with) the widow shall (approach her) at night anointed with clarified butter and silent, (and) beget one son, by no means a second.

Compare also MDh 9.58 (DhK 1064b):

> *jyeṣṭho yavīyaso bhāryām yavīyān vāgrajastriyam*
> *patitau bhavato gatvā niyuktāv apy anāpadi*:

according to Bühler (SBE 25: 337):

> An elder (brother) who approaches the wife of the younger, and a younger (brother who approaches) the wife of the elder, except in times of misfortune, both become outcasts, even though (*they were duly*) *authorised*.

The term *niyukta* is used in the same way be it with regard to different people by Kauṭilya, first in 3.6.24 (DhK 1288a):

kṣetre vā janayed asya niyuktaḥ kṣetrajam sutam
mātṛbandhuḥ sagotro vā tasmai tat pradiśed dhanam;

Kangle (2.246) follows the traditional translation:

Or, *a person appointed,* either a mother's kinsman, or a person of the same gotra, may beget on his wife a kṣetraja son; to him he shall allot that property.

And in 3.7.6 (DhK 1288a):

sagotreṇānyagotreṇa vā niyuktena kṣetrajātaḥ kṣetrajaḥ putraḥ:

in Kangle's translation (2: 247):

A (son) begotten on the wife (of a man) by a *person appointed,* whether of the same gotra or of a different gotra, is a kṣetraja son.

Occasionally the term niyoga is used specifically to indicate the activity of the devara. For instance, in MDh 9.62 (DhK 1066a) the beginning of which corresponds to that of MDh 9.60 quoted earlier:

vidhavāyāṃ niyogārthe nirvṛtte tu yathāvidhi
guruvac ca snuṣāvac ca varteyātāṃ parasparam;

Bühler translates (SBE 25: 338):

But when the purpose of *the appointment* to (cohabit with) the widow has been attained in accordance with the law, those two shall behave towards each other like a father and a daughter- in-law.

However, it is clear from this and similar verses that the line between niyoga as the activity solely of the substitute of the deceased husband and as the combined activities of the two parties involved is a thin one. Not only is the *devara* the substitute of the husband; the act which he performs together with the widow is in itself a substitute for the marriage that has come to an end by the death of the husband. The latter substitution is clearly implied in MDh 9.65ab (DhK 1067b):

nodvāhikeṣu mantreṣu niyogaḥ kīrtyate kvacit;

in Bühler's translation (SBE 25: 339):

> In the sacred texts which refer to marriage *the appointment* (of widows) is nowhere mentioned, ...

Once so far, it is only natural that the term *niyukta* becomes applicable simultaneously to both participants in the single act of niyoga. Hence MDh 9.63 (DhK 1066a):

> *niyuktau yau vidhiṃ hitvā varteyātāṃ tu kāmataḥ*
> *tāv ubhau patitau syātāṃ snuṣāgagurutalpagau;*

Bühler translates (SBE 25: 338):

> If *those two* (*being thus*) *appointed* deviate from the rule and act from carnal desire, they will both become outcasts, (as men) who defile the bed of a daughter or of a Guru,

but, what is really meant, immediately after 9.62 —quoted earlier—, is that they become "like a man and a woman who defile the beds of a daughter-in-law and a father, respectively."

Finally, the widow being as much part of the *niyoga*, as the substitute for her husband, the term *niyuktā*, in the singular, is often applied to her alone. Thus, MDh 9.59 (DhK 1065a):

> *devarād vā sapiṇḍād vā striyā samyaṅ niyuktayā*
> *prajepsitādhigantavyā saṃtānasya parikṣaye;*

Bühler (SBE 25: 337):

> On failure of issue (by her husband) *a woman who has been authorised*, may obtain, (in the) proper (manner prescribed), the desired offspring by (cohabitation with) a brother-in-law or (with some other) Sapiṇḍa (of the husband).

What is true for the past participle *niyuktā* is equally true for other forms of *ni-yuj*, applied solely to the widow. (Notice that Bühler erroneously introduced this concept in his translation of MDh 9.65ab, above.) For instance, MDh 9.64 (DhK 1066b):

> *nānyasmin vidhavā nārī niyoktavyā dvijātibhiḥ*
> *anyasmin hi niyuñjānā dharmam hanyuḥ sanātanam;*

Bühler (SBE 25: 338) again uses the verb "appoint":

> By twice-born men a widow *must not be appointed* to (cohabit with) any other (than her husband); for *they who appoint* (her) to another (man), will violate the eternal law.

Also, MDh 9.68 (DhK 1068b):

tataḥ prabhṛti yo mohāt pramītapatikām striyam
niyojayaty apatyārtham taṃ vigarhanti sādhavaḥ;

Bühler (SBE 25: 339):

Since that (time) the virtuous censure that (man) *who* in his folly *appoints* a woman, whose husband died, to (bear) children (to another man).

The semantic development outlined in the preceding pages shows that the translations "authorised" or "appointed" for *niyuktā*, "he appoints" for *niyojayati*, etc., miss an important point when they are used with reference to widows who participate in a levirate. In reality, *niyuktā* indicates "a widow who performs *niyoga*," *niyojayati* —or even the non-causative *niyunakti*— refers to him "who makes a widow undergo *niyoga*," etc. These equations are obvious from two successive *sūtras* in the VaDh (17.56–57, DhK 1022b):

ūrdhvaṃ ṣaḍbhyo māsebhyaḥ...pitā bhrātā vā
niyogaṃ kārayet;
na sonmādām avaśāṃ vyādhitāṃ vā niyuñjīta.

The simple verbal form *niyuñjīta* corresponds to the compounded form *niyogaṃ kārayet*, and should be interpreted as such. It means that he makes the widow participate in a substitution; in this case: *the* substitution, a levirate to replace the original marriage.

The central place occupied by the institution itself in all forms derived from *ni-yuj* to indicate participants in it —even of the *devara* who is the sole "substitute" in the original sense of *niyukta* as it is used elsewhere in legal literature— is finally, illustrated by the fact that even the deceased husband is, in some way, considered to be connected with it. Again to quote Vasiṣṭha (17.63–64; DhK 1022b):

aniyuktāyām utpanna utpādayituḥ putro bhavatīty āhuh; *syāc cen niyoginoḥ.*

To Bühler's translation (SBE 14: 90–91):

They declare that a son begotten on (a widow who has) not been (duly) appointed, belongs to the begetter. If she was (appointed, the child belongs) to both the males connected with the appointment,

I prefer: If a man begets a son on a woman, the son is his and his alone, unless the woman was performing *niyoga* with him. If that was the case, the son belongs to *both* men connected with the *niyoga*.

39

The Aurasa *Son*

"In modern times the courts generally recognize only two kinds of sons, namely *aurasa* and *dattaka*, the other kinds of sons being held to be obsolete."[774] In fact, the claim that most of the various kinds of sons recognized by the ancient *ṛṣis* had become obsolete is not restricted to "modern times." It goes back far into the past. According to a verse attributed to Bṛhaspati, "present-day" people were no longer able to distinguish between the different kinds of sons introduced by the Seers:

anekadhā kṛtāḥ putrā ṛṣibhiś ca putrātmanaiḥ;
na śakyante 'dhunā kartuṃ śaktahīnair idantanaiḥ. (26.29)

Yet the Dharmaśāstras —including Bṛhaspati's—, the commentators, and the modern treatises on Hindu law prior to 1955/56 went on to list and, in many cases, define and discuss 12 different kinds of sons.[775]

[774] Kane 1930–1962: 3.657. Kane refers to *Nagindas v. Bachoo*, 43 I.A. 56, 57 (1916), and adds: "But two more kinds of sons have been recognized in modern times in certain provinces only, namely the kṛtrima in Mithilā (modern Tirhut) and the putrikāputra among the Nambudri Brāhmaṇas of Malabar." For details, see Kane 3.659–60.

[775] In only very few *smṛtis* is the number of sons different from 12: Baudhāyana (2.2.3.31–33) and Bṛhaspati (26.70–74) list 13, Devala (*Dharmakośa*, I.1373; all references to the DhK are to vol. I: *Vyavahārakāṇḍa*) 15. The view that these were merely apparent deviations from the number 12 is clearly expressed by Nandapaṇḍita (on ViDh 15.2): *yat tu Bṛhaspatinā "putrās trayodaśa proktā Manunā ye 'nupūrvaśa"* (26.77ab) *iti trayodaśatvaṃ, Devalena ca "putrākhyā daśa pañcadaśatvam-uktaṃ, tad avāntarīyabhedamādāya nātyantabhedeneti na virodhaḥ, teṣāṃ apy atrāntarbhāvāt* |

Even though the lists of 12 kinds of sons differ in detail (for comparative lists, see Kane 1930–1962: 3.645; Mayne 1950: 107), there are some features which most of them share:

(1) The different kinds of sons are always listed in descending order of importance. Says Nārada:

pūrvaḥ pūrvaḥ smṛtaḥ śreṣṭho jaghanyo yo ya uttaraḥ. (13.47cd/45cd)[776]

And so does Viṣṇu:

eteṣāṃ pūrvaḥ pūrvaḥ śreyān. (15.28)

(2) Whereas all other sons appear at different places in the several lists, the *aurasa* son invariably occupies the first place. Some texts underscore this position explicitly. Vasiṣṭha's definition (17.13; see below) does not include the term *aurasa*,[777] but is followed by *prathamaḥ*. Viṣṇu's definition (15.2; see below) ends: *aurasaḥ prathamaḥ*. And the second half of the *śloka* in which Manu defines the *aurasa* son (9.166; see below) reads:

tam aurasaṃ vijānīyāt putraṃ prathamakalpitam (or *–kalpakam*).

Being *prathama* "first" in a descending line implies that the *aurasa* is also *mukhya* "most important."[778] Vijñāneśvara introduces Yājñavalkya's list of sons (2.128) as follows:

adhunā mukhyagauṇaputrāṇāṃ dāyagrahaṇavyavasthāṃ darśayiṣyaṃs teṣāṃ svarūpaṃ tāvad āha

Similarly, Nandapaṇḍita introduces Viṣṇu's definition of *aurasa* (15.2): *tatra mukhyaṃ lakṣayati*; and he comments: *prathamo mukhya ity arthaḥ*. More important in the context of this article is the fact that Nandapaṇḍita subsequently introduces his discussion of the other eleven kinds of sons thus: *atha gauṇān lakṣayati*. In other words, the *aurasa* is the single *mukhya* "primary" son;

[776] The first verse refers to Jolly's *Nāradasmṛti* edition (1885), the second to Lariviere's (1989).

[777] The term *aurasa* does occur elsewhere in the text, in connection with the share of an adopted son in case an *aurasa* is born after the adoption: *tasmiṃś* (= *dattake*) *cet pratigṛhīta aurasaḥ putra utpādyate caturbhāgabhāgī syād dattakaḥ* (VaDh 15.9).

[778] BDh (2.2.3.33) quotes the opinion of Aupajaṅghani to the effect that the *aurasa* is the one and only true son: *teṣāṃ prathama evety Aupajaṅghaniḥ*, on which Govidarāja comments: *Aupajaṅghanir ācāryo manyate sma aurasa eva putro na putrikāputrādaya iti.*

all others are *gauṇa* "secondary" sons (cf. Aparārka (on VaDh 17.13, sub YDh 2.128): *prathamo mukhyaḥ tena sa eva putraśabdasya mukhyo 'rthaḥ kṣetrajādis tu gauṇaḥ*).

The idea that the *aurasa* son is different from all other kinds of sons is also expressed in another way. According to Manu:

kṣetrajādīn sutān etān ekādaśa yathoditān
putrapratinidhīn āhuḥ kriyālopān manīṣiṇah (9.180)

Whatever the often discussed meaning of *kriyālopād*,[779] it is clear that any one of the other sons is only a *pratinidhi* "substitute" for the *aurasa*.[780] The fact that, and the reason why, substitute sons are allowed only when a father does not have an *aurasa* son appears in a verse attributed to Atri (DhK 1352):

aputreṇaiva kartavyaḥ putrapratinidhiḥ sadā |
piṇḍodakakriyāhetor yasmāt tasmāt prayatnataḥ||[781]

At this point it is necessary to digress for a moment and look at the peculiar position of one of the "substitutes," the *putrikāputra* "the son of an appointed daughter." In the lists of sons the *putrikāputra* occupies the second place with Baudhāyana,

[779] Eg., *Vyavahāraprakāśa*, p. 480: *kriyālopāt pariṇayādikriyālopād ity arthaḥ kriyālopād iti pratinidhitve hetuḥ | smṛticandrikāyāṃ tu "aurasābhāve tatkartṛkaśrāddhādilopād bibhyato manīṣiṇa ṛṣaya ekādaśa putranidhīn kartavyatvenāhur" iti vyākhyātam |*

[780] Immediately after the list of 12 kinds of sons Manu (9.161) exhibits the following simile:

yādṛśaṃ phalam-āpnoti kuplavaiḥ saṃtarañ jalam |
tādṛśaṃ phalam-āpnoti kuputraiḥ saṃtraṃs tamaḥ ||

Whether or not the term *kuputra* was originally meant to refer to "bad" sons generally, as opposed to "good" sons, the commentators agree that *kuputra* here refers to any son who is not an *aurasa*. E.g. Kullūka: *kuputraiḥ kṣetrajādibhiḥ |*

[781] Cf. a verse attributed, among others, to Yama (DhK 1352):

aputreṇa sutaḥ kāryo yādṛk tādṛk prayatnataḥ |
piṇḍodakakriyāhetor-nāmasaṃkīrtanāya ca ||

Jolly's interpretation of the existence of other sons than the aurasa: "originally an economic motive was perhaps a more important factor in it —to get for the family as many powerful workers as possible" (1928: 156), was dismissed by Kane (Kane 1930–1962: 3.648–49) and Mayne (1950: 114). Kane and Mayne refer to the fact that only in the absence of an *aurasa* son substitute sons could be recurred to. Both also agree that the lists of 12 different kinds of sons were due to "the systematizing habit of Sanskrit writers" (Mayne), or the "the ancient writers' great *penchant* for divisions and sub-divisions based upon very slight differences of circumstances" (Kane).

Yājñavalkya, Bṛhaspati, and Kauṭilya; the third place with Vasiṣṭha,[782] Śaṅkha-Likhita, Nārada, Viṣṇu, and Yama; the fifth place with Hārīta and Devala;[783] the tenth place with Gautama.[784]

Manu's position is ambivalent. The *putrikāputra* is not mentioned in the list of sons. On the other hand, on two occasions the son's son and the daughter's son (whom most commentators interpret as the son of a *putrikā*) are said to be equal:[785]

pautradauhitrayor loke na viśeṣo 'sti dharmataḥ (9.133ab);
pautradauhitrayor loke viśeṣo nopapadyate. (9.139ab)

Yājñavalkya goes farther, and cleary equates the *putrikāputra* with the *aurasa*:

auraso dharmapatnījas tatsamaḥ putrikāsutaḥ. (2.128cd)[786]

And so does Kauṭilya:

tena tulyaḥ putrikāputraḥ. (3.7.5)

When Bṛhaspati illustrates what it means to be a *pratinidhi* type of son, he excludes from that category not only the *aurasa* but the *putrikāputra* as well:

ājyaṃ vinā yathā tailaṃ sadbhiḥ pratinidhīkṛtam |
tathaikādaśa putrās tu pautrikaurasayor vinā || (26.78)

What this means is that the rules regarding the *aurasa* son

[782] ViDh (17.15) lists the *putrikā* rather than the *putrikāputra*: *tṛtīyaḥ putrikā vijñāyate.*

[783] In the enumeration of sons attributed to Devala (Nandapaṇḍita on ViDh 15.27; cf. DhK 1373: *smṛtyantaram*) *putrikāputra* occupies the fifth place, *putrikā* the second.

[784] For an interpretation of this unusual and extreme position at GDh 28.33, see, e.g., the *Mitākṣarā* (on YDh 2.132): *Gautamīye tu pautrikeyasya daśamatvena pāṭho vijātīyaviṣayaḥ.*

[785] Hence Bṛhaspati's statement (26.77) that Manu recognizes 13 kinds of sons:

putrās trayodaśa proktā Manunā ye 'nupūrvaśaḥ |
saṃtānakāraṇaṃ teṣāṃ aurasaḥ putrikā tathā ||

Cf. also Mayne (1950: 107): "Manu mentions the aurasa and the appointed daughter's son as of equal status and then mentions the aurasa and the eleven secondary sons, altogether, thirteen sons."

[786] The *Mitākṣarā* comments: *tatsamaḥ putrikāputraḥ tatsama aurasasamaḥ putrikāyāḥ sutaḥ putrikāsutaḥ,* but also adds an alternative interpretation based on VaDh 17.15 (Cf. note 9): *athavā putrikaiva sutaḥ so 'pyaurasasama eva pitravayavānām alpatvān mātravayavānāṃ bāhulyatvācca.*

that will be discussed in the remaining pages of this article in the opinion of many also apply to the *putrikāputra*.

The *aurasa* being different from and the superior to all other kinds of sons entails that he is entitled to special privileges. Most important are those related to inheritance. Without going into details which are beyond the scope of this study, I will just mention that, according to a number of sources, the *aurasa* alone inherits the paternal property to the exclusion of any other son. According to Manu:

eka evaurasaḥ putraḥ pitryasya vasunaḥ prabhuḥ |
śeṣāṇām ānṛśaṃsyārthaṃ pradadyāt tu prajīvanam || (9.163)

Similarly Bṛhaspati, although again ranking the *putrikāputra* with the *aurasa*:

eka evaurasaḥ pitrye dhane svāmī prakīrtitaḥ |
tattulyaḥ putrikāputro bhartavyās tv apare smṛtāḥ || (26.70)

Nārada lays down the order in which different kinds of sons inherit as follows:

kramād dhy ete prapadyeran mṛte pitari taddhanam |
jyāyaso jyāyaso'bhāve jaghanyas tad avāpnuyāt || (13.49/46)

Yājñavalkya more generally concludes his discussion of the different kinds of sons as follows:

piṇḍado 'ṃśaharaś caiṣāṃ pūrvābhāve paraḥ paraḥ | (2.132cd)

In view of these and other privileges accorded to the *aurasa* son, it is important to define exactly which kind of son qualifies as an *aurasa*. I will now examine the various definitions of the term *aurasa* in the *smṛtis*,[787] and the several ways in which the commentators have tried to reconcile the differences.

A number of *smṛtis* provide remarkably similar definitions for the term *aurasa*:

1. Vasiṣṭha: *svayam utpāditaḥ svakṣetre saṃskṛtāyām* (17.13);
2. Viṣṇu: *svakṣetre saṃskṛtāyām utpāditaḥ svayam* (15.2);

[787] I must mention in passing that some commentators offer etymological explanations for the term *aurasa*. For instance, the *Mitākṣarā* (on YDh 2.128) says that *aurasa* means *uraso jātaḥ*; cf. Aparārka (on the same verse): *urasi bhāvaḥ*. Hence the translation of *aurasa* as "son of the body." According to Rāghavānanda (on MDh 9.166): *svayam udvāhitāyām uraḥsaṃśleṣaṇajātatvād aurasaḥ*; *kṣetraje tadabhāvo Nāradenokto "gātrair gātrāny asaṃspṛśann"* (MDh 12.82d/81d) *ity ādinā* |

3. Manu: *svakṣetre saṃskṛtāyāṃ tu svayam utpādayed dhi yam* (9.166ab);
4. Devala: *saṃskṛtāyāṃ tu bhāryāyāṃ svayam utpādito hi yaḥ* (DhK 1350);
5. Hārīta:[788] *sādhvyāṃ svayam utpāditaḥ* (DhK 1265);
6. Kauṭilya: *svayaṃjātaḥ kṛtakriyāyām.* (3.7.4)

All these definitions basically require only two qualifications for a son to be *aurasa*: (1) he must have been sired by his father, and (2) his mother must be his father's duly wedded wife. Yet, there are other restrictions.

First Restriction

Except for Kauṭilya, who uses the term *jātaḥ*, all other texts quoted so far include either *utpādayet* or *utpāditaḥ* "sire, be sired." As a result, some commentators require that the mother must be the father's duly wedded wife, not only at the time of their son's birth, but also at the time of his conception. For example, Kullūkabhaṭṭa (on MDh 9.166):

svabhāryāyāṃ... kṛtavivāhasaṃskārāyāṃ yaṃ svayam utpādayet ||

That means that, according to Kullūka, a son born after a wedding of his father and his mother, but conceived prior to it, is not *aurasa.*[789]

Second Restriction

According to some commentators, for a son to be *aurasa* he must not only have been conceived after the wedding of his par-

[788] As far as we know from the fragments collected by Jolly (1889), Hārīta does not use the term *aurasa.*

[789] Nevertheless, in *Pedda Amamni v. Zamindar of Marungapuri*, 1 I.A. 282, 293 (1874), the Privy Council decided that the fact that a son was conceived prior to the wedding of his parents does not prevent him from being a "legitimate" son. "That would be a most inconvenient doctrine. If it is the law that law must be administered. Their Lordships, however, do not think that it is the Hindu law. They are of opinion, that the Hindu law is the same in that respect as the English law." This decision drew strong criticism from Gooroodass Banerjee: "with every respect due to the decision of the highest tribunal for India, I may be permitted to say that the doctrine of procreation in lawful wedlock is necessary to constitute legitimacy, is not only supported by the language of the texts cited above, but is also in accordance with the general sprit of Hindu law, by which the nuptial rites are primarily meant only for girls [note: MDh 8.226]; while the necessity of marrying girls before puberty, reduces the practical inconvenience of the doctrine within the narrowest possible limits" (Banerjee 1913: 166).

ents; his mother must also be a virgin at that time. Kullūka's sentence which I quoted earlier in a truncated form reads:

svabhāryāyāṃ kanyāvasthāyām eva kṛtavivāhasaṃskārāyāṃ yaṃ svayam utpādayet.[790]

Third Restriction

At least one Dharmasūtra explicitly requires that the mother of an *aurasa* son be of the same *varṇa* as his father's.[791] Baudhāyana's definition of *aurasa*, although close to the definitions cited above, adds one important word:

savarṇāyāṃ saṃskṛtāyāṃ svayam utpāditam aurasaṃ putraṃ vidyāt (2.2.3.14)

A number of commentators interpret the term *savarṇāyām* literally. For instance, Kullūka (on MDh 9.166) quotes the Baudhāyana text to restrict Manu's definition of the *aurasa* son:

...iti Baudhāyanavacanāt sajātīyāyām eva svayam utpādita auraso jñeyaḥ[792]

Among the commentaries that accepted the requirement that the mother of an *aurasa* son be of the same *varṇa* as his father's is Vijñāneśvara's *Mitākṣarā*, which was to become very influential in Anglo-Indian law. While commenting on Yājñavalkya's requirement that the *aurasa* son be *dharmapatnīja* (2.128a; see above), Vijñāneśvara says:

[790] Although Kullūka does not say so explicitly, he may have been influenced.

[791] One might be tempted to read the same requirement into ĀpDh 2.6.13.1–4, were it not that Āpastamba's is the only text that is brief and vague on the subject of sons, to the extent of not mentioning any of the 12 kinds of sons by name. Yet, Āpastamba distinguishes between two types of sons: (1) sons begotten on a woman who is *savarṇā*, *apūrvā*, and *śāstravihitā*, and (2) sons by a woman who is *pūrvavatī*, by one who is *asaṃskṛtā*, and sons begotten *varṇāntare maithune*. The privileges of the first type of sons (*teṣāṃ karmabhiḥ sambandhaḥ, dāyenāvyatikramaśca*) have been differently interpreted. In the second case there is *doṣa* on the part of the father (or the parents?), and, more important, the son (*tatrāpi doṣavān putra eva*). Based on Pāṇini 5.3.14, according to which the suffix *–tra* in *tatra* can have other meanings than that of the locative, Haradatta interprets the latter sentence as follows: *tābhyām ubhābhyām api putra evātiśayena doṣavān*. This seems to indicate that for Āpastamba and, even more so for his commentator Haradatta, the son of an *asavarṇa* marriage did not qualify as *aurasa*.

[792] Similarly, Sarvajñanārāyaṇa (on the same verse): *svakṣetre svasavarṇakṣetre.*

savarṇā dharmavivāhoḍhā dharmapatnī; tasyāṃ jāta aurasaḥ putro mukhyaḥ[793]

Other commentators adopted a more liberal interpretation. Even Vijñāneśvara's own commentator, Bālambhaṭṭa, argues that the term *dharma* in *dharmapatnīja*, though preventing sons of *pratiloma* marriages to be *aurasa*, does not exclude sons of *anuloma* marriages, including sons of Brahmins, Kṣatriyas, and Vaiśyas by duly wedded Śūdrā wives (538–539).[794]

Similarly, Mitramiśra, who most often supports the views of the *Mitākṣarā*, in this case criticizes Vijñāneśvara for being inconsistent by excluding the sons of *anuloma* marriages, whom he elsewhere in the *Mitākṣarā* declares to be *aurasa*:

"savarṇā dharmavivāhoḍhā dharmapatnī; tasyāṃ jāta aurasaḥ putra" iti Mitākṣarā. vastutas tu nedam evaṃ boddhavyaṃ, (1) *anulomajānāṃ mūrdhāvasiktādīnām auraseṣv antarbhāvād iti svavacanavirodhāt*[795] *—na hi te savarṇāyām utpannāḥ;* (2) *brāhmaṇādiṣu yeṣāṃ yena dharmavivāhas taduḍhotpannānāṃ aurasaprasaṅge teṣu satsv apy anyeṣāṃ dāyagrahaṇaprasaṅgāc ca.* (*Vyavahāraprakāśa* 467)

At the same time Mitramiśra proposes an interesting way of reconciling the *smṛtis* that require the wife to be *savarṇa* with those that do not:

utkarṣābhiprāyaṃ savarṇābhiprāyam.

The idea that a son born to a woman of the same *varṇa* as his father's is a superior (*utkṛṣṭa, prakṛṣṭa*) type of *aurasa* son, but that a son born to a mother of a lower *varṇa* is *aurasa* as well, is formulated even more clearly by Nandapaṇḍita (on ViDh 15.2):

yat tu "savarṇāyāṃ saṃskṛtāyāṃ svayam utpāditam aurasam putraṃ jānīyād" iti Baudhāyanīyaṃ savarṇatvaviśeṣaṇam tad auraseṣu prakṛṣṭaurasapratipādanāya nānyeṣāṃ nirākaraṇāyeti mantavyam.[796]

[793] The term *dharmavivāhoḍhā* may imply that, in Vijñāneśvara's opinion, the parents' wedding must have been one of the "higher," not one of the "lower" types of wedding. Cf. Viśvarūpa's *Bālakrīdā* (on the same verse): *savarṇā brāhmādivivāhasaṃskṛtā dharmapatnī.*

[794] References to the *Bālambhaṭṭī* are according to the Chowkhamba Sanskrit Series (work 41) edition.

[795] This is a reference to a passage in the *Mitākṣarā* (on YDh 2.132cd) where Vijñāneśvara includes sons of *anuloma* marriages among the *aurasa*s and, hence, makes them inherit prior to all other kinds of sons: *anulomajānāṃ mūrdhāvasiktādīnām auraseṣv antarbhāvāt teṣām apy abhāve kṣetrajādīnāṃ dāyaharatvaṃ boddhavyam* |

[796] Cf. Rāghavānanda (on MDh 9.166, after quoting Baudhāyana): *atra*

As one might expect, even among those who accepted the fact that the son born to a duly wedded wife of a lower *varṇa* qualifies as *aurasa*, the question arose whether this extended meaning also applies to the case in which the husband was a twice-born and the wife a Śūdrā.[797] The commentators disagree.

Rāmacandra (on MDh 9.166), without explicitly excluding the son of a Śūdrā, does so indirectly by referring to the *aurasa* as a *dvija*:

> *svakṣetre saṃskṛtāyām ūḍhāyāṃ svayam utpādayed dvijaṃ tam aurasaṃ putraṃ... vijānīyāt* |

In its comment on the term *savarṇā* at ĀpDh 2.2.3.14, the *Pārijāta* (as quoted in the *Vyavahāraprakāśa* 468) is willing to extend the meaning of the term to include any *dvija* female married to any *dvija* male —it is not clear whether or not both *anuloma* and *pratiloma* marriages are included, but for the son of a Śūdrā wife to be *aurasa* his father has to be a Śūdrā:

> *savarṇātra dvijasya dvijā śūdrasya śūdrā na tu brāhmaṇasya brāhmaṇī kṣatriyasya kṣatriyā vaiśyasya vaiśyā. anyathā brāhmaṇādipariṇīta-kṣatriyādiputrāṇāṃ dvādaśavidhaputrāntarbhāvo na syāt* |

In the passage from the *Mitākṣarā* where Vijñāneśvara includes sons of *anuloma* marriages among the *aurasa*s, and, therefore, allows them to claim the entire inheritance prior to any other kinds of sons, he immediately follows up by declaring that sons born of a Śūdrā wife, though *aurasa*, do not enjoy that privilege:

> *śūdrāputras tv auraso 'pi kṛtsnaṃ bhāgam anyābhāve 'pi na labhate* |

Aparārka agrees, and adds a reason why this is so:

> *dharmapatnīśabdena śūdrā vyāvartate, tasyāḥ sahadharmacāritvābhāvāt.*

Bālambhaṭṭa, on the contrary, in the passage quoted earlier, holds that

> *patnītvaṃ mukhyam avivakṣitam iti śūdrāpi tādṛśī dvijānām* (538).

Nandapaṇḍita (on ViDh 15.2) deals with this problem at

savarṇāpadaṃ dvijatvādijātiparam. anyathā kṣatriyāvaiśyāśūdrāsu jātānāṃ viprāditrayapitṛkānāṃ aurasābhāvenāputratvāpatir iti. tatra paraṃ sajātīye mukhyam aurasatvam anyeṣāṃ gauṇam iti bhāvaḥ |

797 Note that a number of *smṛti* texts list the son of a Śūdrā wife separately, invariably at or near the end of their lists.

length. He first mentions an objection to the effect that the son of a Śūdrā cannot qualify as an *aurasa*, because the *śaudra* is listed among the "substitutes" for the *aurasa* (*putrapratinidhitvena tasya gaṇanam*) at MDh 9.160.[798] Nandapaṇḍita retorts that the *śaudra* who is made a substitute (*pratinidhīkriyate*) by Manu is not a son born to a duly wedded Śūdrā woman, but to a Śūdrā who is not his father's wife. And he concludes that nothing prevents the son born to a male *dvija* by his duly wedded Śūdrā wife from being *aurasa*:

> *tasmād ūḍhāyāṃ śūdrāyām utpannasyaurasatve na kiṃcid bādhakam* |

This brief survey of the various definitions of the term *aurasa* in the *smṛtis* and of some of the ways in which the commentators have tried to reconcile the differences clearly shows that the concept of an *aurasa* son in Hindu legal literature is far more varied and complex than the English "legitimate son," the term which is most often used to translate it.

[798] Cf. Aparārka (on YDh 2.128): *ata eva putrapratinidhiṣu ca tam āha Manuḥ*.

40

The Introduction of the Gautamadharmasūtra

This paper deals with the initial *sūtras* of the GDh. In Stenzler's edition (1876) the text reads as follows:

> *vedodharmamūlam*[1] *tadvidāṃcasmṛtiśīle*[2] *dṛṣṭodharmavyatikramaḥ sāhasaṃ ca mahatāṃ na tu dṛṣṭārthe avaradaurbalyāt* [3] *tulyabalavirodhe vikalpaḥ* [4]

Stenzler's text, followed by Bühler's translation (1879), corresponds to that commented on by Maskarin with one difference: in the edition of the *Maskaribhāṣya*, *sūtra* 3 is divided into three parts. Haradatta's *Mitākṣarā* omits the words *na tu dṛṣṭārthe*, and subdivides *sūtra* 3 into two parts. Hence the following concordance:

Stenzler, Bühler	Haradatta	Maskarin
1	1	1
2	2	2
3	3, 4	3, 4, 5
4	5	6

I shall use Stenzler's division of the *sūtras* throughout this article.

Kane refers to GDh 1.3 —and ĀpDh— to show that the Hindu theory of world ages was not yet fully developed at the time of the early Dharmasūtras:

> Both *Gaut.* 1.3–4 and *Āp.Dh.S.* 2.6.13.7–9 give expression to the view that among sages of old transgressions of *dharma* and violent actions are observed, but that on account of their distinguished

> spiritual greatness they incurred no sin, while a person of later days, being weak in spiritual merit, should not imitate them, otherwise he would come to grief. Here a distinction is drawn between very ancient sages and later sages as regards the endowment of spiritual merit, but nothing is said about the names or the theory of the four Yuga-s. (1930–1962: 3.889)

Bühler translates GDh 1.3 as follows: "Transgression of the law and violence are observed (in the case) of (those) great (men); but both are without force (as precedents) on account of the weakness of the men of later ages" (173). Bühler's interpretation is based on Haradatta's commentary. In fact, Bühler adds a lengthy note, in which he recalls "instances of transgression of the law" quoted by way of objection by Haradatta to show that *śīla* in the preceding *sūtra* (GDh 1.2) cannot be a real source of *dharma*: "the adultery of Kataka and Bharadvāja, Vasiṣṭha's marriage with the Cāṇḍālī Akṣamālā, Rāma Jāmadagnya's murder of his mother." He then refers to Haradatta's interpretation of the term *avara*: "Haradatta explains the term '*avara*,' translated 'men of later ages,' to mean 'men like ourselves' (*asmadādi*). In his comment on the parallel passage of Āpastamba he renders it by *idānīṃtana*, 'belonging to our times;' and in his notes on ĀpDh 1.2.5.4, he substitutes *arvācīna kaliyugavartin*, 'men of modern times living in the Kaliyuga.'" Bühler concludes: "The last explanation seems to me the most accurate, if it is distinctly kept in mind that in the times of Gautama the Kaliyuga was not a definite period of calculated duration, but the Iron Age of sin as opposed to the happier times when justice still dwelt on earth." It is clear from this note why Kane in his turn used the GDh and ĀpDh passages to show that the classical Yuga system did not yet exist at the time of the early Dharmasūtras.

Bühler's understanding of Haradatta's commentary of GDh 1.3 cannot be questioned. After Gautama (1.2) has mentioned *śīla* as one of the sources of *dharma*, Haradatta introduces a possible objection: if *śīla* is a source of *dharma*, a number of misdemeanors by famous characters —the ones cited by Bühler— are also sources of *dharma*. Haradatta then interprets 1.3 as a refutation, by Gautama, of this objection: "Such violent acts of the great are to be considered violations of the *dharma*, not *dharma*, for they were based on passion or hate." He concludes: it is not because such things have been done by them that those aspects of *śīla* are sources of law for us. The reason for this is stated in 1.4: "for people like us are weak." Haradatta quotes an anonymous stanza: "they did not commit any fault or offense (*pratyavāya*) because of their special *tejas*; but if we" —the text says: *avarako janaḥ*— "imitate them, we are ruined indeed."

Maskarin essentially agrees with Haradatta: the first two thirds of GDh 1.3 constitute a *pūrvapakṣa*, which is refuted in the last third. The main difference is the addition, within the refutation, of *na tu dṛṣṭārthe*, for which he explicitly rejects the possible interpretation as a dual —with *dharmavyatikramasāhase*— in favour of a locative singular: "when there is a visible purpose *śīla* is not a source of *dharma*." He offers two explanations for *avara*. First, *avara* means "low, overcome by hate," etc.; when one is in such a state one is not capable of separating *dharma* from *adharma*. This eventually happened even to "the great." Hence their acts, in so far as they were due to passion, hate, etc., are not a source of *dharma*. Or, *avara* refers to men of the present, Kali age; they are, by definition, unable to practice *dharma* only.

It is clear from all this that the traditional interpretation and translation of this *sūtra* go back, as far as we can verify, to Haradatta —"between AD 1100–1300, very probably nearer the earlier limit than the later one" (Kane 1930–62: 1.746), or Maskarin— "probably…later than Haradatta"; "certainly not later than 1100 AD….may be assigned to the period 900–1100 AD" (ibid.: 1.36–37). The question remains whether this interpretation was also the one intended by the author of the GDh —who "cannot be placed later than the period between 600–400 bc" (ibid.: 1.36). The fact that I raise the question implies that I believe it does not. I shall start with a few general observations.

First, *sūtra* 1.5, following the passage quoted at the beginning of this paper, clearly introduces a new chapter: *upanayanam*.

Second, *sūtra* 1.4: *tulyabalavirodhe vikalpaḥ*, has invariably and correctly been interpreted as referring to a case of conflict between two injunctions of equal strength. According to Bühler: "If (authorities) of equal force are conflicting, (either may be followed at) pleasure" (173). This *sūtra* reflects a classical view which also appears in other sources; compare, for instance, MDh 2.14:

śrutidvaidhaṃ tu yatra syāt tatra dharmāv ubhau smṛtau,
ubhāv api hi tau dharmau samyag uktau manīṣibhiḥ.

Third, the first two *sūtras* enumerate the sources of *dharma*: *vedo dharmamūlaṃ tadvidāṃ ca smṛtiśīle*. Bühler: "The Veda is the source of the sacred law, and the tradition and practice of those who know the (Veda)" (173). Compare MDh 2.6ab:

vedo 'khilo dharmamūlaṃ smṛtiśīle ca tadvidām,

to which Manu adds two other sources:

ācāraś caiva sādhūnām ātmanas tuṣṭir eva ca.

Finally, if *sūtras* 1 and 2 enumerate the sources of *dharma*, and the last *sūtra* before the long chapter on *upanayana* prescribes what to do in case of conflict between rules —two sources of *dharma*— of equal strength, the logical conclusion is that all *sūtras* before *upanayanam* deal with the sources of *dharma*, and that *sūtra* 1.3 is the connecting link between 1.1–2 and 1.4.

I shall now reproduce the text, dividing it into six separate *sūtras*:

vedo dharmamūlam
tadvidāṃ ca smṛtiśīle
dṛṣṭo dharmavyatikramaḥ
sāhasaṃ ca mahatām
[*na tu dṛṣṭārthe*] *avaradaurbalyāt*
tulyabalavirodhe vikalpaḥ.

It is surprising that no interpreter so far has been struck by the obvious connection between °*daurbalyāt* and *tulyabala*°. This connection is the pivot of my own interpretation which proceeds along the following four steps.

Step 1

"The sources of *dharma* are: the Veda, the *smṛti* and behavior of those who know the Veda."

I shall add the hypothesis that in the expression: *tadvidāṃ ca smṛtiśīle*, the genitive *tadvidām* is not connected with both elements of the *dvandva*, but with its last element only. In other words, there are three sources of *dharma*:

1. *vedaḥ*,
2. *smṛtiḥ*,
3. *vedavidāṃ śīlam.*

This interpretation finds support in MDh 2.6b, quoted earlier: *smṛtiśīle ca tadvidām.* (I shall deal elsewhere with the relations between *sūtra* and *śāstra* styles, and the reasons why I do not hesitate to interpret the "older" Gautama with the help of the "younger" Manu.) Compare also BDh 1.1.1.1–4:

upadiṣṭo dharmaḥ prativedam
tasyānu vyākhyāsyāmaḥ
smārto dvitīyaḥ
tṛtīyaḥ śiṣṭāgamaḥ.

Step 2

"One notices that the great deviate from the *dharma* and commit violent acts."

Given the rigorous structure of *sūtra* texts, I am inclined to divide this sequence, which has been traditionally regarded as a single *sūtra*, into two separate parts:

1. *dṛṣṭo dharmavyatikramaḥ*, "there are evident deviations from the Vedic *dharma*, scil. in the *smṛtis*." MDh 2.10, which defends a different opinion:

śrutis tu vedo vijñeyo dharmaśāstraṃ tu vai smṛtiḥ
te sarvārtheṣv amīmāṃsye tābhyāṃ dharmo hi nirbabhau,

may well represent another approach to *smṛti*, which already appears less explicitly in VaDh 1.4–5:

śrutismṛtivihito dharmaḥ
tadalābhe śiṣṭācāraḥ pramāṇam.

2. *sāhasaṃ ca mahatām*, "violent acts have been and are committed by the great." In other words, the *śīla* of the great occasionally violates the Vedic principles of *dharma*.

Step 3

"Deviation from *dharma* in the *smṛti* and misconduct by those who know the Veda are possible because in the enumeration of the sources of *dharma* the following one (*avara*) is each time less authoritative than the preceding one."

That means that, if a *smṛti* statement conflicts with a Vedic rule, the *smṛti* text is to be considered *dharmavyatikrama*; if a certain behavior, even of a *mahat*, conflicts with the Veda and/or *smṛti*, it is a violation (*sāhasa*) of the *dharma*. Compare Govindasvāmin's commentary on BDh 1.1.1.4, quoted earlier: *sarveṣāṃ vedamūlatve 'pi daurbalyam arthaviprakarṣād veditavyam.*

I am less concerned here with the words *na tu dṛṣṭārthe* which are not commented on by Haradatta, whereas they are by Maskarin. If they were part of the "original" GDh, it means that, as early as Gautama, *smṛti* and *śīla* were not sources of *dharma* "if there is a visible purpose involved"; this could happen in *smṛti* and *śīla* —never in the Veda (!)— because their authoritativeness is less absolute. It may also be an addition introduced by certain teachers of the GDh, in connection with the complex discussions of the Mīmāṃsakas on this subject (PMS 1.3.1–7). More critical work on the text of Gautama will be required to solve this problem. The solution will, however, not alter my interpretation which basically rests on the meaning, in this particular context, of the word *avara*. Instead of the traditional "men later in time and, therefore, less perfect (within the framework of the deteriorating *yugas*)," I take it to mean: "the subsequent items in an established list; in this case: of the sources of *dharma*."

Step 4

"If two sources of the same strength are in conflict —Veda against Veda, *smṛti* against *smṛti*, *śīla* against *śīla*— there is *vikalpa*."

The principal reason for the constant misinterpretation of *avara* in particular and GDh 1.3 in general seems to be ĀpDh 2.6.13.7–9:

> *dṛṣṭo dharmavyatikramaḥ sāhasaṃ ca pūrveṣām* [7] *teṣāṃ tejoviśeṣeṇa pratyavāyo na vidyate* (or *dṛśyate*) [8] *tad anvīkṣya prayuñjānaḥ sīdaty avaraḥ* [9].

In Bühler's translation: "Transgression of the law and violence are found amongst the ancient (sages). They committed no sin on account of the greatness of their lustre. A man of later times who seeing their (deeds) follows them, falls" (131).

It should be noted that in Āpastamba this passage occurs in a totally different context than in Gautama. It follows after the statement that a son belongs to his natural father (*bījin*), not necessarily to his mother's husband. Here again Haradatta uses the passage to give more or less the same examples he quotes in his commentary on GDh 1.3. In this he is remarkably consistent. Besides, his interpretation of *avara* in GDh 1.3 is also consistent with the use of the term in ĀpDh 1.2.5.4:

> *tasmād ṛṣayo avareṣu na jāyante niyamātikramāt*

(Bühler 19 "On account of that (transgression of the rules of studentship) no *Ṛṣis* are born amongst the men of later ages"), and ĀpDh 2.9.24.4:

> *evam avaro 'varaḥ pareṣām*

(Bühler 158 "In this manner each succeeding [generation increases the fame and heavenly bliss] of the preceding ones").

Yet , it should also be noted that the sequence:

> *dṛṣṭo dharmavyatikramaḥ,*

fits the metre of the even *pāda*s of an *anuṣṭubh*, and that, with slight alterations, the sequence:

> *sāhasaṃ ca pūrveṣām* (or *mahatām*),

would fit the metre of the odd *pāda*s. Also, what follows in Āpastamba is a perfect *anuṣṭubh*, if we replace *avaraḥ* by *avarako janaḥ*, which is the reading of the stanza in Haradatta's commentary on Gautama (quoted *supra*).

I therefore suggest that *dṛṣṭo dharmavyatikramaḥ* and *sāhasaṃ ca pūrveṣām/ mahatām* were two, not necessarily originally connected, *pāda*s of the mass of floating verses on *dharma*, which in two different Dharmasūtras could very well be used in very different contexts. It was Haradatta, or some other commentator before him, who gave the identical passages together with their —different (!)— conclusions an identical purpose.

In any event, GDh 1.3 —and the surrounding *sūtra*s— deals with the sources of *dharma*. It has nothing to do with Gautama's concept of the world ages, as suggested by the commentators, via the commentators by Bühler, via Bühler by Kane, etc.

Part Five

Anglo-Hindu and Customary Law

41

Indian Response to Anglo-Hindu Law

Any discussion of Hindu law in the 19th and 20th centuries has first to refer to the often quoted paragraph from the plan which the Committee of Circuit, with Warren Hastings as its president, drew up on August 15, 1772, and which was adopted by the President and Council at Fort William on August 21 of the same year:

> That in all Suits regarding Inheritance, Marriage, Caste and other religious Usages or Institutions, the Laws of Koran with respect to *Mahometans* and those of the Shaster with respect to *Gentoos* shall be invariably adhered to (Forrest, ed. 1910: 295–6).

We might be tempted, two hundred years after these words were written, to consider the decision of the Committee of Circuit as the sole possible and normal course of action. In reality, "the decision was far-sighted policy —not a matter of course" (Rankin 1946: 4), and it was adopted against considerable opposition.[799]

There is no doubt that some of the early British magistrates, who were eager to implement the decision of the Committee, were motivated by highly humanitarian principles. William Jones wrote in a letter to Cornwallis:

> Nothing indeed could be more obviously just, than to determine private contests according to those laws, which the parties themselves had ever considered as the rules of their conduct and engagements in civil life; nor could any thing be wiser than, by a legislative

[799] "To leave the natives entirely to their own laws would be to consign them to anarchy and confusion" (Dow 1792: ci).

> act, to assure the Hindu and Muselman subjects of Great Britain, that the private laws, which they severally hold sacred, and violation of which they would have thought the most grievous oppression, should not be superseded by a new system, of which they could have no knowledge, and which they must have considered as imposed on them by a spirit of rigour and intolerance. (Cannon 1970: 794)

Yet, as the system developed, and the problems which the English magistrates had to cope with became more numerous, their original enthusiasm was replaced by an increasing number of grievances and a general annoyance at the confused legal system they themselves had helped to create. Rankin refers to the overall lack of preparation to administer Hindu law, and recalls his own experience: "Certain I am that when I went in 1918 to India to engage upon the task, I had the smallest amount of information and no real expectation of many facts of great historical importance" (1946: Preface). The judges of the Privy Council complain that they are forced to apply a system of law the sources of which are written in a language to which they have no direct access: "In examining this question their Lordships are again at great disadvantage in not knowing Sanskrit".[800] English translations of Sanskrit texts are inadequate, and do not provide the necessary background to understand the *raison d'être* of the legal rules:

> At the same time it is quite impossible for us to feel any confidence in our opinion, upon a subject like this, when that opinion is founded upon authorities to which we have access only through translations, and when the doctrine themselves, and the reasons by which they are supported, or impugned, are drawn from the religious tradition, ancient usages, and more modern habits of the Hindoos, with which we cannot be familiar.[801]

The Courts and, following them, the jurisprudential literature moved farther and farther away from the original Sanskrit texts, which were supposed to be the basis of the Hindu law. When Burnell tried to derive help from the decisions of the Courts for his translation of the *Manusmṛti*, he wrote in despair: "As the text has been so often referred to by the courts in India, and the ultimate Court of Appeal, the Privy Council in England, it might be expected that some useful help would be got from the law reports; but this is not the case. Most of the cases decided are evidently wrongly decided" (Burnell 1884: xlv). Nelson, whose disappointment with Hindu law is well known, called it "a phantom of the brain, imagined by Sanskritists without law, and lawyers without

[800] *Balusu* v. *Balusu* (1899) 26 I.A. 113, 146 (P.C.).
[801] *Rungamma* v. *Atchamma* (1846) 4 M.I.A. 1, 97–8 (P.C.).

Sanskrit" (Nelson 1877: 2). By the time the British period came to an end, Vesey-FitzGerald pronounced the following verdict:

> There is almost universal dissatisfaction with the present state of Hindu Law. It is rigid without being certain. Judicial precedent, which in the early days of British rule was welcomed as giving the law a previously unknown publicity and an almost forgotten uniformity, is no longer a unifying influence. The multiplication of mutually independent High Courts and the enormous flood of law reports have made it a source of confusion and uncertainty. The case law has become a luxuriant jungle where it is impossible to see the wood for the trees. The evil is far greater than it is in England —or probably even in the United States; and it is lamented by everybody, even by the editors of law reports whose industry does so much to aggravate it. (1947: 2)

Examples of British disenchantment with Hindu law in the 19th and 20th centuries generally, and detailed criticisms of its constituent elements could easily be multiplied. They are, however, not the main purpose of this contribution, which intends to bring out certain Indian reactions to Hindu law as administered by the colonial power.

The least one can say about 19th and 20th century Hindu law is that it was complex. Anyone who is familiar with the introductory chapters of the treatises on Hindu law during the British period —and after Independence— knows the intricacies of their discussions of the sources of law. Anglo-Hindu jurisprudence recognized the traditional sources of law, from the Vedas, via the Dharmasūtras and Dharmaśāstras to the numerous Dharmanibandhas; to these should be added the Arthaśāstra, the Mīmāṃsā rules of interpretation, etc. However, the British introduced a number of changes, and created a structure which every Hindu had to regard as highly unorthodox. Thus, in case of a conflict between the *śruti* and the *smṛti*, the *smṛti* prevailed instead of the *śruti*, contradicting the orthodox view; similarly, in case of a conflict between a *smṛti* and a commentary or *nibandha*, the latter overruled the former; "rules of law" were separated from prescriptions of a religious nature, and became the only rules to be applied in the Courts. Moreover, all these written sources were, under certain circumstances, overruled by unwritten custom.

These changes within the traditional system were, then, supplemented by a number of elements which were totally foreign to Hindu law and Hindu civilization. For all practical purposes, "Hindu law" was implemented only insofar as the Sanskrit texts were available in English translations. The concepts of justice, equity, and good conscience, based upon principles applicable in English society, were often invoked to justify deviations from the original Hindu law. Recognition of judicial precedents as a source of law involved application of the rules of *stare decisis* and *communis error facit ius*, even in cases in which the earlier decisions evidently violated basic principles of Hindu law. Finally, several legislative Acts explicitly introduced fundamental innovations "notwithstanding any rule of Hindu law or custom to the contrary." Many will, therefore, subscribe to Galanter's evaluation: "The development of the modern Indian legal system represents a remarkable instance of the virtually total displacement of a major intellectual and institutional complex in a highly developed civilization with one largely or foreign origin or at least inspiration" (Galanter 1968–69: 215. See also Galanter 1968: 65–91).

The neutral observer can very well understand the reasons for disenchantment with the system on the part of the British. More surprising is the fact that many Indians not only accepted the system as such, but were prepared actively to defend the changes within the traditional system, and the foreign elements introduced into it from English —or Roman— law. Assuredly, not all Indians agreed with the Hindu law as it emerged in the 19th and 20th centuries. The discussions on the Hindu Code Bill saw an active revivalist movement in favor of pure orthodoxy. Besides, a number of objections became stereotyped; for instance, it has been said again and again that the British intervention halted the natural growth of Hindu law, and references to "the petrifying influence of the British Courts of justice"[802] frequently occur in Indian writings. Yet, these understandable objections are countervailed by a number of less expected justifications. I shall give a few examples of various types of justifications, and of the different ways in which they operate.

The most common manifestation of Indians accepting the principles of Anglo-Hindu law are the general jurisprudential manuals composed by Indian authors. When it comes to discussing the relative value of the manifold sources of Hindu law, there are no major differences between treatises written by Western authors, and textbooks prepared by Indian jurists such as S.V. Gupte, D.F. Mulla, G.D. Banerjee, R. Sarvadhikari, and others.

The first type of conscious justification of elements which were not inherent in the traditional Hindu law does not attempt to

[802] Govinda Das, in the preliminary note to the edition of the *Paribhāṣāprakāśa* of the *Vīramitrodaya* (1906: 5). Similar remarks occur in the introductions to the classical treatises (e.g., Mulla 1970: 65). Progressive jurists use this argument to prove that Hindu law, which "has always been dynamic and progressive" in the past, again needs "such changes and modifications...as would bring it in conformity with the felt necessities of the present times and would receive the wholehearted approval of the enlightened social conscience amongst the Hindus" (thus P.B. Gajendragadkar; see Mahajan 1966: 301–2). Cf. J.D.M. Derrett 1968: 315.

deny their foreign origin, but endorses them as such. The principles of justice, equity, and good conscience (Derrett 1963: 114–53), for instance, have been accepted by some, not because they were an integral part of the original Hindu law, but insofar as they incorporated basic concepts of law anywhere in the world, and, therefore, also applicable in India:

> I am of the opinion that the application of the doctrine by the courts of justice in British India need not depend for its authority upon any rule of Hindu law any more than upon any rule of Muhammadan law. The maxim, which owes its origin to Roman jurisprudence, rests upon those principles of justice, equity and good conscience, which we are bound to administer even in dealing with questions of this nature, whenever the substantive rules of the native law furnish no clear and unmistakable guide.[803]

The classical example of an Indian jurist stressing the desirability of giving Hindu law an international background, is Asutosh Mookerjee. In a lecture presented at the Banaras department of legal studies, on August 4, 1923, he insisted that the students read the works of foreign legal authors, acquaint themselves with the principles of foreign legal systems, and make use of this international knowledge in their own legal practice (Mookerjee 1923, especially 50–1; cf. Sinha 1966: 37–8).

Readiness to accept and justify elements of foreign —or universal— law within the Hindu system inevitably led a number of jurists to emphasize less the foreign or universal origin of these elements than to accentuate the basically Indian nature of the new legal system. One way of doing so was to maintain that the extraneous elements had been modified to a large extent and adapted to the legal system in which they were introduced:

> It would be true to say that the foundation of all law in India, civil or criminal, is English law as constituted by the common law and statute law of England and the judicial decisions of its courts. Nevertheless, the principles drawn from these sources have been largely and in numerous matters been subjected to changes to adapt them to Indian conditions so that notwithstanding the main sources from which it is drawn Indian jurisprudence can still be rightly called Indian "in its structure and operation." (Setalvad 1966: 36)

However, in most cases the foreign origin is simply negated, and the foreign element is vindicated as an integral part of the original Hindu law as it existed before the arrival of the British.

[803] Mahmood J., in *Ganga* v. *Lekhraj* (1887) 9 All. 253, 295.

Mr. Justice Chandavarkar more or less formulated the general principle that made this legal fiction possible:

> Hindu law is a jurisprudence by itself and contains, within limits, all the principles necessary for application to any given case … The Hindu law-givers have not indeed laid down a rule in express terms on every conceivable point. But having provided texts for such cases as had arisen before or in their time, they left others to be determined either with reference to certain general principles laid down by them in clear terms or by the analogy of similar cases, governed by express texts.[804]

This principle has been applied in numerous individual cases, and in different ways, as illustrated by the following examples. The woman's right of surrender is generally considered to be "a creation of judicial decisions" and to have been "unknown to Hindu law" (Gharpure 1931: 426).[805] Yet, Asutosh Mookerjee — whose international approach to law has been quoted earlier— has tried to show that the theory of relinquishment finds its origin in a text by Kātyāyana quoted in Jīmūtavāhana's *Dāyabhāga* 11.1.56.[806] KS 921 reads:

> *aputrā śayanaṃ bhartuḥ pālayantī gurau sthitā*
> *bhuñjītā maraṇāt kṣāntā dāyādā ūrdhvam āpnuyuḥ,*
>
> "Let the childless widow, preserving unsullied the bed of her lord, and abiding with her venerable protector, enjoy with moderation the property until her death. After her let the heirs take it."[807]

According to Sir Asutosh this rule is "comprehensive enough to include not merely the case of the death of the widow, but all cases where her right ceases," and the treatises on jurisprudence reflect his opinion:

> …it has been settled that a Hindu widow can renounce the estate in favour of the nearest reversioner if there be only one or of all the reversioners nearest in degree if more than one at the moment; that is to say, she can, so to speak, by a voluntary act bring about

[804] N.G. Chandavarkar, J., in *Kalgavda Tavanappa* v. *Somappa* (1909) 30 Bom. 669, 680. Cf. K. Subha Rao, on December 18, 1966: "The Hindu conception of rule of law is all-comprehensive. The supremacy of Dharma was the central conception of the earlier Hindu political thought. The expression is comprehensive enough to take in law, justice, tradition, custom, righteous conduct and social justice" (Mahajan 1967: II, 3–4).

[805] For these and similar interpretations, see Chaudhary 1961: 71 sqq.

[806] *Debi Pradad* v. *Golap Bhagat* (1913) 40 Cal. 721, 772 (F.B.)

[807] Colebrooke's translation. Cf. Kane 1933: 325. The translation is open to discussion on a few details, but is adequate for our purpose.

> her own civil death. The foundation of the doctrine is the text of Kātyāyana as explained by Jīmūtavāhana. (Aiyar 1950: 785–6)

The maxim of *factum valet*, which "is found in every current English book of legal maxims" (Derrett 1958: 281), and which "in India…started upon its career almost at the commencement of the British period" (ibid.: 294), corresponds to a Sanskrit maxim formulated in India long before the arrival of the Europeans:

> It is a maxim of Hindu law [*Dāyabhāga* 2.30] that "a thing cannot be made otherwise by a hundred texts," that is to say, a fact cannot be altered by a hundred texts. This maxim —one of the Mimamsa rules of interpretation— has played an important part in the interpretation of the texts of Hindu law, particularly those relating to the law of adoption and marriage. (Gupte 1947: 50)

The maxim in *Dāyabhāga* 2.30 is: *vacanaśatenāpi vastuno 'nyathāka-raṇāśakteḥ*. It is quoted there to justify Jīmūtavāhana's interpretation of two passages from the *Vyāsasmṛti*. Although these passages seem to forbid the sale or gift of certain types of property, they do not really invalidate the transactions. They merely refer to cases in which the seller or donor incurs *adharma* because of the transaction which is harmful to the family. The fact (*vastu*) is that they own the property, and that they therefore have a right to dispose of it as they desire (*Dāyabhāga* 2.27: *yatheṣṭa-viniyogārhatvalakṣaṇasya svatvasya*).

The vindication of the principles of justice, equity, and good conscience as foreign but universal elements has been cited earlier in this article. Others claim that they too were implicit in traditional Hindu law:

> The rule of equity and good conscience is implicit in the dicta of Manu and Yājñavalkya on the "feeling of satisfaction, which the good set" (MDh II.6) and what one finds to one's liking (MDh II.12 and YDh I.7). To guard against caprice being taken as equivalent to conscience, the commentators explain that the satisfaction should be that which only those who are both learned in the Vedas and righteous feel, thereby relieving each man of the privilege of deciding what he should do according to his likes and dislikes. Medhātithi points out (ed. Jhā I, pp. 68–9) that the trustworthy character of such learned and good men is the guarantee of its not being misused. "When the learned and good feel satisfied as to the righteousness of an action, it must be taken as right, because such men will never feel satisfied with anything that is wrong." (Rangaswami Aiyangar 1941: 152–3)

The three stanzas referred to in this quotation deal with the sources of the *dharma*. They are, besides the *śruti* and the *smṛti*:

sadācāraḥ (MDh 2.12, YDh 1.7; MDh 2.6: *ācāraḥ sādhūnām*), *svasya priyam ātmanaḥ* (MDh 2.12, YDh 1.7; MDh 2.6: *ātmanas tuṣṭiḥ*), *śīlaṃ tadvidām* (= *vedavidām*) (MDh 2.6), and *samyaksaṃkalpajaḥ kāmaḥ* (YDh 1.7). The commentators have elaborated on these terms to such an extent, that I cannot even summarize their discussions here. It will be enough to say that the terms can easily be interpreted in different ways, and that "justice, equity, and good conscience" is the latest addition to the discussion. Although Rangaswami Aiyangar tries to vindicate the traditional character of justice, equity, and good conscience, he can evidently not agree with the overruling authority they have sometimes been given in the Courts. He continues with the following warning:

> But equity and good conscience cannot over-ride clear law or revealed text. This is made clear by Viśvarūpa (on YDh I.7) who points out that the satisfaction which one feels should not be in action which runs counter to Vedic injunction, or smṛti or is due merely to fidgets. Kullūka (on MDh II.6) lays down that "self-satisfaction" is authoritative only in regard to matters in which an option is open, following the *Mitākṣarā* which rules that the rule of satisfaction applies only to cases in which there are several lawful alternatives open, one of which has to be chosen. This is also the view of the *Smṛticandrikā*. (Samskārakāṇḍa, 5)

The Caste Disabilities Removal Act of 1850 was the first in a long series of enactments by the legislature, which became additional sources of law. There is no doubt, that "most of them are in the direction of reform of Hindu law and some of them supersede Hindu law in certain classes of cases" (Aiyar 1950: 73). Yet, this kind of legislation has not only been accepted but justified as a source of law which was not unknown to the original system:

> As a matter of fact the modern text-writers of the Anglo-Hindu jurisprudence who are most vociferous in subjecting the Sovereign to the jurisdiction of our Smṛtis seem to have entirely forgotten the four heads of law mentioned in our ancient Smṛtis applicable to causes arising for decision before a judicial tribunal and their relative authority in cases of mutual conflict. The superior position assigned to a Sovereign's command as compared with rules of justice, Common law and customary law is only consistent with the theory that the Sovereign represents the ultimate source of law. (Sankararama Sastri 1926: 159–60)

The "four heads of law" are those mentioned in the NS (*Mātṛkā* 1.10):

> *dharmaś ca vyavahāraś ca caritraṃ rājaśāsanam*
> *catuṣpād vyavahāro 'yam uttaraḥ pūrvabādhakāḥ.*

Jolly's translation: "Virtue, a judicial proceeding, documentary evidence, and an edict from the king are the four feet of a lawsuit. *Each following one is superior to the one previously named*" (Jolly 1889: 7, italics mine), seems to confirm that the royal edict supersedes all other sources of law. In addition to the fact that a royal edict and legislation are not synonymous, I have shown elsewhere (Rocher 1964: 217–35, especially 224–8) that Nārada's text implies much more than that, and that it does not refer to anything comparable to the king's legislative power.

In case of justice, equity, and good conscience, Rangaswami Aiyangar made an attempt to keep them within "clear law or revealed text." This was, of course, not possible in the case of modern legislation. Hence, Sankararama Sastri first refers to legislation in conformity with textbooks or custom, but he also casually admits the other alternative in which this condition might not be fulfilled:

> He may be a source of law either because of express legislation or because of recognition given by him by way of enforcement of rules already set forth in text-books or embodied in the customs of the land.[808]

Justifying Anglo-Hindu case law was perhaps the most difficult task of all. It was hardly possible to refer to any element of classical Hindu law as its historical predecessor. Yet, in this case too its modern or foreign character has been denied:

> ...case law did not find a place in the judicial system of the Hindus presumably because the decisions of the Hindu courts, mostly private tribunals, were never recorded in writing. (Banerjee 1923: 14)

The word "presumably" is important. It shows that the author merely wants to put forth a hypothesis. The interesting thing is that he did feel the necessity to formulate such a hypothesis.

I do not wish to examine in this paper why the general public in India received Anglo-Hindu law so favorably and made such a frequent use of it, nor do I want to discuss the reasons why the legal profession attracted so many able young men. I am mainly concerned with the attitude of Indian legal theoreticians toward the new system, and the reasons why *they* were prepared to defend it even in cases where this proved to be difficult.

[808] Continuation of the previous quotation (i.e. Sankararama Sastri 1926: 159–60). Others have approved of modern legislation for different reasons: "It is the bounden duty of the Legislature, to do what it is now doing in the interests of humanity and of the worldly interests of the communities committed to its charge, and for such a purpose as the present to disregard if need be the Hindu Shastras" (thus K.T. Telang; see West 1894: 120).

It would be a mistake to think that those who defended the new legal system failed to see the problem. They realized that Anglo-Hindu law deviated in many respects from "the law of the Shaster" which it was supposed to revive, and they asked themselves the question to what extent they should lend their support to the new tendencies:

> Some of the decisions on Hindu law, though professing to be founded on the written law, have, either from an imperfect understanding of that law, or from a designed non-compliance with its purely religious injunctions, deviated completely from the original rule; and the question arises, how far they are entitled to be followed in preference to the original authorities. (Ibid.: 15)

The answer to this question is informative, and deserves to be quoted in full:

> While, on the one hand, lawyers who set a high value on the uniformity and consistency of the law, maintain that these decisions ought to be followed; on the other hand scholars who have critically studied the subject, and who place an equally high value on the correctness of the law, protest against the perpetuation of error. No doubt, there are arguments in favour of both ideas. Where a decision at variance with the original authorities stands alone and has not been followed, there will be no inconvenience in departing from it when the error is discovered. But where a decision, though erroneous, has been followed as a precedent in a series of cases, the solution of the question involves some difficulty. For, though it is wrong to perpetuate an error, it would hardly be right to rectify the error by unsettling the law and overruling a precedent which might have long been the basis of men's expectations and conduct. Where there has been a uniform current of decisions, notwithstanding that they may be erroneous, the reasons for following them will, on the whole, be found to preponderate, unless the error appears to be so clear as to lead to a fair presumption that the rule laid down in the decisions could not have been uniformly accepted as settled law by the profession or the public. But the question is one of degree. What is meant by a uniform current of decisions, and how clear the error involved must be in order to justify departure from established precedents, are questions for the determination of which no hard-and-fast rule can be laid down. (Ibid.: 15–6)

In short, the Indian's attitude toward Anglo-Hindu law depends on the angle from which he views it, and the theoretical jurist's angle is totally different from that of the legal practitioner. Although "the question is one of degree," the uniformity and consistency of legal practice were given the highest priority, and the jurist was prepared to construe his legal theories accordingly.

42

*Can a Murderer Inherit his Victim's Estate? British Responses to Troublesome Questions in Hindu Law**

Some time in 1914 Chanbasava, a widow from Dharwar District —at the Southern end of what was then the Bombay Presidency— had a quarrel with her late husband Ramanna's brother's son, Hanmappa.[809] Hanmappa filed a suit to claim that he was Chanbasava's —and her late husband's— adopted son. He failed to establish his claim in court, and, within two days, "revenged himself for his failure" by murdering Chanbasava. Hanmappa was convicted of murder and, under Section 302 of the Indian Penal Code, sentenced to transportation for life.

The decision of the criminal court did not, however, solve the civil issue. Hanmappa, the murderer, was also heir to Chanbasava's estate, and he had two sisters, Kenchava and Gangava, who would inherit if Hanmappa was not disqualified as heir to Chanbasava. At the same time there was another nephew, Ramanna's sister's son, Girimallappa, who would inherit, and he alone, if Hanmappa was disqualified. Girimallappa went to the civil courts to establish his claim.

*This text represents a slightly adapted, and annotated, version of the Presidential Address, delivered at the 196th meeting of the American Oriental Society, on March 11, 1986, in New Haven Connecticut.

809

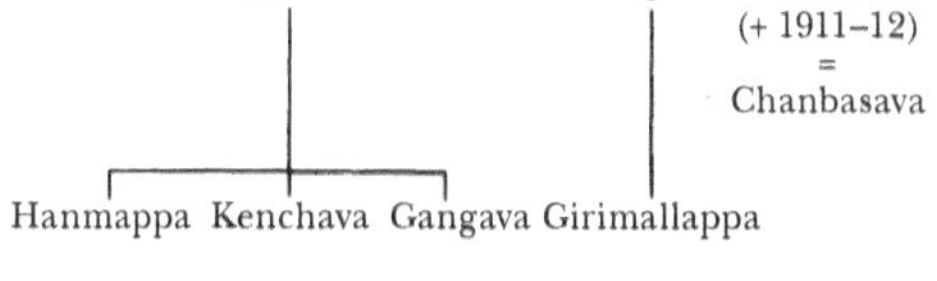

The Anglo-Indian civil courts were faced with the problem: can a murderer inherit his victim's estate? or, even if he loses all beneficial rights personally, is he, for the sake of the inheritance, existent or non-existent? The case was decided by the First Class Subordinate Judge at Dharwar, H.V. Chinmulgund. It was appealed to the High Court in Bombay, before Chief Justice Sir Norman Macleod and Mr. Justice Charles Fawcett. The decision of the Bombay High Court was appealed again, before the Judicial Committee of the Privy Council, at Westminster in London. Their final decision was delivered in 1924, ten years after the murder.

Before describing what happened, in the course of that decade, in the courts of Dharwar, Bombay, and London, and to set the stage for an analysis of the different grounds on which the three decisions were based in the case known as *Kenchava v. Girimallappa Channappa*,[810] I must give a brief account of earlier developments in the history of Hindu law.

Within the long story of the gradual takeover of the administration of justice by the East India Company in the territories under their control,[811] I wish to single out one particular year and one particular event. The year was 1772, the event the adoption, in Calcutta, of a Judicial Plan sponsored by the Governor of Bengal, Warren Hastings. The Judicial Plan of 1772 said, among other things:

> In all suits regarding inheritance, marriage, caste and other religious usages and institutions, the laws of the Koran with respect to Mahomedans and those of the Shaster with respect to the Gentoos shall invariably be adhered to.

I will not deal with the Indian Muslims and the way in which the laws of the Koran were administered to them. I will concentrate on the Hindus, and on Warren Hastings' intent to administer to them the laws of the Shaster, "Shaster" meaning the entire body of the ancient Sanskrit Dharmaśāstras, plus the more recent, voluminous commentaries written on them.

Admittedly, not everyone was enthusiastic about the Judicial Plan. There were warnings, in the same year 1772, that:

> to leave the natives to their own laws would be to consign them to anarchy and confusion...It is therefore absolutely necessary for

[810] For the relevant law reports, see *Kenchava v. Girimallappa Channappa* (1921) 45 Bom. 768; (1924) 51 I.A. 368; A.I.R. 1924 P.C. 209.

[811] For general bibliography on this period, see Derrett 1969. Cf. also, recently, Fisch 1983. Abbreviated references to law reports in this article: All., Bom., Cal., Mad. = Indian Law Reports of the High Courts of Allahabad, Bombay, Calcutta, and Madras, respectively; A.I.R. = All-India Reporter; I.A. = Indian Appeals; M.I.A. = Moore's Indian Appeals.

> the peace and prosperity of the country that the laws of England in so far as they do not oppose prejudice and usages which cannot be relinquished by the natives, should prevail. The measure, besides its equity, is calculated to preserve that influence which conquerors must possess to retain their power. (Dow: *Enquiry into the State of Bengal*: cxliii, quoted by Rankin 1946: 3)

Yet, most Englishmen involved in the administration of justice in India accepted the challenge of the Judicial Plan. A case in point was Sir William Jones, himself a Puisne Judge in the Bengal Supreme Court. In a letter to the Governor General, Lord Cornwallis, on March 19, 1788, wrote:

> Nothing indeed could be more obviously just, than to determine private contests according to those laws, which the parties themselves had ever considered as the rules of their conduct and engagements in civil life; nor could any thing be wiser than, by a legislative act, to assure the Hindu and Muselman subjects of Great Britain, that the private laws, which they severally hold sacred, and a violation of which they would have thought the most grievous oppression, should not be superseded by a new system, of which they could have no knowledge, and which they must have considered as imposed on them by a spirit of rigour and intolerance. (Cannon vol. 2, 1970: 794)

Sir William Jones and others like him are entitled to our admiration for their liberal approach. They tried hard, and, in many ways, they succeeded. Yet, the actual implementation of the 1772 Judicial Plan was a task of epic proportions. What I intend to do in this address is, first, briefly to present some of the factors that made the implementation of the Judicial Plan such a difficult task. Subsequently I will concentrate on some of the reasons why Anglo-Indian law eventually became very different from "the laws of the Shaster" which it honestly tried to apply in the courts. At that time I will return to the case of the murderer Hanmappa from Dharwar District.

If there was any dissatisfaction or discomfort with the system, these feelings were, almost exclusively, unilateral. It was not the Hindus who were unhappy with the working of the Anglo-Indian courts. Indeed not. As far as the litigants were concerned, they resorted to the law courts in droves; and, as I have shown in an article in the Journal of this Society a few years ago, Hindu lawyers and jurists on their part made every attempt to interpret any deviation from the *śāstra*s, however blatant, as an integral part of the original scheme (Rocher 1972). It was the British, mainly the British judges and lawyers directly involved in the administration of Hindu law, who became disillusioned with the system as it developed, under their auspices, in the courts.

Some Englishmen opted for the easiest explanation. They laid the responsibility for the deficiencies in Anglo-Indian law squarely at the feet of the Hindus.

First, as I indicated earlier, the Indians did take their disputes to the courts. In the opinion of some Englishmen they not only did so, they overdid it. One English judge used this argument, in a pamphlet published in 1853, to defend his own performance and that of his confreres on the bench. "It is to be remembered," he said, "that the Hindoos are the most litigious people in the world" (Holloway 1853: 3). The pamphlet went on to say that, for sure, there were a few compulsive litigants in England as well, but there was no comparison: "here the love of litigation is the feeling of a whole people" (ibid.: 15).

Second, not only did Hindus take every minor quarrel to court, not only did they appeal every decision of the lower courts as often and as long as they could; in addition there was the problem of:

> the utter demoralization of the people, high and low, rich and poor. Perjury and forgery are regarded, not only as no crime, but as a perfectly commendable means of gaining a cause. (Ibid.: 21)

As far as the parties to lawsuits were concerned,

> we are to guess amid the perjuries and forgeries of *both sides* at something which we may assume to be facts and of which the legal consequences are apparent; we have in short to strike the balance of probabilities between lies of greater or less magnitude. (Baynes 1853: 74; cf. Norton 1853: 4)

Even if their case was a very strong one, they were never satisfied with adducing genuine evidence only, with the result that:

> we can never in this country confidently take the testimony of one particular witness as a starting point, and say "here at least we have the truth, here is something solid to rest upon." Even men who pass for the best of men, will never hesitate at colouring the facts, and very rarely hesitate in making a purely false statement in aid of the person for whom they are called...After committing a gross act of perjury, he does not sink, in the least, in the eyes of his countrymen. Far from it; the whole transaction is regarded as perfectly legitimate, and if the cause is gained, or the obnoxious individual punished, he will be decidedly raised in their estimation. (Holloway 1853: 21–22)

In addition to the litigants and their witnesses there was one other category of Indians whose role in the judicial process aroused much suspicion. These were the so-called court pandits. It is important to remember that the law to be administered to the Hindus was the law of the *śāstras*. The *śāstras*, however, were written in Sanskrit, and no Englishman knew Sanskrit at that time. The Englishmen who were called upon to sit as judges in lawsuits among Hindus were, in fact, given the task of administering laws the language of which was unknown to them. That was the reason for the appointment, in the Anglo-Indian courts, of court pandits. They were the only members of the court who had access to the Sanskrit law books. They were asked in each case, to consult the *śāstras*, and write down a *vyavasthā* "decision," which was to serve as the basis for the sentence to be pronounced by the British judge. Confidence in the pandits soon diminished. First, the judges were incapable of verifying the answers the pandits provided them with: "we have seen too much of them, not to be satisfied, that they are the authors of many of the irreconcileable contradictions of Hindu law" (Anon., *Quarterly Oriental Magazine*, 1825: 173). Second, the suspicion that the pandits could not always be trusted became widespread. It shows even in a letter from someone like Sir William Jones.

> If we give judgement only from the opinions of the native lawyers and scholars, we can never be sure, that we have not been deceived by them. It would be absurd and unjust to pass an indiscriminate censure on a considerable body of men; but my experience justifies me in declaring, that I could not with an easy conscience concur in a decision, merely on the written opinion of native lawyers, in any cause in which they could have the remotest interest in misleading the court; nor, how vigilant soever we might be, would it be very difficult for them to mislead us. (Cannon vol. 2, 1970: 795)

So far for the criticisms aimed at the Hindus. At the same time, the British were also acutely aware of their own deficiencies in making the system coherent and successful. One lawyer in the Madras Presidency around 1850 complained bitterly about his British compatriots who were acting as judges.

> Throughout the length and breadth of the whole of this Presidency those who occupy the judicial Bench are totally incompetent to the decent fulfillment of their duties. (Norton 1853: 4)

According to him it was the system itself that was at fault, a system in which there was no demarcation between the Judicial and Revenue Departments; a system that considered collecting taxes far more important than rendering justice; a system, therefore, that appointed its best representatives tax collectors, and employed its least deserving members as judges. "It is mainly incompetent Collectors that are turned into judges. In other words, the judges are some kind of 'Sub Collectors'" (ibid.: 5).

Whatever the merits of this sweeping accusation,[812] there was another, far more serious inadequacy on the part of the British, an inadequacy of a linguistic nature, namely the inability of the judiciary to deal with the languages of the land generally, and the language of the law codes in particular.

As far as the local languages are concerned, imagine a will written by a Bengali, in Bengali, but submitted to the Calcutta High Court in English translation. The case I am referring to did not even raise a point of law. It was a simple question of fact: if one particular sentence in the English meant one thing, it was valid; if it meant something else, it was void. The Bench was composed of one Englishman and one Bengali. They sent for the original, Bengali will. The Bengali judge studied the text and concluded that the language of the clause was void. The court even sought the opinion of another experienced Bengali lawyer, who concurred with his countryman. The Calcutta High Court consequently declared the clause void. The defeated party, however, appealed to the Privy Council. Their Lordships at Westminster examined the English translation only and construed the wording of the disputed clause by the rules applicable to English wills. They declared the clause valid and reversed the decision that had so painstakingly been reached in Calcutta (Petherem 1898: 392–93 [Contd. 1899: 173–85; 1900: 77–87, 392–96]).

Not knowing the mother tongues of the parties was one thing; being ignorant of the language of the law books —Sanskrit— was another. Not only was this ignorance far more general; it was also more important and had more far-reaching consequences. I have already referred to the resulting appointment of court pandits and the disappointment of the British with them.

Consider a situation in which the decision of a lawsuit depended to a large extent on the correct interpretation of a passage from the *Vasiṣṭha Dharmasūtra*. By the time the case reached the Privy Council, the meaning of the text had been discussed at great length, back and forth, first in a subordinate court, and again in a High Court. Various interpretations had been defended and rejected. The only thing the Privy Council could do, at the time they had to proclaim an interpretation of their own, was to prefix it with the statement: "In examining this question their Lordships are again at great disadvantage in not knowing Sanskrit."[813]

One good result came out of this situation, though. Some very few —and very courageous— Englishmen decided to seize the

[812] It provoked the responses by Baynes and Holloway which I quoted earlier.

[813] *Sri Balusu Gurlingaswami v. Sri Balusu Ramalakshmamma* (1899) 26 I.A. 113, 146; 22 Mad. 398, 425; 21 All. 460, 489.

bull by the horns. They decided to study Sanskrit for themselves and to translate some of the major Sanskrit law books into English. Perhaps only Indologists can appreciate the magnitude of such a task: no dictionaries; no grammars, at least not of the type Englishmen were used to; teacher with whom they hardly had any means of communication, and whose teaching methods were as foreign as the language itself. Yet, they persevered, and the Sanskrit *śāstras* became available in English translations.

To be sure, it was always possible for an Indian lawyer who knew Sanskrit to place before a nonplussed judge a quotation from a *śāstra* that had not been translated. Even in a session of the Privy Council, in 1940, it happened that "there was a mild flutter when an Indian member of the Judicial Committee of the Privy Council made citations in Sanskrit in a judgment he pronounced" (Rangaswami Aiyangar 1941: 9). As a rule, however, it was the English translations of the śāstric texts that became the law books of the Anglo-Indian courts, in all areas of civil law listed in Warren Hastings' Judicial Plan of 1772. In addition to Sir William Jones' *Laws of Menu* (1794), there was Henry Thomas Colebrooke's *Two Treatises on the Hindu Law of Inheritance* (1810). In this volume Colebrooke translated Jīmūtavāhana's *Dāyabhāga* which became *the* law book on inheritance in Bengal, and a section of Vijñāneśvara's *Mitākṣarā* which became *the* law book on inheritance for the rest of India.

There were translations available then, but, how good were these translations? how useful were they? how comfortable were British judges with them when it came to solving intricate legal problems? The answers to these questions reveal that, notwithstanding the availability of an ever increasing number of Hindu law books in translation, and, in many cases, because of these translations, the Anglo-Indian courts steered Hindu law farther and farther away from the intents and purposes of the original Sanskrit *śāstras*.[814]

In the first place, however good these translations were, considering the state of Sanskrit studies at that time, they were bound to be less than perfect. There are a few instances where Colebrooke misunderstood the intricate reasoning of the authors of the *Mitākṣarā* and *Dāyabhāga*.[815] There also are a few cases in which Colebrooke's

[814] For a rare opinion that criticizing the translations "appears to us wholly unmerited, and, if implicitly credited, calculated to do much more harm," see Anon., *Quarterly Oriental Magazine*, 1825: 177.

[815] See, for instance, the passage from the *Mitākṣarā* discussed by Lord Hobhouse, after his statement: "It is not surprising that conflicts of opinion should have arisen, seeing that the texts of the Mitakshara itself, as translated by Colebrooke, whose translation has long been accepted as correct, are literally in

English text says exactly the opposite of what the Sanskrit authors wanted to convey. It has happened that Indian lawyers pointed out these mistakes, and tried to have the English translation set aside in favor of the original Sanskrit text.[816] Invariably, they failed. The courts conceded that an error might have been made, that the same error might even have been made several times. Yet, in such cases they cited the Latin maxim: *communis error facit ius* "a common error makes law." The principle of *stare decisis* "to stand by what has been decided," which had been imported from Europe, and the search for consistency in legal decisions, overruled the need for conformity with the Sanskrit *śāstras*.[817]

The result was that the law reports remained replete with references to the *śāstras*. Yet, in an overwhelming majority of cases, these references were not to the *śāstras* directly, but to the *śāstras* as they were quoted and with the interpretations they were given in earlier court decisions. In other words, Anglo-Indian law became case law.

The second type of deviation from the *śāstras* resulted from the fact that the British soon came to the conclusion that:

> there is hardly any question arising out of the *Hindoo* law, that may not be either affirmed or denied, under the sanction of texts, which are held to be equal in point of authority.[818]

Inevitably, when the law books contradicted themselves, a choice had to be made. One way of selecting between contradictory solutions offered by the *śāstras* was to investigate current practice: which solution in the law books was accepted practice, for instance, in the province or town the parties came from, or within the caste to which they belonged? In all such cases the courts followed the solutions supported by custom, and the other solutions were set aside. This was reasonable enough.

conflict with one another." *Rao Balwant Singh v. Rani Kishor* (1898) 25 I.A. 54, 67–69; 20 All. 267, 284–85.

[816] E.g., in *Apaji Narhar v. Ramchandra* (1892) 16 Bom. 29, the majority and, hence, the Full Bench followed Colebrooke's translation of the *Mitākṣarā* (1.5.3), and answered a question on partition negatively, even though one judge who knew Sanskrit pointed out that the translation was incorrect and that the original text —and a translation by Julius Jolly— required a positive answer. Said Sargent, C. J.: "We should not be justified in unsettling the law, by overruling the current of authorities by which for so many years the law appears to have been settled, and in accordance with which it appears to have been generally understood and acted upon" (78).

[817] For *stare decisis* in support of wrong precedents, see Derrett 1968: 314.

[818] Macnaghten 1824: Preface, iii. Macnaghten's book carries the following motto on the title page: "*Misera est servitus, ubi jus est vagum aut incertum.*"

In fact, however, it so happened that, in most cases, the British took it upon themselves to make the selection, with the hope that their decision would *become* accepted practice, and that, for the sake of consistency, their decision would become a precedent for similar cases in the future. Faced with the dilemma that, on the one hand, the law books of the Hindus were contradictory and therefore "neutralize the authority of each other," and, on the other hand, "their own is the only law to be administered to them," Macnaghten drew the following conclusion:

> It is our duty to select such parts of the code, as may be most beneficial to the people. These will be confirmed into use, by their undeviating application to cases, which may call for decisions in our Courts of Justice; we may command consistency, at least; we may hope, in time, to cleanse the system of its exaggerated corruptions, and to defecate the impurity of ages. (1824: vi)

There was a third reason why Anglo-Indian law deviated from the law of the *śāstra*s. In the treatise just quoted Macnaghten also made the following confession: "I admit that there is much in the books, which is quite unintelligible" (ibid.). There is, indeed, no doubt —and the British were acutely aware of it— that most of them were totally unprepared for their task. A former Chief Justice of Bengal summarized for the fate of his confreres as follows:

> I have been impressed at times with the peculiarity of the fate of very learned and able friends of mine who, as the reward of exceptional knowledge and skill in the business matters of England and Scotland, are suddenly required to turn a large part of their attention to Indian appeals. What, at first, do they think of them or make of them? What is their approach?...Not many people in this country have any settled notion what we are doing in India administering law to Indians, nor have any means of readily acquiring a well-founded notion of how we come to be doing so or of the principles we apply. Certain I am that when I went in 1918 to India to engage upon the task, I had the smallest amount of information and no real explanation of many facts of great historical importance.[819]

In addition to arriving unprepared, the judges' lifestyle while in India was not such that they would learn to know much about the people. Said one of them:

[819] Rankin 1946: Preface. One of Norton's objections against the system —see above— was that "there is no school for training even those who are primarily destined for the judicial line; and the only means they have of learning law, procedure, practice, evidence, is by trying their 'prentice hand' upon cases which come before them when they first take their seat upon the Bench" (1853: 8).

> The chief administrators in our vast Indian empire are so completely severed from the bulk of the population by colour, race, language, religion, and material interests, that they are often, if not habitually, in complete ignorance of the most patent facts occurring around them. (Perry 1853: Preface, iii)

Yet, once they were in the court rooms, they had to decide some of the most private concerns in the lives of Hindus.

Far more important, however, than their general ignorance of India and Indian life, was, as Macnaghten pointed out, the fact that there was much in the law books that seemed to them unintelligible. These were, indeed, not the kind of law books the British judges were used to. I will illustrate my point with one sentence from Colebrooke's translation of the *Dāyabhāga*. The question is whether a son can request partition of the joint family estate when the father is not yet dead but no longer capable of—or interested in— having other children. The translation reads as follows:

> Here also, to show, that the sons' property in their father's wealth arises from such causes as the extinction of his worldly affections, this one period of partition, known to be at their pleasure, is recited explanatorily: for the recital is conformable to the previous knowledge; and the right of ownership suggests that knowledge. (*Dāyabhāga* 1.34)

This translation, by Colebrooke, is not basically wrong. If one is familiar with Sanskrit technical literature —Mīmāṃsā in this case— and if one reads the original Sanskrit text before turning to the translation, the latter becomes clear enough. In English translation alone, however, the text is totally unintelligible.

British complaints about the law books being ununderstandable abound in the law reports. This is what the Right Hon. T. Pemberto Leigh said, in an important decision of the Privy Council, in 1846:

> It is quite impossible for us to feel any confidence in our opinion, upon a subject like this, when that opinion is founded upon authorities to which we have access only through translations, and when the doctrines, and the reasons by which they are supported, or impugned, are drawn from the religious tradition, ancient usages, and more modern habits of the Hindoos, with which we cannot be familiar.[820]

The inability of British judges to understand the background of the body of Sanskrit texts they were supposed to use as law books,

[820] *Rungamma v. Atchamma* (1846) 4 M.I.A. 1, 97–98.

leads to a fourth reason why Anglo-Indian law gradually deviated from the *śāstras*. Quite naturally, the English found that there were, in the *śāstras*, a number of prescriptions which, to them, did not look like legal prescriptions at all. They concluded that the *śāstras* contained a strange mixture of legal and extra-legal materials.

> All these old text-books and commentaries are apt to mingle religious and moral considerations, not being positive law, with rules intended for positive law.[821]

Since it was their task to administer law, they took it upon themselves to separate the legal rules from the rest.[822]

The legal rules —or what appeared to the British to be legal rules— were binding and had to be enforced. The non-legal rules —or what they interpreted as non-legal rules— were not. If these were followed, they may have made the act in question more deserving or meritorious, mainly from a religious or moral point of view. On the other hand, if such rules were transgressed, the transgression did not make the act illegal and therefore was of no concern to the law court. Whenever a party to a lawsuit claimed that someone had acted against one or the other non-legal rule in the *śāstras*, the British answered with another Latin maxim: *factum valet*, or, more completely, *quod fieri non debuit factum valet* "what ought not to have been done, once it is done, is valid."

We are told, repeatedly, in the law reports and legal treatises (e.g., Gupte 1947: 50), that *factum valet* is not foreign to Hindu law. It was based on a statement in the *Dāyabhāga* to the effect that "a fact cannot be altered by a hundred texts."[823] This is, however, irrelevant for our purpose. What is relevant is that those who decided which rules of the *śāstras* were legal and mandatory, and which rules were moral and advisory, were, in most cases, Englishmen.[824]

[821] *Rao Balwant Singh v. Rani Kishori* (1898) 25 I.A. 69; 20 All. 285.

[822] According to the Privy Council they did so "lest foreign lawyers accustomed to treat as law what they find in authoritative books, and to administer a fixed legal system, should too hastily take for strict law precepts which are meant to appeal to the moral sense, and should thus fetter individual judgments in private affairs, should introduce restrictions into Hindu society, and impart to it an inflexible rigidity, *never contemplated by the original law-givers* [emphasis added] (Balusu's case (1899) 26 I.A. 136; 22 Mad. 416; 21 All. 478–79). The assumption was that "no system of law makes the province of legal obligation co-extensive with that of religious or moral obligation...The Hindu sages doubtless saw this distinction as clearly as we do."

[823] *Dāyabhāga* 2.30: *dānakrayakartavyatāniṣedhāt tatkaraṇāt vidhyatikramo bhavati na tu dānādyaniṣpattiḥ, vacanaśatenāpi vastuno 'nyathākaraṇāsakteḥ.*

[824] Westropp, C. J., was surprised to see "how completely the *pandit* [i.e. the *śāstrī* of Thana] ignored the *factum valet* doctrine." *Gopal Narhar Saffray v. Hanmant Ganesh* (1879) 3 Bom. 273, 295.

Factum valet had a major influence on the development of Anglo-Indian law (see Derrett 1977 [1958]), especially in cases of marriage and adoption. For instance, according to the *śāstras* one integral part of an adoption is a ritual called *dattahoma*. Soon the question arose: is the performance of *dattahoma* a legal or a moral/ religious prescription? The point was discussed endlessly in the Anglo-Indian courts. They realized there was a problem. Said Lord Shaw in the Privy Council:

> In certain circumstances the point might be the subject of a prolonged and very conflicting argument, as the authorities, ancient and modern, are in accord on the point whether this is a legal as well as a religious requisite. There is danger, on the one hand, of not paying due respect to those religious rites which are observed and followed among large classes of Indian belief, while, on the other hand, the danger must also be avoided of carrying these, except when the law is clear, into the legal sphere, so as to affect or impair personal or patrimonial rights.[825]

Throughout these discussions it was clear, however, where British sympathies lay. In more and more cases it was decided that performing the *dattahoma* may make the adoption more morally or religiously meritorious, but that it was immaterial for its legal validity.

> It is...somewhat difficult to see why a ceremony probably intended to give publicity to the fact of adoption in the circle of relations and the community to which the parties belong should now be regarded as a legal requisite for the validity of the adoption itself which is primarily dependent on the giving and taking.[826]

A similar question arose in connection with the validity of the adoption of an only son. Strictly speaking, the adoption of an only son cannot be valid according to the *śāstras*. The person to be protected is neither the adopter nor the adoptee, but the natural father. If he loses his only son, he loses the sole person who can perform the *śrāddha* ceremonies after his death. For some time the courts in India went in different directions. The Madras High Court was in favor of the validity of such adoptions, the other four High Courts were not. At that time the Privy Council stepped in. They dealt simultaneously with two appeals, one from

[825] *Bal Gangadhar Tilak v. Shrinivas Pandit* (1915) 42 I.A. 135, 148–49; 39 Bom. 441, 463–64.

[826] Aiyar 1950: 240. This notwithstanding a statement, two pages earlier: "According to the Dattaka Mimamsa and the Dattaka Chandrika, the *datta homam* or oblation to fire in the most important rite in the case of the three higher classes and is necessary to the establishment of filial relation."

Madras, one from Allahabad. The result was one of the most detailed reports in the history of Anglo-Indian law (*Balusu*'s case). The conclusion, however, was clear and simple:

> The mere fact that a transaction is condemned in books like the Smritis does not necessarily prove it to be void. It raises the question what kind of condemnation is meant.[827]

As could be expected, the shastric rule against the adoption of an only son was considered to be a religious condemnation only. Adopting an only son became an acceptable practice, the *śāstras* notwithstanding. In such cases, the Privy Council added, "the final judiciary authority rests with the Queen in Council."[828]

There was yet a fifth cause of changes in the laws applied to Hindus. The Anglo-Indian courts were occasionally called upon to decide cases for which, rightly or wrongly, they found no solutions in the *śāstras*. The question then was: which source of law to turn to? The intentions were as good as ever. Said Lord Phillimore in the Privy Council, 1870:

> The Hindoo law contains in itself the principles of its own exposition...Nothing from any foreign source should be introduced into it.[829]

To this the Privy Council later added that:

> questions arising under [Hindu law] cannot be determined on abstract reasoning or analogies borrowed from other systems of law.[830]

For all practical purposes, however, the rules of construction and interpretation applied to situations for which the *śāstras* did not offer solutions, were the principles of justice, equity, and good conscience (cf. Derrett 1978: 4.8–27 [1962]; and 1963). As early as 1827 the Bombay Regulation IV, section 26, proclaimed that:

> in the absence of a specific law and usage [the law to be observed in the trial of suits shall be] justice, equity and good conscience alone.

The same principle was reiterated, not only in several local regulations, but also in numerous judicial decisions.[831] When-

[827] 26 I.A. 140; 22 Mad. 419; 21 All. 482.

[828] 26 I.A. 150; 22 Mad. 428–29; 21 All. 493.

[829] *Bhyah Ram Singh v. Bhyah Ugur Singh* (1870) 13 M.I.A. 373, 390.

[830] *Ramchandra Martand Waikar v. Vinayak Venkatesh Kothekar* (1914) 41 I.A. 290, 299; 42 Cal. 384, 406.

[831] For example, "If [the Hindu law of Succession] lays down any definite

ever there was any doubt as to the nature and content of justice, equity, and good conscience, the later law reports unanimously refer to a definition first formulated by Lord Hobhouse in the Privy Council:

> The matter must be decided by equity and good conscience, generally interpreted to mean the rules of English law if found applicable in Indian society and circumstances.[832]

Finally, there was one other situation facing the British judges. There were in the *śāstras* certain rules and prescriptions the enforcement of which was, to them, simply unacceptable.[833] In these cases the British did not hesitate. They all followed the advice Macnaghten gave them in 1824. On the very same page on which Macnaghten said: "their own is the only law to be administered to them," he nevertheless concluded: "where we cannot reconcile, we must abrogate" (Macnaghten 1824: vii).

I now return to widow Chanbasava who was murdered by her nephew Hanmappa.[834] As I indicated earlier, the case was first decided at Dharwar, appealed in Bombay, and finally settled in London. The Indian trial judge at Dharwar, obviously, was uncomfortable with the case. The attorneys for Hanmappa's sisters claimed that there was not in the *śāstras* a single rule that disqualifies the murderer from inheriting his victim's estate. The *śāstras* do contain lists of people who are disqualified from inheritance, but these are individuals who, on account of some physical or mental handicap, are all incapable of performing the necessary ritual for the dead.[835] The murderer is not one of them. The

rule with reference to the question to which the facts of the present case give rise, it is of course not open to this Court to decline to enforce that rule on the ground that it would be more equitable in its opinion so to decline. If, however, in regard to such a question the Hindu law is altogether silent, the rule to be applied would be that of equity, justice and good conscience." *Vedanayaga Mudaliar v. Vedammal* (1904) 27 Mad. 591, 597.

[832] *Waghela Rajsanji v. Sheikh Masludin* (1887) 14 I.A. 89, 96; 11 Bom. 551, 555.

[833] Or they presented the śāstric rules as no longer acceptable to the Hindu community itself. This was done, for instance, in cases involving *devadāsīs* "temple harlots." Said Mr. Justice West, after admitting that theirs "was an occupation of which the Hindu law took cognizance": "Such usage is not law, for over it presides the higher usage of the community at large from whose approval it must have derived any conceivable original validity, and in opposition to which it cannot exist." *Mathura Naikin v. Esu Naikin* (1880) 4 Bom. 545, 550 and 557–58.

[834] *Kenchava v. Girimallappa Channappa* (1921) 45 Bom. 768; (1924) 51 I.A. 368; A.I.R. 1924 P.C. 209. Cf. also Derrett 1977: 3.297–311 [1960].

[835] Reference was made, in the court, to MDh 9.201: "Eunuchs and outcasts, (persons) born blind and deaf, the insane, idiots and the dumb, as well as those deficient in any organ (of action or sensation), receive no share" [Bühler's trans.].

defense concluded: "Thus murder neither entails a forfeiture of inheritance nor does it impress it with any trusts whatever."[836]

Judge Chinmulgund's conscience, however, told him that Hanmappa should not inherit. He applied the principle that Hindu law has its own rules of interpretations, and that, if the *śāstras* are silent on a particular point, one has to construe that silence within the general framework and context of the *śāstras* as a whole.

> On the analogy of texts which prescribe the restoration of property as one of the punishments of robbery accompanied by murder, and the reversal of all dealings brought about by force or deceit, he considered that it might be deduced that the murderer's succession to the estate of the person he murdered should be prevented from becoming effective.[837]

Following a precedent in Madras,[838] he quoted the maxim: *nemo ex suo delicto meliorem suam conditionem facere potest* "no one may improve his own condition as a result of his wrongdoing." He, therefore, disqualified Hanmappa from reaping any benefits from the inheritance, but he did not declare him non-existent. The judge divided the inheritance into three equal parts, one for each of Hanmappa's sisters, and one for their cousin Girimallappa.

Girimallappa was not satisfied with receiving only one third of the estate. He appealed the Dharwar decision to the High Court in Bombay. As I said earlier, there the case was not heard by Indians, but by Sir Norman Macleod, Chief Justice, and Mr. Justice Charles Fawcett. They could not agree with the reasoning by analogy of judge Chinmulgund.[839] They reasoned that, since there was no shastric text by which the murderer was either qualified or disqualified, this was one of those cases in which, in Hindu law, "there is no direct provision bearing on the point we have to decide."[840] They, therefore, referred to the Bombay Regulation IV of 1827 mentioned earlier. For the two justices in Bombay the case was "one which cannot demand much elaboration" (ibid.): the principles of justice, equity, and good conscience dictated not only that Hanmappa, the murderer, should not inherit, but that he be declared non-existent as well. Now Girimallappa got the entire estate, the murderer's sisters nothing.

It was the sisters' turn to be dissatisfied. They took the decision of the Bombay High Court to the Privy Council in Lon-

[836] (1921) 45 Bom. 768, 771.
[837] From the summary by Macleod, C. J., (1921) 45 Bom. 768, 775.
[838] *Vedanayaga Mudaliar v. Vedammal* (1904) 27 Mad. 591, 598–99.
[839] See the long discussion by Fawcett, J., (1921) 45 Bom. 768, 782–84.
[840] Ibid.: 775.

don. Their Lordships agreed with the judge at Dharwar and with the High Court in Bombay that a murderer should not inherit. They discussed the decisions of the lower courts at length. They agreed with Bombay, against Dharwar, that the murderer should be considered non-existent as far as the inheritance was concerned. On the other hand, they agreed with Dharwar, against Bombay, that the *śāstras* did not exclude the murderer from the inheritance. At the same time they rejected Dharwar's reasoning by analogy and concluded that, according to the *śāstras*, Hanappa was indeed not disqualified. However, they also said, simply and directly, that this did not matter in the least. For them this was one of those cases in which the śāstric solution was unacceptable. In such cases the śāstric law, whatever it was, had to be abrogated and declared non-existent.

Ultimately it was, therefore, Girimallappa who claimed victory, via a lawsuit at Dharwar and appeals in Bombay and London, ten years after the fact, when their Lordships of the Privy Council used their supreme power to abrogate a provision of the laws of the Shaster.

Whatever its merits —or lack therof— the system of Hindu civil law elaborated under British rule was carried over unchanged into the law courts of Independent India, in 1947. This lasted until, nearly one decade later, the Indian Parliament passed four Acts, on marriage, on succession, on minority and guardianship, and on adoptions and maintenance. What the British had done reluctantly: abrogate the laws of the *śāstras*, the Indian Parliament did as a matter of principle. To quote the Hindu Succession Act, 1956, Section 4:

> Save as otherwise expressly provided in this Act, —any text, rule of interpretation of Hindu law or any custom or usage as part of that law in force immediately before the commencement of this Act shall cease to have effect with respect to any matter for which provision is made in this Act.

In the words of Derrett, it was the Indian Parliament, not the British, who wrote the "Epitaph for the Rishis" (subtitle of Derrett 1978), the epitaph for the ancient seers who revealed the Dharmaśāstras.

As far as the murderer's right to inherit his victim's estate is concerned, the Hindu Succession Act has foreclosed any further discussion in the future. According to Section 25:

> A person who commits murder or abets the commission of murder shall be disqualified from inheriting the property of the person murdered.

This section has to be read in conjunction with Section 27:

> If any person is disqualified from inheriting any property under this Act, it shall devolve as if such person had died before the intestate.

If the Dharwar case, which was the pivot of this address, were to be tried today, Hanmappa, the murderer, would be disqualified as the "person who commits murder;" he would be considered to have died before his victim. His sisters, however, would remain potential heirs in their own right.

43

Reinterpreting Texts: When Revealed Sanskrit Texts Become Modern Law Books

In 1772, the British East India Company appointed a new governor of Bengal, Warren Hastings, "one of the most remarkable figures in India's history" (see Frykenberg 1988: 38). Hastings did not wait long to promote the adoption of a juridical plan that was to become one of his major legacies on the Indian subcontinent.[841] According to the plan, "in all religious suits regarding inheritance, marriage, caste and all other religious usages and institutions, the laws of the Koran with respect to the Mohamedans and those of the Shaster with respect to the Gentoos shall invariably be adhered to."[842] In other words, in 1772 the British authorities in Calcutta decided that Indian Hindus and Indian Muslims should not be ruled by British laws, which they would not be able to understand, but by their own laws, which

[841] Hastings did so against strong opposition; see Dow 1772: 11, 14: "To leave the natives to their own laws would be to consign them to anarchy and confusion.... It is therefore absolutely necessary for the peace and prosperity of the country that the laws of England in so far as they do not oppose prejudice and usages which cannot be relinquished by the natives should prevail. The measure, besides its equity, is calculated to preserve that influence which conquerors must possess to retain their power."

[842] The plan was drawn up by the Committee of Circuit, of which Hastings was president and was adopted by the president and council at Fort William on August 21, 1772. On April 11, 1780, the paragraph quoted here became law as section 27 of the Administration of Justice Regulation. Note that it exclusively bears on family law and thereby excludes procedure, criminal law, etc., even though these, too, were integral parts of "the Shaster." They were replaced by the Penal Code (1860), the Indian Evidence Act (1872), the Code of Criminal Procedure (1898), and the Code of Civil Procedure (1908).

they had cherished for many centuries.[843] In this essay, I will not deal with the Indian Muslims, who, according to the plan, were to be governed by the laws of the Koran. I will restrict myself to the Hindus, who were to be ruled by the laws of "the Shaster."

The term "Shaster," used in the judicial plan of 1772, corresponds to the Sanskrit term *śāstra*, which is the collective name for the voluminous body of Sanskrit texts (the *śāstra* and their commentaries) dealing with the Hindu *dharma*. The term *dharma* has no appropriate English equivalent; it refers to the aggregate of all the rules by which a Hindu must live, including rules that we would label rules of law. Modern scholarship has established that the several Dharmaśāstras were composed somewhere between 500 BC and 500 AD, but in the Hindu tradition these texts were attributed to ancient *ṛṣis*, that is, "sages" or "seers." They are part of the Vedas, the sacred, revealed texts of Hinduism. Being sacred, the *śāstras* are superhuman and timeless; they proclaim eternal truths, and they should not be interfered with by human beings.[844] One of the adjectives used to describe *dharma* is *sanātana*, "eternal."[845]

From the end of the eighteenth century onward, and throughout the colonial period, the courts of law in India, as well as the highest court of appeal, the Judicial Committee of the Privy Council in London, have indeed, to the best of their abilities, based their judgments in cases involving Hindus on the *śāstras*. The goal of this essay is to show how and why, despite the best intentions to remain faithful to the law of the *śāstras*, the British could not avoid departing from the original intent and meaning of the sacred texts when it came to applying them in the courts of law. As Thomas Babington Macaulay later said, "the decision was farsighted policy —not a matter of course" (cited in Rankin 1946: 4).

[843] See Sir William Jones' letter to Hastings' successor, Cornwallis, dated March 9, 1788, in Cannon, ed., 1970: 794: "Nothing indeed could be more obviously just, than to determine private contests according to those laws, which the parties themselves had ever considered as the rules of their conduct and engagements in civil life; nor could anything be wiser than, by a legislative act, to assure the Hindu and Muselman subjects of Great Britain, that the private laws, which they severally hold sacred , and a violation of which they would have thought the most grievous oppression, should not be superseded by a new system, of which they could have no knowledge, and which they must have considered as imposed on them by a spirit of rigour and intolerance."

[844] The question of whether the Dharmaśāstras actually contained the laws by which Hindus lived in ancient India is still debated; see Rocher 1993.

[845] See Mulla 1970: 3: "It was an article of belief with the ancient Hindu that his law was Revelation, immutable and eternal."

Background

It is important to note that, right from the start, the British found themselves at a triple disadvantage.

The first disadvantage was that the *śāstra* texts were composed in Sanskrit, and no Englishman entrusted with the administration of justice among Hindus had any knowledge whatever of that language.[846] After trying other solutions, which proved unsuccessful,[847] this disadvantage was remedied: some courageous Englishmen decided that there was only one way to administer the law of the *śāstras* properly —namely to study Sanskrit themselves. A very few of them did, and in 1794 Sir William Jones, a judge in the Calcutta Supreme Court, produced an English translation of the most famous of the *śāstras*, a text attributed to Manu, the mythical ancestor of all Hindus (Jones 1794). The text became known as *The Laws of Manu*. Other translations —of commentaries first, of basic texts other than Manu's only later[848]— were to follow, but the shared disadvantage of not having access to the original Sanskrit texts continued to haunt the courts in India and in London. As late as 1899 the Privy Council lamented, "In examining this question their Lordships are again at a great disadvantage in not knowing Sanskrit."[849]

The second disadvantage was that the British not only did not know the language of the *śāstra* but also had no idea of the extent of the texts they were supposed to administer in the courts of law. It was possible, and legal, for the advocate of a party to a lawsuit to present the judge with a śāstric text that neither the advocate of the opposing party nor the judge had ever heard of.

The third disadvantage was that even the translations proved to be of relatively little help. The rules contained in the *śāstras* often were as foreign and unintelligible to the early translators — and, *a fortiori*, to those who had to use the translations— as British law would have been to the Hindus. The *śāstra* was the product of a complex and different civilization with which even the most devoted British enthusiasts at that time were only vaguely familiar.[850]

[846] The situation was different in the case of Indian Muslims. Several Englishmen at the time knew Persian, and some also knew Arabic.

[847] One such solution, adopted in 1772 and abandoned in 1864, was to appoint Indian pandits as "law officers." These pandits consulted the *śāstras*, formulated decisions on the basis of the texts, and handed their decisions over to a British judge to pronounce his verdict. On the growing dissatisfaction with the system, see Jones' letter to Cornwallis in Cannon, ed., 1970: 795.

[848] The reason why commentaries were preferred over the ancient texts will become clear in this essay.

[849] *Sri Balusu v. Sri Balusu* (1899) 26 I.A. 113, 146 (P.C.).

[850] See the testimony, after his return from India, of George C. Rankin, chief

To quote the Privy Council once again, "It is quite impossible for us to feel any confidence in our opinion,...when that opinion is founded upon authorities to which we have access only through translations, and when the doctrines themselves, and the reasons by which they are supported, or impugned, are drawn from the religious tradition, ancient sages, and more modern habits of the Hindus, with which we cannot be familiar."[851]

It is against the background of this triple anomaly —the courts' not having access to and not knowing the extent of the laws they were supposed to administer, and their being ignorant of the historical context in which the *śāstra* had originated— that we must analyze and try to understand the changes that the law of the *śāstra* underwent in Anglo-India.

Changes from Within Traditional Hindu Law

Law versus religion

The British soon realized that the laws contained in the *śāstra* rarely corresponded to their idea of what "law" was supposed to be. Hindu legal texts, they felt, were inextricably mixed with what they called "religion" (see Rocher 1972a). Faced with this situation, the courts decided that it was their duty to administer law, but not religion, with which they were supposed not to interfere. For example, the text of the *śāstra* explicitly declares the adoption of a single son invalid; indeed, if one adopts a single son, one removes him from his natural family in which he is the prime person who can perform the necessary ritual at the time of his father's death. The British gradually came to the conclusion that performing the *śrāddha* ritual at the time of one's father's death belonged to the sphere of religion and was therefore irrelevant with respect to the validity of the "legal" act of adoption. In a landmark decision, the Privy Council wrote, "The British rulers of India have in few things been more careful than in avoiding

justice of Bengal, in the preface to Rankin, *Background to Indian Law*: "I have been impressed at times with the peculiarity of the fate of very learned and able friends of mine who, as the reward of exceptional knowledge and skill in the business matters of England and Scotland, are suddenly required to turn a large part of their attention to Indian appeals. What at first do they think of them or make of them? What is their approach?... Not many people in this country have any settled notion of what we are doing in administering to Indians, nor have any means of readily acquiring a well-founded notion of how we come to be doing so or of the principles we apply. Certain I am that when I went to India In 1918 to engage upon the task I had the smallest amount of information and no real explanation of many facts of historical importance."

[851] *Rungama v. Atchama* (1846) 4 M.I.A. I, 97–98 (P.C.).

interference with the religious tenets of the Indian peoples. They provide for the peace and stability of families by imposing limits on attempts to disturb the possession of property and the personal legal status of individuals. With the religious side of such matters they do not pretend to interfere. But the position is altered if the validity of temporal arrangements on which temporal courts are asked to decide is to be made subordinate to inquiries into religious beliefs" (*Sri Balusu v. Sri Balusu*, cited above). As a result, from 1899 onward treatises on Hindu law have ordained unequivocally that "an only son may be given and taken in adoption" (Mulla 1970: 502). In cases such as this one, the British introduced a nonexistent dichotomy in the text of the *śāstra*, between what they considered to be law and what they considered to be religion. They dutifully applied the legal aspects of the *śāstra* but did not interfere with (that is, they disregarded) the religious aspects of the texts.

Human commentaries outweigh revealed śāstras

Not only was the text of the *śāstra* difficult to understand, often it either was ambiguous, and therefore susceptible of different interpretations, or failed to provide answers to legal questions that the judge had to deal with. In these circumstances, the British learned not only that the Sanskrit commentaries on the original *śāstra*s were more comprehensive, in that they took into consideration the entire *śāstra* literature, but also that each individual commentator had worked out his own coherent system for interpreting the often incoherent and contradictory *śāstra*s. Hence the British turned for help to the commentaries (as indicated earlier, although not a single ancient *śāstra* had been translated in the period that immediately followed the appearance of Jones' *The Laws of Manu*,[852] the commentaries were being translated, in ever-increasing numbers).

Since the commentaries had originated in different parts of India, the British assumed that they represented the way in which the text of the *śāstra* had been interpreted and applied in various parts of India. They introduced the concept of regional schools

[852] Yājñavalkya's Dharmaśāstra was translated more than half a century later (by A.F. Stenzler, in 1849, into German). Most translations still used today were published in F. Max Müller, ed., *The Sacred Books of the East*, vols. 2 (Āpastamba and Gautama, trans. G. Bühler, 1879), 7 (Viṣṇu, trans. J. Jolly, 1880), 14 (Vāsiṣṭha and Baudhāyana, trans. G. Bühler, 1882), 25 (Manu, trans. Bühler, 1886), and 33 (Nārada and Bṛhaspati, trans. J. Jolly, 1889). More recent publications include Richard W. Lariviere, trans., 1989; Doniger and Smith, trans., 1991; and Olivelle, trans., 1999.

of Hindu law, thus admitting that the same *śāstra* text could mean different things in different parts of the subcontinent.[853] "The duty...of an European judge who is under the obligation to administer Hindoo law, is not so much to enquire whether a disputed doctrine is fairly deducible from the earliest authorities, as to ascertain whether it has been received by the particular School which governs the District with which he has to deal."[854] What that meant was a convenient but totally untraditional reversal of authorities; the meaning of the text of the ancient, revealed, and unalterable *śāstra* was now made subordinate to the differing interpretations of human commentators: "It is clear that in the event of a conflict between the ancient text writers and the commentators, the opinion of the latter must be accepted."[855] To be sure, the *śāstras* continued to be quoted in every legal decision, but the judges no longer were under the obligation to inquire what the original *śāstra* texts meant. They could be satisfied with the sometimes forced interpretations the commentators gave the *śāstras*, to make them fit into an overall system. In other words, the courts of law distanced themselves from the texts of the *śāstras* themselves, relying on them only indirectly via the medium of interpretations provided by commentators.

Custom outweighs written texts

The British distanced themselves even further from the text of the *śāstra* by cleverly using a means that the *śāstra* itself provided them with: the *śāstras* indeed do say that, in addition to their own rules, rather unspecified customs of clans, castes, villages, guilds, etc., are valid sources of *dharma* "as long as they are not contrary to the Vedas." The British were only too happy to comply, and soon it became a principle of Anglo-Hindu law that "under the Hindu

[853] On the origin of the schools of Hindu law, see Rocher 1972c: 167–76. The most drastic and far-reaching division within Hindu law pertains to the law of succession and inheritance. The British selected two twelfth-century commentaries as the principal sources on inheritance law: Jīmūtavāhana's *Dāyabhāga* and Vijñāneśvara's *Mitākṣarā*, for Bengal and for the rest of India, respectively. According to the *Mitākṣarā*, every male born into a joint family acquires by birth an undefined but real right of ownership in the family property —a concept that severely restricts the power of the head of the family. The *Dāyabhāga*, working from the same body of *śāstra* texts, concludes that the right of ownership originates only after the disappearance, by death or otherwise, of the previous owner of the property. As a result, in Bengal the head of the joint family was given nearly unlimited rights to dispose of family property as he pleased. Both commentaries were translated in a single volume; see Colebrooke 1810.

[854] *Collector of Madura v. Moottoo Ramalinga* (1868) 12 M.I.A. 397, 436.

[855] *Atmaram v. Bajirao* (1935) 62 I.A. 139, 143 (P.C.).

system of law, clear proof of usage will outweigh the written text of the law."[856] Once again, this did not mean that the *śāstra* texts were easily discarded. They remained at the center of every debate, but their authority was now weighed in the balance against the authority of unwritten custom. The burden of proof that a custom was fully established, and that it ought therefore to overrule the text of the *śāstra*, invariably lay with the party who made such a claim; and yet, once the court had accepted that a custom was "valid," it did outweigh the text of the *śāstra* (see Kane 1950).

Changes from Outside Traditional Hindu Law

The jurisprudential debates in the Anglo-Indian courts of law, and in the Privy Council, debates that centered on the text of the *śāstra* but relied on it in ever more different ways, were preserved in an endless series of law reports. These reports make fascinating reading; many of them are the work of eminent jurists, and some of them run to hundreds of pages. Nevertheless, the law reports were the work of Englishmen —and of an increasing number of British-trained Indian lawyers, who acted exactly as their teachers did[857]— with the result that purely British principles gradually began to infiltrate legal decisions, and purely British principles began to determine the role of the *śāstra* in these decisions.

Precedent

One such principle, borrowed from common law jurisprudence, is that of precedent. In Hindu law, too, it became common practice that if earlier cases had been decided on the basis of a certain interpretation of the *śāstra*, then it was appropriate to apply the same interpretation to the case at hand. Even when the advocate for one of the parties or a member of a Full Bench happened to know Sanskrit and demonstrated in court that the interpretation given to a text of the *śāstra* in earlier decisions had been wrong, a protracted discussion on the correct meaning of the *śāstra* text could be cut short by the Latin maxims of *stare decisis* and *communis error facit ius*.[858] In this connection, we can note that the maxim of *communis error facit ius* has also led to a

[856] *Collector of Madura v. Moottoo Ramalinga*, 397, 436.

[857] They acted as their teachers did, that is, to the extent that Indian jurists were prepared to justify innovations introduced by the British as inherent parts of traditional Hindu law; see Rocher 1972b: 419–24.

[858] See *Apaji Narhar v. Ramchandra* (1891) 16 Bom. 29 (F.B.), in which one judge demonstrated that Colebrooke's translation of a passage from the *Mitākṣarā* was in error. He was overruled by the majority of the Full Bench.

development of a different nature: succession and inheritance in the *śāstras* are intestate, and there are no rules dealing with wills, and yet wills were occasionally recognized in Indian courts of law. When the validity of a will was challenged in 1867, the Privy Council ruled as follows: "It is too late to contend that, because the ancient Hindu treatises make no mention of Wills, a Hindu cannot make a testamentary disposition of his property. Decided cases, too numerous to be questioned, have determined that the testamentary power exits."[859] The undisputed novelty of wills in Hindu law notwithstanding, Indian jurists were prepared to claim them as integral parts of the *śāstra*.[860]

Factum valet

A number of British legal principles that were introduced into the law of the *śāstra* had a long history in British law, and their refinement in British jurisprudence resulted from circumstances inherent in British society. A case in point is the maxim of *factum valet*, or, stated more completely, *quod fieri non debuit factum valet*, "if something that ought not to be done has been done anyway, it becomes law." There is a substantial body of jurisprudence on *factum valet* in Britain, but applying or even adapting that jurisprudence to Indian situations and to Sanskrit *śāstra* texts was bound to lead to some rather hybrid decisions.[861]

Justice, equity, and good conscience

There were also rules in the *śāstra* that, to the British, were incompatible with their principle of "justice, equity and good conscience" (see Derrett 1963). For instance, all *śāstras* agree that inheriting the property of a deceased person involves not only receiving his or her assets but also paying his or her debts, even when the debts exceed the assets, or when there are no assets whatever. A text attributed to the sage Bṛhaspati states, in the most general terms, "The father's debt must be paid first of all, and, after that, a man's own debt" (for this and other *śāstra* texts

[859] *Beer Pertab v. Rajender Pertab* (1867) 12 M.I.A. I, 37–38. Wills among Hindus, including wills written in Indian languages, were officially sanctioned by the Hindu Wills Act (1870). Hindu wills created a complex body of jurisprudence; see Phillips and Trevelyan 1914.

[860] See Kane 1950. For arguments that wills were not unknown in classical India, see Kane 1930–62: 3.816–17. Typically, Kane invokes a *śāstra* that "makes a very near approach to the modern conception of a will."

[861] See Derrett 1958. On the claim that the maxim was referred to in Jīmūtavāhana's *Dāyabhāga*, see Rocher 1995.

to the same effect, see Rocher 1967: 20). The British called this duty on the part of the heir "the pious obligation." They were prepared to accept the principle of the pious obligation as long as the debts did not exceed the assets, but an heir's being forced to pay debts larger than the assets violated their sense of justice, equity, and good conscience: debts were to be paid to the extent of the assets only.

In the case of the pious obligation, the British only narrowed the application of the *śāstra* texts, but the application of justice, equity, and good conscience went farther than that. The *śāstra*s provide detailed rules on who can inherit and who cannot. Those who cannot inherit are those who are physically or mentally incapable of performing the necessary rites for the deceased (*śrāddha*). Inheriting property and performing the rites for the dead are indissolubly linked in the Hindu *śāstra* (see Rocher 1992: 637–49). For instance, according to *The Laws of Manu*, the following are excluded from inheriting property: "No share is given to a man who is impotent or fallen, or blind or deaf from birth, or a madman, an idiot, or a mute, or devoid of virile strength" (Doniger and Smith, trans.: 220). All these are individuals who, for different reasons, are either unable or considered unqualified to perform the rituals for their deceased ancestors.[862]

At one point, two sisters of a murderer claimed the inheritance of their brother's victim. Their lawyers argued that the murderer, according to the *śāstra*, was his victim's heir, that he did not fall within the category of individuals who cannot inherit, and that, therefore, the inheritance belonged to them. Right from the beginning, the question was not so much whether the murderer himself could inherit but rather whether, for the sake of inheritance, he was to be considered existent or nonexistent. The case went from a lower court (which ruled in favor of the sisters), via an appeal to the Bombay High Court (which ruled in favor of their cousin), to the Privy Council in London (see Rocher 1987). Their Lordships discussed the case at great length, once more examining the *śāstra* texts on individuals who were entitled to inherit and on those who were not, but they concluded:

> Before this Board it has been contended that the matter is governed by Hindu law, and that the Hindu law makes no provision disqualifying a murderer from succeeding to the estate of his victim, and therefore it must be taken that according to this law, he can succeed.
> Their Lordships do not take this view... The alternative is between

[862] The scholarly literature on *śrāddha* is vast. For a detailed study, see Kane 1930–62: 4.334–551. See also, more recently, Saindon 1998: 45–71.

the Hindu law being as above stated or being for the purpose non-existent, and in that case the High Court have rightly decided that the principle of equity, justice and good conscience excludes the murderer.[863]

Legislative Acts

The principle of justice, equity, and good conscience presents one example of situations in which the British actually made some texts of the *śāstra* obsolete. This tendency also surfaced in a number of acts that the British imposed on Hindus during the last century of colonial rule. The earliest two, the Caste Disabilities Removal Act (1850) and the Hindu Widow's Remarriage Act (1856), clearly demonstrate the direction in which British interference with the *śāstra* was progressing: taking measures for the protection of the lower castes,[864] against restrictions imposed on women,[865] etc.

Epilogue

The *śāstra* suffered a far greater setback after Indian independence. In 1955–56, the Indian Parliament in Delhi enacted four laws that together overruled much of the *śāstra* and its de-

[863] *Kenshava v. Girimalappa Channappa* (1924) 51 I.A. 368, 372–73 (P.C.). To prevent a murderer or his relatives from using the text of the *śāstra* again to claim the inheritance of the victim, the Hindu Succession Act (1956), even though it abrogates all Hindu law as it existed before the commencement of the act, explicitly disqualifies from inheritance, in section 25, "a person who commits murder or abets the commission of murder."

[864] According to the *śāstra*, any person who became an outcaste lost his right to inherit. The Caste Disabilities Removal Act contains only one article: "So much of any law or usage now in force within the territories subject to the Government of the East India Company as inflicts on any person forfeiture of rights of property, or may be held in any way to impair or affect any right of inheritance by reason of his or her renouncing, or having been excluded from the communion of any religion, or having been deprived of caste, shall cease to be enforced as law in the Courts of the East India Company, and in the Courts established by Royal Charter within the said territories."

[865] According to the *śāstra*, a Hindu widow, even a very young widow whose marriage had not been consummated, was not allowed to remarry; marriage being a lifelong commitment, divorce was prohibited. The Hindu Widows' Remarriage Act is subtitled "An Act to remove all legal obstacles to the marriage of Hindu widows." Article I reads: "No marriage contracted between Hindus shall be invalid, and the issue of no such marriage shall be illegitimate by reason of the woman having been previously married or betrothed to another person who was dead at the time of such marriage, any custom and any interpretation of Hindu law to the contrary notwithstanding."

velopment under British rule.[866] Section 4 of the Hindu Marriage Act unequivocally expresses the purpose of the new legislation:

> Save as otherwise expressly provided in this Act, —
>
> (a) any text, rule of interpretation of Hindu law or any custom or usage as part of that law in force immediately before the commencement of this Act shall cease to have effect with regard to any matter for which provision is made in this Act;
>
> (b) any other law in force immediately before the commencement of this Act shall cease to have effect in so far as it is inconsistent with any of the provisions contained in this Act.[867]

The Hindu Marriage Act[868] provoked a book whose subtitle, *Epitaph for the Rishis*, seemed to suggest that the law of the *śāstra* had come to an end" (Derrett 1978). It had, to a large extent, and yet S.V. Gupte, commenting on section 4 of the Hindu Marriage Act, points out that, notwithstanding its title ("Over-riding effect of the Act"), the section "also means that after the coming into operation of this Act any other law which was in force immediately before the commencement of this Act would continue to be in force provided it has not been repealed by this Act and to the extent to which its provisions are not inconsistent with this Act" (Gupte 1961: 102). Even though, as far as marriage is concerned, "such matters are indeed few" (Mulla 1970: 612), there are broader areas of Hindu family law that remain beyond the purview of the four acts of 1955–56. These aspects continue to be governed by "the Shaster" as I have described it in this essay. Even today the law courts in India decide cases related to the pious obligation, and other cases, according to the law of the *śāstra* as it existed prior to independence.[869]

The laws of Manu and those of the other ancient sages, the *ṛṣis*, may have been interpreted differently in the course of several centuries, and they may have been largely abrogated in more recent times, but they are still on the minds of the legal profession in India. The post-1956 editions of the classical treatises on

[866] These four laws were the Hindu Marriage Act (1955), the Hindu Succession Act (1956), the Hindu Minority and Guardianship Act (1956), and the Hindu Adoptions and Maintenance Act (1956).

[867] The same formula is repeated, in nearly identical terms, in the three acts of 1956.

[868] Or, rather, the Hindu Marriage Act (1955) as amended by the Marriage Law (Amendment) Act (1976).

[869] Mulla 1970: 323: "The pious obligation of sons, grandsons, great-grandsons, to pay the ancestor's debts to the extent of their interest in the joint family property is not abrogated by the Hindu Succession Act, 1956."

Hindu law continue and will continue to devote lengthy introductions to the *śāstra* as long as "the enactments which have so far found place on the statute-book leave an undetermined residue" (ibid.: 69).

44

Father Bouchet's Letter on the Administration of Hindu Law

This paper provides the first complete translation into English of "a most interesting letter written by Father Bouchet in 1714 from Pondicherry to a great man in France" (Nelson 1881: 1188). Except for the first few paragraphs, the letter is entirely devoted to the administration of Hindu law. Although the letter has not remained unnoticed,[870] it has never been made available elsewhere than in its original setting: the *Letters édifiantes et curieuses* and their German and Italian translations.[871]

The author, Jean Venant Bouchet, was born at Fontenay-le-Comte, France, on April 12, 1655.[872] He became a novice in the Society of Jesus on October 1, 1670. In 1688 he left for India, where he was put in charge of Trichinopoly and the surrounding

[870] J.H. Nelson repeatedly refers to it, especially in "Hindu Law at Madras," (1881:208–236). See pp. 221–227 for a summary of contents, and pp. 227–229 for an evaluation. Derrett (1961: 361, n. 21) refers to an "explanation of F. Bouchet's letter of 1714 in a light more consistent with orthodox theory," by Innes (1882).

[871] The letter has been published in the following collections of *Lettres édifiante et curieuse*: Paris, vol. 14, 1720, pp. 321–411; Paris, vol. 12, 1781, pp. 255–313; Paris, vol. 2, 1840, pp. 485–499; Paris, vol. 4, 1843, pp. 485– 499; Lyon, vol. 7, 1819, pp. 152–188. I have used the 1840 edition, pages and columns of which are indicated in brackets in the translation; I have compared the text with the earlier editions of 1720 and 1781. A German translation appeared in Joseph Stöckclein's *Der Neua Welt-Bott*, vol. I. 6, Auzsburg 1728 pp. 87–92. This translation omits the passage: "If am not mistaken, I have read somewhere,..." (p.487a), up to "...I shall not go into it here" (p. 489b); it summarizes the remainder of the letter. I have not seen the ltalian translation, in *Scelta di Lettere Edifconti*, vol. 6, Milan 4 82 9, P9. 5–39.

[872] The following biographical data are based on a variety of sources, in chronological order: Sommervogel 1890 (col. 1864–1866); Jean 1894: 1.132–36; Laucay 1898: 1.xxiv; Jann 1915: 412, 473–474, 480, 482; Besse 1918: 245–246; Streit and Dindinger61931: 6.2; *New Catholic Encyclopedia*, vol. 9, 1967: 98 (V. Cronin).

area. Because of civil troubles in the city he established himself at Ahur, twelve miles south of Trichinopoly. He built a church, and carried on in grand style. In 1702 he was transferred from the Maduré mission to the Carnate mission, of which he became the Superior. He then lived at Tarkolan, in North Arcot District.

On November 6, 1703, Charles de Tournon, papal *legatus a latere*, arrived in Pondicherry, to investigate Jesuit practices. Sickness prevented him from visiting any part of the inland mission. However, until his departure in July 1704, he gathered data on the practices in question, notably from Charles Bertoldi of Maduré, and from Bouchet. In the meanwhile, on June 23, 1704, Tournon signed a decree condemning in sixteen points several usages permitted by the Jesuits; his decree was confirmed by the Holy Office on January 7, 1706. As a result, Bouchet was sent to defend the Jesuit methods to Rome, where he arrived in early July 1707. When his companion, François Laynez, had to return to India as the coadjutor of the bishop of Mylapore —and to become bishop there himself—, Bouchet carried on alone. He obtained from Pope Clement XI, by an *oraculum vivae vocis*, that the missionaries were to observe Tournon's decree only "insofar as the Divine glory and the salvation of souls would permit." Bouchet returned to India in 1709, satisfied with his success.

However, on September 1, 1712, Clement renewed the Holy Office's decree of 1706. In a brief *non sine gravi*, of 17 September 1712, he reprimanded Laynez for failing to take action to carry out Tournon's decree. On July 24, 1715, the cardinal prefect of propaganda sent the brief and the decree of 1706 to Pondicherry; they were promulgated there on January 1, 1716 by Mgr. Claude de Visdelou, Bishop of Claudianopolis and vicar apostolic of Kweichou, and a well known opponent of the Chinese rites. Visdelou threatened Bouchet, then the vice principal of the French Jesuits in India, with excommunication *latae sententiae*, lest he have copies of the brief sent to the provincial of Malabar and the superior of the missions of Maduré, Mysore, and Carnate. On January 15, 1716, Bouchet figures again among those who drafted an answer to Visdelou, and in which they refused to recognize his jurisdiction.

Less often mentioned in Bouchet's biographies are his contributions to cartography. In 1719 he sent to Paris a small map of South India, followed later by other more detailed ones. These maps contributed to greater accuracy in the works of better known French cartographers such as Jean-Baptiste Bourguignon d'Anville, and Guillaume de l'Isle (or Delisle).[873] Only one of these maps appears

[873] Gole 1976: 63–64. D'Anville's map (Herbert 1759: 49) refers to an observation, by Father Bouchet, on the latitude of Cape Comorin (7°58').

to have been published,[874] in a German translation, in Joseph Stocklein's *Der Neue Welt-Bott* (1728: 1.7, 112).

Bouchet died on March 13,1732.

Father Bouchet's letter is addressed to Melchior Cochet de Saint-Vallier (Beaune, 12 December 1664–Paris, 19 December 1738)[875], who, in 1695, became councilor, and, in 1701, president of the Paris *Parlement.* In the letter he is called president of the *Requétes du palais.* He is especially known for his book: *Traité de l'indult du Parlement de Paris, ou du Droit que le chancelier de France, les prisidens, maîtres des requetes, conseillers et autres officiers du Parlement, ont sur les prélatures séculiéres réguliéres du royaume* (first published in 1703, revised edition in 1747).

Translation

[485b] They have neither codes nor digests, nor do they have any books in which are written down the laws to which they have to conform [486a] to solve the disputes that arise in their families. They do have the Vedam, which they regard as a holy book: it is divided into four parts called divine laws, but it is certainly not from these that they draw the maxims that determine their judgments. They have another book called Vinachuram[876]: in it there are many beautiful sentences and a few rules for the different castes, which might very well guide a judge. In it they also relate the highly ingenious way in which certain ancients discovered the truth against attempts to obscure it by various devices. Yet, even though Indians admire the wisdom and sagacity of those judges, it does not occur to them to follow their methods. Finally, an infinite number of beautiful sentences are exhibited in the works of ancient poets, who professed to teach sound morals; but it is again not from them that they draw the principles that determine their decisions.

The equity of all their verdicts is entirely founded on a number of customs which they consider inviolable, and on certain usages which are handed down from father to son. They regard these usages as definite and infallible rules, to maintain peace in the family and to end the suits that arise, not only among private individuals, but also among royal princes. As soon as it has been proven that someone's claim is based on a custom that is

[874] According to Tooley 1955, s.v. Bouchet.

[875] See Roman d'Amat 1961: vol. 9, col. 72.

[876] Possibly Vijñāneśvara, the author of the *Mitākṣarā*. Cf. Nelson 1881: 222. For all Indian names and terms I maintain the spelling used by Bouchet himself. Notice, however, that these transliterations were produced by a French speaker, and have to be read as such.

followed within the caste, and on common usage, that is enough. One does not reason about it; it is the rule, and one has to conform to it. He who would try to demonstrate that a particular custom is not fully established and that it has serious drawbacks, would not gain anything by doing so. Custom invariably prevails over the best arguments.

Among many examples one might mention, I shall select one from the customs observed for marriage. According to a custom accepted in all castes, children of two brothers or two sisters are considered brothers of one another, whereas children of a brother and a sister are only germane cousins. "That is the reason, they say, why the latter are allowed to intermarry, but not the former. Otherwise, it would follow that a brother and a sister could equally well unite themselves in marriage, which would be horrible and totally against common sense." When one tries to convince them [486b] that the degree of relationship is exactly the same between children of two brothers or two sisters as between children of a brother and a sister, since they descend from the same lineage at the same distance, the objection appears to them absurd and they regard those who do it as people who question the most basic principles.

Their unyielding attitude, based on the prejudice of their education and on the continuous application of these maxims, seems to them far more cogent than any kind of demonstration. Consequently, they think that they have convincingly removed all obstacles one opposes to them, as soon as they say: "It is the custom". "For," they continue, "how could we act in disagreement with usages established by the absolute consensus of our ancestors, of those who have followed them in the past and those who are living today? Would one not have to be deprived of reason to revolt against that which has been regulated by so many wise men and has been given authority by uninterrupted practice?"

I have asked them occasionally why they did not collect these customs in books which one might consult if needed. Their answer is that, if these customs were entered into books, only the learned would be able to read them, whereas, if they are handed down from generation to generation through the channel of tradition, everyone is fully informed. "However," they add, "these are only the general laws and universal customs, for, as far as particular customs are concerned, they have been inscribed on copper plates which were guarded with care in a big tower at Cangibouram. Since the Moors have nearly entirely destroyed this large and famous town, no one has been able to find out what happened to these plates; the only thing we know is that they contained everything that relates to any caste in particular and the relations which different castes should observe among one another."

I can vouch for what the Indians say about this, namely that in the past they preserved in Cangibouram everything concerning public deeds. It is, indeed, from Cangibouram that a brame once obtained the copper plate recording the donation of certain tribes, made more than four hundred years ago, by an Indian king to the church of San Thomé. When I arrived in India, the Moors had not yet conquered Cangibouram. In those days, when there was a dispute about caste among Indians, [487a] they said: "Let us go to Cangibouram; we shall find there several brames who possess the laws inscribed on copper plates." Even today, while the city begins to reestablish itself, there are ten or twelve brames there who are often consulted and whose decisions are adhered to. I am not at all convinced that they have read this kind of laws; at least they know more about the tradition than others.

"As far as matters not related to caste are concerned," the Indians say, "these are easily resolved. Common sense and natural insight suffice for anyone who sincerely wishes to decide with equity." As a matter of fact, they have a number of general maxims in lieu of laws, which are known to everybody: the most important ones, on caste, no one ignores. There are no problems except in a few embarrassing cases, which, moreover, present themselves only rarely. I shall relate a few of these maxims, which establish some kind of custom in India.

I remember telling one day a gentleman from Europe what I have now the honor to report to you. He told me that there must certainly be much injustice in India, not only because of the inequity and greed of the judges, but also because there are no sure rules as there are in Europe, in civil law and canon law. I shall not examine here the enormous advantages one pretends to derive from this prodigious multitude of laws; but it seems to me that the Indians are not really to be blamed for not having cared to codify their customs. After all, is it not enough that they posses them perfectly? And, if this is so, what is the good of books? In reality, nothing is better known than these customs: I have seen children ten or twelve years old who knew them perfectly. And when one requires of them something contrary to them, they answer immediately: "Ajaratoucou virodam [*ācārattukku virōtam*] (it is against custom)." If I am not mistaken, I have read somewhere, in a lawbook, that, if customs are accepted by general agreement in a nation, it matters little that they are unwritten; the fact that it is not necessary to write them down is perfect proof of their validity and authority. This maxim fully justifies the practice of the Indians.

[487b] The Indians clearly remember a number of kings who have become famous on account of the equity of decisions they passed, decisions which all peoples have invariably praised. One

of the most remarkable among them was Viéramarken. They say that he was unique in unraveling truth from falsehood, and in disentangling it from the deepest darkness in which one might try to hide it. His reputation was so universally established that not only the princes and kings of his time, but the gods themselves appealed to him to settle their differences. The following happened to the gods of the *chorcam* [*corkkam*] (which is the name of one of their five paradises). These gods had a serious disagreement; unable to solve it themselves, they agreed to let Viéramarken settle it. They provided him with an aerial chariot, and installed him on the throne of Devendiren. His decisions were so well received that they gave him, by way of compensation, the throne on which he had been seated.

However famous this judge was, the Indians hasten to add that he was by far inferior to another named Muiadi-ramen [*Mariyātai-rāman*].[877] In olden times he was considered the head of the castes; some say he was a brame. Never has anyone displayed more acuteness and sagacity than he. People sometimes took pleasure in inventing cases that were specially intricate and puzzling, thinking that he would surely not be able to clear them up. But again and again they were surprised to see how neatly he unraveled the most confused cases, and the ease with which he arrived at decisions which were absolutely unobjectionable. Far be it from me to consider these decisions as admirable as the Indians say they are; if I related them here together with the circumstances that surround them, nothing could be less comfortable to our taste. I shall restrict myself to selecting two of them that have something special. The first one has something in common with Solomon's judgment. It is as follows.

A rich man had married two wives. The first one, who was born without any charms, had nevertheless one advantage over the second, namely that she had a child of her husband, whereas the other had not. On the other hand, the latter was endowed with the kind of beauty that had completely captured her husband's heart. The first wife, incensed by the fact that she was held in disdain while her rival was loved and esteemed, [488a] decided to avenge herself; she resorted to a stratagem as cruel as it is unusual in India. Before realizing her project she made sure to spread the rumor that, of course, she was extremely sensitive to the disdain of her husband who had eyes for her rival only, but that, on the

[877] See Ramachandra Rao 1902. Bouchet's first story corresponds, generally, to "The Child Murderess Detected" (pp. 5–10); details vary, but the solution is identical. Bouchet's second story is similar to another tale, on how to recogize an impostor (pp. 43–47), but in this case even the solution is different: crawling through the neck of a bottle.

other hand, she had a son who meant everything to her. She then showed in every possible way how fond she was of the boy who was still a nursling. "This is the way in which I avenge myself of my rival: I only have to show her this child, and I see painted on her face the grief not to have as much."

After she had convinced everyone how infinitely fond she was of her son, she decided to kill the child —something that sounds unbelievable in India. And indeed, while her husband was absent in a distant town, she wrung the child's neck and took it to the other wife while she was asleep. The next morning, pretending to look for her son, she ran to her rival's room. Seeing the child dead there, she threw herself down, pulled out her hair, and screamed loud enough to be heard by all the people. "O this wretched woman! Look what she has done out of wrath because I have a son and she does not." All the people gathered as she was screaming; suspicion mounted against the other woman. "It is just not possible that a mother would kill her own son. And even if a mother might eventually be carried away to that point, this one can surely not be suspected of having committed such a crime, for she adored her son and regarded him as her sole consolation." The other woman had no other defense except to say that there is no passion more cruel and violent than jealousy, which can lead to the most tragic excesses. There were no witnesses, and no one knew how to find out the truth. After several individuals had tried in vain to decide this obscure case, it was brought before Mariadi-ramen. A date was fixed on which both women were to plead their causes. They did so with the kind of natural eloquence that passion is wont to generate. Mariadi-ramen listened to both of them, and then decided as follows. "The one who is innocent and claims the other one to be guilty of the crime under investigation, shall walk around this assembly hall in the condition which I shall prescribe." [488b] The condition which he indicated was an indecent one and one unworthy of a chaste woman. The mother of the child rose and said boldly: "To show you that it is indeed my rival who is guilty, I not only agree to go around this assembly in the condition which is required of me —I shall do it a hundred times, if necessary." The other woman said: "However innocent I am, even if I were to be convicted of the crime of which I have been falsely accused, and even if I were condemned to die the most cruel death, I shall never do what is required of me here. I shall rather die a hundred times than consent to doing things that are unworthy of a woman who has any honor left at all." The first woman wanted to retort, but the judge told her to remain silent. Raising his voice he declared the second woman innocent and the first one guilty. "For a woman who is so modest as to rather subject herself to a certain death than agree to do something that is ever so slightly indecent, can never have decided to commit so heinous a crime. On the other hand, one who has lost all shame and bashfulness, and subjects herself voluntarily to this kind of indecent behavior, could not indicate more clearly that she is capable of the most heinous crimes." The first woman, ashamed to have been thus exposed, was forced publicly to confess her crime. Everyone in the audience applauded the decision, and Mariadi-ramen's reputation soon spread all over India.

The second example has something strange and rather fabulous to it. As you know, the Indians believe in the existence of lower classes of gods. Although these are, by nature, far inferior to the gods of a higher order, they are nevertheless much more skilful than all mankind put together. This being so, here are the facts. A man by the name of Parjen, known for his strength and his extraordinary skill was married and had, for quite some time, lived peacefully with his wife. One day, I do not know why, he became very angry at her; he abandoned her, and went away to a distant kingdom. In the meanwhile, according to the Indians, one of the lower gods whom I have just mentioned, took the form of Parjen; he came to the house and made peace with his parents-in-law. [489a] When they had thus lived together for about three or four months, the real Parjen arrived. He threw himself at the feet of his parents-in-law, and begged them to return his wife to him. He sincerely acknowledged that it was wrong on his part to get carried way as much as he had been, but that, after all, a first offense ought to be forgiven. The parents-in-law were very surprised to hear him say all this, for they did not understand why Parjen once again asked for the pardon they had given him a few months earlier. And they were even more surprised when the false Parjen arrived. Seeing each other face to face, they began to quarrel together, and they tried to chase one another out of the house. People gathered around, and no one was able to determine which was the true one. They both had the same figure, the same apparel, the same facial expression, and the same tone of voice. In short, to relate in a few words what the Indians are wont to tell at great length, they were exactly like the Sosias described by Plautus.[878] They pleaded before the palleacaren [*palaiyakkāran*], but he confessed that he did not understand anything of the whole matter. They went to the royal palace; the king gatlered his counselors but, after long deliberations, they did not

[878] Reference to Plautus' *Amphitruo*, in which Hermes, disguised as the slave Sosia, keeps away intruders while Zeus, in tbe form of Amphitruo, is with Alkmene. The arrival of the real Rosia leads to all kinds of confusion.

know what to say either. In the end the matter was brought before Mariadi-ramen. He was more than a little puzzled when, after the real Parjen had stated his name, his father's and mother's names, the names of other relatives, the name of the village where he was born, together with other events in his life, the false Parjen said: "He who has just spoken is a cheat; he has inquired about my name, the names of my parents, about my birth, and everything else concerning me, and now he comes and falsely declares that he is Parjen. I am the real one, and I take all those present here as witnesses, especially those who have seen my strength and I my skill". —The true Parjen replied: "Ha! it is me who has done all the things you falsely claim";— The large crowd that heard these declarations thought that this time Mariadi-ramen would not get out of such puzzling business, [not clear in original] but he soon demonstrated that he always had adequate ways of clearing up the most obscure and confused facts. Pointing at an enormously large stone which several men together would have difficulty moving, he said: [489b] "Your respective statements make it difficult for me to come to a decision; and yet, I do have a safe way to find out the truth. The real Parjen is reputed to be unusually strong and skillful; let him prove it by lifting up that stone with his hands". The real Parjen tried his best to move the stone; people were surprised to see that he actually lifted it ever so little, even though the effort made him fall to the ground. He was duly applauded by the full assembly who were convinced that he was the real Parjen. The false Parjen in turn approached the stone, and lifted it up with his hands as if it were a feather. People exclaimed, "There is no doubt, this one is the real Parjen." Mariadi-ramen, on the contrary, decided in favor of the first, who had hardly lifted the stone. He gave his reasons as follows: "He who first lifted the stone did what was humanly possible even when one has extraordinary strength; the second, who lifted the stone without trouble and was ready to throw it up in the air, is undoubtedly a demon or one of the lower gods, who has taken the form of Parjen; for there is not a single mortal who would dare to try what he did." The false Parjen was so ashamed to have been exposed that he disappeared instantly. There is no doubt that this story has been invented to demonstrate the extent of Mariadi-ramen's sagacity. I have left out many details which the Indians add to it; they would be more tiresome than would please you.

There is still another individual, named Apachi[879] of whom the Indians speak very often: he resembles in many ways our own

[879] Appāji (Sājuva Timma), Telugu poet, Brahman minister and friend of Krishna Deva Raya of Vijayanagar (1509–1523). See Sundaram Aiyar 1908.

Aesop. He lived at the court of one of the Indian kings, and was capable of solving even the most obscure riddles which, in those days, kings were wont to propose to one another. For it was mandatory to find the meaning of these riddles, especially those that were proposed by the universal emperor of India; there were penalties for those who did not succeed. However, since this touches only indirectly on the decrees pronounced by the ancients, I shall not go into it here.

These examples clearly illustrate what the Indians consider to be the ideal judge. They exult when they speak of the qualities he is supposed to have; [490a] and, if they were as punctilious in actual practice as they are in their speculations, I think they would not in any way yield to the Europeans. "A judge," they say, "must acquire a good knowledge of the case under consideration; he must know perfectly all maxims that bear upon the law; he must be virtuous; he should be rich so as not to be bought with money; he must be more than twenty years old, not to be inclined to make hurried decisions because of imprudence which is the earmark of youth; he must be less than sixty years old, for the minds of sexagenarians weaken, and they are no longer capable of exerting the same energy; if he is a friend or relative of either party, he must disqualify himself as a judge, lest affection blind him; he shall never decide alone, however good his intentions and knowledge may be." All the things I have just now enumerated are written in grandonic verses, i.e. in the Samouseradam[880] language.

They add that it shall be the judge's principal concern to examine witnesses carefully: they can be easily corrupted and are normally very clever at giving ambiguous answers, in order to exonerate themselves in case they are caught in false testimony. In fact, I may say that even the least intelligent Indians would, in this respect, teach a lesson to those in Europe who are most accustomed to concealing the truth. That is why judges who want to arrive at the full truth, insist on having the responses which witnesses gave to their questions put down in writing; they then dismiss them; two days later they call them again, and ask them the same questions in a somewhat different way; and since the judges are usually as expert as the witnesses themselves, they construe the answers of the witnesses in every possible way, not to allow them later to explain their earlier statements in any other

[880] The same printing error: *Samouseradam*, for *Samonscradam*, also appears in the 1720 and 1781 editions. On the various names used by early European authors to indicate the Sanskrit language —including "Grandonic"—, see Rocher 1977: text pp. 3–4, translation pp. 81–82.

than their common sense. The Indians say that this is what happens when the judge is not corrupt; if he has been won over, he will unfailingly make the witnesses say what he wants them to say.

Other qualities required of a judge are patience, gentleness, and, above all, high regard for what is prescribed by custom. [490b] All Indian verses are replete with invectives against a judge who does not obey the laws. They say, "He is a raging torrent that has shattered its banks and cannot be stopped by anything; he devastates and lays waste anything that comes in his path."

They also have a kind of proverb which they repeat incessantly, namely that the judge shall never look at the faces or hands of pleading parties. They extend the interpretation of this maxim to anything that might establish some kind of connection between the judge and the party, such as birth, alliance, or profession. In connection with the fact that he shall never look at the faces of the parties they quote a quatrain which is to them more or less what Pibrac's quatrains were to us.[881] Its meaning is as follows: "A king who has to decide a lawsuit between one of his subjects and one of the princes, his sons, shall look at the prince, his son, as if he were one of his subjects, and at the subject as if he were his son lest natural affection mislead him; even then it will be quite an accomplishment if, notwithstanding this precaution, his self-esteem, through imperceptible vicissitudes does not mar his best intentions." I have also heard them speak in the highest terms of a king who ruled long ago, at a time when justice was meted out perfectly. He was so afraid of being taken by surprise that each time he climbed on his throne to decide a lawsuit, he had himself blindfolded before the arrival of the parties; and when the parties were present, he explicitly forbade them to say anything that might reveal their identity. They add, "That is also the time when the gods, delighted by the equity of these incorruptible judges, descended on earth to witness it all, and shed showers of flowers on their heads. Alas! our time is so different from those happy days! only fraud and injustice remain."

In the second place, the Indians say, the fact that a judge shall not look at the hands of the parties means that he shall not allow himself to be won by presents, for nothing is more unworthy of a man of that station than giving way to as mean a passion as

[881] Gui du Faur, Seigneur de Pibrac (Toulouse 1529–Paris 1584). His *Cinquante quarrains contenant préceptes et enseignements utiles pour la vie de l'homme, composez á l'imitation de Phocylides, Epicharmus et autres Poëtes grecs,* was first published in 1574; there are numerous later editions, with additions. In the 18th and the first half of the 19th centuries Pibrac's *Quatrains* were included in many civics books for children (Alban Cabos: Guy du Faur de Pibrac, Paris: Champion, 1922, p. 337 n.1).

greed. This is one of their sentences: "When you visit the temple of a god, when you pay your respects to the master who taught you, when you go to see one of your relatives or friends whom you have not met for a long time, [491a] it is appropriate to take them presents, but not when you go to see a judge; to him it would be an insult."

Some time ago I talked to an Indian who was reputed to be very learned among other things we also discussed this particular topic. He told me that the maxim that a judge shall not look at the hands or faces of the parties has indeed a very exalted meaning; however, he said, the opposite maxim has an even more refined and delicate sense. In other words, he held that a judge shall look at the faces and hands of those who plead before him. He shall look at their faces, for in many cases the faces of the parties and witnesses exhibit nearly sure marks of what goes on in their minds, and they provide great opportunities to find out the truth. Passions, he continued, are often so clearly painted in the eyes and all over the face that one easily recognizes hate, love, anger, or whatever other passion the individual tries to conceal. There characteristic marks are often so evident that they contribute a good deal to disclosing what the individual tried hard to conceal. And, even though such marks are not always infallible, they are often extremely useful. The Indians say that the face, which can be seen, is the reflection of the soul which cannot. He added that the judge shall also look at the hands, i.e. the presents one wants to give him. He will thus find out either that the pleader has a poor opinion of his own cause, or that he suspects the equity of the judge. This kind of knowledge may very well guide him later in the proceedings.

The Indian books are full of invectives and imprecations against iniquitous judges who allow themselves to be bribed, and who betray justice. This is the meaning of one of their quatrains: "A bad judge who sentences the innocent will have his family ruined, and his house destroyed; weeds and eroucou [*erukku*] shrubs will grow in the rooms he lived in, and his children will die at a tender age." If I wanted to explore this subject further, I would never have finished; I shall rather pass on to other topics which are not less important.

This is what they think about witnesses who are often to be interrogated by the judges: one ought to be on one's guard against witnesses who are very young or beyond sixty years of age, or who are poor; [491b] as far as women are concerned, they should never be admitted, except in cases of absolute emergency. They have strange ideas about the testimony of one-eyed or hunchbacked people, and of all those who have similar physical disfigurements. "Experience has taught us that the testimony of such people is always very suspect, and that they are much more easily corrupted than others." I must add that Europeans are not at all fit to hear Indians as witnesses, unless they have lived in India for a long time and have fully mastered the language; otherwise they will inevitably be misled by the ambiguous answers they receive.

Each head of a village is the natural judge in suits arising within his village; to make sure that his decisions are as equitable as possible, he selects three or four of the most experienced villagers, who sit as assessors, and who pronounce judgment with him. If the convicted party is not satisfied with the judgment, he may appeal to the maniacarren [*māṇiyakkāran*], who is a kind of chief who has a group of villages under his jurisdiction. He too surrounds himself with two or three individuals who help him examine and decide the the case. Finally, it is possible once more to appeal against this decision to the immediate officers of the prince, who judge in the last resort. If it is a question related to caste, it is the heads of castes who decide. In those cases it is also possible for the relatives to assemble; in general they decide with great equity. The gourous, i.e. the spiritual fathers (for the Gentiles have these as much as the Christians), settle most disputes that arise among their disciples. It happens that parties to a dispute choose arbitrators, whom they give authority to judge their difference; they then comply with the decision without further appeal to other judges.

Of all these judges the maniacarrens are the only ones who take a fee, and even they do not always do so. But there are some who take one tenth of the amount which was the object of the lawsuit; e.g., if the amount is one hundred ecus, one gives ten to the maniacarren. It is normally the party that wins the case who is forced to pay this, for the losing party is already punished enough by having to pay what he owes. [492a] As far as the pagan gourous are concerned, they take, much more; but, according to what they say, this money is not for them: it goes to acts of piety and good works.

After this description of the judges, I must now tell you, Sir, what are the duties of the parties. Those who are engaged in a lawsuit shall plead their cause in person, except when a friend agrees to do so for them. They must maintain a respectful attitude in the presence of their judges; they do not interrupt one another, they merely indicate by a slight movement of the head that they intend to refute what the other party says. When the pleadings are finished, the parties and their witnesses are dismissed. The judge and his counselors deliberate together; and, as soon as they agree on what the judgment shall be, the judge calls in the parties and hands them the decree. You see, Sir, that in this way one avoids the delays caused by chicanery, and that the legal charges amount to very little. In fact, there is no country in the world in which litigation is cheaper than in India: as long as the judges maintain their integrity, one is out of court and out of litigation in no time.

Since most lawsuits in India are about debts and about debts and about borrowed money the remittal of which has been delayed too long, I owe you an explanation of how these sorts of loans are treated. It is customary for the borrower to give a mourrī [*muṟi*], i.e. a bond, in which he pledges to pay his creditor the amount borrowed together with interest. For this document to be authentic it shall be signed by at least three witnesses; it bears the day, month, and year when the money has been received, and states how much interest one has promised to pay per month.

The Indians distinguish three kinds of interest: some interests are virtuous, others are sinful, and others again are neither. These are the expressions they use. The interest called virtuous is of one percent per month, i.e. twelve percent per year. They say that those who do not take more than this perform an act of great virtue, for, they add, with the small profit they make, they relieve the misery of those who are in pressing need. They nearly speak of this way of lending money as if it were almsgiving. The interest called sinful is of four percent per month, i.e. forty-eight percent per year, [492b] which means that after a period of two years and two months the amount is doubled. The interest which is neither virtuous nor sinful is of two percent per month, i.e. twenty-four percent per year. Those who lend money and take no more than the interest which is virtuous, ordinarily do not count the first month nor the month in which payment is made; they are however not forced to make this allowance, and, when they thus relinquish some of their rights, it is pure generosity on their part. In general, it does not occur to them to examine whether or not there is usury in this kind of loan; they believe that they have a right to make the most of their money, and they consider forbidden only that interest which they themselves regard as sinful.

After the creditor has waited for several months, or a year, or two years, he is entitled to arrest his debtor in the name of the prince, and under penalty of being declared a rebel. The debtor is supposed not to disregard this until he has satisfied his creditor. This custom resembles in many ways the *haro* cry which is still in use in Normandy,[882] by means of which one invokes the help

[882] The Old Norman custom of "crying for justice," appears for the first time in France in the *Grand Coutumier de Normandie*; it still survives on the Channel Islands. The wronged party must cry, on his knees and before witnesses: "Haro! haro! haro; à l'aide, mon prince, on me fait tort."

of the judiciary and forces the debtor to go before the judge. In this country the debtor is not yet forced to appear before the judge, for the first passers-by intervene on his behalf and insist that the creditor grant him another few months. Once this term has expired, the creditor is again entitled to arrest the debtor in the name of the prince. it is surprising to see the total submissiveness of those who are thus arrested, for not only would they not dare to run away, but they are not even allowed to drink or eat without the express permission of the creditor. It is then that they are brought before the judge, who again asks for a few months' delay. In the meanwhile the interest continues to accumulate. Finally, if the debtor fails to pay at the prescribed time, the judge convicts him, has him placed in a kind of prison, and has his cattle and furniture sold. It is, however, rare that the entire amount is recovered; one normally induces the creditor to forego part of the interest which he is entitled to.

When someone is accused of theft and there are strong presumptions against him, he is forced to prove his innocence by plunging his hand in a kettle of boiling water. As soon as he withdraws his hand, one wraps it in a piece of cloth, and seals it near the wrist. [493a] Three days later one examines the hand, and if there is no mark of burn, he is declared innocent. This test is quite common in India, and there are many who withdraw their hands uninjured from boiling oil.

To speak of the Christians only, some of them have been forced thus to give evidence of their innocence. Without consulting us they went to public squares, and, in view of everyone, plunged their hands and their arms up to the elbow in boiling oil, without being burned at all. I have examined their hands and their arms without finding any trace of burn.

I once knew a Christian who had a most charming wife; and yet he could not rid himself of the idea that she was unfaithful to him. The deadly reproaches which he constantly addressed to her reduced her to a state of desperation. One day, when the poor woman was overcome by grief, she told her husband that she was prepared to give him any proof he wanted of her innocence. The husband at once locked the door, filled a vessel with oil, boiled it, and ordered his wife to plunge her hand into it; she obeyed immediately, saying that she would not withdraw her hand unless so ordered. The husband was astounded at his wife's determination; he left her a while without saying anything. But then, seeing that she gave no sign of pain and that her hand was not burned at all, he threw himself at her feet, and asked to be forgiven. Four or five days later he came to see me with his wife, and told me the whole story. I mainly questioned the wife, who assured me that she had no more pain than had she put her hand in lukewarm water. Believe what you please; as far as I am concerned, having seen the degree of jealousy of the husband and how fully convinced he was afterwards of his wife's virtuousness, I cannot doubt the veracity of the incident.

In another village a Christian woman, who was suspected by her husband, was accused of infidelity by him before the caste, where the Gentiles hold all power. She was sentenced on the spot to walk twenty steps, carrying in the border of the cloth that covered her head thirty burning coals; if the cloth burned, she was to be declared guilty. [493b] She carried the coal, and, after walking twenty steps, she flung the coal at the accuser. This incident happened before more than two hundred witnesses. I arrived among these people two months after the facts, and I imposed on the husband a penance proportionate to his fault.

I know others who have been forced to lick with their tongues flaming tiles, and who were not burned by it. When the Gentiles impose the ordeal of boiling oil, they first have the accused wash his hands; then they cut his fingernails for fear that there might be a hidden remedy against burns.

They also resort to another ordeal which is quite common. They prepare a large round vessel, something like a big bowl, the entrance to which is so narrow that nothing more than a wrist can pass through it. In the bowl they place one of those big serpents whose bite is fatal if not taken care of immediately; they also drop a ring in it. Subsequently those who are suspected of having committed theft are forced to withdraw the ring from the vessel. The first one who is bitten is declared guilty.

However, before they have recourse to these extremes, they take every precaution not to expose the accused to these types of ordeals too lightly. For instance, if a golden necklace or some similar jewel has been stolen, they hand thirty or forty round vessels in the form of bowls, one to each, so that the thief can secretly deposit the jewel in it. These vessels are made of material that easily dissolves in water. They will go and drop their vessels in a sort of basin, where all bowls are dissolved. One normally finds at the bottom of the basin the stolen object, without having to expose the thief.

When it comes to murder, and the *lex talionis* exists in the caste, this law is observed in all its rigor. Father Martin's letter...[883] gives

[883] The 1840 edition has: "which you can read in one of the collections of these Lettres édifiantes et curieuses." The same formula occurs in the 1781 edition; the 1720 edition refers to "the tenth collection of these Lettrés édifiantes et curieuses." For bibliographical data on the letter from, Father Pierre Martin (1665–1716) to Father de Villette, dated Marava, 8 November 1709, see Streit: *Bibliotheca Missionum*, vol. 6, p. 27, No. 111. English translations in *The Travels of*

several examples of it. One should however not think that the *lex talionis* prevails throughout the caste of thieves: it is practiced only among those in between Marava[884] and Maduré.

Murder is relatively rare all over India; this is probably the reason why there is little justice for this sort of crime. [494a] Provided one gives a certain amount of money to the prince, say one hundred pagodes, he obtains his pardon without difficulty. The surprising thing is that, if an officer of the prince is killed, the murderer will be in the clear by donating one thousand ecus. The law allows a husband to kill his adulterous wife and her accomplice, if he can surprise them together; but he must kill them both, in which case no suit can be brought against him.

It is not exactly fear of punishment that holds them to their duties. During the reign of princess Mangamal[885] who made it her principle not to have anyone die, there was no greater disorder than under the kings who punished the guilty. If there was a state in Europe without any death penalty and in which exile, as is the case in India, consisted of nothing else than leaving the town by one gate and re-entering it by another, one can imagine the excesses in which people would engage!

But whoever the king be, it is never permitted in India to have a brame die, whatever crime he be guilty of; the only way to punish him is to tear his eyes out. I was in the city of Trichirapali when they caught two brames who were performing abominable sacrifices to ensure the death of the queen. The only punishment they got was that their eyes were torn out; and even then this was done against the wishes of the queen who could not conceive that they be punished. On the other hand, one sees in the history of the kings of Maduré, that, when they were unhappy with certain brames, they of course avoided shedding their blood, but they had them confined within a thorny hedge, twelve or fifteen feet across; the hedge was guarded by soldiers; every day the amount of food and drink that was given them was

Several Learned Missioners of the Society of Jesus, London: Gosling; 1714, pp. 126–132; also John Lockman1743, part 2, pp. 408–416, especially pp. 410–413, with disbelieving comments, in the footnotes, by the editor.

[884] Nelson 1881: 227: "by which. ..term I understand the town of Ramnad." However, Lockman (1743: 2.408) translating Father Martin: "Marava is a great Kingdom, tributary to that of Madura. However, the monarch who governs it is only nominally so; his Troops being sufficient to make Head against those of the King of Madura, shou'd the latter pretend to claim the Tribute by Force of arms. The King of Marava reigns with absolute Sway, and several Prioces are subject to him, all whom he dispossesses of their Dominions at Pleasure." On Bouchet's map of South India (see supra) Marava clearly indicates the territory East of Maduré and South of Tanjaor.

[885] Queen Mangammāl, regent of Madura (*Imperial Gazetteer* vol. 16, p. 390).

reduced, and in this way the absence of food slowly caused them to die.

All this, Sir, will give you a general idea of how justice is being administered in India I shall now relate some of their maxims, which are the actual laws that guide them in their judgments.

[494b] First maxim.

When there are several children in a family, the males alone inherit; the girls have no claim at all to the inheritance.

I have often reproached Indians that this maxim appears unjust and contrary to natural law, for daughters have the same father and mother as their brothers. In the first place they came up with the general answer that that was the custom, and that such a custom, introduced as it was by the general consensus of the nation, could not possibly be unjust. They then added that the daughters had no ground for complaint, for their fathers and mothers and, in their absence, their brothers had the obligation to marry them off. In this way, by being transferred into another family with the same rank as their own (for marriages outside the caste are forbidden), the advantages which a daughter encountered in her new family made up for the share in the inheritance she might have been able to claim. I answered, "You can tell that to the Europeans who live on the coast and who have only a very superficial knowledge of your customs, but not to someone like me who has lived with you for many years. After all, is it not the fathers and mothers who profit most from the marriages of their daughters? Is it not to them that the bridegrooms take the money with which they buy the daughters they are about to marry?" For it should be kept in mind that, for the Indians, marrying and buying a wife are the same thing; hence when they want people to know that they are going to get married they normally say that they are going to buy a wife.

However, I must confess that they have a ready answer to this objection of mine. This is what they say: "The sum of money which the bridegroom gives his father-in-law is almost entirely used to buy ornaments for the bride. Indeed, he has earrings made for her, silver bracelets, coral and golden necklaces, golden and silver rings, in accordance with the rank and elevation of their castes (it should be noticed that these rings are worn on the toes as well as on the fingers). Whatever is left over, they add, is used for the wedding banquet; in fact, the expenses imposed on the father of the bride often exceed what he received." [495a] Those who use the money in other ways are looked down upon; for instance, they object to the greed of certain brames who sell their daughters and use hardly anything for them from the amount that is given them. These answer, however, that they do use the money justly, for it serves to marry off their male children.

I remember one day in Europe, when I was explaining this custom of the Indians. There was an outcry that nothing could be more barbarian and contrary to the laws of nature. And yet, we have something similar in our own sacred books. It is said that after the death of Salphad, who had no male children, his daughters called Moses and Eleazar [Numbers 27:1–11] and asked that they be allowed to collect the inheritance. From which the learned Cornelius a Lapide[886] draws the conclusion that among the Jews daughters did not receive any share of their father's inheritance if they had brothers: "From this passage it appears that among Jews, as soon as there was male offspring, they took the entire estate, so that daughters could not collect any share of the inheritance. The reason for this is, the same author adds, that among the Israelites families were named, distinguished, and preserved through the male children only. This distinction was thus made by God's providence, in order that one might recognize the sequence of the heritages and from whom they originated, and in order that one might realize that the Redeemer was born a Jew and in the family of Judah, as promised by God to Jacob." Hence it is that, among the Jews, daughters had nothing to look forward to from their father's estate, as soon as they had brothers; and even when they had none, it is not so clear whether they did have a claim, for we see that when the daughters of Salphad claimed their respective shares, God had to be consulted and his decision, which was favorable, waited for.

Daughters among the Indians are even worse off than among the Jews. At least Jewish daughters had a right to the estate when they had no brothers, whereas among the Indians the exclusion of daughters is absolute, irrespective of whether they have brothers or not. Two brothers marry; one has a son, the other a daughter. [495b] All the goods which naturally should go to the girl go to her uncle, who at the same time contracts the obligation to marry his niece off as well as he can.

There are, however, in India a number of petty kingdoms in which princesses enjoy considerable advantages which place them well ahead of their brothers, for the right of succession is always from the side of the mother. For example, if a king has a

[886] Actually, Cornelius Cornelii a Lapide, translation of Dutch Cornelis Cornelissen van de Steen (1567–1637), Jesuit, biblical scholar. professor at Louvain and the Collegium Romanum. Author of Commentarii in S. Scripturas (1621–1622; lates complete edition, 1871, 25 volumes). See Sommervogel 1893: vol. 4, col. 1511–1526.

daughter of a wife of royal blood, while at the same time having a male child of another wife of the same caste, it is the princess who will succeed and who will receive the inheritance. She can marry whom she pleases; and even if her husband is not of royal blood, her children will be kings, for they have royal blood on their mother's side. Their father does not I count, for, as I said, the right devolves solely from the side of the mother.

Another consequence of the same principle is that, if the reigning princess has a son and a daughter, and if one is unable to find a princess of royal blood to marry the prince, the daughter's children will reign rather than her brother's. And I when both the prince and princess remain childless, as it happened in the kingdom of Travancor, one looks elsewhere to find descendants of the same blood. This practice is followed even when the king has offspring of his own caste, if they are not of royal blood from the side of the mother. When the absolute power rests with queens, there are always six or seven persons who help them carry the burden of government.

Second maxim.

The eldest son of a king or prince, a palleacarren, or head of a village, does not necessarily succeed to the estates or government of his father.

This maxim, which governs the succession of princes, requires some explanation. Indians distinguish two categories of dignities: those that pass from father to son, and those that attach to a certain person without necessarily being passed on to his children. I do not refer here to the latter category, for the prince can dispose of them at will and he can select whom he wants; but I want to speak of the estates that are hereditary. Custom requires that the eldest succeed, if their qualities are such that they are capable of doing so; [496a] but if they are not very intelligent and if they appear unfit to govern well, and if, on the other hand, the younger one seems to be competent to perform the duties of a prince, the king makes the necessary arrangements to pass his estates on to the younger one. If he fails to do so, his relatives assemble upon his death and elect the younger one. And, since the custom is well established, it is less difficult for the eldest to obey it. In fact, his situation is no worse for it; while avoiding the vexations and anguish inherent to royalty, he fully enjoys the pleasures and comforts that go with it. Also, no stone is left unturned to allay the pain he might suffer as a result of his forced submission.

What has been said of kings and princes is also true, proportionately, of palleacarrens and heads of villages. We have observed with admiration how two brothers, the princes of Tanjaour, governed together the country that was left them by their elder brother, who was childless. It is true that experience was to teach them that this common rule troubled their subjects, and that for this reason they divided the kingdom of Tanjaour between themselves. But they do not cease to live together in the same palace, and do so in perfect harmony. They are the children of a brother of the famous Sivaji,[887] who is renowned in India for having shattered the throne of the successors of Tamerlan.

The Mogol princes behave quite differently: he who has the strongest army and who defeats his brothers succeeds to the vast territories of the Mogol; the conquered ones always pay with their lives or imprisonment. They say that when Aureng-zeb was asked to determine which one of his children he considered most capable of succeeding him, he refused to do so, the reason being that that decision had to be made in heaven. He himself acceded to the throne after killing his brothers and imprisoning his father whom, as he put it, he wanted to relieve of the burden of government: strange politics indeed, on the part of the Mogols, when brothers are reduced to the necessity of murdering one another. Our Indian princes abhor so detestable a maxim: there is no other country in which brothers are equally united.

[496b] Third maxim.

If the property has not been divided upon the death of the father, anything that has been acquired by one of the children must be entered into the common stock and divided equally.

This maxim may look strange, but it is universally applied in India; it is also a rule that allows the settlement of numerous lawsuits. An example will help clarify what I mean. Imagine that an Indian, who has five children, leaves at the time of his death one hundred pagodes, which is five hundred livres in our money. If one divided these, each one should receive one hundred livres. But if there is no partition —which is resorted to very rarely, especially when one of the brothers is unmarried —, then, even if the eldest has earned ten thousand pagodes, he has to add this amount to the common stock, for it to be divided equally among all the brothers. All the relatives assemble for that purpose; if there is any resistance on the part of the eldest, he is uniformly denounced on the basis of the maxim I am now explaining.

887 In reality they were the descendants of Śivāji's half-brother, Vyankajī, who established a Maratha dynasty at Tanjore in 1674.

There is another custom, blamed by some, admired by others. When among brothers one is not very intelligent whereas the others are, the share of the former is made larger than that of the latter. They say that the one who is not intelligent is incapable of making the most of what he gets, whereas the others who are ingenious and skilful will soon become far richer than the brother to whom they surrendered the better part of the inheritance.

There are families in which the question of partition never arises: all goods are held in common, and they live in perfect harmony. This happens when someone in the family is clever enough to make it continue. He is the one who manages all expenses; he is, as it were, the superior of the others who have no other worry than working under his orders. He marries off the sons and grandsons of his brothers, he provides for their wants, such as clothing, food, etc. The remarkable thing is that occasionally one finds women who are thus able to manage several families. I have known one who was in charge of eighty individuals whom she provided with every daily need. There are families in which no partition has ever been made, [497a] and which are not for that reason less prosperous than Indians normally are. The number of families that display this kind of unity, are generally greatly respected, and one tries hard to enter into marital alliances with them. The kind of detachment from worldly goods, which one observes among the pagans, is likely to confound so many Christians in Europe, whom the slightest profit divides and engages in endless lawsuits!

Fourth maxim.

Adopted children share equally in the estate with the children of their adoptive fathers and mothers.

When a man is childless, he often chooses a child from the household of one of his relatives, and adopts him. The ceremonies performed on these occasions are worth being described. A meeting is called at the house of the relatives of the adopter. One prepares a large brass vessel shaped like one of our large dishes. It is placed in such a way that the child can put his, two feet in it, and stand up on it if he is strong enough to do so. Then the husband and wife speak more less as follows: "We hereby give notice that, having no children of our own, we wish to adopt the one you see here. We choose him to be our son, so much so that henceforth all our goods will belong to him, as if he were born to us. He shall no longer expect anything from his natural father. In token, whereof we shall drink saffron water, if you agree."

Those present indicate their agreement by moving their heads. Then the husband and his wife bow down and pour water in which saffron has been dissolved; they wash the child's feet with it and drink the water that is left in the vessel. Instantly a document is drafted reporting what happened, and the witnesses sign it. This document is called *manchinircani-chitou.*

If the husband and wife have children of their own at a later time, these children become subordinate to the adopted child, whereas the latter enjoys the privileges of an eldest child; the law does not in any way distinguish between adopted and natural children. It even happens quite often that parents are more fond of the adopted son than of their own children; [497b] they think that the gods, moved by their virtuous act of adopting a child, gave them children and worldly goods which they would not otherwise have.

There is another mode of adoption which does not involve the same advantages, but which is not therefore less peculiar. When a father and a mother who have lost their child meet one that resembles their own, they beg him henceforth to regard them as his father and mother. The child does not normally fail to consent to this; in that case the adoption is a fact. In the language of the land this is called *oppari pirieradou.* The peculiar thing is that, by way of *oppari*, a choutre may take a brame as his son, if the latter resembles one of his deceased children, and the brame will call him his father. However, since they belong to different castes, they are never to eat together.

What has been said of the father and the mother with regard to a son adopted by *oppari*, also applies to brothers and sisters who adopt in the same way him or her who resembles one of their brothers and sisters whom death took away from them. From that moment they treat them like brothers and sisters; they assist them whenever necessary; they share in their good fortunes and misfortunes. The Indians say that in this way people ease to a large extent the grief caused by the loss of their close relatives, for they discover in those they adopt new children, new brothers, new sisters. However, this kind of relationship ends with the death of the adopters; its effects do not pass to their children.

Fifth maxim.

Orphans shall be treated like the children of those to whom they are entrusted.

One of the wisest regulations in India is the one regarding orphans. If they have uncles and aunts, they are raised like the other children of the house, for by law uncles and aunts are considered to be the fathers and mothers of their brothers' and sisters' children. The putative father is held to provide for them in the same way he provides for his other children, to marry them off when they come of age, and to spend whatever is necessary to prepare them for earning a living.

It is as a result of this custom that, when a man loses his wife, he does whatever he can to marry the sister of the deceased. [498a] They consider this an excellent maxim, for, they say, in this way there is no step-mother, and the children of the deceased sister invariably become the children of the living sister. They cannot be convinced of the equity of ecclesiastic law which forbids a man to re-marry the sister of his deceased wife "Do you not see, they tell us, that if the man does not marry his wife's sister, he has to marry another girl, who is bound to be a real step-mother, and who will not fail to wrong her husband's children to favor her own. On the contrary, if the sister of the deceased marries her brother-in-law, who is a widower, the children of the elder sister will always be considered her own."

Finally, if an orphan has neither elder brother, nor uncle, nor aunt, a meeting of relatives is called at which someone is appointed to care for him. They note down what the orphan's father left behind, and one is forced to return it to the orphan as soon as he comes of age. Those who raise orphans make them earn a living as soon as they are able to work; if they are intelligent, they are sent to school, to study reading, writing, and arithmetic.

Sixth maxim.

Whatever crime a child may have committed against his father, he cannot be disinherited.

However strange this maxim may appear, it prevents an infinite number of lawsuits. In Europe it is often very difficult to prove that a father who disinherits his son, does so for a valid reason. Assuredly, this power of the father together with he fear of being disinherited might keep children within the line of duty. Yet, one cannot deny that there are cases in which hate alone makes fathers abuse their powers.

Anyhow, the Indians fancy that their custom is a very wise one, and perfectly equitable. Thus if a son beats his father, if he wounds him, or, even worse, if in a moment of anger he threatens his father's life without however realizing his intentions, the father must nevertheless forgive him. If it happens that a father on his death bed declares that one of his children be excluded from his succession because of bad treatment received from him, [498b] the brothers who claim to execute their father's will

will be convicted by any law court in India. When one tells Indians that it is immoral for a father not to be able to deprive of his rights a son by whom he has been disdained and insulted, they reply that, on the contrary, nothing is more disgraceful than seeing a father die while hating his children. "It is a father's duty, they say, to pardon his son, however ungrateful and wicked he may be. After all, was the son not born from his father? So he is really a part of him. Have you ever seen a man cut off his right hand because it had cut off his left hand?"

For the same reason a child cannot disinherit his father, however unreasonable the latter may have been toward him. Thus if an only son, who is married, dies without leaving children behind but with an important estate, it is his father who becomes his heir; he cannot for any reason be excluded from the inheritance.

Seventh maxim.

The father shall pay all the debts contracted by his children; children shall equally pay all the debts of their father.

This is a general rule, which is very helpful in expediting lawsuits concerning these matters. Yet, the way the Indians explain it, the rule is rather surprising. After all, according to this custom, if a child is dissolute, and if he borrows all over while handing out bonds in due form, the father is bound to pay his debts. It does not serve any purpose to tell them that the son does not deserve pardon, for the money which he borrowed only served to encourage his debauchery; they reply that the father's kindness prevents him from being so rigorous. The same rule also applies to debts contracted by the father: they shall equally be paid by the children. Even if one were to prove that the father had used the money he borrowed for extravagant expenses unworthy of an honest man, and even if the son were to renounce the inheritance, he would still be obliged to pay his father's debts.

The same reasoning applies to debts contracted by one of the brothers before partition of the estate; [499a] the eldest must pay them, and the one who acted wastefully does not, therefore, forfeit his equal share in the common stock. The justification for this kind of behavior lies in another maxim, which the Indians hold in high esteem, namely that, after the father's death, the eldest son becomes like a father to his brothers. In fact, the other brothers throw themselves at his feet, and he regards them as his children. And, even as the father must pay the debts of his children, the eldest brother, who is like a father to his brothers, is equally liable to pay their debts. All this applies before partition only; but then, partition always comes very late. The rule does not extend to daughters: the father is not at all liable to pay their debts, nor is the brother bound by those of his sisters.

It is these general maxims, Sir, that serve as substitutes for laws in India; it is these that are followed in the administration of justice. There are other more specific laws which are applicable within each caste. Since these would lead me too far, they shall be the subject of another letter which I shall be honored to write you.

45

*Jacob Mossel's Treatise on the Customary Laws of the Veḷḷāla Cheṭṭiyārs**

1. On March 8, 1720, at the age of fifteen, Jacob Mossel (November 28, 1704–May 15, 1761) left Texel in Holland *en route* for Batavia, as a young sailor on board "de Haringtuijn" of the Chamber"[888] Enkhuizen. He arrived in Batavia on September 24, 1720.

On May 7, 1721 he sailed westward again, toward Negapatam which had been captured by the Dutch from the Portuguese in 1658 and was to remain one of their main Indian possessions until 1781.[889] He spent about twenty years in this town, building up a successful career which, in 1740, led to the post of "Raad extraordinair van Nederlandsch Indië" (Counsel extraordinary of the Netherlands Indies). Here is a survey of the positions he successively held at Negapatam:

1724 Assistant ("Assistent")
1725 Book-keeper ("Boekhouder")
1730 "Factor"

* I sincerely thank Dr. Holden Furber, who read the manuscript and made a number of most useful and clarifying suggestions. [Ed. note: The present article has been significantly altered from its original published form, notably through the deletion of the critical Dutch text provided by Rocher. Other technical details pertaining to the textual problems of Mossel's writing have also been deleted from the introduction. Thus, a summarized introduction and the entire translation are what appear here.]

[888] The Dutch East India Company was created as a result of the merger of several existing commercial companies. In the cities where the latter had been located, they were replaced by "Kamers," the commanders of which now jointly administered the new Company.

[889] On the capture of Negapatam by the Dutch, cf. Tapan Raychaudhuri 1962:100.

1730 Sub-merchant ("Onderkoopman")
1732 Merchant ("Koopman")
1736 Head Merchant ("Opperkoopman")
1738 First Head Merchant ("Eerste opperkoopman")
1738 Governor and Director of Coromandel ("Gouverneur en Directeur van Coromandel")

An even more brilliant career was to follow after he returned to Batavia in 1742; he was elected Governor-General in 1750. However, this part of Mossel's life, as well as his renewed but unsuccessful contact with India in 1759, lie beyond the scope of this study.[890]

2. At Negapatam —and later— Mossel attached much importance to law and procedure, "the corner-stone of good administration."[891] We may assume that this interest reached its climax during the years 1736–1738 when, in his capacity of head merchant, Mossel was the chairman of the Judiciary Council ("Justitiëele Raad") of Coromandel. Josef van Kan (1935) who deals with Mossel's legal activities in this period, analyzes two treatises composed by the head merchant. The Mackenzie Collection of the India Office Library includes two short manuscripts of another, unpublished treatise by Jacob Mossel; one manuscript is in Dutch, the other in English.[892] This treatise will be the subject-matter of the present paper.

3. Mossel's treatise on *Het Chormandelsch Heijdens Regt Van de Geslagten Wellale & Chittij* is not dated, but everything points to the same period that gave rise to the two texts discussed by van Kan. A reference to the *Civile Rol* for 1737 (XV[i]) may serve as a useful *terminus post quem*; the treatise was written in or after 1737, at a time when the author had lived at Negapatam for at least sixteen consecutive years. On the other hand, we may assume that the year 1742, in which he left the Coromandel Coast, is a reliable *terminus ante quem*. After reading van Kan's analysis, and in view of Mossel's apparent desire to adapt the law to local situations, we are tempted to consider *Het Chormandelsch Heijdens Regt* as a supplement to the *Ordres en Statuten* and the *Ordres rakende schuldenaars*, written shortly after these, probably in 1738.

4. The title of the treatise presents a problem. It distinctly says: "de Geslagten Wellale & Chittij," thereby creating the impression

[890] van der Kloot 1891: 98–100. See also van der Aa 1869: 12.1074; de Graaff and Stibbe: 1918: 2.790. For a recent defense of Mossel, see Coolhaas 1958.

[891] *Memorie van overgave Jacob Mossel* (Coromandel 1744), quoted by van Kan 1930: 1.

[892] Dutch version: I.O.L., Mackenzie Collection, pr 55, 11, pp. 471–511; English version: I.O.L., Mackenzie Collection, Class XIV, 10(f), fo. 82–93.

that the text deals with the laws of two different groups. However, in the text any reference to two distinct castes are definitely absent. Besides, even though the terms Vellālar and Chettiyar have often been employed quite loosely, it is difficult to see why Mossel would have treated together, and separately from all other groups, two castes whose occupations were so basically different. Indeed, "the Vellālas are the great farmer caste of the Tamil country,"[893] whereas "Chetti means trader."[894]

In our opinion, Mossel refers to a single group rather than to two distinct castes. In the first place, it is well known that Chetti is not only a caste name, but often merely indicates an occupation. The sentence from the Census Report 1901, part of which was quoted above, actually says: "Chetti means trader, and is one of those titular or occupational terms, which are often loosely employed as caste names. The weavers, oil pressers, and others use it as a title, and many more tack it on to their names, to denote that trade is their occupation."[895]

In the second place, not all Vellālars are farmers either. It is true that they have been described as "a peace-loving, frugal, and industrious people, and, in the cultivation of rice, betel, tobacco, etc., have perhaps no equals in the world."[896]; and according to the *Madura Manual* too, "most Vellālars support themselves by husbandry, which, according to native ideas, is their only proper means of livelihood."[897] However, there are among the Vellālars a number of local differences which are quite fundamental; we shall only refer to the case of Tanjore District which is of immediate importance when it comes to judging the Vellālars of Negapatam. According to the *Tanjore Manual*, "many Vellālars are found in the Government service, more especially as karnams or village accountants. As accountants they are unsurpassed, and the facility with which, in by-gone days, they used to write on cadjan or palmyra leaves with iron styles, and pick up any information or any given points from a mass of these leaves, by lamp-light no less than daylight, was most remarkable. Running by the side of the Tahsildar's (native revenue officer) palanquin, they could write

[893] H.A. Stuart, in the *Madras Census Report, 1891, and Manual of North Arcol District*, quoted by Edgar Thurston 1909: 7.361.

[894] *Census Report, 1901*, quoted by Thurston 1909: 2.92.

[895] Quoted by Thurston 1909: 2.92. Cf. Georges Olivier: "Les Chettyar, ou *Setti*, fournissent l'exemple typique des erreurs que l'étranger peut commettre: car des groupes totalement différents portent, plus ou moins légitimement, le titre de Chettyar, sans faire partie de la caste du même nom" (1961: 36).

[896] *Madras Census Report, 1871*, quoted by Thurston 1909: 7.370; cf. Olivier 1961: 36–38.

[897] Quoted by Thurston 1909: 7.370.

to dictation, and even make arithmetical calculations with strictest accuracy. In religious observances, they are more strict than the generality of Brāhmans; they abstain from both intoxicating liquors and flesh meat."[898]

After these remarks both on the vague use of Chettiyar and on the great variety that exists among the Vellālars, we shall now refer to a particular Vellālar sub-caste listed by Thurston, which is likely to solve the problem of the title of Mossel's treatise: "Chetti. The members of the Vellālan subdivision of Chetti are 'said to be pure Vellālas, who have taken the title of Chetti. In ancient times, they had the prerogative of weighing the person of kings on occasion of the Tulabhāram ceremony... They were, in fact, the trading class of the Tamil nation in the south.'"[899] In the Madras Census Report, 1901 the "Vellān Chettis" are actually listed as a subdivision of one of the four main divisions of Vellālars, namely of the "Sōliya (or Sōzhia), or men of the Chōla country, the Tanjore and Trichinopoly districts of the present day."[900] Indeed, "the Sōliya Vellālas are sub-divided into the Vellān Chettis, meaning the Vellāla merchants (who are again further split up into three or four other territorial divisions); the Kodikkāls (betel-garden), who grow the betelvine; and the Kānakkilinättār, or inhabitants of Kānakkilinādu."[901] As is the case between members of the four main divisions, "These three similarly may not intermarry, but the last is such a small unit, and girls in it are getting so scarce, that its members are now going to other subdivisions for their brides."[902]

In short, Mossel describes the laws of the Vellālar Chettiyars, "a name, denoting Vellāla merchants, taken by some Vellālas."[903] Judging from the contents of the treatise, they must have been a relatively prosperous group possessing considerable property. This corresponds very well with the general trend among the Vellālars who, although they were, by general consent, regarded as Śūdras, refused to accept this inferior status;[904] within the caste hierarchy they usually take their place immediately after the Brahmins. Moreover, it is but natural that the Dutch had more intense contacts with a group such as the Vellālar Chettiyars than with any other, and that Mossel had a better opportunity to ob-

[898] Quoted by Thurston 1909: 7.371–372; cf. Dupuis 1960: 45.

[899] Thurston 1909: 7.378. The quotation is from the *Madras Census Report, 1891*. Cf. also Dupuis 1960: 43.

[900] Quoted by Thurston 1909: 7.373.

[901] Ibid.: 375.

[902] Ibid.: 375.

[903] Ibid.: 389.

[904] Ibid.: 366.

serve their customs than those of any other caste. The progressive and enterprising Vellālar Chettiyars must have seen in their dealings with the Dutch another occasion to better their status.

5. As indicated above, the text of the treatise is preserved in a version in Dutch, which was its original language, and in an English version which resulted from a translation. The Dutch manuscript preserved at the India Office Library is not the original document prepared by the author.[905] It ends (XV.i) with the words: "Was get [ekend] J:Mossel," i.e., "was signed J. Mossel." The date of the transcript is not known; the date of acquisition within the Mackenzie Collection, April 30, 1823, is the only available *terminus ante quem.*

The Dutch text, as it stands, is in an extremely poor condition. Errors are numerous, and many words and sentences do not make sense at all. However, most mistakes apparently result from pure scribal errors: the copyist was incapable of reading the handwritten text which served as his original. Whether the latter was the true original or not can no longer be determined. In any case, it may have been a correct text; the numerous errors we are faced with may very well have been introduced by the scribe of the copy in our possession. In most cases we were able to analyze the scribal errors, trace their origin, and reconstruct the original readings. It is clear that the copyist of the Dutch version knew very little, if any, Dutch.[906] He copied purely mechanically, and, whenever his original was not extremely clearly written, he often misinterpreted, so as to provide us either with a different Dutch word, or with words that mere not Dutch at all.

6.a. Unlike the Dutch version, the English manuscript offers a very readable text. The handwriting is much more modern, and the document seems to be far more recent than its Dutch counterpart. The subdivisions into paragraphs is much more logical, so much so that, to make the Dutch text better understandable, we often discarded the subdivisions of the Dutch manuscript to replace them by those of the English version.

b. The English scribe was also much more careful than the Dutch copyist. In the Dutch version the cross-references in the text are inaccurate; once again the scribe seems to have copied mechanically anything he found in his original. The English copyist, on the contrary, checked the references as they occurred, and introduced the necessary adaptations.

[905] Dr. M.A.P. Meilink-Roelofsz of the Algemeen Rijksarchief in The Hague was kind enough to inform us that neither the original nor a copy of it are preserved in the Dutch archives.

[906] We suspect that the scribe's mother-tongue was English. Cf. *hair* instead of *haar* (V^c); *actien* instead of *actie* (VI^c); *Civele* instead of *Civile* (XIV^c).

7. So far we mainly dealt with the relationship between the English version and the Dutch manuscript —or any other Dutch manuscript from which it was translated. We shall now add a few remarks about the English text as compared to the Dutch original. The fact that the English version offers a very readable text, the fact also that it proved occasionally useful toward a better understanding of the Dutch manuscript, should not make us overlook the numerous occasions on which it does not render the Dutch original as faithfully as a translation should. The reasons for this may be multiple: although much better than the Dutch manuscript we had to work with, the one used by the English translator may not have been perfectly correct either; some Dutch terms or expressions may have been unknown to the translator; he may not have been well acquainted with the legal situation in India; etc. The fact is that the English translation is likely to create a better impression than it really deserves.

8. Mossel's treatise does not offer a complete description of all the customs of the Vellālar Chettiyars. It deals only with those customs which could be made use of in the Courts. It is no less remarkable that, for that purpose, and as early as 1738, Mossel made a thorough study of the local customary laws on family relations, marriage, inheritance, and the very un-European institution of joint ownership. All this becomes less surprising after one has read van Kan's *Uit de rechtsgeschiedenis der Compagnie*, is which Mossel occupies an important place for his numerous efforts to improve the legal systems of the "*buitencomptoiren*," and to adapt his own Roman-Dutch law to local circumstances. As indicated above, we believe that *Het Chormandels Heijdens Regt* was conceived as the logical supplement, dealing with family law, to his earlier works on judicial procedure and contract law.

The text clearly shows that Mossel was not a professional jurist. He described the local customs as he saw them, without trying to fit them into any preconceived legal framework. As pointed out by van Kan in connection with the *Ordres en Statuten* and the *Ordres rakende schuldenaars*, the language is simple, without any of the legal jargon, complicated sentences and minute casuistry which are characteristic of contemporaneous professional legal writings. All these features appear even more clearly in van Kan's detailed comparisons between the legal texts composed in Holland and their adaptations at Negapatam by the occasional jurist —"den gelegenheidsjurist"— Mossel.

However, notwithstanding its incompleteness and juridical amateurishness, we hope that the legal historian will appreciate this early effort at combining European and Indian law, and that the anthropologist will recognize a few new elements which have not been recorded elsewhere.

Translation

The Heathen Laws of the Vellālar and Chettiyar Castes of Coromandel

I. Men and women, and the differences between them.

a. Unmarried women remain always under the guardianship of the oldest male member of the family, since it is a general rule that men are the absolute masters of everything and women are entirely submissive to them.

b. Married women are under the guardianship of their husbands; they actually are as good as their slaves. It is understood that, to a certain extent, husband and wife are likewise under the authority of the husband's parents or whoever is the oldest in the family and acts as its manager.

c. Widows who have sons remain in their houses; in that case the son becomes the manager of the property when he reaches the age of competence. All this under the authority of the deceased husband's parents, as indicated above (I^{b}). A widow who has no children or only daughters returns to her parents' after her husband's corpse has been carried out, and she comes again under the guardianship of these or any other person who is the manager of the family.

d. However, all unmarried women manage their own property, so that they can also alienate it. Married women, on the contrary, cannot alienate anything nor can they make any transactions, because everything is dependent on the husband even if he decides to spend it all. The only exceptions are the jewels which the wife brings with her at the time of marriage (cf. V^{f}); these the husband cannot touch before she gives birth to a son, or if she commits adultery.

II. Kinship, legitimate and illegitimate offspring.

a. With these peoples kinship is as in Europe, except that again the same restriction applies as before (I^{c}) in case a wife loses her husband without having children, since then the relationship with the husband ceases.

b. Legitimate offspring are children of married parents, either from the one or the other wife, for they may very well marry more than one woman at the same time. It also includes those children who were born after their father's death,[907] provided the following ceremony is observed with regard to them. Before the

[907] For the application of the maxim *nasciturnus pro iam nato* in Hindu law, see Derrett 1963: 32–33. The available evidence from classical Hindu law was discussed by Sir Asutosh Mookerjee, in *Kusum Kumari Dasi v. Dasarathi Sinha* AIR 1921 Cal. 487, 67 I.C. 210–211.

corpse is carried out, the wife who is pregnant at the time of her husband's death takes a large pot with saffron water; she throws into the pot a number of oleander (*alari*) flowers corresponding to the number of months she estimates to be pregnant, and she deposit's the pot in the midst of those who attend; in order that it should be publicly known this is then announced with the sounds of drums and trumpets. Without this public announcement such a child would not be able to inherit anything.

c. Illegitimate offspring, i.e. children begotten without there being a marriage, inherit neither from their father nor from their mother, but these give or bequeath them something at their pleasure. This also applies to adulterine bastards. However, in certain other respects, such as being called as witnesses, holding honorable positions, etc., all illegitimate children enjoy exactly the same rights as legitimate offspring.

III. Those of age and under age, majors and minors.

a. Of age are those who have reached the age of full discretion and wisdom, so that they can be allowed to manage themselves and their property.

b. Senility of elderly people. The beginning of the period of senility depends upon a person's intelligence. At that point, the oldest son or another close relative comes to assist.

c. Under age or minors are males under 25 years, unless it would appear from their intelligence that they are capable to be their own masters; provided, however, they are about 20 years old.[908] Are also considered minors those who are deaf, dumb, mad, foolish, insane, or those who through any other manifest infirmity are unable to manage themselves and their property.

IV. The power of parents over their children and adopted children.

a. During their entire lifetime children are under the authority of their father, and, after their father's death, under the authority of their mother. Provided that the son or the oldest of them, when he attains full age, and on the condition that his father is dead, manages the property and acts for the benefit of the entire family, at his own pleasure.

b. Children do not get married unless their fathers or mothers procure spouses for them. The children are satisfied with these for the simple reason that they are mostly still young and unable to

[908] Accelerated majority between the age of 20 and 25 corresponds to *venia aetatis* in Roman-Dutch law. Cf. Lee 1953: 43–44. see Derrett 1963: 412–413 for a form of grant of *venia aetatis* in Ceylon.

judge. But when the son is able to distinguish what is pretty from what is ugly, which is supposed to happen when he is sixteen years old, and his parents procure him a bride whom he does not like, he may ask for another, provided he does not go beyond his own caste. The father becomes the manager and guardian of the children's property. In the same way the father may enjoy the usufruct of the children's possessions which devolve upon them from the outside.

c. If the children desire a partition of family property after their parents' death, one who is not married may demand in advance, as is feasible, a dowry and marriage expenses. Provided that this right will not pass on to any further members than those who are head participant's in the partition. Consequently, grandsons too may make this advance demand from their uncles with whom they participate in a partition, if these uncles have paid off their own children. But, in that case, they can only claim the smallest among the dowries received by the children who had been paid off by the uncles.

d. Adoption is also in use in this country. It may be made by those who have no sons living; they then acquire a living son from one or the other of their relatives.[909] It may also be a slave child, brought up in the house. About all this there is no other proviso, than that the adopting parent [...];[910] the ceremony is as follows.

e. Husband and wife must in a general reunion apply to all those who are to inherit from them,[911] and have them consent to the adoption, although the latter cannot stop them if the adopted child is a brother's son. The trumpeter[912] washes the child's feet in saffron water, and has all prospective heirs touch it. Then he gives

[909] About the rules of preference in selecting a boy for adoption, see Kane 1930–62: 3.678–679.

[910] The content of the proviso has disappeared from the Dutch ms. The English ms. reads: "provided at all events that the said child is not of a lower caste, than the person, who adopted him" (cf. *supra*, § 6*E* of the introduction). This seems logical, but it might also be a rationalization introduced by the English scribe. The rule that the adopted son must be of the same caste as his adoptive father is well known (Kane: 3.675; Derrett 1963: 114). We have no evidence for the case of the "slave child;" H.W. Tambiah (1958: 134–135) has nothing on this subject. —We do want to mention the possibility that there is no lacuna in the Dutch text, although this solution presents two major difficulties: there is a semi-colon in the Dutch ms. after "de aanneemer;" and the English scribe, even if he used a different original, also thought it necessary to complete the sentence. If there is no lacuna, the text simply means "there is no other proviso than that the adoption ceremony be performed as follows."

[911] For similar adoption ceremonies, see Tambiah 1958:132–134.

[912] Both Andre Béteille and Tapan Raychaudhuri think of the *nadaswaram* player. Béteille adds that there are usually three persons working in a team, two playing the *nadaswaram* pipe and one playing the drum. This description also fits Mossel's statement "with the sounds of drums and trumpets" (II[b]). On the Mēlakkāran caste, members of which play the *nadaswaram* cf. Thurston 1909: 5.59–60.

it to the wife to drink from it, while she in substance speaks as follows: "as it has not pleased God to give us a son, this is our child and heir." But the relatives eventually also force the husband to drink from it. Thus the child is for them as a natural son, whereas he is forever severed from his natural parents and relatives, from whom he cannot inherit anything.

f. Should the adopting parents get another son thereafter, the adoptive son will have the rights of an elder brother, just as if he too was a natural son.

g. A brother's son may be adopted without the drinking of saffron water; in this case it will be enough if he is adopted with the ceremony and if he is brought up in the house of his uncle, whose funeral ceremonies he is also to perform.

h. The authority which the father thus acquires over his sons is permanent, but the latter also remain under the obligation to show obedience and respect to their mother, in accordance with the moral laws. The daughters, however, go out of their parents' power through marriage, at which moment the parents give them something and renounce them forever. From then onward the daughters are under the authority of their husband and the latter's family; unless the husband dies without having a son, in which case she comes again under the authority of her own parents. Although it also happens sometimes that she remains with her parents in law, if they can agree together. Sons become emancipated from the power of their fathers to a certain degree, when they cease to live in their parents' home and under their protection, and can live by themselves, to the extent that they have the power of their fathers, and can acquire property and legally exist by themselves.

i. No dignity or situation can void the authority of the parents.

j. Just as the children have duties toward, and owe obedience to their parents, so the father, or else the oldest of the relatives who manages the family, owes his children support and maintenance according to his means and standard of life; unless the children can maintain themselves by means of some art or trade.

k. In the same way the children have the obligation to maintain their parents who have become indigent; for, although the father always maintains his authority over his children, yet a son who has made circumstances happy for himself retains the management of his property, without the father being able to take it away from him. Except if the father, being of unimpeached conduct and an honest defender of the house, becomes indigent by accident, in which case he can indeed draw upon all his son's property. But if they divide, they each receive one half.

l. Apart from this, a brother is liable to maintain and support his brother, sister, or brother's wife, who become indigent, as long as the estate is undivided, for they always maintain therein their rights as legitimate children. But should the estate be divided, the latter are supposed not to touch the former, provided that the brothers remain under the obligation to marry off their sisters.

m. In an undivided estate the oldest member is liable to provide this kind of support to the entire family, near and remote relatives alike; provided always that female relatives, once they are married, pass into their husbands' families.

n. The terms "support" and "maintenance" not only refer to food and drink, but also include clothing, comfortable shelter, discipline, instruction and education according to one's standard of life.

o. If people live in poverty for lack of maintenance to which they are entitled, they may be boarded out elsewhere by judiciary officers or by the Orphan Chamber,[913] at the charge of those who were liable to maintain them, who shall be forced to this by a special judicial action.[914]

V. Marriage.

a. The parents' power over their children consists principally in arranging the latter's marriages.

b. A man may marry one or more than one woman, but a woman may only marry one man.

c. The husband is not punishable for adultery, but among the natives the wife is punished by cutting the hair off her head; she is put behind on the back of an ass and chased out of town, with her procurer in front of her;[915] but in the country, in accordance with the laws and customs of the caste, such an adulteress is put to death by her husband, parents, or others.

d. Marriage is permitted even to young children, but the parents or the oldest in the family arrange it as seems advisable; they conclude it to all eternity, without in any way informing the young

[913] On the Orphan Chambers, see Lee 1953: 100–101.

[914] For "bij parate excutie" the Dutch dictionary (M. De Vries and L.A. Te Winkel: *Woordenboek der Nederlandsche Taal*, vol. 3, 1920, col. 4316) suggests: "without an order of the Court being necessary to execute the judicial decree." Lee (1953: 201) mentions the expression in connection with the sale of mortgaged property; it then means: "without an order of the Court."

[915] One has to be reminded here of certain rules in the Dharmaśāstras, e.g. VaDh 21.2: "If a Vaiśya approaches a female of the Brāhmana caste, (the king) shall cause the Vaiśya to be tied up in Lohita grass and shall throw him into a fire. He shall cause the head of the Brāhmaṇī to be shaved, and her body to be anointed with butter; placing her naked on a yellowish donkey, he shall cause her to be conducted along the highroad" (transl. G. Bühler, SBE 14, 1882, p. 110).

couple before the celebration. The boy must always be older than the girl; and they come to live together when the bride reaches puberty. However, if the son is sixteen years old, the father must inform him of the marriage.

e. Subsequent wives are most often taken if the first wife bears either no children or only daughters.

f. The priests unite them with ceremonies and admonitions, while the bridegroom ties the *tali*—i.e., a string with a jewel— to the neck of the bride. The bridegroom gives by way of a dowry a certain sum of money to the bride's parents, who use it to have jewels made for their daughter, with which she subsequently comes to her husband. Sometimes the parents of the bride also give something, if it had been stipulated at the marriage. Thus the marriage is formally celebrated, without its being in any way enforced by cohabitation.

g. Should it happen, either before or after cohabitation, that the wife loses her husband without having borne a son, and should she have no adopted son, then her deceased husband's father, brother, or uncle —whoever is alive and his heir —, shall pay the widow in cash a sum of money corresponding to the value of the jewels that had been given as a dowry; with the money and jewels she shall return to her parents', and remain a widow for the rest of her life. And should the jewels have been partly diminished by the husband, this should be fairly redeemed after appraisal of the wife's complaint, and this by preference; cf. *Civil Record* 1719, p. 95.[916] In case the deceased husband leaves daughters, his relatives must marry them off, give them a wedding outfit according to their means, and, moreover, after their marriage give them a present twice a year.

h. After the parents have agreed to the marriage of their children, and after the dowry has been handed to the parents of the bride, should either side decide to take another spouse, then, if the parents of the bride break their word, they shall return twice the amount of the dowry; if the bridegroom's parents do so, they lose the dowry. Thus, the word can be broken up to the moment when the bridegroom brings the *tali* to be tied to the neck of the bride.

i. Ascendants and descendants, brothers and sisters, brothers and brothers' children, brothers and sisters' children, brothers' children and brothers' children and so forth in the male line may not intermarry, but brothers' children and sisters' children may.[917]

[916] Dr. M.A.P. Meilink-Roelofsz informs me that this is probably a reference to the "Civiele Rollen" of the "Raad van Justitie" in Batavia. The "Civiele Rol" for 1719 is not preserved at the Algemen Rijksarchief in The Hague; the "Civiele Rol" for 1737, referred to XV[i], is preserved in the Kamer Zeeland (K.A. 6481 and K.A. 6482; Kamer Zeeland 2224 and 2225). —About the English ms., see § 6*B* of the introduction.

[917] Cf. the Thesawalamai Code, Tambiah 1958: n. 105.

j. If a man has a daughter and his sister a son, the cousins must marry each other at the request of the boy's parents; in case her parents object, they shall settle the affair according to the demand of their nephew's parents. This also applies if the cousin binds the *tali* to his niece's neck, which he may do in case of refusal, if he finds one opportunity of the other; in that case she must marry him, or pay redemption money as stated above.

VI. Divorce.

a. Marriage is for life, and no divorce is allowed unless for adultery of the wife; but the wife may not for any reason complain about her husband.

b. The husband himself shall notify the adultery; nobody can do so in his stead. The adulteress loses her dowry, and she may not remarry, since it is an absolute law that a woman may marry only once.

c. The action follows upon the petition of the injured party, for his divorce is neither founded in fact, by and through the adultery, nor is it granted as of course, but only at the suit of the injured party; and it may not happen without his will. On the other hand, the injured party may forsake his right to a divorce after it was granted him, and he may condone the offense of the adulteress. It is understood that this may also happen tacitly; thus, if the husband, after he finds out about his wife's adultery, desires her carnally, this is taken for tacit condonation, with the result that, if he subsequently files a suit for adultery, he shall not be heard.

d. If a wife is continually mistreated by her husband, she may ask to be separated from him; she then leaves the house, taking her jewels with her, but she shall be maintained by her husband. But they can again reunite with mutual consent . In this case the children remain with the husband, except a nursling who at first follows the wife.

e. The wife may not, however, complain because her husband is impotent. If the sterility is on the wife's side, the husband normally marries a second wife in addition to her.

VII. Guardianship and guardians.

a. Guardianship is the legal administration of somebody's person and property.

b. The father is the guardian of his entire family, except the married daughters; for they belong to their husbands' families.

c. The father being deceased, he is succeeded by his eldest son; he being deceased, by the second son, etc.; all sons being deceased, they are succeeded by the oldest grandson; and so on, each time by the one who is nearest in age. The oldest being incapable, it is always the next one who comes in for his turn. This rule applies as long as the estate is undivided; for if the brothers divide, the house of each brother is again like a family by itself.

d. The mother in the family does not retain guardianship as far as the power to act is concerned; however, the administrators are bound to ask her good advice, to treat her respectfully, and have her treated with respect, except if the sons are minors; cf. the power of parents (IV^h).

e. Notwithstanding the authority of the oldest member of the family, each male member may in his own name negotiate, appear in court, and draw up deeds; but in all items of importance he must have the consent of the oldest of the family.

f. He who has a claim against the estate, shall approach the guardian, but the property of the entire family can be seized in execution.

g. Occasionally other guardians are appointed than the above mentioned, in case there is no son of sufficient age in the family. This then happens mostly orally, by him who managed the family, when he sees death before his eyes; in the presence of a few witnesses he dictates how he wishes to have the estate handled. But the administration is then seldom performed sincerely.

h. The wife retains guardianship if the daughter's son is the heir; after her death it devolves upon him with full authority.

VIII. Estate rights and inheritance.

a. An estate is any property which a deceased person leaves behind, such as a house, a garden, his debts[918] and claims.

b. Estate rights are acquired by inheritance; they include all the benefits and burdens of the deceased, except crimes for which he was liable to corporal punishment. Inheritance is obtained either by will[919] or *ab intestato.*

[918] "His debts" renders "haar schuld" in the Dutch ms. However, it is very well possible that "haar" is a misreading. The English ms. translates "haar schuld" by "effects, debts."

[919] It must be assumed that this reflects the Dutch, rather than the Indian point of view. Wills were unknown in Hindu law; they were introduced, or at least stimulated, by the colonial powers. In 1901, Arthur Philips and Ernst J. Trevelyan wrote: "Its existence can be traced back for a century; and although its development was probably quickened by British example and influence, and still more by the progressive elements of the system with which the Hindus were brought into close contact under British rule, there is reason to believe that the development was largely spontaneous" (1). The occurrence of wills in South India is all the more surprising, because in the British territories they appeared first in Bengal

IX. Last wills and in what they consist.

a. Last wills are either written or unwritten.[920] The written type does not deserve any special mention, since it is made before a secretary and witnesses,[921] and, consequently, the necessary requisites are openly known or can be read elsewhere.

b. In case they leave young children behind, the natives are normally accustomed to declaring their last will in the presence of witnesses. It commonly consists in the appointment of an estate manager, about which they make a statement; moreover, they order some money put aside for so-called charitable institutions. Sometimes a private document is also handed out among them. At all this, whether it happens orally or by means of a private document, the relatives are present; if he is likely to do anything unreasonable, they raise the objections which they might have, and he is forced to listen to reason.

c. There are, however, some wealthy people who have their will written by the secretary. The interpreter Vellappa made his will in this way in favor of his wife, for he apparently felt that his sons would not otherwise live in harmony.

X. By whom and for whom testaments may be made.

a. This is evident from the Dutch laws which may be followed for the most part, in so far as they can be applied.

XI. Testaments, and whom one may or shall appoint as heirs.

a. This too happens among these natives mostly according to the Dutch laws. The following must necessarily be designated as heirs in a reasonable share: *1.* by parents: their children, *2.* by children: their parents. Brothers have no obligation in this respect. But,

—facilitated by the *Dāyabhaga* system—, whereas "it was not apparently till 1859 that the validity of such wills was actually decided in Madras" (Henderson1889: 5).

920 This distinction seems to be inspired by the division of wills into written and nuncupative. Cf. Lee 1953: 356.

921 The English ms. has: "before a Notary and witnesses," which was, of course, a well known way of making one's will in Roman-Dutch law. However, we suspect that in that case Mossel would have said "notaris" rather than "secretaris." On the basis of Lee (1953: 356) we thought of the "secretary of the Court;" cf. Wessels 1908: 197–200. Tapan Raychaudhuri wrote us as follows: "It is not clear to me whether the term 'secretaris' in your manuscript refers to some Indian functionaries or to a functionary of the Company. Each factory or trading establishment of the Company had a Council consisting mainly of the senior actors and the Council invariably had a 'secretaris.' In Negapatam, where the Company acquired some territorial powers, conceivably registration of wills was done by the Secretary to the Council whose office, though clerical, covered a variety of functions. I do not know of any functionary in the Hindu Nayakdoms before whom registration of wills could be done."

failing sons, one of the brothers shall be designated as a heir, and, failing him also, somebody else from the family, who is then also obliged to perform the funeral ceremonies.

b. Disinheritance cannot exist between parents and children, even if there are good reasons for it. But it happens that the testator diminishes the share, for reasons which he announces to his family. The only case of disinheritance, in both directions, is that of a person who forsakes his idolatry. Although it goes without saying that this should not be tolerated in our own territory, in case a heathen becomes a Christian.

c. One shall not impose upon the heir any conditions relative to things which depend on his own free will, such as to marry somebody, not to marry, etc.

XII. The legitim,[922] and statutory portion.

a. This cannot be determined with the natives, except that it shall be a reasonable share, which most of them estimate at about one half of the property pure and free, unless the charge was made for the benefit of the heir or was born out of concern for his welfare.

b. The children's share can be withheld for some time, by placing it in the care of somebody, ordering him to hold it until the heir becomes of age, until his marriage, or until he reaches a certain age.

XIII. Legacies.

a. They can be made in the same way as is the Netherlands, provided that the statutory heir or heirs preserve a reasonable share.

XIV. The law of intestacy, and its succession.

a. Legitimate and adopted sons inherit from their father *per capita*; and, failing these or some of them, the remoter descendants with representation or *per stirpes*.

b. But, if a man leaves sons behind of two wives, the son or sons of one wife shall inherit one half, and the son or sons of the other wife the other half, even if of the one bed there is one son, and of the other two.[923]

c. Are equally included among the children of the male line the sons who were born after their fathers' death, provided at the time of his decease the wife has declared to be pregnant; cf. supra (II^b).

[922] Cf. Lee 1953: 368.

[923] We follow the Dutch ms. which has "twee." However, the English ms. reads "ten"; it is very well possible that "twee" is a scribal error for the original "tien." For a similar case, cf. XV.i "a hundred witnesses."

d. The daughters' sole right is that the heirs shall maintain them and marry them off.

e. The mother's property, consisting solely of the jewels which she received to bring with her at the time of marriage, devolves also in the above said way; and the husband shall be his wife's heir, when he has begotten a son with her, even though the son dies before her. Cf. *Civil Record* 1719.[924]

f. Failing sons and their male offspring, the daughters' sons succeed; failing these, the husband's brothers, and their sons with representation; failing these, half brothers and their sons with representation. After them, father's brothers and father's brother's sons or sons' sons, etc., with representation; and, failing these, father's [father's][925] brothers and their male offspring. These too failing, sisters' sons come in for their turn, and their sons with representation; and, after them, half sisters' sons and their sons representing their fathers.

g. Failing all the above said relatives of the husband, the wife becomes his heir.

h. It is to be observed that the heir shall always have the duty to kindle the firewood for the cremation of the corpse; and he shall burn a doll of hay in his memory after thirty two days, etc. Should he [...],[926] one of the relatives shall do so in his stead; and on his return home, the relative shall hand him some grass to show that he has done it in his stead and that the other person is the legitimate heir.

XV. Joint ownership.

a. Joint ownership is very common among the natives, with silent consent of the brothers; after their father's death they continue to hold their property, not only that which devolved upon them from their father but all other property as well, undivided, sharing the profits and losses. Of this property the eldest brother retains the management, and, at his death, the next one, etc. However, if one of them is not considered capable enough, the father will select another one as the head, or the brothers will settle the matter between themselves.

b. The manager is liable to defend the family, and to look after them as a *bonus paterfamilias.* If the property is of any consequence, an account is kept of it; the account shall be placed before the brothers whenever they should demand it.

[924] The reference to the Civil Record for 1719 must be identical with the one in V.g, which equally concerns the wife's jewels.

[925] See §6*A* of the introduction.

[926] There is no lacuna in the English ms.: "if he neglects it by his absence etc.," which again seems logical but cannot be verified.

c. The sons, together with their sisters, continue to live with their mother according to their obligation. However, when the sons are married, and their wives cannot live in harmony with their mother-in-law, the sons are free to go and live elsewhere, provided they procure their mother and unmarried sisters a yearly, monthly, or daily maintenance of money and clothes, which they shall pay to the manager.[927]

d. If the family property is of no importance, and everybody lives on the products of his own labor, then each son shall procure the maintenance in turn; which is stipulated in advance, and of which a deed is eventually drawn up.

e. Whether the community consists of brothers or cousins, the manager of the family property cannot undertake any business of importance without the consent of his coparceners, nor can he sell immovable property or ships on his own authority; they can prevent him from doing so, even though no ancestral property had been left behind. But if the coparceners consent, he can draw up the deed; except for houses inhabited by the brothers, the deeds of which have to be signed by their inhabitants.

f. Should all the brothers have died, the eldest of the sons' sons should succeed as the manager of the family, etc., as said above; thus it can go on till the seventh degree.

g. There are many families who never partition the property, especially when it is not important; for in that case every one seeks the necessaries of life and his livelihood with the help of his own hands, and he makes use of that which is as it were lent to him with general consent out of the joint property, such as a house, a garden, etc. Even then, every one retains his right to take up the joint estate and claim his own share, up to the seventh degree. But in the eighth they are not related to each other, nor can they claim anything, as every one possesses his property on his own. And this for good reasons, since the heathens mourn the death of their relatives or owe them lamentations up to the seventh degree, but not those of the eighth degree whom they consider as being beyond kinship.

h. Children, children's children, and all others up to the seventh degree may claim the partition of the inherited but still jointly owned estate whenever they desire, and after partition they shall relinquish one another in writing, without which it would be invalid.

i. Should a father leave four sons behind, three of whom remain living together, whereas the fourth goes abroad and earns something by his own industry, on his return home he shall receive an

[927] Or: "which the manager shall share out to them."

equal share of what was earned by the three brothers, but of what he earned himself he shall receive two shares. Cf. *Civil Record* 1737, p. 112.

j. Natives of good repute have declared that partition is indispensable, whether there was something or not, whether the coparceners live separately or together; for they continue to belong together until partition takes place and appears from a written document, up to the seventh degree. Should any one claim that there has to be common property, how can he prove this after some time unless it consists of houses; to what amount shall it be, and who shall prove the debts?

k. In case ceremonies are required, for these too proof shall be produced. Should it be maintained that severance of joint status is a question of fact and of adequate evidence, this is not reasonable, since partition of common property is not valid without a written document, even if there are a hundred witnesses.[928]

l. Those who participate in a partition are entitled to it *per stirpes* and with equal rights, namely: those of the male line, including the adopted sons. However, some may make an advance claim of their wedding expenses; indeed, should one or more of the brothers be unmarried, they claim in advance for their dowry and expenses as much as the others have received. But if brothers divide, some of them having married children, others unmarried, they can no longer receive in advance the expenses and wedding outfit with which a bride is to be bought for the unmarried; cf. what has been said under power of parents (IV^c). And if they marry while the suit is pending, if parties so desire, the expenses shall be counted separately, and be taken out of the share of the father of the married, subject to the aforesaid indemnification.

These Coromandel heathen laws thus after careful investigation compiled by Jacob Mossel.

[928] This paragraph is the only instance where we had to be more explicit than the Dutch text which, due to an excessive use of pronouns rather than substantives, becomes relatively confusing. It evidently deals with the well known presumption referred to in *Palani Ammal v. Muthuvenkatacharla Moniagar* (1925) 52 I.A. 83, 86: "A Mitakshara family is presumed in law to be a joint family until it is proved that the members have separated;" even "the mere fact that the shares of the coparceners have been ascertained does not by itself necessarily lead to an inference that the family had separated." Cf. Derrett: op. cit., p. 317.

Bibliography

Sanskrit Texts

Aparāditya/Aparārka on *Yājñavalkyasmṛti.* 2 vols. Ed. Ānandāśramapaṇḍitāḥ. Ānandāśrama Sanskrit Series (ĀnSS), no. 46, 1904.

Āpastambadharmasūtra. Ed. G. Bühler. Bombay Sanskrit Series (BSS), nos. 44, 50. 3rd ed. Poona: S.K. Belvalkar,1932.

Aṣṭādhyāyī of Pāṇini. Ed and trans. O. Böhtlingk. Leipzig: Haessel, 1887.

Bālakrīḍā of Viśvarūpa on *Yājñavalkyasmṛti.* Ed. T. Gaṇapati Śāstrī. Trivandrum Sanskrit Series (TSS), nos. 74, 81. Trivandrum: Gov't Press, 1922, 1924.

Bālambhaṭṭī. Ed. Nityanand Pant Parvatiya. ChSS 41. Benares: Chowkhamba Sanskrit Series Office, 1914.

Baudhāyanadharmasūtra. Ed. A. Cinnasvamisastri. Benares: Chowkhamba Sanskrit Series Office,1934.

Bhagavad Gītā. Trans. F. Edgerton. Harvard Oriental Series 38. Cambridge, 1952.

Bṛhad-devatā of Śaunaka. Trans. and notes. A.A. MacDonell. Harvard Oriental Series 6. Cambridge, 1904.

Bṛhaspatismṛti. Ed. and trans. K.V. Rangaswami Aiyangar. Gaekwad's Oriental Series (GOS), no. 85. Baroda: Oriental Institute. 1941.

Bṛhaspatismṛti. Trans. J. Jolly. Sacred Books of the East (SBE) 33. Oxford, 1889.

Daṇḍanīti of Keśava Paṇḍita. Ed. V.S. Bendrey. Poona, 1943.

Daṇḍaviveka of Vardhamāna. Ed. Kamalakṛṣṇa Smṛtitīrtha. GOS 52. Baroda, 1931.

Dāyabhāga of Jīmūtavāhana, with the several commentaries. Ed. Bharatacandra Śiromaṇi, 1863.

Dāyabhāganirṇaya. Unpublished ms. from Author's own collation sheets.

Dāya-crama-sangraha: an original treatise on the Hindoo law of inheritance. Trans. P.M. Wynch. Calcutta: Hindoostanee Press, 1818.

Dāyādhikārakramasaṃgraha of Kṛṣṇatarkālaṅkāra. Ed. Lakṣmī Nārāyaṇa Śarmā. Calcutta: Education Press.

Dāyatattva of Raghunandana. Ed. and trans. Golap Chandra Sarkar. 2nd ed. Calcutta: Cambray, 1904.

Dāyatattva of Raghunandana. in *Smṛtitattva.* Ed. Jīvānanda Vidyāsāgara. 2nd ed. Calcutta: Siddheshvar Press,1895.

Dāya-vibhāga. The Law of *Inheritance.* Ed. and trans. A.C. Burnell. Madras: Higginbotham, 1868.

Devalasmṛti. 2 vols. Ed. M.L. Wadekar. Delhi: Koshal Book Depot, 1996–97.

Dharmakośa. Ed. L.S. Jośī. Wai: Prājñapāṭhaśālā Maṇḍala, 1937–38.

Dharmasūtras: The Law Codes of Āpastamba, Gautama, Baudhāyana, and Vasiṣṭha. Trans. Patrick Olivelle. Oxford: Oxford University Press, 1999.

Digest of Hindu Law, on Contracts and Succession. 1786–97. Transl. H.T. Colebrooke. Calcutta: The Honourable Company's Press. [Tr. of Jagannātha Tarkapañcānana's unpublished *Vivāda-bhaṅgārṇava.*]

Dīpakalikā of Śūlapāṇi. Ed. J.R. Gharpure. Collection of Hindu Law Texts 26. Bombay, 1939.

Gautamadharmsūtra. Institutes of Gautama. Ed. A. Stenzler. London: Trübner, 1876.

Halāyudhasmṛti. Ed. Ludo Rocher. *Journal of the Oriental Institute* (Baroda) 3:4, 328–44, 1954 and 4:1, 13–32, 1954.

*Hindu Law Books: the Vyavahára mayúkha, translated by Borrodaile [*i.e. *Borradaile]; the Dáya bhága of Jímúta Váhana, and the Law of inheritance from the Mitákshará, translated by Colebrooke; the Dattaká mímánsá and the Dattaká chandriká, translated by Sutherland.* Edited with notes and an index by Whitley Stokes. Madras: Higginbotham, 1865.

Institutes of Hindu Law; Or, the Ordinances of Menu, According to the Gloss of Culluca, Comprising the Indian System of Duties Religious and Civil Verbally Translated from the Original Sanscrit. Sir William Jones. Printed in Calcutta, by the order of the government, 1794.

Institutes of Vishnu. Trans. J. Jolly. SBE 7, Oxford: Clarendon, 1900.

Kātyāyanasmṛti on Vyavahāra (Law and Procedure). Ed. and trans. P.V. Kane. Poona: Oriental Book Agency, 1933.

Kauṭilīya Arthaśāstra. 3 vols. Crit. ed. and trans. R.P. Kangle. University of Bombay Studies: Sanskrit, Prakrit, and Pali, nos. 1–3. Bombay: University of Bombay, 1960–65. [rpt. Motilal Banarsidass]

Kauṭilīyārthaśāstra. Ed. and trans. R. Shamasastry. Mysore Sanskrit Series, nos. 37, 54 (1st ed. 1906, 2nd ed. 1919. Mysore 1923).

Keśavavaijayantī. see *Viṣṇusmṛti*.

Kṛtyakalpataru. Ed. K.V. Rangaswami Aiyangar. GOS 92, 110, 119, 127. Baroda: Oriental Institute, 1941, 1950, 1953, 1958.

Laws of Manu. Trans. Wendy Doniger and Brian K. Smith. New York: Penguin, 1991.

Lois de Manou. Ed. and trans. A.L. Deslongchamps. Paris: Impr. de Crapelet, 1830–33.

Madanaratnapradīpa. Ed. P.V. Kane. Ganga Oriental Series no. 6. Bikaner: Anup Sanskrit Library,1948.

Maitrāyaṇīyasaṃhitā. Ed. Leopold von Schroeder. 4 vols. Leipzig: DMG, 1881.

Mānavadharmaśāstra (The Institutes of Manu). Ed. and trans. G.C. Haughton. London: Cox and Baylis, 1825.

Mānavadharmaśāstra (The Laws of Manu). Trans. G. Bühler. SBE 25. Oxford: Clarendon, 1886.

Mānavadharmaśāstra. Ed. J. Jolly. London: Trübner, 1887.

Mānava-Dharma-Śāstra: Institutes of Manu: with the commentaries of Medhātithi, Sarvajñanarāyaṇa, Kullūka, Rāghavānanda, Nandana, and Rāmacandra and an appendix. 3 Vols. Ed. V.N. Mandlik. Bombay, 1886.

Manubhāvārthacandrikā of Rāmacandra. See *Mānava-Dharma-Śāstra*. Ed. Mandlik.

Manu-Smrti: the Laws of Manu with Bhāsya of Mēdhātithi. Ed. and trans. G. Jha. Calcutta: University of Calcutta, 1920–26. [rpt. Motilal Banarsidass]

Manusmṛti: with the commentary Manvarthamuktāvali of Kullūka. 10th ed. Ed. Nārāyana Rāmācārya. Bombay: Nirnaya Sagar, 1946.

Manusmṛtivivaraṇa of Bhāruci. Ed. and trans. J.D.M. Derrett. 2 vols. Wiesbaden: Franz Steiner, 1975.

Manvarthacandrikā of Rāghavānanda. See *Mānava-Dharma-Śāstra*. Ed. Mandlik.

Manvarthamuktāvalī of Kullūkabhaṭṭa. See *Mānava-Dharma-Śāstra*. Ed. Mandlik.

Manvarthanibandha of Sarvajñanārāyaṇā. See *Mānava-Dharma-Śāstra*. Ed. Mandlik.

Maskaribhāṣya of Maskarin on *Gautamadharmasūtra*. Ed. Veda Mitra. New Delhi, 1969.

Mīmāṃsādarśanam, with the *Śābarabhāṣya* of Śabara, *Tantravārttika* and *Ṭupṭikā* of Kumārilabhaṭṭa. 7 vols. Ed. K.V. Abhyankar and G.A. Joshi. Trivandrum: Ānandāśrama Sanskrit Series 97, 1970–76 [1930–34].

Minor Law-Books. Part 1: Nārada, Bṛhaspati. Trans. J. Jolly. SBE 33. Oxford: Clarendon, 1889.

Mitākṣarā of Haradatta on *Gautamadharmasūtra*. Ed. Gaṇeśa Śāstrī Gokhale. ĀnSS 61. 2nd ed., 1931.

Mitākṣarā of Vijñāneśvara on *Yājñavalkyasmṛti*. Ed. V.L. Paṇaśīkara. 4th ed. 1936.

Mitākṣarā: with Viśvarūpa and commentaries of Subodhinī and Bālambhaṭṭī. Ed. S.S. Setlur. Georgetown: Brahmavadin Press, 1912.

Nandinī of Nandana. See *Mānava-Dharma-Śāstra*. Ed. Mandlik.

Nāradasmṛti. Ed. J. Jolly. BI 102. Calcutta, 1885–86. Trans. *The Minor Law-Books*, SBE 33. Oxford, 1889.

Nāradasmṛti. Ed. and trans. Richard W. Larivière. 2 vols. Philadelphia: Department of South Asia Regional Studies, University of Pennsylvania, 1989.

Nāradīyamanusaṃhitā, with the Bhāṣya of Bhavasvāmin. Ed. K. Sāmbaśiva Śāstri. TSS, no. 97. Trivandrum, 1929.

Nṛsiṃhaprasāda, Vyavahārasāra of Dalapatirāja. Ed. V.S. Ṭillū. Sarasvatībhavana Series 53. Benares: Gov't Sanskrit Library, 1934.

Ordinances of Manu, Translated from the Sanskrit. Trans. A.C. Burnell. London: Trübner, 1884.

Pāṇini. see *Aṣṭādhyāyī*.

Parāśaramādhavīya. Ed. Śrīcandrakānta Tarkalaṅkāra. Bibliotheca Indica 298, 303. 3 vols. in 2. 1893, 1899; also Bombay Sanskrit and Prakrit Series nos. 67, 74. Bombay: Gov't Central Press, 1911, 1919.

Paribhāṣāprakāśa. Ed. Govinda Das. ChSS no. 30, vol. 2, 1906, see *Vīramitrodaya*.

Pitāmaha. Die Fragmente des Pītamaha: Text und Übersetzung. Ed. Karl Scriba. Leipzig: Drugulin, 1902.

Rājadharmakaustubha of Anantadeva. Ed. Kamalakṛṣṇa Smṛtitīrtha. GOS 72. Baroda: Oriental Institute, 1935.

Ṛgveda. Die Hymnen des Rigveda. Ed. Th. Aufrecht. Bonn, 1877; and *Der Rig-Veda, aus dem Sanskrit ins Deutsche übers. und mit einem laufenden Kommentar versehen*. Trans. K.F. Geldner. Harvard Oriental Series 33–36. Cambridge, 1952.

Śabarabhāṣya on the *Mīmāṃsāsūtra* of Jaimini. Trans. Ganganatha Jha. 3 vols. GOS 66, 70, 73. Baroda: Oriental Institute, 1933–36.

Sacred Books of the East. Translated by various Oriental scholars and edited by F. Max Müller. Oxford, Clarendon Press, 1879–1910: Āpastamba and Gautama (vol. 2, transl. Georg Bühler 1879), Viṣṇu (vol. 7, transl. Jolly, 1880), Vasiṣṭha and Baudhāyana (vol. 14, transl. Bühler, 1882), Manu (vol. 25, transl. Bühler, 1886), Nārada and Bṛhaspati (vol. 33, transl. Jolly, 1889).

Śaṅkha-Likhita Smṛti. Ed. P.V. Kane. *Annals of the Bhandarkar Ori-*

ental Research Institute 7–8,1926–27.

Sarasvatīvilāsa, Vyavahārakāṇḍa. Ed. R. Shamasastry. Bibliotheca Sanskrita 71. Mysore: Gov't Branch Press, 1927.

Śatapathabrāhmaṇa. Ed. A. Weber. Berlin: Dümmler, 1855; trans. J. Eggeling. SBE 12, 26, 41, 43, 44. Oxford: Clarendon, 1882–1900.

Smṛticandrikā of Devaṇabhaṭṭa. Ed. L. Srinivasacharya. Vyavahārakāṇḍa. Gov't Oriental Library Series. Bibliotheca Sanskrita No. 45, 48. Mysore: Gov't Branch Press, 1914–16.

Smṛticintāmaṇi of Gaṅgāditya. Ed. L. Rocher. GOS 161. Baroda: Oriental Institute,1976.

Subodhinī of Viśveśvarabhaṭṭa. Ed. S.S. Setlur. Madras: Brahmavadin Press, 1912; trans. (on inheritance) J.R. Gharpure. *The Collection of Hindu Law Texts* 4. Bombay, 1930.

Śukranītisāra. Ed. G. Oppert. Madras: Gov't Press, 1882. Trans. B.K. Sarkar. Sacred Books of the Hindus 13. Allahabad: Pāṇini Office, 1914.

Taittirīyasaṃhitā. Ed. A. Weber. 2 vols. Leipzig: Brockhaus, 1871–72; trans. A.B. Keith. Harvard Oriental Series 18, 19. 1914.

The Sacred Laws of the Āryas: as taught in the schools of Āpastamba, Gautama, Vāsishtha, and Baudhāyana. Trans. G. Bühler. SBE 2, 14. Oxford: Clarendon, 1879, 1882.

The Vyavahāramayūkha of Bhaṭṭa Nīlakaṇṭha. Ed. and trans. P.V. Kane. Poona: Bhandarkar Oriental Research Institute, 1926.

Two Treatises on the Hindu Law of Inheritance. Trans. H.T. Colebrooke. Calcutta: Hindoostanee Press. 1810.

Vasiṣṭhadharmasūtra. Ed. A. Führer. BSS 23. Bombay, 1930.

Vira Mitrodaya, a treatise on Hindu Law. Mitra Miśra. Ed. and publ. by Pandit Jibananda Vidyasagara. Calcutta, 1875.

Vīramitrodaya by Mm Pandit Mitra Miśra. Ed. Parvatīya Nityānanda Śarma Pant and Pandit Viṣṇu Prasāda Śarmā Bhandari. 8 vols. ChSS no. 30. Benares, 1906–32.

Vīramitrodaya of Mitramiśra. Ed. Jagannatha Sastri Hoshing. ChSS 62. Benares: Chowkhamba Sanskrit Series Office, 1930.

Viṣṇusmṛti, with the commentary *Keśavavaijayantī* of Nandapaṇḍita. Ed. V. Krishnamacharya. Adyar: Adyar Library, 1964.

Viṣṇusmṛti. Ed. J. Jolly. Bibliotheca Indica 91. Calcutta: Asiatic Society, 1881.

Vivādachintāmaṇi of Vāchaspati Mishra. Trans. Ganganatha Jha. Baroda: Oriental Institute, 1942.

Vivādacintāmaṇi of Vācaspatimiśra. Ed. L.K. Jha. Patna: United Press, 1937.

Vivādacintāmaṇi. Ed. Rāmacandra Vidyāvāgīśa. Calcutta, 1837.

Vivādaratnākara. Ed. Mm. Kamalakṛṣṇa Smṛtitīrtha. Bibliotheca Indica no. 103. Reissue. Calcutta, 1931.

Vivādārṇavasetu. Bombay: Śrīvenkaṭeśvara Press, 1888.

Vivādatāṇḍava of Kamalākara. Ed. M.N. Dvivedī. Baroda: Lakṣmīvilāsa Press,1901; ed. Heramba Chatterjee. *Our Heritage* 7:2, 1–23; 8:2, 25–37; 11:1, 39–50; 13:1, 51–58, 1959–65.

Vyāsasmṛti. in 2 parts. Ed. Batakrishna Ghosh. *Zeitschrift für Indologie und Iranistik* 9, 1933, 78–92 and *Wilhelm Geiger Commemoration Volume,* 1967, 108–21.

Vyavahāracintāmaṇi: a digest on Hindu legal procedure. Crit. ed. and trans. Ludo Rocher. Gent, 1956.

Vyavahārakalpataru. see *Kṛtyakalpataru.*

Vyavahāramayūkha of Bhaṭṭa Nīlakaṇṭha. Ed. P.V. Kane. BSS no. 80. 1926. Transl. Kane and S.G. Patwardan. 1933.

Vyavahāranirṇaya of Varadarāja. *The law of partition and succession from the ms. Sanskrit text of Varadarāja's* Vyavahāranirṇaya. Ed. and trans. A.C. Burnell. Mangalore: C. Stol,1872.

Vyavahāranirṇaya. Ed. K.V. Rangaswami Aiyangar and A.N. Krishna Aiyangar. Adyar: Adyar Library,1942.

Vyavahāraprakāśa. See *Vīramitrodaya.* ChSS no. 30, vol. 7,1929.

Yājñavalkyadharmaśāstram. Yājñavalkya's Gesetzbuch. Sanskrit und Deutsch. 2 vols. Ed. and trans. Adolf Friedrich Stenzler. Berlin: Dümmler, 1849.

Yājñavalkyasmṛti: with the commentary Mitākṣarā of Vijñanesvara. Ed. Narayan Ram Acharya. Bombay: Nirnaya Sagar, 1936.

Table of Cases

Apaji Narhar v. Ramchandra, 16 Bom. 29 (1892)

Atmaram Abhimanji v. Bajirao Janrao, 62 I.A. 139 (1935)

Bal Gangadhar Tilak v. Shrinivas Pandit, 42 I.A. 135 (1915); 39 Bom. 441 (1915)

Bal Rajaram v. Maneklal, 56 Bom. 36 (1932)

Beer Pertab v. Rajender Pertab, 12 M.I.A. 1, 37 (1867)

Bhyah Ram Singh v. Bhyah Ugur Singh, 13 M.I.A. 373 (1870)

Binda v. Kaunsilia, I.L.R. 13 All. 126 (1891)

Chandika Bakhsh v. Muna Kunwar, 24 All. 273 (1901)

Chhakauri Mahton v. Ganga Prasad, 39 Cal. 862 (1912)

Collector of Madura v. Moottoo Ramalinga, 12 M.I.A. 397 (1868)

Commissioner of Income Tax v. Lakshminarayana, A.I.R. Nag. 128 (1949)

Din Tarini Debi v. Krishna Gopal Bagchi, 36 Cal. 149 (1909)

Durbar v. Khachar, 32 Bom. 348 (1908)

Ganga v. Lekhraj, 9 All. 253 (1887)

Gopal Narhar Saffray v. Hanmant Ganesh, 3 Bom. 273 (1879)

Govind Prasad v. Raghunath Prasad, 63 Bom. 533 (1939)

Guru Gobind Shaha Mandal v. Anand Lal Ghose Mazumdar, 5 B.L.R. 15 (1870)

Hemraj v. Kem Chand, 70 I.A. 171 (1943)

Hyman v. Hyman, A.C. 601 (1929)
Jakati v. Borkar, A.S.C. 282 (1959)
Jatra Shekh v. Reazat Shekh, I.L.R. 20 Cal. 483 (1892)
Jukni v. Queen Empress, I.L.R. 19 Cal. 627 (1892)
Kalgavda Tavanappa v. Somappa, 30 Bom. 669 (1909)
Kameswara Sastri v. Veeracharlu, I.L.R. 34 Madras 422 (1911)
Kamulammal v. Vishwanathaswami, 50 I.A. 32 (1923)
Kenchava v. Girimallappa Channappa, 45 Bom. 768 (1921); 51 I.A. 368, 373 (1924); A.I.R. P.C. 209 (1924)
Kusum Kumari Dasi v. Dasarathi Sinha, A.I.R. Cal. 487 (1921); 67 I.C. 210 (1921)
Mathura Naikin v. Esu Naikin, 4 Bom. 545 (1880)
Modi Nathubhai Motilal v. Chotubhai Manibhal Desei, A.I.R. Guj. 68 (1962)
Mushusami Mudaliar v. Masilamani, I.L.R. 33 Mad. 342 (1910)
Nachimson v. Nachimson P. (C.A.) 85, 217 (1930)
Narayan Bharthi v. Laving Bharthi, I.L.R. 2 Bom. 140 (1877)
Norendra Nath Sircar v. Kamatbesini Dasi, 23 Cal. P.C. 563 (1896)
Parami v. Mahadevi, I.L.R. 34 Bom. 282 (1909)
Pedda Amamni v. Zamindar of Marungapuri, 1 I.A. 282 (1874)
Purshottamdas v. Purshottamdas, I.L.R. 21 Bom. 23 (1897)
Radha v. Income Tar Commissioner, A.I.R. Mad. 538 (1950)
Rahi v. Govinda, I.L.R. 1 Bom. 97 (1875)
Rajani Nath v. Nitai Chandra, I.L.R. 48 Cal. 643 (1921)
Raman Nadar Viswanathan Nadar v. Snehappoo Rasalamma, 2 S.C.J. 738 (1970); A.I.R. S.C. 1759 (1970)
Ramchandra Martand Waikar v. Vinayak Venkatesh Kothekar, 41 I.A. 290 (1914); 42 Cal. 384 (1914)
Ranoji v. Kandoji, I.L.R. 8 Madras 557 (1885)
Rao Balwant Singh v. Rani Kishori, 25 I.A. 54 (1898); 20 All. 267 (1897)
Reg. v. Bai Rupa, 2 Bom. H.C.R. 117 (1864)
Reg. v. Karsan Goja, 2 Bom. H.C.R. 124 (1864)
Reg. v. Sambhu Raghu, I.L.R. 1 Bom. 347 (1876)
Runchordas v. Parvatibai, 26 I.A. 71 (1899); 23 Bom. 725 (1899)
Rungama v. Atchama, 4 M.I.A. 1 (1846)
Sankaralingam Chetti v. Subhan Chetti, I.L.R. 17 Mad. 479 (1894)
Sheo Shankar Lal v. Debi Sahai, 30 I.A. 202 (1903)
Sri Balusu Gurlingaswami v. Sri Balusu Ramalakshmamma, 26 I.A. 113, 131 (1899); 22 Mad. 398 P.C. (1899); 21 All. 460 (1899)
State of Bombay v. Narsu Appa Mali, 59 Bom. 775 (1951)
Uji v. Hathi Lalu, 7 Bom. H.C.R. 133 (1870)
Vedanayaga Mudaliar v. Vedammal, 27 Mad. 591 (1904)
Venugopala v. Ramanadhan, 37 Mad. 458 (1914)
Waghela Rajsanji v. Sheikh Masludin, 14 I.A. 89 (1887); 11 Bom. 551 (1887)

Secondary Literature

"G". 1925. "Hindu Theories of the Origin of Kingship and Mr. K.P. Jayaswal." *Indian Historical Quarterly* I, 577–78.
Aa, A.J. van der. 1869. *Biographisch Woordenboek der Nederlanden* 12. Haarlem: J.J. van Brederode.
Aiyar, N. Chandrasekhara. 1950. *Mayne's Treatise of Hindu Law and Usage.* 11th ed. Madras: Higginbotham.
Aiyar, T.M. Sundaram. 1908. *The Story of Raya and Appaji: 16 Amusing and Instructive Stories.* Madras: G.A. Natesan.
Alexandrowicz, Charles Henry. 1958. *A Bibliography of Indian Law.* London: Oxford University Press.
Altekar, A.S. 1939. "Divinity of King in Hindu Polity." *Journal of the Gujarat Research Society* 1, no. 4, 152–57.
Altekar, A.S. 1955. *State and Government in Ancient India.* 2nd ed. Benares: Motilal Banarsidass.
Anantanarayanan, M. and G.C. Venkata Subba Rao. 1957. "Influence of English Common Law and Equity upon law in India: the areas influenced, and reasons therefore." *Revisata del Instituto de Derecho Comparedo* 8–9, 118–27.
Anderson, J.N.D. 1963. *Changing Law in Developing Countries.* London: Allen-Unwin.
Anon. 1825. *Observations on the Law and Constitution of India, on the Nature of Landed Tenures, and on the System of Revenue and Finance, as established by the Moohummudum Law and Moghul Government.* London: Kingsbury, Parbury and Allen.
Anon. 1825. *The Quarterly Oriental Magazine, Review, and Register* 3, nos. 5–6, Jan.–June.
Auboyer, Jeannine. 1938. "The Symbolism of Sovereignty in India according to Iconography (Parasols-Thrones)." *Indian Art and letters* 12, no. 1, 26–36.
Auboyer, Jeannine. 1949. *Le trône et son symbolisme dans l'lnde ancienne.* Paris: Presses Universitaires de France.
Banerjea, Tara Prossono. 1893. "The Bengal School." *A Manual of Hindu Law of Succession* 1. Calcutta: Calcutta Central Press.
Banerjee, Gooroodass. 1923. *The Hindu law of Marriage and Stridhan (being the Tagore Law Lectures for 1878).* 5th ed. Calcutta: Lahari.
Basu, N. 1957. *The Law of Succession, containing the Indian Successton Act (XXXIX) of 1925 and the Hindu Succession Act (XXX) of 1956.* Calcutta: Eastern Law House.
Baynes, C.R. 1853. *A Plea for the Madras Judges. Upon the Charges Proffered Against Them, by J.B. Norton, Esq.* Madras: Higginbotham.
Benfey, Th. 1869. *Geschichte der Sprachwissenschaft und orientalischen Philologie in Deutschland seit dem Anfange des 19. Jahrhunderts mit einem Rückblick auf die früheren Zeiten.* München.

Bernhöft, Franz. 1891. "Altindische Familienorganisation." *Zeitschrift für vergleichende Rechtswissenschaft* 9, 1–45.
Besse, Léon. 1918. *Father Beschi, of the Society of Jesus.* Trichinopoly: St. Joseph's Industrial School Press.
Bhattacharya, Batuknath. 1943. *The Kalivarjyas or Prohibitions in the Kali Age, their Origin and Evolution and their Present Legal Bearing.* Calcutta: University of Calcutta.
Blochmann, H., *The Ain-i-Akbarī.* Calcutta, 1873.
Böhtlingk, Otto and Rudolph Roth. 1855–75. *Sanskrit-Wörterbuch.* St. Petersburg: Kaiserliche Akademie der Wissenschaften.
Böhtlingk, Otto. 1870–73. *Indische Sprüche.* 2nd ed. 3 vols. St. Petersburg: Kaiserliche Akademie der Wissenschaften.
Böhtlingk, Otto. 1909. *Sanskrit-Chrestomathie.* Leipzig: H. Haessel.
Bongert, Y. 1963. "Réflexions sur le problème de l'esclavage dans l'Inde ancienne." *Bulletin de l'École française d'Extrême-Orient* 51, 143–94.
Bose, Jogendra Chunder. 1917. *The Principles of Hindu Law.* 3rd ed. Calcutta: Audrey.
Boulnois, Ch. and Rattigan, W.H. 1876. *Notes on Customary Law as Administered in the Courts of the Punjab.* Lahore: Albert Press.
Bradke, P. von. 1882. "Über das Mānava-Gṛhyasūtra." *Zeitschrift der deutschen morgenländischen Gesellschaft*, 36, 417–77.
Brinkhaus, Horst. 1978. *Die altindischen Mischkastensysteme.* Wiesbaden: Steiner.
Buckland, W.W. 1939. A *Manual of Roman Private Law.* 2nd ed. Cambridge: Cambridge University Press.
Cannon, Garland, ed. 1970. *The Letters* of *Sir William Jones.* Oxford: Clarendon Press.
Cannon, Garland. 1979. *Sir William Jones: A Bibliography of Primary and Secondary Sources.* Amsterdam: Benjamins.
Chakravarti, Monmohan. 1915. "Contributions to the history of Smṛti in Bengal and Mithilā." *Journal of the Asiatic Society of Bengal* 11, 311–75, 377–406.
Chanana, Dev Raj. 1960. *Slavery in Ancient India, as Depicted in Pali and Sanskrit Texts.* New Delhi: People's Publishing House. Translation of *L'esclavage dans l'Inde ancienne d'après les textes palis et sanscrits.* Pondichéry: Institut Français d'Indologie, 1957.
Chatterjee, Heramba. 1971. *The Law of Debt in Ancient India.* Calcutta: Sanskrit College.
Chaudary, R.L. 1961. *Hindu Woman's Right to Property (Past and Present).* Calcutta: Firma K.L. Mukhopadhyay.
Colebrooke, Henry Thomas. 1810. *Two Treatises on the Hindu Law of Inheritance.* Calcutta: Hidoostanee Press.
Colebrooke, Henry Thomas. 1874 [1786–97]. *Digest of Hindu Law on Contracts and Successions.* Madras: Higginbotham.

Coolhaas, W.P. 1958. "Zijn de Gouverneurs-generaal Van Imhoff en Mossel juist beoordeeld?" In *Bijdragen tot de taal-, land- en volkenkunde van Nederlandsch-Indië* 114, 29–54.

Corbett, P.E. 1930. *The Roman Law of Marriage*. Oxford: Clarendon Press.

Dahlmann, Joseph. 1899. *Das altindische Volkstum und seine Bedeutung für die Gesellsaftskunde*. Köln, 1899.

Dahlmann, Joseph. *Das Mahābhārata als Epos und als Rechtsbuch* (Berlin, 1895).

Dahlmann, Joseph. 1899. *Das altindische Volkstum und seine Bedeutung für die Gesellschaftskunde*. Cologne: Bachem.

D'Amat, Roman. 1961. *Dictionnaire de Biographie Française*. 9, col. 72. Paris: Letouzey et Ané.

D'Anville, Jean B.B. 1759. *A Geographical Illustration of the map of India*. Trans. William Herbert. London: Printed for the Editor. Translation of *Éclaircissemens géographiques sur la carte de l'Inde*. Paris: L'Imprimerie royale, 1753.

Das, Govinda. 1906. "Preliminary Note." Parvatiya Nityananda Sarma, ed. *Vīramitrodaya*. Benares: Chowkhamba Sanskrit Book-Depot.

Das, Govinda. 1914. "The Real Character of Hindu Law," Intro. to *Vyavahāra-bālambhaṭṭī: the extensive commentary on the Mitāksharā, with the original*. Ed. Parvatiya Nityananda Sarma. Banaras: Chowkhamba Sanskrit Book-depot.

Das, R.M. 1962. *Women in Manu and His Seven Commentators*. Varanasi: Kanchana Publications.

de Graaff, S. and D.G. Stibbe, ed. 1918. *Encyclopaedie van Nederlandsch-Indië* 2. 2nd ed.

De Vries, M. and L.A. Te Winkel. 1920. *Woordenboek der Nederlandsche Taal*. Vol. 3.

Derrett, J. Duncan M. 1952. "The Relative Antiquity of the Mitāksharā and the Dāyabhāga," *Madras Law Journal* 2, 9–14. Mylapore: Madras Law Journal Press. Reprinted in *Essays in Classical and Modern Hindu Law* 1. Leiden: Brill, 1976. 198–206.

Derrett, J. Duncan M. 1956a. "Hindu Law: The Dharmaśāstra and Anglo-Hindu Law." *Zeitschrift für vergleichende Rechtswissenschaft* 58, 199–245.

Derrett, J. Duncan M. 1956b. "Kamalākara on Illegitimates." *Bombay Law Reporter* 58, 177–87. Reprinted in *Essays in Classical and Modern Hindu Law* 3. Leiden: Brill, 1977.

Derrett, J. Duncan M., 1956c. "An Indian Contribution to the Study of Property." *Bulletin of the School of Oriental and African Studies* 18, 475–98.

Derrett, J. Duncan M. 1957. "The Codification of Personal Law in India: Hindu Law." *Indian Year Book of International Affairs* 6, 189–211.

Derrett, J. Duncan M. 1957. *Hindu Law Past and Present*. Calcutta: Mukherjee.
Derrett, J. Duncan M.1958. "Factum Valet: The Adventures of a Maxim." *The International and Comparative Law Quarterly* 7. Reprinted in *Essays in Classical and Modern Hindu Law* 3. Leiden: Brill, 1977.
Derrett, J. Duncan M. 1959a. "Sir Henry Maine and Law in India." *The Juridical Review*, 40–55.
Derrett, J. Duncan M. 1959b. "Hindu Succession Act, 1956: An Experiment in Social Legislation." *American Journal of Comparative Law* 8, no. 4, 485–501.
Derrett, J. Duncan M. 1960. "The Slayer's Bounty." *University of Ceylon Law Review* 1. Reprinted in *Essays in Classical and Modern Hindu Law* 3. Leiden: Brill, 1977.
Derrett, J. Duncan M. 1961a. "Sanskrit Legal Treatises Compiled at the Instance of the British." *Zeitschrift für vergleichende Rechtswissenschaft* 63, 72–117.
Derrett, J. Duncan M. 1961b. "Illegitimates: A Test for Modern Hindu Family Law." *Journal of the American Oriental Society* 81, 251–61.
Derrett, J. Duncan M. 1961c. "J.H. Nelson: A Forgotten Administrator-Historian of India." C.H. Philips, ed. *Historians of India, Pakistan and Ceylon*. London: Oxford University Press.
Derrett, J. Duncan M. 1961d. "The Administration of Hindu Law by the British." *Comparative Studies in Society and History* 4, 225–30.
Derrett, J. Duncan M. 1962a. "The Development of the Concept of Property in India, c. AD 800–1800". *Essays in Classical and Modern Hindu Law*. Vol. 2, 8–130. Leiden: Brill, 1976.
Derrett, J. Duncan M. 1962b. "Justice, Equity and Good Conscience in India." *Bombay Law Reporte, Journal* 64. Reprinted in J.N.D. Anderson, ed. *Changing Law in Developing Countries*. London: Allen & Unwin, 1963. Reprinted in *Essays in Classical and Modern Hindu Law* 4, 1978.
Derrett, J. Duncan M. 1963a. "Justice, Equity, and Good Conscience." In J.N.D. Anderson. *Changing Law in Developing Countries*, 114–53. London: Allen-Unwin.
Derrett, J. Duncan M. 1963b. "Divorce by caste custom." *Bombay Law Reporter, Journal* 65, 161–69.
Derrett, J. Duncan M. 1963c. *Introduction to Modern Hindu Law*. London: Oxford University Press.
Derrett, J. Duncan M. 1968a. "A Juridical Fabrication of Early British India: The *Mahānirvāṇa-Tantra*." *Zeitschrift für Vergleichende Rechtswissenschaft* 69. Reprinted in *Essays in Classical and Modern Hindu Law* 2, 197–242. Leiden: Brill, 1977.
Derrett, J. Duncan M. 1968b. "The British as Patrons of the

Śāstra." J.D.M. Derrett, ed. *Religion, Law and the State in India*, 225–69. London: Faber and Faber.

Derrett, J. Duncan M. 1968c. *Religion, Law and the State in India*. London: Faber and Faber.

Derrett, J. Duncan M. 1969. "The Indian Subcontinent under European Influence." John Gilissen, ed. *Bibliographical Introduction to Legal History and Ethnography*, fasc. E/8. Brussel: University.

Derrett, J. Duncan M. 1971. "A want of legal history in the Supreme Court." *Madras Law Journal (Journal)* 1. Reprinted in *Essays in Classical and Modern Hindu Law* 4, 1978.

Derrett, J. Duncan M. 1978a. Foreword. Heramba Caṭṭopādhyāya Śāstrī, ed. *Dāyabhāga* I. Howrah: Howrah Saṃskṛta Sāhitya Samāja.

Derrett, J. Duncan M. 1978b. *The Death of a Marriage Law. Epitaph for the Rishis*. New Delhi: Vikas Publishing House.

Desai, Sunderlal T., ed. 1966. *Mulla's Principles of Hindu Law*. 13th ed. Bombay: N.M. Tripathi. Reprinted 1970.

Deshpande, V.V. 1943. *Dharma-shastra and the Proposed Hindu Code*. Benares: Benares Hindu University Press.

Dow, Alexander. 1792. "Enquiry into the State of Bengal." *The history of Hindostan, translated from the Persian* 3, XXXIX–CXIV. London: John Murray.

Drekmeier, Charles. 1962. *Kingship and Community in Early India*. Stanford: Stanford University Press.

Dumont, Louis. 1962. "The Conception of Kingship in Ancient India." *Contributions to Indian Sociology* 6. 48–77.

Dumont, Louis. 1986. *A South Indian Subcaste: Social Organization and Religion of the Pramalai Kallar*. French Studies in South Asian Society and Culture 1. Trans. Michael Moffatt and L. Morton, and A. Morton. Delhi: Oxford University Press. Translation of *Une sous-caste de l'Inde du Sud: organisation sociale et religion des Pramalai Kallar*. Paris: Mouton, 1957.

Dumont, Louis. 1980. *Homo Hierarchicus: The Caste System and Its Implications*. trans. M. Sainsbury, *et al.* Chicago: University of Chicago Press.

Duncan, Johnathan. 1785. *Regulations for the administration of justice in the courts of Dewannee Adaulut, passed in Council, the 5th July 1783*. Calcutta: At the Honorable Co.'s Press.

Emeneau, M.B. and B.A. van Nooten. 1991. "The Young Wife and Her Husband's Brother: *Ṛgveda* 10.42.2 and 10.85.44." *Journal of the American Oriental Society* 111:3, 481–94.

Fawcett, Charles. 1934. *The First Century of British Justice in India. An Account of the Court of judicature at Bombay, established in 1672, and of other courts of justice in Madras, Calcutta and Bombay, from 1661 to the latter part of the eighteenth century*. Oxford: Clarendon Press.

Fisch, Jörg. 1983. *Cheap Lives and Dear Limbs. The British Transformation of the Bengal Criminal Law 1769–1817*. Beiträge zur Südasienforschung 79. Wiesbaden: Franz Steiner Verlag.

Forrest, G.W., ed. 1910. *Selections from the State Papers of the Governors-General of India* 2, Warren Hastings Documents. Oxford: B.H. Blackwell.

Foy, Willy. 1895. *Die königliche Gewalt nach den altindischen Rechtsbüchern, den Dharmasūtren und älteren Dharmaśāstren*. Leipzig: Haessel.

Foy, Willy. 1895. *Die königliche Gewalt nach den altindischen Rechtbüchern, den Dharmasūtren und älteren Dharmaśāstren*. Leipzig.

Frykenberg, Robert E. 1988. "Warren Hastings." In Ainslie T. Embree, ed. *Encyclopedia of Asian History* 2. New York: Scribner.

Gadamer, Hans-Georg. 1989. *Truth and Method*. 2nd rev. ed. Trans. Joel Weinsheimer and Donald G. Marshall. New York: Continuum.

Galanter, Marc. 1968. "The Displacement of Traditional Law in Modern India." *Journal of Social Issues* 24, 65–91.

Galanter, Marc. 1968–69. "The Study of the Indian Legal Profession." *Law and Society Review* 3, no. 2, 201–17.

Galanter, Marc. 1971. "Hinduism, Secularism, and the Indian Judiciary." *Philosophy East and West* 21, no. 4. Reprinted in Rajeev Dhavan, ed. *Law and Society*. Bombay: Oxford University Press, 1989.

Galanter, Marc. 1972. "The Aborted Restoration of 'Indigenous' Law in India," *Comparative Studies in Society and History* 14, no. 1, 53–70.

Gampert, Wilhelm. 1939. *Sühnezeremonien in der altindischen Rechtsliteratur*. Prague: Orientalisches Institut.

Gans, Eduard. 1824–25. *Das Erbrecht in weltgeschichtlicher Entwickelung*. Stuttgart: J.G. Cotta.

Geldner, K.F. 1901. "Wurzel yat." *Vedische Studien* 3. Stuttgart: Kohlhammer.

Gellius, Aulus. 1960. *Attic Nights (Noctes Atticae)*. Trans. J.C. Rolfe. Loeb Classical Library. London: W. Heinemann.

Gharpure, J.R. 1931. *Hindu Law*. 4th ed. Bombay: Office of the Collection of Hindu Law Texts.

Ghose, N.N. 1901. *Memoirs of Maharaja Nubkissen Bahadur*. Calcutta: K.B. Basu.

Ghoshal, U.N. 1927. *A History of Hindu Political Theories*. London: Oxford University Press.

Glasenapp, Helmutt von. 1922. *Der Hinduismus: Religion und Gesellschaft im heutigen Indien*. Munich: K. Wolff.

Gledhill, A. 1954. "The Influence of Common Law and Equity on Hindu Law since 1800." *The International and Comparative Law Quarterly, 4th series*, 576–603.

Goldstücker, Th. 1871. *On the Deficiencies in the Present Administration of Hindu Law.* London.

Gole, Susan. 1976. *Early Maps of India.* New Delhi: Sanskriti/Arnold-Heinemann.

Gonda, Jan. 1941. "Achtergrond en karakter der Oud-Indische wetboeken." *De Indische Gids* 63, 545–69.

Gonda, Jan. 1943. *Het Hindoeisme.* Den Haag: Servire.

Gonda, Jan. 1955. "*Purohita.*" Otto Spies, ed. *Studia Indologica, Festschrift für Willibald Kirfel*, 107–24. Bonn: Selbstverlag des Orientalischen Seminars der Universität.

Gonda, Jan. 1956–57. "Ancient Indian kingship from the religious point of view." *Numen* 3–4, 24–58.

Gonda, Jan. 1957. *Some Observations on the Relations between Gods and Powers in the Veda, apropos of the phrase sūnuḥ sahasaḥ.* The Hague: Mouton.

Gosvamy, K.G. 1938. "Hindu Conception of Law". *Calcutta Review*, 69, 194–202.

Gray, Louis H. 1914. "King (Indian)." Hastings, James, ed. *Encyclopedia of Religion and Ethics* 7. New York: Scribner.

Gupte, Shankar Vinayak. 1947. *Hindu Law in British India.* 2nd ed. Bombay: N.M. Tripathi.

Gupte, Shankar Vinayak. 1961. *Hindu Law of Marriage.* Bombay: N.M. Tripathi.

Halhed, N.B. 1776. *A Code of Gentoo Laws, Or, Ordinations of the Pundits from a Persian Translation, Made from the Original, Written in the Shanscrit Language.* London.

Hastings, Warren. 1777–80. *Two letters; one to Mr. Justice Chambers, containing a plan for the administration of justice in Bengal, and one to M'clean concerning Alexander Elliott.* East India Company.

Heesterman, J.C. 1957. *The Ancient Indian Royal Consecration. The Rājasūya described according to the Yajus Texts and Annotated.* The Hague: Mouton.

Henderson, G.S. 1889. *The Law of Testamentary Devise as Administered in India.* Calcutta: Thacker. Spink & Co.

Hillebrandt, Alfred. 1923. *Altindische Politik.* Jena: Fischer.

Hoffman, Karl. 1953. "Die Begriffe für 'König' und 'Herrschaft' im indischen Kulturkreis." *Saeculum* 4, 334–39.

Holloway, William. 1853. *Notes on Madras Judicial Administration.* Madras: Higginbotham.

Hopkins, E.W. 1889. "The Social and Military Position of the Ruling Caste in Ancient India as Revealed by the Sanskrit Epic." *Journal of the American Oriental Society* 13, 57–376.

Hopkins, E.W. 1931. "The Divinity of Kings." *Journal of the American Oriental Society* 51, 267–90.

Ingalls, Daniel H.H. 1954. "Authority and Law in Ancient India." *Journal of the American Oriental Society* 74 (suppl. 17), 34–47.

Innes, L.C. 1882. *Examination of Mr. Nelson's Views of Hindu Law in a letter to the Right Hon. Mountstuart Elphinstone Grunt Duff, Governor of Madras.* Madras: Higginbotham.

Jacob, G.A. 1907 [1983]. *Laukikanyāyāñjaliḥ: A Handful of Popular Maxims Current in Sanskrit Literature.* Parts 1–3. Delhi: Nīrājanā.

Jacobi, H. 1910. "Cakravartin." Hastings, James, ed. *Encyclopedia of Religion and Ethics* 7, 336–37. New York: Scribner.

Jacobi, H. 1912. "Ueber die Echtheit des Kauṭilīya". *Sitzungsberichte der Akademie der Wissenschaften*, 832–49.

Jain, M.P. 1951. *Outlines of Indian Legal History.* Delhi: Dhanvantra Bookhouse.

Jann, Adelhelm. 1915. *Die katholischen Missionen in Indien, China und Japan.* Paderborn: Schöningh.

Jayaswal, K.P. 1930. *Manu and Yājñavalkya: A Comaparison and a Contrast: A Treatise on the Basic Hindu Law (Tagore Law Lectures 1917).* Calcutta: Butterworth.

Jayaswal, K.P. 1943. *Hindu Polity: A Constitutional History of India in Hindu Times.* 2nd ed. Bangalore: Bangalore Print. & Pub. Co.

Jean, Auguste 1894. *Le Maduré. L'ancienne et la nouvelle mission* 1. Bruges: Desclée de Brouwer.

Jesuits. 1714. *The Travels of Several Learned Missioners of the Society of Jesus into Divers Parts of the Archipelago, India, China, and America.* London: Gosling. Trans. of *Lettres édifiantes et curieuses: Ecrites des missions etrangeres*, 9–10. Paris: Barbou, 1711–13.

Jha, Chakradar. 1987. *History and Sources of Law in Ancient India.* Delhi: Ashish Publishing House.

Jha, D.N. 1967. *Revenue System in Post-Maurya and Gupta Times.* Calcutta: Punthi Pustak.

Jha, Ganganatha. 1942. *Pūrva-Mīmāṃsā in its sources.* Benares: Benares Hindu University.

Jolly, Julius. 1878. "Über die Systematik des indischen Rechts." *Zeitschrift für vergleichende Rechtwissenschaft* 1, 234–60.

Jolly, Julius. 1882–83. "Die juristischen Abschnitte aus dem Gesetzbuch des Manu." *Zeitschrift für vergleichende Rechtswissenschaft* 3–4, 232–83, 321–61.

Jolly, Julius. 1885. *Outlines of an History of Hindu Law of Partition, Inheritance, and Adoption. as contained in the original Sanskrit treatises (Tagore Law Lectures, 1883).* Calcutta: Thacker, Spink, and Co.

Jolly, Julius. 1890. "Beitrage Zur Indischen Rechtsgeschichte." *Zeitschrift Der Deutschen Morgenländischen Gesellschaft* 44, 339–62.

Jolly, Julius. 1913. "Arthaśāstra und Dharmaśāstra." *Zeitschrift der deutschen morgenländischen Gesellschaft* 67, 49–96.

Jolly, Julius. 1914. "Kollectaneen zum Kauṭilīya Arthaśāstra." *Zeitschrift Der Deutschen Morgenländischen Gesellschaft* 68, 345–59.

Jolly, Julius. 1928. *Hindu Law and Custom*. Trans. B.K. Ghosh. Calcutta: Greater India Society. Translation of *Recht und Sitte: Einschliesslich der einheimischen Litteratur*. Strasburg: K.J. Trübner, 1896.

Kan, Josef van. 1930. *Uit de rechtsgeschiedenis der Compagnie* 1. Batavia: De Unie.

Kan, Josef van. 1935. *Uit de rechtsgeschiedenis der Compagnie* 2. Bandoeng: Nix.

Kane, P.V., *Vedic Basis of Hindu Law*. Dharwar, 1936.

Kane, Pandurang Vaman. 1921–23. "Vedic Basis of Hindu Law." *Journal of the Bombay Branch of the Royal Asiatic Society* 26, 57–82.

Kane, Pandurang Vaman. 1925. "The Predecessors of Vijñāneśvara." *Journal of the Bombay Branch of the Royal Asiatic Society, New Series* 1, 193–224.

Kane, Pandurang Vaman. 1930–62. *History of Dharmaśāstra: Ancient and Mediæval Religious and Civil Law*. 5 vols. Poona: Bhandarkar Oriental Research Institute.

Kane, Pandurang Vaman. 1950. *Hindu Customs and Modern Law*. Bombay: University of Bombay.

Kapadia, K.M. 1958. *Marriage and Family in India*. 2nd ed. Bombay: Oxford University Press.

Katre, S.M. and P.K. Gode. 1954. *Introduction to Indian Textual Criticism*. 2nd ed. Poona: S.M. Katre.

Keith, Arthur Barriedale. 1920. *A History of Sanskrit Literature*. Oxford UP.

Keith, Arthur Barriedale. 1921. *Indian Logic and Atomism*. Oxford: Clarendon Press.

Kloot, M.A. van Rhede van der. 1891. *De Gouverneurs-Generaal van Nederlandsch Indië 1610–1888*. The Hague: van Stockum.

Kohler, Joseph. 1891. *Altindisches Prozeßrecht: mit einem Anhang, Altindischer Eigenthumserwerb*. Stuttgart: F. Enke.

Kohler, Joseph. 1910. "Das älteste Lehrbuch der juristischen Auslegungs- und Methodenlehre. Jaiminis Mīmānsā-Regeln." *Archiv für Rechts- und Wirtschaftsphilosophie* 4, 235–43.

Lariviere, Richard W. 1984. "A Sanskrit Jayapattra from 18th Century Mithilā." In *Studies in Dharmaśāstra*. Ed. R.W. Lariviere. Calcutta: Firma KLM, 49–80.

Lariviere, Richard W. 2004. "Dharmaśāstra, Custom, 'Real Law,' and 'Apocryphal' Smṛtis." *Journal of Indian Philosophy* 32, nos. 5–6, 611–27.

Laucay, Adrien Ch. 1898. *Histoire des missions de l'Inde* 1. Paris: Douniol.

Lee, R.W. 1953. *An Introduction to Roman-Dutch Law*. Oxford: Clarendon Press.

Lindsay, Benjamin. 1941. "Law." L.S.S. O'Malley, ed. *Modern India and the West*. London: Oxford University Press.

Lingat, Robert. 1962. "Les quatre pieds du procès." *Journal Asiatique* 250. 489–503.
Lingat, Robert. 1973. *The Classical Law of India.* Trans. J.D.M. Derrett. Berkeley: University of California Press. Translation of *Sources du droit dans le système traditionnel de l'Inde.* La Haye: Mouton and Co, 1967.
Lipstein, K. 1957. "The Reception of Western Law in a Country of a Different Social and Economic Background (India)." *The Indian Year Book of International Affairs* 6, 277–93.
Lockman, John. 1743. *Travels of the Jesuits.* London: John Noon.
Losch, Hans. 1927. *Die Yājñavalkyasmṛti. Ein Beitrag zur Quellenkunde des indischen Rechts.* Leipzig.
Lüders, Heinrich. 1917. "Eine arische Anschauung über den Vertragsbruch." *Sitzundsberichte der Akademie die Wissenschaften.* Berlin, 347–74. Reprinted in *Philologica Indica. Ausgewählte kleine Schriften.* Göttingen: Vandenhoeck & Ruprecht, 1940.
Macdonell, Arthur A. 1900. *A History of Sanskrit Literature.* London.
Macnaghten, Francis Workman. 1824. *Considerations on the Hindoo Law, As It Is Current in Bengal.* Serampore: Mission Press.
Mahajan, V.D. 1966. *Chief Justice Gajendragadkar: His Life, Ideas, Papers and Addresses.* Delhi: S. Chand.
Mahajan, V.D.1967. *Chief Justice K. Subha Rao, Defender of Liberties.* Delhi: S. Chand.
Maine, H.S. 1920. *Ancient Law, its connection with the early history of society, and its relation to modern ideas.* 10th ed. London: John Murray. Reprinted in *The Worlds Classics* 362. London: Geoffrey Cumberlege, Oxford University Press, 1954.
Maine, Sir Henry Summer. 1886. "The Sacred Laws of the Hindus." *Dissertations on Early Law and Custom.* New York: Holt. [rpt. New York: Arno Press, 1975.]
Majumdar, R.C. 1960. *The Classical Accounts of India.* Calcutta: K.L. Mukhopadhyay.
Makrydimas, Démètre. 1932. *La royauté hindoue d'après les codes brahmaniques.* Trieste: Morterra and Co.
Mayne, J.D. 1950. *Treatise on Hindu Law and Usage.* 11th Ed. N. Chandrasekhara Aiyar. Madras: Higginbotham.
Mayr, Aurel. 1873. *Das indische Erbrecht.* Vienna: Becksche Universitäts-Buchhandlung.
Mayrhofer, Manfred. 1963. *Kurzgefasstes etymologisches Wörterbuch des Altindischen* 2. Heidelberg: C. Winter.
McDonald, William J., ed. 1967. *New Catholic Encyclopedia* 9. New York: McGraw-Hill.
Meyer, J.J. 1925–26. *Das altindische Buch vom Welt- und Staatsleben. Das Arthaçāstra des Kauṭilya.* 6 vols. Hannover: H. Lafaire.
Meyer, J.J. 1926. *Das altindische Buch Vom Welt- und Staalseben.* Leipzig: Harrassowitz.

Meyer, J.J. 1929. *Gesetzbuch und Purāṇa*. Breslau.
Mill, James. 1817. *History of British India*. London: Baldwin, Cradock, and Joy. 2nd ed. London: Baldwin, Cradock, and Joy, 1820. Reprinted Delhi: Associated Publishing House, 1972.
Miller, J. 1828. *On the Administration of Justice in the British Colonies in the East-Indies*. London: Parbury-Allen.
Misra, B.B. 1959. *The Central Administration of the East India Company 1773–1834*. Manchester: Manchester University Press.
Mitra, Sarada Charan. 1906. "Origin and Development of the Bengal School of Hindu Law." *Law Quarterly Review* 21–22.
Mitra, Trailokyanath. 1881. *The Law Relating to the Hindu Widow (Tagore Law Lectures for 1879)*. Calcutta: Thacker, Spink, and Co.
Mitter, Dwarkanath. 1913. *The Position of Women in Hindu Law*. Calcutta: University.
Mookerji, Radha Kumud. 1969. *Ancient Indian Education (Brahmanical and Buddhist)*. 4th ed. Delhi: Motilal Banarsidass.
Morley, W.H. 1858. *The Administration of Justice in British India: its past history and present state: comprising an account of the laws pecular to India*. London: Williams and Norgate.
Mulla, Dinshah Fardunji. 1959. *Principles of Hindu Law*. 12th ed. Bombay: N.M. Tripathi.
Mulla, Dinshah Fardunji. 1970. *Principles of Hindu Law*. 13th ed. Sunderlal T. Desai. Bombay: N.M. Tripathi.
Müller, Friedrich Max. 1859. *A History of Ancient Sanskrit Literature so far as it illustrates the primitive religion of the Brahmans*. London: Williams & Norgate.
Nataraja Ayyar, A.S. 1952. *Mimāmsa Jurisprudence (The Sources of Hindu Law)*. Allahabad: Ganganatha Jha Research Institute.
Nelson, James Henry. 1877. *A View of the Hindū Law as administered by the High Court of Judicature at Madras*. Madras: Higginbotham.
Nelson, J.H. 1881a. "Hindu Law at Madras." *Journal of the Royal Asiatic Society, New Series* 13, 208–36.
Nelson, J.H. 1881b. *A Prospectus of the Scientific Study of the Hindu Law*. London: Kegan Paul.
Nelson, James Henry. 1887. *Indian Usage and Judge-Made Law in Madras*. London: Kegan Paul.
Newton, C.T. 1880. *Essays on Art and Archaeology*. London: Macmillan.
Norton, John Bruce. 1853. *The Administration of Justice in Southern India*. Madras–London: Athenaeum Press.
Oldenberg, Hermann. 1897. "Zur Geschichte des indischen Kastenwesens." *Zeitschrift der deutschen morgenländischen Gesellschaft* 51, 267–90.
Olivelle, Patrick (ed. and trans.) 2005. *Manu's Code of Law: a Critical Edition and Translation of the Mānava-Dharmaśāstra*. South Asia Research Series. New York: Oxford UP.

Olivelle, Patrick. 2004. *The Law Code of Manu*. New York: Oxford UP.

Olivier, Georges. 1961. *Anthropologie des tamouls du sud de l'Inde*. Paris: Ecole Française d'Extrême Orient.

O'Malley, L.S.S., ed. 1941. *Modern India and the West*. London: Oxford University Press.

Padfield, J.D. 1908. *The Hindu at Home. Being Sketches of Hindu Dairy Life*. 2nd ed. Madras: S.P.C.K. Depository.

Pal, Radhabinod. 1929. *The History of Primogeniture with special Reference to India, Ancient and Modern (Tagore Law Lectures, 1925)*. Calcutta: University of Calcutta.

Pargiter, F.E. 1922. *Ancient Indian Historical Tradition*. London.

Perry, Sir Erskine. 1853. *Cases Illustrative of Oriental Life, and The Application of English Law to India, in H.M. Supreme Court at Bombay*. London: S. Sweet.

Petherem, W.C. 1898–1900. "English Judges and Hindu Law." *Law Quarterly Review* 14–16: 14, 392–404; 15, 173–85; 16, 77–87, 392–96.

Philips, Arthur and Trevelyan, Ernst J. 1901. *The Law Relating to Hindu Wills*. London: W. Thacker & Co.

Phillip, A. and Trevelyan, E.J. 1914. *The law of Hindu Wills including the Hindu Wills Act and the Probate and Administration Act*. London: Thacker.

Phillips, C.H., ed. 1961. *Historians of India, Pakistan and Ceylon*. Oxford: Oxford University Press.

Phillips, C.H., ed. 1977. *The Correspondence of Lord William Cavendish Bentinck, Governor-General of India, 1828–1835*. Oxford: Oxford University Press.

Pollock, Sheldon. 1989. "The Idea of Śāstra in Traditional India." In A.L. Dallapiccola, ed., *Shastric Traditions in Indian Arts*, 17–26. Wiesbaden: Steiner.

Raghavan, V. 1962. "The Manu Saṃhitā." In *The Cultural Heritage of India*. 2nd ed. Calcutta: The Ramakrishna Institute of Culture, 2: 335–63.

Raju, V.B. 1957. *Commentary on the Penal Code*. Bombay: The Author.

Ramachandra Rao, P.. 1902. *Indian Tales of Fun, Folly, and Folklore; a collection of the Tales of Tennali Raman, Tales of Mariada Raman, Tales of Raja Birbal, Komati wit and Wisdom, The son-in-law abroad, New Indian Tales of Raya and Appaji, Folklore of the Telugus*. Madras: G.A. Natesan.

Ramaswami, V. 1948. "Law of Nations in Ancient India." *Journal of the Bihar and Orissa Research Society* 34, 43–48.

Ramaswami, V. 1961. "Hindu Law and English Judges." In *Studies in Law (Patna Law College Jubilee Commemoration Volume)*. Bombay: Asia Publishing House.

Rancchodas, Ratanlal and Dhirajlal Keshavlal Thakore, eds. 1939. *The Indian Penal Code.* Bombay: The Bombay Law Reporter.

Rangaswami Aiyangar, K.V. 1941. *Rajadharma.* Adyar: Adyar Library.

Rangaswami Aiyangar, K.V. 1952. *Some aspects of the Hindu view of life according to Dharmaśāstra.* Baroda: Oriental Institute.

Rangaswami Aiyangar, K.V. 1958. *Introduction to Vyavahārakāṇḍa of Kṛtyakalpataru.* Baroda: Oriental Institute.

Rankin, G. 1946. *Background to Indian Law.* Cambridge: Cambridge University Press.

Rankin, George Claus. 1946. *Background to Indian Law.* Cambridge: Cambridge University Press.

Raychaudhuri, Tapan. 1962. *Jan Company in Coromondel 1605–1690.* The Hague: Nijhoff.

Renou, Louis. 1950. *La civilisation de l'Inde ancienne, d'après les textes sanskrits.* Paris: Flammarion.

Renou, Louis. 1956. *Études védiques et pāṇinéennes* 11. Paris: E. de Boccard.

Renou, Louis. 1963. "Notes sur la Bṛhaspatismṛti." *Indo-Iranian Journal* 6, no. 2, 82–102.

Ricoeur, Paul. 1981. *Hermeneutics and the Human Sciences : Essays on Language, Action, and Interpretation.* Ed. and trans. J.B. Thompson. Cambridge UP.

Rocher, Ludo. 1951–52. "The Place of Vardhamāna's *Daṇḍaviveka* in Sanskrit Dharma-nibandha-literature." *Journal of Oriental Institute of Baroda* 1, 214–24.

Rocher, Ludo. 1952. "De bronnen van het Hindoe-recht." *Archives du Droit Oriental et Revue Internationale des Droits de l'Antiquité* 1, 87–104.

Rocher, Ludo. 1954. "Het Positieve Recht in het Oude Indië: zijn plaats in de dharma en zijn vertakkingen." *Indonesië* 7, 296–319.

Rocher, Ludo. 1955. "Ancient Hindu Criminal Law." *Journal of Oriental Research, Madras* 24, 15–34.

Rocher, Ludo. 1955. "The Technical Term 'Anubandha' in Sanskrit Legal Literature." *Annals of the Bhandarkar Oriental Research Institute* 35, 221–28.

Rocher, Ludo. 1956. "Caṇḍeśvara's *Vyavahāraratnākara.*" *Journal of the Oriental Institute, Baroda* 5, 249–65.

Rocher, Ludo. 1956. "The Reply in Hindu Legal Procedure: Mitra Miśras's Criticism of the *Vyavahāracintāmaṇi.*" *Adyar Library Bulletin* 20, 1–19.

Rocher, Ludo. 1956–57. "Megasthenes on Indian Lawbooks." *Journal of the Oriental Institute Baroda* 6, 125–28.

Rocher, Ludo. 1957. "De historische grondslagen van het Oudindische recht." *Indonesië* 10, 472–95.

Rocher, Ludo. 1961. "The Problem of the Mixed Reply in Ancient Hindu Law." *Studies in Law (Patna Law College Jubilee Commemoration Volume)*, Bombay: Asia Publishing House.

Rocher, Ludo. 1962. "La sacralité du pouvoir dans l'Inde ancienne d'après les texts de Dharma." Luc de Heusch, ed. *Le Pouvoir et le Sacré*, 123-37. Bruxelles: Université libre de Bruxelles.

Rocher, Ludo. 1964. "*Anumāna* als bewijsmiddel in de Hindoese rechtspleging." *Orientalia Gandensia* 1, 217–35.

Rocher, Ludo. 1965. "Bibliographic du droit hindou ancient." In *Introduction bibliographique à l'histoire du droit et à l'ethnologie juridique.* J. Gilissen, ed. Brussels: Université libre de Bruxelles.

Rocher, Ludo. 1967. "Hindu Law of Succession: from the Śāstras to Modern Law." *Revue du sud-est asiatique* 6, 1–47.

Rocher, Ludo. 1969. "'Lawyers' in Classical Hindu Law." *Law and Society Review* 3, 383–402.

Rocher, Ludo.1971. "*Janmasvatvavāda* and *uparamasvatvavāda*." *Our Heritage* 19, 1-13.

Rocher, Ludo. 1972. Review of *D.N. Jha, Revenue System in Post-Maurya and Gupta Times. Indo-Iranian Journal* 13, 287–89.

Rocher, Ludo. 1972a. "Hindu Law and Religion. Where to draw the line?". *Malik Ram Felicitation Volume*, 167–94. New Delhi: Malik Ram Felicitation Committee.

Rocher, Ludo. 1972b. "Indian response to Anglo-Hindu law." *Journal of the American Oriental Society* 92, 419–24.

Rocher, Ludo. 1972c. "Schools of Hindu law." *India Maior (Gonda Volume)*, 167–76. Leiden.

Rocher, Ludo. 1975a. "*Anumāna* in the *Bṛhapastismṛti*." *Silver Jubilee Volume: Annals of Oriental Research, University of Madras*, 34–42. Madras: University of Madras.

Rocher, Ludo.1975b. "Caste and Occupation in Classical India: The Normative Texts." *Contributions to Indian Sociology, New Series* 9, 139–51.

Rocher, Ludo. 1977. *Paulinus à S. Bartholomaeo: Dissertation on the Sanskrit Language.* Amsterdam studies in the theory and history of linguistic science: Series 3, Studies in the history of linguistics 12. Amsterdam: Benjamins.

Rocher, Ludo. 1978. "Hindu Conceptions of Law." *The Hastings Law Journal* 29, 1284–1305.

Rocher, Ludo.1979. "The Sūtras and Śāstras on the Eight Types of Marriage." J.P. Sinha, ed. *Ludwik Sternbach Felicitation Volume*, 207-214. Lucknow: Akhila Bharatiya Sanskrit Parishad.

Rocher, Ludo. 1980–81. "Notes on Mixed Castes in Classical India." *The Adyar Library Bulletin (Dr. K. Kunjunni Raja Felicitation Volume)*, 44–45, 132–46.

Rocher, Ludo. 1984a. "Changing Patterns of Diversification in Hindu law." Peter Gaeffke and David A. Utz, ed. *Identity and*

Division in Cults and Sects in South Asia. Proceedings of the South Asia Seminar 1, 31–44. Philadelphia: Dept of South Asia Regional Studies.

Rocher, Ludo. 1984b. "Father Bouchet's Letter on the Administration of Hindu Law." Richard W. Lariviere, ed. *Studies in Dharmaśāstra,* 14–48. Calcutta: K.L. Mukhopadhyay.

Rocher, Ludo. 1987. "Can a Murderer Inherit His Victim's Estate? British Responses to Troublesome Questions in Hindu Law." *Journal of the American Oriental Society* 107, 1–10.

Rocher, Ludo.1992. "Inheritance and Śrāddha: The Principle of Spiritual Benefit." A.W. Van Hoek *et al.*, eds. *Ritual, State and History in South Asia: Essays in Honour of J.C. Heesterman,* 637–49. Leiden: Brill.

Rocher, Ludo. 1993. "Law Books in an Oral Culture: The Indian Dharmasastras." *Proceedings of the American Philosophical Society* 137, 254–67.

Rocher, Ludo. 1994. *Orality and Textuality in the Indian Context.* Victor Mair, ed. Sino-Platonic Papers 49. Philadelphia: University of Pennsylvania.

Rocher, Ludo.1995. "Jīmūtavāhana's *Dāyabhāga* and the Maxim *factum valet.*" *Adyar Library Bulletin* 59, 83–96.

Rocher, Ludo. 2002. *Jīmūtavāhana's Dāyabhāga: The Hindu Lawof Inheritance in Bengal.* New York: Oxford UP.

Rocher, Ludo and Rosane Rocher. 2001. "Ownership by Birth: The *Mitākṣarā* Stand." *Journal of Indian Philosophy* 29, 241–55.

Rocher, Rosane. 1983. *Orientalism, Poetry, and the Millennium: The Checkered Life of Nathaniel Brassey Halhed 1751–1830.* Delhi: Motilal Banarsidass.

Rocher, Rosane. 1993. "British Orientalism in the Eighteenth Century: The Dialectics of Knowledge and Government." C.A. Breckenridge and P. van der Veer, eds. *Orientalism and the Postcolonial Predicament,* 215–49. Philadelphia: University of Pennsylvania Press.

Rocher, Rosane and Ludo Rocher. 2011. *The Making of Western Indology: Henry Thomas Colebrooke and the East India Company.* New York: Routledge.

Sahay, N.K. 1931. *A Short History of the Indian Bar.* Patna: Bhaktiniketan.

Said, Edward. 1994 [1979]. *Orientalism.* New York: Random House.

Said, Edward. 2004. *Humanism and Democratic Criticism.* New York: Columbia University Press.

Saindon, Marcelle. 1998. *Le Pitṛkalpa du Harivaṃśa.* Sainte-Foy: Presses de l'Université Laval.

Saletore, Bhasker Anand. 1963. *Ancient Indian Political Thought and Institutions.* London: Asia Pub. House.

Sarkar, B.K. 1937. *The Positive Background of Hindu Sociology*. The Sacred Books of the Hindus Series 16. Allahabad.
Sarkar, Golap Chandra. 1910. *Treatise on Hindu Law*. 4th ed., Calcutta: R. Banerjee. 6th ed. Calcutta: R. Banerjee, 1927.
Sarkar, Jadunath 1920. "Mughal Administration." *Patna University Lectures 1920*. 2nd ed. 1924.
Sarkar, Kisori Lal. 1909. *The Mimansa Rules of Interpretation as applied to Hindu Law (Tagore Law Lectures, 1905)*. Calcutta: Thacker, Spink, and Co.
Sarkar, U.C. 1958. *Epochs in Hindu Legal History*. Hoshiarpur: Vishveshvaranand Vedic Research Institute.
Sarma, D.S. 1941. *What is Hinduism?* 2nd ed. Mylapore.
Sarvadhikari, R. 1922. *The Principles of the Hindu Law of Inheritance (Tagore Law Lectures 1880)*. 2nd rev. ed. J.P. Sarvadhikari. Madras: Law Books Depot.
Sastri, C. Sankararama. 1926. *Fictions in the Development of the Hindu Law Texts*. Adyar: Vasanta Press.
Scheftelowitz, I. 1931. "Die bedeutungsvolle Zahl 108 im Hinduismus und Buddhismus." *Studia Indo-Iranica. Ehrengabe für Wilhelm Geiger*. Leipzig.
Schlerath, Bernfried. 1960. *Das Königtum im Rig und Atharvaveda: ein Beitrag zur indogermanischen Kulturgeschichte. Abhandlungen fur die Kunde des Morgenlandes* 33, no. 3. Wiesbaden: F. Steiner.
Schmidt, Richard. 1902. *Beiträge zur indischen Erotik*. Leipzig: Lotus-verlag. 3rd ed. 1922. Berlin: Barsdorf.
Schrader, Otto. 1909. "Aryan Religion." Hastings, James, ed. *Encyclopedia of Religion and Ethics* 2. New York: Scribner.
Schroeder, Leopold von. 1887. *Indiens Literatur und Cultur in historischer Entwicklung*. Leipzig: Haessel.
Schwanbeck, E.A. 1846. *Megasthenis Indica. Fragmenta collegit commentationem et indices addidit*. Bonn: Pleimes.
Sen, Priyanath. 1918. *The General Principles of Hindu Jurisprudence* (*Tagore Law Lectures for 1909*). Calcutta: University.
Senart, Emile. 1896. *Les castes dans L'Inde. Les faits et le système*. Annales du Musée Guimet. Bibliothèque de vulgarisation, tome 10. Paris: E. Leroux. 2nd ed. 1927. Paris: Geuthner.
Sen-Gupta, Nares Chandra. 1953. *Evolution of Ancient Indian Law (Tagore Law Lectures 1950)*. London: Probsthain.
Setalvad, Motilal Chimanlal. 1966. *The Role of English Law in India*. London: Oxford University Press.
Setalvad. M.C. 1960. *The Common Law in India*. London: Stevens and Sons.
Setlur, S.S. 1911. *A Complete Collection of Hindu Law Books on Inheritance Translated into English*. Madras: V. Kalyanaram Iyer and Co.
Setlur, Śrinivāsa. 1907. "Bengal School of Hindu Law." *Law Quarterly Review* 23, 202–19.

Singh, S.N., *History of Tirhut. From the Earliest Times to the End of the Nineteenth Century*. Calcutta, 1922.

Smith, Graham and J. Duncan M. Derrett. "Hindu Judicial Administration in Pre-British Times and its Lesson for Today." *Journal of the American Oriental Society* 95, no. 3, 417–23.

Smith, V.A. 1905. "Consular Officers in India and Greece." *Indian Antiquary* 34, 200–3.

Sommer, Ferdinand. 1905. *Griechische Lautstudien*. Strassburg: J. Trübner.

Sommervogel, Carlos. 1890. *Bibliothéque de la Compagnie de Jésus*. Brussels: Schepens. Paris: Picard.

Sontheimer, Günther-Dietz. 1977. *The Joint Hindu Family: Its Evolution as a Legal Institution*. New Delhi: Munshiram Manoharlal.

Spellman, John W. 1964. *Political Theory of Ancient India. A Study of Kingship from the earliest times to circa A D. 300*. Oxford: Clarendon Press.

Srinivas, M.N. 1952. *Religion and Society among the Coorgs of South India*. Oxford: Clarendon.

Stein, O. 1936. "The numeral 18." *The Poona Orientalist* 1, 1–37.

Stenzler, Adolf Friedrich. 1849. *Yājñavalkyadharmaśāstram. Yājña-valkya's Gesetzbuch. Sanskrit und Deutsch*. 2 vols. Berlin: Dümmler.

Stenzler, Adolf Friedrich.1850. "Zur Literatur der indischen Gesetzbücher." In *Indische Studien* 1, 232–46. Albrecht Weber, ed. Berlin: Dümmler.

Sternbach, Ludwik. 1942. "The harmonising of law with the requirements of economic conditions according to the ancient Indian Dharmaśāstras, Arthaśāstras and Gṛhyasūtras." *Annals of the Bhandarkar Oriental Research Institute* 23, 528–43.

Sternbach, Ludwik. 1953. *Texts on Courtezans in Classical Sanskrit*. Hoshiapur: VVRI.

Sternbach, Ludwik. 1965. *Juridical Studies in Ancient Hindu Law*. 2 vols. Delhi: Motilal Banarsidass.

Sternbach, Ludwik. 1973. *Bibliography on Dharma and Artha in Ancient and Mediaeval India*. Wiesbaden: Harrasowitz.

Sternbach, Ludwik. 1987. Introduction to Jha, Chakradar. *History and Sources of Law in Ancient India*. Delhi: Ashish Publishing House.

Stokes, W. 1865. *Hindu Law Books*. Madras: Higginbotham.

Stokes, W. 1887–1888. *The Anglo-Indian Codes*. 2 vols. Oxford: Clarendon Press.

Strabo. 1930. *The Geography of Strabo*. Ed. and trans. Horace Leonard Jones. Loeb Classical Library, vol. 7. London: W. Heinemann.

Strange, Thomas. 1825. *Elements of Hindu Law; referable to British Judicature*. 2 vols. London: Payne & Foss.

Strauch, Ingo. 2002. *Die Lekhapaddhati-Lekhapañcāśikā: Briefe und Urkunden im mittelalterlichen Gujarat.* Berlin: Dietrich Reimar Verlag.

Streit, Robert and Dindinger, Johannes. 1931. *Bibliotheca Missionum.* Aachen: Franciscus Xaverius Missionsverein. Vol. 6.

Tambiah, H.W. 1958. *The Laws and Customs of the Tamils of Jaffna.* Colombo: The Times of Ceylon.

Teignmouth, J.S. 1835. *Memoirs of the life, writing, and correspondence of Sir William Jones.* London: John Parker.

Thakur, A. 1937. *Hindu Law of Evidence According to the Smrtis.* Calcutta: University.

Thurston, Edgar. 1909. *Castes and Tribes of Southern India* 2. Madras: Government Press.

Thurston, Edgar. 1909. *Castes and Tribes of Southern India* 7. Madras: Government Press.

Timmer, Barbara Catharina Jacoba. 1930. *Megasthenes en de Indische Maatschappij.* Amsterdam: H.J. Paris.

Tooley, R.V. 1955. *A Dictionary of Mapmakers: including cartographers, publishers, engravers,* etc. *from the earliest times to 1900.* London: Map Collectors' Circle.

Trautmann, Thomas R. 1997. *Aryans and British India.* Berkeley: University of California Press.

Vaidya, P.L. 1948. *Ṭoḍarānandam. An encyclopaedic work on Dharmaśāstra compiled under the patronage of Rājā Ṭoḍar Mal.* Bikaner: Anup Sanskrit Library.

Varadachariar, S. 1946. *The Hindu Judicial System.* Lucknow: Lucknow University.

Varro, Marcus. 1958. *On the Latin Language.* Trans. Roland G. Kent. Loeb Classical Library. London: W. Heinemann.

Vasu, Śrīśa Chandra. (1891). *The Ashṭādhyāyayī of Pāṇini.* Allahabad, Indian Press. Reprinted 1962. Delhi: Motilal Banarsidass.

Venkataraman, S. 1957. "Influence of Common Law and Equity on the Personal law of the Hindus." In *Revisata del Institutu de Derecho Comparedo* 8–9, 118–27.

Vesey-FitzGerald. 1947. *The Projected Codification of Hindu Law.* London.

Viswanatha, S.V. 1925. *International Law in Ancient India.* Bombay: Longmans, Green & Co.

Weber, Albrecht. 1868. "Collectanea über die Kastenverhältnisse in den Brāhmaṇa und Sūtra." *Indischen Studien* 10.

Weber, Albrecht. 1868. *Literarisches Centralblatt* 30. Reprinted in Albrecht Weber. 1869. *Indische Streifen* 2. Berlin: Nicolai.

Weber, Albrecht. 1893. *Über die Königsweihe, den Rājasūya.* Abhandlungen der Preussischen Akademie der Wissenschaften. Berlin: Reimer.

Wessels, J.W. 1908. *History of the Roman-Dutch Law.* Grahamstown: African Book Co.

West, Raymond & Georg Bühler. 1919. *A Digest of the Hindu Law of Inheritance, Partition, and Adoption.* 4th ed. London: Sweet and Maxwell.

West, Raymond. 1894. "Mr. Justice Telang." *Journal of the Royal Asiatic Society* 18, 103–47.

Westermarck, Edward. 1922. *History of Human Marriage.* New York: Allerton Book Co.

Whitney, William Dwight. 1884. "The Study of Hindu Grammar and the Study of Sanskrit." *American Journal of Philology* 5. Reprinted in J.F. Staal, ed. 1992. *A Reader in the Sanskrit Grammarians,* 142–54. Cambridge: MIT Press.

Wilhelm, Friedrich. 1966. "Die Beziehungen zwischen Kāmasūtra and Arthaśāstra." *Zeitschrift der Deutchen Morgenländischen Gesellschaft* 116, 291–310.

Williams, Sir Monier. 1883. *Religious Thought and Life in India. Pt. 1. Vedism, Brāhmanism, and Hindūism.* London: J. Murray.

Wilson, Horace H. 1825. "Review of Francis Workman Macnaghten's *Considerations of the Hindoo Law, As It is Current in Bengal* (1824)." *Quarterly Oriental Magazine* 3. Reprinted in Reinhold Rost, ed. 1865. *Select works of H.H. Wilson* 5, 1–98. London: Trübner.

Windisch, E. 1917–20. *Geschichte der Sanskrit-Philologie und indischen Altertumskunde.* Strassburg-Berlin: K.J. Trübner.

Winternitz, Maurice. 1908–22. *Geschichte der indischen litteratur.* 3 vols. Leipzig: C.F. Ameland.

Winternitz, Maurice. 1967. *History of Indian Literature* 3. Trans. Subhadra Jhā. Delhi: Motilal Banarsidass. Translation of 1908–22. *Geschichte der indischen litteratur.* 3 vols. Leipzig: C.F. Ameland.

Zimmer, Heinrich. 1879. *Altindisches Leben. Die Cultur der vedischen Arier nach den Saṁhitā dargestellt.* Berlin: Weidmann.

Index

Abu'l Fazl 75
abusing 540, 541
ācāra 25, 70, 75, 77, 166, 182, 188, 271, 273–74, 327, 352, 419, 428–29, 720, 723, 740
Acts: Guardianship Act 99, 140, 197, 671; Hindu Adoptions Act 99, 140, 197, 671; Hindu Gains of Learning Act 175; Hindu Marriage Act 90, 99, 140, 197, 671; Hindu Minority Act 99, 140, 197, 671; Hindu Succession Act 44, 93–94, 99, 140, 163–165, 197, 200, 305, 658, 670–671, 726, 729; Indian Evidence Act 57, 79, 661; Maintenance Act 99, 140, 197, 671
adhikaraṇa 148, 463, 466, 468, 490–91
adopter 654, 694
adultery 48, 147, 157–59, 293–99, 303, 344, 374, 387, 417, 492, 541, 545, 565, 624, 705, 709, 711
Āīn-i-Akbarī. See Abu'l Fazl
Aiyar 43, 64, 74, 76, 107, 167, 639–40, 654, 681, 726, 735
Akbar 74–75
Alexander the Great 110, 730, 732
Altekar 220, 317, 328, 726
amercement 377, 478, 566–67, 570
anubandha 29–31, 473–79
anuloma 256–58, 261, 264, 493, 503, 620–21
anumāna 6, 435, 440–41, 738–39
Āpaddharma 90
Aparāditya 14, 276–77, 536–37, 719
Aparārka 14, 276, 437, 449, 454–55, 615, 617, 621–22, 719. See also Aparāditya
Āpastamba 13, 45–46, 105–106, 169, 202, 211, 241–42, 255, 323, 361, 368, 454, 539, 551, 555, 587, 619, 624–29, 665, 720, 722–23

Āpastambadharmasūtra 13, 168–69, 178, 202–203, 205, 210–11, 287, 344, 354, 356, 367, 372, 377, 386, 454, 513, 519, 547, 555, 572, 578, 619, 621, 623–24, 628
appropriation 19, 21, 31, 33, 499, 565
artha 69, 70, 333, 338, 340, 341, 348, 453–54, 481–86, 587
Arthaśāstra 13, 30, 45–46, 61, 69–71, 89, 116, 148, 220, 223–25, 228, 230–31, 246, 255–56, 258–63, 281, 291, 293, 319–20, 331, 333, 335–37, 340–42, 344, 346, 348, 350–51, 353–55, 427, 45–54, 456, 470–71, 476, 482–83, 485, 487, 492, 509, 515, 569–70, 581–85, 589, 600–601, 635, 720, 733, 743. See also Kauṭilya
arthavāda 78, 327, 352, 440, 455, 457, 459, 467, 470
Ārya 108, 241–42
Aryan 129, 232, 743
Asahāya 157, 245, 419, 433, 529, 538, 599, 600
asceticism 465–67
ascetics 89, 123, 169, 221, 373, 392, 427, 556
assassin 452–62, 464–70
assault 48, 66, 147, 157–59, 293–94, 374, 387, 425, 513, 565–66, 570
assessor 356, 603
Aṣṭādhyāyī 14, 274, 369, 482, 719, 722. See also Pāṇini
aśvamedha 466, 469
asvāmivikraya 147
Atharvaveda 64, 337–38, 455, 741
Atri 615
Aulus Gellius 573–74
aurasa 242, 508, 613–22
Aureng-zeb 693
avyāvahārika debt 30, 31, 193, 582–84

bāla 235–36, 238–40, 246–47
Baudhāyana 13, 45, 46, 88, 105, 202–3, 209–10, 238, 244, 256, 258, 262, 265, 284, 361, 539, 587, 613, 615, 619–20, 665, 720, 722–23
Baudhāyanadharmasūtra 13, 113, 167, 178, 202–4, 209, 255, 369, 372–73, 376–77, 461, 513, 559, 572, 578, 614, 626–27, 719
Bhagavadgītā 48, 134, 348, 467
bhāṣā 364, 584
bhukti 382, 436–38
Bouchet, Father 7, 24, 55, 111–14, 132, 141, 673–75, 678, 689, 739
brahmacarya 486–87, 489
Brāhmaṇa 46, 62–63, 66, 131, 155, 179, 202–6, 209–13, 228, 241, 256–57, 259, 262–63, 294, 321, 323–24, 329, 339, 344, 352, 355–57, 441, 452–53, 455–56, 458, 460–70, 487, 506, 531, 539, 545, 547, 551–53, 560, 571–72, 604, 605, 743. See also Brahmin
Brahmanical rule 66
Brahmin 41–42, 50, 66, 71, 76, 107–9, 241, 319, 323–24, 326, 329, 389, 419–20, 491, 501, 503, 506, 509, 546, 561
Bṛhaddevatā 336
Bṛhaspati 13, 45, 52, 65,

67–68, 89–90, 105, 114, 126, 149, 152, 169–71, 178, 249, 251–54, 299–301, 303, 342, 362, 364, 368, 370, 390, 396, 419, 423–25, 428, 436–38, 440, 445, 448–50, 465, 477, 487, 504–5, 521, 523, 530, 569–71, 597–98, 613, 616–17, 665, 668, 721–22
Bṛhaspatismṛti 6, 114, 116, 148–49, 161, 249, 435, 719, 738
British Indian Courts 95
brother 47, 50, 64, 112, 115, 129–30, 135, 168, 173, 181, 183, 192, 199, 240, 270–71, 275, 276, 302, 309, 336–37, 418, 422–23, 432, 609, 611, 643, 669, 676, 692, 693–94, 696–98, 707, 708, 710, 712, 715

cakravartin 350, 351
caṇḍāla 258–59, 264, 546
Caṇḍeśvara 14, 121, 300, 307, 516–17, 600–1, 738
Candragupta Maurya 45, 69, 70, 110, 215, 220
cara 221–22, 350. See also *dūta*
caritra 348, 439–40, 597–602
Chief Judge 113, 370–71, 376, 431
childless 171, 175–76, 638, 692–94
child 55, 80, 168, 235–36, 238, 240–43, 249, 254, 337, 379, 384, 455, 469, 501, 511, 612, 678–79, 692, 694–97, 706–8
children 112–13, 178, 193, 240–43, 252, 290, 296, 341, 384, 389, 392, 426, 479, 612, 652, 676–77, 683–84, 690–97, 705–11, 713–14, 716–17
Christians 198, 479, 687–88, 714
Code of Gentoo Laws 79, 120, 124, 186, 417, 732
Colebrooke, Henry Thomas 21–23, 30–31, 33, 79, 119–26, 138, 141, 164, 168–69, 172–73, 186–89, 249–54, 277, 281, 293, 297, 305, 478, 498–99, 500, 504–8, 510–11, 527, 529, 534–35, 537–38, 582–84, 638, 649–50, 652, 666–67, 720, 723, 727, 740
confession 405–6
conjugal intercourse 297
consumption 561
contradiction 32, 77–78, 135, 155, 209, 307, 356, 373–74, 400, 453–60, 464, 469–71, 499
cow-slayer 562
Criminal Procedure Code 57, 303
criminal liability 451–52

daṇḍa 335–36, 346, 348, 406, 407, 566–67
daṇḍapāruṣya 66, 147, 149–52, 156–58, 514, 527
Daśaratha 338
Das, Govinda 52, 62, 65, 69, 74, 78, 109, 116, 132–33, 191, 289, 636, 722, 727–28, 731, 734–35, 741
dāsī 506–12
dattahoma 43, 97, 654
dattaka 613
dattasyānapākarma 147
daughter 50, 91, 130, 176, 192, 199–200, 237, 267, 270–71, 282, 287, 290,

311, 336–37, 506, 508, 610–11, 615–16, 690–92, 710–12
Dāyabhāga 6, 13, 21, 22, 77, 120–27, 136, 138–39, 141, 187–88, 192, 249–54, 267, 269, 271–77, 305–12, 497–98, 501, 512, 527, 638–39, 649, 652–53, 666, 668, 719, 728, 730, 740
dāyavibhāga 274, 527
death 43, 49, 60, 64, 72, 77, 88, 91–92, 112, 114, 130, 163, 169, 170–72, 176, 180–81, 183, 186, 192–93, 199, 230, 241, 249–54, 272, 283, 288, 302, 311–12, 326, 337, 344, 346, 348, 351, 376–77, 381–82, 389, 431, 456, 462, 464, 497, 506–8, 511, 529–30, 534–36, 553–59, 610, 638–39, 654, 664, 666, 679–80, 689, 691–97, 705–9, 712, 714–16; after death 91, 92, 283, 344, 346, 377, 389, 431, 553, 556, 558–59; father's death 43, 64, 163, 170–71, 180, 183, 193, 253, 497, 506–8, 511, 529–30, 534–35, 664, 697, 705–6, 715
deposition 369–78, 387
detention 228–30
dharma 19–28, 39–56, 60, 61, 63, 67, 69–73, 76, 86–87, 93, 96, 97–98, 100, 102, 104–6, 115–17, 125, 145, 166, 202, 203, 205–7, 209–10, 212, 215, 226, 272, 280, 291, 319, 322, 324–26, 333, 336, 338, 340–44, 347–49, 35–56, 361–64, 377, 386, 389, 390, 403, 430, 432–33, 439, 453–54, 474, 476, 479, 481–86, 489–90, 492, 494–95, 513–14, 521, 540, 552, 555, 587, 597, 599, 620, 623–29, 639, 662, 666, 738
dharmanibandha 159
Dharmaśāstra 6, 11–34, 41, 51–52, 54, 56, 61–62, 56, 68, 70–72, 76, 86–87, 92, 97–100, 102, 104,
Dharmasūtra 13, 14, 46, 51, 62, 64, 136, 172, 255, 274, 619, 648
Vasiṣṭha Dharmasūtra 14, 64, 648
dharmya 311–12
Digest 121–24, 186, 293, 297, 583, 720, 727, 743. See also Colebrooke
discrimination 98
disturbed persons 426
divorce 302, 711, 729
dumbness 336, 561
Dumont, Louis 25, 333, 730
dūta 219–28, 230, 232, 350
dyspepsia 561
dyūtasamāhvaya 147

envoy 219, 220, 222, 224–28, 230–32. See also *dūta*
Epitaph for the Rishis 658, 671, 730. See also Hindu Marriage Act
equity 44
evil 151, 283, 285, 292, 307, 311, 325, 348, 352, 373, 377, 417, 491, 541, 558, 635
expiation 88, 377, 456, 559, 561, 572

fallacies 406
false doctrines 540, 541
family 21, 47, 64, 73, 77, 88,

93, 95–98, 101, 111–12, 115–16, 136–38, 163, 166–76, 180–84, 189, 192–93, 198, 200, 224, 242, 244, 246, 272–73, 277, 287, 297, 302–7, 310, 324, 333, 337, 341, 343, 372–73, 426, 433, 460, 465, 497, 500, 516, 520–21, 523, 534, 555, 609, 615, 639, 652, 661, 664, 666, 671, 675, 684, 690–91, 694, 704–17
forbidden food 208, 425, 521, 552, 559

Galanter, Mark 32, 116, 636, 731
Gampert, Wilhelm 89, 461, 731
Gaṇeśvaramiśra 516
gati 554–56
Gauḍīyas 140
Gautama 13, 45, 46, 51, 52, 105, 168, 170–72, 183, 202, 204, 207, 209, 211, 237, 240, 242–43, 255–56, 265, 300, 323–24, 343, 361, 368, 371, 388, 504–5, 530–31, 535, 537, 539, 555, 559, 571, 573, 575–76, 587, 616, 624, 626–29, 665, 720, 722–23
Gautama Dharmasūtra 13, 51, 168, 170–73, 175, 178, 183, 202–5, 207, 209, 211, 246, 255, 296, 323, 343–44, 347, 349, 354–55, 371–72, 374, 377, 383–84, 388–89, 475–76, 487, 504, 509, 511, 514, 530–31, 537, 555, 559, 571, 616, 623–29
Geldner, Karl Friedrich 113, 575, 578, 722, 731
gift 9, 21, 35, 97, 147, 175, 181, 195, 205, 241, 282, 290, 306–8, 379, 409–10, 498–501, 533, 639. See also *dāna*
Glasenapp, Helmut von 100, 731
god 283, 325–27, 348, 545, 577, 684
Gṛhyasūtra 587, 589, 727
Gupte, Shankar Vinayak 43, 83, 90, 164–65, 191, 198, 636, 639, 653, 671, 732

Harinātha 275
Hārīta 168, 397–402, 616, 618
Hastings, Warren 56, 86, 103, 105, 117, 124, 137–38, 184–86, 633, 644, 649, 661–62, 730–32, 739, 741
Hindu Code Bill 57, 97–98, 140, 146, 197, 636
Hopkins, Edward W. 116, 320, 329, 333–34, 732
husband 47, 50, 91–92, 115, 129–30, 147, 175–76, 179, 192–93, 237, 242, 256, 268, 281–93, 296–303, 310, 327, 448, 490, 493, 503, 509, 553, 609–12, 621, 628, 643, 678–79, 687–89, 692, 694–96, 705–11, 715

idiots 44, 94, 246, 426, 560, 656
ignorance 111, 177, 377, 381, 433, 648, 652
illness 242, 375, 391, 562
imprisoning 693
incest 425
Indian Constitution 40, 57
Indica 110, 117, 215, 722, 723, 735, 741. See also Megasthenes
inference 386, 407, 435–38, 440, 463, 598, 717

inheritance 39, 43–44, 48–49, 77, 80, 86, 93–96, 103, 112–16, 119, 125, 127, 131–38, 147, 164–68, 170, 175–97, 200, 202, 238, 243–45, 267–78, 305, 311, 367, 411, 486–87, 503–7, 527, 530, 534, 538, 617, 621, 644, 649, 656–58, 661, 666, 668–70, 690–94, 697, 704, 712, 720, 723
injuring creatures 541
injustice 112, 344, 377, 556, 677, 683
innocence 25, 295, 390, 391, 431, 679, 684, 687
insult 147, 157, 158, 159, 293, 566, 684

jayapattra 27, 366, 378
Jayaswal, Kashi Prasad 30, 53, 65, 66, 134, 148, 298, 317, 342, 418–20, 421, 473, 474, 475, 476, 479, 725, 733
Jha, Ganganatha 39, 49, 116, 127, 152, 300, 511, 572, 721–23, 733, 736, 739, 742
Jīmūtavāhana 6, 13, 21, 22, 120, 125, 127, 136, 138, 249–54, 267–71, 273–77, 300, 305–13, 497–501, 512, 527–38, 638–39, 649, 666, 668, 719, 740
jīva 554, 556
jīvikā 202–6
Jones, Sir Williams 23, 39, 56, 78, 79, 86, 104–5, 107–8, 110–11, 185–86, 280, 504–5, 507–10, 633, 645, 647, 649, 662–63, 665, 720, 727, 742
justice 18, 20, 44, 55, 57, 94, 100, 104–5, 111, 113, 117, 132, 147, 184, 188–91, 196, 242, 253, 263, 299–301, 323, 343, 345, 347, 356, 368, 375–77, 385, 389, 392, 431, 440, 492, 581, 583, 604, 608, 624, 635–41, 644–45, 647, 655–57, 663–64, 668–70, 683–84, 686, 689–90, 698, 730, 732

Kali age. See Kaliyuga
Kālidāsa 59, 60, 340
Kaliyuga 51, 344, 624
kalpa 354–55
kāma 70, 481, 483–86, 488–89, 491–95, 594
Kāmasūtra 6, 481–95, 743. See also Vātsyāyana
Kane, Pandurang Vaman 13, 21, 26, 32, 40, 45, 60, 64, 73, 86, 95, 106, 114, 116, 123, 125–26, 145, 147–48, 157, 166, 174–75, 177, 194, 222, 235–36, 242, 244–46, 255, 260, 269, 271, 27–77, 282, 286, 299, 332–57, 362, 364, 367, 388–90, 393, 395, 419, 424–25, 429–30, 433, 435, 446, 449–50, 452–53, 455, 457–58, 469, 477, 493, 497, 501, 508–9, 511, 514, 521–22, 523–24, 527, 529, 532, 538, 567–68, 570–72, 582, 599–601, 604, 606–8, 613–15, 623–25, 633, 638, 667–69, 707, 720–24, 734
Kangle, R.P. 45, 89, 116, 237–45, 333, 335–37, 340, 346, 350–51, 355, 427, 476–77, 487, 514, 569–70, 582–83, 585, 601, 610, 720

kaṇṭakaśodhana 148
karma 153, 155, 476, 499, 539–42, 545, 552–53, 557–59, 561, 565, 568, 591, 594
Kātyāyana 13, 28, 45, 46, 68, 89, 95, 148, 175, 236, 238, 244–46, 354, 362, 375, 391, 397, 399–402, 419, 424, 430, 432, 435, 465–70, 522, 598–601, 638
Kātyāyanasmṛti 116, 148, 326, 333, 362, 720
Kauṭilya 6, 13, 45, 46, 69–71, 89, 116, 152, 220–24, 226–30, 232, 237, 239, 240–46, 255–56, 259, 262, 265, 284–86, 291, 293, 297, 319–20, 335–37, 340, 344, 427, 431, 482, 492, 509, 569, 570, 581, 583, 587, 600–1, 610, 616, 618, 720, 735. See also *Arthaśāstra*
Keith, Arthur Barriedale 61, 406, 572, 723, 734
killing 41, 42, 91, 227–28, 230, 337, 352, 355, 453, 455–70, 545, 679, 689, 693; killing a Brāhmaṇa 352, 456, 458, 463, 469–70, 545
king 300–1, 317, 322, 336, 689, 726, 732; king's duty 344; king's responsibilities 345
kingdom 72, 149, 203, 320, 325, 328, 333, 335, 337, 344, 349, 354–55, 357, 577, 680, 692–93
kingship 317, 351, 725, 730, 742. See also royal power
Koran 86, 103, 184, 633, 644, 661–62
krayavikrayānuśaya 147, 149
Kṣatriya 50, 72, 77, 108, 131, 155, 202–3, 205–6, 208–12, 241, 256–59, 262, 264, 321, 334, 341, 348–49, 355, 389, 463, 487, 547, 551, 572
Kullūka 171, 179, 204, 337, 605, 615, 618–19, 640, 721
kusīda 149, 203, 206

Lariviere, Richard W. 5, 10, 12, 19–20, 27, 134, 274, 614, 665, 734, 739
law: eternal law 50, 130, 611; criminal law 70, 74, 79, 88–90, 97–98, 146–49, 151–52, 159, 161, 294, 372, 374, 451–52, 479, 661; law book. See *dharmaśāstra*;
law cases:
Apaji Narhar v. Ramchandra 188, 650, 667, 724
Bal Gangadhar Tilak v. Shrinivas Pandit 43, 654, 724
Bal Rajaram v. Maneklal 582, 724
Bhyah Ram Singh v. Bhyah Ugur Singh 655, 724
Chhakauri Mahton v. Ganga Prasad 582, 724
Collector of Madura v. Moottoo Ramalinga 188, 666–67, 724
Durbar v. Khachar 582, 724
Ganga Sahai v. Lekhraj Singh 120
Gopal Narhar Saffray v. Hanmant Ganesh 653, 724
Govind Prasad v. Raghunath Prasad 582, 724
Guru Gobind Shaha Mondal v. Anand Lal Ghose 267
Hemraj v. Kem Chand 582, 724

Hyman v. Hyman 302, 724
Jakati v. Borkar 583, 724
Kenchava v. Girimallappa Channappa 44, 93, 644, 656, 725
Mathura Naikin v. Esu Naikin 656, 725
Purshottamdas v. Purshottamdas 91, 725
Ramchandra Martand Waikar v. Vinayak Venkatesh Kothekar 655, 725
Rao Balwant Singh v. Rani Kishori 43, 84, 653, 725
Reg. v. Sambhu Raghu 301, 302, 725
Rungamma v. Atchamma 634, 652
Sri Balusu Gurlingaswami v. Sri Balusu Ramalakshmamma 83–85, 96, 100, 454, 634, 648, 653, 655, 663, 665, 725
State of Bombay v. Narsu Appa Mali 101, 725
Vedanayaga Mudaliar v. Vedammal 656–57, 725
Venugopala v. Ramanadhan 582, 725
Laws of Manu 39, 60, 86, 131, 134, 138, 145, 362–63, 665, 669, 721. See also *Mānavadharmaśāstra, Manusmṛti*
learning 45, 76–78, 87, 107, 109, 125, 135, 163, 175, 182, 185, 224, 290, 339, 386, 395, 432, 475, 485–86, 501, 651
legal practice 52
legal procedure 26, 27, 29, 30, 113, 148, 226, 304, 348, 362–64, 382, 386, 400, 405, 417, 421, 428–29, 431, 569, 583–84, 608, 724
leprosy 336, 393, 560–61
levirate 50–51, 114–17, 129–31, 134–35, 138, 609, 612. See also *niyoga*
Lingat, Robert 11, 22, 26, 55, 115, 439, 597, 599, 734
Lord Cornwallis 78, 645
Losch, Hans 66–67, 735

Macdonell, Arthur Anthony 59, 336, 735
madmen 426
Mahābhārata 13, 48, 71, 72, 134, 224, 228, 230, 316, 318–19, 325–26, 328, 334, 336–37, 340–41, 353, 355, 485, 575–76, 728
Maheśvara 253, 529
Mānavadharmaśāstra 13, 30, 42–44, 48–50, 66, 130, 147–57, 160–61, 168–76, 178–79, 183, 202, 205, 210–11, 224–26, 230–31, 237, 250–51, 255, 268, 276, 282–86, 288, 290, 293, 302, 309, 311–12, 322, 335, 337, 340–41, 343–49, 352–57, 369, 371–77, 379, 381, 383–84, 388–89, 393, 418, 420–21, 431, 447, 454–60, 462, 464–68, 470, 473–79, 487, 488, 490–92, 503–14, 519, 531, 533, 536, 539–42, 545, 551–61, 565–67, 570–71, 578, 605–6, 609–12, 617–22, 625–27, 639–40, 656. See also *Manusmṛti*
Manusmṛti 67–68, 70, 104–5, 108, 114–15, 186, 201–2, 204, 209, 213, 268, 318–19, 321, 482, 539–40, 565, 569, 634, 721. See also *Mānavadharmaśāstra*

manslaughter 146, 157, 159
Manu 19, 39, 42, 44–46, 48–50, 53–54, 56, 60, 65–69, 71, 86, 88–94, 100, 104–5, 107–8, 114–16, 122, 127, 131–35, 138, 145, 152, 154, 156–58, 169–70, 172–73, 183, 202–13, 225, 237, 239–46, 251, 256, 261–62, 265, 268–69, 283, 285, 288–97, 300–3, 318–19, 322–25, 328, 335, 337, 341–44, 357, 362–63, 370–71, 388, 390, 418, 420–21, 435–36, 457–59, 462, 465, 467, 473, 482, 487, 490, 494, 504–12, 524, 539–41, 545–62, 565, 570–73, 579, 587, 605, 614–19, 622, 625–26, 639, 663, 665, 669, 671, 721–22, 728, 733, 736–37
marriage 6, 90, 99, 101, 140, 191, 197, 282, 286, 289, 302–3, 587, 633, 671, 709, 711, 726–27, 730, 732, 734, 739, 743; Hindu Marriage Act. See Acts Matrimonial Causes 6, 279
maryādā 25, 70, 75, 77, 166, 182, 188, 271, 273–74, 327, 352, 419, 428–29, 720, 723, 740
Maurya kings 69, 216
Medhātithi 13, 122, 153–54, 171, 288–89, 309, 337, 347, 353, 393, 447, 457, 474–75, 508, 512, 639, 721
Megasthenes 5, 24, 110–11, 132, 215–18, 220, 227, 738, 743. See also *Indica*
Meyer, Johann Jacob 45, 67, 226, 228, 335, 346, 569–70, 581, 583–85, 602, 735
Mīmāṃsā 14, 21, 48, 77–78, 122, 140, 182, 288–89, 309, 327, 635, 652, 733
Mitākṣarā 13–14, 22, 77, 94, 120, 122–27, 135–36, 138–39, 141, 156, 169, 172–73, 187–93, 199–200, 221–24, 268, 271, 272–74, 305, 365, 388, 400–1, 453, 475–76, 527, 529, 603, 616–23, 640, 649, 650, 666–67, 675, 721–22, 724, 740
Mithilā 75, 137–39, 516, 613, 727, 734
Mitra Miśra 6, 14, 137, 267, 271–73, 405–7, 409, 411–16, 452, 721, 723, 736, 738
mixed caste 262–63
mobility 207–8, 211
Mogol 693
monocracy 6, 331, 333
Mossel, Jacob 7, 699–704, 707, 713, 717, 727
Muhammadan law 74, 287, 637
Müller, Max 46, 62, 105–6, 665, 736
murder 44, 71, 88, 93, 352, 417, 425, 452, 456, 458–66, 468–70, 547, 624, 643–44, 657–70, 688
Muslim law 56, 120, 139, 141, 182

nāgaraka 487–88
Nandapaṇḍita 14, 96, 341, 613–14, 616, 620–22
Nārada 14, 45, 48, 54, 65, 68, 94–95, 105, 152, 156–61, 167–70, 172, 175–76, 183–84, 235–36, 238–39,

242, 245, 251, 289–303, 306, 345–46, 354, 362–65, 368–70, 378, 411–12, 419, 421–23, 432, 435, 477, 514, 533, 587, 599–601, 607, 614, 616–17, 641, 665, 721–22
Nārada Smṛti 14, 105, 113, 148, 153, 156–58, 160, 167–69, 171, 172, 174–76, 178, 183–84, 226, 235, 245, 251, 274, 287, 291–94, 296, 306, 312, 319, 341, 343, 345, 351–52, 354, 362, 367, 369–93, 412–13, 419, 421, 424, 429, 438, 478, 490, 514–24, 528, 534, 566, 568, 570, 601, 609, 614, 640, 722
Nāradīyamanusaṃhitā 14, 156, 599, 601, 722
Nearchus 110
nibandha 56, 74, 76, 124, 134, 305, 445, 452, 477, 510, 534, 635, 738
nikṣepa 147
Nirukta 336, 339
niyoga 6, 50–51, 115–16, 130, 422, 426, 429, 430, 432, 603, 607–8, 610–12
niyukta 419, 423–26, 430, 432, 603–12
non-payment of debts 48, 147, 152, 159–60, 569
Nyāya 25, 70, 75–77, 122, 166, 182, 188, 271, 273–74, 327, 352, 395, 408, 415, 419, 428–29, 453, 488, 720, 723, 740

oaths 388
offspring 50, 64, 92, 96, 130, 177, 238, 241–42, 262, 268, 276, 282, 286, 463, 479, 492–93, 504, 509, 511, 611, 691–92, 705–6, 715
oligarchy 333–34
Olivelle, Patrick 2, 12, 19, 20, 39, 150–51, 504, 665, 720, 736
ordeal 70, 389
orientalism 33–36, 740
orphan 696
outcast 169, 178, 286, 291
ownership 21, 48–49, 77–78, 136, 164, 167, 180–81, 184, 189, 250, 272, 283, 306–7, 382–85, 437, 446–50, 498–500, 530–35, 538, 652, 666, 704, 715

paiśāca 494, 588–89
Paiṭhīnasi 311
paṇa 53
Panikkar, Kalavam Madhava 74, 77
Pāṇini 14, 21, 45, 334, 369, 483, 487–98, 499, 500, 506, 602, 619, 719, 722–23, 743.
parents 91, 114–15, 169–70, 172, 178, 183, 236–37, 249–50, 252–54, 276, 286, 290, 536, 618–20, 680–81, 695, 705–14, 717
partition 163, 171, 244, 733, 743
Patañjali 216
Penal Code 57, 79, 146, 149, 160, 296, 303, 451–52, 643, 661, 737
penance 89–90, 123, 240, 284, 454, 459–65, 470, 559, 688
Pitāmaha 67, 362, 389–92, 426, 428, 446–47, 599, 608, 722
pogaṇḍa 235–36, 246
Pokorny, Julius 574
Pollock, Sheldon 27, 737

prakṛta 481
pratiloma 256–58, 261, 264, 493, 620–21
pretas 552
prince 277, 337, 683, 685–87, 689, 692
princess 283, 689, 692
private defence 451–52
Privy Council 43, 44, 83–85, 87, 96, 140, 181, 188–90, 194–96, 506, 582, 618, 634, 644, 648–49, 652–58, 662–64, 667–69
profession 72, 287, 418–20, 422, 425, 429–30, 433, 463, 607, 641–42, 671, 683
proof 6, 361, 365, 368–69, 377, 382, 385, 387–89; means of proof 345, 365, 368–69, 371, 378, 380, 382–86, 440, 453
property 149, 192, 242, 245, 268, 532, 727–29
punishment 30, 42, 66, 71–72, 77, 88–90, 131, 134, 153–55, 159–60, 230, 240–41, 244, 284, 294, 296, 300–2, 326, 345–46, 354, 375, 383, 390, 406, 422–23, 425, 429, 431, 452, 456–57, 459, 460, 465, 473–75, 477–79, 488, 491, 518, 531, 553, 567–71, 578–79, 689, 712
purchase 48, 147, 242, 379
purohita 324, 357
Puruṣasūkta 321

Quran 103

rājadharma 72–73, 89, 325–26, 336, 353, 431
rājan 203, 329, 339–40, 349–50
Rājanya 321. See also *kṣatriya*
rākṣasa 494, 588–89
Rāma 227, 325, 338, 340, 343, 624
Rāmāyaṇa 14, 72, 224, 227, 230, 316, 325–27, 337–38, 341–42
Rangaswami Aiyangar, K.V. 24, 72, 76, 98, 249, 342, 362, 396, 436–37, 445, 477, 567–600, 639–41, 649, 719, 721, 724, 737
rank 56, 206–7, 209, 270, 343, 370, 374, 392, 452, 467, 468–70, 494, 690; elevated rank 468–70
rāṣṭra 335
rebirth 42, 70, 72, 539–42, 545, 546, 550–55, 557, 559, 561
remuneration 351, 426, 433
Renou, Louis 150–51, 340, 436, 600, 738
Ṛgveda 46–48, 64, 66, 113, 206, 321, 337, 389, 461, 574, 576–78, 722, 730
ṛṇādāna 147, 569
robbery 48, 293, 417, 565–66, 657
Rocher, Ludo 3, 9, 10–12, 15, 17–36, 40, 60, 66, 68, 73, 80, 89, 109–11, 113–14, 117, 132, 182, 185, 187, 226, 267, 272, 299, 305, 311, 319, 345, 356–57, 366, 372, 396, 423, 430, 482, 487, 490, 493–94, 517, 527, 598, 600, 641, 645, 662, 664, 666–69, 699, 720, 723–24, 738–40
Roman law 279–80, 287, 290, 309
royal grant 455
royal messenger 222. See also *cara*, *dūta*
royal power 6, 315, 339. See also kingship
Sacred Books of the East 14,

105–6, 131, 361, 539, 665, 719, 722
sacrifice 61–62, 89, 205, 242, 282, 324, 466, 468, 531–32, 552, 559, 607
sāhasa 147, 149, 151–62, 293–94, 298, 565, 566–71, 574, 577–79, 627
samaya 25, 70, 75, 77, 166, 182, 188, 271, 273–74, 327, 352, 419, 428–29, 720, 723, 740
saṃbhūyasamutthāna 147
Saṃhitā 14, 46, 62–63, 737; *Maitrāyaṇiyasaṃhitā* 441; *Taittirīyasaṃhitā* 113, 457, 723
saṃsāra 540, 545, 555–57
saṃvidvyatikrama 147
sapiṇḍa 50, 130, 267–68, 270, 288, 446, 448–49
Sarkar, Golap Chandra 25, 70, 75, 77, 166, 182, 188, 271–74, 327, 352, 419, 428–29, 720, 723, 740
śāstra 20, 22, 27, 29, 39, 56, 62, 86, 113, 117, 185, 481, 484, 489, 495, 530, 587, 626, 649, 662–72, 743
Sātavāhanas 66
satī 79
Sāyaṇa 572, 574, 576–77
scholasticism 76
sedition 425
Senart, Émile 106, 108–9, 741
servant 95, 291, 299, 426, 504, 509, 511. See also slave
sexual intercourse 425
Sharia 103
Śilāhāras 277
sīmāvivāda 147
sin 42, 44, 88–91, 150–52, 169, 228, 240, 282, 293, 295, 344, 356, 376–77, 383, 457, 465–66, 468, 470, 521–23, 541, 545–46, 552–54, 558–59, 572, 624, 628, 686; mortal sin 521–23, 545–46; sinful act 344, 553–54
sister 112–13, 192, 199, 520–22, 643, 676, 696, 708, 711
slave 95, 174, 239, 241, 302, 508–12, 530, 680, 707
smṛti 47, 55, 63–69, 72–73, 77–78, 104, 110, 122, 127, 134–35, 180, 223, 231, 272, 283, 306, 308, 310–11, 407, 413, 454, 463, 477, 501, 528, 535, 570, 597–98, 621, 626–28, 635, 640; *smṛti* rules 66, 127, 310–11; *smṛti* texts 77, 308, 310, 413, 627
snātaka 262, 323
son 30–31, 43–44, 47, 64, 77, 84, 88, 92–97, 101, 111, 113–15, 129–33, 138, 159, 163, 167–68, 171–83, 189, 192–94, 199, 200, 207, 237, 239, 242, 245–46, 251, 262, 267–68, 270–72, 275–77, 284–86, 299, 302, 311–12, 316, 336–38, 340, 342, 348–49, 418, 422–23, 428, 432, 448, 463, 490, 497, 503–13, 533–35, 562, 577, 584, 609–23, 628, 643, 652, 654–55, 664–65, 675, 679, 683, 691–97, 705–8, 710–16, 726, 737
śrāddha 43, 94, 96, 168, 269–70, 273–77, 654, 664, 669
Śrīkara 275–76
Śrīkṛṣṇa 121, 250–52, 312, 529, 535
śruti 47, 51, 63, 104, 122, 218,

223, 309, 441, 465, 590, 605, 625, 627, 635, 639
steya 147, 149, 152–58, 565
Strabo 110, 215, 218, 742
strīdhana 163, 175–76
strīpuṃdharma 147
strīsaṃgrahaṇa 147, 157, 158. See also adultery
Succession. See Hindu Succession Act
Śūdra 66, 77, 108, 131, 155, 203–8, 211–12, 241, 256–57, 259, 262, 264, 321, 389, 463, 487, 503–12, 519, 551–52, 572–73
Śūlapāṇi 137, 465, 467–69, 720
Sumantu 240, 457, 460–62, 467, 470
sūta 258–60, 264
svadharma 41, 72, 343
svāmin 335
svāminpālavivāda 147

Taittirīyabrāhmaṇa 441
Taittirīyāraṇyaka 441
teacher 76, 168, 240, 243, 299, 343, 454, 458–59, 465–67, 649
theft 48, 147–59, 215, 354, 374, 392, 425, 455, 547, 550–51, 565, 569, 687–88
Ṭoḍaramalla 74–75
Ṭoḍarānanda 74–75
trivarga 481–88
truth 182, 212, 217, 233, 348, 363, 371–77, 386, 388–90, 395, 406, 414, 440, 453, 646, 675, 678–79, 681–84
twice-born 50, 89–90, 97, 116, 130, 202–3, 207–8, 322, 503–5, 510, 519, 558, 611, 621
untruthfulness 376; speaking untruth 540
upanayana 91, 310, 341, 625
Uśanas 30–31, 582–84

Vācaspati Miśra 14, 28, 137, 152, 401–16
Vaiśya 50, 77, 108, 131, 155, 202–12, 241, 256–59, 262, 264, 290, 321, 389, 463, 487, 547, 551, 572–73, 709
vākpāruṣya 147, 149–52, 156–58, 513–25, 527
vānaprasthin 486
Vardhamāna 13, 159, 161, 516, 520, 524, 719, 738
varṇa 41, 50, 88, 172, 201, 207, 238, 256, 263, 295, 320–21, 343, 349, 377, 492–95, 503, 551, 557–58, 619–21. See also caste
Vasiṣṭha 14, 43, 47–48, 174, 178–79, 202–5, 208, 210–11, 255, 286, 343, 356, 372, 373, 376, 383–84, 455, 460, 476, 491, 513–14, 519, 553, 558–59, 612, 614–16, 627, 709
Vasiṣṭha Dharmasūtra 14, 43–48, 64, 71, 96, 105, 163, 174, 202, 243, 256, 258, 265, 311, 319–20, 323, 389, 460, 464, 539, 560, 587, 612, 614–17, 624, 648, 720, 722
Veda 47–49, 52, 63–64, 73, 77, 98, 116, 203–4, 282, 316, 321–24, 341, 347, 355, 356, 380, 455, 458, 460, 469, 470, 475, 556–58, 561, 574, 625–28, 675, 721–22, 732
Vedic school 62–63, 432; Maitrāyaṇīya 46; Vājasaneyi 46

Vellālar 699, 701–5
vibhāga 147, 528–30, 533, 536–37, 720. See also inheritance
vidyā 475–76, 486
Vijñāneśvara 14, 28, 122–26, 136, 138, 187, 223–24, 231, 240, 268, 272–74, 305, 365, 400–3, 454–60, 475, 518, 527–38, 603, 614, 619–21, 649, 666, 675, 722, 734
violence 48, 66, 151, 155, 158–59, 227, 374, 459, 565–66, 569, 570, 624, 628
Viṣṇu 14, 45, 105, 163, 173, 175, 178, 202, 207–8, 237, 240, 256, 258, 261, 263, 265, 296, 302, 329, 341, 343, 435, 533, 539, 547–50, 555, 560–62, 587, 614–17, 665, 722–23
Viṣṇu Smṛti 14, 173, 175–76, 178, 202–4, 243, 255, 311, 335, 340–44, 348–49, 366–67, 369, 371–72, 374, 376–79, 381–83, 388–93, 476, 491–92, 503, 514, 551–52, 561, 566, 570, 604, 613, 616, 620, 622
Viśvarūpa 14, 276, 317, 454, 533, 620, 640, 719, 722
vivādapada 48, 152, 156, 160, 362, 569
von Schroeder, Leopold 61–62, 106, 575, 721
Vyāsa 14, 30–31, 306–8, 362, 365, 382, 385, 395–96, 407, 425, 432, 447–48, 461, 582–84, 597, 606
vyavahāra 24, 26, 30–31, 56, 72, 147–48, 239, 300, 348, 364–65, 400, 405, 428, 432, 439, 445, 473, 583–84, 597, 600

warrior 348. See also Kṣatriya
weapon 386, 455–57, 469, 571
widow 91–92, 130, 244, 343, 611–12, 670
wife 48, 64, 91–92, 95–96, 120, 147, 167, 172, 174, 177, 179, 193, 207, 239, 242, 244, 251, 256, 268, 281–303, 327, 337, 343, 350, 386, 389, 425, 448, 455–56, 483, 489–90, 493, 503–4, 508, 522, 533, 541, 545–46, 552–53, 561, 566, 609–10, 618–22, 678–80, 687–90, 692, 694–96, 705–16
witness 146, 297, 329, 369, 370–78, 386, 388, 393, 417, 438, 646, 683
woman 47, 50, 88, 92, 129, 175–76, 191–92, 237, 241, 243, 246, 256–57, 262–63, 268, 282, 284–91, 295–97, 301–3, 323, 355, 379, 385, 417, 489–93, 504–8, 511–12, 549, 553, 562, 611–12, 619–22, 638, 670, 679–80, 687–88, 705, 709, 711; pregnant women 343. See also wife

Yājñavalkya 14, 45–48, 53–54, 65–68, 71, 91, 105, 134, 152, 156, 168–69, 172–77, 209, 223, 225, 239–40, 256, 261–62, 265, 276, 297, 306, 317, 333, 362, 400, 421, 435, 473, 505–11, 527, 534, 545–50, 553, 561–62, 570, 587, 614, 616–17, 619, 639, 665, 724, 733
Yājñavalkya Dharmaśāstra 14,

47, 66, 91, 160, 169, 172–78, 202–5, 208, 211, 221–22, 226, 236, 246, 255, 285, 305–6, 335, 341, 344, 346, 350, 354, 365–68, 371–84, 389–93, 400, 411, 437, 440, 453–56, 475–78, 492, 503, 507–8, 510–14, 533, 536, 540–45, 552, 554–55, 557, 559–61, 566, 568, 570, 603–4, 615–17, 620, 622, 639, 640. See also *Yājñavalkyasmṛti*
Yājñavalkyasmṛti 24, 64, 67–68, 126, 134–35, 148, 268, 276, 719, 722, 724, 735
Yajurveda 46
Yama 318–19, 325, 328, 575–76, 615–16

www.ingramcontent.com/pod-product-compliance
Lightning Source LLC
Chambersburg PA
CBHW030101010526
44116CB00005B/49
9781783083152